Tolley's

hips: The New

Be   Legislation

by

Douglas Armour, Partner
of
David Venus and Company

Limited Liability Partnership Agreement

by

Simon Young, Partner
of
Veitch Penny Solicitors

R A member of the Reed Elsevier plc group

Whilst every care has been taken to ensure the accuracy of the contents of this work, no responsibility for loss occasioned to any person acting or refraining from action as a result of any statement in it can be accepted by any of the authors, editors or the publishers.

Published by
Tolley
2 Addiscombe Road
Croydon Surrey CR9 5AF
England

Printed in Great Britain by
Hobbs the Printers, Southampton

Preface

The limited liability partnership (LLP) is a new type of corporate entity which came into effect on 6 April 2001. The purpose of this book is to bring together within one work the principal legislation relating to LLPs, accompanied by a commentary. The Limited Liability Partnerships Act 2000, together with related regulations (in particular the Limited Liability Partnerships Regulations 2001), adopt much of the Companies Act 1985 and the Insolvency Act 1986, as well as the Company Directors Disqualification Act 1986 and sundry sections from other Acts. These basic provisions have been specifically modified in numerous instances, as well as being subject to general modifications such as that which provides that 'company' shall include 'limited liability partnership'.

The appendices to this book contain the full text of the Acts and Regulations referred to above, as they apply to LLPs, with all the specific and general modifications included so far as possible. In addition, specimens of the forms prescribed for use by LLPs are also reproduced, and a draft LLP agreement is also included. The commentary outlines the main provisions of the legislation applying to LLPs, including basic concepts of company law and insolvency law (for example, accounting and audit, and winding up). Thus whilst helpful, a prior knowledge of these concepts is not essential for using this book.

The book is not intended to be a comprehensive guide to the working of the legislation, but a handy first guide to its provisions. At the time of writing, a companion work is being finalised which will provide detailed guidance to the legislation, with practical insight and precedents dealing with the relevant procedures.

I must also express my thanks to Sally Moss at the DTI, for drawing our attention to various statutory instruments (in particular, the regulations relating to Scotland) and for her assistance in interpreting various modifications to the existing legislation, and to Ami Chilvers and Stephen Barc of Butterworths Tolley for their invaluable help in putting together the text of the legislation, with all the modifications, and for acting as a sounding board to assess the effect of certain of the modifications.

Douglas Armour

April 2001

Abbreviations and References

BNA 1985	Business Names Act 1985
CA 1985	Companies Act 1985
CA 1989	Companies Act 1989
CDDA 1986	Company Directors Disqulification Act 1986
FSA 1986	Financial Services Act 1986
IA 1986	Insolvency Act 1986
ICTA 1988	Income and Corporation Taxes Act 1988
LLP	Limited Liability Partnerships
LLPA 2000	Limited Liability Partnerships Act 2000
LLPR 2001	Limited Liability Partnerships Regulations 2001
TCGA 1992	Taxation of Chargeable Gains Act 1992

Contents

1 – General	**1–2**
2 – Incorporation	**3–9**
Matters to consider when incorporating an LLP	3
Name of the LLP	3
Control of LLP names	3
Registration of LLPs	4
Partnership agreement	5
Change of name	6
Business names	7
Registered office	8
LLP letterheads	8
Annual return	9
3 – Membership	**11–16**
Introduction	11
Members	11
Authority	11
Changes in membership	12
Designated members	13
Disqualification of members	14
Disqualification for unfitness	14
Disqualification on conviction	14
Disqualification for breach of statutory obligations	15
Disqualification for fraudulent or wrongful trading	15
Disqualification in the public interest	15
Unfair prejudice	16
4 – Accounts and Audit	**17–36**
Introduction	17
Duty to keep accounting records	17
Accounting reference date	18
Form and content of accounts	19
Group accounts	19
Approval and signing of accounts	21
Auditors' report	21
Duties of auditors in preparing auditors' report	22
Publication and delivery of accounts	22
Small and medium-sized LLPs	24
Small and medium-sized groups	25
Exemptions for accounts filing and preparation	25
Small LLPs	25
Medium-sized LLPs	26
Audit exemption	26
Audit exemption for dormant subsidiaries	28

Contents

Audit exemption for dormant LLPs   28
Delivery and publication of unaudited accounts   28
Dormant LLPs   28
Revisions   29
Appointment of auditors   30
Eligibility   31
Exemption from obligation to appoint auditors   32
Rights of auditors   32
Remuneration   33
Auditors ceasing to hold office   33
   Notification to Companies House   34
Resignation of auditors   34
Removal or non-re-appointment of auditors   35
Rights of auditors who are removed or not re-appointed   36

5 – Taxation   **37–42**
Introduction   37
Income and capital gains tax   37
   Additions to ICTA 1988   38
   Additions to TCGA 1992   39
Inheritance tax   40
   Addition to Inheritance Tax Act 1984   41
Transfer of business   41
Stamp duty   41
National insurance   42

6 – Charges   **43–49**
Issue of debentures   43
Types of debenture   43
Secured debentures   44
Issue of debenture stock   45
Unsecured loan stock   46
Redemption of debentures   47
Charges   47
Satisfaction or release of charge   48
Rectification of register of charges   48
LLP's register of charges   48

7 – Insolvency   **51–75**
Winding up – introduction   51
Methods of winding up   51
   Members' voluntary winding up   52
   Creditors' voluntary winding up   52
   Winding up the court   52
Initial procedures   53
   Members' voluntary winding up   53
   Creditors' voluntary winding up   54
   Winding up by the court   56
Liquidator   56

Qualifiactions of liquidators 57
Duties and powers of liquidators 57
Members 59
Investigations, preferneces, fraud and criminal offences 59
Member's contribution to assets 60
Determination of creditors' claims 61
Distribution and release 61
Voluntary winding-up 61
Winding up by the court 62
Dissolution without liquidation 63
Winding up in Scotland 63
LLP voluntary arrangements 64
Procedure 64
Remuneration, expenses and completion of the voluntary
arrangement 66
Administration orders 66
Effect of the administration order 68
Administrator 68
Powers of an administrator 69
Duties of an administrator 69
Discharge or variation of the order 69
Vacation of office 70
Receiverships – England and Wales 70
Qualification and remuneration 70
Appointment by the court 71
Appointment by debenture holders 71
The employees' legal position 73
Powers, liabilities and responsibilities 74
Priority in distribution of funds 74
Arrangements and reconstructions 74
Compromise or arrangement 74
Reconstruction 75

Appendix 1 – Limited Liability Partnership Agreement **77**

Appendix 2 – Legislation **101**

Appendix 3 – Companies House Forms **623**

1 – General

The long awaited Limited Liability Partnerships Act 2000 (LLPA 2000, the Act) received Royal Assent on 20 July 2000. The Act creates a new form of legal identity known as a limited liability partnership (LLP) and will be available for incorporation in England and Wales and Scotland by any two or more persons who wish to set up in business together.

The Act came into force on 6 April 2001 (by virtue of the Limited Liability Partnerships Act 2000 (Commencement) Order 2000 (SI 2000 No 3316)). On the same date, the Limited Liability Partnerships Regulations 2001 (LLPR 2001) (SI 2001 No 1090), in which the bulk of the legislation is contained, also came into effect (together with separate regulations dealing with those parts of companies and insolvency legislation devolved to the Scottish Parliament, the Limited Liability Partnerships (Scotland) Regulations 2001 (SSI 2001 No 128)). In addition, fees charged by Companies House in relation to LLPs are prescribed by the Limited Liability Partnerships (Fees) (No 2) Regulations 2001 (SI 2001 No 969).

An LLP combines the organisational flexibility and taxation treatment of a partnership but with limited liability for its members. The price to pay for this limited liability is that, for the purposes of accounts and insolvency, an LLP will be subject to broadly the same requirements as a limited company. Indeed the regulations adopt provisions of the Companies Act 1985, the Insolvency Act 1986 and the Company Directors Disqualification Act 1986, together with appropriate amendment, virtually unchanged. The full text of the Companies Act 1985 and the Insolvency Act 1986, as adopted and modified by LLPR 2001, is set out in **Appendix 2**. Forms to be used under the provisions of the Companies Act 1985 which apply to LLPs are prescribed by the Limited Liability Partnerships (Forms) Regulations 2001 (SI 2001 No 927); other forms, to be used under the LLPA 2000, have been approved by the Registrar of Companies. All the forms are reproduced in **Appendix 3**.

This is the first legislation concerning the operation of partnerships since the Partnership Act 1890. The Partnership Act 1890 established rules for the liability of partners of the firm to those persons trading with them. All partners in the firm are jointly liable, and in Scotland severally also, with their fellow partners for all the debts and obligations of the partnership whilst they remain as partners. Additionally all partners are jointly and

1

severally liable for all losses or damages arising from the acts or omissions of the partners incurred in the ordinary course of business or with the consent of the partners.

In general, partnership works well for small partnerships where all the partners are known to each other and work closely with each other. However, the growing sizes of professional partnerships, particularly solicitors and accountants, and the increasingly litigious environment has exposed a weakness in the structure of partnerships. The problem is that an individual partner's personal assets are at risk from a claim arising out of the actions of an unknown partner, perhaps located in a different country, which exceeds not only the firm's insurance cover but also the ability of the firm to meet the quantum of the claim from its own resources, the so called 'doomsday' claim.

The members of an LLP benefit from limited liability and so their own personal assets will be protected whilst those of the LLP will be at risk, as is the case with a limited company. A negligent member's assets will however still be at risk since, under the general law, professional people owe a duty of care to their clients which cannot be avoided.

Unlike a partnership an LLP has unlimited capacity and accordingly is a legal entity in its own right separate from its members.

Unlike a limited company there is no distinction between the owners of the company (its shareholders) and its managers (the directors). An LLP only has members, who are free to regulate their internal affairs as they see fit. The majority of LLPs are expected to adopt a formal agreement regulating their affairs and a suggested agreement is set out in **Appendix 1**. There is no obligation to adopt a formal written agreement. As will be seen, there is no requirement for the internal agreement (if any) to be made public. Where no agreement is adopted, or where such an agreement is silent on specific matters, Regs 7 and 8 of the LLPR 2001 set out default provisions concerning the rights of members between themselves and with the LLP.

Broadly speaking the members of an LLP will be taxed as if the LLP were a partnership. Accordingly a decision to transfer the business of a partnership into an LLP should be tax neutral (see **Chapter 5**).

2 – Incorporation

Matters to consider when incorporating an LLP   2.1

- Are the owners and managers the same people without exception?
- Are their at least two members?
- Is it intended to raise funding from the public?
- Is the LLP to trade for profit or to be a charitable or non-profit making body such as an association?
- Is the liability of the members to be limited or unlimited? Some professional associations require their members to trade without limited liability.
- Is it preferred not to disclose financial information of the business?

In addition to these considerations, appropriate professional advice should be sought concerning the differing taxation provisions relating to companies, LLPs and partnerships.

Name of the LLP   2.2

The name must terminate with the word 'limited liability partnership' or either abbreviation 'llp' or 'LLP'. If the registered office of the LLP is situated in Wales the name may end with the Welsh equivalents 'partneriaeth atebolrwydd cyfyngedig', 'pac' or 'PAC' (LLPA 2000 Sch, para 2).

The LLP's name must be 'painted or affixed' outside every office or place of the LLP. In addition it must appear on all business letters and other specified documents. (CA 1985, ss 348, 349 as modified). Equivalent requirements apply in the case of LLPs incorporated outside Great Britain which have a place of business in Great Britain ('oversea LLPs') (CA 1985, s 693 as modified).

Control of LLP names   2.3

There is no procedure for obtaining approval of a name in advance, and it is for the persons forming the LLP to check the index of company names (including LLP names) maintained by the Registrar of Companies pursuant to section 714 of the Companies Act 1985. In particular the following should be noted.

- An LLP will not be registered by the Registrar of Companies if the name would be 'the same as' an existing name on the index of names or where it does not bear the appropriate status, i.e. 'limited liability partnership' (or an abbreviation).
- A name will not be registered if it would be offensive or constitute a criminal offence to use it (LLPA 2000, Sch, para 3(1)).
- A name would not be approved if it gave the impression that the LLP was connected with central or local government or contained an expression which may only be used with the approval of the Secretary of State unless written approval has been obtained from the appropriate authority (LLPA 2000, Sch, para 3(2)).
- Where an LLP has been registered with a name which is 'the same as' or 'too like' a name shown on the index of names maintained by the Registrar of Companies, the LLP may be directed in writing by the Secretary of State within 12 months of the registration to change its name within such period as he may specify (LLPA 2000, Sch, para 4(2). This period is extended to five years after registration where the LLP has provided, for the purpose of registration, information which is misleading or which has not fulfilled assurances given at the time of registration (LLPA 2000, Sch, para 4(3)). At any time after registration, the Secretary of State may direct an LLP to change its name within such period as he may allow, where the LLP's name is so misleading in regard to the nature of its activities as to be likely to cause harm to the public (LLPA 2000, Sch, para 4(4)).
- There are detailed guidance notes (GBLLP1) on the provisions regarding LLP names which may be obtained from the Registrar of Companies on request or downloaded from the Companies House website (www.companieshouse.gov.uk).
- LLPs are subject to the provisions of the Business Names Act 1985 as amended by paragraphs 10 and 11 of Schedule 5 to the LLPR 2001 (see **2.7** below).

Registration of LLPs 2.4

Registration of an LLP is the process by which the LLP is formed and becomes a separate legal entity from its owners (the members).

Any two or more persons associated for the carrying on of a lawful business with a view to profit may form an LLP (LLPA 2000, s 2) as follows.

- The names of the first members, differentiating between designated and non-designated members (for the relevance of this distinction, see **3.5** below) and intended place of the registered office of the LLP must be submitted on form LLP2. This form incorporates a consent to be signed by the persons to become the first members. The form must also be signed by a member or an agent/solicitor acting on the members' behalf.
- The formal approval of the name of the LLP (if required).
- A cheque payable to Companies House for the registration fee of £95.

If all is in order, the Registrar of Companies will issue a certificate of incorporation (LLPA 2000, s 3), bearing the date of incorporation, the LLP's registered number and stating that the LLP is a limited liability partnership. The certificate should be very carefully preserved since it may at some time be necessary to produce it. However, it is possible to obtain duplicate certificates of incorporation from the Registrar of Companies for a fee. An LLP may commence business as soon as it has been incorporated.

Partnership agreement 2.5

Although not required by the Act it is likely that most LLPs will adopt an agreement regulating the relationship between its members, rather than relying upon any verbal agreements as to division of profits and office holders (if any). In the absence of any written agreement, or where the agreement does not deal with a particular issue, default provisions are set out in Regulations 7 and 8 of the LLPR 2001 which modify those set out in section 24 of the Partnership Act 1890. The default provisions are as follows.

- All members entitled to have equal share of capital and profit.
- LLP to indemnify members in respect of expenses incurred in relation to the LLP.
- All members to participate in management.
- Members not entitled to remuneration in respect of management duties carried out for the LLP.
- All existing members to agree to admit new members or to assignment of interest by another member.
- Member cannot be expelled without express agreement of all members.
- Decisions of the members to be by majority decision, other than changes to nature of business which require consent of all members.

- All members entitled to have access to books and records of the LLP.
- Members cannot compete against LLP without consent.

The default provisions are set out in full in **Appendix 2** (pages 123-124).

The partnership agreement, if any, is not a public document and a copy is not required to be filed with the Registrar of Companies.

Typically the LLP agreement will deal with the following matters.

- Nature of the business.
- LLP's name.
- Property and place of business.
- Banking.
- Members' shares and contributions.
- Profit and losses.
- Drawings.
- Members' duties.
- Holiday entitlement.
- Management.
- Limits on members' authority.
- Admission of new members.
- Retirement.
- Expulsion.
- Termination/winding up.
- Covenants.

A suggested form of LLP agreement is contained in **Appendix 1**.

Change of name   2.6

Provided the partnership agreement contains appropriate authority, the members of an LLP may resolve to change the LLP's name at any time subject only to the restrictions noted above (LLPA 2000, Sch, para 4(1)).

Once the necessary resolution has been passed, notice must be given to the Registrar of Companies on form LLP3 (see **Appendix 3**), signed by a designated member (see **3.5** below), and accompanied by a cheque in the sum of £20 in respect of the change of name fee payable. Any such cheque should be made payable to Companies House.

Provided that he is happy that the name is satisfactory, the Registrar will issue a certificate of incorporation on change of name.

Business names 2.7

Where an LLP carries on business under a name which is not its registered name, it is necessary to comply with the provisions of the Business Names Act 1985 (BNA 1985) (as amended by LLPR 2001, Sch 5, paras 10 and 11). These are as follows.

- Although the controls on 'same' or 'too like' names do not apply in relation to business names, names implying connection with central or local government or containing certain words and expressions may only be used with the written approval of the Secretary of State (BNA 1985, ss 2 and 3). If the business name is used on business letters, written orders for goods, invoices, etc., the corporate name of the LLP and the name of each member (subject to the exception set out below) must also be stated and an address given within Great Britain at which service of any document relating to the business will be effective (BNA 1985, s 4(1)(a)).
- The name of each member need not be set out in any document issued by an LLP with more than 20 members which maintains a list of members at its principal place of business, provided that:
  - none of the members' names appears in the document otherwise than in the text or as a signatory, and
  - the document states in legible characters the address of the principal place of business of the LLP, and that the list of the members' names is open to inspection at that place.

  Any person may inspect the list during office hours (BNA 1985, s 4(3A)(4A)).
- Additional information must also be shown on business letters, as stated in **2.9** below.
- The corporate name of the LLP, and the name of each member, must also be shown in all premises where the business is carried on under the business name so that customers or suppliers may refer to it, and this information must also be given immediately in writing to any person doing business with the LLP who may request it (BNA 1985, s 4(1)(b)).

Failure to comply with any of the above provisions renders any member of the LLP responsible liable to criminal penalties, and the LLP may suffer difficulties in enforcing contracts made under the business name where the provisions have not been complied with (BNA 1985, ss 4(6)(7), 5 and 7).

Although, as noted above, the restrictions on LLP names do not also apply to business names, care must be taken not to infringe any trade marks or to use an existing name of a company or LLP operating in the same or similar industry which might lead to an action for passing off. Passing off is where one business is seen to be benefiting from the reputation of another established business by using the same or very similar name and 'passing itself off' as that other business.

Registered office   2.8

The incorporation document LLP2 (see **Appendix 3**) states the country within Great Britain in which the registered office is situated (with special provisions applying where the situation of the registered office is in Wales), and stipulates the address of the initial registered office. When the address is changed, notice must be given to the Registrar on Form LLP287 (see **Appendix 3**). The change in address is only effective once registered by the Registrar. However, the registered office of an LLP must be situated within the country specified in the incorporation document LLP2 , so that an LLP registered in England and Wales may not have its registered office situated in Scotland and the converse position applies in the case of LLPs registered in Scotland (LLPA 2000, Sch, paras 9, 10).

The situation of the registered office is determined by the members and any change is made by resolution of the members.

Where the registered office is changed, it is necessary to amend the LLP headed stationery and to amend any signage outside its registered office within 14 days of the change. Service of any document may still be made at the old registered office for a period of 14 days following registration of the change by the Registrar. (CA 1985, s 287 as modified.)

The LLP must display its name outside every office or place in which its business is carried on. The name must be in a conspicuous place and the letters must be legible. (CA 1985, s 348 as modified.)

LLP letterheads   2.9

The LLP's full name must be shown on all business letters and other documents as specified in CA 1985, s 349 (as modified). The place of registration and the registered number of the LLP as shown on the certificate of incorporation must also be shown on business letters and order forms, together with the address of the registered office (CA 1985, s 351 as modified).

Where the LLP uses a trade name which is different from its registered name this can be shown on the headed paper. However, the LLP's full name as registered must also be shown, usually in small print at the foot of the page (see also **2.7** above).

Where the LLP has 20 or less members, the names of all the members must be shown on all headed paper. Where the LLP has more than 20 members, the LLP can choose not to show the names but to state an address at which the list of members names can be viewed.

Annual return   2.10

LLPs are required to make an annual return (form LLP363 – see **Appendix 3**) to the Registrar of Companies (CA 1985, s 363 as modified). The return is made up to a date not more than 12 months after the previous return, or 12 months after incorporation (the 'return date') although an LLP may choose to make it up to an earlier date. The annual return must be filed with the Registrar of Companies within 28 days of the return date, together with a fee of £35.

The annual return has been designed as a 'shuttle' document in that the form, with information pre-printed on it from the LLP's records at Companies House, is sent to LLPs about two weeks before the return date. The form must be checked, amended as necessary and signed by a designated member.

The contents of the annual return are as follows (CA 1985, s 364 as modified).

- The name of the LLP.
- The registered number of the LLP.
- The address of the LLP's registered office.
- The address where the register of debenture holders, if any, is kept, if this is not kept at the LLP's registered office.
- The name and address of every member and distinguishing which, if not all, are designated members.

3 – Membership

Introduction

As with partnerships, the Act contains the minimum of regulations or provisions regarding the admission and expulsion of members. Although as mentioned in **2.5** above, default provisions are set out in Regulations 7 and 8 of the LLPR 2001, in the absence of an LLP agreement there are few other provisions regarding the internal regulation of an LLP. It is very much for the members to agree how to regulate their own affairs as is the case with partnerships (LLPA 2000, s 5(1)).

Members 3.2

On incorporation the first members of an LLP are those persons who have subscribed their names to the incorporation document, form LLP2 (LLPA 2000, s 4(1)).

Subject to any LLP agreement or by agreement with the existing members, additional members may be admitted. Admission of new members will usually require an amendment or variation of the existing agreement to take account of any different share of capital and/or division of profit. Membership can cease through dissolution of the LLP, death of the member or by agreement with the other members. Specific power must be contained in the LLP agreement, or by a separate agreement, to enable members to expel one of their number for breach of the LLP agreement or other serious misconduct.

If, for any reason, the number of members of an LLP falls to one for a period of six months or more then that person is liable jointly and severally with the LLP for payment of its debts contracted during that period (CA 1985, s 24 as modified by LLPR 2001, Sch 2).

Authority 3.3

Every member of an LLP is an agent of the LLP (LLPA 2000, s 6(1)). In dealings with a third party, each member is presumed to have the necessary power and authority to bind the LLP to any contract unless the member in fact has no such authority, and that third party (i) knows that that member has no authority or (ii) does not know or believe that that person is a member (LLPA 2000, s 6(2)).

Where a person has ceased, for whatever reason, to be a member of the LLP a third party may still regard that person as a member and accordingly bind the LLP to a contract, unless the third party has been notified that the member is an ex-member or notice has been delivered to the Registrar on form LLP 288b (see **Appendix 3**), notifying the cessation of membership of that member (LLPA 2000, s 6(3)).

The LLP is jointly and severally liable for the liability of any member as regards any wrongful act or omission by him in the course of the business of the LLP, or other act or omission carried out by him with its authority, except where that liability is to another member of the LLP (LLPA 2000, s 6(4)).

Changes in membership 3.4

Where any person becomes or ceases to be a member of an LLP, the LLP must give notice of that fact to the Registrar within 14 days on forms LLP 288a or LLP 288b respectively (LLPA 2000, s 9).

The form LLP 288a or LLP 288b must be signed by a designated member (see **3.5** below). Unless all members of the LLP are to be regarded as designated members, the form must give notice of whether the appointment or cessation relates to their appointment or cessation to act as a designated member as well as a member.

In the case of a new appointment, the form must be signed (or authenticated) by the appointee, confirming his consent to become a member or a designated member (as the case may be).

It will be seen that where an LLP has both designated and non-designated members, notice of resignation must be filed with the Registrar where a designated member ceases to be a designated member but remains as a non-designated member. Equally, notification will be required where an existing member is appointed as a designated member.

Where there is any change in the name or address of a member, notice must be given on form LLP 288c within 28 days of the change (LLPA 2000, s 9(1)(a)). Form LLP 288c must be signed by the member it relates to and must be countersigned by an existing designated member. (For notification of change of status of a member or designated member, see **3.5** below.)

Designated members   3.5

On incorporation of an LLP, those members specified as such in the incorporation document shall be the designated members (LLPA 2000, s 8(1)). If however there is no notification of designated members, or there would only be one designated member, all members of the LLP shall be designated members (LLPA 2000, s 8(2)).

The incorporation document may state that every person who from time to time is a member of the LLP shall be regarded as a designated member, in which case no separate notification is required. In addition, an LLP may give notice to the Registrar (i) that specified members are to be designated members, or (ii) that all members from time to time of the LLP shall be regarded as designated members. Once such a notice is delivered, (i) or (ii) (as the case may be) will have effect as if stated in the incorporation document (LLPA 2000, s 8(4)(5)).

Where not all members of the LLP are designated members, a designated member can cease to be a designated member and a member can become a designated member by agreement with the other members of the LLP or as provided for in the LLP agreement. Changes in status of members and designated members must be notified to the Registrar on form LLP 288c within 14 days of the change in status of the member (LLPA 2000, s 9(1)(b)).

All members have the same rights and duties towards the LLP and these are governed by the Act and by the LLP agreement, if any. The Act places additional duties on designated members.

The additional duties of the designated members, for which they are legally responsible, are as follows.

- Appointing an auditor.
- Signing the LLP's accounts.
- Delivery of accounts to the Registrar of Companies.
- Notifying the Registrar of Companies of any changes in membership, registered office address or LLP's name.
- Preparation, signing and filing the LLP's annual return.
- Acting on behalf of the LLP if it is wound up and dissolved.

Disqualification of members 3.6

Members may be disqualified under the Company Directors Disqualification Act 1986 (as applied to LLPs by LLPR 2001, Reg 4 and Sch 2,
Part II) either as an automatic disqualification resulting from a defined
event or where application has been made to the court that a person is
unfit to be a member of an LLP. A person who has been disqualified
may not, during the period of disqualification, be a member of an
LLP, company director, liquidator, administrator, receiver or manager
of an LLP, whether directly or indirectly, without the consent of the
court.

Contravention of a disqualification order is a criminal offence punishable
on indictment by up to two years' imprisonment or an unlimited
fine. Application for disqualification is made under the appropriate
provision of the CDDA 1986, and disqualification may be automatic
(where the ground is unfitness – see **3.7** below) or discretionary.

Disqualification for unfitness 3.7

The court is obliged to disqualify a person who was or is a member of an
insolvent LLP where his conduct as a member makes him unfit to be
involved in the management of an LLP (CDDA 1986, s 6). A member
may be found to be unfit as a result of his actions or as a result of inaction.
When determining unfitness for this purpose, the court is required to
have regard in particular to the matters set out in CDDA 1986, Sch 1. The
minimum period of disqualification under section 6 is two years, and the
maximum period is 15 years.

Disqualification on conviction 3.8

The courts may make a disqualification order if a person has been convicted (either on indictment or summarily) of an indictable offence in
connection with the management, promotion, formation or liquidation
of an LLP (CDDA 1986, s 2). The maximum period of disqualification
under section 2 is five years where the disqualification order is made by
a magistrates' court, and 15 years in any other case.

Disqualification for breach of statutory obligations 3.9

A disqualification order may be made for persistent failure to file accounts or annual returns or other documents required to be filed with Companies House (CDDA 1986, s 3). There is a separate ground for disqualification in CDDA 1986, s 5 where a member is convicted of a summary offence in consequence of failing to file accounts or annual returns or other documents with Companies House, and during the five years ending with the date of the conviction, the member has had made against him (or has been convicted of) not less than three default orders (or offences) counting for the purposes of that section. Under both sections 3 and 5, the maximum period of disqualification is five years.

Disqualification for fraudulent or wrongful trading 3.10

A disqualification order may be made against a person if, during the course of a winding up, it appears that:

- he has been guilty of an offence under CA 1985, s 458 as modified (fraudulent trading), or
- while a member or liquidator of the LLP, or receiver or manager of its property, he has been guilty of any breach of duty as such, or of any fraud in relation to the LLP (CDDA 1986, s 4).

In addition, there is a separate ground of disqualification in CDDA 1986, s 10 where the court makes a declaration under the Insolvency Act 1986, s 213 (fraudulent trading) or 214 (wrongful trading) that a person is liable to contribute to the LLP's assets. The maximum period of disqualification under both sections 4 and 10 is 15 years.

Disqualification in the public interest 3.11

The Secretary of State has power to apply to the courts for a disqualification order on the grounds of public interest (CDDA 1986, s 8). This would usually follow from an enquiry by DTI inspectors. The maximum period of disqualification under section 8 is 15 years.

Unfair prejudice 3.12

Any member of an LLP may petition the court for an order that the affairs of the LLP are being conducted in way that is unfair to the interests of the members generally or to some group of the members including himself. A petition for an order may also be made in circumstances where any act or failure to take any act is or would be prejudicial. (CA 1985, s 459 as modified.)

The Secretary of State may also petition for such an order if after enquiring into the affairs of the LLP, he is satisfied that the business of the LLP is or might conducted in such a manner that is or might be prejudicial to the members or any of them. (CA 1985, s 460 as modified.)

If the court is satisfied that the petition is well founded, it may make such an order it thinks fit in respect of the petition including the following (CA 1985, s 461 as modified).

- Regulating the conduct of the affairs of the LLP.
- Requiring the LLP to refrain from doing or continuing an act complained of by the petitioner, or to do an act which the petitioner has complained it has omitted to do.
- Authorise civil proceedings to be brought in the name of the LLP by the petitioners.
- Require the LLP or specified members to buy the shares in the LLP held by other specified members.

The members of the LLP may, by written agreement amongst themselves, exclude the right to petition the court on the grounds of unfair prejudice for such period as shall be agreed. (CA 1985, s 459(1A) as modified.)

4 – Accounts and Audit

Introduction 4.1

This chapter outlines the main provisions relating to accounts and audit of LLPs. LLPR 2001, Reg 3 and Sch 1 apply to LLPs Part VII of the Companies Act 1985 (accounts and audit), and relevant Schedules (4, 4A, 5, 7, 8, 8A and 10A; 6 applies only for limited purposes) with appropriate modifications. Where a provision of Part VII or one of those Schedules is not specifically mentioned in LLPR 2001, Sch 1, that provision or Schedule applies without modification. Part VII of the Companies Act 1985, incorporating those modifications, can be found in **Appendix 2**.

This chapter also outlines the main provisions relating to the appointment of auditors of LLPs (and exemption from the requirement to do so), as well as provisions relating to the rights of auditors whilst in office, their remuneration, and their removal and resignation (see **4.20 *et seq.***). These can be found in LLPR 2001, Sch 2, which applies to LLPs various provisions of the Companies Act 1985 other than Part VII referred to above (including provisions relating to auditors, set out in Chapter V of Part XI of CA 1985), with appropriate modifications. However, by contrast with Sch 1 referred to above, only the sections of CA 1985 specifically referred to in Sch 2 apply. This means that in relation to auditors, any section within Chapter V of Part XI of CA 1985 which is omitted from LLPR 2001, Sch 2, will not apply to LLPs.

In this chapter, any references to modified sections of CA 1985 are references to that Act (as modified by LLPR 2001 in the manner outlined above).

Duty to keep accounting records 4.2

All LLPs are required to keep records of the LLP's financial transactions. The records must contain sufficient detail to enable the financial position of the LLP to be determined at any time and so that the members can ensure that any profit and loss account or balance sheet complies with the requirements of the Act (CA 1985, s 221 as modified).

The records should contain all details of any income and expenditure and a record of the LLP's assets and liabilities. If a parent LLP has a subsidiary undertaking not registered under the Act or the Companies Act 1985 it must ensure that sufficient records are maintained by or for the subsidiary so as to ensure that the profit and loss account and balance sheet of the parent LLP comply with the provisions of the Act. If the LLP fails to comply with any provision of CA 1985, s 221 (as modified), every member who is in default commits an offence (punishable by imprisonment or a fine) unless he shows that he acted honestly and that, in the circumstances in which the LLP's business was carried on, the default was excusable (CA 1985, s 221(5)(6) as modified).

The records must be kept by the LLP for a period of three years (CA 1985, s 222(5) as modified). A member is liable to imprisonment or a fine or both if he does not take reasonable steps to comply with the requirements of CA 1985, s 222(5) (as modified) or intentionally causes default by the LLP.

Accounting reference date   4.3

An LLP's first financial year begins on the first day of its 'accounting reference period' and ends with the last day of that period (or a date not more than seven days before or after the end of that period, as the members may determine). Each subsequent financial year begins with the day following the end of the LLP's previous financial year and ends with the last day of its next accounting reference period (again with the flexibility of the seven-day period referred to above) (CA 1985, s 223 as modified). This flexibility is allowed to enable an LLP to arrange a year end stock count at a suitable time.

For a new LLP, its first accounting reference period starts on the day of incorporation and ends on the last day of the month on which the anniversary of its incorporation falls. The date on which an accounting reference period ends is known as the LLP's 'accounting reference date'. An LLP may change its accounting reference date, including its automatically allocated one, provided that the resulting accounting reference period is no longer than eighteen months. An LLP can alter its accounting reference date to as short a period as it wishes, except that its first accounting reference period must be at least six months. (CA 1985, ss 224, 225 as modified.)

A change in accounting reference date is made by notice to the Registrar. An LLP can change its accounting reference date at any time so as to take effect either:

- in relation to the current accounting reference period (and subsequent periods); or
- in relation to the immediately preceding accounting reference period (and subsequent periods), provided that the period for filing the accounts for that period has not expired.

Except in certain specified circumstances, an LLP cannot extend its accounting reference period more than once in any five-year period (CA 1985, s 225(4) as modified). If the LLP becomes a subsidiary undertaking or a parent LLP the accounting periods for the two entities must coincide. In these circumstances, if necessary, an LLP may extend its accounting reference period even if it has, in the previous five years, extended that period previously (CA 1985, s 225(4) as modified).

The members will determine any change in the LLP's accounting reference date and must notify the Registrar on form LLP225 (see **Appendix 3**).

Form and content of accounts   4.4

Pursuant to CA 1985, s 226 (as modified) an LLP's individual accounts must comply with the provisions of CA 1985, Sch 4 (as modified) with respect to the form and content of the profit and loss account, balance sheet and any additional information that is required to be given. There is an overriding requirement that the accounts must give a true and fair view of the state of affairs of the LLP as at the end of the financial year (CA 1985, s 226(2) as modified). In circumstances where it is necessary to depart from the provisions of CA 1985, Sch 4 (as modified) or other provisions in order to give a true and fair view, such departure and the reasons for it must be noted in the accounts (CA 1985, s 226(5) as modified). In addition to the requirements of CA 1985, Sch 4 (as modified), accounts must be prepared in accordance with accounting standards issued by the Accounting Standards Board. The Accounting Standards Board is expected to issue separate accounting standards for LLPs.

Certain exemptions from and exceptions to the above requirements apply to small and medium-sized LLPs; see 4.10 below.

Group accounts   4.5

In addition to the requirement to prepare individual accounts, the members of an LLP must also, if the LLP was a parent LLP at the financial year end, prepare group accounts complying with CA 1985, Sch 4A (as modified) in terms of form and content (CA 1985, s 227 as modified). These group accounts consist of a consolidated balance sheet and a consolidated profit and loss account.

A parent LLP is a parent undertaking which is an LLP. A parent undertaking is one which, in relation to another LLP or company (a subsidiary undertaking):

- holds the majority of the voting rights in the subsidiary undertaking;
- is a member of the subsidiary undertaking and has the right to remove or appoint a majority of its members or (as the case may be) directors;
- has the right to exercise dominant control over the subsidiary undertaking, either by a right contained in that undertaking's LLP agreement or (as the case may be) its memorandum or articles of association, or by a contractual arrangement;
- is a member of the subsidiary undertaking, and controls a majority of the voting rights by agreement with other members or shareholders, as appropriate; or
- has a participating interest in the subsidiary undertaking, and either exercises dominant control or the affairs of both undertakings are managed together.

These definitions of parent and subsidiary undertakings contained in CA 1985, s 258 (supplemented by CA 1985, Sch 10A as modified) apply only for the purposes of determining whether group accounts should be prepared. In all other instances the definitions of parent and subsidiary companies are those contained in CA 1985, ss 736 and 736A as modified.

The parent LLP of a group qualifying as small or medium-sized (see **4.10** below) may claim exemption from preparing group accounts in terms of CA 1985, s 248 as modified.

Exemptions from the requirement to prepare group accounts are given by CA 1985, s 228(1) (as modified) where the parent undertaking is itself a subsidiary undertaking of an undertaking registered in an EC member state.

Where the requirement to prepare group accounts applies, all the subsidiary undertakings of the parent LLP must be included in the consolidation unless one of the exceptions set out in CA 1985, s 229 (as modified) applies – these exceptions are set out below.

A subsidiary undertaking may be excluded from consolidation if its inclusion is not material for the purpose of giving a true and fair view (CA 1985, s 229(2) as modified). Additional exemptions apply where the exercise of control by the parent is substantially restricted on a long-term basis, the necessary information for the preparation of group accounts cannot be obtained without unreasonable expense or undue delay, or the parent holds the shares with a view to resale and the undertaking has not previously been included in any consolidated accounts of the parent (CA 1985, s 229(3) as modified). In addition, the accounts of a subsidiary must be excluded from the consolidation if it carries out a substantially different activity from those of other undertakings to be included in the consolidation, so that to consolidate the results would result in the true and fair view being obscured (CA 1985, s 229(4) as modified).

Approval and signing of accounts   4.6

An LLP's annual accounts must be approved by the members, and signed, on the balance sheet, on behalf of all the members by a designated member. Every copy of the balance sheet which is circulated, published or issued must state the name of the signatory. The copy of the balance sheet which is delivered to the Registrar must also be signed on behalf of the members by a designated member. Non-compliance with these requirements is an offence. (CA 1985, s 233 as modified.)

Auditors' report   4.7

The LLP's accounts are to be submitted to its auditors, who are required to make a report on them to the LLP's members (CA 1985, s 235(1) as modified). (For appointment of auditors, see **4.20** below; note that certain LLPs are exempt from the requirement to have their accounts audited, and hence are also not required to appoint auditors; see **4.14** below.)

The report of the auditors must state the following (CA 1985, s 235(2) as modified):

- Whether the accounts have been properly prepared in accordance with the Act.
- Whether a true and fair view has been given:
  - ○   in respect of the balance sheet, of the state of affairs of that LLP at the end of the financial year;

❍ in respect of the profit and loss account, of the profit or loss of the LLP in respect of the financial year;

❍ in respect of group accounts, of the state of affairs of the group at the end of the financial year, and the profit and loss account for the financial year, of the undertakings included in the consolidation as a whole, so far as concerns members of the LLP.

Where an LLP prepares group accounts (see **4.5** above), the auditors are not required to report on that LLP's individual profit and loss account (CA 1985, s 230(3) as modified).

The auditors' report must state the name of the auditors and be signed by them. Every copy which is circulated, published or issued must also state the auditors' names. The copy of the auditors' report which is submitted to the Registrar of Companies must also state the name of the auditors and be signed by them. Non-compliance with these requirements is an offence. (CA 1985, s 236 as modified.)

Duties of auditors in preparing auditors' report   4.8

In preparing their report, the auditors must carry out whatever investigations are necessary in order to form an opinion as to whether (i) proper accounting records have been maintained by the LLP, and (ii) proper and adequate returns have been received from branches not visited by them, and (iii) the LLP's accounts are in agreement with those records and returns. If the auditors are of opinion that any of (i) to (iii) do not apply, this fact must be stated in their report, giving such details of the omissions or inconsistencies as are appropriate in the circumstances (CA 1985, ss 237(1) and (2) as modified).

Publication and delivery of accounts   4.9

Within one month of the LLP's accounts being signed in accordance with CA 1985, s 233 as modified (see **4.6** above), and in any event not later than 10 months after the end of the relevant accounting reference period (see **4.3** above), a copy of those accounts (together with a copy of the auditors' report – see **4.7** above) must be sent to every member of the LLP and every holder of the LLP's debentures. ('Sending' also includes (i) sending the documents to the member electronically at an address notified by him to the LLP, or (ii) by agreement with the member, publishing them on a specified web site.) Non-compliance with these requirements is an offence. (CA 1985, s 238 as modified.) (Note that members and debenture holders also have a separate right to be sent copies of the LLP's last accounts and auditors' report – CA 1985, s 239 as modified.)

In addition, the designated members of the LLP must send a copy of the accounts (again accompanied by the auditors' report) to the Registrar by the end of 'the period allowed for the delivering the accounts and the auditors' report' (CA 1985, s 242(1) as modified). This period is stipulated as 10 months after the end of the relevant accounting reference period (CA 1985, s 244(1) as modified), subject to the following exceptions.

- If the accounting reference period is the LLP's first and is a period of greater than 12 months, the period allowed is 10 months from the first anniversary of the incorporation of the LLP or 3 months from the end of the accounting reference period, whichever expires last (CA 1985, s 244(2) as modified).
- If the LLP trades outside the UK, Channel Islands or the Isle of Man the designated members may apply for an extension of 3 months to the period using Form LLP244 (CA 1985, s 244(3) as modified).
- If the LLP's accounting reference date has been changed by notice under CA 1985, s 225 as modified (see **4.3** above), resulting in a shorter period, the period allowed for delivery of the accounts is the normal 10-month period referred to above, or 3 months from the date of the notice, whichever occurs last (CA 1985, s 244(4) as modified).
- Under CA 1985, s 244(5) (as modified), the Secretary of State may grant an extension to the period for delivery of the accounts if there is sufficient cause. Any application must be made before the expiry of the period for delivery of the accounts. The application is made in writing, there being no statutory form.

If accounts are delivered to the Registrar outside the period allowed for delivery in accordance with the provisions of CA 1985, s 244 (as modified), the designated members are each guilty of an offence (subject to a statutory defence that the person charged took reasonable steps to secure compliance), and they can also be made liable by court order to make good the default within 14 days (CA 1985, s 242(2)-(5) as modified). In addition, the LLP itself is subject to a late filing penalty calculated as follows (CA 1985, s 242A as modified):

	Amount of penalty
Not more than 3 months late	£100
More than 3 and not more than 6 months late	£250
More than 6 and not more than 12 months late	£500
More than 12 months late	£1,000

Small and medium-sized LLPs   4.10

LLPs falling within the definitions of either small or medium-sized may deliver abbreviated accounts to the Registrar of Companies (see **4.12** below). In addition, small LLPs are entitled to certain exemptions in preparing their accounts (see **4.12** below). Also, certain (but not all) small LLPs may be exempt from the requirement to prepare audited accounts in accordance with CA 1985, s 249A as modified (see **4.14** below).

The provisions relating to the qualification of an LLP as small or medium-sized are contained in CA 1985, s 247 (as modified). However, note that LLPs do not qualify as small or medium-sized if at any time during the financial year they were:

- authorised under the Financial Services Act 1986;
- an LLP which is a member of a group containing:
  - a public company,
  - a corporate body that can offer its shares or debentures to the public,
  - an authorised institution under the Banking Act 1987, an insurance company subject to the Insurance Companies Act 1982 or a company authorised under the Financial Services Act 1986.

(CA 1985, s 247A as modified).

A small LLP is one which satisfies any two of the following conditions (CA 1985, s 247(3) as modified):

- turnover must not exceed £2,800,000;
- balance sheet total must not exceed £1,400,000;
- average number of employees must not exceed 50.

A medium-sized LLP is one which satisfies any two of the following conditions (CA 1985, s 247(3) as modified):

- turnover must not exceed £11,200,000;
- balance sheet total must not exceed £5,600,000;
- average number of employees must not exceed 250.

If an LLP qualifies as small or medium-sized in one financial year but not in the next, it may still file abbreviated accounts in that second year, unless disqualified under CA 1985, s 247A (as modified). It will not be able to file abbreviated accounts in the third year unless it qualifies in that year as either small or medium-sized.

Small and medium-sized groups 4.11

A parent LLP need not prepare, or deliver, group accounts if the group qualifies as either small or medium-sized. It will so qualify if the aggregate figures for turnover, balance sheet total and average number of employees (i.e. those figures in respect of each member of the group, added together) qualify it as either small or medium-sized.

The qualifying criteria for small or medium-sized groups are slightly modified as compared with those for small or medium-sized LLPs shown above. In order to qualify, the group must satisfy any two of the following conditions.

For a small group (CA 1985, s 249(3) as modified):

* turnover must not exceed £2,800,000 (net) £3,360,000 (gross);
* balance sheet total must not exceed £1,400,000 (net) £1,680,000 (gross);
* average number of employees must not exceed 50.

For a medium-sized group (CA 1985, s 249(3) as modified):

* turnover must not exceed £11,200,000 (net) £13,440,000 (gross);
* balance sheet total must not exceed £5,600,000 (net) £6,720,000 (gross);
* average number of employees must not exceed 250.

The reference to net means those aggregate figures for turnover and balance sheet total with the set offs and other adjustments made in accordance with CA 1985, Sch 4A (as modified). The reference to gross turnover or balance sheet total means those aggregate figures prior to any set off or other adjustment. The group accounts must satisfy the appropriate conditions on either a net or gross basis, but cannot do so by using one net figure and one gross figure (CA 1985, s 249(4) as modified).

Exemptions for accounts filing and preparation 4.12

Small LLPs

An LLP that qualifies as a small LLP may file abbreviated accounts consisting of the following.

- An abbreviated version of the balance sheet (in one of the formats set out in LLPR Sch 1 Sch 8A) together with abbreviated notes (no profit and loss account need be filed), and a statement immediately above the signature(s) of the designated member(s) that he has relied upon the exemptions available to the LLP as a small LLP (CA 1985, s 246 as modified).
- A special auditors' report stating that the requirements for qualifying as a small LLP have been met (CA 1985, s 247B as modified). A copy of this statement must be included in the full accounts issued to members.

In addition to these exemptions, small LLPs and small groups may take advantage of exemptions relating to the full accounts that are submitted to their members. The exemptions modify and omit some details from the prescribed formats for the balance sheet and notes to the accounts; the form and content of accounts prepared by small companies, giving effect to these exemptions, are set out in CA 1985, Sch 8 (as modified).

Medium-sized LLPs   4.13

An LLP that qualifies as a medium-sized LLP may file abbreviated accounts consisting of the following.

- A balance sheet together with notes (no exemptions are available for medium-sized LLPs in this respect, unlike small LLPs), with a statement immediately above the signature(s) of the designated member(s) that he has relied upon the exemptions available to the LLP as a medium-sized LLP (CA 1985, s 246A(4) as modified).
- A profit and loss account which can be abbreviated and does not need to disclose turnover (CA 1985, s 246A(3) as modified).
- A special auditors' report stating that the requirements for qualifying as medium-sized have been met (CA 1985, s 247B as modified). A copy of this statement must be included in the full accounts issued to members.

In addition, a medium-sized LLP's full accounts need not state whether the accounts have been prepared in accordance with accounting standards (CA 1985, s 246A(2) as modified).

Audit exemption   4.14

Except as set out below, small LLPs with a turnover of £1,000,000 or less are exempt from the obligation to have their accounts audited (CA 1985, s 249A as modified) (and from the obligation to appoint auditors (CA 1985, s 388A as modified – see **4.20** below).

Not every LLP automatically qualifies to take advantage of the exemption from audit under CA 1985, s 249A as modified (referred to below as 'the audit exemption'). The following conditions must be observed:

- the LLP must not be in a category specified in CA 1985, s 249B(1) (as modified); and
- the LLP must not have been a parent LLP or subsidiary undertaking at any time during the financial year (but see below).

Small groups consisting only of LLPs or private companies may still qualify for audit exemption if the following conditions can be satisfied:

- aggregate turnover for the year does not exceed £1,000,000 net (£1,200,000 gross before deduction of intra group set-offs required by CA 1985, Sch 4A); and
- aggregate balance sheet total for the year does not exceed £1.4m net (£1.68m gross before deduction of intra group set-offs required by CA 1985, Sch 4A).

The group must qualify as a small group in accordance with CA 1985, s 249 as modified (see **4.11** above) and must not be, or have been during the year, an ineligible group as set out in CA 1985, s 248(2) (as modified).

If a group satisfied the conditions in the previous year but not in the current year, it will continue to be treated as a small group in the current year. However, for any subsequent year, the group will only re-qualify as a small group when the conditions can be met in full once more.

A group is ineligible under CA 1985, s 248(2) (as modified) if any of the group companies or LLPs is:

- a public company or a body corporate which is entitled to offer its shares or debentures to the public; or
- a banking or insurance company; or
- an authorised body under the FSA 1986.

For the above purpose, the wide accounting definition of a group, contained in CA 1985, s 258 and Sch 10A as modified (see **4.5** above) applies.

Where the members of the LLP have taken advantage of the audit exemption, CA 1985, ss 238 and 239 as modified (see **4.9** above) apply with the omission of references to the auditors' report, and no auditors' report need be delivered to the Registrar (CA 1985, s 249E as modified).

Audit exemption for dormant subsidiaries   4.15

CA 1985, s 249B(1A) (as modified) permits an LLP, which would otherwise not be entitled to the audit exemption because it was a subsidiary undertaking for any period in that year, to claim that exemption provided it was dormant throughout that period (For the meaning of 'dormant', see **4.18** below.)

Audit exemption for dormant LLPs   4.16

Under CA 1985, s 249A(6A) (as modified), an LLP which has been dormant (see **4.18** below) since incorporation, or dormant since the end of the previous financial year, is nevertheless entitled to the audit exemption.

Delivery and publication of unaudited accounts   4.17

A qualifying LLP which prepares unaudited accounts must, in the normal manner (see **4.9** above), file a copy of those accounts with the Registrar of Companies (which can be abbreviated if appropriate) and must also circulate full unaudited accounts to its members. The LLP will not be entitled to the audit exemption unless, immediately above the signature(s) of the designated member(s) on the balance sheet, there is a statement by the members (CA 1985, s 249B(4)(5) as modified) that:

- for the year in question, the LLP is eligible to prepare unaudited accounts and qualifies for audit exemption; and
- they acknowledge their responsibilities to maintain proper accounting records and to prepare accounts which give a true and fair view of the LLP's position and have been prepared in accordance with the provisions of CA 1985, Part VII (as modified).

Dormant LLPs   4.18

An LLP is 'dormant' during any period in which it has had no significant accounting transaction (CA 1985, s 249AA(4) as modified). This is defined as a transaction which is required to be entered in the LLP's accounting records (see **4.2** above), except a transaction which consists of paying a penalty for failure to deliver accounts, or paying a fee to the Registrar on a change of name or for the registration of an annual return (CA 1985, s 249AA(5)(7) as modified).

An LLP is entitled to audit exemption (see **4.14** above) and is exempt from the obligation to appoint auditors (see **4.20** below) in respect of a financial year if it has been dormant since its formation. It is also entitled to those exemptions if it has been dormant since the end of its previous financial year and it is entitled to prepare its individual accounts for the financial year in question as a small LLP (see **4.12** above) (or would be so entitled but for being a member of an ineligible group at any time during that financial year) (CA 1985, s 249AA(2) as modified).

However, an LLP which at any time during the financial year in question was an authorised person under the FSA 1986 is not entitled to those exemptions even if it is a dormant LLP (CA 1985, s 249AA(3) as modified).

The grant of the exemption does not relieve the LLP of its obligation to send a copy of its accounts to its members but if it is a small LLP it is entitled to the exemptions available to small LLPs (see **4.12** above).

If the LLP ceases to be dormant and, therefore, no longer eligible for the exemption from audit under section 249AA, the obligation to appoint auditors applies again immediately unless the LLP is eligible for audit exemption under section 249A. The designated members must make the necessary appointment but, if they do not do so, the appointment may be made by the members (see **4.20** below).

Where a dormant LLP has acted as an agent for another person or corporate body during the financial year, this fact must be stated in the accounts.

Revisions 4.19

The members of an LLP are permitted to prepare and issue revised accounts to replace accounts which they believe are defective. If the original accounts have been filed with the Registrar of Companies, then the only modifications permitted are in respect of those matters within the accounts that do not comply with the requirements of the Act and any consequential amendments. (CA 1985, s 245 as modified.) Provision has been made by regulations in relation to revised accounts, which apply to LLPs by virtue of LLPR 2001, Sch 6, Part I (see Companies (Revision of Defective Accounts and Report) Regulations 1990 (SI 1990 No 2570), as amended).

Where an LLP's accounts have been filed with the Registrar of Companies, and it appears to the Secretary of State that the accounts may not comply with the provisions of the Act, he may issue a notice giving the members a period of not less that one month in which to give an explanation of the accounts or to prepare revised accounts (CA 1985, s 245A as modified). If the members do not give a satisfactory explanation or do not prepare revised accounts the Secretary of State may make an application to the court for an order directing the preparation of revised accounts (CA 1985, s 245B as modified).

Appointment of auditors   4.20

The LLP is under a duty to appoint auditors (CA 1985, s 384 as modified), unless it is exempt from doing so by virtue of CA 1985, s 388A as modified (see **4.22** below). The appointment is to be made by the designated members, who must appoint auditors in respect of the first financial year before the end of that financial year. The auditor holds office until the expiration of two months following the approval of the accounts for that financial year. (CA 1985, s 385(3) as modified). For subsequent financial years, the designated members must appoint or re-appoint auditors no later than two months following the approval of the accounts for the previous financial year. (CA 1985, s 385(2) as modified). If the designated members fail to appoint auditors, the members may do so in a meeting of the LLP convened for the purpose (CA 1985, s 385(4) as modified).

The designated members may also appoint an auditor to fill a casual vacancy caused by the resignation or death of the previous auditor (CA 1985, s 388 as modified).

If the LLP does not appoint or re-appoint an auditor before the end of the time for appointing auditors, the LLP must give notice of that fact to the Secretary of State within seven days. The Secretary of State may then appoint an auditor pursuant to CA 1985, s 387 (as modified) to fill the vacancy.

The provisions of Part II of the Companies Act 1989 (eligibility for appointment as company auditor – see also **4.21** below) have been applied to LLPs as if they were incorporated under the Companies Act 1985 (CA 1985, s 384(5)). Accordingly, unless there is a clear statement to the contrary, the appointment of a partnership as auditor is an appointment of the partnership and not the individual partners (CA 1989, s 26(2)). Where the partnership ceases, the appointment is treated as having been extended to:

- any person who succeeds to that partnership having previously carried it on in that partnership and is an eligible person (see **4.21** below); and
- any partnership which is eligible and succeeds the partnership that has ceased.

A partnership is treated as succeeding another partnership only if the partners are substantially the same, or if the new partnership takes over substantially the whole of the business of the previous partnership.

A partnership established under the laws of England and Wales or Northern Ireland (or any other country where partnerships do not constitute a legal person) ceases whenever there is a change not only on a dissolution but also a change in partners. Partnerships established under the law of Scotland do constitute a legal person and do not cease on a change of partners.

Eligibility   4.21

A person or firm may only be appointed as an auditor if, were the LLP a limited company registered under the Companies Act 1985, he would be eligible for appointment under Part II of the Companies Act 1989 (CA 1985, s 384(4) as modified). Section 25(1) of CA 1989 provides that in order to be so eligible, he must:

- be a member of a recognised supervisory body; or
- be eligible for appointment under the rules of that body. A firm may be a partnership or a corporate body.

A person is prohibited by CA 1989, s 27(1) as modified (applied by CA 1985, s 384(5) as modified) from acting as auditor to any LLP of which he:

- is a member or employee;
- is a partner or employee of such a person or a member of a partnership of which that person is a partner.

However, where an auditor is deemed to be an officer or employee of the LLP by virtue of any provision of the Act, the auditor is not prohibited from acting as auditor by virtue of such provision.

Exemption from obligation to appoint auditors   4.22

An LLP that is exempt from audit (see **4.14** above) is also exempt from the obligation to appoint auditors (CA 1985, s 388A as modified). An LLP may lose that exemption (for example, if its business grows or if it becomes part of an ineligible group as set out in CA 1985, s 248(2) as modified (see **4.14** above) or if it ceases to be dormant and is not otherwise exempt). In such a situation, the designated members may appoint auditors, and the auditors will hold office until the expiration of two months following approval of the accounts for the financial year in respect of which they were appointed. (CA 1985, s 388A(3) as modified). If, in these circumstances, the designated members fail to exercise their power to appoint auditors, the members of the LLP may do so in a meeting convened for the purpose (CA 1985, s 388A(5) as modified).

Rights of auditors   4.23

The auditors of the LLP enjoy certain statutory rights in connection with the exercise of their duty. These include the following.

- The auditors have a right of access at all time to the LLP's books, accounts and vouchers and to require from the LLP's officers such information and explanations as the auditor thinks necessary for the performance of their duties (CA 1985, s 389A(1) as modified).
- It is the duty of subsidiary undertakings incorporated in Great Britain and their auditors to give the auditors of the parent LLP such information and explanations as those auditors may reasonably require for the purposes of their duties as auditors of the parent (CA 1985, s 389A(3) as modified).
- The auditors are entitled to attend any meetings of the LLP, and to receive all notices and other communications relating to any meeting, where the meeting or any part of it concerns them as auditors. They may also speak on any business of the meeting which concerns them as auditors (CA 1985, s 390(1) as modified).
- A parent LLP, having a subsidiary undertaking which is not a body incorporated in Great Britain shall, if its auditors require, take all such steps as are reasonably open to it to obtain from the subsidiary

such information and explanations as its auditors may reasonably require (CA 1985, s 389A(4) as modified).

- It is an offence (punishable by fine and/or imprisonment) for an officer of the LLP, in conveying information and explanations required by the LLP's auditors, to make a statement which he knows is misleading, false or deceptive in a material particular (CA 1985, s 389A(2) as modified).

Remuneration 4.24

Remuneration of auditors appointed by the LLP shall be fixed by the designated members or in such other manner as the members of the LLP may choose (CA 1985, s 390A(1) as modified).

The amount of the auditors' remuneration in their capacity as auditors including any expenses must be disclosed as a note to the accounts (CA 1985, s 390A(3) as modified). Remuneration includes the cash value of any benefits in kind given to the auditors (CA 1985, s 390A(5) as modified). In addition to remuneration for audit services companies are required to disclose amounts paid to auditors and their associates for non-audit services such as financial or taxation services (CA 1985, s 390B as modified; Companies Act 1985 (Disclosure of Remuneration for Non-Audit Work) Regulations 1991 (SI 1991 No 2128)). LLPs qualifying as small LLPs are exempt from the obligation to disclose auditors' remuneration (CA 1985, s 246(6) as modified) and LLPs qualifying as either small or medium-sized are exempt from the obligation to disclose non-audit remuneration (SI 1991 No 2128, reg 4).

Auditors ceasing to hold office 4.25

Where for any reason an auditor ceases to hold office, he must send to the LLP at its registered office a statement of any circumstances connected with his ceasing to hold office which he considers should be brought to the attention of the members or creditors of the LLP or, alternatively, a statement that there are no such circumstances to be reported to them (CA 1985, s 394(1) as modified). In the case of a resigning auditor (see **4.27** below), the statement must be deposited with the notice of resignation. If the auditor is not seeking reappointment, the statement should be delivered not less than 14 days before the end of the period allowed for next appointing auditors. In any other circumstances, the statement should be deposited not later than the end of 14 days beginning with the date on which the auditor ceases to hold office (CA 1985, s 394(2) as modified).

If the statement contains details of circumstances that the auditor considers should be brought to the attention of the members or creditors, the LLP must, within 14 days of it being deposited, send copies of the statement to those persons entitled to receive copies of the audited accounts pursuant to CA 1985, s 238 as modified (see **4.9** above). However, the LLP may instead apply to the court if the LLP believes the statement is defamatory or seeking needless publicity (CA 1985, s 394(3) as modified).

If application is made to the court, the LLP must notify the auditor of the application (CA 1985, s 394(4) as modified). If the court upholds the LLP's contentions, it may direct that copies of the statement need not be sent out, and may order costs against the auditor in full or in part. Within 14 days of the judgement, the LLP must send a statement setting out the effect of the court's decision to those persons entitled to receive copies of the audited accounts (CA 1985, s 394(6) as modified). If the court upholds the auditors' statement, the LLP must within 14 days of the court's decision (i) issue the statement to those persons entitled to receive copies of the accounts, and (ii) notify the auditor of the decision (CA 1985, s 394(3)(b) as modified).

Notification to Companies House   4.26

Unless the auditor receives notification within 21 days of depositing the statement that an application is to be made by the LLP to the court pursuant to CA 1985, s 394(3)(b) as modified (see **4.25** above), he must send to the Registrar a copy of his statement within a further seven days. If an application to the court is made and rejected, the auditor must send to the Registrar a copy of his statement within seven days of being notified of the court's decision by the LLP.

Resignation of auditors   4.27

Under CA 1985, s 392 (as modified) an auditor may resign his office by depositing a notice in writing to the LLP at its registered office. In doing so, he must also deposit with the LLP the statement required by CA 1985, s 394 as modified (see **4.25** above) and the notice of resignation will not be effective unless it is accompanied by such a statement. In practice, where the LLP's registered office is not also its head office, it may be desirable to send a copy of the resignation letter and statement to both the registered office address and the head office address.

An effective notice of resignation brings the auditor's term of office to an end on the date on which the notice is deposited, or on such later date as is specified in the notice (CA 1985, s 392(2) as modified). Within 14 days of the deposit of the notice of resignation, a copy must be sent to the Registrar of Companies by the LLP (CA 1985, s 392(3) as modified).

CA 1985, s 392A (as modified) confers rights on a resigning auditor, whose notice of resignation is accompanied by a statement of circumstances which he considers should be brought to the attention of members and creditors of the LLP. He may lodge, with his notice of resignation, a requisition calling on the designated members to convene a meeting of the LLP to consider his explanation of the circumstances connected with his resignation. Within 21 days of the deposit of the requisition, the designated members must convene a meeting, to be held on a date not more than 28 days from the date of convening the meeting. In addition, the auditor may request that a statement (not exceeding a reasonable length) of the circumstances connected with his resignation must be sent to the members of the LLP with the notice of the meeting; if it is received too late for this to be done, the auditor may require that the statement be read out at the meeting. As with the statement under CA 1985, s 394 as modified (see **4.25** above) the statement need not be sent (or read out at the meeting) if on the application of the LLP, the court is of the opinion that the provisions of section 392A are being used by the auditor to secure needless publicity for defamatory matter.

Notwithstanding his resignation, the auditor is entitled to receive notice and to attend and speak at the meeting convened on his requisition (CA 1985, s 392A(8) as modified).

Removal or non-re-appointment of auditors   4.28

An auditor can be replaced by a new auditor pursuant to a decision of the designated members not to re-appoint him and to appoint auditor in his place (CA 1985, s 391 as modified).

Notice must be given to the Registrar of Companies within 14 days on the prescribed form (LLP391 – see **Appendix 3**). The new auditor would usually be appointed by the designated members at the same meeting although it would be in order for them to fill the casual vacancy at some later date.

Rights of auditors who are removed or not re-appointed 4.29

Where the designated members propose to remove or not re-appoint an auditor, seven days' prior notice must be sent forthwith by the designated members to the person proposed to be removed as auditor (CA 1985, s 391A(1) as modified).

The auditor proposed to be removed or not re-appointed may make representations in writing to the LLP on the proposal and may ask the LLP to circulate that representation to the members. The LLP must comply with that request within 21 days of receipt (CA 1985, s 391A(3)(4) as modified).

If a copy of the representations is not sent out, the LLP and any designated member in default commits an offence (CA 1985, s 391A(5) as modified). However, the representations need not be sent out if on the application of either the LLP or any other person claiming to be aggrieved, the court is satisfied that the rights conferred on the auditor proposed to be removed or not re-appointed are being abused to secure needless publicity of defamatory matter (CA 1985, s 391A(5)(6) as modified).

The auditor proposed to be removed or not re-appointed is also entitled to receive notice of, and to attend and speak at any meeting of the LLP's members at which his term of office would otherwise have expired, or at which it is proposed to fill the vacancy caused by his removal, on any matters concerning him as a former auditor (CA 1985, s 391(4) as modified).

5 – Taxation

Introduction 5.1

Sections 10 to 13 of the Act set out the provisions relating to the taxation of LLPs.

Following the enactment of the Act, the Inland Revenue set out guidance on the taxation of LLPs in its December 2000 Tax Bulletin. It confirmed this guidance in an announcement on 8 March 2001, in which it stated that LLPs will, in general, be treated for tax purposes as a partnership. The announcement also confirmed that legislation will be brought forward to ensure that no tax loss is incurred when the new structure is used as an alternative to existing business structures.

Thus, unlike other corporate bodies, the profits or gains made by an LLP will not be subject to corporation tax assessed on the LLP. Provided the LLP carries on the business of a trade or profession, it is transparent for tax purposes and each member will be assessed on his shares of any income or gain of the LLP such that individual members will be assessed to tax in accordance with section 111 of the Income and Corporation Taxes Act 1988 (ICTA 1988) and corporate members will be liable to corporation tax in accordance with section 114 of ICTA 1988.

LLPs that do not carry on business of a trade or profession such as an investment company will be subject to corporation tax.

Income and capital gains tax 5.2

Section 10 of LLPA 2000 inserts new sections 118ZA to 118ZD in the Income and Corporation Taxes Act 1988 (ICTA 1988) and new sections 59A and 156A in the Taxation of Chargeable Gains Act 1992 (TCGA 1992). The effect of these is to treat an LLP as if it were a partnership for all purposes of those two Acts. These new sections are reproduced in full below.

The existing rules for calculating the taxable profit of a professional business set out in Tax Bulletin No 38 will be applied to the computation of the Case II schedule D profit of an LLP for the purposes of establishing the income tax liability of the members.

New sections 118ZC-118ZD set out the application of loss relief to an LLP which carries business of a trade to the members of an LLP in respect of undrawn profits. The availability of undrawn profit for loss relief will depend upon provisions in the LLP agreement providing that undrawn profits stands as part of a member's capital account. An LLP that carries on business of a profession will be entitled to loss relief under the existing loss relief provisions.

Additions to ICTA 1988   **5.3**

'Limited liability partnerships

118ZA Treatment of limited liability partnerships
For the purposes of the Tax Acts, a trade, profession or business carried on by a limited liability partnership with a view to profit shall be treated as carried on in partnership by its members (and not by the limited liability partnership as such); and, accordingly, the property of the limited liability partnership shall be treated for those purposes as partnership property.

118ZB Restriction on relief
Sections 117 and 118 have effect in relation to a member of a limited liability partnership as in relation to a limited partner, but subject to sections 118ZC and 118ZD.

118ZC Member's contribution to trade
(1) Subsection (3) of section 117 does not have effect in relation to a member of a limited liability partnership.
(2) But, for the purposes of that section and section 118, such a member's contribution to a trade at any time ("the relevant time") is the greater of –
    (a) the amount subscribed by him, and
    (b) the amount of his liability on a winding up.
(3) The amount subscribed by a member of a limited liability partnership is the amount which he has contributed to the limited liability partnership as capital, less so much of that amount (if any) as –
    (a) he has previously, directly or indirectly, drawn out or received back,
    (b) he so draws out or receives back during the period of five years beginning with the relevant time,
    (c) he is or may be entitled so to draw out or receive back at any time when he is a member of the limited liability partnership, or
    (d) he is or may be entitled to require another person to reimburse to him.

(4)   The amount of the liability of a member of a limited liability partnership on a winding up is the amount which –
  (a)   he is liable to contribute to the assets of the limited liability partnership in the event of its being wound up, and
  (b)   he remains liable so to contribute for the period of at least five years beginning with the relevant time (or until it is wound up, if that happens before the end of that period).

118ZD Carry forward of unrelieved losses
(1)   Where amounts relating to a trade carried on by a member of a limited liability partnership are, in any one or more chargeable periods, prevented from being given or allowed by section 117 or 118 as it applies otherwise than by virtue of this section (his "total unrelieved loss"), subsection (2) applies in each subsequent chargeable period in which –
  (a)   he carries on the trade as a member of the limited liability partnership, and
  (b)   any of his total unrelieved loss remains outstanding.
(2)   Sections 380, 381, 393A(1) and 403 (and sections 117 and 118 as they apply in relation to those sections) shall have effect in the subsequent chargeable period as if –
  (a)   any loss sustained or incurred by the member in the trade in that chargeable period were increased by an amount equal to so much of his total unrelieved loss as remains outstanding in that period, or
  (b)   (if no loss is so sustained or incurred) a loss of that amount were so sustained or incurred.
(3)   To ascertain whether any (and, if so, how much) of a member's total unrelieved loss remains outstanding in the subsequent chargeable period, deduct from the amount of his total unrelieved loss the aggregate of –
  (a)   any relief given under any provision of the Tax Acts (otherwise than as a result of subsection (2)) in respect of his total unrelieved loss in that or any previous chargeable period, and
  (b)   any amount given or allowed in respect of his total unrelieved loss as a result of subsection (2) in any previous chargeable period (or which would have been so given or allowed had a claim been made).'

Additions to TCGA 1992   **5.4**

'59A Limited liability partnerships
(1)   Where a limited liability partnership carries on a trade or business with a view to profit –
  (a)   assets held by the limited liability partnership shall be treated for the purposes of tax in respect of chargeable gains as held by its members as partners, and

(b) any dealings by the limited liability partnership shall be treated for those purposes as dealings by its members in partnership (and not by the limited liability partnership as such),

and tax in respect of chargeable gains accruing to the members of the limited liability partnership on the disposal of any of its assets shall be assessed and charged on them separately.

(2) Where subsection (1) ceases to apply in relation to a limited liability partnership with the effect that tax is assessed and charged –

(a) on the limited liability partnership (as a company) in respect of chargeable gains accruing on the disposal of any of its assets, and

(b) on the members in respect of chargeable gains accruing on the disposal of any of their capital interests in the limited liability partnership,

it shall be assessed and charged on the limited liability partnership as if subsection (1) had never applied in relation to it.

(3) Neither the commencement of the application of subsection (1) nor the cessation of its application in relation to a limited liability partnership is to be taken as giving rise to the disposal of any assets by it or any of its members.

156A Cessation of trade by limited liability partnership

(1) Where, immediately before the time of cessation of trade, a member of a limited liability partnership holds an asset, or an interest in an asset, acquired by him for a consideration treated as reduced under section 152 or 153, he shall be treated as if a chargeable gain equal to the amount of the reduction accrued to him immediately before that time.

(2) Where, as a result of section 154(2), a chargeable gain on the disposal of an asset, or an interest in an asset, by a member of a limited liability partnership has not accrued before the time of cessation of trade, the member shall be treated as if the chargeable gain accrued immediately before that time.

(3) In this section "the time of cessation of trade", in relation to a limited liability partnership, means the time when section 59A(1) ceases to apply in relation to the limited liability partnership.'

Inheritance tax   5.5

Section 11 of LLPA 2000 inserts a new section 267A in the Inheritance Tax Act 1984, set out at **5.6** below, the effect of which is to treat an LLP as if it were a partnership for all purposes relating to inheritance tax.

The transfer is deemed to be a transfer made by the members of the LLP and not the LLP itself. Accordingly liability under section 94 of the Inheritance Tax Act 1984 cannot arise even in circumstances where the LLP would otherwise be a close company.

Addition to Inheritance Tax Act 1984   5.6

'267A Limited liability partnerships

For the purposes of this Act and any other enactments relating to inheritance tax –

(a) property to which a limited liability partnership is entitled, or which it occupies or uses, shall be treated as property to which its members are entitled, or which they occupy or use, as partners,

(b) any business carried on by a limited liability partnership shall be treated as carried on in partnership by its members,

(c) incorporation, change in membership or dissolution of a limited liability partnership shall be treated as formation, alteration or dissolution of a partnership, and

(d) any transfer of value made by or to a limited liability partnership shall be treated as made by or to its members in partnership (and not by or to the limited liability partnership as such).'

Transfer of business   5.7

Where an existing partnership transfers its business to an LLP this transfer will not constitute a disposal by the partners of their interest in the partnership for the purposes of capital gains tax. Additionally the transfer of assets to an LLP does not affect the availability of indexation allowance, the period of ownership for retirement relief or the holding period for taper relief.

Stamp duty   5.8

Section 12 of the Act states that stamp duty will not be chargeable on an instrument that transfers property from a person to an LLP, in connection with its incorporation, within one year of the date of incorporation if:

- that person is a partner in a partnership comprised of all the members or proposed members of the LLP (and no-one else); or
- that person holds the property being transferred as nominee or bare trustee for one or more partners in the partnership; and
- the members of the LLP are entitled to the same proportion of that property as they were when partners of the partnership; or
- no difference in that proportion has arisen out of a scheme or arrangement of which the main purpose or one of the main purposes is avoidance of liability to any duty or tax.

Although an instrument transferring property which qualifies for exemption from stamp duty under section 12 of the Act is not liable to stamp duty, it must be stamped by the Inland Revenue stamp office with a stamp denoting that it is not chargeable.

Although transfer of property to a newly incorporated LLP at the same time as either the admission of new partners and or retirement of partners would be liable to stamp duty, the Inland Revenue have confirmed that relief will remain available if the change in partners takes place the instant before or after incorporation. The stamp office will need to review the documentation relating to the transfer and incorporation to satisfy themselves that relief may be given.

National insurance   5.9

Section 13 of LLPA 2000 inserts a new subsection 3A into section 15 of both the Social Security Contributions and Benefits Act 1992 and the Social Security Contributions and Benefits (Northern Ireland) Act 1992 (Class 4 contributions) as follows:

> '(3A) Where income tax is (or would be) charged on a member of a limited liability partnership in respect of profits or gains arising from the carrying on of a trade or profession by the limited liability partnership, Class 4 contributions shall be payable by him if they would be payable were the trade or profession carried on in partnership by the members.'

The effect of the new subsection is to make any profit or gain arising out of the business of an LLP attributable to any particular member liable to Class 4 national insurance contributions.

6 – Charges

Issue of debentures 6.1

The legislation governing the issue of debentures and the creation of charges by an LLP are contained in CA 1985, ss 190–196 and ss 395– 423 respectively, as modified. The requirements relating to registration of charges is based upon the provisions of the Companies Act 1985, which were to have been radically amended by new provisions introduced by the Companies Act 1989 (sections 92–104) as new sections 395–420. These provisions have not been brought into effect and, as time passes, it seems unlikely that they will. If the Companies Act provisions are changed, this will lead to a consequential change to the provisions relating to the registration of charges for an LLP.

The members have power to borrow money on behalf of the LLP under their general powers to manage the business of the LLP, subject to the provisions of the Act and the partnership agreement, if any.

If the partnership agreement restricts the members' borrowing powers it must be carefully followed, since if they were to borrow in excess of the limit specified they might find themselves personally liable. The position of third parties acting in good faith would not, however, be affected by any restriction imposing a limit on the members' powers to borrow on behalf of the LLP.

The ways in which the LLP may borrow money may be in the form of debentures of various types, unsecured loan stocks and convertible loan stocks, apart from borrowing from a bank by way of overdraft for the LLP's day-to-day business.

Types of debenture 6.2

CA 1985, s 744 as modified defines a 'debenture' as including debenture stock, bonds and any other securities of the LLP, whether constituting a charge on the assets of the LLP or not. In effect a debenture is a document which creates a debt or acknowledges a debt and it may, therefore, be an unsecured promise to pay, or a promise to pay secured by a mortgage or charge over the property of the LLP.

Although it would be possible to issue debentures in bearer form, it is more common to issue a series of debentures in registered form, and the conditions relating to interest, redemption or security will be printed on the reverse of each debenture issued. Registered debentures may be transferable on stock transfer forms under the Stock Transfer Act 1963 and such transfers are exempt from stamp duty (with a few exceptions). When a debenture or one of a series of debentures is transferred, the name and address of the new holder are endorsed on the debenture itself by the LLP.

If the LLP keeps a register of debenture holders, the transfer should be recorded in the register, and if it creates a charge over the undertaking or any property of the LLP, an entry should be made in the LLP's register of charges (see **6.10** below) and the charge registered with the Registrar of Companies within 21 days (CA 1985, s 395 as modified) using form LLP397 (see **6.3** below).

Secured debentures 6.3

The security for a mortgage debenture may be either a *fixed charge* or a *floating charge* or a combination of the two. Fixed charges are equivalent to mortgages, and the LLP is restricted in dealing with the asset or assets charged, without the prior consent of the debenture holder or of the trustee for the debenture stock. The difference in the case of a floating charge is that this extends over the whole of the undertaking of the LLP and is not restricted to particular assets. This enables the LLP to deal with its assets in the ordinary course of its business. It is possible for a fixed charge to be given over an asset which is already the subject of a floating charge and this would then take priority over the floating charge, although it would be usual to expect the terms of issue of a debenture creating a floating charge to prohibit the LLP from doing this.

A floating charge crystallises and becomes a fixed charge if an event should happen which allows the debenture holders or the trustee to take possession of the security or to appoint a receiver. The circumstances in which this may happen will be specified in the debenture or the trust deed. Usually, of course, amongst the specified circumstances will be the non-payment of interest within a specified time from the due date, or if a resolution should be passed to wind up the LLP. Subject to the rights of preferential creditors, on the crystallisation of a floating charge the debenture holders have priority, to the extent of the security held, over the ordinary and other secured creditors. (In Scotland, a floating charge only crystallises on the commencement of a winding-up or the appointment of a receiver – see CA 1985, s 462, as modified by Sch 1 to the LLP (Scotland) Regulations 2001.) Notice of the appointment of a receiver or manager of an LLP's property must also be notified to the Registrar within seven days of the appointment (CA 1985, s 405 as modified) on form LLP 405(1) (see **Appendix 3**).

Particulars of a charge to secure any issue of debentures in Great Britain must be registered with the Registrar of Companies within 21 days of the creation of the charge (CA 1985, s 397(1) as modified) on form LLP 397. Further, the LLP must deliver to the Registrar particulars in the prescribed form of the date on which any debentures of the issue were taken up, and of the amount of the issue taken up, and to do so within 21 days after the date on which they were taken up (CA 1985, s 397 as modified).

Particulars of charges registered with the Registrar must be entered in the LLP's own register of charges which must be kept at its registered office (CA 1985, s 407 as modified) (see **6.10** below).

It is necessary to send to the Registrar with the particulars the original of the charge document (CA 1985, s 395(1) as modified) so he can check the particulars, and he may reject particulars which he considers to be unregistrable. It is obviously important to the debenture holders that the particulars of a charge created by an issue of debentures is registered with the Registrar of Companies, since a charge is void unless particulars are filed with the Registrar within 21 days of its creation (CA 1985, s 395(1) as modified). It is usual, therefore, for the trustee for the debenture holders to attend to the registration under the authority contained in CA 1985, s 399 (as modified), which provides that registration of a charge may be effected on the application of any person interested in it. However, in the absence of such application, that section also imposes a duty on the LLP itself to register the charge (see **6.7** below).

Where a charge has not been registered within the 21-day period, in certain circumstances the court may extend the time for registration or order the rectification of the register of charges kept by the Registrar – see **6.9** below.

Issue of debenture stock   6.4

A trust deed to secure the issue of debenture stock will usually cover the following matters.

- Details of the stock, terms of issue, payment of principal and interest, any conversion rights and stock certificates.
- The provisions constituting the charges of assets of the LLP in favour of the trustee(s), stipulating the events on the occurrence of which the security becomes enforceable.
- Trustees' powers to concur with the LLP in dealings with the charged assets.
- Covenants by the LLP in relation to its business and to the charged assets.
- The trustees' remuneration.
- Where a floating charge is constituted, a prohibition on the issue of any other security ranking ahead of the stock without the consent of the holder.
- Schedules to the trust deed containing the form of stock certificate, the detailed conditions of redemption in whole or in part by drawings or purchase and of any conversion rights, regulations with the regard to the register of debenture holders, provisions governing the transfer and transmission of the stock, and regulations governing meetings of holders of the stock.

The holder of debenture stock is entitled to be supplied with a copy of the trust deed at his request on payment of a fee. The register of debenture holders maintained by an LLP must be available for inspection by any holder (and any member of the LLP) without fee and by any other person on payment of the prescribed fee, currently £2.50 per hour or part thereof. (CA 1985, s 191 as modified; SI 1991 No 1998, applied to LLPs by LLPR 2001, Sch 6, Part I.)

Unsecured loan stock   6.5

Loan stock which is unsecured obviously carries a higher risk for investors and to compensate for this it is usual for such stocks to bear a higher rate of interest than would be appropriate if the stock were a secured debenture stock.

The trust deed constituting unsecured loan stock will usually cover the following matters.

- Details of the terms of issue, and payment of principal and interest attached to the stock.
- Restrictions on issuing further unsecured loan stock.
- Restrictions on further borrowing.
- Restrictions on disposal of the business or specified assets.

- Events in which the whole of the stock becomes immediately payable (e.g. default in payment of interest or ceasing to carry on business).
- The trustees' remuneration.
- Schedules will be attached to the trust deed containing the form of stock certificate, the detailed conditions for redemption in whole or in part by drawings or purchase, regulations regarding the register of holders of the stock, arrangements for transfer and transmission of the stock, and regulations governing meetings of holders of the stock.

Redemption of debentures   6.6

Although debentures may be reissued (CA 1985, s 194 as modified), this is unusual and in practice debentures and debenture stock are redeemable not later than a fixed future date.

The LLP should give notice of its intention to redeem the stock to every holder. The money for the redemption may come from a new issue of securities, out of profits, or out of a combination of the two.

Where debentures or debenture stock, secured by a registered charge over the LLP's property or any part of it, are redeemed or converted in whole or in part, a memorandum of satisfaction that the property ceases to be affected by the registered charge may be filed for registration with the Registrar of Companies in the prescribed form (LLP 403a – see **Appendix 3**) signed by or on behalf of the LLP and the chargee (CA 1985, s 403 as modified). Although this procedure is not obligatory under the section (which provides that such a memorandum *may* be delivered), it is, however, in the best interests of the LLP for charges to be deleted from the public register immediately they are satisfied in whole or in part. This is to avoid misleading any banks or other creditors, who would otherwise form an unduly adverse view of the LLP's credit. It will also be necessary to make the appropriate entries in the LLP's own register of charges (see **6.10** below).

Charges   6.7

As with debentures (see **6.3** above), it is the duty of an LLP to register with the Registrar of Companies details of any other charges it creates over its assets (CA 1985, s 399 as modified) on form LLP395 within 21 days of the date of creation. (CA 1985, s 395 as modified). Such charges would usually be created to secure bank borrowing and overdraft facilities but could be created to secure any other form of borrowing or indebtedness. Although it is the duty of the LLP to register details of the charge, this does not prevent any other interested party from registering the details in place of the LLP. In practice, the bank or other lender will usually undertake the registration process in order to ensure that the 21-day deadline is met. However, where this does not happen, breach of the LLP's duty to effect registration is punishable by a fine (and, for continued contravention, a daily default fine) on the LLP and every member of it who is in default.

Upon receipt of the particulars, the Registrar will note the details on the LLP's file at Companies House and issue a certificate of registration to the LLP.

Satisfaction or release of charge   6.8

Again as with debentures (see **6.6** above), a memorandum of satisfaction or release, given on the prescribed form (LLP403a), may be delivered to the Registrar of Companies once the debt for which any other category of registrable charge was given has been paid or satisfied, whether in whole or in part only.

Rectification of register of charges   6.9

On application of the LLP or some other interested party, the court has certain powers if it is satisfied that the omission to register a charge within 21 days, or the omission or mis-statement of any particular with respect to the charge or in a memorandum of satisfaction, was accidental, or due to inadvertence, or would not prejudice the rights of any creditors or the members of the LLP, or that on other grounds it is just and equitable to grant relief. In such circumstances, the court may order (on such terms and conditions as it considers expedient) that the time for registering a charge be extended or, as the case may be, that the omission or mis-statement be rectified. (CA 1985, s 404 as modified.)

LLP's register of charges   6.10

Every LLP is required to keep at its registered office a copy of every instrument creating or evidencing a charge, and a register of charges. The register must contain entries relating to all charges specifically affecting the LLP's property, and all floating charges on the LLP's undertaking or any of its property. In each case, the entry must contain a brief description of the property charged, the amount secured by the charge and the names of those entitled to the benefit of the charge. (CA 1985, ss 406, 407 as modified).

Copies of all instruments creating or evidencing a charge, together with the register of charges, must be open to inspection (for at least two hours in each day during business hours) by any creditor or member of the LLP without charge, or by any other person on payment of such fee (not exceeding 5p per inspection) as the LLP may prescribe (CA 1985, s 408 as modified).

7 – Insolvency

Winding up – introduction   7.1

Section 14 of the LLPA 2000 provides that regulations are to apply Parts I to IV, VI and VII of the Insolvency Act 1986 (IA 1986) to LLPs with such modifications as are appropriate. This is given effect by LLPR 2001, Reg 5. Reg 5(1), in addition to applying those Parts of the IA 1986 to LLPs, also applies to LLPs sections 386 to 444 of the IA 1986, referred to in that Act as the 'Third Group of Parts' (miscellaneous matters). Reg 5(2) sets out some general modifications to the IA 1986 provisions, while LLPR 2001, Sch 3 sets out specific modifications to a number of sections of the IA 1986. In this chapter, any references to modified sections of the IA 1986 are therefore references to that Act as modified by LLPR 2001, Reg 5(2) and (if applicable) Sch 3. The full text of the applicable IA 1986 provisions as modified by LLPR 2001, Reg 5(2) and Sch 3 is set out in **Appendix 2**.

In relation to winding up, the modifications are broadly limited to procedural amendments related to the holding of meetings of the members of the LLP to determine that the LLP be wound up. The significant modifications to the provisions are the introduction of a new section 214A and amendments to section 74 of the IA 1986, under which present and past members of a LLP might be liable to contribute to the assets of the LLP on a winding up.

Methods of winding up   7.2

There are three methods of winding up:

- members' voluntary winding up;
- creditors' voluntary winding up;
- winding up by the court.

A voluntary winding up of either type is deemed to commence at the time when the LLP determines that it be wound up voluntarily (IA 1986, s 86 as modified).

Members' voluntary winding up   7.3

This is a solvent winding up under which the designated members must make a statutory declaration that, having made full inquiry, they are of the opinion that the LLP will be able to pay its debts in full with interest at the official rate within a period not exceeding twelve months from commencement of the winding up (IA 1986, s 89 as modified). The statutory declaration must be made within the five weeks immediately preceding the determination by the LLP that it be wound up voluntarily. The declaration must embody a statement of the LLP's assets and liabilities as at the latest practicable date before the making of the declaration. If a designated member makes a declaration without reasonable grounds for his opinion that the LLP will be able to pay its debts (plus interest) within the specified period, he is liable to a fine or imprisonment or both. If the debts and interest are not paid within the specified period, the burden of proving reasonable grounds is on the designated member (IA 1986, s 89(4)(5) as modified).

The determination to wind up voluntarily is coupled with the appointment of a liquidator (IA 1986, s 91 as modified) who is required, should he form the opinion during the course of the winding up that the LLP will be unable to pay its liabilities in full within the stipulated time, to call a meeting of creditors within 28 days of forming that opinion, thereby converting the winding up into a creditors' voluntary winding up. (IA 1986, ss 95, 96 as modified).

Creditors' voluntary winding up   7.4

This may be appropriate where a declaration of solvency cannot be made, and the LLP is wound up as a creditors' voluntary winding up. A meeting of the creditors must be called and held within 14 days of the determination by the LLP that it be wound up voluntarily (IA 1986, s 98 as modified).

Winding up by the court   7.5

An LLP may be wound up by the court in the following circumstances.

- The LLP determines that it be wound up by the court.
- The LLP is unable to pay its debts. (An LLP is deemed unable to pay its debts where:

○ in England and Wales, execution or other process issued on a judgment, decree or other court order in favour of a creditor is returned unsatisfied either in whole or in part (there are equivalent provisions relating to Scotland and Northern Ireland), or

○ a creditor (whether a judgment creditor or otherwise) petitions the court, where an amount in excess of £750 has not been paid within three weeks of a written demand for payment having been served on the LLP at its registered office in the prescribed form, or

○ the court is satisfied that the value of the LLP's assets is less than the amount of its liabilities, or

○ it is proved to the court's satisfaction that the LLP is unable to pay its debts as they fall due (IA 1986, s 123 as modified).)

● The court is of the opinion that it is just and equitable for the LLP to be wound up.

● The LLP does not commence its business within a year of incorporation or suspends its business for a whole year.

● The number of members of the LLP falls below two (IA 1986, s 122 as modified).

A contributory, the Official Receiver, the Secretary of State, the Bank of England and the Attorney General may present a petition under various statutory provisions even if the LLP is solvent.

Initial procedures 7.6

Members' voluntary winding up

● The designated members make a declaration of solvency, which must embody a statement of assets and liabilities and be made within five weeks immediately before the determination of the LLP to wind up. The declaration has to be filed with the Registrar of Companies within 15 days of the determination to wind up (IA 1986, ss 89 and 90 as modified).

● The members' determination to wind up the LLP must be made in such manner as is specified by the LLP's partnership agreement.

● If the determination is made, it will be necessary to appoint a liquidator.

● A copy of the determination should be published in the *London Gazette* or the *Edinburgh Gazette,* as appropriate, within 14 days of being passed (IA 1986, s 85 as modified) and must also be filed within 15 days with the Registrar of Companies (IA 1986, s 84 as modified).

- The liquidator must, within 14 days of his appointment, advertise his appointment in each *Gazette* and give notice to the Registrar of Companies (IA 1986, s 109 as modified).

The subsequent procedure is similar to that for a creditors' voluntary winding up set out below, except that meetings of, and notices to, creditors are not required.

Creditors' voluntary winding up   7.7

- A meeting of the creditors must be called by the LLP, to be held within 14 days of the determination of the LLP that it be wound up (IA 1986, s 98 as modified). At least seven days' notice of the meeting must be given to the creditors. Notice of the creditors' meeting must be advertised in the appropriate *Gazette* and two local newspapers (IA 1986, s 98(1)(b)(c) as modified).
- The notice must state either:
  - the name and address of the insolvency practitioner who will give such information to the creditors before the meeting takes place as they may reasonably require; or
  - a place in the principal area of business of the LLP where a list of names and addresses of the LLP 's creditors will be available for inspection without charge.
- The designated members must make out a statement of affairs of the LLP in the prescribed form, and have that statement laid before the creditors' meeting. The designated members must also appoint one of their number to attend the meeting, and that person must then attend the meeting and preside over it. (IA 1986, s 99 as modified.) (Any liquidator appointed by the LLP (see below) must also attend the creditors' meeting.) At the creditors' meeting, the designated member presiding over the meeting (or other designated members) may answer questions put by the creditors concerning the administration of the LLP, although there is no legal requirement for him or them to do so.
- The liquidator shall be the person nominated by the creditors at their meeting or, where no other person has been so nominated, the person (if any) nominated by the LLP. Where different persons are nominated, any member or creditor of the LLP may apply to the court within seven days of the date of the creditors' nomination for an order that the person nominated by the members shall remain liquidator instead of, or jointly with, the person nominated by the creditors, or that some other person be appointed liquidator. (IA 1986, s 100 as modified.)

- The creditors at their meeting have the power to appoint a liquidation committee of not more than five persons. The LLP may (when it determines that it be wound up voluntarily or any time thereafter) may appoint up to five persons to be members of the committee. However, the creditors may resolve that all or any of the LLP's appointees ought not to be members of the committee, in which case the persons mentioned in the resolution will not be members unless the court resolves otherwise. (IA 1986, s 101 as modified.)
- On the appointment of a liquidator, all the powers of the members cease unless their continuance is sanctioned by the liquidation committee (or the creditors, where there is no such committee) (IA 1986, s 103 as modified).
- The remuneration of the liquidator is fixed by the liquidation committee or, if there is no committee, by the creditors, failing which it is based on the scales applicable to the Official Receiver.
- Upon his appointment in a voluntary winding up (of either type), the liquidator should immediately see to the following matters:
  - if not already done, arrange for the redirection of mail;
  - if thought necessary, change the registered office address;
  - take over all books and records of the LLP;
  - make a formal report to each creditor enclosing a copy of the designated members' statement of affairs, and a copy of any statement made by the designated members at the creditors' meeting – creditors must be informed of the appointment of the liquidator and invited to forward a statement of their claims;
  - advertise for claims at the appropriate time;
  - inform the appropriate sheriffs and bailiffs of the winding-up resolution and of the appointment of the liquidator;
  - take into protective custody the LLP's assets and ensure that there is adequate insurance cover;
  - open in the name of the liquidator separate bank accounts – any sums not immediately required may and should be transferred into a deposit account in the liquidator's name or in another suitable interest-bearing security;
  - consider the position of secured creditors – if necessary, this should be discussed and negotiated with them;
  - consider the position of any landlords, particularly any distress warrants;
  - consider the most appropriate way of disposing of the LLP's assets and discuss this with appointed agents;
  - make a demand for the LLP's outstanding book debts and consider the position as to work in progress;
  - consider, and discuss with the LLP's solicitors, any pending or future litigation outstanding against the LLP.

Winding up by the court 7.8

- When the court makes a winding-up order, the Official Receiver becomes the liquidator (IA 1986, s 136(2) as modified).
- The Official Receiver may require officers of the LLP, or other persons as specified, to prepare and submit a statement of affairs (verified by affidavit) within 21 days (IA 1986, s 131 as modified).
- Separate meetings of creditors and contributories may be summoned by the Official Receiver, at his discretion, for the appointment of some other person to be liquidator of the LLP (IA 1986, s 136(4) as modified). ('Contributories' are defined by IA 1986, s 79 (as modified) but are usually synonymous with the term 'members'.) The Official Receiver remains liquidator if another person is not appointed. The Official Receiver *must* summon a meeting for the appointment of another liquidator if one-quarter in value of the creditors request him to do so.
- The creditors and contributories may nominate as liquidator any person who is qualified to act as an insolvency practitioner (IA 1986, s 139 as modified). The creditors' nominee will be the liquidator except in the absence of a nomination by the contributories, in which case the contributories' nominee (if any) will be the liquidator.
- Where different persons are nominated, any contributory or creditor may apply to the court within seven days of the creditors' nomination being made. The court may appoint the contributories' nominee instead of, or jointly with, the creditors' nominee, or appoint some other person to be liquidator. (IA 1986, s 139(4) as modified.)
- At any time the Official Receiver may apply to the Secretary of State for the appointment of a liquidator in his place. Any such liquidator must send notice of his appointment to the creditors, or (if the court allows) advertise his appointment as the court may direct. (IA 1986, s 137 as modified.)

Liquidator 7.9

In a winding-up by the court, the liquidator should deal with the following matters:

- take over responsibility for the assets of the LLP together with its books and records;
- take other necessary steps to protect and realise the assets, as indicated above in the case of a creditors' voluntary winding up;

- disclaim any onerous property or unprofitable contracts (IA 1986, s 178 as modified); and
- provide the Official Receiver with information, access to books or such other assistance as he may reasonably require.

The winding-up order halts any proceedings against the LLP except by leave of the court (IA 1986, s 130(2) as modified).

As to the matters with which the liquidator should deal in a voluntary winding up, see **7.7** above.

Qualifications of liquidators   7.10

A liquidator must be a person who is qualified to act as an insolvency practitioner (IA 1986, s 390 as modified). The Secretary of State may give authority for a person to act as an insolvency practitioner or authorise another competent authority to do so (IA 1986, s 392 as modified).

There are detailed provisions in IA 1986, ss 390–398 as modified as to who may be regarded as a fit and proper person, and as to the necessary education, practical training and experience, for appointment as a licensed insolvency practitioner. A person who is adjudged bankrupt or who is subject to a disqualification order under the CDDA 1986 is not qualified to act as an insolvency practitioner.

Duties and powers of liquidators   7.11

The IA 1986, ss 165 to 170 and Sch 4 (as modified), specify the duties and powers of a liquidator in all categories of winding up. The principal duties and powers are as follows.

(a) The liquidator's primary duty is to realise the LLP's assets to the best advantage, to determine the claims against the LLP and to distribute the funds realised, to the creditors and contributories, after payment of the costs and expenses in the order of priority laid down by regulation. In a voluntary winding up, the liquidator is specifically required to pay the LLP's debts and adjust the rights of the contributories amongst themselves (IA 1986, s 165(4) as modified).

(b) In carrying out his duties, the liquidator has considerable powers, although the exercise of some of them requires specific sanctions.

No sanction is necessary in respect of the following matters (IA 1986, Sch 4 Part III as modified):

- ❍ to sell the LLP's assets and transfer title on behalf of the LLP;
- ❍ to execute deeds, receipts and documents and affix the LLP's seal, if it has one, where necessary;
- ❍ to prove, rank and claim in the bankruptcy or insolvency of any contributory;
- ❍ to draw, accept and endorse bills of exchange or promissory notes in the name, and on behalf, of the LLP;
- ❍ to raise money on security of the LLP's assets;
- ❍ to take out letters of administration to the estate of a deceased contributory;
- ❍ to appoint agents (although in practice the sanction of any liquidation committee is usually sought);
- ❍ to do all such other things as may be necessary for winding up the LLP's affairs and disposing of its assets.

(c) In the case of a voluntary winding up, but not in the case of a winding up by the court, the liquidator may:

- ❍ exercise the court's powers to settle a list of contributories, and of making calls; and
- ❍ convene meetings of the members of the LLP to obtain their sanction or for any other purpose he may think fit (IA 1986, s 165(4) as modified).

(d) In the case of winding up by the court, but not in the case of a voluntary winding-up, the liquidator requires sanction of the court or the liquidation committee (IA 1986, Sch 4 Part II as modified) to:

- ❍ bring or defend actions or other legal proceedings;
- ❍ carry on the business for beneficial winding-up.

(e) Sanction is required in all cases (IA 1986, Sch 4 Part I as modified) to:

- ❍ pay any class of creditor in full;
- ❍ make any compromise or arrangement with creditors or contributories;
- ❍ make any compromise affecting the assets of winding-up of the LLP, take security for the discharge of any debt and give a discharge in respect of it.

(f) In a winding up by the court, sanction for matters in (d) above is usually sought from the liquidation committee except for matters which are reserved to the court. If there is no liquidation committee the Secretary of State may exercise its functions except where they are exercised by the Official Receiver (IA 1986, s 141 as modified).

(g) In the case of a creditors' voluntary winding up, the liquidation committee's sanction for the matters in (e) above is usually sought or, if there is no such committee, it is sought from the creditors.

Members 7.12

A report must be made forthwith to the Secretary of State under section 7(3) of the Company Directors Disqualification Act 1986 (CDDA 1986) (applied to LLPs by LLPR 2001, Reg 4(2)) if in the winding-up proceedings, it appears to the Official Receiver (where the winding up is by the court) or the liquidator (in the case of a creditors' or members' voluntary winding up) that the conduct of a member of the LLP is such as to render him unfit to be concerned in the management of an LLP or limited company, or where it appears to the Official Receiver or liquidator or that a member might have been trading fraudulently or wrongfully (IA 1986, ss 213 and 214 as modified). (For disqualification, see **3.6** to **3.11** above.)

Investigations, preferences, fraud and criminal offences 7.13

The liquidator must investigate the records of the LLP to establish whether any of the following have occurred:

- transactions at an undervalue (IA 1986, s 238 as modified);
- preferences (IA 1986, s 239 as modified);
- floating charges created in favour of a connected person within two years of commencement of the liquidation (or within one year, if created in favour of any other person), or created between the time of presentation of a petition for an administration order and the making of the order (IA 1986, s 245 as modified);
- fraudulent trading (IA 1986, ss 213 and 215 as modified);
- wrongful trading (IA 1986, ss 214 and 215 as modified);
- withdrawal of property from LLP by a member (IA 1986, s 214A as modified) (see **7.14** below);
- any misfeasance by any director or manager (IA 1986, s 212 as modified);
- failure to register any charge under CA 1985, ss 395–398 as modified (see **6.7** above).

Under the IA 1986, s 218(4) as modified (as amended by the Insolvency Act 2000) the liquidator has a statutory duty in a voluntary winding-up to report any fraud or criminal act he discovers to the Secretary of State (or, in Scotland, the Lord Advocate).

Member's contribution to assets   7.14

A member of an LLP, or any person who has been a member within the period of two years immediately prior to the commencement of the winding up of the LLP, who during that period withdrew any property of the LLP may be liable to contribute to its assets to meet creditors' claims. (IA 1986, s 214A as modified.) 'Property' includes any asset of the LLP and in most instances would be the profit share actually withdrawn by any individual member.

In order for a member to be liable, the liquidator must prove to the satisfaction of the court that at the time of the withdrawal of property, the member(s) concerned:

● knew or had reasonable grounds of believing that the LLP was unable to pay its debts in terms of IA 1986, s 123 as modified (see **7.5** above); or
● knew or had reasonable grounds to believe that the LLP would become unable to meet its debts as a result of that withdrawal taken together with any other withdrawals made (or contemplated) at the same time.

If the court is satisfied that these conditions are met, it may issue a declaration that the member(s) concerned contribute to the assets of the LLP in such manner as the court sees fit.

The court will not make a declaration in relation to any member which would require that member to contribute an amount which exceeds the aggregate of the amounts or values of all the withdrawals made by that member within the period of two years immediately prior to the commencement of the winding up.

The court shall not make a declaration under section 214A with respect to any member unless that person knew (or ought to have concluded) that after each withdrawal there was no reasonable prospect that the LLP would avoid going into insolvent liquidation. For this purpose, the facts that a member ought to have known or ascertained are those which would be known or ascertained by a reasonably diligent person having both:

● the general knowledge, skill and experience that may be expected of a person carrying out the same functions as are carried out by that member in relation to the LLP; and
● the general knowledge, skill and experience that that member has.

For the purposes of section 214A, (i) an LLP goes into insolvent liquidation at a time when its assets are insufficient for the payment of its debts and other liabilities together with the expenses of the winding up, and (ii) 'member' includes a shadow member.

Determination of creditors' claims   7.15

In a winding-up by the court, creditors must submit ('prove') their claims in writing, on a 'proof of debt' form. In the case of voluntary liquidations, the liquidator may require a creditor to prove his claim in writing but no specific form is provided for this. If the liquidator rejects a proof in whole or in part, he must send to the creditor a written statement of his reasons for doing so. A creditor has 21 days from receipt of that statement to apply to the court for the decision to be reversed or varied. (See Rules 4.73 to 4.85 of the Insolvency Rules 1986 (SI 1986 No 1925), applied to LLPs by LLPR 2001, Sch 6, Part II.)

Distributions and release   7.16

Voluntary winding-up

After payment of relevant fixed charges, the order of priority for payment is as follows.

- Costs and expenses of the winding-up (see Rule 4.218 of the Insolvency Rules 1986).
- Preferential claims as defined in the IA 1986, s 386 and Schedule 6 as modified, the principal categories being:
  - O PAYE deductions and national insurance contributions relating to 12 months prior to the relevant date,
  - O VAT relating to six months prior to the relevant date,
  - O employees' unpaid salary or wages for four months prior to the relevant date limited to the amount fixed by delegated legislation (currently £800),
  - O employees' accrued holiday remuneration,
  - O sums paid by third parties on behalf of the LLP to discharge debts which would have been preferential had the third parties not paid them and which remain outstanding to such third parties.
- Creditors who have a floating charge (IA 1986, s 175(2)(b) as modified).
- Admitted ordinary unsecured creditors.

(The 'relevant date' is defined in the IA 1986, s 387 as modified. Where the LLP is being wound up by the court, it usually means the date of appointment of the provisional liquidator, or if no provisional liquidator has been appointed, the date of the winding-up order. If the LLP is being wound up voluntarily, the 'relevant date' will usually be the date on which the LLP made the determination that it be wound up voluntarily.)

After settlement of all debts and costs, any surplus should be paid to contributories (i.e. the members) (IA 1986, s 107 as modified).

Upon completion of a creditors' voluntary winding up, the liquidator should call meetings of the members of the LLP and of the creditors, to lay an account of his administration before the meetings and to give any explanations which are necessary. At least 28 days' notice of the meetings must be given to all creditors who have proved their debts (Insolvency Rules 1986, Rule 4.126) which must also be published in the appropriate Gazette at least one month beforehand (IA 1986, s 106(2) as modified). Within one week of the meetings being held, he must send a copy of the accounts, and a return of the holding of the meetings and of their dates, to the Registrar of Companies. If the meeting resolves against the liquidator having his release, he must apply for it to the Secretary of State. Three months after the registration of the return with the Registrar of Companies, the LLP is deemed to be dissolved (IA 1986, s 201(2) as modified).

Similar provisions to the above apply in the case of a members' voluntary winding up except that meetings of creditors are not necessary. (See IA 1986, s 94 as modified.)

Winding up by the court 7.17

- The order of distribution is generally the same as in the case of a voluntary winding up.
- Upon the completion of the winding-up, the liquidator should proceed as follows.
  - He must send to all creditors who have proved their debts 28 days' notice of a final meeting to receive the liquidator's report and grant his release. Notice must also be gazetted at least one month before the meeting (IA 1986, s 146 as modified; Insolvency Rules 1986, Rule 4.125).
  - He must file with the court and the Registrar of Companies notice that the final meeting has been held under IA 1986, s 146 as modified, together with a copy of his report, stating whether he has been given his release.

- ○ If the creditors have not objected to the liquidator's release, he vacates office and his release is effective from that time.
- ○ If the final meeting resolves against the release of the liquidator, the liquidator must apply to the Secretary of State to determine the outcome.
- ○ If there should be no quorum at the final meeting, it is deemed to have been held and the creditors not to have resolved against the liquidator's release.

Dissolution without liquidation 7.18

An LLP may apply to the Registrar of Companies to be struck off the Register. This is an alternative to formal liquidation by the members, creditors or the court, and is a simpler and more convenient method of dissolving an LLP which is not trading and has no assets or liabilities, i.e. a defunct LLP. An LLP may become defunct if it was formed to carry on any business which did not come to fruition, or if the business for which the LLP was formed has ended and it is left with neither assets or liabilities (CA 1985, ss 652A to 652C as modified).

To effect the dissolution of the LLP, two or more designated members must complete and sign form LLP 652a – see **Appendix 3**. This form must be submitted to Companies House together with a filing fee of £10.

A copy of the form must also be sent, within 7 days of the application being made, to every person who on the date of the application is a member, employee or creditor of the LLP, or the manager or trustee of any employee pension fund, and to any other person of a description specified by regulations made by the Secretary of State (CA 1985, s 652B(6) as modified).

Winding up in Scotland 7.19

Certain provisions relating to winding up in Scotland are peculiar to Scottish law, although many of the provisions of the Insolvency Act 1986 applicable to England and Wales also apply to Scotland. Those provisions which deal with matters applicable to LLPs in England and Wales and in Scotland are set out in LLPR 2001, Sch 3.

LLPR 2001, Sch 4 excludes, in relation to LLPs in Scotland, the application of various provisions of the Insolvency Act 1986, in relation to which the power to legislate has been devolved to Scotland. The provisions which deal with these devolved matters are applied to LLPs in Scotland (subject to certain modifications) by the LLP (Scotland) Regulations 2001, and with one exception exactly mirror the provisions excluded by LLPR 2001, Sch 4. The one exception relates to the modification of IA 1986, s 416 and this is believed to be a drafting error.

It should be noted that floating charges in Scotland are dealt with in sections 462 to 466 of the Companies Act 1985, as modified by LLPR 2001, Sch 2 (non-devolved matters) and LLP (Scotland) Regulations 2001, Sch 1 (devolved matters).

LLP voluntary arrangements   7.20

IA 1986, ss 1 to 7, as modified, enable the designated members of an LLP, an administrator, or a liquidator, as appropriate, to make a proposal to the LLP's creditors for a composition in satisfaction of its debts or a scheme of arrangement of its affairs, known as a voluntary arrangement.

A proposal must provide for some person ('the nominee'), who is qualified to act as an insolvency practitioner in relation to the LLP, to act in relation to the voluntary arrangement either as trustee or for the purpose of supervising its implementation. The procedure outlined below assumes that the proposal has been made by the LLP itself (i.e. that the LLP is not being wound up or subject to an administration order), so that the nominee is not a liquidator or administrator. (A slightly different procedure applies where the proposal is made by the liquidator or administrator, which is subject to separate modifications in LLPR 2001, Sch 3.)

Procedure   7.21

Where the proposal is made by the LLP, the following procedure must be followed.

● The designated members prepare a document setting out the terms of the proposed arrangement, incorporating a statement of affairs, and submit it to the nominee (IA 1986, s 2 as modified). The nominee will endorse the notice with his consent to act and must submit a report to the court, within 28 days, stating whether in his opinion, a meeting of the creditors should be summoned to consider the proposal and, if applicable, the date, the time and place at which the meeting should be held. The date on which the meeting is to be held shall not be less than 14 or more than 28 days from the date on which the nominee's report is filed in court (IA 1986, s 3(1) as modified; Insolvency Rules 1986, Rule 1.9). The nominee is required to send notice of the creditors' meeting, at least 14 days before the day fixed for it to be held, to all creditors of whom he is aware. With the notice of the meeting, the nominee must send:

O   the proposal;

O   a statement of affairs; and

O   the nominee's comments.

- At the creditors' meeting, a majority in excess of three-quarters in value of those present in person or by proxy is required for approval of the proposal (Rule 1.19). The meeting may propose modifications which may include conferring the nominee's proposed functions on another person qualified to act as an insolvency practitioner in relation to the LLP. The meeting cannot approve a proposal or any modification under which the rights of preferential creditors are altered without their concurrence (IA 1986, s 4 as modified). Before the conclusion of the meeting, the chairman of the meeting is required to ascertain from the LLP whether it accepts any proposed modifications. If, before the meeting is concluded, the LLP has failed to respond to a proposed modification, it will be presumed not to have agreed to it (IA 1986, s 4(5A) as modified).

- The votes of certain creditors must be left out of account and any resolution is invalid if those voting against it include more than one half in value of qualifying votes (Rule 1.19(4)).

- After the conclusion of the meeting, the chairman must report the result of the meeting to the court (including the response of the LLP to any proposed modifications) and, immediately after reporting to the court, notify the result of the meeting to the LLP (IA 1986, s 4(6) as modified).

- Approval of the voluntary arrangement by the meeting binds every person who had notice of, and was entitled to vote at, either of the meetings (IA 1986, s 5(2)(b) as modified).

- If on the day of the meeting of the creditors, the requisite majority is not obtained, the chairman may, and shall if so resolved, adjourn the meeting for not more than 14 days (Rule 1.21).

- An application may be made to the court by a member of the LLP, a creditor, or the nominee that the voluntary arrangement is unfairly prejudicial or that there has been some material irregularity in relation to either of the meetings (IA 1986, s 6 as modified).

Remuneration, expenses and completion of the voluntary arrangement 7.22

Once the voluntary arrangement is approved, the person carrying out the functions conferred on the nominee (whether the nominee, or a person on whom the nominee's functions have been conferred by virtue of IA 1986, s 2 or s 4 as modified) is known as the 'supervisor' of the voluntary arrangement (IA 1986, s 7 as modified).

The following fees, costs, charges and expenses may be incurred in connection with the voluntary arrangement (Insolvency Rules 1986, Rule 1.28):

- disbursements by the nominee prior to approval of the arrangement, and agreed remuneration for his services;
- disbursements, remuneration, expenses and any payments sanctioned by the terms of the arrangement or which would be payable in an administration or winding-up.

The supervisor must, within 28 days of full implementation of the arrangement, or within such extended time as may be allowed by the court, send notice to that effect to the Registrar of Companies, the court, and all creditors and members of the LLP who were bound by it. With the notice there must be included a report by the supervisor summarising all receipts and payments made by him in pursuance of the arrangement and, if applicable, an explanation of any material disparity between the anticipated and the actual result (Insolvency Rules 1986, Rule 1.29).

Administration orders 7.23

The court may make an administration order in relation to an LLP if it is satisfied that the LLP is or is likely to become unable to pay its debts, as defined in IA 1986, s 123 as modified (see **7.5** above), and that it is likely to achieve one or more of the following purposes (IA 1986, s 8 as modified):

- the survival of the LLP as a going concern, in whole or in part;
- the approval of a voluntary arrangement;
- the sanction of an arrangement under CA 1985, s 425 as modified; or
- a more beneficial realisation of the LLP's assets than would be effected in the event of winding-up.

An administration order is an order directing that, during the period for which it is in force, the affairs, business and property of the LLP shall be managed by an 'administrator' appointed by the court (IA 1986, s 8(2) as modified).

An application to the court for an administration order is made by petition, which may be presented by the members, a creditor or creditors, or any combination of them (IA 1986, s 9(1) as modified). The supervisor of a voluntary arrangement may also present a petition (IA 1986, s 7(4)(b) as modified).

It is advisable to support the application for an administration order with a report from by an independent person concluding that the appointment of an administrator is expedient (Insolvency Rules 1986, Rule 2.2). The report may be prepared by the insolvency practitioner proposed as administrator, or by any person having adequate knowledge of the LLP's affairs, not being a member or employee of the LLP. The report must specify the purposes which may be achieved for the LLP by the making of an administration order, being purposes specified in IA 1986, s 8(3) as modified (see above).

Any person who has appointed, or who is entitled to appoint, an administrative receiver must be given notice of the application. If there is an administrative receiver in office, the application will be dismissed unless consent is given by the appointor of the receiver. An application may not be withdrawn except with the leave of the court. (IA 1986, s 9(2)(3) as modified).

Between the presentation of an application and its hearing, resulting in the making of an order or the dismissal of the application (IA 1986, s 10(1), as modified (as amended by the Insolvency Act 2000)):

- no determination may be made, or order made, for the winding up of the LLP although a petition for its winding up may be presented;
- no landlord (or other person to whom rent is payable) may exercise any right of forfeiture by peaceable re-entry in relation to premises let to the LLP in respect of a failure by the LLP to comply with any term or condition of its tenancy, except with the leave of the court;
- no steps may be taken to enforce any security over the LLP's property or to repossess goods under any hire purchase agreement without the leave of the court; and
- no other proceedings and execution or other legal process may be commenced or continued, and no distress may be levied against the LLP or its property, without the leave of the court.

Effect of the administration order   **7.24**

The making of an administration order has certain immediate effects, notably that:

- any petition for the winding-up of the LLP is dismissed;
- any administrative receiver of the LLP must vacate office;
- any receiver of part of the LLP's property must vacate office on being required to do so by the administrator (IA 1986, s 11(1) and (2) as modified).

In addition, during the period for which an administration order is in force (IA 1986, s 11(3) as modified, as amended by the Insolvency Act 2000):

- no determination or order may be made for the winding up of the LLP;
- no administrative receiver of the LLP may be appointed;
- no landlord (or other person to whom rent is payable) may exercise any right of forfeiture by peaceable re-entry in relation to premises let to the LLP in respect of a failure by the LLP to comply with any term or condition of its tenancy, except with the leave of the court;
- no other steps may be taken to enforce any security over the LLP's property, or to repossess goods in the LLP's possession under any hire purchase agreement, except with the consent of the administrator or the leave of the court;
- no other proceedings and no execution or other legal process may be commenced or continued, and no distress may be levied, against the LLP or its property except with the consent of the administrator or the leave of the court.

Administrator   **7.25**

An administrator shall be a person authorised to act as an insolvency practitioner. Any person acting as an administrator who is not so qualified is liable to imprisonment or to a fine, or both (IA 1986, s 389 as modified). (As noted in **7.10** above there are detailed provisions set out in IA 1986, ss 390–398 (as modified) regarding the qualification of insolvency practitioners.) An administrator's remuneration may be determined by a creditors' committee (if there is one – see generally Insolvency Rules 2.32–2.46A) or, if there is no such committee, or it does not make the requisite determination, his remuneration may be fixed by a resolution of a creditors' meeting or, ultimately, by the court (Rule 2.47).

Powers of an administrator 7.26

In general, an administrator of an LLP has power to do all such things as may be necessary for the management of the affairs, business and property of the LLP. The powers are specified in IA 1986, ss 14 and 15 and Sch 1 (as modified) and include the following:

- power to hold meetings of the members or creditors of the LLP;
- power to deal with property of the LLP subject to a floating charge, as if it were not charged, without the leave of the court – however, the property directly or indirectly representing property so disposed shall be subject to the security in the same priority as the disposed property;
- power to deal with any other charged property, or goods subject to a hire-purchase agreement, with the consent of the court subject to a condition that the net proceeds of the disposal are applied towards discharging the sums secured by the security or payable under the hire-purchase agreement.

Duties of an administrator 7.27

On his appointment, the administrator must take into his custody or under his control all the property to which the LLP is or appears to be entitled (IA 1986, s 17 as modified). He is required to manage the affairs, business and property of the LLP, in accordance with proposals made by him under IA 1986, s 23 (as modified) and approved by a creditors' meeting under IA 1986, s 24 (as modified). (Before those proposals are approved, the administrator's management must be in accordance with any directions given by the court.) The administrator is required to summon a meeting of the LLP's creditors if he is requested to do by one-tenth in value of those creditors, or directed to do so by the court (see Rules 2.18 to 2.30 of the Insolvency Rules 1986).

The administrator also has a duty to report to the Secretary of State under section 7(3) of the CDDA 1986, where it appears to him that the circumstances set out in that subsection are satisfied (see **7.12** above).

Discharge or variation of the order 7.28

The administrator may, as specified by IA 1986, s 18 (as modified), at any time apply to the court for the order to be discharged or to be varied. He must make such an application if it appears that the purposes specified in the order have either been achieved or are incapable of achievement, or if he is required to do so by a meeting of creditors. On the hearing of such an application, the court may discharge or vary the administration order and make such other order as it thinks fit. Where the administration order is discharged or varied, the administrator must, within 14 days, send an office copy of that order to the Registrar of Companies.

Vacation of office 7.29

An administrator may be removed by order of the court and may resign by giving notice to the court. An administrator vacates office if he ceases to be qualified to act as an insolvency practitioner or the administration order is discharged, or upon death (IA 1986, s 19 as modified).

Receiverships – England and Wales 7.30

Qualification and remuneration

Under IA 1986, s 390 (as modified), only a qualified insolvency practitioner may act as an administrative receiver of a floating charge and any person acting as such who is not so qualified is liable to imprisonment or to a fine, or both (IA 1986, s 389 as modified). As noted in **7.10** above there are detailed provisions set out in IA 1986, ss 390 to 398 (as modified) regarding the qualification of licensed insolvency practitioners.

In the case of receivers appointed under a fixed charge, it is desirable to appoint as receiver only professionally competent persons because of the administrative and legal tasks involved. It should be noted that in the case of both types of receiver, a corporate body may not be appointed as a receiver (IA 1986, s 30 as modified). It is usual for debentures to specify the maximum rate of remuneration for the receiver or that it shall be agreed between the receiver and the debenture holder. If the receiver is appointed by the court, the receiver's remuneration will be determined by the court. In addition, a liquidator of an LLP may apply to the court to determine the receiver's remuneration (IA 1986, s 36 as modified).

Appointment by the court   7.31

A court may appoint a receiver on the application of a mortgagee or a debenture holder in the following circumstances:

- where repayment of principal and/or interest is in arrears;
- when the security has become crystallised into a specific charge by the making of a winding-up order or passing of a resolution to wind up; or
- where the security of the mortgagee or the debenture holder is in jeopardy.

A receiver may also be appointed by the court on the application either of a contributory (i.e. a person liable to contribute to the assets of the LLP in the event of its being wound up) or of the LLP itself.

Appointment by debenture holders   7.32

The appointment is made under a deed executed by the debenture holder and is, together with the debenture, evidence of his capacity. The appointment of a receiver usually arises in the following circumstances:

- failure to pay the principal and/or interest in accordance with the terms of the debenture;
- where a borrowing limit has been exceeded and has not been reduced within a specified period; or
- a breach of some other provisions in the debenture or trust deed.

The debenture usually confers fixed and floating charges on the assets of an LLP. (For debentures generally, see **6.1** above.) It is possible, however, for the security to be simply a fixed or a floating charge. It is therefore important to consider the following at the commencement of a receivership.

- Under a fixed charge, a receiver will not normally have power to manage the business and may only call in and realise the relevant assets for the purpose of redeeming the debt due to the debenture holder.
- An appointment under a floating charge may be made as 'receiver' or 'administrative receiver'. The former cannot be appointed with the powers of the latter unless the deed contains such provision.

- A 'receiver' will have power to manage if such right is given to him by the debenture deed containing a charge on the goodwill of business of the LLP.

The appointment as receiver or manager must be accepted before the end of the next business day following receipt of the instrument of appointment and shall be deemed to be effective from the time and date the instrument of appointment was received (IA 1986, s 33 as modified).

The receiver must advertise notice of his appointment in the London Gazette and an appropriate newspaper (IA 1986, s 46(1) as modified; Insolvency Rules 1986, Rule 3.2). The receiver or manager should attend to the undermentioned matters following his appointment.

- Examine the deed of appointment and a copy of the debenture (or trust deed) in order to consider the validity of the debenture and his appointment.
- Ensure that his appointment has been registered with the Registrar of Companies by the debenture holder within seven days on Form LLP405(1).
- Advise the LLP of his appointment and take possession of the appropriate assets.
- Ensure that adequate insurance is in force.
- Notify the appointment to the LLP's bankers and open an account in the name of the receiver or manager, as appropriate.
- Consider the position of employees, in particular whether they should be dismissed or retained (see **7.33** below).
- Check arrangements for the receipt and dispatch of goods and collect the book debts.
- Ensure that all documents bearing the LLP's name leaving the LLP's premises contain a statement that a receiver has been appointed (IA 1986, s 39(1) as modified).
- Consider the position of current contracts, whether they should be completed or whether the business should be disposed of in whole or in part and, if applicable, the mode of disposal.
- Ensure that the LLP's books are written up to the date of his appointment, if appropriate.
- Inform all creditors within 28 days (IA 1986, s 46 as modified) of his appointment as receiver and, in particular, notify judgment creditors, persons who have issued writs against the LLP, and their solicitors, if known. The position of other secured creditors, hire-purchase agreements and claims by landlords should also be considered.
- Maintain proper records and books of account of the receivership.

- Require officers of the LLP and/or other relevant persons to prepare and submit to the receiver within 21 days a statement of affairs verified by affidavit (IA 1986, s 47 as modified).
- Within three months of his appointment (or such longer period as the Court may allow), an administrative receiver must send to the Registrar of Companies, to any trustees for secured creditors and to all such creditors (so far as he is aware of their addresses) a report giving details of the following matters (IA 1986, s 48(1) as modified):
  - ○ the events leading to his appointment;
  - ○ disposal or proposed disposal of any property and the continuation or proposed continuation of the business;
  - ○ the amounts of principal and interest payable to the debenture holders who appointed him and the amounts due to preferential creditors; and
  - ○ the amount likely to be available for payment to other creditors.
- The administrative receiver must also, within the same time limit, send a copy of the report to all unsecured creditors (or publish a notice of availability) and, unless the court directs otherwise, and summon a meeting of the unsecured creditors on not less than 14 days' notice to receive the same (IA 1986, s 48(2) as modified). An administrative receiver is not required to comply with subsection (2) if the LLP has gone or goes into liquidation, provided that a copy of the report is sent to the liquidator within the three-month time limit referred to above (IA 1986, s 48(4) as modified).

The employees' legal position   **7.33**

The appointment of a receiver does not automatically terminate the employment of the LLP's employees. However, the receiver will not be taken to have adopted any contract of employment by reason of anything done (or omitted to be done) within 14 days after his appointment. In respect of contracts of employment adopted by him in the carrying out of his functions, he will be personally liable on such contracts (subject to a right of indemnity out of the assets of the LLP – see **7.34** below) only to the extent of any 'qualifying liability'. A qualifying liability is a liability incurred to pay wages, salary or a contribution to an occupational pension scheme, incurred while the administrative receiver is in office, and which is in respect of services rendered wholly or partly after the adoption of the contract (IA 1986, s 44 as modified).

As to the receiver's agency and liability on other contracts, see **7.34** below.

Powers, liabilities and responsibilities   7.34

An administrative receiver has the powers which the debenture holders have conferred on him which are deemed to include the powers listed in IA 1986, Sch 1 (IA 1986 s 42 as modified). On application to the court, a receiver may seek authority to dispose of any of the LLP's property as if it were not subject to the security (IA 1986, s 43(1) as modified).

An administrative receiver is deemed to be the LLP's agent until the commencement of liquidation and, unless the contract provides otherwise, is personally liable on any contract entered into by him in carrying out his functions albeit that he is normally entitled to indemnity out of the assets of the LLP (IA 1986, s 44(1) as modified). If the administrative receiver enters into contracts without authority, his liability is unlimited with no right of indemnity.

Priority in distribution of funds   7.35

- The proceeds realised from specific assets charged under a fixed charge must be used first to meet the costs of realisation, then the receiver's remuneration and then the claims of the debenture holders. If there is any surplus, it is to be distributed in accordance with the priorities for floating charges.
- The order of priority for distribution of funds arising from a floating charge are as follows:
  - costs of realisation;
  - other outgoings and costs of the receivership;
  - the receiver's remuneration;
  - preferential debts listed in Schedule 6 to the IA 1986 (as modified), for example, money owed to the Inland Revenue for income tax and national insurance contributions deducted at source, VAT, remuneration, etc. of employees all being subject to limits specified in that Schedule;
  - interest due under the debenture subject to the debenture's terms;
  - principal sum secured by the debenture.

Arrangements and reconstructions   7.36

Compromise or arrangement

Where a scheme of compromise or arrangement under CA 1985, ss 425 to

427 (as modified) is proposed between an LLP and its members or creditors, the court may on application of any member, creditor, administrator or liquidator of the LLP order that a meeting of the members or creditors be summoned to consider the proposal (CA 1985, s 425 as modified)

If the proposal is approved by 75% in value of the creditors (or, as the case may be, of 75% in value of the members) present in person or by proxy, the terms of the compromise or arrangement will be binding on all parties if sanctioned by the court and has effect when an office copy of the court order has been delivered to the Registrar of Companies.

A statement setting out the effect of the arrangement must accompany each notice issued to members or creditors and, where the meeting is convened by advertisement, must contain a note of the place at which copies of the statement may be obtained (CA 1985, s 426 as modified).

Reconstruction   7.37

A reconstruction is a form of compromise or arrangement involving the transfer of all or part of an LLP's property or assets to another LLP or a company, or the amalgamation of two or more LLPs or companies, and may also involve the winding up of the transferor LLP(s) (CA 1985, s 427 as modified).

Either by the order sanctioning the reconstruction, or by any subsequent order, the court may make provision regarding the transfer of any of the property, assets or liabilities of the LLP, allotting or appropriating any debentures of the LLP, the continuance or otherwise of any proceedings against the LLP and the dissolution without winding up of the transferor LLP.

The reconstruction takes effect as set out in the court order(s), and every LLP in respect of which an order has been made must deliver an office copy of the order to the Registrar of Companies within seven days of the order being made.

Appendix 1

Limited Liability Partnership Agreement

Limited Liability Partnership Agreement

THIS AGREEMENT is made the   day of

BETWEEN each of the Members and all others of them and the LLP

WHEREBY it is agreed as follows:

1.   Definitions and interpretation

1.1   In this Agreement the following expressions have the following meanings:

'the LLP' means the limited liability partnership [to be] incorporated under the Name which the Members [shall seek to register at Companies House] or [have registered at Companies House with number *(number)*]

'the Initial Members' means the persons (whether individuals limited liability partnerships or limited companies) whose names and addresses appear in the first schedule

'the Members' means those of the Initial Members and/or such other or additional persons as may from time to time be appointed in accordance with the provisions hereof whose membership of the LLP has not been determined in accordance with the provisions hereof

'the Name' means *(name)* [limited liability partnership] or [LLP] or [llp][1] or such other name as shall from time to time be registered by the LLP at Companies House as its name

['the Former Partnership' shall mean the partnership known as *(name)* carried on by [certain of] the Members [and others] known as *(name)*]

['the Transfer Agreement' means an agreement dated the *(date)* and made between the partners in the Former Partnership of the one part and the LLP of the other part whereby it was agreed to transfer the assets and liabilities of the Former Partnership to the LLP]

'the Registered Office' means *(address)* or such other address as shall from time to time be registered by the LLP at Companies House as its registered office

'the Designated Members' means [all the Members] or [those Members whose names and addresses appear in Part 1 of the first schedule] or such of the Members for the time being of the LLP as shall be designated in accordance with the provisions hereof

'the Initial Auditors' means *(name and address)*

'the Auditors' means the Initial Auditors or such other auditors as may from time to time be appointed in accordance with the provisions hereof
'the Initial Bank' means *(name and address)*
'the Bank' means the Initial Bank or such other bank as may from time to time be appointed as the lead bank of the LLP in accordance with the provisions hereof
'the Business' means the profession trade or business of *(nature of business)* to be carried on by the LLP [in succession to the Former Partnership]
'the Act' means the Limited Liability Partnerships Act 2000
'the Insolvency Act' means the Insolvency Act 1986 as amended by the Act
'the Employment Rights Act' means the Employment Rights Act 1996 as amended by (inter alia) the Employment Relations Act 1999
'the Commencement Date' means [*(date)*] *or* [the date upon which the transfer of the Business pursuant to the Transfer Agreement [shall be] *or* [was] effected]
'the Initial Property' means the freehold or leasehold property or properties [to be] owned or occupied by the LLP for the purposes of the Business details of which are set out in the second schedule
'the Property' means the Initial Property and/or such additional or replacement property or properties as may from time to time be owned or occupied by the LLP for the purpose of the Business
'the Intellectual Property' means all industrial and intellectual property rights of the Seller including without limitation domain names patents trade marks and/or service marks (whether registered or unregistered) registered designs unregistered designs and copyrights and any applications for any of the same owned by the LLP and used in connection with the Business and all Know-how and confidential information so owned and used
'Know-how' means all information (including that comprised in or derived from data disks tapes manuals source codes flow-charts manuals and instructions) relating to the Business and the services provided by it
'the Year End Date' means *(date)* or such other date as may be determined in accordance with the provisions hereof
'an Accounting Year' means a year ending on a Year End Date
'the Capital' means the net capital of the LLP as shown in any balance sheet prepared in accordance with the provisions hereof as belonging to the Members and being the excess of the assets of the LLP over its liabilities
'a Member's Share' means a Member's share and interest of and in the Capital

'a Contribution' means any money or assets paid into the accounts of or transferred into the ownership of the LLP by a Member (other than by way of a loan for which specific written arrangements between him and the LLP shall have been made) less any liabilities attaching thereto which shall be assumed by the LLP in substitution for him

'Drawings' means sums drawn by any Member on account of any anticipated profits of the LLP and any other sums paid or assets applied for his personal benefit by the LLP (other than for any such expenses as shall be provided for in this agreement) including in particular but without limitation any Tax paid on his behalf by the LLP

'the Initial Drawings Amount' means the monthly sum of *(amount)* pounds

'the Interest Rate' shall mean a rate of *(rate)* per cent [above the base rate for the time being of the Bank]

'the Primary Percentage' means *(rate)* per cent

'the Weekly Sum' means *(amount)* pounds per week

'a Payment Date' shall mean the *(date)* in each month or if the same shall not be a Working Day then the Working Day immediately [preceding] *or* [following] the same

'Tax' means any Income Tax Capital Gains Tax or National Insurance Contribution payable by any Member in respect of his status as a member of the LLP or his share of the profits of the LLP or the proceeds from the disposal of any of the assets of the LLP

'the Chairman' means *(name)*

'the Chief Executive' means *(name)*

'the Members' Quorum' means *(number)* Members

'the Designated Members' Quorum' means *(number)* Designated Members

'the Expenditure Limit' means *(amount)* pounds

'the Requisite Number' means *(number)* Members

'the Authority Limit' means *(amount)* pounds

'the Notice Period' means a period of *(number)* months

'the Retirement Age' means the age of *(number)* years

'the Payment Period' means a period of *(number)* years

'the Cessation Date' means in respect of any Member the date of the retirement deemed retirement or expulsion of that Member

'the Radius' means a radius of *(number)* miles

'a Working Day' means any day from Monday to Friday inclusive save for any such day which is a bank or statutory holiday

'Month' means calendar month

'Holiday Weeks' mean *(number)* weeks per year

1.2 Reference to any profits or losses of the LLP include a reference to profits and losses of a capital nature

1.3   Reference to the death of any Member shall in the case of any Member being a body corporate include reference to the winding up dissolution or striking off the register of that Member unless the context otherwise requires

1.4   Reference to any statute or statutory provision includes a reference to that statute or provision as from time to time amended extended re-enacted or consolidated and to all statutory instruments or orders made under it

1.5   Words denoting the singular number only include the plural and vice versa

1.6   Words denoting any gender include all genders and words denoting persons include firms and corporations and vice versa

1.7   Unless the context otherwise requires reference to any clause sub-clause paragraph or schedule is to a clause sub-clause paragraph or schedule (as the case may be) of or to this Agreement

1.8   The headings in this document are inserted for convenience only and shall not affect the construction or interpretation of this Agreement

2.   Incorporation

[2.1   The Members shall complete and deliver to Companies House all such documents and pay all such fees as shall be necessary to lead to the incorporation of the LLP in accordance with the Act][2]

2.2   The certificate of registration of the LLP under the Act [to be] issued to it shall be kept at the Registered Office

3.   Commencement and duration

3.1   The provisions of this agreement shall [take effect] *or* [be deemed to have taken effect] on the Commencement Date

3.2   The LLP shall carry on the Business and/or carry on such other or additional trade profession or business as the Members shall from time to time determine

3.3   The LLP shall subsist until wound up in accordance with the provisions of the Act[3]

[3.4   In the event that any Member may be personally liable under any contract entered into by him prior to the incorporation of the LLP which was for the benefit of the LLP and with the express or implied consent of the other Members then the LLP shall on incorporation be deemed to ratify that contract and shall indemnify that Member from and against all claims liabilities and costs in connection with it]

4.   Name and Registered Office

4.1   The [Designated] Members may from time to time determine upon a change in the Name and/or the Registered Office

4.2   Upon any change in the Name and/or the Registered Office it shall be the responsibility of the Designated Members to notify Companies House of any such change in accordance with the Act

5.   Property and place of business

5.1   The Business shall be carried on by the LLP from the Property

5.2   In the event that any property from time to time comprised within the Property shall be vested in any one or more of the Members (or any nominees for them) those Members (or nominees):

   5.2.1   shall as from the Commencement Date be deemed to have held them in trust for the LLP and the LLP shall indemnify them and their respective estates and effects against all liability in respect thereof after the Commencement Date

   5.2.2   shall upon service upon them of any notice requesting them so to do and on receipt of any necessary mortgagees' and/or landlord's consents permitting them so to do convey transfer or assign the same to the LLP at the cost of the LLP and upon the LLP indemnifying them and their respective estates and effects against all future liability in respect thereof after the date of conveyance transfer or assignment

   PROVIDED that for the purposes of this clause liability shall include in particular but without limitation all liability in respect of any outgoings payable in respect of the relevant property any restrictive covenants relating thereto any rent falling due in respect thereof and the performance and observance of any lessees' covenants relating thereto

5.3   The Property the Intellectual Property and all computers and ancillary equipment office equipment furniture books stationery and other property and equipment in or about the Property and used for the purposes of the Business shall be the property of the LLP

6.   Accounts

6.1   It shall be the responsibility of the Members to ensure that proper books of account giving a true and fair view of the Business and the affairs of the LLP shall be kept properly posted

6.2   Such books of account shall be:

   6.2.1   kept at the Registered Office or at such other place as the Members may from time to time determine

   6.2.2   open to inspection by the Members

6.3   The Designated Members shall (acting where appropriate in accordance with the requirements of the Act):

6.3.1   be deemed hereby to appoint the Initial Auditors as auditors of the LLP for the next ensuing Accounting Year thereof

6.3.2   each year appoint Auditors

6.3.3   have power to remove the Auditors from office

6.3.4   have power to fix the remuneration of the Auditors

6.4   The Members may from time to time determine to amend the Year End Date

6.5   A profit and loss account shall be taken in every year on the Year End Date and a balance sheet [(taking no account of goodwill)] shall be prepared and the same shall be audited in accordance with all relevant Statements of Standard Accounting Practice and in such format and giving such information notes and disclosure of the interests therein of the Members as may be required by the Act

6.6   The accounts to be prepared in accordance with clause 6.5 shall be:

6.6.1   approved by the Members in accordance with the Act at a meeting and shall thereafter become binding on all Members save that any Member may request the rectification of any manifest error discovered in any such accounts within three months of receipt of the same and

6.6.2   distributed to all Members as required by the Act

7.   Banking arrangements

7.1   The bankers shall be the Bank and/or such other bank as the [Designated] Members may from time to time determine [and notify to all Members] as being the lead bank or subsidiary bank of the LLP

7.2   All monies cheques and drafts received by or on behalf of the LLP solely shall be paid promptly into the bank account of the LLP and all securities for money shall be promptly deposited in the name of the LLP with the Bank

7.3   In the event that it shall be a normal part of the Business to receive monies on behalf of any client or third party the LLP shall open a separate client account or accounts with the Bank and:

7.3.1   all monies cheques and drafts received by or on behalf of such clients or third parties shall be paid promptly into such client account(s) and all securities for money shall be promptly deposited in the name of the clients or third parties with the Bank

7.3.2   any such account or accounts shall at all times be operated by the LLP strictly in accordance with any rules or regulations of any professional or regulatory body which may exercise relevant jurisdiction over the LLP

7.4 All cheques drawn on or instructions for the electronic transfer of monies from any such account as is mentioned in this clause 7 shall be in the name of the LLP and may be drawn or given by any [[Designated] Member] *or* [two [Designated] Members] and in the case of any instructions for electronic transfer written confirmation thereof shall be signed by the authorising Member[s]

8. Members' Shares and Contributions

8.1 Each of the Initial Members shall acquire as at the Commencement Date a Member's Share equal to [the amount specified in the Transfer Agreement] *or* [the amount shown as being the value of his capital in the Former Partnership in the cessation accounts [to be] prepared in respect thereof as at the day before the Commencement Date] *or* [the amount or value of any Contribution made by him on the Commencement Date]

8.2 Any Member making any Contribution at any time after the Commencement Date shall acquire a new Member's Share or augment his previous Member's Share by an amount equal to the amount or value of that Contribution

8.3 There shall be added to or subtracted from each Member's Share any share of the profit or loss of the LLP to which he is entitled or which is to be borne by him in accordance with clause 9 after allowing for any Drawings to be charged to him in accordance with clause 10

8.4 The [Designated] Members may from time to time require the Members or any of them to make such Contribution as is necessary for the Business and shall in that event specify the time within which such Contribution is to be made

[8.5 No Member shall be entitled to any interest on the amount for time being of his Member's Share]

9. Profits and losses

[9.1 Before the division of the profits of the LLP as set out below there shall be paid interest upon the amounts for the time being of each Member's Share as follows:

    9.1.1 interest at the Interest Rate in force on the Year End Date on the amount of the Member's Share (before adding any share of profit or deducting any Drawings for the year in question) at that date shall be payable on that Date

    9.1.2 in the event that the aggregate of the amounts of interest payable to Members in accordance with clause 9.1.1 shall exceed the profits of the LLP for the year in question then the several amounts of interest so payable shall abate rateably

9.1.3   in the event that the accounts of the LLP for any year shall show a loss then no such interest shall be payable or credited to any Member]

[9.2   Before the division of any [such] profits of the LLP [after allowing for any amounts payable in accordance with clause 9.1] there shall be payable to each of the Members named in the third schedule out of such profits the prior share of profit specified in that schedule for him provided that:

9.2.1   in the event that the aggregate of such prior shares of profit payable to Members in accordance with clause 9.1.2 shall exceed the profits of the LLP for the year in question so available for payment then such prior shares so payable shall abate rateably

9.2.2   in the event that there shall be no profits so available for payment no such prior shares of profit shall be payable or credited to any Member]

9.3   The profits and losses of the LLP [after allowing for any amounts payable in accordance with clause 9.1 [or clause 9.2]] shall be payable by the LLP to the Members or by the Members to the LLP (as the case may be) [in equal shares] *or* [in the proportions set out in the fourth schedule] *or* [as follows:

9.3.1   as to the Primary Percentage of any profits or as to the total of any losses in the proportions set out in the fourth schedule

9.3.2   as to the residue of any profits as set out in the fifth schedule

9.4   Notwithstanding the provisions of clauses 9.2 and 9.3 where during any Accounting Year any member was prevented by reason of ill-health or accident from devoting his or her full time and attention to the Business (except during holiday leave, maternity leave, parental leave or family leave, as provided for in clauses 12 to 14) for a period of more than 13 successive weeks or for any lesser period commencing within 26 weeks after the Member in question shall have resumed normal duties following a period of such absence exceeding 13 weeks then the share of profits to which such Member is entitled shall thereafter be reduced by the Weekly Sum for every complete week of incapacity until he or she shall resume normal duties and the share of the profits of the other Members shall be increased by a like sum and be divided between them [equally] *or* [in the proportions set out in the fourth schedule]

10.   Drawings

10.1   There shall be paid to each Member on the Payment Date in each month the Initial Drawings Amount or such other sum as the [Designated] Members may from time to time agree in respect either of all Members or such Members as may thus be determined [and notification of any such change shall be given by the Designated Members to all Members]

10.2   Any further payments to be made to or on behalf of any Member and any assets to be transferred to or for the benefit of any Member shall only be made transferred or applied with the consent of the [Designated] Members [and notification of any such payment transfer or application shall be given by the Designated Members to all Members]

10.3   The LLP shall on the taking of the annual accounts provided for in clause 6 reserve out of profits before distribution[:

       10.3.1   any amounts of Tax estimated by the Auditors to be payable by Members during the next following Accounting Year and each Member shall be charged with his due proportion of such Tax and

       10.3.2] such amount as the [Designated] Members shall determine in order to provide further working capital for the Business

[10.4   The LLP shall pay for the benefit of each Member such amounts of Tax as shall be payable by him][4]

10.5   If on the taking of any such annual accounts they shall show that in the relevant Accounting Year any Member drew pursuant to the provisions of this clause 10 in excess of his share of the profits for that Accounting Year then such Member shall repay the excess forthwith together with interest on the excess or such part thereof as shall from time to time be outstanding at the Interest Rate from a date being one month after the receipt by him of such accounts to the date of repayment

10.6   Subject to clause 10.3 each Member shall be entitled to be paid by the LLP the balance (if any) of his actual share of any profits shown in the accounts for any Accounting Year at any time after the same has been approved in accordance with clause 6.6.1

11.   Members' obligations and duties

11.1   Each Member shall at all times:

       11.1.1   devote his whole time and attention to the Business except during holiday leave, maternity leave, parental leave, family leave (as provided for in clauses 12 to 14) or incapacity due to illness injury or other substantial cause

       11.1.2   not without the consent of the [Designated] Members engage in any business other than the Business or accept (otherwise than in a voluntary or honorary capacity) any office or appointment [unless that other Business or the office or appointment is not in competition with the Business] (and in the event of any breach of this sub-clause the Member shall account to the LLP for any profit derived by him from the business office or appointment in question)

11.1.3 not without the consent of the [Designated] Members derive any benefit from the use of the Name or the property or the business connection of the LLP (and in the event of any breach of this sub-clause the Member shall account to the LLP for any profit derived by him from the use in question)

11.1.4 conduct himself in a proper and responsible manner and use his best skill and endeavour to promote the Business

11.1.5 comply with all statutes regulations professional standards and other provisions as may from time to time govern the conduct of the Business [or be determined by the [Designated] Members as standards to be voluntarily applied by the LLP to the Business][5]

[11.2 Each Member shall at all times show the utmost good faith to the LLP] *or*

[11.2 For the avoidance of doubt the Members shall not owe fiduciary duties to each other or to the LLP (save for such fiduciary duties to the LLP as are implied by their status as agents of the LLP)][6]

12. Holiday leave

12.1 Each member shall be entitled in each calendar year to a number of weeks' leave equal to the Holiday Weeks in addition to statutory or public holidays

12.2 Not more than two weeks' holiday leave shall be taken consecutively (ignoring statutory or public holidays) without the consent of the [Designated] Members

12.3 Members shall be entitled to carry forward not more than one week of untaken holiday leave from one calendar year to the next

12.4 Each Member shall give notice to the LLP of his intended dates of holiday leave and shall be responsible for ensuring that those dates do not conflict with dates of any form of leave already notified to the LLP by such other Members or senior employees of the LLP as may be appropriate having regard to the work undertaken by the Member

13. Maternity leave

13.1 Each female Member shall be entitled to such maternity leave as she would be under the Employment Rights Act if she were an employee of the LLP having more than one year's continuous service with the LLP

13.2 During maternity leave the Member shall be entitled to her normal share of the profits of the LLP

13.3   As soon as reasonably practical a Member who becomes pregnant shall notify the LLP of her expected week of confinement and of the date upon which she expects to commence her maternity leave and as soon as reasonably practical after the commencement of her confinement she shall notify the LLP of the date on which she expects to resume her duties

14.   Parental and family leave

14.1   Each Member shall be entitled to such parental leave and family leave as he would be under the Employment Rights Act if he were an employee of the LLP having more than one year's continuous service with the LLP

14.2   During parental leave and/or family leave the Member shall be entitled to his normal share of the profits of the LLP

14.3   Each Member shall give notice to the LLP of his intended dates of parental or family leave and shall be responsible so far as possible for ensuring that those dates do not conflict with dates of any form of leave already notified to the LLP by such other Members or senior employees of the LLP as may be appropriate having regard to the work undertaken by the Member

15.   Management

15.1   Meetings of the Designated Members and the Members respectively shall be held at least four times a year and shall normally be convened by the Chief Executive but may also be convened by the Chairman or not less than three Designated Members or Members as the case may be (or by any liquidator of the LLP appointed under the Insolvency Act)

15.2   Not less than one month's notice of any such meeting shall be given to all those entitled to attend the same provided that any resolution passed at a meeting of which shorter notice or no notice has been given shall be deemed to have been duly passed if it is afterwards ratified by the required majority of the Designated Members or the Members as the case may be at a meeting thereof which has been duly convened

15.3   Meetings of either the Designated Members or the Members shall be chaired by the Chairman or by the Chief Executive in the Chairman's absence or if neither of them shall be present then by such Designated Member or Member as shall be appointed for the purpose by those present at the meeting

15.4   No business shall be conducted at a meeting of the Designated Members or the Members as the case may be unless the Designated Members' Quorum or the Members' Quorum shall respectively be present in person provided that any resolution passed at an inquorate meeting shall be deemed to have been duly passed if it is afterwards ratified by the required majority of the Designated Members or the Members as the case may be at a quorate meeting thereof duly convened

15.5 Proxy voting shall not be permitted

15.6 Any matters which are by reason of the Act or by this Agreement reserved for the decision of the Designated Members shall be determined by them [by a simple majority] *or* [by unanimous vote] at a duly convened meeting provided that a resolution in writing signed as approved by [a majority] *or* [all] of the Designated Members shall be as valid as a resolution passed at such a meeting

15.7 Any matters not either:

    15.7.1 reserved as above for the decision of the Designated Members (or which have been thus reserved but in respect of which the Designated Members shall have defaulted or shall appear likely to default in exercising their powers or taking any decision or other step required of them by the Act or any other statute within any time limit prescribed therefor) or

    15.7.2 delegated as below for the decision of a committee shall be determined by the Members by their votes at a duly convened meeting (save that any such decision taken in anticipation of any default by the Designated Members in acting as above shall only take effect upon the expiry of the time prescribed by law for that action if the Designated Members shall not in fact have acted appropriately by that time)

15.8 At any meeting of the Members a decision may be taken by a simple majority save that:

    15.8.1 a majority of not less than seventy five per cent of the Members present and voting shall be required for any of the following purposes

        15.8.1.1 any determination to be made under the Insolvency Act including in particular but without limitation any determination to propose for a Voluntary Arrangement in respect of or a voluntary winding-up of the LLP

        15.8.1.2 any resolution to appoint any Member(s) as delegates empowered on behalf of the LLP to approve or reject under Section 4(5A) of the Insolvency Act any modifications to any proposed Voluntary Arrangement in respect of the LLP

        15.8.1.3 any resolution to appoint remove or fill a vacancy in the office of a liquidator of the LLP

15.8.1.4 any resolution to give or withhold any sanction required under the Insolvency Act including in particular but without limitation any sanction under Section 110(3) or Section 165(2) thereof

15.8.2 a unanimous vote of the Members present and voting shall be required for any of the following purposes:

15.8.2.1 the opening or closing of any place of business of the LLP

15.8.2.2 the admission or expulsion of any Member or the passing of a resolution authorising the service or revocation of any notice requiring any Member to retire in accordance with clause 20.3

15.8.2.3 the appointment of any Member as a Designated Member or the revocation of any such appointment

15.8.2.4 the appointment of all Members for the time being as Designated Members or any reversal of any such resolution

15.8.2.5 the purchase of any capital item or connected items of equipment having (in the aggregate where appropriate) a cost in excess of the Expenditure Limit

15.8.2.6 the borrowing or lending by the LLP or the giving of any guarantee or undertaking by the LLP of or in respect of any sum or connected sums being (in the aggregate where appropriate) in excess of the Expenditure Limit

15.8.2.7 the delegation (or revocation of such delegation) of powers to a committee in accordance with sub-clause 15.9

15.8.2.8 a change in the nature of the Business

15.9 The Members may from time to time delegate (or revoke the delegation of) any of their powers of managing or conducting the affairs of the LLP to a committee or committees consisting of such Members [and employees of the LLP] as are appointed in the appropriate resolution provided that such delegation may be made subject to such conditions as the resolution may prescribe

15.10 The procedure for the conduct of any such committee as is formed in accordance with sub-clause 15.9 shall be as prescribed by the resolution establishing it or in default thereof shall be as determined by a majority of that committee

15.11 For the avoidance of doubt no Member who is at any time within any of the circumstances prescribed by Section 7(1) of the Act shall have an entitlement to attend any meeting of the Members or the Designated Members or any committee thereof or have any vote at any such meeting and any reference to a resolution requiring to be signed by Members shall be deemed to exclude reference to signature by any such Member

16. Limitations on Members' powers as agents

16.1 No Member shall without the consent of at least the Requisite Number of Members

16.1.1 engage or dismiss any employee of the LLP

16.1.2 except in the ordinary course of the business of the LLP and for the benefit thereof and if the Authority Limit shall not be exceeded pledge the credit of the LLP or incur any liability or lend any monies on behalf of the LLP

16.1.3 give any guarantee or undertaking on behalf of the LLP in respect of any sum or connected sums exceeding (in the aggregate where appropriate) the Authority Limit

16.1.4 compromise or compound or (except on payment in full) release or discharge any debt or connected debts due to the LLP where the same exceed (in the aggregate where appropriate) the Authority Limit

16.2 No Member shall

16.2.1 have any dealings with any person partnership limited liability partnership or limited company with whom or which the Members have previously resolved not to deal

16.2.2 procure that the LLP shall enter into any bond or become bail or surety for any person

16.2.3 knowingly cause or permit or suffer to be done anything whereby the property of the LLP may be taken in execution or otherwise endangered

16.2.4 assign mortgage or charge his interest in the Capital

17. Indemnity and expenses

17.1 The LLP shall indemnify each Member from and against any claims costs and demands arising out of payments made by him or liabilities incurred by him in the performance by him of his duties as a Member in the normal course of the operation of the Business or in respect of anything necessarily done by him for the preservation of the Business or the property of the LLP

17.2 Each Member shall be entitled to charge and be refunded all out-of-pocket expenses properly incurred by him in connection with the Business provided that:

17.2.1 All expenses shall be vouched by an appropriate receipt and VAT invoice where appropriate

17.2.2 If the LLP shall provide a credit card for the use of a Member for such expenses he shall provide the copies of the vouchers for all expenditure charged to such card

17.2.3 The Members may from time to time resolve to place upper limits on any category or categories of expenses of which reimbursement may be claimed by Members

18. Cars

18.1 Each Member shall be provided by the LLP with a car of his choice which shall be the property of the LLP

18.2 The [Designated] Members shall from time to time determine:

18.2.1 a limit or limits to be placed upon the cost of such cars (whether in terms of their price or the cost of any financing arrangements to be entered into in respect of them) and

18.2.2 a policy as to the ability of any Member personally to provide any excess of the cost of his chosen car over and above such limit as above and as to the consequences thereof with regard to the future ownership of the car and the accounting entries thus required

18.2.3 a policy for the periodic replacement of such cars

18.3 Each Member shall be entitled to be reimbursed for the full running cost of the car acquired for him as above including excise tax insurance premiums fuel maintenance and repairs

19. Insurances

19.1 The LLP shall maintain policies of insurance for such respective amounts as the [Designated] Members may from time to time determine in respect of:

19.1.1 the Property

19.1.2 all plant equipment and other chattels belonging to or used by the LLP

19.1.3 all cars and other vehicles belonging to or used by the LLP

19.1.4 employers' liability

19.1.5 public liability

19.1.6 professional negligence

19.1.7 loss of profits consequent upon destruction of or damage to the Property

19.1.8 loss of profits consequent upon destruction of or damage to or theft of any plant equipment chattels cars and other vehicles including in the case of any computers or ancillary equipment any virus or corruption or loss of any software or data

19.1.9 permanent health in respect of the Members [and any such employees of the LLP as the [Designated] Members may determine]

93

19.2   The LLP shall procure at its expense that there shall be in force in respect of each Member a policy of insurance which shall provide that in the event of his being incapacitated by illness or injury and prevented from attending to his duties as a Member for a period of more than 13 successive weeks (or for any lesser period commencing within 26 weeks after a Member shall have resumed normal duties following an absence of more than 13 weeks by reason of illness or injury) the Weekly Sum shall be paid to him for each complete week of incapacity in excess of the said period of 13 weeks

19.3   The LLP shall at its expense effect and maintain for its own benefit such life insurance policies in such sums on the lives of such of the Members as the [Designated] Members shall from time to time determine and Members shall cooperate in the obtaining of such policies and in particular but without limitation shall undergo such medical examination(s) in respect thereof as shall be reasonable

20.   Retirement

20.1   A Designated Member may resign his designation upon giving notice to the LLP and to the other Members such notice to take effect [forthwith] *or* [upon the expiry of the Notice Period from the date of the said notice] save that in the event that such resignation would reduce the number of Designated Members of the LLP to one then the notice shall not take effect until the Members shall have appointed a new Designated Member to fill the vacancy to be created by the said notice

20.2   If any Member shall give to the LLP and to the other Members notice of his intention to retire from the LLP provided that such notice shall be of a duration not less than the Notice Period then on [the Year End Date next following] the expiry of the notice he shall retire from the LLP

20.3   A Member shall be deemed to retire from the LLP:

20.3.1   on the Year End Date next following the birthday upon which he attains the Retirement Age [(or if before that birthday the LLP shall have agreed with the Member in question to substitute a later birthday then upon the Year End Date next following that birthday)]

20.3.2   on the expiry of not less than three months' notice requiring him to retire given to him by the LLP at a time when by reason of illness injury or other cause he has been unable to perform his duties as a Member and has been so unable throughout the period of at least twelve months immediately preceding the service of the notice or for an aggregate period of at least twelve months during the period of twenty-four months immediately preceding such service provided that:

20.3.2.1 there shall be excepted from the calculation of any such period any period(s) of maternity leave, parental leave or family leave (as provided for in clauses 13 and 14) and

20.3.2.2 a notice under this sub-clause shall be of no effect if before it expires the Member upon whom it has been served satisfactorily resumes his duties as a Member and the LLP accordingly resolves to withdraw the notice

20.3.3 forthwith on the service upon him of notice in writing requiring him to retire given by the LLP at any time after he has become a patient within the meaning of the Mental Health Act 1983 Section 94(2) or Section 145(1)

21. Expulsion

21.1 The LLP shall be netitled to expel any Member forthwith by notice in writing given to him if he shall:

21.1.1 commit any grave breach or persistent breaches of this Agreement or

21.1.2 have a bankruptcy order made against him or

21.1.3 fail to pay any monies owing by him to the LLP within 14 days of being requested in writing by the LLP so to do or

21.1.4 be guilty of any conduct likely to have a serious adverse effect upon the Business or

21.1.5 cease to hold any professional qualification or certification required for the normal performance of his duties as a member of the LLP

21.2 Any such notice as is referred to in clause 21.1 shall give sufficient details of the alleged breach or breaches to enable the same to be properly identified.

21.3 If the Member on whom such notice is served shall within fourteen days of the date of service of the said notice serve on the LLP a counter-notice denying the allegations and shall within the said period of fourteen days refer the dispute to Arbitration the operation of the said notice shall be suspended until written notice of acceptance by the Member on whom the said notice has been served is served on the LLP or the decision of the appropriate arbitrator and any reference in this Agreement to a date of cessation of membership consequent upon such a notice of dissolution shall be deemed to be a reference to the date of the notice of acceptance or the decision of the arbitrator as the case may be

22. Provisions relating to death retirement or expulsion

22.1 In the event that any Member shall die or retire or be deemed to retire or shall be expelled on a date other than an Year End Date then

22.1.1   he shall not be entitled to receive any share of the profit of the LLP from the date of his ceasing to be a Member

22.1.2   the LLP shall not be obliged to prepare any accounts other than the accounts which would normally prepared as at the next Year End Date

22.1.3   for the purpose of ascertaining the amount of the interest in the LLP of the Member in question the profits of the LLP in such accounts shall be apportioned on a time basis in respect of the periods before and after his death retirement or expulsion [provided that interest calculated in accordance with Clause 9.1 shall be credited to the relevant Member's Share]

22.2   In the event of the death retirement or expulsion of any Member there shall be due to him from the LLP the amount of his Member's Share as shown in the accounts thereof for the Year End Date next following such death retirement or expulsion or upon which the same shall take effect [(and for the avoidance of doubt there shall be no goodwill payable to him)]

23.   Payments following death retirement or expulsion

23.1   In the event of the death of any Member being an individual the LLP shall:

23.1.1   pay on the first day of each of the three months next following that Member's death an amount equal to the normal monthly drawings then applicable in accordance with Clause 10.1 such payments to be made to the deceased Member's personal representatives or widow or to such other person as the LLP shall at its absolute discretion determine (provided that the LLP shall not be concerned as to whether the recipient(s) of such payments shall in due course prove to be the person(s) entitled at law to the deceased Member's estate)

23.1.2   pay the appropriate Member's Share (after allowing for any such payments as are referred to in clause 23.1.1) to the deceased Member's personal representatives as soon as may be reasonably practical but in any event within one year of his death (together with interest at the Interest Rate on the aggregate amount or the balance thereof from time to time remaining unpaid)

23.2   In the event of any retirement deemed retirement or expulsion of any Member or in the event of the dissolution winding up or striking off of any Member being a body corporate then that Member's Share together with interest at the Interest Rate upon the balance thereof for the time being outstanding shall be paid by the LLP to the retiring or expelled Member or any liquidator appointed in respect of the Member or the Secretary of State (as the case may be) by equal half yearly instalments over the Payment Period (the first such payment being due on the Year End Date occurring next after the retirement expulsion dissolution winding up or striking off takes effect) PROVIDED that the LLP shall be entitled at any time to make such payments at any such earlier time as it thinks fit at its absolute discretion

24.   Other provisions following death retirement or expulsion

24.1   Any Member who shall have retired or been deemed to retire or been expelled shall, not before the second Year End Date following the Cessation Date:

24.1.1   solicit business from canvass for or accept instructions to supply goods or services to or for any person firm or company which has habitually introduced clients or customers to the LLP or was a client or customer of the LLP during the period of one year preceding the Cessation Date

24.1.2   solicit or induce or endeavour to solicit or induce any person who is at the Cessation Date an employee in any capacity whatever of or a Member in the LLP to cease working for or providing services to or membership of the LLP whether or not any such person would thereby commit a breach of contract

24.1.3   employ or otherwise engage anyone who is at the Cessation Date an employee in any capacity whatever or a Member of the LLP

24.1.4   engage in any business of a nature similar to that of the Business (whether on his own account or as a partner or member in or an employee of or consultant to any other person partnership limited liability partnership or limited company) within the Radius of any place of business of the LLP at the Cessation Date

PROVIDED that each of the separate paragraphs of this sub-clause 24.1 shall constitute an entirely separate and independent restriction so that if one or more of them are held to be invalid for any reason whatever then the remaining paragraphs shall nonetheless be valid[7]

24.2   Any member who shall have retired or been deemed to retire or been expelled shall:

24.2.1   forthwith pay into the LLP's bank account all sums due from him to the LLP and any sums not so paid shall be recoverable by the LLP from him as a debt

24.2.2   deliver to the LLP all such books of account records letters and other documents in his possession relating to the LLP as may be required for the continuing conduct of the Business but during any subsequent period in which there shall still be monies owed to him by the LLP the retired or expelled Member or his duly authorised agents shall be permitted to inspect by appointment the books of account records letters and other documents of the LLP insofar as they relate to any period preceding the Cessation Date

24.2.3 sign execute and do all such documents deeds acts and things as the LLP may reasonably request for the purpose of conveying assigning or transferring to them any property or assets which immediately prior to the Cessation Date were vested in the retired or expelled Member as nominee for or in trust for the LLP

25. Winding up

25.1 For the avoidance of doubt no Member has agreed with the other Members or with the LLP that he shall in the event of the winding up of the LLP contribute in any way to the assets of the LLP in accordance with Section 74 of the Insolvency Act

25.2 In the event of the winding up of the LLP then any surplus of assets of the LLP over its liabilities remaining at the conclusion of the winding up after payment of all monies due to the creditors of the LLP and all expenses of the winding up shall be payable by the liquidator to the Members in such proportions as their respective Members' Shares shall have borne to each other on the [day] *or* [the last Year End Date] before the commencement of the winding up

[25.3 In the event that any Court makes a declaration or declarations under Section 214A of the Insolvency Act requiring any Member or Members to make any contribution to the assets of the LLP then the other Member(s) shall indemnify the Member(s) in respect of whom the said declaration(s) shall have been made in such manner that the amount or aggregate amounts payable in accordance with the said declaration(s) shall be borne by the Members in the proportions set out in the fourth schedule][8]

26. Notices

26.1 Any notice herein referred to shall be in writing and shall be sufficiently given to or served on the person to whom it is addressed if it is delivered to or sent in a prepaid first class letter by the Recorded Delivery Service addressed (in the case of notice to the LLP) to its Registered Office or (in the case of notice to any Member) to him at his residential address as registered for the time being with Companies House and shall be deemed to have been delivered in the ordinary course of post

26.2   For the purposes of this Agreement any notice shall be deemed to have been given to the personal representatives of a deceased Member notwithstanding that no grant of representation has been made in respect of his estate in England if the notice is addressed to the deceased Member by name or to his personal representatives by title and is sent by prepaid letter by the Recorded Delivery Service to the residential address as registered for the time being with Companies House of the deceased at his death

27.   Arbitration

Any dispute under or arising out of this Agreement shall be referred in accordance with the Arbitration Acts 1950 to 1996 to a single arbitrator to be appointed in default of agreement by the President for the time being of the [Chartered Institute of Arbitrators[9]] and the decision of the arbitrator shall be final and binding on all parties

AS WITNESS etc

FIRST SCHEDULE
Member's names and residential addresses
[Part 1 : Designated members
Part 2 : Other members]
(set out details)

SECOND SCHEDULE
Initial Property
(set out details)

THIRD SCHEDULE
Prior shares of profit
(set out details)

FOURTH SCHEDULE
Primary Percentage division of profits and losses
(set out details)

FIFTH SCHEDULE
Secondary profit share principles (if any)
(set out details)

Signed by all Members and on behalf of the LLP

NOTES

1. Or their Welsh equivalents 'partneriaeth atebolrwydd cyfyngedig', 'PAC' or 'pac'
2. Omit if already registered
3. It is quite possible for an LLP to be formed for a specific duration or venture, but this has not been provided for here
4. Whilst this is not legally necessary, as members have personal liability for tax, many LLPs will find this a prudent way to avoid members getting into difficulties with the Inland Revenue
5. This would include an obligation not to breach quality assurance standards adopted by the LLP such as Investors in People or ISO 9000
6. The question of whether such duties should or should not be owed by members to each other was probably the most contentious single issue during the passage through Parliament of the Act
7. All constituent parts of this clause should be carefully considered to ensure that they are reasonable and will not be void as being in restraint of trade
8. This clause should be omitted if it is felt that the making of any declaration requiring a contribution will necessarily require a degree of culpability against which it is not appropriate for other Members to offer an indemnity
9. Substitute a relevant professional body where possible

Appendix 2

Legislation

Limited Liability Partnerships Act 2000

2000 Chapter 12

An Act to make provision for limited liability partnerships.

[20th July 2000]

BE IT ENACTED by the Queen's most Excellent Majesty, by and with the advice and consent of the Lords Spiritual and Temporal, and Commons, in this present Parliament assembled, and by the authority of the same, as follows–

INTRODUCTORY

1. – (1)   There shall be a new form of legal entity to be known as a limited liability partnership.

(2)   A limited liability partnership is a body corporate (with legal personality separate from that of its members) which is formed by being incorporated under this Act; and–
- (a)   in the following provisions of this Act (except in the phrase "oversea limited liability partnership"), and
- (b)   in any other enactment (except where provision is made to the contrary or the context otherwise requires),

references to a limited liability partnership are to such a body corporate.

(3)   A limited liability partnership has unlimited capacity.

(4)   The members of a limited liability partnership have such liability to contribute to its assets in the event of its being wound up as is provided for by virtue of this Act.

(5)   Accordingly, except as far as otherwise provided by this Act or any other enactment, the law relating to partnerships does not apply to a limited liability partnership.

(6)   The Schedule (which makes provision about the names and registered offices of limited liability partnerships) has effect.

INCORPORATION

2. – (1)   For a limited liability partnership to be incorporated–
- (a)   two or more persons associated for carrying on a lawful business with a view to profit must have subscribed their names to an incorporation document,
- (b)   there must have been delivered to the registrar either the incorporation document or a copy authenticated in a manner approved by him, and

(c) there must have been so delivered a statement in a form approved by the registrar, made by either a solicitor engaged in the formation of the limited liability partnership or anyone who subscribed his name to the incorporation document, that the requirement imposed by paragraph (a) has been complied with.

(2) The incorporation document must–
   (a) be in a form approved by the registrar (or as near to such a form as circumstances allow),
   (b) state the name of the limited liability partnership,
   (c) state whether the registered office of the limited liability partnership is to be situated in England and Wales, in Wales or in Scotland,
   (d) state the address of that registered office,
   (e) state the name and address of each of the persons who are to be members of the limited liability partnership on incorporation, and
   (f) either specify which of those persons are to be designated members or state that every person who from time to time is a member of the limited liability partnership is a designated member.

(3) If a person makes a false statement under subsection (1)(c) which he–
   (a) knows to be false, or
   (b) does not believe to be true,
he commits an offence.

(4) A person guilty of an offence under subsection (3) is liable–
   (a) on summary conviction, to imprisonment for a period not exceeding six months or a fine not exceeding the statutory maximum, or to both, or
   (b) on conviction on indictment, to imprisonment for a period not exceeding two years or a fine, or to both.

3. – (1) When the requirements imposed by paragraphs (b) and (c) of subsection (1) of section 2 have been complied with, the registrar shall retain the incorporation document or copy delivered to him and, unless the requirement imposed by paragraph (a) of that subsection has not been complied with, he shall–
   (a) register the incorporation document or copy, and
   (b) give a certificate that the limited liability partnership is incorporated by the name specified in the incorporation document.

(2) The registrar may accept the statement delivered under paragraph (c) of subsection (1) of section 2 as sufficient evidence that the requirement imposed by paragraph (a) of that subsection has been complied with.

(3) The certificate shall either be signed by the registrar or be authenticated by his official seal.

(4) The certificate is conclusive evidence that the requirements of section 2 are complied with and that the limited liability partnership is incorporated by the name specified in the incorporation document.

MEMBERSHIP

4. – (1)   On the incorporation of a limited liability partnership its members are the persons who subscribed their names to the incorporation document (other than any who have died or been dissolved).

(2)   Any other person may become a member of a limited liability partnership by and in accordance with an agreement with the existing members.

(3)   A person may cease to be a member of a limited liability partnership (as well as by death or dissolution) in accordance with an agreement with the other members or, in the absence of agreement with the other members as to cessation of membership, by giving reasonable notice to the other members.

(4)   A member of a limited liability partnership shall not be regarded for any purpose as employed by the limited liability partnership unless, if he and the other members were partners in a partnership, he would be regarded for that purpose as employed by the partnership.

5. – (1)   Except as far as otherwise provided by this Act or any other enactment, the mutual rights and duties of the members of a limited liability partnership, and the mutual rights and duties of a limited liability partnership and its members, shall be governed–
> (a)   by agreement between the members, or between the limited liability partnership and its members, or
> (b)   in the absence of agreement as to any matter, by any provision made in relation to that matter by regulations under section 15(c).

(2)   An agreement made before the incorporation of a limited liability partnership between the persons who subscribe their names to the incorporation document may impose obligations on the limited liability partnership (to take effect at any time after its incorporation).

6. – (1)   Every member of a limited liability partnership is the agent of the limited liability partnership.

(2)   But a limited liability partnership is not bound by anything done by a member in dealing with a person if–
> (a)   the member in fact has no authority to act for the limited liability partnership by doing that thing, and
> (b)   the person knows that he has no authority or does not know or believe him to be a member of the limited liability partnership.

(3)   Where a person has ceased to be a member of a limited liability partnership, the former member is to be regarded (in relation to any person dealing with the limited liability partnership) as still being a member of the limited liability partnership unless–
> (a)   the person has notice that the former member has ceased to be a member of the limited liability partnership, or

(b) notice that the former member has ceased to be a member of the limited liability partnership has been delivered to the registrar.

(4) Where a member of a limited liability partnership is liable to any person (other than another member of the limited liability partnership) as a result of a wrongful act or omission of his in the course of the business of the limited liability partnership or with its authority, the limited liability partnership is liable to the same extent as the member.

7. – (1) This section applies where a member of a limited liability partnership has either ceased to be a member or–
  (a) has died,
  (b) has become bankrupt or had his estate sequestrated or has been wound up,
  (c) has granted a trust deed for the benefit of his creditors, or
  (d) has assigned the whole or any part of his share in the limited liability partnership (absolutely or by way of charge or security).

(2) In such an event the former member or–
  (a) his personal representative,
  (b) his trustee in bankruptcy or permanent or interim trustee (within the meaning of the Bankruptcy (Scotland) Act 1985) or liquidator,
  (c) his trustee under the trust deed for the benefit of his creditors, or
  (d) his assignee,
may not interfere in the management or administration of any business or affairs of the limited liability partnership.

(3) But subsection (2) does not affect any right to receive an amount from the limited liability partnership in that event.

8. – (1) If the incorporation document specifies who are to be designated members–
  (a) they are designated members on incorporation, and
  (b) any member may become a designated member by and in accordance with an agreement with the other members,
and a member may cease to be a designated member in accordance with an agreement with the other members.

(2) But if there would otherwise be no designated members, or only one, every member is a designated member.

(3) If the incorporation document states that every person who from time to time is a member of the limited liability partnership is a designated member, every member is a designated member.

(4) A limited liability partnership may at any time deliver to the registrar–
  (a) notice that specified members are to be designated members, or
  (b) notice that every person who from time to time is a member of the limited liability partnership is a designated member,

and, once it is delivered, subsection (1) (apart from paragraph (a)) and subsection (2), or subsection (3), shall have effect as if that were stated in the incorporation document.

(5)   A notice delivered under subsection (4)–
    (a) shall be in a form approved by the registrar, and
    (b) shall be signed by a designated member of the limited liability partnership or authenticated in a manner approved by the registrar.

(6)   A person ceases to be a designated member if he ceases to be a member.

9. – (1)   A limited liability partnership must ensure that–
    (a) where a person becomes or ceases to be a member or designated member, notice is delivered to the registrar within fourteen days, and
    (b) where there is any change in the name or address of a member, notice is delivered to the registrar within 28 days.

(2)   Where all the members from time to time of a limited liability partnership are designated members, subsection (1)(a) does not require notice that a person has become or ceased to be a designated member as well as a member.

(3)   A notice delivered under subsection (1)–
    (a) shall be in a form approved by the registrar, and
    (b) shall be signed by a designated member of the limited liability partnership or authenticated in a manner approved by the registrar,
and, if it relates to a person becoming a member or designated member, shall contain a statement that he consents to becoming a member or designated member signed by him or authenticated in a manner approved by the registrar.

(4)   If a limited liability partnership fails to comply with subsection (1), the partnership and every designated member commits an offence.

(5)   But it is a defence for a designated member charged with an offence under subsection (4) to prove that he took all reasonable steps for securing that subsection (1) was complied with.

(6)   A person guilty of an offence under subsection (4) is liable on summary conviction to a fine not exceeding level 5 on the standard scale.

TAXATION

10. – (1) In the Income and Corporation Taxes Act 1988, after section 118 insert–

"Limited liability partnerships

118ZA Treatment of limited liability partnerships
For the purposes of the Tax Acts, a trade, profession or business carried on by a limited liability partnership with a view to profit shall be treated as carried on in partnership by its members (and not by the limited liability partnership as such); and, accordingly, the property of the limited liability partnership shall be treated for those purposes as partnership property.

118ZB Restriction on relief
Sections 117 and 118 have effect in relation to a member of a limited liability partnership as in relation to a limited partner, but subject to sections 118ZC and 118ZD.

118ZC Member's contribution to trade
(1) Subsection (3) of section 117 does not have effect in relation to a member of a limited liability partnership.
(2) But, for the purposes of that section and section 118, such a member's contribution to a trade at any time ("the relevant time") is the greater of–
 (a) the amount subscribed by him, and
 (b) the amount of his liability on a winding up.
(3) The amount subscribed by a member of a limited liability partnership is the amount which he has contributed to the limited liability partnership as capital, less so much of that amount (if any) as –
 (a) he has previously, directly or indirectly, drawn out or received back,
 (b) he so draws out or receives back during the period of five years beginning with the relevant time,
 (c) he is or may be entitled so to draw out or receive back at any time when he is a member of the limited liability partnership, or
 (d) he is or may be entitled to require another person to reimburse to him.
(4) The amount of the liability of a member of a limited liability partnership on a winding up is the amount which–
 (a) he is liable to contribute to the assets of the limited liability partnership in the event of its being wound up, and
 (b) he remains liable so to contribute for the period of at least five years beginning with the relevant time (or until it is wound up, if that happens before the end of that period).

118ZD Carry forward of unrelieved losses
(1) Where amounts relating to a trade carried on by a member of a limited liability partnership are, in any one or more chargeable periods, prevented from being given or allowed by section 117 or 118 as it applies otherwise than by virtue of this section (his "total unrelieved loss"), subsection (2) applies in each subsequent chargeable period in which–
 (a) he carries on the trade as a member of the limited liability partnership, and
 (b) any of his total unrelieved loss remains outstanding.
(2) Sections 380, 381, 393A(1) and 403 (and sections 117 and 118 as they apply in relation to those sections) shall have effect in the subsequent chargeable period as if–
 (a) any loss sustained or incurred by the member in the trade in that chargeable period were increased by an amount equal to so much of his total unrelieved loss as remains outstanding in that period, or
 (b) (if no loss is so sustained or incurred) a loss of that amount were so sustained or incurred.

(3) To ascertain whether any (and, if so, how much) of a member's total unrelieved loss remains outstanding in the subsequent chargeable period, deduct from the amount of his total unrelieved loss the aggregate of–

    (a) any relief given under any provision of the Tax Acts (otherwise than as a result of subsection (2)) in respect of his total unrelieved loss in that or any previous chargeable period, and

    (b) any amount given or allowed in respect of his total unrelieved loss as a result of subsection (2) in any previous chargeable period (or which would have been so given or allowed had a claim been made)."

(2) In section 362(2)(a) of that Act (loan to buy into partnership), after "partner" insert "in a limited partnership registered under the Limited Partnerships Act 1907".

(3) In the Taxation of Chargeable Gains Act 1992, after section 59 insert–

"59A Limited liability partnerships

(1) Where a limited liability partnership carries on a trade or business with a view to profit–

    (a) assets held by the limited liability partnership shall be treated for the purposes of tax in respect of chargeable gains as held by its members as partners, and

    (b) any dealings by the limited liability partnership shall be treated for those purposes as dealings by its members in partnership (and not by the limited liability partnership as such),

and tax in respect of chargeable gains accruing to the members of the limited liability partnership on the disposal of any of its assets shall be assessed and charged on them separately.

(2) Where subsection (1) ceases to apply in relation to a limited liability partnership with the effect that tax is assessed and charged–

    (a) on the limited liability partnership (as a company) in respect of chargeable gains accruing on the disposal of any of its assets, and

    (b) on the members in respect of chargeable gains accruing on the disposal of any of their capital interests in the limited liability partnership,

it shall be assessed and charged on the limited liability partnership as if subsection (1) had never applied in relation to it.

(3) Neither the commencement of the application of subsection (1) nor the cessation of its application in relation to a limited liability partnership is to be taken as giving rise to the disposal of any assets by it or any of its members."

(4) After section 156 of that Act insert–

"156A Cessation of trade by limited liability partnership

(1) Where, immediately before the time of cessation of trade, a member of a limited liability partnership holds an asset, or an interest in an asset, acquired by him for a consideration treated as reduced under section 152 or 153, he shall be treated as if a chargeable gain equal to the amount of the reduction accrued to him immediately before that time.

(2) Where, as a result of section 154(2), a chargeable gain on the disposal of an asset, or an interest in an asset, by a member of a limited liability partnership has not accrued before the time of cessation of trade, the member shall be treated as if the chargeable gain accrued immediately before that time.

(3) In this section "the time of cessation of trade", in relation to a limited liability partnership, means the time when section 59A(1) ceases to apply in relation to the limited liability partnership."

11. In the Inheritance Tax Act 1984, after section 267 insert–

"267A Limited liability partnerships

For the purposes of this Act and any other enactments relating to inheritance tax–

(a) property to which a limited liability partnership is entitled, or which it occupies or uses, shall be treated as property to which its members are entitled, or which they occupy or use, as partners,

(b) any business carried on by a limited liability partnership shall be treated as carried on in partnership by its members,

(c) incorporation, change in membership or dissolution of a limited liability partnership shall be treated as formation, alteration or dissolution of a partnership, and

(d) any transfer of value made by or to a limited liability partnership shall be treated as made by or to its members in partnership (and not by or to the limited liability partnership as such)."

12. – (1) Stamp duty shall not be chargeable on an instrument by which property is conveyed or transferred by a person to a limited liability partnership in connection with its incorporation within the period of one year beginning with the date of incorporation if the following two conditions are satisfied.

(2) The first condition is that at the relevant time the person–

(a) is a partner in a partnership comprised of all the persons who are or are to be members of the limited liability partnership (and no-one else), or

(b) holds the property conveyed or transferred as nominee or bare trustee for one or more of the partners in such a partnership.

(3) The second condition is that–

(a) the proportions of the property conveyed or transferred to which the persons mentioned in subsection (2)(a) are entitled immediately after the conveyance or transfer are the same as those to which they were entitled at the relevant time, or

(b) none of the differences in those proportions has arisen as part of a scheme or arrangement of which the main purpose, or one of the main purposes, is avoidance of liability to any duty or tax.

(4) For the purposes of subsection (2) a person holds property as bare trustee for a partner if the partner has the exclusive right (subject only to satisfying any outstanding charge, lien or other right of the trustee to resort to the property for

payment of duty, taxes, costs or other outgoings) to direct how the property shall be dealt with.

(5)   In this section "the relevant time" means–
    (a)   if the person who conveyed or transferred the property to the limited liability partnership acquired the property after its incorporation, immediately after he acquired the property, and
    (b)   in any other case, immediately before its incorporation.

(6)   An instrument in respect of which stamp duty is not chargeable by virtue of subsection (1) shall not be taken to be duly stamped unless–
    (a)   it has, in accordance with section 12 of the Stamp Act 1891, been stamped with a particular stamp denoting that it is not chargeable with any duty or that it is duly stamped, or
    (b)   it is stamped with the duty to which it would be liable apart from that subsection.

13.   In section 15 of the Social Security Contributions and Benefits Act 1992 and section 15 of the Social Security Contributions and Benefits (Northern Ireland) Act 1992 (Class 4 contributions), after subsection (3) insert–

"(3A)   Where income tax is (or would be) charged on a member of a limited liability partnership in respect of profits or gains arising from the carrying on of a trade or profession by the limited liability partnership, Class 4 contributions shall be payable by him if they would be payable were the trade or profession carried on in partnership by the members."

REGULATIONS

14. – (1)   Regulations shall make provision about the insolvency and winding up of limited liability partnerships by applying or incorporating, with such modifications as appear appropriate, Parts I to IV, VI and VII of the Insolvency Act 1986.

(2)   Regulations may make other provision about the insolvency and winding up of limited liability partnerships, and provision about the insolvency and winding up of oversea limited liability partnerships, by–
    (a)   applying or incorporating, with such modifications as appear appropriate, any law relating to the insolvency or winding up of companies or other corporations which would not otherwise have effect in relation to them, or
    (b)   providing for any law relating to the insolvency or winding up of companies or other corporations which would otherwise have effect in relation to them not to apply to them or to apply to them with such modifications as appear appropriate.

(3)   In this Act "oversea limited liability partnership" means a body incorporated or otherwise established outside Great Britain and having such connection with Great Britain, and such other features, as regulations may prescribe.

15.   Regulations may make provision about limited liability partnerships and oversea limited liability partnerships (not being provision about insolvency or winding up) by–

(a)   applying or incorporating, with such modifications as appear appropriate, any law relating to companies or other corporations which would not otherwise have effect in relation to them,

(b)   providing for any law relating to companies or other corporations which would otherwise have effect in relation to them not to apply to them or to apply to them with such modifications as appear appropriate, or

(c)   applying or incorporating, with such modifications as appear appropriate, any law relating to partnerships.

16. – (1) Regulations may make in any enactment such amendments or repeals as appear appropriate in consequence of this Act or regulations made under it.

(2)   The regulations may, in particular, make amendments and repeals affecting companies or other corporations or partnerships.

17. – (1) In this Act "regulations" means regulations made by the Secretary of State by statutory instrument.

(2)   Regulations under this Act may in particular–

(a)   make provisions for dealing with non-compliance with any of the regulations (including the creation of criminal offences),

(b)   impose fees (which shall be paid into the Consolidated Fund), and

(c)   provide for the exercise of functions by persons prescribed by the regulations.

(3)   Regulations under this Act may–

(a)   contain any appropriate consequential, incidental, supplementary or transitional provisions or savings, and

(b)   make different provision for different purposes.

(4)   No regulations to which this subsection applies shall be made unless a draft of the statutory instrument containing the regulations (whether or not together with other provisions) has been laid before, and approved by a resolution of, each House of Parliament.

(5)   Subsection (4) applies to–

(a)   regulations under section 14(2) not consisting entirely of the application or incorporation (with or without modifications) of provisions contained in or made under the Insolvency Act 1986,

(b)   regulations under section 15 not consisting entirely of the application or incorporation (with or without modifications) of provisions contained in or made under Part I, Chapter VIII of Part V, Part VII, Parts XI to XIII, Parts XVI to XVIII, Part XX or Parts XXIV to XXVI of the Companies Act 1985,

(c)   regulations under section 14 or 15 making provision about oversea limited liability partnerships, and

(d)   regulations under section 16.

(6)   A statutory instrument containing regulations under this Act shall (unless a draft of it has been approved by a resolution of each House of Parliament) be subject to annulment in pursuance of a resolution of either House of Parliament.

SUPPLEMENTARY

18.   In this Act—

"address", in relation to a member of a limited liability partnership, means—
(a)   if an individual, his usual residential address, and
(b)   if a corporation or Scottish firm, its registered or principal office,

"business" includes every trade, profession and occupation,

"designated member" shall be construed in accordance with section 8,

"enactment" includes subordinate legislation (within the meaning of the Interpretation Act 1978),

"incorporation document" shall be construed in accordance with section 2,

"limited liability partnership" has the meaning given by section 1(2),

"member" shall be construed in accordance with section 4,

"modifications" includes additions and omissions,

"name", in relation to a member of a limited liability partnership, means—
(a)   if an individual, his forename and surname (or, in the case of a peer or other person usually known by a title, his title instead of or in addition to either or both his forename and surname), and
(b)   if a corporation or Scottish firm, its corporate or firm name,

"oversea limited liability partnership" has the meaning given by section 14(3),

"the registrar" means –
(a)   if the registered office of the limited liability partnership is, or is to be, situated in England and Wales or in Wales, the registrar or other officer performing under the Companies Act 1985 the duty of registration of companies in England and Wales, and
(b)   if its registered office is, or is to be, situated in Scotland, the registrar or other officer performing under that Act the duty of registration of companies in Scotland, and

"regulations" has the meaning given by section 17(1).

19. – (1) The preceding provisions of this Act shall come into force on such day as the Secretary of State may by order made by statutory instrument appoint; and different days may be appointed for different purposes.

(2)   The Secretary of State may by order made by statutory instrument make any transitional provisions and savings which appear appropriate in connection with the coming into force of any provision of this Act.

(3)   For the purposes of the Scotland Act 1998 this Act shall be taken to be a pre-commencement enactment within the meaning of that Act.
(4)   Apart from sections 10 to 13 (and this section), this Act does not extend to Northern Ireland.

(5)   This Act may be cited as the Limited Liability Partnerships Act 2000.

SCHEDULE
NAMES AND REGISTERED OFFICES

PART I
NAMES

Index of names

1.   In section 714(1) of the Companies Act 1985 (index of names), after paragraph (d) insert–
     "(da) limited liability partnerships incorporated under the Limited Liability Partnerships Act 2000,".

Name to indicate status

2. – (1)   The name of a limited liability partnership must end with–
     (a)   the expression "limited liability partnership", or
     (b)   the abbreviation "llp" or "LLP".

(2)   But if the incorporation document for a limited liability partnership states that the registered office is to be situated in Wales, its name must end with–
     (a)   one of the expressions "limited liability partnership" and "partneriaeth atebolrwydd cyfyngedig", or
     (b)   one of the abbreviations "llp", "LLP", "pac" and "PAC".

Registration of names

3. – (1)   A limited liability partnership shall not be registered by a name–
     (a)   which includes, otherwise than at the end of the name, either of the expressions "limited liability partnership" and "partneriaeth atebolrwydd cyfyngedig" or any of the abbreviations "llp", "LLP", "pac" and "PAC",
     (b)   which is the same as a name appearing in the index kept under section 714(1) of the Companies Act 1985,
     (c)   the use of which by the limited liability partnership would in the opinion of the Secretary of State constitute a criminal offence, or
     (d)   which in the opinion of the Secretary of State is offensive.

(2)   Except with the approval of the Secretary of State, a limited liability partnership shall not be registered by a name which–
    (a)   in the opinion of the Secretary of State would be likely to give the impression that it is connected in any way with Her Majesty's Government or with any local authority, or
    (b)   includes any word or expression for the time being specified in regulations under section 29 of the Companies Act 1985 (names needing approval),

and in paragraph (a) "local authority" means any local authority within the meaning of the Local Government Act 1972 or the Local Government etc (Scotland) Act 1994, the Common Council of the City of London or the Council of the Isles of Scilly.

Change of name

4. – (1)   A limited liability partnership may change its name at any time.

(2)   Where a limited liability partnership has been registered by a name which–
    (a)   is the same as or, in the opinion of the Secretary of State, too like a name appearing at the time of registration in the index kept under section 714(1) of the Companies Act 1985, or
    (b)   is the same as or, in the opinion of the Secretary of State, too like a name which should have appeared in the index at that time,

the Secretary of State may within twelve months of that time in writing direct the limited liability partnership to change its name within such period as he may specify.

(3)   If it appears to the Secretary of State–
    (a)   that misleading information has been given for the purpose of the registration of a limited liability partnership by a particular name, or
    (b)   that undertakings or assurances have been given for that purpose and have not been fulfilled,

he may, within five years of the date of its registration by that name, in writing direct the limited liability partnership to change its name within such period as he may specify.

(4)   If in the Secretary of State's opinion the name by which a limited liability partnership is registered gives so misleading an indication of the nature of its activities as to be likely to cause harm to the public, he may in writing direct the limited liability partnership to change its name within such period as he may specify.

(5)   But the limited liability partnership may, within three weeks from the date of the direction apply to the court to set it aside and the court may set the direction aside or confirm it and, if it confirms it, shall specify the period within which it must be complied with.

(6)   In sub-paragraph (5) "the court" means–
    (a)   if the registered office of the limited liability partnership is situated in England and Wales or in Wales, the High Court, and
    (b)   if it is situated in Scotland, the Court of Session.

(7)   Where a direction has been given under sub-paragraph (2), (3) or (4) specifying a period within which a limited liability partnership is to change its name, the Secretary of State may at any time before that period ends extend it by a further direction in writing.

(8)   If a limited liability partnership fails to comply with a direction under this paragraph–
    (a)   the limited liability partnership, and
    (b)   any designated member in default,
commits an offence.

(9)   A person guilty of an offence under sub-paragraph (8) is liable on summary conviction to a fine not exceeding level 3 on the standard scale.

Notification of change of name

5. – (1)   Where a limited liability partnership changes its name it shall deliver notice of the change to the registrar.

(2)   A notice delivered under sub-paragraph (1)–
    (a)   shall be in a form approved by the registrar, and
    (b)   shall be signed by a designated member of the limited liability partnership or authenticated in a manner approved by the registrar.

(3)   Where the registrar receives a notice under sub-paragraph (2) he shall (unless the new name is one by which a limited liability partnership may not be registered)–
    (a)   enter the new name in the index kept under section 714(1) of the Companies Act 1985, and
    (b)   issue a certificate of the change of name.

(4)   The change of name has effect from the date on which the certificate is issued.

Effect of change of name

6.   A change of name by a limited liability partnership does not–
    (a)   affect any of its rights or duties,
    (b)   render defective any legal proceedings by or against it,
and any legal proceedings that might have been commenced or continued against it by its former name may be commenced or continued against it by its new name.

Improper use of "limited liability partnership" etc

7. – (1)   If any person carries on a business under a name or title which includes as the last words–
    (a)   the expression "limited liability partnership" or "partneriaeth atebolrwydd cyfyngedig", or

116

(b)   any contraction or imitation of either of those expressions,
that person, unless a limited liability partnership or oversea limited liability
partnership, commits an offence.

(2)   A person guilty of an offence under sub-paragraph (1) is liable on summary
conviction to a fine not exceeding level 3 on the standard scale.

Similarity of names

8.   In determining for the purposes of this Part whether one name is the same
as another there are to be disregarded–
(1)   the definite article as the first word of the name,
(2)   any of the following (or their Welsh equivalents or abbreviations of them or
their Welsh equivalents) at the end of the name–

"limited liability partnership",

"company",

"and company",

"company limited",

"and company limited",
"limited",

"unlimited",

"public limited company", and

"investment company with variable capital", and

(3)   type and case of letters, accents, spaces between letters and punctuation marks,
and "and" and "&" are to be taken as the same.

PART II
REGISTERED OFFICES

Situation of registered office

9. – (1)   A limited liability partnership shall–
(a)   at all times have a registered office situated in England and Wales or in
Wales, or
(b)   at all times have a registered office situated in Scotland,
to which communications and notices may be addressed.

(2)   On the incorporation of a limited liability partnership the situation of its
registered office shall be that stated in the incorporation document.

(3)   Where the registered office of a limited liability partnership is situated in Wales, but the incorporation document does not state that it is to be situated in Wales (as opposed to England and Wales), the limited liability partnership may deliver notice to the registrar stating that its registered office is to be situated in Wales.

(4)   A notice delivered under sub-paragraph (3)–
   (a)   shall be in a form approved by the registrar, and
   (b)   shall be signed by a designated member of the limited liability partnership or authenticated in a manner approved by the registrar.

Change of registered office

10. – (1)   A limited liability partnership may change its registered office by delivering notice of the change to the registrar.

(2)   A notice delivered under sub-paragraph (1)–
   (a)   shall be in a form approved by the registrar, and
   (b)   shall be signed by a designated member of the limited liability partnership or authenticated in a manner approved by the registrar.

Limited Liability Partnerships Regulations 2001

(SI 2001 No 1090)

Made: 19th March 2001
Coming into force: 6th April 2001

Whereas a draft of these Regulations has been approved by a resolution of each House of Parliament pursuant to section 17(4) of the Limited Liability Partnerships Act 2000;

Now, therefore, the Secretary of State, in exercise of the powers conferred on him by sections 14, 15, 16 and 17 of the Limited Liability Partnerships Act 2000 and all other powers enabling him in that behalf hereby makes the following Regulations:

PART I
CITATION, COMMENCEMENT AND INTERPRETATION

Citation and commencement

1. These Regulations may be cited as the Limited Liability Partnerships Regulations 2001 and shall come into force on 6th April 2001.

Interpretation

2. In these Regulations–

"the 1985 Act" means the Companies Act 1985;

"the 1986 Act" means the Insolvency Act 1986;

"the 2000 Act" means the Financial Services and Markets Act 2000;

"devolved", in relation to the provisions of the 1986 Act, means the provisions of the 1986 Act which are listed in Schedule 4 and, in their application to Scotland, concern wholly or partly, matters which are set out in Section C.2 of Schedule 5 to the Scotland Act 1998 as being exceptions to the reservations made in that Act in the field of insolvency;

"limited liability partnership agreement", in relation to a limited liability partnership, means any agreement express or implied between the members of the limited liability partnership or between the limited liability partnership and the members of the limited liability partnership which determines the mutual rights and duties of the members, and their rights and duties in relation to the limited liability partnership;

"the principal Act" means the Limited Liability Partnerships Act 2000; and

"shadow member", in relation to limited liability partnerships, means a person in accordance with whose directions or instructions the members of the limited liability partnership are accustomed to act (but so that a person is not deemed a shadow member by reason only that the members of the limited partnership act on advice given by him in a professional capacity).

PART II
ACCOUNTS AND AUDIT

Application of the accounts and audit provisions of the 1985 Act to limited liability partnerships

3. – (1)   Subject to paragraph (2), the provisions of Part VII of the 1985 Act (Accounts and Audit) shall apply to limited liability partnerships.

(2)   The enactments referred to in paragraph (1) shall apply to limited liability partnerships, except where the context otherwise requires, with the following modifications–

   (a) references to a company shall include references to a limited liability partnership;
   (b) references to a director or to an officer of a company shall include references to a member of a limited liability partnership;
   (c) references to other provisions of the 1985 Act and to provisions of the Insolvency Act 1986 shall include references to those provisions as they apply to limited liability partnerships in accordance with Parts III and IV of these Regulations;
   (d) the modifications set out in Schedule 1 to these Regulations; and
   (e) such further modifications as the context requires for the purpose of giving effect to those provisions as applied by this Part of these Regulations.

PART III
COMPANIES ACT 1985 AND COMPANY DIRECTORS
DISQUALIFICATION ACT 1986

Application of the remainder of the provisions of the 1985 Act and of the provisions of the Company Directors Disqualification Act 1986 to limited liability partnerships

4. – (1)   The provisions of the 1985 Act specified in the first column of Part I of Schedule 2 to these Regulations shall apply to limited liability partnerships, except where the context otherwise requires, with the following modifications–

   (a) references to a company shall include references to a limited liability partnership;
   (b) references to the Companies Acts shall include references to the principal Act and regulations made thereunder;
   (c) references to the Insolvency Act 1986 shall include references to that Act as it applies to limited liability partnerships by virtue of Part IV of these Regulations;

(d) references in a provision of the 1985 Act to other provisions of that Act shall include references to those other provisions as they apply to limited liability partnerships by virtue of these Regulations;

(e) references to the memorandum of association of a company shall include references to the incorporation document of a limited liability partnership;

(f) references to a shadow director shall include references to a shadow member;

(g) references to a director of a company or to an officer of a company shall include references to a member of a limited liability partnership;

(h) the modifications, if any, specified in the second column of Part I of Schedule 2 opposite the provision specified in the first column; and

(i) such further modifications as the context requires for the purpose of giving effect to that legislation as applied by these Regulations.

(2)   The provisions of the Company Directors Disqualification Act 1986 shall apply to limited liability partnerships, except where the context otherwise requires, with the following modifications–

(a) references to a company shall include references to a limited liability partnership;

(b) references to the Companies Acts shall include references to the principal Act and regulations made thereunder and references to the companies legislation shall include references to the principal Act, regulations made thereunder and to any enactment applied by regulations to limited liability partnerships;

(d) references to the Insolvency Act 1986 shall include references to that Act as it applies to limited liability partnerships by virtue of Part IV of these Regulations;

(e) references to the memorandum of association of a company shall include references to the incorporation document of a limited liability partnership;

(f) references to a shadow director shall include references to a shadow member;

(g) references to a director of a company or to an officer of a company shall include references to a member of a limited liability partnership;

(h) the modifications, if any, specified in the second column of Part II of Schedule 2 opposite the provision specified in the first column; and

(i) such further modifications as the context requires for the purpose of giving effect to that legislation as applied by these Regulations.

PART IV
WINDING UP AND INSOLVENCY

Application of the 1986 Act to limited liability partnerships

5. – (1)   Subject to paragraphs (2) and (3), the following provisions of the 1986 Act, shall apply to limited liability partnerships–

(a) Parts I, II, III, IV, VI and VII of the First Group of Parts (company insolvency; companies winding up),

121

   (b) the Third Group of Parts (miscellaneous matters bearing on both company and individual insolvency; general interpretation; final provisions).

(2)   The provisions of the 1986 Act referred to in paragraph (1) shall apply to limited liability partnerships, except where the context otherwise requires, with the following modifications–

   (a) references to a company shall include references to a limited liability partnership;

   (b) references to a director or to an officer of a company shall include references to a member of a limited liability partnership;

   (c) references to a shadow director shall include references to a shadow member;

   (d) references to the 1985 Act, the Company Directors Disqualification Act 1986, the Companies Act 1989 or to any provisions of those Acts or to any provisions of the 1986 Act shall include references to those Acts or provisions as they apply to limited liability partnerships by virtue of the principal Act;

   (e) references to the memorandum of association of a company and to the articles of association of a company shall include references to the limited liability partnership agreement of a limited liability partnership;

   (f) the modifications set out in Schedule 3 to these Regulations; and

   (g) such further modifications as the context requires for the purpose of giving effect to that legislation as applied by these Regulations.

(3)   In the application of this regulation to Scotland, the provisions of the 1986 Act referred to in paragraph (1) shall not include the provisions listed in Schedule 4 to the extent specified in that Schedule.

PART V
FINANCIAL SERVICES AND MARKETS

Application of provisions contained in Parts XV and XXIV of the 2000 Act to limited liability partnerships

6. – (1)   Subject to paragraph (2), sections 215(3), (4) and (6), 356, 359(1) to (4), 361 to 365, 367, 370 and 371 of the 2000 Act shall apply to limited liability partnerships.

(2)   The provisions of the 2000 Act referred to in paragraph (1) shall apply to limited liability partnerships, except where the context otherwise requires, with the following modifications–

   (a) references to a company shall include references to a limited liability partnership;

   (b) references to body shall include references to a limited liability partnership; and

   (c) references to the 1985 Act, the 1986 Act or to any of the provisions of those Acts shall include references to those Acts or provisions as they apply to limited liability partnerships by virtue of the principal Act.

PART VI
DEFAULT PROVISION

Default provision for limited liability partnerships

7.   The mutual rights and duties of the members and the mutual rights and duties of the limited liability partnership and the members shall be determined, subject to the provisions of the general law and to the terms of any limited liability partnership agreement, by the following rules:

(1)   All the members of a limited liability partnership are entitled to share equally in the capital and profits of the limited liability partnership.

(2)   The limited liability partnership must indemnify each member in respect of payments made and personal liabilities incurred by him–
      (a)   in the ordinary and proper conduct of the business of the limited liability partnership; or
      (b)   in or about anything necessarily done for the preservation of the business or property of the limited liability partnership.

(3)   Every member may take part in the management of the limited liability partnership.

(4)   No member shall be entitled to remuneration for acting in the business or management of the limited liability partnership.

(5)   No person may be introduced as a member or voluntarily assign an interest in a limited liability partnership without the consent of all existing members.

(6)   Any difference arising as to ordinary matters connected with the business of the limited liability partnership may be decided by a majority of the members, but no change may be made in the nature of the business of the limited liability partnership without the consent of all the members.

(7)   The books and records of the limited liability partnership are to be made available for inspection at the registered office of the limited liability partnership or at such other place as the members think fit and every member of the limited liability partnership may when he thinks fit have access to and inspect and copy any of them.

(8)   Each member shall render true accounts and full information of all things affecting the limited liability partnership to any member or his legal representatives.

(9)   If a member, without the consent of the limited liability partnership, carries on any business of the same nature as and competing with the limited liability partnership, he must account for and pay over to the limited liability partnership all profits made by him in that business.

(10)   Every member must account to the limited liability partnership for any benefit derived by him without the consent of the limited liability partnership from any

transaction concerning the limited liability partnership, or from any use by him of the property of the limited liability partnership, name or business connection.

Expulsion

8.   No majority of the members can expel any member unless a power to do so has been conferred by express agreement between the members.

PART VII
MISCELLANEOUS

General and consequential amendments

9. – (1)   Subject to paragraph (2), the enactments mentioned in Schedule 5 shall have effect subject to the amendments specified in that Schedule.

(2)   In the application of this regulation to Scotland–
   (a)   paragraph 15 of Schedule 5 which amends section 110 of the 1986 Act shall not extend to Scotland; and
   (b)   paragraph 22 of Schedule 5 which applies to limited liability partnerships the culpable officer provisions in existing primary legislation shall not extend to Scotland insofar as it relates to matters which have not been reserved by Schedule 5 to the Scotland Act 1998.

Application of subordinate legislation

10 – (1)   The subordinate legislation specified in Schedule 6 shall apply as from time to time in force to limited liability partnerships and–
   (a)   in the case of the subordinate legislation listed in Part I of that Schedule with such modifications as the context requires for the purpose of giving effect to the provisions of the Companies Act 1985 which are applied by these Regulations;
   (b)   in the case of the subordinate legislation listed in Part II of that Schedule with such modifications as the context requires for the purpose of giving effect to the provisions of the Insolvency Act 1986 which are applied by these Regulations; and
   (c)   in the case of the subordinate legislation listed in Part III of that Schedule with such modifications as the context requires for the purpose of giving effect to the provisions of the Business Names Act 1985 and the Company Directors Disqualification Act 1986 which are applied by these Regulations.

(2)   In the case of any conflict between any provision of the subordinate legislation applied by paragraph (1) and any provision of these Regulations, the latter shall prevail.

SCHEDULE 1

Regulation 3

MODIFICATIONS TO PROVISIONS OF PART VII OF THE 1985 ACT
APPLIED BY THESE REGULATIONS

Provision of Part VII	*Modification*
Section 222 (Where and for how long accounting records to be kept)	
subsection (5)	In paragraph (a), omit the words "in the case of a private company," and the word "and". Omit paragraph (b).
Section 224 (accounting reference periods and accounting reference date)	
subsections (2) and (3)	Omit subsections (2) and (3).
subsection (3A)	Omit the words "incorporated on or after 1st April 1996".
Section 225 (alteration of accounting reference date)	
subsection (5)	For the words "laying and delivering accounts and reports" substitute "delivering the accounts and the auditors' report".
Section 228 (exemption for parent companies included in accounts of larger group)	Omit subsection (4).
Section 231 (disclosure required in notes to accounts: related undertakings)	
subsection (3)	Omit the words from "This subsection" to the end.
Section 232 (disclosure in notes to accounts: emoluments etc of directors and others)	Omit section 232, save that Schedule 6 shall apply for the purpose of paragraph 56A of Schedule 4, as inserted by this Schedule.

Section 233 (approval and signing of accounts)	
subsection (1)	For subsection (1) substitute: "(1) A limited liability partnership's annual accounts shall be approved by the members, and shall be signed on behalf of all the members by a designated member.".
subsection (3)	Omit the words from "laid before" to "otherwise", and for the words "the board" substitute "the members of the limited liability partnership".
subsection (4)	For the words "the board by a director of the company" substitute "the members by a designated member".
subsection (6)	In paragraph (a), omit the words "laid before the company, or otherwise".
Sections 234 (duty to prepare directors' report) and 234A (approval and signing of directors' report)	Omit sections 234 and 234A.
Section 235 (auditors' report)	
subsection (1)	For subsection (1) substitute: "(1) The limited liability partnership's annual accounts shall be submitted to its auditors, who shall make a report on them to the members of the limited liability partnership.".
subsection (3)	Omit subsection (3).
Section 236 (signature of auditors' report)	
subsection (2)	For subsection (2) substitute: "(2) Every copy of the auditors' report which is circulated, published or issued shall state the names of the auditors.".
subsection (4)	In paragraph (a) omit the words "laid before the company, or otherwise".
Section 237 (duties of auditors)	

subsection (4)	Omit subsection (4).
Section 238 (persons entitled to receive copies of accounts and report)	
subsection (1)	For subsection (1) substitute: "(1) A copy of the limited liability partnership's annual accounts, together with a copy of the auditors' report on those accounts, shall be sent to every member of the limited liability partnership and to every holder of the limited liability partnership's debentures, within one month of their being signed in accordance with section 233(1) and in any event not later than 10 months after the end of the relevant accounting reference period."
subsection (2)	(a) In paragraph (a), omit the words from "who is" to "meetings and", and (b) in paragraph (b) and (c), omit the words "shares or" in both places where they occur.
subsections (3) and (4)	Omit subsections (3) and (4).
subsection (4A)	Omit the words ", of the directors' report".
subsections (4C) to (4E)	Omit subsections (4C) to (4E).
Section 239 (right to demand copies of accounts and report)	
subsection (1)	Omit the words "and directors' report".
subsection (2B)	Omit subsection (2B).
Section 240 (requirements in connection with publication of accounts)	
subsection (1)	Omit the words from "or, as the case may be," to the end.
subsection (3)	(a) In paragraph (c) omit the words from "and, if no such report has been made," to "any financial year", (b) in paragraph (d), omit the words "or whether any report made for the purposes of section 249A(2) was qualified", and

	(c) omit the words "or any report made for the purposes of section 249A(2)".
Section 241 (accounts and report to be laid before general meeting)	Omit section 241.
Section 242 (accounts and report to be delivered to registrar)	
subsection (1)	(a) For the words "The directors of a company" substitute "The designated members of a limited liability partnership", (b) omit the words "a copy of the directors' report for that year and", (c) for the words "or reports" substitute "or that report", and (d) for the words "the directors shall annex" substitute "the designated members shall annex".
subsection (2)	(a) For the words "laying and delivering accounts and reports", substitute "delivering the accounts and the auditors' report", and (b) for the word "director" substitute the words "designated member".
subsection (3)	For the words "the directors" in each place where they occur substitute the words " the designated members".
subsection (4)	For the words "laying and delivering accounts and reports", substitute "delivering the accounts and the auditors' report".
Section 242A (civil penalty for failure to deliver accounts)	
subsection (1)	(a) For the words "laying and delivering accounts and reports" substitute "delivering the accounts and the auditors' report", and (b) for the words "the directors" substitute "the designated members".
subsection (2)	(a) For the words "laying and delivering accounts and reports" substitute "delivering the accounts and the auditors' report", (b) omit the words ", and whether the company is a public or private company,",

	(c) omit the heading "*Public company*" and all entries under it, and (d) for the heading "*Private company*" substitute "*Amount of penalty*".
Section 242B (delivery and publications of accounts in euros)	
subsection (2)	For the words "the directors of a company" substitute "the designated members of a limited liability partnership".
Section 243 (accounts of subsidiary undertakings to be appended in certain cases)	
subsection (4)	For the words "the directors" substitute "the designated members".
Section 244 (period allowed for delivering accounts and report)	
subsection (1)	For subsection (1), substitute the following: "(1) The period allowed for delivering the accounts and the auditors' report is 10 months after the end of the relevant accounting reference period. This is subject to the following provisions of this section."
subsection (2)	In paragraph (a), omit the words "or 7 months, as the case may be,".
subsection (3)	(a) For the words "the directors" substitute "the designated members", and (b) in paragraph (b), for the words "laying and delivering accounts and reports" substitute "delivering the accounts and the auditors' report".
subsection (4)	For the words "laying and delivering accounts" substitute "delivering the accounts and the auditors' report".
Section 245 (voluntary revision of accounts)	

subsection (1)	Omit the words ", or any directors' report," and the words "or a revised report".
subsection (2)	(a) Omit the words " or report" in both places where they occur, and (b) omit the words "laid before the company in general meeting or".
subsection (3)	Omit the words "or a revised directors' report".

subsection (4)	(a) In paragraph (a), omit the words "or report",
	(b) in paragraph (b), omit the words "or reporting accountant" and the words "or report", and
	(c) in paragraph (c):
	    (i) for the words "previous accounts or report" substitute "previous accounts",
	    (ii) omit sub-paragraph (ii), and
	    (iii) omit the words from ",or where a summary financial statement" to the end.

Section 245A (Secretary of State's notice in respect of annual accounts)	
subsection (1)	For the words from "copies of" to "general meeting or" substitute "a copy of a limited liability partnership's annual accounts has been".
Section 245B (application to court in respect of defective accounts)	
subsection (3)	Omit paragraph (b).
Section 246 special provisions for small companies)	
subsection (3)	Omit paragraph (a), and paragraph (b) (ii), (iii) and (iv).
subsection (4)	Omit subsection (4).
subsection (5)	(a) For the words "the directors of the company" substitute "the designated members of the limited liability partnership", and (b) omit paragraph (b).

subsection (6)	Omit paragraphs (b) and (c).
subsection (8)	Omit paragraph (b) and the words ", in the report" and ", 234A".
Section 246A (special provisions for medium-sized companies)	
subsection (3)	(a) For the words "The company" substitute "The designated members", and (b) for paragraph (a), substitute the following: "(a) which includes a profit and loss account in which the following items listed in the profit and loss account formats set out in Part I of Schedule 4 are combined as one item under the heading "gross profit or loss" Items 1 to 3 and 6 in Format 1 Items 1 to 5 in Format 2."
Section 247 (qualification of company as small or medium-sized)	
subsection (5)	In paragraph (a), for the words "items A to D" substitute "items B to D".
Section 247A (cases in which special provisions do not apply)	
subsection (1)	Omit paragraphs (a)(i) and (ii).
Section 247B (special auditors' report)	
subsection (1)	(a) In paragraph (a), for the words "the directors of a company" substitute "the designated members of a limited liability partnership", and (b) in paragraph (b) omit the words "or (2)".
Section 249A (exemptions from audit)	
subsection (2)	Omit subsection (2).
subsection (3A)	Omit subsection (3A).

subsection (4)	Omit subsection (4).
subsection (6)	Omit the words "or gross income".
subsection (6A)	Omit the words "or (2)".
subsection (7)	Omit the words from ", and 'gross income'" to the end.
Section 249AA (dormant companies)	
subsection (1)	For the words "section 249B(2) to (5)" substitute "section 249B (4) and (5)".
subsection (2)	In paragraph (a), for the words "section 247A(1)(a)(i) or (b)" substitute "section 247A(1)(b)".
subsection (3)	Omit paragraph (a).
subsection (5)	In paragraph (b), omit the words "(6) or".
subsection (6)	Omit subsection (6).
subsection (7)	In paragraph (a), for the words "section 28 (change of name)" substitute "paragraph 5 of the Schedule to the Limited Liability Partnerships Act 2000". Omit paragraph (b).
Section 249B (cases where audit exemption not available)	
subsection (1)	Omit the words "or (2)" and paragraphs (a) and (b).
subsection (1C)	For paragraph (b), substitute "that the group's aggregate turnover in that year (calculated in accordance with section 249) is not more than £1 million net (or £1.2 million gross),".
subsections (2) and (3)	Omit subsections (2) and (3).
subsection (4)	(a) Omit the words "or (2)" in both places where they occur, and (b) omit paragraph (b).
Sections 249C (the report required for the purposes of	Omit sections 249C and 249D.

section 249A(2)) and 249D (the reporting accountant)	
Section 249E (effect of exemption from audit)	
subsection (1)	(a) In paragraph (b) omit the words from "or laid" to the end, and (b) omit paragraph (c).
subsection (2)	Omit subsection (2).
Section 251 (provision of summary financial statement by listed public companies)	Omit section 251.
Sections 252 and 253 (private company election to dispense with laying of accounts and reports)	Omit sections 252 and 253.
Section 254 (exemption for unlimited companies from requirement to deliver accounts and reports)	Omit section 254.
Section 255 (special provisions for banking and insurance companies)	Omit section 255.
Section 255A (special provisions for banking and insurance groups)	Omit section 255A.
Section 255B (modification of disclosure requirements in relation to banking company or group)	Omit section 255B.
Section 255D (power to apply provisions to banking partnerships)	Omit section 255D.
Section 257 (power of Secretary of State to alter accounting requirements)	Omit section 257.
Section 260 (participating interests)	

subsection (6)	For the words from ", Schedule 8A," to "Schedule 9A" substitute the words "and Schedule 8A".
Section 262 (minor definitions)	
subsection (1)	(a) Omit the definitions of "annual report", and "credit institution", and (b) insert the following definition at the appropriate place: ""limited liability partnership" means a limited liability partnership formed and registered under the Limited Liability Partnerships Act 2000;".
subsection (2)	Omit subsection (2).
Section 262A (index of defined expressions)	In the index of defined expressions: (a) the entries relating to "annual report" "credit institution" and "reporting accountant", and all entries relating to sections 255 and 255A and to Schedules 9 and 9A, shall be omitted, and (b) the following entry shall be inserted at the appropriate place: ""limited liability partnership" section 262".
Schedule 4 (form and content of company accounts)	
Paragraph 1	In sub-paragraph (1)(b), for the words "any one of" substitute "either of".
Paragraph 3	In sub-paragraph (2)(b), omit the words "shares or". Omit sub-paragraph (7)(b) and (c).
Balance Sheet Format 1	Omit the following items and the notes on the balance sheet formats which relate to them: (a) item A (called up share capital not paid), (b) item B.III.7 (own shares), (c) item C.II.5 (called up share capital not paid), and (d) item C.III.2 (own shares). For item K (capital and reserves) substitute: "**K.** Loans and other debts due to members *(12)*

	L. Members' other interests I Members' capital II Revaluation reserve III Other reserves."
Balance Sheet Format 2	Omit the following items and the notes on the balance sheet format which relate to them: (a) Assets item A (called up share capital not paid), (b) Assets item B.III.7 (own shares), (c) Assets item C.II.5 (called up share capital not paid), and (d) Assets item C.III.2 (own shares). For Liabilities item A (capital and reserves) substitute: "**A.** Loans and other debts due to members *(12)* **AA.** Members' other interests I Members' capital II Revaluation reserve III Other reserves."
Notes on the balance sheet formats	
Note *(12)*	Substitute the following as Note *(12)*: "*(12) Loans and other debts due to members* (Format 1, item K and Format 2, item A) The following amounts shall be shown separately under this item– (a) the aggregate amount of money advanced to the limited liability partnership by the members by way of loan, (b) the aggregate amount of money owed to members by the limited liability partnership in respect of profits, (c) any other amounts."
Profit and Loss Account Formats	In Format 1, for item 20 (profit or loss for the financial year) substitute: "**20.** Profit or loss for the financial year before members' remuneration and profit shares" In Format 2, for item 22 (profit or loss for the financial year) substitute: "**22.** Profit or loss for the financial year before members' remuneration and profit shares" Omit Profit and Loss Account Formats 3 and 4 and the notes on the profit and loss account formats which relate to them.

Notes on the profit and loss account formats	
Note *(15)* (income from other fixed asset investments: other interest receivable and similar income)	At the end of Note *(15)* insert the words "Interest receivable from members shall not be included under this item."
Note *(16)* (interest payable and similar charges)	At the end of Note *(16)* insert "Interest payable to members shall not be included under this item."
Accounting principles and rules	
Paragraph 12	In sub-paragraph (b) omit the words "on behalf of the board of directors".
Paragraph 34	Omit sub-paragraph (3), (3A) and (3B).
Notes to the accounts	
Paragraph 37	For the words "38 to 51" substitute the words "41 to 51(1)".
Insertion of new paragraph after paragraph 37	Insert the following new paragraph after paragraph 37: " *Loans and other debts due to members* **37A.** The following information shall be given– (a) the aggregate amounts of loans and other debts due to members as at the date of the beginning of the financial year, (b) the aggregate amounts contributed by members during the financial year, (c) the aggregate amounts transferred to or from the profit and loss account during that year, (d) the aggregate amounts withdrawn by members or applied on behalf of members during that year, (e) the aggregate amount of loans and other debts due to members as at the balance sheet date, and (f) the aggregate amount of loans and other debts due to members that fall due after one year."
Paragraphs 38 to 40	Omit paragraphs 38 to 40.

Paragraphs 49 and 51(2)	Omit paragraphs 49 and 51(2).

Paragraph 56	Insert the following paragraph after paragraph 56:
	"Particulars of members
	56A.
	(1) Particulars shall be given of the average number of members of the limited liability partnership in the financial year, which number shall be determined by dividing the relevant annual number by the number of months in the financial year.
	(2) The relevant annual number shall be determined by ascertaining for each month in the financial year the number of members of the limited liability partnership for all or part of that month, and adding together all the monthly numbers.
	(3) Where the amount of the profit of the limited liability partnership for the financial year before members' remuneration and profit shares exceeds £200,000, there shall be disclosed the amount of profit (including remuneration) which is attributable to the member with the largest entitlement to profit (including remuneration).
	For the purpose of determining the amount to be disclosed, "remuneration" includes any emoluments specified in paragraph 1(1)(a), (c) or (d) of Schedule 6 to this Act which are paid by or receivable from–
	    (i) the limited liability partnership; and
	    (ii) the limited liability partnership's subsidiary undertakings; and
	    (iii) any other person.".".

Paragraph 58	Omit sub-paragraph (3)(c).
Special provisions where the company is an investment company	
Paragraphs 71 to 73	Omit paragraphs 71 to 73.
Schedule 4A (form and content of group accounts)	
Paragraph 1	Omit sub-paragraph (3).

Paragraph 10	Omit sub-paragraph (1)(a) to (c). Omit sub-paragraph (2).
Paragraph 11	For sub-paragraph (1), substitute: "(1) Where a limited liability partnership adopts the merger method of accounting, it must comply with this paragraph, and with generally accepted accounting principles or practice." Omit sub-paragraphs (5) to (7).
Paragraph 17	(a) In sub-paragraph (2)(a), for the words "item K" substitute "item L", (b) in sub-paragraph (2)(b), for the words "item A" substitute "item AA", and (c) In sub-paragraphs (3) and (4), omit paragraphs (c) and (d).
Paragraph 21	In sub-paragraph (3), omit paragraphs (c) and (d).
Schedule 5 (disclosure of information: related undertakings)	
Paragraph 6	Omit paragraph 6.
Paragraph 9A	Omit paragraph 9A.
Paragraph 20	Omit paragraph 20.
Paragraph 28A	Omit paragraph 28A.
Schedule 8 (form and content of accounts prepared by small companies)	
Paragraph 1	In sub-paragraph (1)(b), for the words "any one of" substitute "either of".
Paragraph 3	In sub-paragraph (2)(b), omit the words "shares or". Omit sub-paragraph (7)(b).
Balance Sheet Format 1	Omit item A (called up share capital not paid) and note (1) on the balance sheet format. For item K (capital and reserves) substitute: "**K.** Loans and other debts due to members(9)

	L. Members' other interests
	    I Members' capital
	    II Revaluation reserve
	    III Other reserves".

Balance Sheet Format 2	Omit Assets item A (called up share capital not paid) and note (1) on the balance sheet format. For Liabilities item A (capital and reserves) substitute:
	"**A.** Loans and other debts due to members (9)
	AA. Members' other interests
	    I Members' capital
	    II Revaluation reserve
	    III Other reserves".

Notes on the balance sheet formats	
Note *(4)* (Others: Other investments)	Omit Note *(4)*.

Note *(9)*	Substitute the following as Note *(9)*:
	"*(9) Loans and other debts due to members*
	(Format 1, item K and Format 2, item A)
	The following amounts shall be shown separately under this item–
	    (a) the aggregate amount of money advanced to the limited liability partnership by the members by way of loan,
	    (b) the aggregate amount of money owed to members by the limited liability partnership in respect of profits,
	    (c) any other amounts.".

Profit and Loss Account Formats	In Format 1, for item 20 (profit or loss for the financial year) substitute: "**20.** Profit or loss for the financial year before members' remuneration and profit shares" In Format 2, for item 22 (profit or loss for the financial year) substitute: "**22.** Profit or loss for the financial year before members' remuneration and profit shares" Omit Profit and Loss Account Formats 3 and 4 and the notes on the profit and loss account formats which relate to them.
Notes on the profit and loss account formats	

Note *(12)* (income from other fixed asset investments: other interest receivable and similar income)	At the end of Note *(12)* insert the words "Interest receivable from members shall not be included under this item."
Note *(13)* (interest payable and similar charges)	At the end of Note *(13)* insert "Interest payable to members shall not be included under this item.".
Accounting principles and rules	
Paragraph 12	In sub-paragraph (b), omit the words "on behalf of the board of directors".
Paragraph 34	Omit sub-paragraphs (3), (4) and (5).
Notes to the accounts	
Paragraph 37	For the words "Paragraphs 38 to 47" substitute "Paragraphs 40 to 47".
Insertion of new paragraph after paragraph 37	Insert the following new paragraph after paragraph 37: "*Loans and other debts due to members* **37A.** The following information shall be given— (a) the aggregate amount of loans and other debts due to members as at the date of the beginning of the financial year, (b) the aggregate amounts contributed by members during the financial year, (c) the aggregate amounts transferred to or from the profit and loss account during that year, (d) the aggregate amounts withdrawn by members or applied on behalf of members during that year, (e) the aggregate amount of loans and other debts due to members as at the balance sheet date, and (f) the aggregate amount of loans and other debts due to members that fall due after one year."
Paragraphs 38 and 39	Omit paragraphs 38 and 39.
Paragraph 45	Omit paragraph 45.

Paragraph 51	Omit sub-paragraph (3)(c).
Schedule 8A (form and content of abbreviated accounts of small companies delivered to registrar)	
Balance Sheet Format 1	Omit item A (called up share capital not paid). For item K (capital and reserves) substitute: "**K.** Loans and other debts due to members **L.** Members' other interests I Members' capital II Revaluation reserve III Other reserves".
Balance Sheet Format 2	Omit Assets item A (called up share capital not paid). For Liabilities item A (capital and reserves) substitute: "**A.** Loans and other debts due to members **AA.** Members' other interests I Members' capital II Revaluation reserve III Other reserves".
Notes to the accounts	
Paragraphs 5 and 6	Omit paragraphs 5 and 6.
Paragraph 9	Omit sub-paragraph (3)(c).

SCHEDULE 2

Regulation 4

PART I
MODIFICATIONS TO PROVISIONS OF THE 1985 ACT APPLIED TO LIMITED LIABILITY PARTNERSHIPS

Provisions	*Modifications*
Formalities of carrying on business	
24 (minimum membership for carrying on business)	In the first paragraph omit the words ", other than a private company limited by shares or by guarantee,".
36 (company contracts England and Wales)	

36A (execution of documents	In subsection (4) for "a director and the secretary of a company, or by two directors of a company," substitute "two members of a limited liability partnership". In subsection (6) for "a director and the secretary of a company, or by two directors of the company" substitute "two members of a limited liability partnership".
36C (pre-incorporation contracts, deeds and obligations)	
37 (bills of exchange and promissory notes)	
38 (execution of deeds abroad)	
39 (power of company to have official seal for use abroad)	In subsection (1), omit the words "whose objects require or comprise the transaction of business in foreign countries may, if authorised by its articles" and before the word "have" insert the word "may".
41 (authentication of documents)	For "director, secretary or other authorised officer" substitute "member".
42 (events affecting a company's status)	
subsection (1)	In subsection (1), for "other persons" substitute "persons other than members of the limited liability partnership".
subsection (1)(b)	In subsection (1)(b) omit the words "or articles".
subsection (1)(c)	Omit subsection (1)(c).
Miscellaneous provisions about shares and debentures	
183 (transfer and registration)	
subsection (1)	Subsection (1), omit the words "shares in or". For the words "company's articles" substitute "limited liability partnership agreement.".
subsection (2)	Subsection (2), omit the words "shareholder or" together with the words "shares in or".

subsection (3)	Omit subsection (3).
subsection (4)	Omit subsection (4).
subsection (5)	Omit the words "shares or".
184 (certification of transfers)	
subsection (1)	Subsection (1), omit the words "shares in or" together with the words "shares or".
185 (duty of company as to issue of certificates)	
subsection (1)	Subsection (1), omit the words "shares," in each of the four places that it occurs.
subsection (3)	Omit subsection (3).
subsection (4)	Omit the words "shares or" together with the words "shares,".
Debentures	
190 (register of debenture holders)	
191 (right to inspect register)	
subsection (1)	In subsection (1), paragraph (a), for the words "or any holder of shares in the company" substitute "or any member of the limited liability partnership".
subsection (2)	In subsection (2), delete "or holder of shares".
subsection (6)	In subsection (6), delete the words "in the articles or".
192 (liability of trustees of debentures)	
193 (perpetual debentures)	
194 (power to re-issue redeemed debentures)	
subsection (1)(a)	In subsection (1)(a), omit the words "in the articles or".

subsection (1)(b)	In subsection (1)(b), for "passing a resolution" substitute "making a determination".
195 (contract to subscribe for debentures)	
196 (payment of debts out of assets subject to floating charge (England and Wales))	
Officers and registered office	
287 (registered office)	For section 287 there shall be substituted: "(1) The change of registered office takes effect upon the notice of change of registered office (delivered to the registrar in accordance with paragraph 10 of the Schedule to the Limited Liability Partnerships Act 2000), being registered by the registrar, but until the end of the period of 14 days beginning with the date on which it is registered a person may validly serve any document on the limited liability partnership at its previous registered office. (2) Where a limited liability partnership unavoidably ceases to perform at its registered office any duty to keep at its registered office any register, index or other document or to mention the address of its registered office in any document in circumstances in which it was not practicable to give prior notice to the registrar of a change in the situation of the registered office, but– (a) resumes performance of that duty at other premises as soon as practicable, and (b) gives notice accordingly to the registrar of a change in the situation of its registered office within 14 days of doing so it shall not be treated as having failed to comply with that duty".
288 (register of directors and secretaries)	For section 288 there shall be substituted: "Where a person becomes a member or designated member of a limited liability partnership the notice to be delivered to the registrar under section 9(1)(a) of the Limited Liability Partnerships Act 2000 shall contain the following particulars with respect to that person– (1) name, which–

	(a) in the case of an individual means his forename and surname (or, in the case of a peer or other person usually known by a title, his title instead of or in addition to either or both his forename and surname), and (b) if a corporation or a Scottish firm, its corporate or firm name; and (2) address, which– (a) in the case of an individual means his usual residential address; and (b) if a corporation or a Scottish firm, its registered or principal office; and (3) in the case of an individual, the date of his birth."
Company identification	
348 (company name to appear outside place of business)	
349 (company's name to appear in its correspondence)	
350 (company seal)	
351 (particulars in correspondence etc.)	In subsection (1) for paragraph (c) substitute the words "in the case of a limited liability partnership, whose name ends with the abbreviation "llp", "LLP", "pac" or "PAC", the fact that it is a limited liability partnership or a partneriaeth atebolrwydd cyfyngedig." Also in subsection (1) delete paragraph (d) and delete subsection (2).
Annual return	
363 (duty to deliver annual returns)	Section 363 of the 1985 Act shall apply to a limited liability partnership being modified so as to read as follows: "(1) Every limited liability partnership shall deliver to the registrar successive annual returns each of which is made up to a date not later than the date which is from time to time the "return date" of the limited liability partnership, that is–

	(a) the anniversary of the incorporation of the limited liability partnership, or
	(b) if the last return delivered by the limited liability partnership in accordance with this section was made up to a different date, the anniversary of that date.
	(2) Each return shall–
	    (a) be in a form approved by the registrar,
	    (b) contain the information required by section 364, and
	    (c) be signed by a designated member of the limited liability partnership.
	(3) If a limited liability partnership fails to deliver an annual return in accordance with this section before the end of the period of 28 days after the return date, the limited liability partnership is guilty of an offence and liable on summary conviction to a fine not exceeding level 5 on the standard scale. The contravention continues until such time as an annual return made up to that return date and complying with the requirements of subsection (2) (except as to date of delivery) is delivered by the limited liability partnership to the registrar.
	(4) Where a limited liability partnership is guilty of an offence under subsection (3) every designated member of the limited liability partnership is similarly liable unless he shows that he took all reasonable steps to avoid the commission of or the continuance of the offence."

364 (contents of annual return: general)	For section 364 substitute the following:
	"Every annual return shall state the date to which it is made up and shall contain the following information–
	    (a) the address of the registered office of the limited liability partnership,
	    (b) the names and usual residential addresses of the members of the limited liability partnership and, if some only of them are designated members, which of them are designated members, and
	    (c) if any register of debenture holders (or a duplicate of any such register or a part of it) is not kept at the registered office of the limited liability partnership, the address of the place where it is kept."

Auditors	
384 (duty to appoint auditors)	
subsection (2)	In subsection (2), for the words from "(appointment at general meeting at which accounts are laid)" to the end substitute the words "(appointment of auditors)".
subsection (3)	In subsection (3), omit the words from "or 385A(2)" to the end.
subsection (4)	For subsection (4) substitute the following subsection: "(4) A person is eligible for appointment by a limited liability partnership as auditor only if, were the limited liability partnership a company, he would be eligible under Part II of the Companies Act 1989 for appointment as a "company auditor"."
subsection (5)	Insert a new subsection (5): "(5) Part II of the Companies Act 1989 shall apply in respect of auditors of limited liability partnerships as if the limited liability partnerships were companies formed and registered under this Act, and references in Part II to an officer of a company shall include reference to a member of a limited liability partnership."
385 (appointment at general meeting at which accounts laid)	
title to the section	In the title to the section for the existing wording substitute "Appointment of auditors".
subsection (1)	Omit subsection (1).
subsection (2)	For subsection (2) substitute: "(2) The designated members of a limited liability partnership shall appoint the auditors for the first financial year in respect of which auditors are appointed before the end of that financial year and thereafter before the expiration of not more than two months following the approval of the accounts for the preceding financial year in accordance with section 233.".

subsection (3)	For subsection (3) substitute: "(3) The auditor of a limited liability partnership shall hold office until not later than the expiration of two months following the approval in accordance with section 233 of the accounts for the financial year in respect of which the auditor was appointed."
subsection (4)	For subsection (4) substitute: "(4) If the designated members fail to exercise their powers under subsection (2), the powers may be exercised by the members of the limited liability partnership in a meeting convened for the purpose".
387 (appointment by Secretary of State in default of appointment by company)	
subsection (1)	In subsection (1), omit the words "re-appointed or deemed to be re-appointed".
subsection (2)	In subsection (2), for the word "officer" substitute the words "designated member".
388 (filling of casual vacancies)	
subsection (1)	In subsection (1), for "directors, or the company in general meeting," substitute "designated members".
subsection (3)	Omit subsection (3).
subsection (4)	Omit subsection (4).
388A (certain companies exempt from obligation to appoint auditors)	
subsection (3)	For subsection (3) substitute: "(3) The designated members may appoint auditors and the auditors so appointed shall hold office until the expiration of two months following the approval in accordance with section 233 of the accounts for the financial year in respect of which the auditor was appointed."
subsection (4)	Omit subsection (4).

subsection (5)	For subsection (5) substitute: "(5) If the designated members fail to exercise their powers under subsection (3), the powers may be exercised by the members of the limited liability partnership in a meeting convened for the purpose."
389A (rights to information)	
390 (right to attend company meetings)	
subsection (1)	In paragraph (a), (b) and (c) of subsection (1) omit the word "general" in each place where it occurs. At the end of paragraph (a) add the words "and where any part of the business of the meeting concerns them as auditors." At the end of paragraph (b) add the words "where any part of the business of the meeting concerns them as auditors."
subsection (1A)	Omit subsection (1A).
subsection (2)	Omit subsection (2).
390A (remuneration of auditors)	
subsection (1)	For subsection (1) substitute: "The remuneration of auditors appointed by the limited liability partnership shall be fixed by the designated members or in such manner as the members of the limited liability partnership may determine".
subsection (2)	In subsection (2), omit the words "directors or the", in both places where they occur, and omit the words "as the case may be".
390B (remuneration of auditors or their associates for non-audit work)	
391 (removal of auditors)	
subsection (1)	In subsection (1), for the words "A company may by ordinary resolution" substitute "The designated members of a limited liability

	partnership may" and for the words "between it and" substitute "with".
subsection (2)	(a) In subsection (2), for the words "a resolution removing an auditor is passed at a general meeting of a company, the company" substitute the words "the designated members of the limited liability partnership have made a determination to remove an auditor, the designated members". (b) For the words "every officer of it who is in default" substitute "every designated member of it who is in default".
subsection (4)	In subsection (4), omit the word "general".
391A (rights of auditors who are removed or not re-appointed)	
subsection (1)	For subsection (1) substitute: "The designated members shall give seven days' prior written notice to– (a) any auditor whom it is proposed to remove before the expiration of his term of office; or (b) a retiring auditor where it is proposed to appoint as auditor a person other than the retiring auditor."
subsection (2)	Omit subsection (2).
subsection (3)	In subsection (3), for the words "intended resolution" substitute the word "proposal" and omit the words "of the company".
subsection (4)	Omit the words "(unless the representations are received by it too late for it to do so)". Omit subsection (4)(a). In subsection (4)(b), for the words "of the company to whom notice in writing of the meeting is or has been sent." substitute "within twenty one days' of receipt.".
subsection (5)	For subsection (5) substitute: "If a copy of the representations is not sent out as required by subsection (4), then unless subsection (6) applies, the limited liability partnership and any designated

	member in default commits an offence. A person guilty of an offence under this section is liable on summary conviction to a fine not exceeding level 3 on the standard scale."
subsection (6)	In subsection (6), the words "and the representations need not be read at the meeting" shall be omitted.
392 (resignation of auditors)	
subsection (3)	In the second paragraph of subsection (3) for "and every officer of it who is in default" substitute "and every designated member of it who is in default".
392A (rights of resigning auditors)	
subsection (2)	In subsection (2), for "directors" substitute "designated members" and for "an extraordinary general meeting of the company" substitute "a meeting of the members of the limited liability partnership".
subsection (3)	In subsection (3), omit ",or" from paragraph (a) and omit paragraph (b).
subsection (5)	In subsection (5), for "directors" substitute "designated members" and for "director" substitute "designated member".
subsection (8)	In subsection (8), omit the word "general" and the phrase "(a) or (b)".
394 (statement by person ceasing to hold office as auditor)	
394A (offences of failing to comply with section 394)	

Registration of charges

The following references are to sections of the 1985 Act which were replaced by section 92 of the Companies Act 1989. They will apply to limited liability partnerships until the said section 92 is commenced.

395 (certain charges void if not registered)	
396 (charges which have to be registered)	In subsection (1) delete paragraphs (b) and (g).
397 (formalities of registration (debentures))	In subsection (1), paragraph (b) for the word "resolutions" substitute "determinations of the limited liability partnership".
398 (verification of charge on property outside United Kingdom)	
399 (company's duty to register charges it creates)	
400 (charges existing on property acquired)	
401 (register of charges to be kept by registrar of companies)	
402 (endorsement of certificate on debentures)	
403 (entries of satisfaction and release)	In subsection (1A), after "of the company" insert "or designated member, administrator or administrative receiver of the limited liability partnership".
404 (rectification of register of charges)	In subsection (1), omit the words "or shareholders".
405 (registration of enforcement of security)	
406 (companies to keep copies of instruments creating charges)	
407 (company's register of charges)	In subsection (1), for "limited company" substitute "company (including limited liability partnership)".
408 (right to inspect instruments which create charges etc.)	In subsection (1) delete "in general meeting".

410 (charges void unless registered)	In subsection (4) delete paragraph (b) and sub-paragraph (ii) of paragraph (c). In subsection (5) for "an incorporated company" substitute "a limited liability partnership".
411 (charges on property outside the United Kingdom)	
412 (negotiable instrument to secure book debts)	
413 (charges associated with debentures)	In subsection (2)(b), for the word "resolutions" substitute "determinations of the limited liability partnership".
414 (charge by way of ex facie absolute disposition, etc.)	
415 (company's duty to register charges created by it)	
416 (duty to register charges existing on property acquired)	
417 (register of charges to be kept by registrar of companies)	
418 (certificate of registration to be issued)	
419 (entries of satisfaction and relief)	In subsection (1A), after the words "of the company" insert "or a designated member, liquidator, receiver or administrative receiver of the limited liability partnership".
420 (rectification of the register)	Omit the words "or shareholders".
421 (copies of instruments creating charges to be kept by the company)	
422 (company's register of charges)	
423 (right to inspect copies of instruments, and the company's register)	In subsection (1) delete "in general meeting".

Arrangements and reconstructions	
425 (power of company to compromise with creditors and members)	
subsection (3)	Omit the words "and a copy of every such order shall be annexed to every copy of the company's memorandum issued after the order has been made or, in the case of a company not having a memorandum, of every copy so issued of the instrument constituting the company or defining its constitution." For the semi-colon after the word "registration" substitute a full stop.
subsection (6)	Omit subsection (6).
426 (information as to compromise to be circulated)	
subsection (2)	Omit the words "as directors or".
427 (provisions for facilitating company reconstruction or amalgamation)	
subsection (3)	In paragraph (b) for the words "policies or other like interests" substitute "policies, other like interests or, in the case of a limited liability partnership, property or interests in the limited liability partnership".
subsection (6)	For the words ""company" includes only a company as defined in section 735(1)" substitute ""company" includes only a company as defined in section 735(1) or a limited liability partnership".
Investigation of companies and their affairs: Requisition of documents	
431 (investigation of a company on its own application or that of its members)	For subsection (2) substitute the following: "(2) The appointment may be made on the application of the limited liability partnership or on the application of not less than one-fifth in number of those who appear from notifications made to the registrar of companies to be currently members of the limited liability partnership."

432 (other company investigations)	
subsection (4)	For the words "but to whom shares in the company have been transferred or transmitted by operation of law" substitute "but to whom a member's share in the limited liability partnership has been transferred or transmitted by operation of law."
433 (inspectors' powers during investigation)	
434 (production of documents and evidence to inspectors)	
436 (obstruction of inspectors treated as contempt of court)	
437 (inspectors' reports)	
438 (power to bring civil proceedings on company's behalf)	
439 (expenses of investigating a company's affairs)	
subsection (5)	Omit paragraph (b) together with the word "or" at the end of paragraph (a).
441 (inspectors' report to be evidence)	
447 (Secretary of State's power to require production of documents)	
448 (entry and search of premises)	
449 (provision for security of information obtained)	
450 (punishment for destroying, mutilating etc. company documents)	In subsection (1), omit the words ", or of an insurance company to which Part II of the Insurance Companies Act 1982 applies,".

451 (punishment for furnishing false information)	
451A (disclosure of information by Secretary of State or inspector)	In subsection (1), for the words "sections 434 to 446" substitute "sections 434 to 441". Omit subsection (5).
452 (privileged information)	In subsection (1), for the words "sections 431 to 446" substitute "sections 431 to 441". In subsection (1A), for the words "sections 434, 443 or 446" substitute "section 434".
Fraudulent trading	
458 (punishment for fraudulent trading)	
Protection of company's members against unfair prejudice	
459 (order on application of company member)	At the beginning of subsection (1), insert the words: "Subject to subsection (1A),". After subsection (1) insert as subsection (1A): "The members of a limited liability partnership may by unanimous agreement exclude the right contained in subsection 459(1) for such period as shall be agreed. The agreement referred to in this subsection shall be recorded in writing." Omit subsections (2) and (3).
460 (order on application of Secretary of State)	In subsection (1) omit the words "or, section 43A or 44(2) to (6) of the Insurance Companies Act 1982 …,". Omit subsection (2).
461 (provisions as to orders and petitions under this Part)	In subsection (2)(d) for the words "the shares of any members of the company by other members or by the company itself and, in the case of a purchase by the company itself, the reduction of the company's capital accordingly" substitute the words "the shares of any members in the limited liability partnership by other members or by the limited liability partnership itself.". In subsection (3) for the words "memorandum or articles" substitute the words "limited liability partnership agreement". For the existing words of subsection (4) substitute the words "Any alteration in the limited liability

	partnership agreement made by virtue of an order under this Part is of the same effect as if duly agreed by the members of the limited liability partnership and the provisions of this Act apply to the limited liability partnership agreement as so altered accordingly.". Omit subsection (5).

Floating charges and receivers (Scotland)

464 (ranking of floating charges)	In subsection (1), for the words "section 462" substitute "the law of Scotland".
466 (alteration of floating charges)	Omit subsections (1), (2), (3) and (6).
486 (interpretation for Part XVIII generally)	For the current definition of "company" substitute" "company" means a limited liability partnership;" Omit the definition of "Register of Sasines".
487 (extent of Part XVIII)	

Matters arising subsequent to winding up

651 (power of court to declare dissolution of company void)	
652 (registrar may strike defunct company off the register)	In subsection (6) paragraph (a) omit the word "director".
652A (registrar may strike private company off the register on application)	In this section the references to "a private company" shall include a reference to "a limited liability partnership".
subsection (1)	In subsection (1) the following shall be substituted for the existing wording: "On application by two or more designated members of a limited liability partnership, the registrar of companies may strike the limited liability partnership's name off the register". Omit subsection 2(a) and in subsection 2(b) after the word "be" insert the word "made". In subsection (6), omit the word "director".
652B (duties in connection with making an application under section 652A)	In paragraph (a) of subsection (5) for "no meetings are" substitute "no meeting is". In paragraph (b) of subsection (5) for

157

	"meetings summoned under that section fail" substitute "the meeting summoned under that section fails". In paragraph (c) of subsection (5) for "meetings" substitute "a meeting". In paragraph (d) of subsection (5) for "at previous meetings" substitute "at a previous meeting".
652C (directors' duties following application under section 652A)	In subsection (2), for the words "is a director of the company" substitute "is a designated member of the limited liability partnership". In subsection (2) omit paragraph (d). In subsection (5) for the words "is a director of the company" substitute "is a designated member of the limited liability partnership". In subsection (6), omit paragraph (d).
652D (sections 652B and 652C: supplementary provisions)	
652E (sections 652B and 652C: enforcement)	
652F (other offences connected with section 652A)	
653 (objection to striking off by person aggrieved)	
654 (property of dissolved company to be bona vacantia)	
655 (effect on section 654 of company's revival after dissolution)	
656 (crown disclaimer of property vesting as bona vacantia)	
657 (effect of crown disclaimer under section 656)	
658 (liability for rentcharge on company's land after dissolution)	

Oversea limited liability partnerships	
693 (obligation to state name and other particulars)	For the wording of subsection (1) there shall be substituted the following words: "Every oversea limited liability partnership shall– (a) in every prospectus inviting subscriptions for its debentures in Great Britain, state the country in which the limited liability partnership is incorporated, (b) conspicuously exhibit on every place where it carries on business in Great Britain the name of the limited liability partnership and the country in which it is incorporated, (c) cause the name of the limited liability partnership and the country in which it is incorporated to be stated in legible characters in all bill heads, letter paper, and in all notices and other official publications and communications of the limited liability partnership." For subsection (2) there shall be substituted the following words: "For the purposes of this section "oversea limited liability partnership" means a body incorporated or otherwise established outside Great Britain whose name under its law of incorporation or establishment includes the words "limited liability partnership."". Subsections (3) and (4) shall be omitted.
The Registrar of Companies: His functions and offices	
704 (registration offices)	
705 (companies' registered numbers)	Omit subsection (5).
706 (delivery to the registrar of documents in legible form)	In subsection (2)(a), omit the words from "and, if the document is delivered" to the end of that paragraph.
707A (the keeping of company records by the registrar)	Omit subsection (4).
707B (delivery to the registrar using electronic communications)	In subsection (3), omit the "or" at the end of paragraph (a) and omit paragraph (b).

708 (fees payable to the registrar)	
709 (inspection of records kept by the registrar)	
710 (certificate of incorporation)	
710A (provision and authentication by registrar of documents in non-legible form)	
710B (documents relating to Welsh companies)	In subsection (7), omit the words "272(5) and 273(7) and paragraph 7(3) of Part II of Schedule 9".
711 (public notice by registrar of receipt and issue of certain documents)	In subsection (1) delete "or articles" in paragraph (b) and delete paragraphs (d) to (j), (l), (m) and (s) to (z).
713 (enforcement of company's duty to make returns)	In subsection (1), in the penultimate line for "any officer" substitute "any designated member". In subsections (2) and (3) for "officers" substitute "designated members".
714 (registrar's index of company and corporate names)	
715A (interpretation)	
Miscellaneous and supplementary provisions	
721 (production and inspection of books where offence suspected)	In subsection (2)(b), for the words "the secretary of the company or such other" substitute "such".
722 (form of company registers, etc.)	
723 (use of computers for company records)	Omit subsection (2).
723A (obligations of company as to inspections of registers, & etc.)	

725 (service of documents)	In subsection (2), for the words "other head officer" substitute "a designated member".
726 (costs and expenses in actions by certain limited companies)	References to a "limited company" shall include references to a "limited liability partnership".
727 (power of court to grant relief in certain cases)	In subsection (1) delete the words "an officer of a company or" and "officer or". In subsection (2), delete the words "officer or".
728 (enforcement of High Court orders)	
729 (annual report by Secretary of State)	
730 (punishment of offences)	
731 (summary proceedings)	
732 (prosecution by public authorities)	Delete the references to sections 210, 324, 329 and 455. Omit subsection (2) paragraphs (a) and (c). In subsection (2)(b), for the words "either one of those two persons" substitute "either the Secretary of State, the Director of Public Prosecutions". Omit subsection (3).
733 (offences by bodies corporate)	
subsection (1)	In subsection (1), delete the references to section 210 and 216(3).
subsection (2)	In subsection (2), omit the word "secretary".
subsection (3)	Omit subsection (3).
734 (criminal proceedings against unincorporated bodies)	
Interpretation	
735A (relationship of this Act to the Insolvency Act)	In subsection (1), delete all the references to provisions of the 1985 Act other than the references to sections 425(6)(a), 460(2) and 728.

736 ("subsidiary", "holding company", and "wholly-owned subsidiary")	

subsection (1)	For subsection (1) there shall be substituted the following words:
	"(1) Subject to subsection (1A), a company is a subsidiary of a limited liability partnership, its "holding company", if that limited liability partnership–
	    (a) holds a majority of the voting rights in it, or
	    (b) is a member of it and has the right to appoint or remove a majority of its board of directors, or
	    (c) is a member of it and controls alone, pursuant to an agreement with other shareholders or members, a majority of the voting rights in it,
	or if it is a subsidiary of a company or limited liability partnership which is itself a subsidiary of that other company."

subsection (1A)	Insert as subsection (1A):
	"(1A) A limited liability partnership is a subsidiary of a company or a subsidiary of another limited liability partnership, (such company or limited liability partnership being referred to in this section as its "holding company") if that company or limited liability partnership–
	    (a) holds a majority of the voting rights in it;
	    (b) is a member of it and has the right to appoint or remove a majority of other members; or
	    (c) is a member of it and controls, alone or pursuant to an agreement with other members, a majority of voting rights in it,
	or if it is a subsidiary of a company or limited liability partnership which is itself a subsidiary of that holding company".

subsection (2)	For subsection (2) substitute: "A company or a limited liability partnership is a "wholly-owned subsidiary" of another company or limited liability partnership if it has no members except that other and that

	other's wholly-owned subsidiaries or persons acting on behalf of that other or its wholly-owned subsidiaries."
736A (provisions supplementing section 736)	After subsection (1) insert a new subsection (1A) in the following form: "(1A) In section 736(1A)(a) and (c) the references to the voting rights in a limited liability partnership are to the rights conferred on members in respect of their interest in the limited liability partnership to vote on those matters which are to be decided upon by a vote of the members of the limited liability partnership." After subsection (2) insert the new subsection (2A) in the following form: "(2A) In section 736(1A)(b) the reference to the right to appoint or remove a majority of the members of the limited liability partnership is to the right to appoint or remove members holding a majority of the voting rights referred to in subsection (1A) and for this purpose– (a) a person shall be treated as having the right to appoint a member if (i) a person's appointment as member results directly from his appointment as a director or member of the holding company, or (ii) the member of the limited liability partnership is the company or limited liability partnership which is the holding company; and (b) a right to appoint or remove which is exercisable only with the consent or concurrence of another person shall be left out of account." In subsection (7) after the words "Rights attached to shares" insert the words "or to a member's interest in a limited liability partnership". In subsection (8) after the words "held by a company", in both places where they occur, insert "or a limited liability partnership". In subsection (9) after the words "in the interest of company" insert "or a limited liability partnership" and after the words "that company" in both places where they occur

	insert "or limited liability partnership". In subsection (10) after the words "a company" insert the words "or a limited liability partnership" and after the words "by the company" insert the words "or the limited liability partnership". In subsection (12) for the existing words substitute "In this section "company" includes a body corporate other than a limited liability partnership."
739 ("non-cash asset")	
740 ("body corporate" and "corporation")	
741 ("director" and "shadow director")	Omit subsection (3).
742 (expressions used in connection with accounts)	
743A (meaning of "office copy" in Scotland)	
744 (expressions used generally in this Act)	Delete the definitions of expressions not used in provisions which apply to limited liability partnerships and insert the following definitions: ""limited liability partnership" has the meaning given it in section 1(2) of the Limited Liability Partnerships Act 2000 "shadow member" has the same meaning as it has in the Limited Liability Partnerships Regulations 2000."
744A (index of defined expressions)	Delete the references to expressions not used in provisions which apply to limited liability partnerships including, in particular, the following expressions: Allotment (and related expressions) Section 738 Annual general meeting Section 366 Authorised minimum Section 118 Called up share capital Section 737(1) Capital redemption reserve Section 170(1) Elective resolution Section 379A Employees' share scheme Section 743 Existing company Section 735(1) Extraordinary general meeting Section 368

	Extraordinary resolution Section 378(1) The former Companies Acts Section 735(1) The Joint Stock Companies Acts Section 735(3) Overseas branch register Section 362 Paid up (and related expressions) Section 738 Registered office (of a company) Section 287 Resolution for reducing share capital Section 135(3) Share premium account Section 130(1) Share warrant Section 188 Special notice (in relation to a resolution) Section 379 Special resolution Section 378(2) Uncalled share capital Section 737(2) Undistributable reserves Section 264(3) Unlimited company Section 1(2) Unregistered company Section 718
SCHEDULE 24 (PUNISHMENT OF OFFENCES UNDER THIS ACT)	Delete the references to those sections which are not applied to limited liability partnerships including, in particular, the following sections: Section 6(3) company failing to deliver to the registrar notice or other document, following alteration of its objects; Section 18(3) company failing to register change in memorandum or articles; Section 19(2) company failing to send to one of its members a copy of the memorandum or articles, when so required by the member; Section 20(2) where company's memorandum altered, company issuing copy of the memorandum without the alteration; Section 28(5) company failing to change name on direction of Secretary of State; Section 31(5) company altering its memorandum or articles, so ceasing to be exempt from having "limited" after its name; Section 31(6) company failing to change name, on Secretary of State's direction, so as to have "limited" (or Welsh equivalent) at the end; Section 32(4) company failing to comply with the Secretary of State's direction to change its name, on grounds that the name is misleading; Section 33 trading under misleading name (use of "public limited company" or Welsh equivalent when not so entitled); purporting to be a private company; Section 34 trading or carrying on business with improper use of "limited" or "cyfyngedig";

Section 54(10) public company failing to give notice, or copy of court order, to registrar, concerning application to re-register as private company;
Section 80(9) directors exercising company's power of allotment without the authority required by section 80(1);
Section 81(2) private company offering shares to the public, or allotting shares with a view to their being so offered;
Section 82(5) allotting shares or debentures before third day after issue of prospectus;
Section 86(6) company failing to keep money in separate bank account, where received in pursuance of prospectus stating that stock exchange listing is to be applied for;
Section 87(4) offeror of shares for sale failing to keep proceeds in separate bank account;
Section 88(5) officer of company failing to deliver return of allotments, etc. to the registrar;
Section 95(6) knowingly or recklessly authorising or permitting misleading, false or deceptive material in statement by directors under section 95(5);
Section 97(4) company failing to deliver to registrar the prescribed form disclosing amount or rate of share commission;
Section 110(2) making misleading, false or deceptive statement in connection with valuation under section 103 or 104;
Section 111(3) officer of company failing to deliver copy of asset valuation report to registrar;
Section 111(4) company failing to deliver to registrar copy of resolution under Section 104(4), with respect to transfer of an asset as consideration for allotment;
Section 114 contravention of any of the provisions of sections 99 to 104, 106;
Section 117(7) company doing business or exercising borrowing powers contrary to section 117;
Section 122(2) company failing to give notice to registrar of reorganisation of share capital;
Section 123(4) company failing to give notice to registrar of increase of share capital;
Section 127(5) company failing to forward to registrar copy of court order, when application

made to cancel resolution varying shareholders' rights;

Section 128(5) company failing to send to registrar statement or notice required by section 128 (particulars of shares carrying special rights);

Section 129(4) company failing to deliver to registrar statement or notice required by section 129 (registration of newly created class rights);

Section 141 officer of company concealing name of creditor entitled to object to reduction of capital, or wilfully misrepresenting the nature or amount of debt or claim, etc.;

Section 142(2) director authorising or permitting non-compliance with section 142 (requirement to convene company meeting to consider serious loss of capital);

Section 143(2) company acquiring its own shares in breach of section 143;

Section 149(2) company failing to cancel its own shares acquired by itself, as required by section 146(2); or failing to apply for re-registration as private company as so required in the case there mentioned;

Section 151(3) company giving financial assistance towards acquisition of its own shares;

Section 156(6) company failing to register statutory declaration under section 155;

Section 156(7) director making statutory declaration under section 155, without having reasonable grounds for opinion expressed in it;

Section 169(6) default by company's officer in delivering to registrar the return required by section 169 (disclosure by company of purchase of its own shares);

Section 169(7) company failing to keep copy of contract, etc., at registered office; refusal of inspection to person demanding it;

Section 173(6) director making statutory declaration under section 173 without having reasonable grounds for the opinion expressed in the declaration;

Section 175(7) refusal of inspection of statutory declaration and auditor's report under section 173, etc.;

Section 176(4) company failing to give notice to registrar of application to court under section 176, or to register court order;

Section 183(6) company failing to send notice of refusal to register a transfer of shares or debentures;

Section 185(5) company default in compliance with section 185(1) (certificates to be made ready following allotment or transfer of shares, etc.);

Section 189(1) offences of fraud and forgery in connection with share warrants in Scotland;

Section 189(2) unauthorised making of, or using or possessing apparatus for making share warrants in Scotland;

Section 210(3) failure to discharge obligation of disclosure under Part VI; other forms of non-compliance with that Part;

Section 211(10) company failing to keep register of interests disclosed under Part IV; other contraventions of section 211;

Section 214(5) company failing to exercise powers under section 212, when so required by the members;

Section 215(8) company default in compliance with section 215 (company report of investigation of shareholdings on members' requisition);

Section 216(3) failure to comply with company notice under section 212; making false statement in response etc.;

Section 217(7) company failing to notify a person that he has been named as a shareholder; on removal of name from register, failing to alter associated index;

Section 218(3) improper removal of entry from register of interests disclosed; company failing to restore entry improperly removed;

Section 219(3) refusal of inspection of register or report under Part VI; failure to send copy when required;

Section 232(4) default by director or officer of a company in giving notice of matters relating to himself for purposes of Schedule 6 Part I;

Section 234(5) non-compliance with Part VII as to directors' report and its content; directors individually liable;

Section 234A(4) laying, circulating or delivering directors' report without required signature;

Section 241(2) failure to lay accounts and reports before the company in general meeting before the end of the period allowed for doing this;

Section 251(6) failure to comply with requirements in relation to summary financial statements;
Section 288(4) default in complying with section 288 (keeping register of directors and secretaries, refusal of inspection);
Section 291(5) acting as director of a company without having the requisite share qualification;
Section 294(3) director failing to give notice of his attaining retirement age; acting as director under appointment invalid due to his attaining it;
Section 305(3) company default in complying with section 305 (directors' name to appear on company correspondence, etc.);
Section 306(4) failure to state that liability of proposed director or manager is unlimited; failure to give notice of that fact to person accepting office;
Section 314(3) director failing to comply with section 314;
Section 317(7) director failing to disclose interest in contract;
Section 318(8) company in default in complying with section 318(1) or (5);
Section 322B(4) terms of unwritten contract between sole member of a private company limited by shares or by guarantee and the company not set out in a written memorandum or recorded in minutes of a directors' meeting;
Section 323(2) director dealing in options to buy or sell company's listed shares or debentures;
Section 324(7) director failing to notify interest in company's shares; making false statement in purported notification;
Section 326(2), (3), (4) and (5) various defaults in connection with company register of directors' interests;
Section 328(6) director failing to notify company that members of his family etc. have or have exercised options to buy shares or debentures; making false statement in purported notification;
Section 329(3) company failing to notify investment exchange of acquisition of its securities by a director;
Section 342(1) director or relevant company authorising or permitting company to enter

into transaction or arrangement, knowing or suspecting it to contravene section 330;
Section 342(2) relevant company entering into transaction or arrangement for a director in contravention of section 330;
Section 342(3) procuring a relevant company to enter into transaction or arrangement known to be contrary to section 330;
Section 343(8) company failing to maintain register of transactions etc. made with and for directors and not disclosed in company accounts; failing to make register available at registered office or at company meeting;
Section 352(5) company default in complying with section 352 (requirement to keep register of members and their particulars);
Section 352A(3) company default in complying with section 352A (statement that company has only one member);
Section 353(4) company failing to send notice to registrar as to place where register of members is kept;
Section 354(4) company failing to keep index of members;
Section 356(5) refusal of inspection of members' register; failure to send copy on requisition;
Section 364(4) company without share capital failing to complete and register annual return in due time;
Section 366(4) company default in holding annual general meeting;
Section 367(3) company default in complying with Secretary of State's direction to hold a company meeting;
Section 367(5) company failing to register resolution that meeting held under section 367 is to be its annual general meeting;
Section 372(4) failure to give notice, to member entitled to vote at company meeting, that he may do so by proxy;
Section 372(6) officer of company authorising or permitting issue of irregular invitations to appoint proxies;
Section 376(7) officer of company in default as to circulation of members' resolutions for company meeting;
Section 380(5) company failing to comply with section 380 (copies of certain resolutions etc. to be sent to registrar of companies);

Section 380(6) company failing to include copy of resolution to which section 380 applies in articles; failing to forward copy to member on request;

Section 381B(2) director or secretary of company failing to notify auditors of proposed written resolution;

Section 382(5) company failing to keep minutes of proceedings at company and board meetings, etc.;

Section 382B(2) failure of sole member to provide the company with a written record of a decision;

Section 383(4) refusal of inspection of minutes of general meeting; failure to send copy of minutes on member's request;

Section 389(10) person acting as a company auditor knowing himself to be disqualified: failing to give notice vacating office when he becomes disqualified;

Section 429(6) offeror failing to send copy of notice or making statutory declaration knowing it to be false etc.;

Section 430A(6) offeror failing to give rights to minority shareholder;

Section 444(3) failing to give Secretary of State, when required to do so, information about interests in shares etc.; giving false information;

Section 455(1) exercising a right to dispose of, or vote in respect of, shares which are subject to restrictions under Part XV; failing to give notice in respect of shares so subject; entering into agreement void under section 454(2), (3);

Section 455(2) issuing shares in contravention of restrictions under Part XV;

Section 461(5) failure to register office copy of court order under Part XVII altering, or giving leave to alter, company's memorandum;

Section 697(1) oversea company failing to comply with any of sections 691 to 693 or 696;

Section 697(2) oversea company contravening section 694(6) (carrying on business under its corporate name after Secretary of State's direction);

Section 697(3) oversea company failing to comply with section 695A or Schedule 21A;

Section 703(1) oversea company failing to comply with requirements as to accounts and reports;

	Section 703D(5) oversea company failing to deliver particulars of charge to registrar; Section 703R(1) company failing to register winding up or commencement of insolvency proceedings etc.; Section 703R(2) liquidator failing to register appointment, termination of winding up or striking off of company; Section 720(4) insurance company etc. failing to send twice yearly statement in form of Schedule 23; Schedule 14, Pt II, paragraph 1(3) company failing to give notice of location of overseas branch register, etc.; Schedule 14, Pt II, paragraph 4(2) company failing to transmit to its registered office in Great Britain copies of entries in overseas branch register or to keep duplicate of overseas branch register.; Schedule 21C, Pt I, paragraph 7 credit or financial institution failing to deliver accounting documents; Schedule 21C, Pt II, paragraph 15 credit or financial institution failing to deliver accounts and reports; Schedule 21D, Pt I, paragraph 5 company failing to deliver accounting documents; Schedule 21D, Pt I, Paragraph 13 company failing to deliver accounts and reports.

PART II
MODIFICATIONS TO THE COMPANY DIRECTORS
DISQUALIFICATION ACT 1986

Part II of Schedule I	After paragraph 8 insert: "8A The extent of the member's and shadow members' responsibility for events leading to a member or shadow member, whether himself or some other member or shadow member, being declared by the court to be liable to make a contribution to the assets of the limited liability partnership under section 214A of the Insolvency Act 1986."

	Omit the word "and" at the end of paragraph (b) and omit paragraph (c).
subsection (3)	For "each of the reports" substitute "the report".
subsection (4)	For subsection (4) substitute the following: "(4) Where on such an application the court is satisfied as to either of the grounds mentioned in subsection (1), it may do one or both of the following, namely— (a) revoke or suspend the approval given by the meeting; (b) give a direction to any person for the summoning of a further meeting to consider any revised proposal the limited liability partnership may make or, in a case falling within subsection (1)(b), a further meeting to consider the original proposal.".
subsection (5)	For the first "meetings" substitute "a meeting", for the second "meetings" substitute "meeting" and for "person who made the original proposal" substitute "limited liability partnership".
Section 7 (implementation of proposal)	
subsection (1)	For "meetings" substitute "meeting".

The following modifications to sections 2 and 3 apply where a proposal under section 1 has been made, where an administration order is in force in relation to the limited liability partnership, by the administrator or, where the limited liability partnership is being wound up, by the liquidator.

Section 2 (procedure where the nominee is not the liquidator or administrator)	
subsection (2)	In paragraph (a) for "meetings of the company" substitute "meetings of the members of the limited liability partnership".
Section 3 (summoning of meetings)	

subsection (2)	For "meetings of the company" substitute "a meeting of the members of the limited liability partnership".
Section 8 (power of court to make order)	
subsection (1A)	Omit subsection (1A).
subsection (4)	Omit subsection (4).
Section 9 (application for order)	
subsection (1)	Delete ", or the directors".
Section 10 (effect of application)	
subsection (1)	In paragraph (a) for "no resolution may be passed" to the end of the subsection substitute "no determination may be made or order made for the winding up of the limited liability partnership.".
Section 11 (effect of order)	
subsection (3)	In paragraph (a) for "no resolution may be passed" to the end of the subsection substitute "no determination may be made or order made for the winding up of the limited liability partnership.".
Section 13 (appointment of administrator)	
subsection (3)	In paragraph (c) delete "or the directors".
Section 14 (general powers)	
subsection (2)	For paragraph (a) substitute: "(a) to prevent any person from taking part in the management of the business of the limited liability partnership and to appoint any person to be a manager of that business, and"; and at the end add the following: "Subsections (3) and (4) of section 92 shall apply for the purposes of this subsection as they apply for the purposes of that section."

Section 73 (alternative modes of winding up)	
subsection (1)	Delete ",within the meaning given to that expression by section 735 of the Companies Act,".
Section 74 (liability as contributories of present and past members)	For section 74 there shall be substituted the following: "**74.** When a limited liability partnership is wound up every present and past member of the limited liability partnership who has agreed with the other members or with the limited liability partnership that he will, in circumstances which have arisen, be liable to contribute to the assets of the limited liability partnership in the event that the limited liability partnership goes into liquidation is liable, to the extent that he has so agreed, to contribute to its assets to any amount sufficient for payment of its debts and liabilities, and the expenses of the winding up, and for the adjustment of the rights of the contributories among themselves. However, a past member shall only be liable if the obligation arising from such agreement survived his ceasing to be a member of the limited liability partnership."
Sections 75 to 78	Delete sections 75 to 78.
Section 79 (meaning of "contributory")	
subsection (1)	In subsection (1) for "every person" substitute: "(a) every present member of the limited liability partnership and (b) every past member of the limited liability partnership".
subsection (2)	After "section 214 (wrongful trading)" insert" or 214A (adjustment of withdrawals)".
subsection (3)	Delete subsection (3).
Section 83 (companies registered under Companies Act, Part XXII, Chapter II)	Delete section 83.

Section 84 (circumstances in which company may be wound up voluntarily)	
subsection (1)	For subsection (1) substitute the following: "(1) A limited liability partnership may be wound up voluntarily when it determines that it is to be wound up voluntarily."
subsection (2)	Omit subsection (2).
subsection (3)	For subsection (3) substitute the following: "(3) Within 15 days after a limited liability partnership has determined that it be wound up there shall be forwarded to the registrar of companies either a printed copy or else a copy in some other form approved by the registrar of the determination."
subsection (4)	After subsection (3) insert a new subsection (4): "(4) If a limited liability partnership fails to comply with this regulation the limited liability partnership and every designated member of it who is in default is liable on summary conviction to a fine not exceeding level 3 on the standard scale."
Section 85 (notice of resolution to wind up)	
subsection (1)	For subsection (1) substitute the following: "(1) When a limited liability partnership has determined that it shall be wound up voluntarily, it shall within 14 days after the making of the determination give notice of the determination by advertisement in the Gazette."
Section 86 (commencement of winding up)	Substitute the following new section: "**86.** A voluntary winding up is deemed to commence at the time when the limited liability partnership determines that it be wound up voluntarily.".
Section 87 (effect on business and status of company)	
subsection (2)	In subsection (2), for "articles" substitute "limited liability partnership agreement".

Section 88 (avoidance of share transfers, etc. after winding-up resolution)	For "shares" substitute "the interest of any member in the property of the limited liability partnership".
Section 89 (statutory declaration of solvency)	For "director(s)" wherever it appears in section 89 substitute "designated member(s)";
subsection (2)	For paragraph (a) substitute the following: "(a) it is made within the 5 weeks immediately preceding the date when the limited liability partnership determined that it be wound up voluntarily or on that date but before the making of the determination, and".
subsection (3)	For "the resolution for winding up is passed" substitute "the limited liability partnership determined that it be wound up voluntarily".
subsection (5)	For "in pursuance of a resolution passed" substitute "voluntarily".
Section 90 (distinction between "members" and "creditors" voluntary winding up)	For "directors'" substitute "designated members'".
Section 91 (appointment of liquidator)	
subsection (1)	Delete "in general meeting".
subsection (2)	For the existing wording substitute: "(2) On the appointment of a liquidator the powers of the members of the limited liability partnership shall cease except to the extent that a meeting of the members of the limited liability partnership summoned for the purpose or the liquidator sanctions their continuance." After subsection (2) insert: "(3) Subsections (3) and (4) of section 92 shall apply for the purposes of this section as they apply for the purposes of that section."
Section 92 (power to fill vacancy in office of liquidator)	
subsection (1)	For "the company in general meeting" substitute "a meeting of the members of the limited liability partnership summoned for the purpose".

subsection (2)	For "a general meeting" substitute "a meeting of the members of the limited liability partnership".
subsection (3)	In subsection (3), for "articles" substitute "limited liability partnership agreement".
new subsection (4)	Add a new subsection (4) as follows: "(4) The quorum required for a meeting of the members of the limited liability partnership shall be any quorum required by the limited liability partnership agreement for meetings of the members of the limited liability partnership and if no requirement for a quorum has been agreed upon the quorum shall be 2 members."
Section 93 (general company meeting at each year's end)	
subsection (1)	For "a general meeting of the company" substitute "a meeting of the members of the limited liability partnership".
new subsection (4)	Add a new subsection (4) as follows: "(4) subsections (3) and (4) of section 92 shall apply for the purposes of this section as they apply for the purposes of that section."
Section 94 (final meeting prior to dissolution)	
subsection (1)	For "a general meeting of the company" substitute "a meeting of the members of the limited liability partnership".
new subsection (5A)	Add a new subsection (5A) as follows: "(5A) Subsections (3) and (4) of section 92 shall apply for the purposes of this section as they apply for the purposes of that section."
subsection (6)	For "a general meeting of the company" substitute "a meeting of the members of the limited liability partnership".
Section 95 (effect of company's insolvency)	
subsection (1)	For "directors'" substitute "designated members'".

subsection (7)	For subsection (7) substitute the following: "(7) In this section 'the relevant period' means the period of 6 months immediately preceding the date on which the limited liability partnership determined that it be wound up voluntarily."
Section 96 (conversion to creditors' voluntary winding up)	
paragraph (a)	For "directors'" substitute "designated members'".
paragraph (b)	Substitute a new paragraph (b) as follows: "(b) the creditors' meeting was the meeting mentioned in section 98 in the next Chapter;".
Section 98 (meeting of creditors)	
subsection (1)	For paragraph (a) substitute the following: "(a) cause a meeting of its creditors to be summoned for a day not later than the 14th day after the day on which the limited liability partnership determines that it be wound up voluntarily;".
subsection (5)	For "were sent the notices summoning the company meeting at which it was resolved that the company be wound up voluntarily" substitute "the limited liability partnership determined that it be wound up voluntarily".
Section 99 (directors to lay statement of affairs before creditors)	
subsection (1)	For "the directors of the company" substitute "the designated members" and for "the director so appointed" substitute "the designated member so appointed".
subsection (2)	For "directors" substitute "designated members".
subsection (3)	For "directors" substitute "designated members" and for "director" substitute "designated member".
Section 100 (appointment of liquidator)	

subsection (1)	For "The creditors and the company at their respective meetings mentioned in section 98" substitute "The creditors at their meeting mentioned in section 98 and the limited liability partnership".
subsection (3)	Delete "director,".
Section 101 (appointment of liquidation committee)	
subsection (2)	For subsection (2) substitute the following: "(2) If such a committee is appointed, the limited liability partnership may, when it determines that it be wound up voluntarily or at any time thereafter, appoint such number of persons as they think fit to act as members of the committee, not exceeding 5."
Section 105 (meetings of company and creditors at each year's end)	
subsection (1)	For "a general meeting of the company" substitute "a meeting of the members of the limited liability partnership".
new subsection (5)	Add a new subsection (5) as follows: "(5) Subsections (3) and (4) of section 92 shall apply for the purposes of this section as they apply for the purposes of that section."
Section 106 (final meeting prior to dissolution)	
subsection (1)	For "a general meeting of the company" substitute "a meeting of the members of the limited liability partnership".
new subsection (5A)	After subsection (5) insert a new subsection (5A) as follows: "(5A) Subsections (3) and (4) of section 92 shall apply for the purposes of this section as they apply for the purposes of that section."
subsection (6)	For "a general meeting of the company" substitute "a meeting of the members of the limited liability partnership".

Section 110 (acceptance of shares, etc., as consideration for sale of company property)	For the existing section substitute the following:
	"(1) This section applies, in the case of a limited liability partnership proposed to be, or being, wound up voluntarily, where the whole or part of the limited liability partnership's business or property is proposed to be transferred or sold to another company whether or not it is a company within the meaning of the Companies Act ("the transferee company") or to a limited liability partnership ("the transferee limited liability partnership").
	(2) With the requisite sanction, the liquidator of the limited liability partnership being, or proposed to be, wound up ("the transferor limited liability partnership") may receive, in compensation or part compensation for the transfer or sale, shares, policies or other like interests in the transferee company or the transferee limited liability partnership for distribution among the members of the transferor limited liability partnership.
	(3) The sanction required under subsection (2) is–
	    (a) in the case of a members' voluntary winding up, that of a determination of the limited liability partnership at a meeting of the members of the limited liability partnership conferring either a general authority on the liquidator or an authority in respect of any particular arrangement, (subsections (3) and (4) of section 92 to apply for this purpose as they apply for the purposes of that section), and
	    (b) in the case of a creditor's voluntary winding up, that of either court or the liquidation committee.
	(4) Alternatively to subsection (2), the liquidator may (with the sanction) enter into any other arrangement whereby the members of the transferor limited liability partnership may, in lieu of receiving cash, shares, policies or other like interests (or in addition thereto), participate in the profits, or receive any other benefit from the transferee company or the transferee limited liability partnership.
	(5) A sale or arrangement in pursuance of this section is binding on members of the transferor limited liability partnership.

	(6) A determination by the limited liability partnership is not invalid for the purposes of this section by reason that it is made before or concurrently with a determination by the limited liability partnership that it be wound up voluntarily or for appointing liquidators; but, if an order is made within a year for winding up the limited liability partnership by the court, the determination by the limited liability partnership is not valid unless sanctioned by the court."
Section 111 (dissent from arrangement under section 110)	
subsections (1)–(3)	For subsections (1)–(3) substitute the following: "(1) This section applies in the case of a voluntary winding up where, for the purposes of section 110(2) or (4), a determination of the limited liability partnership has provided the sanction requisite for the liquidator under that section. (2) If a member of the transferor limited liability partnership who did not vote in favour of providing the sanction required for the liquidator under section 110 expresses his dissent from it in writing addressed to the liquidator and left at the registered office of the limited liability partnership within 7 days after the date on which that sanction was given, he may require the liquidator either to abstain from carrying the arrangement so sanctioned into effect or to purchase his interest at a price to be determined by agreement or arbitration under this section. (3) If the liquidator elects to purchase the member's interest, the purchase money must be paid before the limited liability partnership is dissolved and be raised by the liquidator in such manner as may be determined by the limited liability partnership."
subsection (4)	Omit subsection (4).
Section 117 (high court and county court jurisdiction)	

subsection (2)	Delete "Where the amount of a company's share capital paid up or credited as paid up does not exceed £120,000, then (subject to this section)".
subsection (3)	Delete subsection (3).
Section 120 (court of session and sheriff court jurisdiction)	
subsection (3)	Delete "Where the amount of a company's share capital paid up or credited as paid up does not exceed £120,000,".
subsection (5)	Delete subsection (5).
Section 122 (circumstances in which company may be wound up by the court)	
subsection (1)	For subsection (1) substitute the following: "(1) A limited liability partnership may be wound up by the court if– (a) the limited liability partnership has determined that the limited liability partnership be wound up by the court, (b) the limited liability partnership does not commence its business within a year from its incorporation or suspends its business for a whole year, (c) the number of members is reduced below two, (d) the limited liability partnership is unable to pay its debts, or (e) the court is of the opinion that it is just and equitable that the limited liability partnership should be wound up."
Section 124 (application for winding up)	
subsections (2), (3) and (4)(a)	Delete these subsections.
Section 124A (petition for winding-up on grounds of public interest)	
subsection (1)	Omit paragraph (b).

Section 126 (power to stay or restrain proceedings against company)	
subsection (2)	Delete subsection (2).
Section 127 (avoidance of property dispositions, etc.)	For "any transfer of shares" substitute "any transfer by a member of the limited liability partnership of his interest in the property of the limited liability partnership".
Section 129 (commencement of winding up by the court)	
subsection (1)	For "a resolution has been passed by the company" substitute "a determination has been made" and for "at the time of the passing of the resolution" substitute "at the time of that determination".
Section 130 (consequences of winding-up order)	
subsection (3)	Delete subsection (3).
Section 148 (settlement of list of contributories and application of assets)	
subsection (1)	Delete ", with power to rectify the register of members in all cases where rectification is required in pursuance of the Companies Act or this Act,".
Section 149 (debts due from contributory to company)	
subsection (1)	Delete "the Companies Act or".
subsection (2)	Delete subsection (2).
subsection (3)	Delete ", whether limited or unlimited,".
Section 160 (delegation of powers to liquidator (England and Wales))	
subsection (1)	In subsection (1)(b) delete "and the rectifying of the register of members".

subsection (2)	For subsection (2) substitute the following: "(2) But the liquidator shall not make any call without the special leave of the court or the sanction of the liquidation committee."
Section 165 (voluntary winding up)	
subsection (2)	In paragraph (a) for "an extraordinary resolution of the company" substitute "a determination by a meeting of the members of the limited liability partnership".
subsection (4)	For paragraph (c) substitute the following: " (c) summon meetings of the members of the limited liability partnership for the purpose of obtaining their sanction or for any other purpose he may think fit."
new subsection (4A)	Insert a new subsection (4A) as follows: "(4A) Subsections (3) and (4) of section 92 shall apply for the purposes of this section as they apply for the purposes of that section."
Section 166 (creditors' voluntary winding up)	
subsection (5)	In paragraph (b) for "directors" substitute "designated members".
Section 171 (removal, etc. (voluntary winding up))	
subsection (2)	For paragraph (a) substitute the following: "(a) in the case of a members' voluntary winding up, by a meeting of the members of the limited liability partnership summoned specially for that purpose, or".
subsection (6)	In paragraph (a) for "final meeting of the company" substitute "final meeting of the members of the limited liability partnership" and in paragraph (b) for "final meetings of the company" substitute "final meetings of the members of the limited liability partnership".
new subsection (7)	Insert a new subsection (7) as follows: "(7) Subsections (3) and (4) of section 92 are

	to apply for the purposes of this section as they apply for the purposes of that section."
Section 173 (release (voluntary winding up))	
subsection (2)	In paragraph (a) for "a general meeting of the company" substitute "a meeting of the members of the limited liability partnership".
Section 183 (effect of execution or attachment (England and Wales))	
subsection (2)	Delete paragraph (a).
Section 184 (duties of sheriff (England and Wales))	
subsection (1)	For "a resolution for voluntary winding up has been passed" substitute "the limited liability partnership has determined that it be wound up voluntarily".
subsection (4)	Delete "or of a meeting having been called at which there is to be proposed a resolution for voluntary winding up," and "or a resolution is passed (as the case may be)".
Section 187 (power to make over assets to employees)	Delete section 187.
Section 194 (resolutions passed at adjourned meetings)	After "contributories" insert "or of the members of a limited liability partnership".
Section 195 (meetings to ascertain wishes of creditors or contributories)	
subsection (3)	Delete "the Companies Act or".
Section 206 (fraud, etc. in anticipation of winding up)	
subsection (1)	For "passes a resolution for voluntary winding up" substitute "makes a determination that it be wound up voluntarily".

Section 207 (transactions in fraud of creditors)	
subsection (1)	For "passes a resolution for voluntary winding up" substitute "makes a determination that it be wound up voluntarily".
Section 210 (material omissions from statement relating to company's affairs)	
subsection (2)	For "passed a resolution for voluntary winding up" substitute "made a determination that it be wound up voluntarily".
Section 214 (wrongful trading)	
subsection (2)	Delete from "but the court shall not" to the end of the subsection.
After section 214	Insert the following new section 214A: **"214A Adjustment of withdrawals** (1) This section has effect in relation to a person who is or has been a member of a limited liability partnership where, in the course of the winding up of that limited liability partnership, it appears that subsection (2) of this section applies in relation to that person. (2) This subsection applies in relation to a person if— (a) within the period of two years ending with the commencement of the winding up, he was a member of the limited liability partnership who withdrew property of the limited liability partnership, whether in the form of a share of profits, salary, repayment of or payment of interest on a loan to the limited liability partnership or any other withdrawal of property, and (b) it is proved by the liquidator to the satisfaction of the court that at the time of the withdrawal he knew or had reasonable ground for believing that the limited liability partnership— (i) was at the time of the withdrawal unable to pay its debts within the meaning of section 123, or

(ii) would become so unable to pay its debts after the assets of the limited liability partnership had been depleted by that withdrawal taken together with all other withdrawals (if any) made by any members contemporaneously with that withdrawal or in contemplation when that withdrawal was made.

(3) Where this section has effect in relation to any person the court, on the application of the liquidator, may declare that that person is to be liable to make such contribution (if any) to the limited liability partnership's assets as the court thinks proper.

(4) The court shall not make a declaration in relation to any person the amount of which exceeds the aggregate of the amounts or values of all the withdrawals referred to in subsection (2) made by that person within the period of two years referred to in that subsection.

(5) The court shall not make a declaration under this section with respect to any person unless that person knew or ought to have concluded that after each withdrawal referred to in subsection (2) there was no reasonable prospect that the limited liability partnership would avoid going into insolvent liquidation.

(6) For the purposes of subsection (5) the facts which a member ought to know or ascertain and the conclusions which he ought to reach are those which would be known, ascertained, or reached by a reasonably diligent person having both–

(a) the general knowledge, skill and experience that may reasonably be expected of a person carrying out the same functions as are carried out by that member in relation to the limited liability partnership, and

(b) the general knowledge, skill and experience that that member has.

(7) For the purposes of this section a limited liability partnership goes into insolvent liquidation if it goes into liquidation at a time when its assets are insufficient for the payment of its debts and other liabilities and the expenses of the winding up.

	(8) In this section "member" includes a shadow member. (9) This section is without prejudice to section 214."
Section 215 (proceedings under ss 213, 214)	
subsection (1)	Omit the word "or" between the words "213" and "214" and insert after "214" "or 214A".
subsection (2)	For "either section" substitute "any of those sections".
subsection (4)	For "either section" substitute "any of those sections".
subsection (5)	For "Sections 213 and 214" substitute "Sections 213, 214 or 214A".
Section 218 (prosecution of delinquent officers and members of company)	
subsection (1)	For "officer, or any member, of the company" substitute "member of the limited liability partnership".
subsections (3), (4) and (6)	For "officer of the company, or any member of it," substitute "officer or member of the limited liability partnership".
Section 233 (supplies of gas, water, electricity etc.)	
subsection (1)	For paragraph (c) substitute the following: "(c) a voluntary arrangement under Part I has taken effect in accordance with section 5".
subsection (4)	For paragraph (c) substitute the following: "(c) the date on which the voluntary arrangement took effect in accordance with section 5".
Section 247 ("insolvency" and "go into liquidation")	
subsection (2)	For "passes a resolution for voluntary winding up" substitute "makes a determination that it

	be wound up voluntarily" and for "passing such a resolution" substitute "making such a determination".
Section 249 ("connected with a company")	For the existing words substitute: "For the purposes of any provision in this Group of Parts, a person is connected with a company (including a limited liability partnership) if– (a) he is a director or shadow director of a company or an associate of such a director or shadow director (including a member or a shadow member of a limited liability partnership or an associate of such a member or shadow member); or (b) he is an associate of the company or of the limited liability partnership."
Section 250 ("member" of a company)	Delete section 250.
Section 251 (expressions used generally)	Delete the word "and" appearing after the definition of "the rules" and insert the word "and" after the definition of "shadow director". After the definition of "shadow director" insert the following: ""shadow member", in relation to a limited liability partnership, means a person in accordance with whose directions or instructions the members of the limited liability partnership are accustomed to act (but so that a person is not deemed a shadow member by reason only that the members of the limited liability partnership act on advice given by him in a professional capacity);"
Section 386 (categories of preferential debts)	
subsection (1)	In subsection (1), omit the words "or an individual".
subsection (2)	In subsection (2), omit the words "or the individual".
Section 387 ("the relevant date")	

subsection (3)	In paragraph (c) for "passing of the resolution for the winding up of the company" substitute "making of the determination by the limited liability partnership that it be wound up voluntarily".
subsection (5)	Omit subsection (5).
subsection (6)	Omit subsection (6).
Section 388 (meaning of "act as insolvency practitioner")	
subsection (2)	Omit subsection (2).
subsection (3)	Omit subsection (3).
subsection (4)	Delete ""company" means a company within the meaning given by section 735(1) of the Companies Act or a company which may be wound up under Part V of this Act (unregistered companies);" and delete ""interim trustee" and "permanent trustee" mean the same as the Bankruptcy (Scotland) Act 1985".
Section 389 (acting without qualification an offence)	
subsection (1)	Omit the words "or an individual".
Section 402 (official petitioner)	Delete section 402.
Section 412 (individual insolvency rules (England and Wales))	Delete section 412.
Section 415 (Fees orders (individual insolvency proceedings in England and Wales))	Delete section 415.
Section 416 (monetary limits (companies winding up))	
subsection (1)	In subsection (1), omit the words "section 117(2) (amount of company's share capital determining whether county court has

	jurisdiction to wind it up);" and the words "section 120(3) (the equivalent as respects sheriff court jurisdiction in Scotland);".
subsection (3)	In subsection (3), omit the words "117(2), 120(3) or".
Section 418 (monetary limits (bankruptcy))	Delete section 418.
Section 420 (insolvent partnerships)	Delete section 420.
Section 421 (insolvent estates of deceased persons)	Delete section 421.
Section 422 (recognised banks, etc.)	Delete section 422.
Section 427 (parliamentary disqualification)	Delete section 427.
Section 429 (disabilities on revocation or administration order against an individual)	Delete section 429.
Section 432 (offences by bodies corporate)	
subsection (2)	Delete "secretary or".
Section 435 (meaning of "associate")	
new subsection (3A)	Insert a new subsection (3A) as follows: "(3A) A member of a limited liability partnership is an associate of that limited liability partnership and of every other member of that limited liability partnership and of the husband or wife or relative of every other member of that limited liability partnership.".
subsection (11)	For subsection (11) there shall be substituted: "(11) In this section "company" includes any body corporate (whether incorporated in Great Britain or elsewhere); and references to directors and other officers of a company and to voting power at any general meeting of a

	company have effect with any necessary modifications."
Section 436 (expressions used generally)	The following expressions and definitions shall be added to the section: ""designated member" has the same meaning as it has in the Limited Liability Partnerships Act 2000; "limited liability partnership" means a limited liability partnership formed and registered under the Limited Liability Partnerships Act 2000; "limited liability partnership agreement", in relation to a limited liability partnership, means any agreement, express or implied, made between the members of the limited liability partnership or between the limited liability partnership and the members of the limited liability partnership which determines the mutual rights and duties of the members, and their rights and duties in relation to the limited liability partnership."
Section 437 (transitional provisions, and savings)	Delete section 437.
Section 440 (extent (Scotland))	
subsection (2)	In subsection (2), omit paragraph (b).
Section 441 (extent (Northern Ireland))	Delete section 441.
Section 442 (extent (other territories))	Delete section 442.
Schedule 1	
Paragraph 19	For paragraph 19 substitute the following; "**19.** Power to enforce any rights the limited liability partnership has against the members under the terms of the limited liability partnership agreement."
Schedule 10	
Section 85(2)	In the entry relating to section 85(2) for "resolution for voluntary winding up"

	substitute "making of determination for voluntary winding up".
Section 89(4)	In the entry relating to section 89(4) for "Director" substitute "Designated member".
Section 93(3)	In the entry relating to section 93(3) for "general meeting of the company" substitute "meeting of members of the limited liability partnership".
Section 99(3)	In the entries relating to section 99(3) for "director" and "directors" where they appear substitute "designated member" or "designated members" as appropriate.
Section 105(3)	In the entry relating to section 105(3) for "company general meeting" substitute "meeting of the members of the limited liability partnership".
Section 106(6)	In the entry relating to section 106(6) for "final meeting of the company" substitute "final meeting of the members of the limited liability partnership".
Sections 353(1) to 362	Delete the entries relating to sections 353(1) to 362 inclusive.
Section 429(5)	Delete the entry relating to section 429(5).

SCHEDULE 4

[Schedule 4 excludes, in relation to LLPs in Scotland, the application of various provisions of the Insolvency Act 1986, in relation to which the power to legislate has been devolved to the Scottish Ministers under the Scotland Act 1998. The Scottish Ministers have enacted the Limited Liability Partnerships (Scotland) Regulations 2001, which apply to LLPs in Scotland the provisions excluded by Schedule 4. In effect, these provisions therefore apply to LLPs in both England and Wales, and Scotland. It is therefore unnecessary to set out the provisions of Schedule 4, and consequently they have been omitted.]

SCHEDULE 5

Regulation 9

GENERAL AND CONSEQUENTIAL AMENDMENTS IN OTHER LEGISLATION

The Bills of Sale Act (1878) Amendment Act 1882 c. 43

1.   In section 17, after "incorporated company" insert "or by any limited liability partnership" and after "such company" insert "or a limited liability partnership".

The Third Parties (Rights Against Insurers) Act 1930 c. 25

2.   After section 3, insert–

"**Application to limited liability partnerships**
3A. – (1) This Act applies to limited liability partnerships as it applies to companies.

(2) In its application to limited liability partnerships, references to a resolution for a voluntary winding-up being passed are references to a determination for a voluntary winding-up being made."

The Corporate Bodies' Contracts Act 1960 c. 46

3.   In section 2, insert at the end "or to a limited liability partnership".

The Criminal Justice Act 1967 c. 80

4.   In section 9(8)(d), insert at the end–

"; and in paragraph (d) of this subsection references to the secretary, in relation to a limited liability partnership, are to any designated member of the limited liability partnership."

The Solicitors Act 1974 c. 47

5.   In section 87, after the definition of "non-contentious business", insert–

""officer", in relation to a limited liability partnership, means a member of the limited liability partnership;".

The Sex Discrimination Act 1975 c. 65

6.   In section 11, insert at the end–

"(6) This section applies to a limited liability partnership as it applies to a firm; and, in its application to a limited liability partnership, references to a partner in a firm are references to a member of the limited liability partnership."

The Race Relations Act 1976 c. 74

7. In section 10, insert at the end–

"(5) This section applies to a limited liability partnership as it applies to a firm; and, in its application to a limited liability partnership, references to a partner in a firm are references to a member of the limited liability partnership."

The Betting and Gaming Duties Act 1981 c. 63

8. After section 32, insert–

"**Application to limited liability partnerships**
32A – (1) This Act applies to limited liability partnerships as it applies to companies.

(2) In its application to a limited liability partnership, references to a director of a company are references to a member of the limited liability partnership."

The Companies Act 1985 c. 6

9. In section 26, in subsection (1), after paragraph (bb) insert–

"(bbb) which includes, at any place in the name, the expression "limited liability partnership" or its Welsh equivalent ("partneriaeth atebolrwydd cyfyngedig");".

The Business Names Act 1985 c. 7

10. In section 1, in subsection (1), insert at the end–

"(d) in the case of a limited liability partnership, does not consist of its corporate name without any addition other than one so permitted."

11. – (1) Section 4 is amended as follows.

(2) In subsection (1)(a), for "subject to subsection (3)" substitute "subject to subsections (3) and (3A)", omit the word "and" at the end of sub-paragraph (iii) and after that sub-paragraph insert–

"(iiia) In the case of a limited liability partnership, its corporate name and the name of each member, and".

(3) In subsection (2), for "the subsection next following" substitute "subsection (3) or (3A)".

(4) After subsection (3) insert–

"(3A) Subsection (1)(a) does not apply in relation to any document issued by a limited liability partnership with more than 20 members which

maintains at its principal place of business a list of the names of all the members if–
> (a) none of the names of the members appears in the document otherwise than in the text or as a signatory; and
> (b) the document states in legible characters the address of the principal place of business of the limited liability partnership and that the list of the members' names is open to inspection at that place."

(5)   After subsection (4) insert–

"(4A) Where a limited liability partnership maintains a list of the members' names for the purposes of subsection (3A), any person may inspect the list during office hours."

(6)   In subsection (7), after "subsection (4)" insert "or (4A)" and after "any partner of the partnership concerned" insert ",or any member of the limited liability partnership concerned,".

The Administration of Justice Act 1985 c. 61

12.   In section 9(8), after the definition of "multi-national partnership", insert–

""officer", in relation to a limited liability partnership, means a member of the limited liability partnership;".

13.   In section 39(1), after the definition of "the Council", insert–

""director", in relation to a limited liability partnership, means a member of the limited liability partnership;".

14.   In paragraph 1(3) of Schedule 2, insert at the end–

"; and references in this Schedule to a director, in relation to a limited liability partnership, are references to a member of the limited liability partnership."

The Insolvency Act 1986 c. 45

15. – (1)   Section 110 is amended as follows.

(2)   In subsection (1), after "sold" insert "(a)" and at the end insert–

", or (b) to a limited liability partnership (the "transferee limited liability partnership")."

(3)   In subsection (2), for the words "sale," onwards substitute–

"sale–
> (a) in the case of the transferee company, shares, policies or other like interests in the transferee company for distribution among the members of the transferor company, or

(b) in the case of the transferee limited liability partnership, membership in the transferee limited liability partnership for distribution among the members of the transferor company."

(4)   In subsection (4), for the words "company may," onwards substitute–

"company may–
(a) in the case of the transferee company, in lieu of receiving cash, shares, policies or other like interests (or in addition thereto) participate in the profits of, or receive any other benefit from, the transferee company, or
(b) in the case of the transferee limited liability partnership, in lieu of receiving cash or membership (or in addition thereto), participate in some other way in the profits of, or receive any other benefit from, the transferee limited liability partnership."

The Building Societies Act 1986 c. 53

16.   In paragraph 1(2) of Schedule 21, after "In this Schedule - ", insert–

"director", in relation to a limited liability partnership, means a member of the limited liability partnership;".

The Courts and Legal Services Act 1990 c. 41

17.   In section 119(1), after the definition of "multi-national partnership" insert–

"officer", in relation to a limited liability partnership, means a member of the limited liability partnership;".

The Employment Rights Act 1996 c. 18

18. – (1) Section 166 is amended as follows.

(2)   In subsection (5), omit the word "and" at the end of paragraph (a), and insert at the end of paragraph (b)–

", and
(c) where the employer is a limited liability partnership, if (but only if) subsection (8) is satisfied."

(3)   After subsection (7) insert–

"(8) This subsection is satisfied in the case of an employer which is a limited liability partnership–
(a) if a winding-up order, an administration order or a determination for a voluntary winding-up has been made with respect to the limited liability partnership,
(b) if a receiver or (in England and Wales only) a manager of the undertaking of the limited liability partnership has been duly appointed,

or (in England and Wales only) possession has been taken, by or on behalf of the holders of any debentures secured by a floating charge, of any property of the limited liability partnership comprised in or subject to the charge, or

(c) if a voluntary arrangement proposed in the case of the limited liability partnership for the purpose of Part I of the Insolvency Act 1986 has been approved under that Part of that Act."

19. – (1) Section 183 is amended as follows.

(2) In subsection (1), omit the word "and" at the end of paragraph (a), and insert at the end of paragraph (b)–

", and
(c) where the employer is a limited liability partnership, if (but only if) subsection (4) is satisfied."

(3) After subsection (3) insert–

"(4) This subsection is satisfied in the case of an employer which is a limited liability partnership–
(a) if a winding-up order, an administration order or a determination for a voluntary winding-up has been made with respect to the limited liability partnership,
(b) if a receiver or (in England and Wales only) a manager of the undertaking of the limited liability partnership has been duly appointed, or (in England and Wales only) possession has been taken, by or on behalf of the holders of any debentures secured by a floating charge, of any property of the limited liability partnership comprised in or subject to the charge, or
(c) if a voluntary arrangement proposed in the case of the limited liability partnership for the purposes of Part I of the Insolvency Act 1986 has been approved under that Part of that Act."

The Contracts (Rights of Third Parties) Act 1999 c. 31

20. In section 6, after subsection (2) insert–

"(2A) Section 1 confers no rights on a third party in the case of any incorporation document of a limited liability partnership or any limited liability partnership agreement as defined in the Limited Liability Partnerships Regulations 2001 (S.I. No. 2001/1090)."

The Financial Services and Markets Act 2000 c. 8

21. In each of sections 177(2), 221(2) and 232(2) insert at the end–

"; and "officer", in relation to a limited liability partnership, means a member of the limited liability partnership."

Culpable officer provisions

22. – (1) A culpable officer provision applies in the case of a limited liability partnership as if the reference in the provision to a director (or a person purporting to act as a director) were a reference to a member (or a person purporting to act as a member) of the limited liability partnership.

(2)   A culpable officer provision is a provision in any Act or subordinate legislation (within the meaning of the Interpretation Act 1978) to the effect that where–
  (a)   a body corporate is guilty of a particular offence, and
  (b)   the offence is proved to have been committed with the consent or connivance of, or to be attributable to the neglect on the part of, (among others) a director of the body corporate,
he (as well as the body corporate) is guilty of the offence.

SCHEDULE 6

Regulation 10

APPLICATION OF SUBORDINATE LEGISLATION

Part I
Regulations made under the 1985 Act

1.   The Companies (Revision of Defective Accounts and Report) Regulations 1990

2.   The Companies (Defective Accounts) (Authorised Person) Order 1991

3.   The Accounting Standards (Prescribed Body) Regulations 1990

4.   The Companies (Inspection and Copying of Registers, Indices and Documents) Regulations 1991

5.   The Companies (Registers and other Records) Regulations 1985

6.   Companies Act 1985 (Disclosure of Remuneration for Non-Audit Work) Regulations 1991

Part II
Regulations made under the 1986 Act

1.   Insolvency Practitioners Regulations 1990

2.   The Insolvency Practitioners (Recognised Professional Bodies) Order 1986

3.   The Insolvency Rules 1986 and the Insolvency (Scotland) Rules 1986 (except in so far as they relate to the exceptions to the reserved matters specified in section C.2 of Part II of Schedule 5 to the Scotland Act 1998)

4.   The Insolvency Fees Order 1986

5.   The Co-operation of Insolvency Courts (Designation of Relevant Countries and Territories) Order 1986

6.   The Co-operation of Insolvency Courts (Designation of Relevant Countries and Territories) Order 1996

7.   The Co-operation of Insolvency Courts (Designation of Relevant Country) Order 1998

8.   Insolvency Proceedings (Monetary Limits) Order 1986

9.   Insolvency Practitioners Tribunal (Conduct of Investigations) Rules 1986

10.   Insolvency Regulations 1994

11.   Insolvency (Amendment) Regulations 2000

Part III
Regulations made under other legislation

1.   Company and Business Names Regulations 1981

2.   The Companies (Disqualification Orders) Regulations 1986

3.   The Insolvent Companies (Disqualification of Unfit Directors) Proceedings Rules 1987

4.   The Contracting Out (Functions of the Official Receiver) Order 1995

5.   The Uncertificated Securities Regulations 1995

6.   The Insolvent Companies (Reports on Conduct of Directors) Rules 1996

7.   The Insolvent Companies (Reports on Conduct of Directors)(Scotland) Rules 1996

EXPLANATORY NOTE
(This note is not part of the Regulations)

The Limited Liability Partnerships Act 2000 provided for the creation of Limited Liability Partnerships (LLPs) and for the making of regulations concerning them. These Regulations regulate LLPs by applying to them, with appropriate modifications, the appropriate provisions of the existing law which relate to companies and partnerships.

The Regulations are structured in seven parts accompanied by six schedules. They apply to LLPs, with appropriate modifications to reflect the structure of LLPs, a large number of the provisions contained within the Companies Acts 1985 and 1989, the Insolvency Act 1986 and the Company Directors Disqualification Act 1986.

The Regulations amend the relevant primary legislation by way of general modifications which, provide that references to a company include references to a limited liability partnership, and references to a director or officer include a reference to a member of an LLP. Throughout the Schedules to the Regulations there are references to designated members. This category of member is responsible for a number of administrative and filing duties of the LLP but is also representative of the LLP and its membership in circumstances such as the appointment, removal and remuneration of auditors.

Part I of the Regulations contains the citation, commencement and interpretation provisions to be applied to the Regulations, and gives the date on which they come into force.

Part II of, and Schedule 1 to, the Regulations apply the provisions of Part VII of the Companies Act 1985 (accounts and audit) and its attendant Schedules to LLPs with appropriate modifications. Schedule 1 lists only those sections contained in Part VII of the Companies Act 1985, (including the Schedules related to those sections), which have been modified in their application to LLPs or not applied to LLPs. Therefore, if Schedule 1 does not refer to a particular section, which is contained in Part VII of the Companies Act 1985, or paragraph of a relevant Schedule, then that section or paragraph will apply to LLPs, subject only to the general amendments set out in regulation 3. The accounts and audit provisions, as applied by Part II of, and Schedule 1 to, the Regulations, impose accounting requirements on LLPs which are similar to those for companies. They require that LLPs file annual accounts with the registrar of companies, and place audit requirements on LLPs similar to those imposed on companies. They also define the form and content of the accounts, and allow derogations for small and medium sized LLPs.

Part III of and Schedule 2 to the Regulations apply to LLPs the remainder of the provisions of the Companies Act 1985 together with Part II of the Companies Act 1989 with appropriate modifications. Schedule 2 lists all those sections which apply to LLPs. If Schedule 2 does not refer to a particular section of the Companies Act 1985 then that section will not apply to LLPs. Part III of and Schedule 2 to the Regulations regulate an LLP by applying provisions, many of which are the same as or similar to those imposed on companies, but which reflect the different nature and structure of LLPs. They include provision for:

the execution of documents including bills of exchange and promissory notes and the execution of deeds abroad;

the registration of debenture holders including, a right for the holders of debentures issued by an LLP to inspect the register, the liability of trustees of debentures and perpetual debentures;

the officers and registered office including a requirement to register changes in the registered office of an LLP with the registrar of companies;

company identification – the name of an LLP is to appear outside its place of business and on correspondence, in addition an LLP may have a common seal;

annual return – this part of the regulations provides that it is the duty of an LLP to deliver an annual return to the registrar of companies and sets out requirements as to the content of the annual return;

auditors – an LLP is, in general, required to appoint auditors, provision is made for the appointment of auditors by the Secretary of State where an LLP is in default, the auditors have various rights including the right to have access to an LLP's books, accounts and information as necessary, the right to attend meetings of the LLP, and certain rights in the event of being removed or not being re-appointed, provision is also made for the resignation of auditors and the making of a statement by a person ceasing to hold office as auditor;

registration of charges – sections 395 to 408, 410 to 423 of the Companies Act 1985, will apply to LLPs, with modifications, until section 92 of the Companies Act 1989 is commenced or some other amendment is made;

arrangements and reconstructions – an LLP will have the power to compromise with its creditors and members, the sections set out detailed provisions concerning the circulation of information on any compromise together with provisions for facilitating an LLP's reconstruction or amalgamation;

investigation of LLPs and their affairs – an investigation of an LLP may be made following its own application of that of its members, the sections set out detailed provisions concerning investigations, the production of documents and evidence, contempt of court, inspectors' reports and the use of inspectors' reports as evidence;

fraudulent trading is punished in the case of an LLP in the same was as a company;

unfair prejudice – Schedule 2 applies the Companies Act 1985 so that, in general, there is a remedy for the members of an LLP should they suffer unfair prejudice, the members of a limited liability partnership may, however, by unanimous agreement exclude the right contained in section 459 (1) for such period as may be agreed;

matters arising subsequent to winding up – the provisions deal with various matters including the power of the court to declare the dissolution of a company void, the striking out by the registrar of companies of a defunct company and crown disclaimer of property vesting as bona vacantia;

registrar of companies – Schedule 2 sets out the registrar's functions and offices in relation to LLPs;

miscellaneous and supplementary provisions – the provisions deal with various matters including the form of company registers etc., the use of computers for company records, the service of documents, the powers of a court to grant relief in certain cases, and the punishment of offences.

Part III of the Regulations also applies the provisions of the Company Directors Disqualification Act 1986 to limited liability partnerships with appropriate modifications. These provide that members of an LLP will be subject to the same penalties that currently apply to company directors under the CDDA 1986 and may be disqualified from being the member of an LLP or a director of a company under those provisions.

Part IV of, and Schedule 3 to, the Regulations apply to LLPs the First and Third Groups of Parts of the Insolvency Act 1986, with appropriate modifications. Schedule 3 lists only those sections contained in the First or Third Group of Parts which have been modified or omitted in their application to LLPs. If there is no reference in Schedule 3 to a particular section contained in the First or Third Group of Parts of the Insolvency Act 1986 then that section will apply to LLPs subject to the general modifications contained in Regulation 5. The insolvency provisions as applied to LLPs include provisions for voluntary arrangements, administration orders, receivership, winding-up and liquidations. The most notable modifications of the provisions which apply to companies are, an additional section, section 214A and the re-worded section 74.

The new Section 214A provides that withdrawals made by members during the two years prior to the commencement of winding-up will be subject to claw back if it is proved that at the time of the withdrawal the member knew or had reasonable grounds for believing that the LLP was, or would be made, insolvent. The modified section 74 provides that in the event that an LLP is wound up, both past and present members of the LLP are liable to contribute to the assets of the LLP to the extent that they have agreed to do so with the other members, in the limited liability partnership agreement.

Part V of the Regulations apply the provisions contained in Parts XV and XXIV of the Financial Services and Markets Act 2000 to LLPs. These Parts provide for insolvency arrangements of LLPs which are authorised under FSMA 2000. In addition, these Parts give the Authority powers to ask the courts to wind up, or initiate other insolvency procedures against, authorised and certain other persons. It also enables the Authority to be heard by the court when such proceedings are commenced by third parties.

Part VI of the Regulations provides for default provisions governing the rights and duties of members, which modify those contained in section 24 of the Partnership Act 1890. They will apply when there is no existing limited liability partnership agreement, or where the agreement does not wholly deal with a particular issue.

Schedule 4 to the Regulations lists those provisions contained in the First and Third Group of Parts of the Insolvency Act 1986 which are not applied to Scotland. The provisions wholly or partly concern matters which are set out in Section C.2 of the Fifth Schedule of the Scotland Act 1998 as being exceptions to the reservation.

Part VII of, and Schedule 5 to, the Regulations apply a number of general and consequential amendments to other Acts of Parliament.

Part VII of, and Schedule 6 to, the Regulations apply to LLPs certain pieces of subordinate legislation made under the Companies Act 1985, the Insolvency Act 1986 and other primary legislation.

Limited Liability Partnerships (Scotland) Regulations 2001

(SSI 2001 No 128)

Made: 28th March 2001
Coming into force: 6th April 2001

Whereas a draft of these Regulations has been approved by a resolution of the Scottish Parliament pursuant to section 17(4) of the Limited Liability Partnerships Act 2000;

Now, therefore, the Scottish Ministers, in exercise of the powers conferred by sections 14, 15, 16 and 17 of the Limited Liability Partnerships Act 2000 and all other powers enabling them in that behalf hereby makes the following Regulations:

PART I
CITATION, COMMENCEMENT AND INTERPRETATION

Citation, commencement and extent

1. – (1)   These Regulations may be cited as the Limited Liability Partnerships (Scotland) Regulations 2001 and shall come into force on 6th April 2001.

(2)   These Regulations extend to Scotland only.

Interpretation

2. – (1)   In these Regulations–

"the 1985 Act" means the Companies Act 1985;

"the 1986 Act" means the Insolvency Act 1986;

"limited liability partnership agreement", in relation to a limited liability partnership, means any agreement express or implied between the members of the limited liability partnership or between the limited liability partnership and the members of the limited liability partnership which determines the mutual rights and duties of the members, and their rights and duties in relation to the limited liability partnership;

"the principal Act" means the Limited Liability Partnerships Act 2000; and

"shadow member", in relation to limited liability partnerships, means a person in accordance with whose directions or instructions the members of the limited liability partnership are accustomed to act (but so that a person is not deemed a shadow member by reason only that the members of the limited liability partnership act on advice given by him in a professional capacity).

(2)   In these Regulations, unless the contrary intention appears, expressions which are also used in the principal Act shall have the same meanings as in that Act.

PART II
COMPANIES ACT

Application of the provisions of the 1985 Act to limited liability partnerships

3.   The provisions of the 1985 Act specified in the first column of Schedule 1 to these Regulations shall apply to limited liability partnerships, except where the context otherwise requires, with the following modifications–
- (a) references to a company shall include references to a limited liability partnership;
- (b) references to the Companies Acts shall include references to the principal Act and regulations made thereunder;
- (c) references to the Insolvency Act 1986 shall include references to that Act as it applies to limited liability partnerships by virtue of Part III of these Regulations;
- (d) references in a provision of the 1985 Act to other provisions of that Act shall include references to those other provisions as they apply to limited liability partnerships by virtue of these Regulations; and
- (e) the modifications, if any, specified in the second column of Schedule 1 opposite the provision specified in the first column.

PART III
WINDING UP AND INSOLVENCY

Application of the 1986 Act to limited liability partnerships

4. – (1)   Subject to paragraph (2), the provisions of the 1986 Act listed in Schedule 2 to the extent that they concern matters which are set out in section C2 of Schedule 5 to the Scotland Act 1998 as being exceptions to the reservation of insolvency, shall apply in relation to limited liability partnerships as they apply in relation to companies.

(2)   The provisions of the 1986 Act referred to in paragraph (1) shall apply to limited liability partnerships, except where the context otherwise requires, with the following modifications–
- (a) references to a company shall include references to a limited liability partnership;
- (b) references to a director or to an officer of a company shall include references to a member of a limited liability partnership;
- (c) references to a shadow director include references to a shadow member;

(d) references to the 1985 Act, the Company Directors Disqualification Act 1986, the Companies Act 1989 or to any provisions of those Acts or to any provisions of the 1986 Act shall include references to those Acts or provisions as they apply to limited liability partnerships by virtue of the principal Act; and

(e) the modifications set out in Schedule 3 to these Regulations.

PART IV
MISCELLANEOUS

General and consequential amendments

5. The enactments mentioned in Schedule 4 shall have effect subject to the amendments specified in that Schedule.

Application of subordinate legislation

6. – (1) The subordinate legislation specified in Schedule 5 shall apply to limited liability partnerships as from time to time in force and with such modifications as the context requires for the purpose of giving effect to the provisions of the Insolvency Act 1986 which are applied by these Regulations.

(2) In the case of any conflict between any provision of the subordinate legislation applied by paragraph (1) and any provision of these Regulations, the latter shall prevail.

Regulation 3
SCHEDULE 1
MODIFICATIONS TO PROVISIONS OF THE 1985 ACT

Formalities of carrying on business

36B (execution of documents by companies)

Floating charges and receivers (Scotland)

462 (power of incorporated company to create floating charge) In subsection (1), for the words "an incorporated company (whether a company within the meaning of this Act or not)," substitute "a limited liability partnership", and the words "(including uncalled capital) are omitted.

463 (effect of floating charge on winding up)
466 (alteration of floating charges)
Subsections (1), (2), (3) and (6)
486 (interpretation for Part XVIII generally) For the current definition of "company" substitute ""company" means a limited liability partnership;".

487 (extent of Part XVIII)

SCHEDULE 2

[Schedule 2 applies to LLPs in Scotland various provisions of the Insolvency Act 1986, in relation to which the power to legislate has been devolved to the Scottish Ministers under the Scotland Act 1998, and the application of which were therefore excluded in relation to LLPs in Scotland by the Limited Liability Partnerships Regulations 2001. In effect, these provisions therefore apply to LLPs in both England and Wales, and Scotland. It is therefore unnecessary to set out the provisions of Schedule 2, and consequently they have been omitted.]

SCHEDULE 3

[Schedule 3 sets out specific modifications to the provisions of the Insolvency Act 1986 which are applied to LLPs in Scotland by Schedule 2 referred to above. As these modifications are virtually identical to the modifications of those same provisions as they apply to LLPs in England and Wales, set out in Schedule 3 to the Limited Liability Partnerships Regulations 2001, it is unnecessary to set out these modifications separately here. Consequently, the provisions of Schedule 3 have been omitted.]

Regulation 5
SCHEDULE 4
GENERAL AND CONSEQUENTIAL AMENDMENTS IN OTHER LEGISLATION

The Insolvency Act 1986 c. 45

1. – (1) Section 110 is amended as follows.

(2) In subsection (1), after "sold" insert "(a)" and at the end insert–

", or (b) to a limited liability partnership (the "transferee limited liability partnership")."

(3) In subsection (2), for the words "sale", onwards substitute:

"sale–
   (a) in the case of the transferee company, shares, policies or other like interests in the company for distribution among the members of the transferor company, or
   (b) in the case of the transferee limited liability partnership, membership in the limited liability partnership for distribution among the members of the transferor company.".

(4) In subsection (4), for the words "may," onwards substitute:

"may–
   (a) in the case of the transferee company, in lieu of receiving cash, shares, policies or other like interests (or in addition thereto) participate in the profits of, or receive any other benefit from, the company, or
   (b) in the case of the transferee limited liability partnership, in lieu of receiving cash, or membership (or in addition thereto) participate in

some other way in the profits of, or receive any other benefit from, the limited liability partnership."

Criminal Procedure (Scotland) Act 1995 c. 46

1.   In section 70 (8) insert at the end–

"; and "officer" and "any person having or being one of the persons having the management of the affairs of the body corporate", in relation to a limited liability partnership, means a member of the limited liability partnership".

2.   In section 141(2), insert at the end–

"; and in sub paragraph (b)(i) of this subsection references to the director or secretary or other official, in relation to a limited liability partnership, are to any member of the limited liability partnership".

3.   In section 143(3), insert at the end–

"; and in sub paragraph 3(b) of this subsection references to the managing director or the secretary, in relation to a limited liability partnership, are to any member of the limited liability partnership".

Requirements of Writing (Scotland) Act 1995 c. 7

4.   In section 7 (7) after "companies," insert "limited liability partnerships,".

5.   After paragraph 3 of Schedule 2, insert–

"Limited Liability Partnerships

3A. – (1)   Except where an enactment expressly provides otherwise, where a granter of a document is a limited liability partnership, the document is signed by the limited liability partnership if it is signed on its behalf by a member of the limited liability partnership.

(2) This Act is without prejudice to paragraph 9 of Schedule 1, paragraph 9 of Schedule 2, and paragraph 7 of Schedule 4, to the Insolvency Act 1986.

(3) Sub-paragraphs (1) and (2) of this paragraph apply in relation to the signing of an alteration made to a document as they apply in relation to the signing of a document.

(4) Where a granter of a document is a limited liability partnership, section 3 of and Schedule 1 to this Act shall have effect subject to the modifications set out in sub-paragraphs (5) and (6) below.

(5) In section 3–
    (a) for subsection (1) there shall be substituted the following subsections–

"(1) Subject to subsections (1A) to (7) below, where–

(a) a document bears to have been subscribed on behalf of a limited liability partnership by a member of the limited liability partnership;

(b) the document bears to have been signed by a person as a witness of the subscription of the member of the limited liability partnership and to state the name and address of the witness; and

(c) nothing in the document, or in the testing clause or its equivalent, indicates–

(i) that it was not subscribed on behalf of the limited liability partnership as it bears to have been so subscribed; or

(ii) that it was not validly witnessed for any reason specified in paragraphs (a) to (e) of subsection (4) below,

the document shall be presumed to have been subscribed by the limited liability partnership.

(1A) Where a document does not bear to have been signed by a person as a witness of the subscription of the member of the limited liability partnership it shall be presumed to have been subscribed by the limited liability partnership if it bears to have been subscribed on behalf of the limited liability partnership by two members of the limited liability partnership.

(1B) A presumption under subsection (1) or (1A) above as to subscription of a document does not include a presumption that a person bearing to subscribe the document as a member of the limited liability partnership was such member. ";

(b) in subsection (4) after paragraph (g) there shall be inserted the following paragraph–

"(h) if the document does not bear to have been witnessed, but bears to have been subscribed on behalf of the limited liability partnership by two of the members of the limited liability partnership, that a signature bearing to be the signature of a member is not such a signature, whether by reason of forgery or otherwise;".

(6) In paragraph 1 of Schedule 1–

(a) for sub-paragraph (1) there shall be substituted the following sub-paragraphs–

"(1) Subject to sub-paragraphs (1A) to (7) below, where–

(a) an alteration to a document bears to have been signed on behalf of a limited liability partnership by a member of the limited liability partnership;

(b) the alteration bears to have been signed by a person as a witness of the signature of the member of the limited liability partnership and to state the name and address of the witness; and

(c) nothing in the document or alteration, or in the testing clause or its equivalent, indicates–

(i) that the alteration was not signed on behalf of the limited liability partnership as it bears to have been so signed; or

(ii) that the alteration was not validly witnessed for any reason specified in paragraphs (a) to (e) of sub-paragraph (4) below,

the alteration shall be presumed to have been signed by the limited liability partnership.

(1A) Where an alteration does not bear to have been signed by a person as a witness of the signature of the member of the limited liability partnership it shall be presumed to have been signed by the limited liability partnership if it bears to have been signed on behalf of the limited liability partnership by two members of the limited liability partnership.

(1B) A presumption under sub-paragraph (1) or (1A) above as to signing of an alteration to a document does not include a presumption that a person bearing to sign the alteration as a member of the limited liability partnership was such member";

(b) in sub-paragraph (4) after paragraph (g) there shall be inserted the following paragraph–

"(h) if the alteration does not bear to have been witnessed, but bears to have been signed on behalf of the limited liability partnership by two of the members of the limited liability partnership, that a signature bearing to be the signature of a member is not such a signature, whether by reason of forgery or otherwise;".

Culpable officer provision

6. – (1)   A culpable officer provision applies in the case of a limited liability partnership as if the reference in the provision to a director (or a person purporting to act as a director) were a reference to a member (or a person purporting to act as a member) of the limited liability partnership.

(2)   A culpable officer provision is a devolved provision in any Act or subordinate legislation (within the meaning of the Interpretation Act 1978 or the Scotland Act 1998 (Transitory and Transitional Provisions) (Publication and Interpretation etc. of Acts of the Scottish Parliament) Order 1999 to the effect that where–

(a)   a body corporate is guilty of a particular offence, and

(b)   the offence is proved to have been committed with the consent or connivance of, or to be attributable to the neglect on the part of, (among others) a director of the body corporate,

he (as well as the body corporate) is guilty of the offence.

(3)   In this paragraph "devolved provision" means any provision that would be within devolved competence for the purposes of section 54 [section 101] of the Scotland Act.

Regulation 6

SCHEDULE 5
APPLICATION OF SUBORDINATE LEGISLATION

Regulations made under the 1986 Act

1.   The Insolvency (Scotland) Rules 1986 (in so far as they relate to the exceptions to the reserved matters specified in section C.2 of Part II of Schedule 5 to the Scotland Act 1998 (c.46)).

EXPLANATORY NOTE
(This note is not part of the Regulations)

The Limited Liability Partnerships Act 2000 c.12. provided for the creation of Limited Liability Partnerships (LLPs) and for the making of regulations concerning them. These Regulations regulate LLPs by applying to them, with appropriate modifications, the appropriate provisions of the existing law which relate to companies and partnerships.

The Act is of GB application. Section 19(3) of the Act provides that the Act shall be a pre-commencement enactment for the purposes of the Scotland Act 1998. Specifically, the Act makes provision that would impact on legislation within the competence of the Scottish Parliament so as to:

Allow for registration of LLPs with the registrar of companies in Scotland;

Apply Scots law in relation to winding up and insolvency of LLPs;

Extend certain provisions of the Companies Act 1985, as appropriate, to LLPs registered in Scotland to ensure that such an LLP should be able to create floating charges over its assets.

The Regulations are structured in four parts accompanied by five schedules. They apply to LLPs, with appropriate modifications to reflect the structure of LLPs, a large number of the provisions contained within the Companies Acts 1985 and the Insolvency Act 1986.

The Regulations amend the relevant primary legislation by way of general modifications which, provide that references to a company includes references to a limited liability partnership , and references to director or officer include a reference to a member of an LLP. Throughout the Schedules to the Regulations there are references to designated members. This category of member is responsible for a number of administrative and filing duties of the LLP but is also representative of the LLP and its membership in circumstances such as the appointment, removal and remuneration of auditors.

Part I of the Regulations contains the citation, commencement, extent and interpretation provisions to be applied to the Regulations, and gives the date on which they come into force.

Part II of and Schedule 1 to the Regulations apply to certain provisions of the Companies Act 1985.

Part III of and Schedules 2 and 3 to the Regulations apply to LLPs the provisions of the First and Third Groups of Parts of the Insolvency Act 1986, with appropriate modifications. **Schedule 2 to the Regulations** lists those provisions contained in the First and Third Group of Parts of the Insolvency Act 1986 which are devolved to Scotland. Schedule 3 lists those sections contained in **Schedule 3** which have been modified or omitted in their application to LLPs.

The provisions are devolved matters in relation to Scotland because they wholly or partly concern matters which are set out in Section C.2 of the Fifth Schedule of the Scotland Act 1998 as not being reserved.

The insolvency provisions as applied to LLPs include provisions for voluntary arrangements, receivership, winding-up and liquidations. The most notable modification of the provisions which apply to companies is, an additional section, Section 214A.

The new Section 214A provides that withdrawals made by members during the two years prior to the commencement of winding-up will be subject to claw back if it is proved that at the time of the withdrawal the member knew or had reasonable grounds for believing that the LLP was, or would be made, insolvent.

Part IV of and Schedule 4 to the Regulations apply a number of general and consequential amendments to other enactments.

Part IV of and Schedule 5 to the Regulations apply to LLPs the Insolvency (Scotland) Rules 1986.

Note on the modified legislation

Set out on the following pages are the provisions of the Companies Act 1985 (CA 1985), Company Directors Disqualification Act 1986 (CDDA 1986) and Insolvency Act 1986 (IA 1986), as they are applied to limited liability partnerships. Except where otherwise stated (as to which, see under *Scotland* below), these provisions are set out with the modifications applied to them by the Limited Liability Partnerships Regulations 2001 (LLPR 2001). These modifications consist of general and specific modifications, which can be found in the LLPR 2001 as set out below.

Title of Act	General modifications	Specific modifications
CA 1985	LLPR 2001, Regs 3, 4(1)	LLPR 2001, Sch 1, Sch 2, Part I
CDDA 1986	LLPR 2001, Reg 4(2)	LLPR 2001, Sch 2, Part II
IA 1986	LLPR 2001, Reg 5	LLPR 2001, Sch 3

Specific additions made by the LLPR 2001 are shown within square brackets. Specific deletions are marked with elipses (i.e. ....).

Since the general modifications are not always precise (there are references to 'such further modifications as the context requires ...'), and to apply all of them literally would in some cases render certain provisions almost unreadable, the legislation as set out below is *for guidance only*. It cannot be and is not intended to be definitive. **It is believed to be correct as at 6 April 2001.**

Scotland. Separate regulations, the Limited Liability Partnerships (Scotland) Regulations 2001 (the 'Scottish Regulations'), have been made which apply to limited liability partnerships in Scotland certain provisions of the Companies Act 1985 and the Insolvency Act 1986, in relation to which the power to legislate has been devolved to the Scottish Ministers under the Scotland Act 1998. In most instances, the provisions applied, and the modifications made to them, are identical to those applied to limited liability partnerships in England and Wales by the LLPR 2001 mentioned above. Where such is the case, this is not separately noted. However, certain provisions of the Companies Act 1985 (sections 36B, 462, 463, and 466) and the Insolvency Act 1986 (Schedule 2, paragraph 17) applicable to Scotland only are modified separately by the Scottish Regulations. This is noted in relation to each of these provisions.

Companies Act 1985

1985 Chapter 6

Provisions of the Companies Act 1985 with modifications as they apply to Limited Liability Partnerships

PART I
FORMATION AND REGISTRATION OF LIMITED LIABILITY PARTNERSHIPS; JURIDICAL STATUS AND MEMBERSHIP

CHAPTER I
LIMITED LIABILITY PARTNERSHIP FORMATION

1–23

24 Minimum membership for carrying on business

If a limited liability partnership ... carries on business without having at least two members and does so for more than six months, a person who, for the whole or any part of the period that it so carries on business after those six months–
 (a) is a member of the limited liability partnership, and
 (b) knows that it is carrying on business with only one member,
is liable (jointly and severally with the limited liability partnership) for the payment of the limited liability partnership's debts contracted during the period or, as the case may be, that part of it.

25–34

CHAPTER III
A LIMITED LIABILITY PARTNERSHIP'S CAPACITY; FORMALITIES OF CARRYING ON BUSINESS

35–35B

36 Limited liability partnership contracts: England and Wales

Under the law of England and Wales a contract may be made–
 (a) by a limited liability partnership, by writing under its common seal, or
 (b) on behalf of a limited liability partnership, by any person acting under its authority, express or implied;
and any formalities required by law in the case of a contract made by an individual also apply, unless a contrary intention appears, to a contract made by or on behalf of a limited liability partnership.

36A Execution of documents: England and Wales

(1)   Under the law of England and Wales the following provisions have effect with respect to the execution of documents by a limited liability partnership.

(2)   A document is executed by a limited liability partnership by the affixing of its common seal.

(3)   A limited liability partnership need not have a common seal, however, and the following subsections apply whether it does or not.

(4)   A document signed by [two members of a limited liability partnership], and expressed (in whatever form of words) to be executed by the limited liability partnership has the same effect as if executed under the common seal of the limited liability partnership.

(5)   A document executed by a limited liability partnership which makes it clear on its face that it is intended by the person or persons making it to be a deed has effect, upon delivery, as a deed; and it shall be presumed, unless a contrary intention is proved, to be delivered upon its being so executed.

(6)   In favour of a purchaser a document shall be deemed to have been duly executed by a limited liability partnership if it purports to be signed by [two members of a limited liability partnership], and, where it makes it clear on its face that it is intended by the person or persons making it to be a deed, to have been delivered upon its being executed.
       A "purchaser" means a purchaser in good faith for valuable consideration and includes a lessee, mortgagee or other person who for valuable consideration acquires an interest in property.

36B Execution of documents by limited liability partnerships

(1)   Notwithstanding the provisions of any enactment, a limited liability partnership need not have a limited liability partnership seal.

(2)   For the purposes of any enactment–
       (a) providing for a document to be executed by a limited liability partnership by affixing its common seal; or
       (b) referring (in whatever terms) to a document so executed,
a document signed or subscribed by or on behalf of the limited liability partnership in accordance with the provisions of the Requirements of Writing (Scotland) Act 1995 shall have effect as if so executed.

(3)   In this section "enactment" includes an enactment contained in a statutory instrument.

[Section 36B, as modified by the Limited Liability Partnerships (Scotland) Regulations 2001]

36C Pre-incorporation contracts, deeds and obligations

(1) A contract which purports to be made by or on behalf of a limited liability partnership at a time when the limited liability partnership has not been formed has effect, subject to any agreement to the contrary, as one made with the person purporting to act for the limited liability partnership or as agent for it, and he is personally liable on the contract accordingly.

(2) Subsection (1) applies–
(a) to the making of a deed under the law of England and Wales, and
(b) to the undertaking of an obligation under the law of Scotland,
as it applies to the making of a contract.

37 Bills of exchange and promissory notes

A bill of exchange or promissory note is deemed to have been made, accepted or endorsed on behalf of a limited liability partnership if made, accepted or endorsed in the name of, or by or on behalf or on account of, the limited liability partnership by a person acting under its authority.

38 Execution of deeds abroad

(1) A limited liability partnership may, by writing under its common seal, empower any person, either generally or in respect of any specified matters, as its attorney, to execute deeds on its behalf in any place elsewhere than in the United Kingdom.

(2) A deed executed by such an attorney on behalf of the limited liability partnership has the same effect as if it were executed under the limited liability partnership's common seal.

(3) This section does not extend to Scotland.

39 Power of limited liability partnership to have official seal for use abroad

(1) A limited liability partnership which has a common seal [may] have for use in any territory, district, or place elsewhere than in the United Kingdom, an official seal, which shall be a facsimile of its common seal, with the addition on its face of the name of every territory, district or place where it is to be used.

(2) The official seal when duly affixed to a document has the same effect as the limited liability partnership's common seal.

(2A) Subsection (2) does not extend to Scotland.

(3) A limited liability partnership having an official seal for use in any such territory, district or place may, by writing under its common seal, or as respects Scotland by writing in accordance with the Requirements of Writing (Scotland)

Act 1995 authorise any person appointed for the purpose in that territory, district or place to affix the official seal to any deed or other document to which the limited liability partnership is party in that territory, district or place.

(4)   As between the limited liability partnership and a person dealing with such an agent, the agent's authority continues during the period (if any) mentioned in the instrument conferring the authority, or if no period is there mentioned, then until notice of the revocation or determination of the agent's authority has been given to the person dealing with him.

(5)   The person affixing the official seal shall certify in writing on the deed or other instrument to which the seal is affixed the date on which and the place at which it is affixed.

40

41 Authentication of documents

A document or proceeding requiring authentication by a limited liability partnership is sufficiently authenticated for the purposes of the law of England and Wales by the signature of a [member] of the limited liability partnership.

42 Events affecting a limited liability partnership's status

(1)   A limited liability partnership is not entitled to rely against [persons other than members of the limited liability partnership] on the happening of any of the following events–
  (a) the making of a winding-up order in respect of the limited liability partnership, or the appointment of a liquidator in a voluntary winding up of the limited liability partnership, or
  (b) any alteration of the limited liability partnership's incorporation document …, or
  (c) …
  (d) (as regards service of any document on the limited liability partnership) any change in the situation of the limited liability partnership's registered office,
if the event had not been officially notified at the material time and is not shown by the limited liability partnership to have been known at that time to the person concerned, or if the material time fell on or before the 15th day after the date of official notification (or, where the 15th day was a non-business day, on or before the next day that was not) and it is shown that the person concerned was unavoidably prevented from knowing of the event at that time.

(2)   In subsection (1)–
  (a) "official notification" and "officially notified" have the meanings given by section 711(2) (registrar of companies to give public notice of the issue or receipt by him of certain documents), and
  (b) "non-business day" means a Saturday or Sunday, Christmas Day, Good Friday and any other day which is a bank holiday in the part of Great Britain where the limited liability partnership is registered.

CHAPTER VIII
MISCELLANEOUS PROVISIONS ABOUT SHARES AND DEBENTURES

182

183 Transfer and registration

(1)   It is not lawful for a limited liability partnership to register a transfer of ... debentures of the limited liability partnership unless a proper instrument of transfer has been delivered to it, or the transfer is an exempt transfer within the Stock Transfer Act 1982 or is in accordance with regulations made under section 207 of the Companies Act 1989.

This applies notwithstanding anything in the [limited liability partnership agreement].

(2)   Subsection (1) does not prejudice any power of the limited liability partnership to register as ... debenture holder a person to whom the right to any ... debentures of the limited liability partnership has been transmitted by operation of law.

(3),(4) ...

(5)   If a limited liability partnership refuses to register a transfer of ... debentures, the limited liability partnership shall, within two months after the date on which the transfer was lodged with it, send to the transferee notice of the refusal.

(6)   If default is made in complying with subsection (5), the limited liability partnership and every member of it who is in default is liable to a fine and, for continued contravention, to a daily default fine.

184 Certification of transfers

(1)   The certification by a limited liability partnership of any instrument of transfer of any ... debentures of the limited liability partnership is to be taken as a representation by the limited liability partnership to any person acting on the faith of the certification that there have been produced to the limited liability partnership such documents as on their face show a prima facie title to the ... debentures in the transferor named in the instrument.

However, the certification is not to be taken as a representation that the transferor has any title to the shares or debentures.

(2)   Where a person acts on the faith of a false certification by a limited liability partnership made negligently, the limited liability partnership is under the same liability to him as if the certification had been made fraudulently.

(3)   For purposes of this section–
    (a) an instrument of transfer is deemed certificated if it bears the words "certificate lodged" (or words to the like effect);

    (b) the certification of an instrument of transfer is deemed made by a limited liability partnership if–
        (i) the person issuing the instrument is a person authorised to issue certificated instruments of transfer on the limited liability partnership's behalf, and
        (ii) the certification is signed by a person authorised to certificate transfers on the limited liability partnership's behalf or by a member or servant either of the limited liability partnership or of a body corporate so authorised;
    (c) a certification is deemed signed by a person if–
        (i) it purports to be authenticated by his signature or initials (whether handwritten or not), and
        (ii) it is not shown that the signature or initials was or were placed there neither by himself nor by a person authorised to use the signature or initials for the purpose of certificating transfers on the limited liability partnership's behalf.

185 Duty of limited liability partnership as to issue of certificates

(1)   Subject to the following provisions, every limited liability partnership shall–
    (a) within two months after the allotment of any of its ... debentures or debenture stock, and
    (b) within two months after the date on which a transfer of any such ... debentures or debenture stock is lodged with the limited liability partnership,

complete and have ready for delivery the certificates of all ... the debentures and the certificates of all debenture stock allotted or transferred (unless the conditions of issue of the ... debentures or debenture stock otherwise provide).

(2)   For this purpose, "transfer" means a transfer duly stamped and otherwise valid, or an exempt transfer within the Stock Transfer Act 1982, and does not include such a transfer as the limited liability partnership is for any reason entitled to refuse to register and does not register.

(3)   ...

(4)   A limited liability partnership of which ... debentures are allotted or debenture stock is allotted to a recognised clearing house or a nominee of a recognised clearing house or of a recognised investment exchange, or with which a transfer is lodged for transferring any ... debentures or debenture stock of the limited liability partnership to such a clearing house or nominee, is not required, in consequence of the allotment or the lodging of the transfer, to comply with subsection (1); but no person shall be a nominee for the purposes of this section unless he is a person designated for the purposes of this section in the rules of the recognised investment exchange in question.
      "Recognised clearing house" means a recognised clearing house within the meaning of the Financial Services Act 1986 acting in relation to a recognised investment exchange and "recognised investment exchange" has the same meaning as in that Act.

(5)   If default is made in complying with subsection (1), the limited liability partnership and every member of it who is in default is liable to a fine and, for continued contravention, to a daily default fine.

(6)   If a limited liability partnership on which a notice has been served requiring it to make good any default in complying with subsection (1) fails to make good the default within 10 days after service of the notice, the court may, on the application of the person entitled to have the certificates or the debentures delivered to him, exercise the power of the following subsection.

(7)   The court may make an order directing the limited liability partnership and any member of it to make good the default within such time as may be specified in the order; and the order may provide that all costs of and incidental to the application shall be borne by the limited liability partnership or by a member of it responsible for the default.

186–189

190 Register of debenture holders

(1)   A limited liability partnership registered in England and Wales shall not keep in Scotland any register of holders of debentures of the limited liability partnership or any duplicate of any such register or part of any such register which is kept outside Great Britain.

(2)   A limited liability partnership registered in Scotland shall not keep in England and Wales any such register or duplicate as above-mentioned.

(3)   Neither a register of holders of debentures of a limited liability partnership nor a duplicate of any such register or part of any such register which is kept outside Great Britain shall be kept in England and Wales (in the case of a limited liability partnership registered in England and Wales) or in Scotland (in the case of a limited liability partnership registered in Scotland) elsewhere than–
  (a) at the limited liability partnership's registered office; or
  (b) at any office of the limited liability partnership at which the work of making it up is done; or
  (c) if the limited liability partnership arranges with some other person for the making up of the register or duplicate to be undertaken on its behalf by that other person, at the office of that other person at which the work is done.

(4)   Where a limited liability partnership keeps (in England and Wales or in Scotland, as the case may be) both such a register and such a duplicate, it shall keep them at the same place.

(5)   Every limited liability partnership which keeps any such register or duplicate in England and Wales or Scotland shall send to the registrar of companies notice (in the prescribed form) of the place where the register or duplicate is kept and of any change in that place.

(6)   But a limited liability partnership is not bound to send notice under subsection (5) where the register or duplicate has, at all times since it came into existence, been kept at the limited liability partnership's registered office.

191 Right to inspect register

(1)   Every register of holders of debentures of a limited liability partnership shall, except when duly closed, be open to the inspection–
  (a)   of the registered holder of any such debentures [or any member of the limited liability partnership] without fee; and
  (b)   of any other person on payment of such fee as may be prescribed.

(2)   Any such registered holder of debentures ..., or any other person, may require a copy of the register of the holders of debentures of the limited liability partnership or any part of it, on payment of such fee as may be prescribed.

(3)   A copy of any trust deed for securing an issue of debentures shall be forwarded to every holder of any such debentures at his request on payment of such fee as may be prescribed.

(4)   If inspection is refused, or a copy is refused or not forwarded, the limited liability partnership and every member of it who is in default is liable to a fine, and for continued contravention, to a daily default fine.

(5)   Where a limited liability partnership is in default as above-mentioned, the court may by order compel an immediate inspection of the register or direct that the copies required be sent to the person requiring them.

(6)   For purposes of this section, a register is deemed to be duly closed if closed in accordance with provisions contained ... in the debentures or, in the case of debenture stock, in the stock certificates, or in the trust deed or other document securing the debentures or debenture stock, during such period or periods not exceeding in the whole 30 days in any year, as may be therein specified.

(7)   Liability incurred by a limited liability partnership from the making or deletion of an entry in its register of debenture holders, or from a failure to make or delete any such entry, is not enforceable more than 20 years after the date on which the entry was made or deleted or, in the case of any such failure, the failure first occurred.
    This is without prejudice to any lesser period of limitation.

192 Liability of trustees of debentures

(1)   Subject to this section, any provision contained–
  (a)   in a trust deed for securing an issue of debentures, or
  (b)   in any contract with the holders of debentures secured by a trust deed,
is void in so far as it would have the effect of exempting a trustee of the deed from, or indemnifying him against, liability for breach of trust where he fails to show the degree of care and diligence required of him as trustee, having

regard to the provisions of the trust deed conferring on him any powers, authorities or discretions.

(2)   Subsection (1) does not invalidate–
   (a)   a release otherwise validly given in respect of anything done or omitted to be done by a trustee before the giving of the release; or
   (b)   any provision enabling such a release to be given–
      (i)   on the agreement thereto of a majority of not less than three-fourths in value of the debenture holders present and voting in person or, where proxies are permitted, by proxy at a meeting summoned for the purpose, and
      (ii)   either with respect to specific acts or omissions or on the trustee dying or ceasing to act.

(3)   Subsection (1) does not operate–
   (a)   to invalidate any provision in force on 1st July 1948 so long as any person then entitled to the benefit of that provision or afterwards given the benefit of that provision under the following subsection remains a trustee of the deed in question; or
   (b)   to deprive any person of any exemption or right to be indemnified in respect of anything done or omitted to be done by him while any such provision was in force.

(4)   While any trustee of a trust deed remains entitled to the benefit of a provision saved by subsection (3), the benefit of that provision may be given either–
   (a)   to all trustees of the deed, present and future; or
   (b)   to any named trustees or proposed trustees of it,
by a resolution passed by a majority of not less than three-fourths in value of the debenture holders present in person or, where proxies are permitted, by proxy at a meeting summoned for the purpose in accordance with the provisions of the deed or, if the deed makes no provision for summoning meetings, a meeting summoned for the purpose in any manner approved by the court.

193 Perpetual debentures

A condition contained in debentures, or in a deed for securing debentures, is not invalid by reason only that the debentures are thereby made irredeemable or redeemable only on the happening of a contingency (however remote), or on the expiration of a period (however long), any rule of equity to the contrary notwithstanding.
    This applies to debentures whenever issued, and to deeds whenever executed.

194 Power to re-issue redeemed debentures

(1)   Where (at any time) a limited liability partnership has redeemed debentures previously issued, then–
   (a)   unless provision to the contrary, whether express or implied, is contained … in any contract entered into by the limited liability partnership; or
   (b)   unless the limited liability partnership has, by [making a determination] to that effect or by some other act, manifested its intention that the debentures shall be cancelled,

the limited liability partnership has, and is deemed always to have had, power to re-issue the debentures, either by re-issuing the same debentures or by issuing other debentures in their place.

(2)   On a re-issue of redeemed debentures, the person entitled to the debentures has, and is deemed always to have had, the same priorities as if the debentures had never been redeemed.

(3)   Where a limited liability partnership has (at any time) deposited any of its debentures to secure advances from time to time on current account or otherwise, the debentures are not deemed to have been redeemed by reason only of the limited liability partnership's account having ceased to be in debit while the debentures remained so deposited.

(4)   The re-issue of a debenture or the issue of another debenture in its place under the power which by this section is given to or deemed to be possessed by a limited liability partnership is to be treated as the issue of a new debenture for purposes of stamp duty; but it is not to be so treated for the purposes of any provision limiting the amount or number of debentures to be issued.
          This applies whenever the issue or re-issue was made.

(5)   A person lending money on the security of a debenture re-issued under this section which appears to be duly stamped may give the debenture in evidence in any proceedings for enforcing his security without payment of the stamp duty or any penalty in respect of it, unless he had notice (or, but for his negligence, might have discovered) that the debenture was not duly stamped; but in that case the limited liability partnership is liable to pay the proper stamp duty and penalty.

195 Contract to subscribe for debentures

A contract with a limited liability partnership to take up and pay for debentures of the limited liability partnership may be enforced by an order for specific performance.

196 Payment of debts out of assets subject to floating charge (England and Wales)

(1)   The following applies in the case of a limited liability partnership registered in England and Wales, where debentures of the limited liability partnership are secured by a charge which, as created, was a floating charge.

(2)   If possession is taken, by or on behalf of the holders of any of the debentures, of any property comprised in or subject to the charge, and the limited liability partnership is not at that time in course of being wound up, the limited liability partnership's preferential debts shall be paid out of assets coming to the hands of the person taking possession in priority to any claims for principal or interest in respect of the debentures.

(3)   "Preferential debts" means the categories of debts listed in Schedule 6 to the Insolvency Act; and for the purposes of that Schedule "the relevant date" is the date of possession being taken as above mentioned.

(4)   Payments made under this section shall be recouped, as far as may be, out of the assets of the limited liability partnership available for payment of general creditors.

197–220

PART VII
ACCOUNTS AND AUDIT

CHAPTER I
PROVISIONS APPLYING TO LIMITED LIABILITY PARTNERSHIPS
GENERALLY

221 Duty to keep accounting records

(1)   Every limited liability partnership shall keep accounting records which are sufficient to show and explain the limited liability partnership's transactions and are such as to–
    (a)   disclose with reasonable accuracy, at any time, the financial position of the limited liability partnership at that time, and
    (b)   enable the members to ensure that any balance sheet and profit and loss account prepared under this Part complies with the requirements of this Act.

(2)   The accounting records shall in particular contain–
    (a)   entries from day to day of all sums of money received and expended by the limited liability partnership, and the matters in respect of which the receipt and expenditure takes place, and
    (b)   a record of the assets and liabilities of the limited liability partnership.

(3)   If the limited liability partnership's business involves dealing in goods, the accounting records shall contain–
    (a)   statements of stock held by the limited liability partnership at the end of each financial year of the limited liability partnership,
    (b)   all statements of stocktakings from which any such statement of stock as is mentioned in paragraph (a) has been or is to be prepared, and
    (c)   except in the case of goods sold by way of ordinary retail trade, statements of all goods sold and purchased, showing the goods and the buyers and sellers in sufficient detail to enable all these to be identified.

(4)   A parent limited liability partnership which has a subsidiary undertaking in relation to which the above requirements do not apply shall take reasonable steps to secure that the undertaking keeps such accounting records as to enable the members of the parent limited liability partnership to ensure that any balance sheet and profit and loss account prepared under this Part complies with the requirements of this Act.

(5)   If a limited liability partnership fails to comply with any provision of this section, every member of the limited liability partnership who is in default is guilty of an offence unless he shows that he acted honestly and that in the

circumstances in which the limited liability partnership's business was carried on the default was excusable.

(6)   A person guilty of an offence under this section is liable to imprisonment or a fine, or both.

222 Where and for how long records to be kept

(1)   A limited liability partnership's accounting records shall be kept at its registered office or such other place as the members think fit, and shall at all times be open to inspection by the limited liability partnership's members.

(2)   If accounting records are kept at a place outside Great Britain, accounts and returns with respect to the business dealt with in the accounting records so kept shall be sent to, and kept at, a place in Great Britain, and shall at all times be open to such inspection.

(3)   The accounts and returns to be sent to Great Britain shall be such as to–
   (a)   disclose with reasonable accuracy the financial position of the business in question at intervals of not more than six months, and
   (b)   enable the members to ensure that the limited liability partnership's balance sheet and profit and loss account comply with the requirements of this Act.

(4)   If a limited liability partnership fails to comply with any provision of subsections (1) to (3), every member of the limited liability partnership who is in default is guilty of an offence, and liable to imprisonment or a fine or both, unless he shows that he acted honestly and that in the circumstances in which the limited liability partnership's business was carried on the default was excusable.

(5)   Accounting records which a limited liability partnership is required by section 221 to keep shall be preserved by it–
   (a)   ... for three years from the date on which they are made, ...
   (b)   ...
   This is subject to any provision contained in rules made under section 411 of the Insolvency Act 1986 (limited liability partnership insolvency rules).

(6)   A member of a limited liability partnership is guilty of an offence, and liable to imprisonment or a fine or both, if he fails to take all reasonable steps for securing compliance by the limited liability partnership with subsection (5) or intentionally causes any default by the limited liability partnership under that subsection.

223 A limited liability partnership's financial year

(1)   A limited liability partnership's "financial year" is determined as follows.

(2)   Its first financial year begins with the first day of its first accounting reference period and ends with the last day of that period or such other date,

not more than seven days before or after the end of that period, as the members may determine.

(3)   Subsequent financial years begin with the day immediately following the end of the limited liability partnership's previous financial year and end with the last day of its next accounting reference period or such other date, not more than seven days before or after the end of that period, as the members may determine.

(4)   In relation to an undertaking which is not a limited liability partnership, references in this Act to its financial year are to any period in respect of which a profit and loss account of the undertaking is required to be made up (by its constitution or by the law under which it is established), whether that period is a year or not.

(5)   The members of a parent limited liability partnership shall secure that, except where in their opinion there are good reasons against it, the financial year of each of its subsidiary undertakings coincides with the limited liability partnership's own financial year.

224 Accounting reference periods and accounting reference date

(1)   A limited liability partnership's accounting reference periods are determined according to its accounting reference date.

(2),(3) ...

(3A)   The accounting reference date of a limited liability partnership ... is the last day of the month in which the anniversary of its incorporation falls.

(4)   A limited liability partnership's first accounting reference period is the period of more than six months, but not more than 18 months, beginning with the date of its incorporation and ending with its accounting reference date.

(5)   Its subsequent accounting reference periods are successive periods of twelve months beginning immediately after the end of the previous accounting reference period and ending with its accounting reference date.

(6)   This section has effect subject to the provisions of section 225 relating to the alteration of accounting reference dates and the consequences of such alteration.

225 Alteration of accounting reference date

(1)   A limited liability partnership may by notice in the prescribed form given to the registrar specify a new accounting reference date having effect in relation to—

   (a)   the limited liability partnership's current accounting reference period and subsequent periods; or
   (b)   the limited liability partnership's previous accounting reference period and subsequent periods.

A limited liability partnership's "previous accounting reference period" means that immediately preceding its current accounting reference period.

(3)   The notice shall state whether the current or previous accounting reference period–
- (a)   is to be shortened, so as to come to an end on the first occasion on which the new accounting reference date falls or fell after the beginning of the period, or
- (b)   is to be extended, so as to come to an end on the second occasion on which that date falls or fell after the beginning of the period.

(4)   A notice under subsection (1) stating that the current or previous accounting reference period is to be extended is ineffective, except as mentioned below, if given less than five years after the end of an earlier accounting reference period of the limited liability partnership which was extended by virtue of this section.
This subsection does not apply–
- (a)   to a notice given by a limited liability partnership which is a subsidiary undertaking or parent undertaking of another EEA undertaking if the new accounting reference date coincides with that of the other EEA undertaking or, where that undertaking is not a limited liability partnership, with the last day of its financial year, or
- (b)   where an administration order is in force under Part II of the Insolvency Act 1986,
or where the Secretary of State directs that it should not apply, which he may do with respect to a notice which has been given or which may be given.

(5)   A notice under subsection (1) may not be given in respect of a previous accounting reference period if the period allowed for [delivering the accounts and the auditors' report] in relation to that period has already expired.

(6)   An accounting reference period may not in any case, unless an administration order is in force under Part II of the Insolvency Act 1986, be extended so as to exceed 18 months and a notice under this section is ineffective if the current or previous accounting reference period as extended in accordance with the notice would exceed that limit.

(7)   In this section "EEA undertaking" means an undertaking established under the law of any part of the United Kingdom or the law of any other EEA State.

226 Duty to prepare individual limited liability partnership accounts

(1)   The members of every limited liability partnership shall prepare for each financial year of the limited liability partnership–
- (a)   a balance sheet as at the last day of the year, and
- (b)   a profit and loss account.

Those accounts are referred to in this Part as the limited liability partnership's "individual accounts".

(2)   The balance sheet shall give a true and fair view of the state of affairs of the limited liability partnership as at the end of the financial year; and the profit and

loss account shall give a true and fair view of the profit or loss of the limited liability partnership for the financial year.

(3)   A limited liability partnership's individual accounts shall comply with the provisions of Schedule 4 as to the form and content of the balance sheet and profit and loss account and additional information to be provided by way of notes to the accounts.

(4)   Where compliance with the provisions of that Schedule, and the other provisions of this Act as to the matters to be included in a limited liability partnership's individual accounts or in notes to those accounts, would not be sufficient to give a true and fair view, the necessary additional information shall be given in the accounts or in a note to them.

(5)   If in special circumstances compliance with any of those provisions is inconsistent with the requirement to give a true and fair view, the members shall depart from that provision to the extent necessary to give a true and fair view.
        Particulars of any such departure, the reasons for it and its effect shall be given in a note to the accounts.

227 Duty to prepare group accounts

(1)   If at the end of a financial year a limited liability partnership is a parent limited liability partnership the members shall, as well as preparing individual accounts for the year, prepare group accounts.

(2)   Group accounts shall be consolidated accounts comprising–
    (a) a consolidated balance sheet dealing with the state of affairs of the parent limited liability partnership and its subsidiary undertakings, and
    (b) a consolidated profit and loss account dealing with the profit or loss of the parent limited liability partnership and its subsidiary undertakings.

(3)   The accounts shall give a true and fair view of the state of affairs as at the end of the financial year, and the profit or loss for the financial year, of the undertakings included in the consolidation as a whole, so far as concerns members of the limited liability partnership.

(4)   A limited liability partnership's group accounts shall comply with the provisions of Schedule 4A as to the form and content of the consolidated balance sheet and consolidated profit and loss account and additional information to be provided by way of notes to the accounts.

(5)   Where compliance with the provisions of that Schedule, and the other provisions of this Act, as to the matters to be included in a limited liability partnership's group accounts or in notes to those accounts, would not be sufficient to give a true and fair view, the necessary additional information shall be given in the accounts or in a note to them.

(6)   If in special circumstances compliance with any of those provisions is inconsistent with the requirement to give a true and fair view, the members shall depart from that provision to the extent necessary to give a true and fair view. Particulars of any such departure, the reasons for it and its effect shall be given in a note to the accounts.

228 Exemption for parent limited liability partnerships included in accounts of larger group

(1)   A limited liability partnership is exempt from the requirement to prepare group accounts if it is itself a subsidiary undertaking and its immediate parent undertaking is established under the law of a member State of the European Economic Community, in the following cases–
- (a)   where the limited liability partnership is a wholly-owned subsidiary of that parent undertaking;
- (b)   where that parent undertaking holds more than 50 per cent of the shares in the limited liability partnership and notice requesting the preparation of group accounts has not been served on the limited liability partnership by shareholders holding in aggregate–
   - (i)   more than half of the remaining shares in the limited liability partnership, or
   - (ii)   5 per cent of the total shares in the limited liability partnership.

Such notice must be served not later than six months after the end of the financial year before that to which it relates.

(2)   Exemption is conditional upon compliance with all of the following conditions–
- (a)   that the limited liability partnership is included in consolidated accounts for a larger group drawn up to the same date, or to an earlier date in the same financial year, by a parent undertaking established under the law of a member State of the European Economic Community;
- (b)   that those accounts are drawn up and audited, and that parent undertaking's annual report is drawn up, according to that law, in accordance with the provisions of the Seventh Directive (83/349/EEC) (where applicable as modified by the provisions of the Bank Accounts Directive (86/635/EEC)or the Insurance Accounts Directive (91/674/EEC));
- (c)   that the limited liability partnership discloses in its individual accounts that it is exempt from the obligation to prepare and deliver group accounts;
- (d)   that the limited liability partnership states in its individual accounts the name of the parent undertaking which draws up the group accounts referred to above and–
   - (i)   if it is incorporated outside Great Britain, the country in which it is incorporated,
   - (ii)   and
   - (iii)   if it is unincorporated, the address of its principal place of business;
- (e)   that the limited liability partnership delivers to the registrar, within the period allowed for delivering its individual accounts, copies of

those group accounts and of the parent undertaking's annual report, together with the auditors' report on them; and

(f)   (subject to section 710B(6) (delivery of certain Welsh documents without translation)) that if any document comprised in accounts and reports delivered in accordance with paragraph (e) is in a language other than English, there is annexed to the copy of that copy document delivered a translation of it into English, certified in the prescribed manner to be a correct translation.

(3)   The exemption does not apply to a limited liability partnership any of whose securities are listed on a stock exchange in any member State of the European Economic Community.

(4)   ...

(5)   For the purposes of subsection (1)(b) shares held by a wholly-owned subsidiary of the parent undertaking, or held on behalf of the parent undertaking or a wholly-owned subsidiary, shall be attributed to the parent undertaking.

(6)   In subsection (3) "securities" includes–
   (a)   shares and stock,
   (b)   debentures, including debenture stock, loan stock, bonds, certificates of deposit and other instruments creating or acknowledging indebtedness,
   (c)   warrants or other instruments entitling the holder to subscribe for securities falling within paragraph (a) or (b), and
   (d)   certificates or other instruments which confer–
      (i)   property rights in respect of a security falling within paragraph (a),(b) or (c),
      (ii) any right to acquire, dispose of, underwrite or convert a security, being a right to which the holder would be entitled if he held any such security to which the certificate or other instrument relates, or
      (iii) a contractual right (other than an option) to acquire any such security otherwise than by subscription.

229 Subsidiary undertakings included in the consolidation

(1)   Subject to the exceptions authorised or required by this section, all the subsidiary undertakings of the parent limited liability partnership shall be included in the consolidation.

(2)   A subsidiary undertaking may be excluded from consolidation if its inclusion is not material for the purpose of giving a true and fair view; but two or more undertakings may be excluded only if they are not material taken together.

(3)   In addition, a subsidiary undertaking may be excluded from consolidation where–
   (a)   severe long-term restrictions substantially hinder the exercise of the rights of the parent limited liability partnership over the assets or management of that undertaking, or

(b) the information necessary for the preparation of group accounts cannot be obtained without disproportionate expense or undue delay, or

(c) the interest of the parent limited liability partnership is held exclusively with a view to subsequent resale and the undertaking has not previously been included in consolidated group accounts prepared by the parent limited liability partnership.

The reference in paragraph (a) to the rights of the parent limited liability partnership and the reference in paragraph (c) to the interest of the parent limited liability partnership are, respectively, to rights and interests held by or attributed to the limited liability partnership for the purposes of section 258 (definition of "parent undertaking") in the absence of which it would not be the parent limited liability partnership.

(4) Where the activities of one or more subsidiary undertakings are so different from those of other undertakings to be included in the consolidation that their inclusion would be incompatible with the obligation to give a true and fair view, those undertakings shall be excluded from consolidation.

This subsection does not apply merely because some of the undertakings are industrial, some commercial and some provide services, or because they carry on industrial or commercial activities involving different products or provide different services.

(5) Where all the subsidiary undertakings of a parent limited liability partnership fall within the above exclusions, no group accounts are required.

230 Treatment of individual profit and loss account where group accounts prepared

(1) The following provisions apply with respect to the individual profit and loss account of a parent limited liability partnership where–
(a) the limited liability partnership is required to prepare and does prepare group accounts in accordance with this Act, and
(b) the notes to the limited liability partnership's individual balance sheet show the limited liability partnership's profit or loss for the financial year determined in accordance with this Act.

(2) The profit and loss account need not contain the information specified in paragraphs 52 to 57 of Schedule 4 (information supplementing the profit and loss account).

(3) The profit and loss account must be approved in accordance with section 233(1) (approval by members) but may be omitted from the limited liability partnership's annual accounts for the purposes of the other provisions below in this Chapter.

(4) The exemption conferred by this section is conditional upon its being disclosed in the limited liability partnership's annual accounts that the exemption applies.

231 Disclosure required in notes to accounts: related undertakings

(1)   The information specified in Schedule 5 shall be given in notes to a limited liability partnership's annual accounts.

(2)   Where the limited liability partnership is not required to prepare group accounts, the information specified in Part I of that Schedule shall be given; and where the limited liability partnership is required to prepare group accounts, the information specified in Part II of that Schedule shall be given.

(3)   The information required by Schedule 5 need not be disclosed with respect to an undertaking which–
    (a)   is established under the law of a country outside the United Kingdom, or
    (b)   carries on business outside the United Kingdom,
if in the opinion of the members of the limited liability partnership the disclosure would be seriously prejudicial to the business of that undertaking, or to the business of the limited liability partnership or any of its subsidiary undertakings, and the Secretary of State agrees that the information need not be disclosed.
   …

(4)   Where advantage is taken of subsection (3), that fact shall be stated in a note to the limited liability partnership's annual accounts.

(5)   If the members of the limited liability partnership are of the opinion that the number of undertakings in respect of which the limited liability partnership is required to disclose information under any provision of Schedule 5 to this Act is such that compliance with that provision would result in information of excessive length being given, the information need only be given in respect of–
    (a)   the undertakings whose results or financial position, in the opinion of the members, principally affected the figures shown in the limited liability partnership's annual accounts, and
    (b)   undertakings excluded from consolidation under section 229(3) or (4).

(6)   If advantage is taken of subsection (5)–
    (a)   there shall be included in the notes to the limited liability partnership's annual accounts a statement that the information is given only with respect to such undertakings as are mentioned in that subsection, and
    (b)   the full information (both that which is disclosed in the notes to the accounts and that which is not) shall be annexed to the limited liability partnership's next annual return.
For this purpose the "next annual return" means that next delivered to the registrar after the accounts in question have been approved under section 233.

(7)   If a limited liability partnership fails to comply with subsection (6)(b), the limited liability partnership and every member of it who is in default is liable to a fine and, for continued contravention, to a daily default fine.

Appendix 2 – CA 1985 as modified

232 …

[Section 232 is omitted save that Schedule 6 shall apply for the purpose of paragraph 56A of Schedule 4]

233 Approval and signing of accounts

[(1)   A limited liability partnership's annual accounts shall be approved by the members, and shall be signed on behalf of all the members by a designated member.]

(2)   The signature shall be on the limited liability partnership's balance sheet.

(3)   Every copy of the balance sheet which is … circulated, published or issued, shall state the name of the person who signed the balance sheet on behalf of [the members of the limited liability partnership].

(4)   The copy of the limited liability partnership's balance sheet which is delivered to the registrar shall be signed on behalf of [the members by a designated member].

(5)   If annual accounts are approved which do not comply with the requirements of this Act, every member of the limited liability partnership who is party to their approval and who knows that they do not comply or is reckless as to whether they comply is guilty of an offence and liable to a fine.
For this purpose every member of the limited liability partnership at the time the accounts are approved shall be taken to be a party to their approval unless he shows that he took all reasonable steps to prevent their being approved.

(6)   If a copy of the balance sheet–
  (a)   is … circulated, published or issued, without the balance sheet having been signed as required by this section or without the required statement of the signatory's name being included, or
  (b)   is delivered to the registrar without being signed as required by this section,
the limited liability partnership and every member of it who is in default is guilty of an offence and liable to a fine.

234, 234A   …

235 Auditors' report

[(1)   The limited liability partnership's annual accounts shall be submitted to its auditors, who shall make a report on them to the members of the limited liability partnership.]

(2)   The auditors' report shall state whether in the auditors' opinion the annual accounts have been properly prepared in accordance with this Act, and in particular whether a true and fair view is given–
  (a)   in the case of an individual balance sheet, of the state of affairs of the limited liability partnership as at the end of the financial year,

(b) in the case of an individual profit and loss account, of the profit or loss of the limited liability partnership for the financial year,

(c) in the case of group accounts, of the state of affairs at the end of the financial year, and the profit or loss for the financial year, of the undertakings included in the consolidation as a whole, so far as concerns members of the limited liability partnership.

(3) ...

236 Signature of auditors' report

(1) The auditors' report shall state the names of the auditors and be signed by them.

[(2) Every copy of the auditor's report which is circulated, published or issued, shall state the names of the auditors.]

(3) The copy of the auditors' report which is delivered to the registrar shall state the names of the auditors and be signed by them.

(4) If a copy of the auditors' report–
(a) is ... circulated, published or issued, without the required statement of the auditors' names, or
(b) is delivered to the registrar without the required statement of the auditors' names or without being signed as required by this section,
the limited liability partnership and every member of it who is in default is guilty of an offence and liable to a fine.

(5) References in this section to signature by the auditors are, where the office of auditor is held by a body corporate or partnership, to signature in the name of the body corporate or partnership by a person authorised to sign on its behalf.

237 Duties of auditors

(1) A limited liability partnership's auditors shall, in preparing their report, carry out such investigations as will enable them to form an opinion as to–
(a) whether proper accounting records have been kept by the limited liability partnership and proper returns adequate for their audit have been received from branches not visited by them, and
(b) whether the limited liability partnership's individual accounts are in agreement with the accounting records and returns.

(2) If the auditors are of opinion that proper accounting records have not been kept, or that proper returns adequate for their audit have not been received from branches not visited by them, or if the limited liability partnership's individual accounts are not in agreement with the accounting records and returns, the auditors shall state that fact in their report.

(3)   If the auditors fail to obtain all the information and explanations which, to the best of their knowledge and belief, are necessary for the purposes of their audit, they shall state that fact in their report.

(4)   ...

(4A) If the members of the limited liability partnership have taken advantage of the exemption conferred by section 248 (exemption for small and medium-sized groups from the need to prepare group accounts) and in the auditors' opinion they were not entitled so to do, the auditors shall state that fact in their report.

238 Persons entitled to receive copies of accounts and reports

[(1)   A copy of the limited liability partnership's accounts, together with a copy of the auditors' report on those accounts, shall be sent to every member of the limited liability partnership and to every holder of the limited liability partnership's debentures, within one month of their being signed in accordance with section 233(1) and in any event not later than ten months after the end of the relevant accounting reference period.]

(2)   Copies need not be sent–
   (a) to a person ... of whose address the limited liability partnership is unaware, or
   (b) to more than one of the joint holders of ... debentures none of whom is entitled to receive such notices, or
   (c) in the case of joint holders of ... debentures some of whom are, and some not, entitled to receive such notices, to those who are not so entitled.

(3),(4) ...

(4A) References in this section to sending to any person copies of a limited liability partnership's annual accounts, ... and of the auditors' report include references to using electronic communications for sending copies of those documents to such address as may for the time being be notified to the limited liability partnership by that person for that purpose.

(4B) For the purposes of this section copies of those documents are also to be treated as sent to a person where–
   (a) the limited liability partnership and that person have agreed to his having access to the documents on a web site (instead of their being sent to him);
   (b) the documents are documents to which that agreement applies; and
   (c) that person is notified, in a manner for the time being agreed for the purpose between him and the limited liability partnership, of–
      (i)   the publication of the documents on a web site;
      (ii) the address of that web site; and
      (iii) the place on that web site where the documents may be accessed, and how they may be accessed.

(5)   If default is made in complying with this section, the limited liability partnership and every member of it who is in default is guilty of an offence and liable to a fine.

(6)   Where copies are sent out under this section over a period of days, references elsewhere in this Act to the day on which copies are sent out shall be construed as references to the last day of that period.

239 Right to demand copies of accounts and reports

(1)   Any member of a limited liability partnership and any holder of a limited liability partnership's debentures is entitled to be furnished, on demand and without charge, with a copy of the limited liability partnership's last annual accounts ... and a copy of the auditors' report on those accounts.

(2)   The entitlement under this section is to a single copy of those documents, but that is in addition to any copy to which a person may be entitled under section 238.

(2A)   Any obligation by virtue of subsection (1) to furnish a person with a document may be complied with by using electronic communications for sending that document to such address as may for the time being be notified to the limited liability partnership by that person for that purpose.

(2B)   ...

(3)   If a demand under this section is not complied with within seven days, the limited liability partnership and every member of it who is in default is guilty of an offence and liable to a fine and, for continued contravention, to a daily default fine.

(4)   If in proceedings for such an offence the issue arises whether a person had already been furnished with a copy of the relevant document under this section, it is for the defendant to prove that he had.

240 Requirements in connection with publication of accounts

(1)   If a limited liability partnership publishes any of its statutory accounts, they must be accompanied by the relevant auditors' report under section 235 ...

(2)   A limited liability partnership which is required to prepare group accounts for a financial year shall not publish its statutory individual accounts for that year without also publishing with them its statutory group accounts.

(3)   If a limited liability partnership publishes non-statutory accounts, it shall publish with them a statement indicating–
   (a)   that they are not the limited liability partnership's statutory accounts,
   (b)   whether statutory accounts dealing with any financial year with which the non-statutory accounts purport to deal have been delivered to the registrar,

(c) whether the limited liability partnership's auditors have made a report under section 235 on the statutory accounts for any such financial year …, and

(d) whether any auditors' report so made was qualified or contained a statement under section 237(2) or (3) (accounting records or returns inadequate, accounts not agreeing with records and returns or failure to obtain necessary information and explanations) …;

and it shall not publish with the non-statutory accounts any auditors' report under section 235 …

(4)   For the purposes of this section a limited liability partnership shall be regarded as publishing a document if it publishes, issues or circulates it or otherwise makes it available for public inspection in a manner calculated to invite members of the public generally, or any class of members of the public, to read it.

(5)   References in this section to a limited liability partnership's statutory accounts are to its individual or group accounts for a financial year as required to be delivered to the registrar under section 242; and references to the publication by a limited liability partnership of "non-statutory accounts" are to the publication of–

(a) any balance sheet or profit and loss account relating to, or purporting to deal with, a financial year of the limited liability partnership, or

(b) an account in any form purporting to be a balance sheet or profit and loss account for the group consisting of the limited liability partnership and its subsidiary undertakings relating to, or purporting to deal with, a financial year of the limited liability partnership,

otherwise than as part of the limited liability partnership's statutory accounts.

(6)   A limited liability partnership which contravenes any provision of this section, and any member of it who is in default, is guilty of an offence and liable to a fine.

241   …

242 Accounts and reports to be delivered to the registrar

(1)   The [designated members of a limited liability partnership] shall in respect of each financial year deliver to the registrar a copy of the limited liability partnership's annual accounts together with a … copy of the auditors' report on those accounts.

     If any document comprised in those accounts [or that report] is in a language other than English then, subject to section 710B(6) (delivery of certain Welsh documents without a translation)), [the designated members shall annex] to the copy of that document delivered a translation of it into English, certified in the prescribed manner to be a correct translation.

(2)   If the requirements of subsection (1) are not complied with before the end of the period allowed for [delivering the accounts and the auditors' report], every person who immediately before the end of that period was a [designated member]

of the limited liability partnership is guilty of an offence and liable to a fine and, for continued contravention, to a daily default fine.

(3)   Further, if [the designated members] of the limited liability partnership fail to make good the default within 14 days after the service of a notice on them requiring compliance, the court may on the application of any member or creditor of the limited liability partnership or of the registrar, make an order directing [the designated members] (or any of them) to make good the default within such time as may be specified in the order.

The court's order may provide that all costs of and incidental to the application shall be borne by [the designated members].

(4)   It is a defence for a person charged with an offence under this section to prove that he took all reasonable steps for securing that the requirements of subsection (1) would be complied with before the end of the period allowed for [delivering the accounts and the auditors' report].

(5)   It is not a defence in any proceedings under this section to prove that the documents in question were not in fact prepared as required by this Part.

242A Civil penalty for failure to deliver accounts

(1)   Where the requirements of section 242(1) are not complied with before the end of the period allowed for [delivering the accounts and the auditors' report], the limited liability partnership is liable to a civil penalty.

This is in addition to any liability of [the designated members] under section 242.

(2)   The amount of the penalty is determined by reference to the length of the period between the end of the period allowed for [delivering the accounts and the auditors' report] and the day on which the requirements are complied with, … as follows–

Length of period	*Amount of penalty*
Not more than 3 months	£100
More than 3 months but not more than 6 months	£250
More than 6 months but not more than 12 months	£500
More than 12 months	£1,000

(3)   The penalty may be recovered by the registrar and shall be paid by him into the Consolidated Fund.

(4)   It is not a defence in proceedings under this section to prove that the documents in question were not in fact prepared as required by this Part.

242B Delivery and publication of accounts in ECUs

(1)   The amounts set out in the annual accounts of a limited liability partnership may also be shown in the same accounts translated into ECUs.

(2)   When complying with section 242, [the designated members of a limited liability partnership] may deliver to the registrar an additional copy of the limited liability partnership's annual accounts in which the amounts have been translated into ECUs.

(3)   In both cases–
    (a)   the amounts must have been translated at the relevant exchange rate prevailing on the balance sheet date, and
    (b)   that rate must be disclosed in the notes to the accounts.

(4)   For the purposes of section 240 any additional copy of the limited liability partnership's annual accounts delivered to the registrar under subsection (2) shall be treated as statutory accounts of the limited liability partnership and, in the case of such a copy, references in section 240 to the auditors' report under section 235 shall be read as references to the auditors' report on the annual accounts of which it is a copy.

(5)   In this section–

"ECU" means a unit with a value equal to the value of the unit of account known as the ecu used in the European Monetary System, and

"relevant exchange rate" means the rate of exchange used for translating the value of the ecu for the purposes of that System.

243 Accounts of subsidiary undertakings to be appended in certain cases

(1)   The following provisions apply where at the end of the financial year a parent limited liability partnership has a subsidiary undertaking–
    (a)   a body corporate incorporated outside Great Britain which does not have an established place of business in Great Britain, or
    (b)   an unincorporated undertaking,
which is excluded from consolidation in accordance with section 229(4) (undertaking with activities different from the undertakings included in the consolidation).

(2)   There shall be appended to the copy of the limited liability partnership's annual accounts delivered to the registrar in accordance with section 242 a copy of the undertaking's latest individual accounts and, if it is a parent undertaking, its latest group accounts.
    If the accounts appended are required by law to be audited, a copy of the auditors' report shall also be appended.

(3)   The accounts must be for a period ending not more than twelve months before the end of the financial year for which the parent limited liability partnership's accounts are made up.

(4)   If any document required to be appended is in a language other than English then, subject to section 710B(6) (delivery of certain Welsh documents without a translation)), [the designated members] shall annex to the copy of that document

delivered a translation of it into English, certified in the prescribed manner to be a correct translation.

(5)   The above requirements are subject to the following qualifications–

(a)   an undertaking is not required to prepare for the purposes of this section accounts which would not otherwise be prepared, and if no accounts satisfying the above requirements are prepared none need be appended;

(b)   a document need not be appended if it would not otherwise be required to be published, or made available for public inspection, anywhere in the world, but in that case the reason for not appending it shall be stated in a note to the limited liability partnership's accounts;

(c)   where an undertaking and all its subsidiary undertakings are excluded from consolidation in accordance with section 229(4), the accounts of such of the subsidiary undertakings of that undertaking as are included in its consolidated group accounts need not be appended.

(6)   Subsections (2) to (4) of section 242 (penalties, &c in case of default) apply in relation to the requirements of this section as they apply in relation to the requirements of subsection (1) of that section.

244 Period allowed for laying and delivering accounts and reports

[(1)   The period allowed for delivering the accounts and the auditors' report is ten months after the end of the relevant accounting reference period.
This is subject to the following provisions of this section.]

(2)   If the relevant accounting reference period is the limited liability partnership's first and is a period of more than twelve months, the period allowed is–

(a)   ten months ... from the first anniversary of the incorporation of the limited liability partnership, or

(b)   three months from the end of the accounting reference period,
whichever last expires.

(3)   Where a limited liability partnership carries on business, or has interests, outside the United Kingdom, the Channel Islands and the Isle of Man, [the designated members] may, in respect of any financial year, give to the registrar before the end of the period allowed by subsection (1) or (2) a notice in the prescribed form–

(a)   stating that the limited liability partnership so carries on business or has such interests, and

(b)   claiming a three-month extension of the period allowed for [delivering the accounts and the auditors' report];
and upon such a notice being given the period is extended accordingly.

(4)   If the relevant accounting period is treated as shortened by virtue of a notice given by the limited liability partnership under section 225 (alteration of accounting reference date), the period allowed for [delivering the accounts and the auditors' report] is that applicable in accordance with the above

provisions or three months from the date of the notice under that section, whichever last expires.

(5)   If for any special reason the Secretary of State thinks fit he may, on an application made before the expiry of the period otherwise allowed, by notice in writing to a limited liability partnership extend that period by such further period as may be specified in the notice.

(6)   In this section "the relevant accounting reference period" means the accounting reference period by reference to which the financial year for the accounts in question was determined.

245 Voluntary revision of annual accounts

(1)   If it appears to the members of a limited liability partnership that any annual accounts of the limited liability partnership …, did not comply with the requirements of this Act, they may prepare revised accounts.

(2)   Where copies of the previous accounts … have been laid before the limited liability partnership in general meeting or delivered to the registrar, the revisions shall be confined to–
    (a)   the correction of those respects in which the previous accounts … did not comply with the requirements of this Act, and
    (b)   the making of any necessary consequential alterations.

(3)   The Secretary of State may make provision by regulations as to the application of the provisions of this Act in relation to revised annual accounts …

(4)   The regulations may, in particular–
    (a)   make different provision according to whether the previous accounts … are replaced or are supplemented by a document indicating the corrections to be made;
    (b)   make provision with respect to the functions of the limited liability partnership's auditors … in relation to the revised accounts …;
    (c)   require the members to take such steps as may be specified in the regulations where the [previous accounts] have been–
        (i)   sent out to members and others under section 238(1),
        (ii)   …, or
        (iii) delivered to the registrar,
    …
    (d)   apply the provisions of this Act (including those creating criminal offences) subject to such additions, exceptions and modifications as are specified in the regulations.

(5)   Regulations under this section shall be made by statutory instrument which shall be subject to annulment in pursuance of a resolution of either House of Parliament.

245A Secretary of State's notice in respect of annual accounts

(1)   Where [a copy of a limited liability partnerships' annual accounts has been] delivered to the registrar, and it appears to the Secretary of State that there is, or may be, a question whether the accounts comply with the requirements of this Act, he may give notice to the members of the limited liability partnership indicating the respects in which it appears to him that such a question arises, or may arise.

(2)   The notice shall specify a period of not less than one month for the members to give him an explanation of the accounts or prepare revised accounts.

(3)   If at the end of the specified period, or such longer period as he may allow, it appears to the Secretary of State that no satisfactory explanation of the accounts has been given and that the accounts have not been revised so as to comply with the requirements of this Act, he may if he thinks fit apply to the court.

(4)   The provisions of this section apply equally to revised annual accounts, in which case the references to revised accounts shall be read as references to further revised accounts.

245B Application to court in respect of defective accounts

(1)   An application may be made to the court–
    (a)   by the Secretary of State, after having complied with section 245A, or
    (b)   by a person authorised by the Secretary of State for the purposes of this section,
for a declaration or declarator that the annual accounts of a limited liability partnership do not comply with the requirements of this Act and for an order requiring the members of the limited liability partnership to prepare revised accounts.

(2)   Notice of the application, together with a general statement of the matters at issue in the proceedings, shall be given by the applicant to the registrar for registration.

(3)   If the court orders the preparation of revised accounts, it may give directions with respect to–
    (a)   the auditing of the accounts,
    (b)   ...
    (c)   the taking of steps by the members to bring the making of the order to the notice of persons likely to rely on the previous accounts,
and such other matters as the court thinks fit.

(4)   If the court finds that the accounts did not comply with the requirements of this Act it may order that all or part of–
    (a)   the costs (or in Scotland expenses) of and incidental to the application, and
    (b)   any reasonable expenses incurred by the limited liability partnership in connection with or in consequence of the preparation of revised accounts,
shall be borne by such of the members as were party to the approval of the defective accounts.

For this purpose every member of the limited liability partnership at the time the accounts were approved shall be taken to have been a party to their approval unless he shows that he took all reasonable steps to prevent their being approved.

(5)   Where the court makes an order under subsection (4) it shall have regard to whether the members party to the approval of the defective accounts knew or ought to have known that the accounts did not comply with the requirements of this Act, and it may exclude one or more members from the order or order the payment of different amounts by different members.

(6)   On the conclusion of proceedings on an application under this section, the applicant shall give to the registrar for registration an office copy of the court order or, as the case may be, notice that the application has failed or been withdrawn.

(7)   The provisions of this section apply equally to revised annual accounts, in which case the references to revised accounts shall be read as references to further revised accounts.

245C Other persons authorised to apply to court

(1)   The Secretary of State may authorise for the purposes of section 245B any person appearing to him–
  (a) to have an interest in, and to have satisfactory procedures directed to securing, compliance by limited liability partnerships with the accounting requirements of this Act,
  (b) to have satisfactory procedures for receiving and investigating complaints about the annual accounts of limited liability partnerships, and
  (c) otherwise to be a fit and proper person to be authorised.

(2)   A person may be authorised generally or in respect of particular classes of case, and different persons may be authorised in respect of different classes of case.

(3)   The Secretary of State may refuse to authorise a person if he considers that his authorisation is unnecessary having regard to the fact that there are one or more other persons who have been or are likely to be authorised.

(4)   Authorisation shall be by order made by statutory instrument which shall be subject to annulment in pursuance of a resolution of either House of Parliament.

(5)   Where authorisation is revoked, the revoking order may make such provision as the Secretary of State thinks fit with respect to pending proceedings.

(6)   Neither a person authorised under this section, nor any officer, servant or member of the governing body of such a person, shall be liable in damages for anything done or purporting to be done for the purposes of or in connection with–
  (a) the taking of steps to discover whether there are grounds for an application to the court,

(b)   the determination whether or not to make such an application, or

(c)   the publication of its reasons for any such decision,

unless the act or omission is shown to have been in bad faith.

CHAPTER II
EXEMPTIONS, EXCEPTIONS AND SPECIAL PROVISIONS

246 Special provisions for small limited liability partnerships

(1)   Subject to section 247A, this section applies where a limited liability partnership qualifies as a small limited liability partnership in relation to a financial year.

(2)   If the limited liability partnership's individual accounts for the year–

(a)   comply with the provisions of Schedule 8, or

(b)   fail to comply with those provisions only in so far as they comply instead with one or more corresponding provisions of Schedule 4,

they need not comply with the provisions or, as the case may be, the remaining provisions of Schedule 4; and where advantage is taken of this subsection, references in section 226 to compliance with the provisions of Schedule 4 shall be construed accordingly.

(3)   The limited liability partnership's individual accounts for the year–

(a)   ...

(b)   need not give the information required by–

(i)   paragraph 4 of Schedule 5 (financial years of subsidiary undertakings);

(ii),(iii),(iv)   ...

(4)   ...

(5)   Notwithstanding anything in section 242(1), [the designated members of the limited liability partnership] need not deliver to the registrar any of the following, namely–

(a)   a copy of the limited liability partnership's profit and loss account for the year;

(b)   ...

(c)   if they deliver a copy of a balance sheet drawn up as at the last day of the year which complies with the requirements of Schedule 8A, a copy of the limited liability partnership's balance sheet drawn up as at that day.

(6)   Neither a copy of the limited liability partnership's accounts for the year delivered to the registrar under section 242(1), nor a copy of a balance sheet delivered to the registrar under subsection (5)(c), need give the information required by–

(a)   paragraph 4 of Schedule 5 (financial years of subsidiary undertakings);

(b),(c)   ...

(d)   section 390A(3) (amount of auditors' remuneration).

(7)   The provisions of section 233 as to the signing of the copy of the balance sheet delivered to the registrar apply to a copy of a balance sheet delivered under subsection (5)(c).

(8)   Subject to subsection (9), each of the following, namely–
   (a)   accounts prepared in accordance with subsection (2) or (3),
   (b)   …
   (c)   a copy of accounts delivered to the registrar in accordance with subsection (5) or (6),

shall contain a statement in a prominent position on the balance sheet … or, as the case may be, on the copy of the balance sheet, above the signature required by section 233 … or subsection (7), that they are prepared in accordance with the special provisions of this Part relating to small limited liability partnerships.

(9)   Subsection (8) does not apply where the members of the limited liability partnership have taken advantage of the exemption from audit conferred by section 249AA (dormant limited liability partnerships).

246A Special provisions for medium-sized limited liability partnerships

(1)   Subject to section 247A, this section applies where a limited liability partnership qualifies as a medium-sized limited liability partnership in relation to a financial year.

(2)   The limited liability partnership's individual accounts for the year need not comply with the requirements of paragraph 36A of Schedule 4 (disclosure with respect to compliance with accounting standards).

(3)   [The designated members] may deliver to the registrar a copy of the limited liability partnership's accounts for the year–
   [(a)   which includes a profit and loss account in which the following items listed in the profit and loss account format set out in Part I of Schedule 4 are combined as one item under the heading "gross profit or loss"–
      Items 1 to 3 and 6 in Format 1
      Items 1 to 5 in Format 2]
   (b)   which does not contain the information required by paragraph 55 of Schedule 4 (particulars of turnover).

(4)   A copy of accounts delivered to the registrar in accordance with subsection (3) shall contain a statement in a prominent position on the copy of the balance sheet, above the signature required by section 233, that the accounts are prepared in accordance with the special provisions of this Part relating to medium-sized limited liability partnerships.

247 Qualification of limited liability partnership as small or medium-sized

(1)   A limited liability partnership qualifies as small or medium-sized in relation to a financial year if the qualifying conditions are met–
   (a)   in the case of the limited liability partnership's first financial year, in that year, and
   (b)   in the case of any subsequent financial year, in that year and the preceding year.

(2) A limited liability partnership shall be treated as qualifying as small or medium-sized in relation to a financial year–
- (a) if it so qualified in relation to the previous financial year under subsection (1) above or was treated as so qualifying under paragraph (b) below; or
- (b) if it was treated as so qualifying in relation to the previous year by virtue of paragraph (a) and the qualifying conditions are met in the year in question.

(3) The qualifying conditions are met by a limited liability partnership in a year in which it satisfies two or more of the following requirements–

Small limited liability partnership

1 Turnover	Not more than £2.8 million
2 Balance sheet total	Not more than £1.4 million
3 Number of employees	Not more than 50

Medium-sized limited liability partnership

1 Turnover	Not more than £11.2 million
2 Balance sheet total	Not more than £5.6 million
3 Number of employees	Not more than 250

(4) For a period which is a limited liability partnership's financial year but not in fact a year the maximum figures for turnover shall be proportionately adjusted.

(5) The balance sheet total means–
- (a) where in the limited liability partnership's accounts Format 1 of the balance sheet formats set out in Part I of Schedule 4 or Part I of Schedule 8 is adopted, the aggregate of the amounts shown in the balance sheet under the headings corresponding to items A to D in that Format, and
- (b) where Format 2 is adopted, the aggregate of the amounts shown under the general heading "Assets".

(6) The number of employees means the average number of persons employed by the limited liability partnership in the year (determined on a monthly basis).

That number shall be determined by applying the method of calculation prescribed by paragraph 56(2) and (3) of Schedule 4 for determining the corresponding number required to be stated in a note to the limited liability partnership's accounts.

247A Cases in which special provisions do not apply

(1) Nothing in section 246 or 246A shall apply where–
- (a) the limited liability partnership is, or was at any time within the financial year to which the accounts relate–
  - (i),(ii) ...
  - (iii) an authorised person under the Financial Services Act 1986; or
- (b) the limited liability partnership is, or was at any time during that year, a member of an ineligible group.

(2)   A group is ineligible if any of its members is–
  (a)   a public company or a body corporate which (not being a company) has power under its constitution to offer its shares or debentures to the public and may lawfully exercise that power,
  (b)   an authorised institution under the Banking Act 1987,
  (c)   an insurance company to which Part II of the Insurance Companies Act 1982 applies, or
  (d)   an authorised person under the Financial Services Act 1986.

(3)   A parent limited liability partnership shall not be treated as qualifying as a small limited liability partnership in relation to a financial year unless the group headed by it qualifies as a small group, and shall not be treated as qualifying as a medium-sized limited liability partnership in relation to a financial year unless that group qualifies as a medium-sized group (see section 249).

247B Special auditors' report

(1)   This section applies where–
  (a)   [the designated members of a limited liability partnership] propose to deliver to the registrar copies of accounts ("abbreviated accounts") prepared in accordance with section 246(5) or (6) or 246A(3) ("the relevant provision"),
  (b)   the members have not taken advantage of the exemption from audit conferred by section 249A(1) … or section 249AA

(2)   If abbreviated accounts prepared in accordance with the relevant provision are delivered to the registrar, they shall be accompanied by a copy of a special report of the auditors stating that in their opinion–
  (a)   the limited liability partnership is entitled to deliver abbreviated accounts prepared in accordance with that provision, and
  (b)   the abbreviated accounts to be delivered are properly prepared in accordance with that provision.

(3)   In such a case a copy of the auditors' report under section 235 need not be delivered, but–
  (a)   if that report was qualified, the special report shall set out that report in full together with any further material necessary to understand the qualification; and
  (b)   if that report contained a statement under–
    (i)   section 237(2) (accounts, records or returns inadequate or accounts not agreeing with records and returns), or
    (ii)   section 237(3) (failure to obtain necessary information and explanations),
the special report shall set out that statement in full.

(4)   Section 236 (signature of auditors' report) applies to a special report under this section as it applies to a report under section 235.

(5)   If abbreviated accounts prepared in accordance with the relevant provision are delivered to the registrar, references in section 240 (requirements in connection

with publication of accounts) to the auditors' report under section 235 shall be read as references to the special auditors' report under this section.

248 Exemption for small and medium-sized groups

(1)   A parent limited liability partnership need not prepare group accounts for a financial year in relation to which the group headed by that limited liability partnership qualifies as a small or medium-sized group and is not an ineligible group.

(2)   A group is ineligible if any of its members is–
   (a)   a public company or a body corporate which (not being a company) has power under its constitution to offer its shares or debentures to the public and may lawfully exercise that power,
   (b)   an authorised institution under the Banking Act 1987,
   (c)   an insurance company to which Part II of the Insurance Companies Act 1982 applies, or
   (d)   an authorised person under the Financial Services Act 1986.

248A Group accounts prepared by small limited liability partnership

(1)   This section applies where a small limited liability partnership–
   (a)   has prepared individual accounts for a financial year in accordance with section 246(2) or (3), and
   (b)   is preparing group accounts in respect of the same year.

(2)   If the group accounts–
   (a)   comply with the provisions of Schedule 8, or
   (b)   fail to comply with those provisions only in so far as they comply instead with one or more corresponding provisions of Schedule 4,
they need not comply with the provisions or, as the case may be, the remaining provisions of Schedule 4; and where advantage is taken of this subsection, references in Schedule 4A to compliance with the provisions of Schedule 4 shall be construed accordingly.

(3)   For the purposes of this section, Schedule 8 shall have effect as if, in each balance sheet format set out in that Schedule, for item B III there were substituted the following item–
   "B III Investments
   1   Shares in group undertakings
   2   Interests in associated undertakings
   3   Other participating interests
   4   Loans to group undertakings and undertakings in which a participating interest is held
   5   Other investments other than loans
   6   Others."

(4)   The group accounts need not give the information required by the provisions specified in section 246(3).

(5)   Group accounts prepared in accordance with this section shall contain a statement in a prominent position on the balance sheet, above the signature required by section 233, that they are prepared in accordance with the special provisions of this Part relating to small limited liability partnerships.

249 Qualification of group as small or medium-sized

(1)   A group qualifies as small or medium-sized in relation to a financial year if the qualifying conditions are met–
    (a) in the case of the parent limited liability partnership's first financial year, in that year, and
    (b) in the case of any subsequent financial year, in that year and the preceding year.

(2)   A group shall be treated as qualifying as small or medium-sized in relation to a financial year–
    (a) if it so qualified in relation to the previous financial year under subsection (1) above or was treated as so qualifying under paragraph (b) below; or
    (b) if it was treated as so qualifying in relation to the previous year by virtue of paragraph (a) and the qualifying conditions are met in the year in question.

(3)   The qualifying conditions are met by a group in a year in which it satisfies two or more of the following requirements–

	Small group
1. Aggregate turnover	Not more than £2.8 million net (or £3.36 million gross)
2. Aggregate balance sheet total	Not more than £1.4 million net (or £1.68 million gross)
3. Aggregate number of employees	Not more than 50

	Medium-sized group
1. Aggregate turnover	Not more than £11.2 million net (or £13.44 million gross)
2. Aggregate balance sheet total	Not more than £5.6 million net (or £6.72 million gross)
3. Aggregate number of employees	Not more than 250

(4)   The aggregate figures shall be ascertained by aggregating the relevant figures determined in accordance with section 247 for each member of the group.
In relation to the aggregate figures for turnover and balance sheet total, "net" means with the set-offs and other adjustments required by Schedule 4A in the case of group accounts and "gross" means without those set-offs and other adjustments; and a limited liability partnership may satisfy the relevant requirement on the basis of either the net or the gross figure.

(5)   The figures for each subsidiary undertaking shall be those included in its accounts for the relevant financial year, that is–

(a) if its financial year ends with that of the parent limited liability partnership, that financial year, and

(b) if not, its financial year ending last before the end of the financial year of the parent limited liability partnership.

(6)   If those figures cannot be obtained without disproportionate expense or undue delay, the latest available figures shall be taken.

249A Exemptions from audit

(1)   Subject to section 249B, a limited liability partnership which meets the total exemption conditions set out below in respect of a financial year is exempt from the provisions of this Part relating to the audit of accounts in respect of that year.

(2)   ...

(3)   The total exemption conditions are met by a limited liability partnership in respect of a financial year if–
(a) it qualifies as a small limited liability partnership in relation to that year for the purposes of section 246,
(b) its turnover in that year is not more than £1 million, and
(c) its balance sheet total for that year is not more than £1.4 million.

(3A),(4)   ...

(6)   For a period which is a limited liability partnership's financial year but not in fact a year the maximum figures for turnover ... shall be proportionately adjusted.

(6A)   A limited liability partnership is entitled to the exemption conferred by subsection (1) ... notwithstanding that it falls within paragraph (a) or (b) of section 249AA(1).

(7)   In this section–

"balance sheet total" has the meaning given by section 247(5), ...

249AA Dormant limited liability partnerships

(1)   Subject to [section 249B(4) and (5)], a limited liability partnership is exempt from the provisions of this Part relating to the audit of accounts in respect of a financial year if–
(a) it has been dormant since its formation, or
(b) it has been dormant since the end of the previous financial year and subsection (2) applies.

(2)   This subsection applies if the limited liability partnership–
(a) is entitled in respect of its individual accounts for the financial year in question to prepare accounts in accordance with section 246, or would be so entitled but for the application of [section 247A(1)(b)], and
(b) is not required to prepare group accounts for that year.

(3)   Subsection (1) does not apply if at any time in the financial year in question the limited liability partnership was–

(a)   …

(b)   an authorised person for the purposes of the Financial Services Act 1986.

(4)   A limited liability partnership is "dormant" during any period in which it has no significant accounting transaction.

(5)   "Significant accounting transaction" means a transaction which–

(a)   is required by section 221 to be entered in the limited liability partnership's accounting records; but

(b)   is not a transaction to which subsection … (7) applies.

…

(7)   This subsection applies to a transaction consisting of the payment of–

     (a)   a fee to the registrar on a change of name under [paragraph 5 of the Schedule to the Limited Liability Partnerships Act 2000],

     (b)   …

     (c)   a penalty under section 242A (penalty for failure to deliver accounts), or

     (d)   a fee to the registrar for the registration of an annual return under Chapter III of Part XI.

249B Cases where exemptions not available

(1)   Subject to subsection (1A) to (1C), a limited liability partnership is not entitled to the exemption conferred by subsection (1) … of section 249A in respect of a financial year if at any time within that year–

     (a),(b)   …

     (c)   it was enrolled in the list maintained by the Insurance Brokers Registration Council under section 4 of the Insurance Brokers (Registration) Act 1977,

     (d)   it was an authorised person or an appointed representative under the Financial Services Act 1986,

     (e)   it was a special register body as defined in section 117(1) of the Trade Union and Labour Relations (Consolidation) Act 1992 or an employers' association as defined in section 122 of that Act, or

     (f)   it was a parent limited liability partnership or a subsidiary undertaking.

(1A)   A limited liability partnership which, apart from this subsection, would fall within subsection (1)(f) by virtue of its being a subsidiary undertaking for any period within a financial year shall not be treated as so falling if it is dormant (within the meaning of section 249AA) throughout that period.

(1B)   A limited liability partnership which, apart from this subsection, would fall within subsection (1)(f) by virtue of its being a parent limited liability partnership or a subsidiary undertaking for any period within a financial year, shall not be treated as so falling if throughout that period it was a member of a group meeting the conditions set out in subsection (1C).

(1C)   The conditions referred to in subsection (1B) are–
- (a)   that the group qualifies as a small group, in relation to the financial year within which the period falls, for the purposes of section 249 (or if all bodies corporate in such group were companies, would so qualify) and is not, and was not at any time within that year, an ineligible group within the meaning of section 248(2),
- (b)   [that the group's aggregate turnover in that year (calculated in accordance with section 249) is not more than £1 million net (or £1.2 million gross)], and
- (c)   that the group's aggregate balance sheet total for that year (calculated in accordance with section 249) is not more than £1.4 million net (or £1.68 million gross).

(2),(3) …

(4)   A limited liability partnership is not entitled to the exemption conferred by subsection (1) … of section 249A or by subsection (1) of section 249AA unless its balance sheet contains a statement by the members–
- (a)   to the effect that for the year in question the limited liability partnership was entitled to exemption under subsection (1) … of section 249A or subsection (1) of section 249AA,
- (b)   …
- (c)   to the effect that the members acknowledge their responsibilities for–
  - (i)   ensuring that the limited liability partnership keeps accounting records which comply with section 221, and
  - (ii)   preparing accounts which give a true and fair view of the state of affairs of the limited liability partnership as at the end of the financial year and of its profit or loss for the financial year in accordance with the requirements of section 226, and which otherwise comply with the requirements of this Act relating to accounts, so far as applicable to the limited liability partnership.

(5)   The statement required by subsection (4) shall appear in the balance sheet above the signature required by section 233.

249C, 249D …

249E Effect of exemptions

(1)   Where the members of a limited liability partnership have taken advantage of the exemption conferred by section 249A(1) or section 249AA(1)–
- (a)   sections 238 and 239 (right to receive or demand copies of accounts and reports) shall have effect with the omission of references to the auditors' report;
- (b)   no copy of an auditors' report need be delivered to the registrar …;
- (c)   …

(1A)   Where the members of a limited liability partnership have taken advantage of the exemption conferred by section 249AA, then for the purposes of that section the limited liability partnership shall be treated as a limited liability partnership entitled to prepare accounts in accordance with section 246 even though it is a member of an ineligible group.

(2)   …

251, 252, 253, 254, 255, 255A, 255B, 255D   …

CHAPTER III
SUPPLEMENTARY PROVISIONS

256 Accounting standards

(1)   In this Part "accounting standards" means statements of standard accounting practice issued by such body or bodies as may be prescribed by regulations.

(2)   References in this Part to accounting standards applicable to a limited liability partnership's annual accounts are to such standards as are, in accordance with their terms, relevant to the limited liability partnership's circumstances and to the accounts.

(3)   The Secretary of State may make grants to or for the purposes of bodies concerned with–
   (a)   issuing accounting standards,
   (b)   overseeing and directing the issuing of such standards, or
   (c)   investigating departures from such standards or from the accounting requirements of this Act and taking steps to secure compliance with them.

(4)   Regulations under this section may contain such transitional and other supplementary and incidental provisions as appear to the Secretary of State to be appropriate.

257   …

258 Parent and subsidiary undertakings

(1)   The expressions "parent undertaking" and "subsidiary undertaking" in this Part shall be construed as follows; and a "parent limited liability partnership" means a parent undertaking which is a limited liability partnership.

(2)   An undertaking is a parent undertaking in relation to another undertaking, a subsidiary undertaking, if–
   (a)   it holds a majority of the voting rights in the undertaking, or
   (b)   it is a member of the undertaking and has the right to appoint or remove a majority of its board of directors, or
   (c)   it has the right to exercise a dominant influence over the undertaking–
      (i)   by virtue of provisions contained in the undertaking's memorandum or articles, or
      (ii)   by virtue of a control contract, or

(d) it is a member of the undertaking and controls alone, pursuant to an agreement with other shareholders or members, a majority of the voting rights in the undertaking.

(3)   For the purposes of subsection (2) an undertaking shall be treated as a member of another undertaking–
(a) if any of its subsidiary undertakings is a member of that undertaking, or
(b) if any shares in that other undertaking are held by a person acting on behalf of the undertaking or any of its subsidiary undertakings.

(4)   An undertaking is also a parent undertaking in relation to another undertaking, a subsidiary undertaking, if it has a participating interest in the undertaking and–
(a) it actually exercises a dominant influence over it, or
(b) it and the subsidiary undertaking are managed on a unified basis.

(5)   A parent undertaking shall be treated as the parent undertaking of undertakings in relation to which any of its subsidiary undertakings are, or are to be treated as, parent undertakings; and references to its subsidiary undertakings shall be construed accordingly.

(6)   Schedule 10A contains provisions explaining expressions used in this section and otherwise supplementing this section.

259 Meaning of "undertaking" and related expressions

(1)   In this Part "undertaking" means–
(a) a body corporate or partnership, or
(b) an unincorporated association carrying on a trade or business, with or without a view to profit.

(2)   In this Part references to shares–
(a) in relation to an undertaking with a share capital, are to allotted shares;
(b) in relation to an undertaking with capital but no share capital, are to rights to share in the capital of the undertaking; and
(c) in relation to an undertaking without capital, are to interests–
(i) conferring any right to share in the profits or liability to contribute to the losses of the undertaking, or
(ii) giving rise to an obligation to contribute to the debts or expenses of the undertaking in the event of a winding up.

(3)   Other expressions appropriate to limited liability partnerships shall be construed, in relation to an undertaking which is not a limited liability partnership, as references to the corresponding persons, officers, documents or organs, as the case may be, appropriate to undertakings of that description.
This is subject to provision in any specific context providing for the translation of such expressions.

(4)   References in this Part to "fellow subsidiary undertakings" are to undertakings which are subsidiary undertakings of the same parent undertaking but are not parent undertakings or subsidiary undertakings of each other.

(5)   In this Part "group undertaking", in relation to an undertaking, means an undertaking which is–
> (a)   a parent undertaking or subsidiary undertaking of that undertaking, or
> (b)   a subsidiary undertaking of any parent undertaking of that undertaking.

260 Participating interests

(1)   In this Part a "participating interest" means an interest held by an undertaking in the shares of another undertaking which it holds on a long-term basis for the purpose of securing a contribution to its activities by the exercise of control or influence arising from or related to that interest.

(2)   A holding of 20 per cent or more of the shares of an undertaking shall be presumed to be a participating interest unless the contrary is shown.

(3)   The reference in subsection (1) to an interest in shares includes–
> (a)   an interest which is convertible into an interest in shares, and
> (b)   an option to acquire shares or any such interest;

and an interest or option falls within paragraph (a) or (b) notwithstanding that the shares to which it relates are, until the conversion or the exercise of the option, unissued.

(4)   For the purposes of this section an interest held on behalf of an undertaking shall be treated as held by it.

(5)   For the purposes of this section as it applies in relation to the expression "participating interest" in section 258(4) (definition of "subsidiary undertaking")–
> (a)   there shall be attributed to an undertaking any interests held by any of its subsidiary undertakings, and
> (b)   the references in subsection (1) to the purpose and activities of an undertaking include the purposes and activities of any of its subsidiary undertakings and of the group as a whole.

(6)   In the balance sheet and profit and loss formats set out in Part I of Schedule 4, Part I of Schedule 8 [and Schedule 8A] "participating interest" does not include an interest in a group undertaking.

(7)   For the purposes of this section as it applies in relation to the expression "participating interest"–
> (a)   in those formats as they apply in relation to group accounts, and
> (b)   in paragraph 20 of Schedule 4A (group accounts: undertakings to be accounted for as associated undertakings),

the references in subsection (1) to (4) to the interest held by, and the purposes and activities of, the undertaking concerned shall be construed as references to the interest held by, and the purposes and activities of, the group (within the meaning of paragraph 1 of that Schedule).

261 Notes to the accounts

(1)   Information required by this Part to be given in notes to a limited liability partnership's annual accounts may be contained in the accounts or in a separate document annexed to the accounts.

(2)   References in this Part to a limited liability partnership's annual accounts, or to a balance sheet or profit and loss account, include notes to the accounts giving information which is required by any provision of this Act, and required or allowed by any such provision to be given in a note to limited liability partnership accounts.

262 Minor definitions

(1)   In this Part—

"annual accounts" means—
(a)   the individual accounts required by section 226, and
       (b)   any group accounts required by section 227,
(but see also section 230 (treatment of individual profit and loss account where group accounts prepared);

"balance sheet date" means the date as at which the balance sheet was made up;

"capitalisation", in relation to work or costs, means treating that work or those costs as a fixed asset;

"fixed assets" means assets of a limited liability partnership which are intended for use on a continuing basis in the limited liability partnership's activities, and "current assets" means assets not intended for such use;

"group" means a parent undertaking and its subsidiary undertakings;

"included in the consolidation", in relation to group accounts, or "included in consolidated group accounts", means that the undertaking is included in the accounts by the method of full (and not proportional) consolidation, and references to an undertaking excluded from consolidation shall be construed accordingly;

["limited liability partnership" means a limited liability partnership formed and registered under the Limited Liability Partnerships Act 2000;]

"purchase price", in relation to an asset of a limited liability partnership or any raw materials or consumables used in the production of such an asset, includes any consideration (whether in cash or otherwise) given by the limited liability partnership in respect of that asset or those materials or consumables, as the case may be;

"qualified", in relation to an auditors' report, means that the report does not state the auditors' unqualified opinion that the accounts have been properly prepared in accordance with this Act or, in the case of an undertaking not required to prepare accounts in accordance with this Act, under any corresponding legislation under which it is required to prepare accounts;

"true and fair view" refers–

    (a)   in the case of individual accounts, to the requirement of section 226(2), and

    (b)   in the case of group accounts, to the requirement of section 227(3);

"turnover", in relation to a limited liability partnership, means the amounts derived from the provision of goods and services falling within the limited liability partnership's ordinary activities, after deduction of–

    (i)   trade discounts,

    (ii) value added tax, and

    (iii) any other taxes based on the amounts so derived.

(2)   …

(3)   References in this Part to "realised profits" and "realised losses", in relation to a limited liability partnership's accounts, are to such profits or losses of the limited liability partnership as fall to be treated as realised in accordance with principles generally accepted, at the time when the accounts are prepared, with respect to the determination for accounting purposes of realised profits or losses.

    This is without prejudice to–

    (a)   the construction of any other expression (where appropriate) by reference to accepted accounting principles or practice, or

    (b)   any specific provision for the treatment of profits or losses of any description as realised.

262A Index of defined expressions

The following Table shows the provisions of this Part defining or otherwise explaining expressions used in this Part (other than expressions used only in the same section or paragraph)–

accounting reference date and accounting reference period	section 224
accounting standards and applicable accounting standards	section 256
annual accounts (generally)	section 262(1)
(includes notes to the accounts)	section 261(2)
associated undertaking (in Schedule 4A)	paragraph 20 of that Schedule
balance sheet (includes notes)	section 261(2)
balance sheet date	section 262(1)
capitalisation (in relation to work or costs)	section 262(1)
current assets	section 262(1)

fellow subsidiary undertaking	section 259(4)
financial year	section 223
fixed assets	section 262(1)
group	section 262(1)
group undertaking	section 259(5)
historical cost accounting rules	
–in Schedule 4	paragraph 29 of that Schedule
–in Schedule 8	paragraph 29 of that Schedule
included in the consolidation and related expressions	section 262(1)
individual accounts	section 262(1)
land of freehold tenure and land of leasehold tenure (in relation to Scotland)	
–in Schedule 4	paragraph 93 of that Schedule
lease, long lease and short lease	
–in Schedule 4	paragraph 83 of that Schedule
limited liability partnership	section 262
listed investment	
–in Schedule 4	paragraph 84 of that Schedule
–in Schedule 8	paragraph 54 of that Schedule
notes to the accounts	section 261(1)
parent undertaking (and parent limited liability partnership)	section 258 and Schedule 10A
participating interest	section 260
pension costs	
–in Schedule 4	paragraph 94(2) of that Schedule
–in Schedule 8	paragraph 59(2) of that Schedule
period allowed for laying and delivering accounts and reports	section 244
profit and loss account	
(includes notes)	section 261(2)
(in relation to a limited liability partnership not trading for profit)	section 262(2)
provision	
–in Schedule 4	paragraphs 88 and 89 of that Schedule
–in Schedule 8	paragraphs 57 and 58 of that Schedule
purchase price	section 262(1)
qualified	section 262(1)
realised losses and realised profits	section 262(3)

shares	section 259(2)
social security costs	
–in Schedule 4	paragraph 94(1) and (3) of that Schedule
–in Schedule 8	paragraph 59(1) and (3) of that Schedule
subsidiary undertaking	section 258 and Schedule 10A
true and fair view	section 262(1)
turnover	section 262(1)
undertaking and related expressions	section 259(1) to (3)

263–281

PART IX
A LIMITED LIABILITY PARTNERSHIP'S MANAGEMENT;
MEMBERS; THEIR QUALIFICATIONS, DUTIES AND
RESPONSIBILITIES

282–286

287 Registered office

[(1)   The change of registered office takes effect upon the notice of change of registered office (delivered to the registrar in accordance with paragraph 10 of the Schedule to the Limited Liability Partnerships Act 2000), being registered by the registrar, but until the end of the period of 14 days beginning with the date on which it is registered a person may validly serve any document on the limited liability partnership at its previous registered office.

(2)   Where a limited liability partnership unavoidably ceases to perform at its registered office any duty to keep at its registered office any register, index or other document or to mention the address of its registered office in any document in circumstances in which it was not practicable to give prior notice to the registrar of a change in the situation of the registered office, but–
    (a)   resumes performance of that duty at other premises as soon as practicable, and
    (b)   gives notice accordingly to the registrar of a change in the situation of its registered office within 14 days of doing so it shall not be treated as having failed to comply with that duty.]

288 Register of members

[Where a person becomes a member or designated member of a limited liability partnership the notice to be delivered to the registrar under section 9(1)(a) of the Limited Liability Partnerships Act 2000 shall contain the following particulars with respect to that person:

(1)   name, which

(a) in the case of an individual means his forename and surname (or, in the case of a peer or other person usually known by a title, his title instead of or in addition to either or both his forename and surname), and

(b) if a corporation or a Scottish firm, its corporate or firm name; and

(2) address, which
(a) in the case of an individual means his usual residential address; and
(b) if a corporation or a Scottish firm, its registered or principal office; and

(3) in the case of an individual, the date of his birth.]

289–347

PART XI
LIMITED LIABILITY PARTNERSHIP ADMINISTRATION AND
PROCEDURE

CHAPTER I
LIMITED LIABILITY PARTNERSHIP IDENTIFICATION

348 Limited liability partnership name to appear outside place of business

(1) Every limited liability partnership shall paint or affix, and keep painted or affixed, its name on the outside of every office or place in which its business is carried on, in a conspicuous position and in letters easily legible.

(2) If a limited liability partnership does not paint or affix its name as required above, the limited liability partnership and every member of it who is in default is liable to a fine; and if a limited liability partnership does not keep its name painted or affixed as so required, the limited liability partnership and every member of it who is in default is liable to a fine and, for continued contravention, to a daily default fine.

349 Limited liability partnership's name to appear in its correspondence, etc

(1) Every limited liability partnership shall have its name mentioned in legible characters–
(a) in all business letters of the limited liability partnership,
(b) in all its notices and other official publications,
(c) in all bills of exchange, promissory notes, endorsements, cheques and orders for money or goods purporting to be signed by or on behalf of the limited liability partnership, and
(d) in all its bills of parcels, invoices, receipts and letters of credit.

(2) If a limited liability partnership fails to comply with subsection (1) it is liable to a fine.

(3)   If an member of a limited liability partnership or a person on its behalf–
  (a) issues or authorises the issue of any business letter of the limited liability partnership, or any notice or other official publication of the limited liability partnership, in which the limited liability partnership's name is not mentioned as required by subsection (1), or
  (b) issues or authorises the issue of any bill of parcels, invoice, receipt or letter of credit of the limited liability partnership in which its name is not so mentioned,
he is liable to a fine.

(4)   If an member of a limited liability partnership or a person on its behalf signs or authorises to be signed on behalf of the limited liability partnership any bill of exchange, promissory note, endorsement, cheque or order for money or goods in which the limited liability partnership's name is not mentioned as required by subsection (1), he is liable to a fine; and he is further personally liable to the holder of the bill of exchange, promissory note, cheque or order for money or goods for the amount of it (unless it is duly paid by the limited liability partnership).

350 Limited liability partnership seal

(1)   A limited liability partnership which has a common seal shall have its name engraved in legible characters on the seal; and if it fails to comply with this subsection it is liable to a fine.

(2)   If an member of a limited liability partnership or a person on its behalf uses or authorises the use of any seal purporting to be a seal of the limited liability partnership on which its name is not engraved as required by subsection (1), he is liable to a fine.

351 Particulars in correspondence etc

(1)   Every limited liability partnership shall have the following particulars mentioned in legible characters in all business letters and order forms of the limited liability partnership, that is to say–
  (a) the limited liability partnership's place of registration and the number with which it is registered,
  (b) the address of its registered office,
  (c) [in the case of a limited liability partnership, whose name ends with the abbreviation "llp", "LLP", "pac" or "PAC", the fact that it is a limited liability partnership or a partneriaeth atebolrwydd cyfyngedig.]
  (d) ...

(2)   ...

(5)   As to contraventions of this section, the following applies–
  (a) if a limited liability partnership fails to comply with subsection (1) or (2), it is liable to a fine,
  (b) if an member of a limited liability partnership or a person on its behalf issues or authorises the issue of any business letter or order form not complying with those subsections, he is liable to a fine.

352–362

CHAPTER III
ANNUAL RETURN

363 Duty to deliver annual returns

[(1)   Every limited liability partnership shall deliver to the registrar successive annual returns each of which is made up to a date not later than the date which is from time to time the "return date" of the limited liability partnership, that is–
- (a)   the anniversary of the incorporation of the limited liability partnership, or
- (b)   if the last return delivered by the limited liability partnership in accordance with this section was made up to a different date, the anniversary of that date.

(2)   Each return shall–
- (a)   be in a form approved by the registrar,
- (b)   contain the information required by section 364, and
- (c)   be signed by a designated member of the limited liability partnership.

(3)   If a limited liability partnership fails to deliver an annual return in accordance with this section before the end of the period of 28 days after the return date, the limited liability partnership is guilty of an offence and liable on summary conviction to a fine not exceeding level 5 on the standard scale. The contravention continues until such time as an annual return made up to that return date and complying with the requirements of subsection (2) (except as to date of delivery) is delivered by the limited liability partnership to the registrar.

(4)   Where a limited liability partnership is guilty of an offence under subsection (3) every designated member of the limited liability partnership is similarly liable unless he shows that he took all reasonable steps to avoid the commission of or the continuance of the offence.]

364 Contents of annual return: general

[Every annual return shall state the date to which it is made up and shall contain the following information:
- (a)   the address of the registered office of the limited liability partnership,
- (b)   the names and usual residential addresses of the members of the limited liability partnership and, if some only of them are designated members, which of them are designated members.
- (c)   if any register of debenture holders (or a duplicate of any such register or part of it) is not kept at the registered office of the limited liability partnership, the address of the place where it is kept.]

366–383

CHAPTER V
AUDITORS

384 Duty to appoint auditors

(1)   Every limited liability partnership shall appoint an auditor or auditors in accordance with this Chapter.
    This is subject to section 388A (certain limited liability partnerships exempt from obligation to appoint auditors).

(2)   Auditors shall be appointed in accordance with section 385 [(appointment of auditors)].

(3)   References in this Chapter to the end of the time for appointing auditors are to the end of the time within which an appointment must be made under section 385(2) …

[(4)   A person is eligible for appointment by a limited liability partnership as auditor only if, were the limited liability partnership a company, he would be eligible under Part II of the Companies Act 1989 for appointment as a "company auditor".]

[(5)   Part II of the Companies Act 1989 shall apply in respect of auditors of limited liability partnerships as if limited liability partnerships were companies formed and registered under this Act, and references in Part II to an officer of a company shall include references to a member of a limited liability partnership.]

385 [Appointment of auditors]

(1)   …

[(2)   The designated members of a limited liability partnership shall appoint the auditors for the first financial year in respect of which auditors are appointed before the end of that financial year and thereafter before the expiration of not more than two months following the approval of the accounts for the preceding financial year in accordance with section 233.]

[(3)   The auditor of a limited liability partnership shall hold office until not later than the expiration of two months following the approval in accordance with section 233 of the accounts for the financial year in respect of which the auditor was appointed.]

[(4)   If the designated members fail to exercise their powers under subsection (2), the powers may be exercised by the members of the limited liability partnership in a meeting convened for the purpose.]

385A–386

387 Appointment by Secretary of State in default of appointment by limited liability partnership

(1)   If in any case no auditors are appointed ... before the end of the time for appointing auditors, the Secretary of State may appoint a person to fill the vacancy.

(2)   In such a case the limited liability partnership shall within one week of the end of the time for appointing auditors give notice to the Secretary of State of his power having become exercisable.
    If a limited liability partnership fails to give the notice required by this subsection, the limited liability partnership and every [designated member] of it who is in default is guilty of an offence and liable to a fine and, for continued contravention, to a daily default fine.

388 Filling of casual vacancies

(1)   The [designated members] may fill a casual vacancy in the office of auditor.

(2)   While such a vacancy continues, any surviving or continuing auditor or auditors may continue to act.

(3),(4) ...

388A Certain limited liability partnerships exempt from obligation to appoint auditors

(1)   A limited liability partnership which by virtue of section 249A (certain categories of small limited liability partnership) or section 250 (dormant limited liability partnerships) is exempt from the provisions of Part VII relating to the audit of accounts is also exempt from the obligation to appoint auditors.

(2)   The following provisions apply if a limited liability partnership which has been exempt from those provisions ceases to be so exempt.

[(3)   The designated members may appoint auditors and the auditors so appointed shall hold office until the expiration of two months following the approval in accordance with section 233 of the accounts for the financial year in respect of which the auditor was appointed.]

(4)   ...

[(5)   If the designated members fail to exercise their powers under subsection (3), the powers may be exercised by the members of the limited liability partnership in a meeting convened for the purpose.]

389A Rights to information

(1)   The auditors of a limited liability partnership have a right of access at all times to the limited liability partnership's books, accounts and vouchers, and are

entitled to require from the limited liability partnership's members such information and explanations as they think necessary for the performance of their duties as auditors.

(2)   A member of a limited liability partnership commits an offence if he knowingly or recklessly makes to the limited liability partnership's auditors a statement (whether written or oral) which–
  (a) conveys or purports to convey any information or explanations which the auditors require, or are entitled to require, as auditors of the limited liability partnership, and
  (b) is misleading, false or deceptive in a material particular.
   A person guilty of an offence under this subsection is liable to imprisonment or a fine, or both.

(3)   A subsidiary undertaking which is a body corporate incorporated in Great Britain, and the auditors of such an undertaking, shall give to the auditors of any parent limited liability partnership of the undertaking such information and explanations as they may reasonably require for the purposes of their duties as auditors of that limited liability partnership.
   If a subsidiary undertaking fails to comply with this subsection, the undertaking and every officer of it who is in default is guilty of an offence and liable to a fine; and if an auditor fails without reasonable excuse to comply with this subsection he is guilty of an offence and liable to a fine.

(4)   A parent limited liability partnership having a subsidiary undertaking which is not a body corporate incorporated in Great Britain shall, if required by its auditors to do so, take all such steps as are reasonably open to it to obtain from the subsidiary undertaking such information and explanations as they may reasonably require for the purposes of their duties as auditors of that limited liability partnership.
   If a parent limited liability partnership fails to comply with this subsection, the limited liability partnership and every member of it who is in default is guilty of an offence and liable to a fine.

(5)   Section 734 (criminal proceedings against unincorporated bodies) applies to an offence under subsection (3).

390 Right to attend limited liability partnership meetings

(1)   A limited liability partnership's auditors are entitled–
  (a) to receive all notices of, and other communications relating to, any … meeting which a member of the limited liability partnership is entitled to receive [and where any part of the business of the meeting concerns them as auditors];
  (b) to attend any … meeting of the limited liability partnership [where any part of the business of the meeting concerns them as auditors]; and
  (c) to be heard at any … meeting which they attend on any part of the business of the meeting which concerns them as auditors.

(1A),(2)   ...

(3)   The right to attend or be heard at a meeting is exercisable in the case of a body corporate or partnership by an individual authorised by it in writing to act as its representative at the meeting.

390A Remuneration of auditors

(1)   [The remuneration of auditors appointed by the limited liability partnership shall be fixed by the designated members or in such manner as the members of the limited liability partnership may determine.]

(2)   The remuneration of auditors appointed by the ... Secretary of State shall be fixed by the ... Secretary of State ...

(3)   There shall be stated in a note to the limited liability partnership's annual accounts the amount of the remuneration of the limited liability partnership's auditors in their capacity as such.

(4)   For the purposes of this section "remuneration" includes sums paid in respect of expenses.

(5)   This section applies in relation to benefits in kind as to payments in cash, and in relation to any such benefit references to its amount are to its estimated money value.
The nature of any such benefit shall also be disclosed.

390B Remuneration of auditors or their associates for non–audit work

(1)   The Secretary of State may make provision by regulations for securing the disclosure of the amount of any remuneration received or receivable by a limited liability partnership's auditors or their associates in respect of services other than those of auditors in their capacity as such.

(2)   The regulations may–
    (a)   provide that "remuneration" includes sums paid in respect of expenses,
    (b)   apply in relation to benefits in kind as to payments in cash, and in relation to any such benefit require disclosure of its nature and its estimated money value,
    (c)   define "associate" in relation to an auditor,
    (d)   require the disclosure of remuneration in respect of services rendered to associated undertakings of the limited liability partnership, and
    (e)   define "associated undertaking" for that purpose.

(3)   The regulations may require the auditors to disclose the relevant information in their report or require the relevant information to be disclosed in a note to the limited liability partnership's accounts and require the auditors to supply the members of the limited liability partnership with such information as is necessary to enable that disclosure to be made.

(4)   The regulations may make different provision for different cases.

(5)   Regulations under this section shall be made by statutory instrument which shall be subject to annulment in pursuance of a resolution of either House of Parliament.

391 Removal of auditors

(1)   [The designated members of a limited liability partnership may] at any time remove an auditor from office, notwithstanding anything in any agreement [with] him.

(2)   Where [the designated members of the limited liability partnership have made a determination to remove an auditor, the designated members] shall within 14 days give notice of that fact in the prescribed form to the registrar.
If a limited liability partnership fails to give the notice required by this subsection, the limited liability partnership and [every designated member of it who is in default] is guilty of an offence and liable to a fine and, for continued contravention, to a daily default fine.

(3)   Nothing in this section shall be taken as depriving a person removed under it of compensation or damages payable to him in respect of the termination of his appointment as auditor or of any appointment terminating with that as auditor.

(4)   An auditor of a limited liability partnership who has been removed has, notwithstanding his removal, the rights conferred by section 390 in relation to any … meeting of the limited liability partnership–
      (a)   at which his term of office would otherwise have expired, or
      (b)   at which it is proposed to fill the vacancy caused by his removal.
In such a case the references in that section to matters concerning the auditors as auditors shall be construed as references to matters concerning him as a former auditor.

391A Rights of auditors who are removed or not re-appointed

(1)   [The designated members shall give seven days' prior written notice to–
      (a)   any auditor whom it is proposed to remove before the expiration of his term of office; or
      (b)   a retiring auditor where it is proposed to appoint as auditor a person other than the retiring auditor.]

(2)   …

(3)   The auditor proposed to be removed or (as the case may be) the retiring auditor may make with respect to the [proposal] representations in writing to the limited liability partnership (not exceeding a reasonable length) and request their notification to members …

(4)   The limited liability partnership shall …–
      (a)   …

(b) send a copy of the representations to every member [within twenty one days' of receipt].

(5) [If a copy of the representations is not sent out as required by subsection (4), then unless subsection (6) applies, the limited liability partnership and any designated member in default commits an offence. A person guilty of an offence under this section is liable on summary conviction to a fine not exceeding level 3 on the standard scale.]

(6) Copies of the representations need not be sent out ... if, on the application either of the limited liability partnership or of any other person claiming to be aggrieved, the court is satisfied that the rights conferred by this section are being abused to secure needless publicity for defamatory matter; and the court may order the limited liability partnership's costs on the application to be paid in whole or in part by the auditor, notwithstanding that he is not a party to the application.

392 Resignation of auditors

(1) An auditor of a limited liability partnership may resign his office by depositing a notice in writing to that effect at the limited liability partnership's registered office.
  The notice is not effective unless it is accompanied by the statement required by section 394.

(2) An effective notice of resignation operates to bring the auditor's term of office to an end as of the date on which the notice is deposited or on such later date as may be specified in it.

(3) The limited liability partnership shall within 14 days of the deposit of a notice of resignation send a copy of the notice to the registrar of companies.
  If default is made in complying with this subsection, the limited liability partnership [and every designated member of it who is in default] is guilty of an offence and liable to a fine and, for continued contravention, a daily default fine.

392A Rights of resigning auditors

(1) This section applies where an auditor's notice of resignation is accompanied by a statement of circumstances which he considers should be brought to the attention of members or creditors of the limited liability partnership.

(2) He may deposit with the notice a signed requisition calling on the [designated members] of the limited liability partnership forthwith duly to convene [a meeting of the members of the limited liability partnership] for the purpose of receiving and considering such explanation of the circumstances connected with his resignation as he may wish to place before the meeting.

(3) He may request the limited liability partnership to circulate to its members–
  (a) before the meeting convened on his requisition ...
  (b) ...

a statement in writing (not exceeding a reasonable length) of the circumstances connected with his resignation.

(4)   The limited liability partnership shall (unless the statement is received too late for it to comply)–

    (a) in any notice of the meeting given to members of the limited liability partnership, state the fact of the statement having been made, and

    (b) send a copy of the statement to every member of the limited liability partnership to whom notice of the meeting is or has been sent.

(5)   If the [designated members] do not within 21 days from the date of the deposit of a requisition under this section proceed duly to convene a meeting for a day not more than 28 days after the date on which the notice convening the meeting is given, every [designated member] who failed to take all reasonable steps to secure that a meeting was convened as mentioned above is guilty of an offence and liable to a fine.

(6)   If a copy of the statement mentioned above is not sent out as required because received too late or because of the limited liability partnership's default, the auditor may (without prejudice to his right to be heard orally) require that the statement be read out at the meeting.

(7)   Copies of a statement need not be sent out and the statement need not be read out at the meeting if, on the application either of the limited liability partnership or of any other person who claims to be aggrieved, the court is satisfied that the rights conferred by this section are being abused to secure needless publicity for defamatory matter; and the court may order the limited liability partnership's costs on such an application to be paid in whole or in part by the auditor, notwithstanding that he is not a party to the application.

(8)   An auditor who has resigned has, notwithstanding his resignation, the rights conferred by section 390 in relation to any such … meeting of the limited liability partnership as is mentioned in subsection (3) …

    In such a case the references in that section to matters concerning the auditors as auditors shall be construed as references to matters concerning him as a former auditor.

393

394 Statement by person ceasing to hold office as auditors

(1)   Where an auditor ceases for any reason to hold office, he shall deposit at the limited liability partnership's registered office a statement of any circumstances connected with his ceasing to hold office which he considers should be brought to the attention of the members or creditors of the limited liability partnership or, if he considers that there are no such circumstances, a statement that there are none.

(2)   In the case of resignation, the statement shall be deposited along with the notice of resignation; in the case of failure to seek re-appointment, the statement

shall be deposited not less than 14 days before the end of the time allowed for next appointing auditors; in any other case, the statement shall be deposited not later than the end of the period of 14 days beginning with the date on which he ceases to hold office.

(3)　If the statement is of circumstances which the auditor considers should be brought to the attention of the members or creditors of the limited liability partnership, the limited liability partnership shall within 14 days of the deposit of the statement either–
>　(a)　send a copy of it to every person who under section 238 is entitled to be sent copies of the accounts, or
>　(b)　apply to the court.

(4)　The limited liability partnership shall if it applies to the court notify the auditor of the application.

(5)　Unless the auditor receives notice of such an application before the end of the period of 21 days beginning with the day on which he deposited the statement, he shall within a further seven days send a copy of the statement to the registrar.

(6)　If the court is satisfied that the auditor is using the statement to secure needless publicity for defamatory matter–
>　(a)　it shall direct that copies of the statement need not be sent out, and
>　(b)　it may further order the limited liability partnership's costs on the application to be paid in whole or in part by the auditor, notwithstanding that he is not a party to the application;

and the limited liability partnership shall within 14 days of the court's decision send to the persons mentioned in subsection (3)(a) a statement setting out the effect of the order.

(7)　If the court is not so satisfied, the limited liability partnership shall within 14 days of the court's decision–
>　(a)　send copies of the statement to the persons mentioned in subsection (3)(a), and
>　(b)　notify the auditor of the court's decision;

and the auditor shall within seven days of receiving such notice send a copy of the statement to the registrar.

394A Offences of failing to comply with s 394

(1)　If a person ceasing to hold office as auditor fails to comply with section 394 he is guilty of an offence and liable to a fine.

(2)　In proceedings for an offence under subsection (1) it is a defence for the person charged to show that he took all reasonable steps and exercised all due diligence to avoid the commission of the offence.

(3)　Sections 733 (liability of individuals for corporate default) and 734 (criminal proceedings against unincorporated bodies) apply to an offence under subsection (1).

(4)   If a limited liability partnership makes default in complying with section 394, the limited liability partnership and every member of it who is in default is guilty of an offence and liable to a fine and, for continued contravention, to a daily default fine.

PART XII
REGISTRATION OF CHARGES

CHAPTER I
REGISTRATION OF CHARGES (ENGLAND AND WALES)

395 Certain charges void if not registered

(1)   Subject to the provisions of this Chapter, a charge created by a limited liability partnership registered in England and Wales and being a charge to which this section applies is, so far as any security on the limited liability partnership's property or undertaking is conferred by the charge, void against the liquidator or administrator and any creditor of the limited liability partnership, unless the prescribed particulars of the charge together with the instrument (if any) by which the charge is created or evidenced, are delivered to or received by the registrar of companies for registration in the manner required by this Chapter within 21 days after the date of the charge's creation.

(2)   Subsection (1) is without prejudice to any contract or obligation for repayment of the money secured by the charge; and when a charge becomes void under this section, the money secured by it immediately becomes payable.

396 Charges which have to be registered

(1)   Section 395 applies to the following charges–
  (a)   a charge for the purpose of securing any issue of debentures,
  (b)   …
  (c)   a charge created or evidenced by an instrument which, if executed by an individual, would require registration as a bill of sale,
  (d)   a charge on land (wherever situated) or any interest in it, but not including a charge for any rent or other periodical sum issuing out of the land,
  (e)   a charge on book debts of the limited liability partnership,
  (f)   a floating charge on the limited liability partnership's undertaking or property,
  (g)   …
  (h)   a charge on a ship or aircraft, or any share in a ship,
  (j)   a charge on goodwill, or on any intellectual property.

(2)   Where a negotiable instrument has been given to secure the payment of any book debts of a limited liability partnership, the deposit of the instrument for the purpose of securing an advance to the limited liability partnership is not, for purposes of sections 395, to be treated as a charge on those book debts.

(3)   The holding of debentures entitling the holder to a charge on land is not for purposes of this section deemed to be an interest in land.

(3A)   The following are "intellectual property" for the purposes of this section–
(a)   any patent, trade mark, registered design, copyright or design right;
(b)   any licence under or in respect of any such right.

(4)   In this Chapter, "charge" includes mortgage.

397 Formalities of registration (debentures)

(1)   Where a series of debentures containing, or giving by reference to another instrument, any charge to the benefit of which the debenture holders of that series are entitled pari passu is created by a limited liability partnership, it is for purposes of section 395 sufficient if there are delivered to or received by the registrar, within 21 days after the execution of the deed containing the charge (or, if there is no such deed, after the execution of any debentures of the series), the following particulars in the prescribed form–
(a)   the total amount secured by the whole series, and
(b)   the dates of the [determinations of the limited liability partnership] authorising the issue of the series and the date of the covering deed (if any) by which the security is created or defined, and
(c)   a general description of the property charged, and
(d)   the names of the trustees (if any) for the debenture holders,
together with the deed containing the charge or, if there is no such deed, one of the debentures of the series:
Provided that there shall be sent to the registrar of companies, for entry in the register, particulars in the prescribed form of the date and amount of each issue of debentures of the series, but any omission to do this does not affect the validity of any of those debentures.

(2)   Where any commission, allowance or discount has been paid or made either directly or indirectly by a limited liability partnership to a person in consideration of his–
(a)   subscribing or agreeing to subscribe, whether absolutely or conditionally, for debentures of the limited liability partnership, or
(b)   procuring or agreeing to procure subscriptions, whether absolute or conditional, for such debentures,
the particulars required to be sent for registration under section 395 shall include particulars as to the amount or rate per cent of the commission, discount or allowance so paid or made, but omission to do this does not affect the validity of the debentures issued.

(3)   The deposit of debentures as security for a debt of the limited liability partnership is not, for the purposes of subsection (2), treated as the issue of the debentures at a discount.

398 Verification of charge on property outside United Kingdom

(1)   In the case of a charge created out of the United Kingdom comprising property situated outside the United Kingdom, the delivery to and the receipt by the registrar of companies of a copy (verified in the prescribed manner) of the instrument by which the charge is created or evidenced has the same effect for purposes of sections 395 to 398 as the delivery and receipt of the instrument itself.

(2)   In that case, 21 days after the date on which the instrument or copy could, in due course of post (and if despatched with due diligence), have been received in the United Kingdom are substituted for the 21 days mentioned in section 395(2) (or as the case may be, section 397(1)) as the time within which the particulars and instrument or copy are to be delivered to the registrar.

(3)   Where a charge is created in the United Kingdom but comprises property outside the United Kingdom, the instrument creating or purporting to create the charge may be sent for registration under section 395 notwithstanding that further proceedings may be necessary to make the charge valid or effectual according to the law of the country in which the property is situated.

(4)   Where a charge comprises property situated in Scotland or Northern Ireland and registration in the country where the property is situated is necessary to make the charge valid or effectual according to the law of that country, the delivery to and receipt by the registrar of a copy (verified in the prescribed manner) of the instrument by which the charge is created or evidenced, together with a certificate in the prescribed form stating that the charge was presented for registration in Scotland or Northern Ireland (as the case may be) on the date on which it was so presented has, for purposes of sections 395 to 398, the same effect as the delivery and receipt of the instrument itself.

399 Limited liability partnership's duty to register charges it creates

(1)   It is a limited liability partnership's duty to send to the registrar of companies for registration the particulars of every charge created by the limited liability partnership and of the issues of debentures of a series requiring registration under sections 395 to 398; but registration of any such charge may be effected on the application of any person interested in it.

(2)   Where registration is effected on the application of some person other than the limited liability partnership, that person is entitled to recover from the limited liability partnership the amount of any fees properly paid by him to the registrar on the registration.

(3)   If a limited liability partnership fails to comply with subsection (1), then, unless the registration has been effected on the application of some other person, the limited liability partnership and every member of it who is in default is liable to a fine and, for continued contravention, to a daily default fine.

400 Charges existing on property acquired

(1)   This section applies where a limited liability partnership registered in England and Wales acquires property which is subject to a charge of any such kind as would, if it had been created by the limited liability partnership after the acquisition of the property, have been required to be registered under this Chapter.

(2)   The limited liability partnership shall cause the prescribed particulars of the charge, together with a copy (certified in the prescribed manner to be a correct copy) of the instrument (if any) by which the charge was created or is evidenced, to be delivered to the registrar of companies for registration in manner required by this Chapter within 21 days after the date on which the acquisition is completed.

(3)   However, if the property is situated and the charge was created outside Great Britain, 21 days after the date on which the copy of the instrument could in due course of post, and if despatched with due diligence, have been received in the United Kingdom is substituted for the 21 days above-mentioned as the time within which the particulars and copy of the instrument are to be delivered to the registrar.

(4)   If default is made in complying with this section, the limited liability partnership and every member of it who is in default is liable to a fine and, for continued contravention, to a daily default fine.

401 Register of charges to be kept by registrar of companies

(1)   The registrar of companies shall keep, with respect to each limited liability partnership, a register in the prescribed form of all the charges requiring registration under this Chapter; and he shall enter in the register with respect to such charges the following particulars–
   (a) in the case of a charge to the benefit of which the holders of a series of debentures are entitled, the particulars specified in section 397(1),
   (b) in the case of any other charge–
      (i)   if it is a charge created by the limited liability partnership, the date of its creation, and if it is a charge which was existing on property acquired by the limited liability partnership, the date of the acquisition of the property, and
      (ii) the amount secured by the charge, and
      (iii) short particulars of the property charged, and
      (iv) the persons entitled to the charge.

(2)   The registrar shall give a certificate of the registration of any charge registered in pursuance of this Chapter, stating the amount secured by the charge.
   The certificate–
   (a) shall be either signed by the registrar, or authenticated by his official seal, and
   (b) is conclusive evidence that the requirements of this Chapter as to registration have been satisfied.

(3)   The register kept in pursuance of this section shall be open to inspection by any person.

402 Endorsement of certificate on debentures

(1)   The limited liability partnership shall cause a copy of every certificate of registration given under section 401 to be endorsed on every debenture or certificate of debenture stock which is issued by the limited liability partnership, and the payment of which is secured by the charge so registered.

(2)   But this does not require a limited liability partnership to cause a certificate of registration of any charge so given to be endorsed on any debenture or certificate of debenture stock issued by the limited liability partnership before the charge was created.

(3)   If a person knowingly and wilfully authorises or permits the delivery of a debenture or certificate of debenture stock which under this section is required to have endorsed on it a copy of a certificate of registration, without the copy being so endorsed upon it, he is liable (without prejudice to any other liability) to a fine.

403 Entries of satisfaction and release

(1)   Subject to subsection (1A), the registrar of companies, on receipt of a statutory declaration in the prescribed form verifying, with respect to a registered charge,–
    (a)   that the debt for which the charge was given has been paid or satisfied in whole or in part, or
    (b)   that part of the property or undertaking charged has been released from the charge or has ceased to form part of the limited liability partnership's property or undertaking,
may enter on the register a memorandum of satisfaction in whole or in part, or of the fact that part of the property or undertaking has been released from the charge or has ceased to form part of the limited liability partnership's property or undertaking (as the case may be).

(1A)   The registrar of companies may make any such entry as is mentioned in subsection (1) where, instead of receiving such a statutory declaration as is mentioned in that subsection, he receives a statement by a director, secretary, administrator or administrative receiver of the company [or designated member, administrator or administrative receiver of the limited liability partnership] which is contained in an electronic communication and that statement–
    (a)   verifies the matters set out in paragraph (a) or (b) of that subsection,
    (b)   contains a description of the charge,
    (c)   states the date of creation of the charge and the date of its registration under this Chapter,
    (d)   states the name and address of the chargee or, in the case of a debenture, trustee, and
    (e)   where paragraph (b) of subsection (1) applies, contains short particulars of the property or undertaking which has been released from the charge, or which has ceased to form part of the limited liability partnership's property or undertaking (as the case may be).

(2)   Where the registrar enters a memorandum of satisfaction in whole, he shall if required furnish the limited liability partnership with a copy of it.

(2A)   Any person who makes a false statement under subsection (1A) which he knows to be false or does not believe to be true is liable to imprisonment or a fine, or both.

404 Rectification of register of charges

(1)   The following applies if the court is satisfied that the omission to register a charge within the time required by this Chapter or that the omission or mis-statement of any particular with respect to any such charge or in a memorandum of satisfaction was accidental, or due to inadvertence or to some other sufficient cause, or is not of a nature to prejudice the position of creditors … of the limited liability partnership, or that on other grounds it is just and equitable to grant relief.

(2)   The court may, on the application of the limited liability partnership or a person interested, and on such terms and conditions as seem to the court just and expedient, order that the time for registration shall be extended or, as the case may be, that the omission or mis-statement shall be rectified.

405 Registration of enforcement of security

(1)   If a person obtains an order for the appointment of a receiver or manager of a limited liability partnership's property, or appoints such a receiver or manager under powers contained in an instrument, he shall within seven days of the order or of the appointment under those powers, give notice of the fact to the registrar of companies; and the registrar shall enter the fact in the register of charges.

(2)   Where a person appointed receiver or manager of a limited liability partnership's property under powers contained in an instrument ceases to act as such receiver or manager, he shall, on so ceasing, give the registrar notice to that effect, and the registrar shall enter the fact in the register of charges.

(3)   A notice under this section shall be in the prescribed form.

(4)   If a person makes default in complying with the requirements of this section, he is liable to a fine and, for continued contravention, to a daily default fine.

406 Limited liability partnerships to keep copies of instruments creating charges

(1)   Every limited liability partnership shall cause a copy of every instrument creating a charge requiring registration under this Chapter to be kept at its registered office.

(2)   In the case of a series of uniform debentures, a copy of one debenture of the series is sufficient.

407 Limited liability partnership's register of charges

(1)   Every [company (including limited liability partnership)] shall keep at its registered office a register of charges and enter in it all charges specifically affecting property of the limited liability partnership and all floating charges on the limited liability partnership's undertaking or any of its property.

(2)   The entry shall in each case give a short description of the property charged, the amount of the charge and, except in the case of securities to bearer, the names of the persons entitled to it.

(3)   If a member of the limited liability partnership knowingly and wilfully authorises or permits the omission of an entry required to be made in pursuance of this section, he is liable to a fine.

408 Right to inspect instruments which create charges, etc

(1)   The copies of instruments creating any charge requiring registration under this Chapter with the registrar of companies, and the register of charges kept in pursuance of section 407, shall be open during business hours (but subject to such reasonable restrictions as the limited liability partnership … may impose, so that not less than two hours in each day be allowed for inspection) to the inspection of any creditor or member of the limited liability partnership without fee.

(2)   The register of charges shall also be open to the inspection of any other person on payment of such fee, not exceeding 5 pence, for each inspection, as the limited liability partnership may prescribe.

(3)   If inspection of the copies referred to, or of the register, is refused, every member of the limited liability partnership who is in default is liable to a fine.

(4)   If such a refusal occurs in relation to a limited liability partnership registered in England and Wales, the court may by order compel an immediate inspection of the copies or register.

409

CHAPTER II
REGISTRATION OF CHARGES (SCOTLAND)

410 Charges void unless registered

(1)   The following provisions of this Chapter have effect for the purpose of securing the registration in Scotland of charges created by limited liability partnerships.

(2)   Every charge created by a limited liability partnership, being a charge to which this section applies, is, so far as any security on the limited liability partnership's property or any part of it is conferred by the charge, void against the

liquidator or administrator and any creditor of the limited liability partnership unless the prescribed particulars of the charge, together with a copy (certified in the prescribed manner to be a correct copy) of the instrument (if any) by which the charge is created or evidenced, are delivered to or received by the registrar of companies for registration in the manner required by this Chapter within 21 days after the date of the creation of the charge.

(3)   Subsection (2) is without prejudice to any contract or obligation for repayment of the money secured by the charge; and when a charge becomes void under this section the money secured by it immediately becomes payable.

(4)   This section applies to the following charges–
(a)   a charge on land wherever situated, or any interest in such land (not including a charge for any rent, ground annual or other periodical sum payable in respect of the land, but including a charge created by a heritable security within the meaning of section 9(8) of the Conveyancing and Feudal Reform (Scotland) Act 1970),
(b)   ...
(c)   a security over incorporeal moveable property of any of the following categories–
(i)   the book debts of the limited liability partnership,
(ii)   ...
(iii)   goodwill,
(iv)   a patent or a licence under a patent,
(v)   a trade mark,
(vi)   a copyright or a licence under a copyright,
(vii) a registered design or a licence in respect of such a design,
(viii)   a design right or a licence under a design right,
(d)   a security over a ship or aircraft or any share in a ship, and
(e)   a floating charge.

(5)   In this Chapter "limited liability partnership" ... means [a limited liability partnership] registered in Scotland; "registrar of companies" means the registrar or other officer performing under this Act the duty of registration of limited liability partnerships in Scotland; and references to the date of creation of a charge are–
(a)   in the case of a floating charge, the date on which the instrument creating the floating charge was executed by the limited liability partnership creating the charge, and
(b)   in any other case, the date on which the right of the person entitled to the benefit of the charge was constituted as a real right.

411 Charges on property outside United Kingdom

(1)   In the case of a charge created out of the United Kingdom comprising property situated outside the United Kingdom, the period of 21 days after the date on which the copy of the instrument creating it could (in due course of post, and if despatched with due diligence) have been received in the United Kingdom is substituted for the period of 21 days after the date of the creation of the charge

as the time within which, under section 410(2), the particulars and copy are to be delivered to the registrar.

(2)   Where a charge is created in the United Kingdom but comprises property outside the United Kingdom, the copy of the instrument creating or purporting to create the charge may be sent for registration under section 410 notwithstanding that further proceedings may be necessary to make the charge valid or effectual according to the law of the country in which the property is situated.

412 Negotiable instrument to secure book debts

Where a negotiable instrument has been given to secure the payment of any book debts of a limited liability partnership, the deposit of the instrument for the purpose of securing an advance to the limited liability partnership is not, for purposes of section 410, to be treated as a charge on those book debts.

(1)   The copies and the register referred to in section 411 shall be open to the inspection of any creditor or member of the limited liability partnership without fee; and to the inspection of any other person on payment of such fee as may be prescribed.

(2)   Any person may request the limited liability partnership to provide him with a copy of–
    (a) any instrument creating or evidencing a charge over the limited liability partnership's property, or
    (b) any entry in the register of charges kept by the limited liability partnership, on payment of such fee as may be prescribed.
This subsection applies to any charge, whether or not particulars are required to be delivered to the registrar for registration.

(3)   The limited liability partnership shall send the copy to him not later than ten days after the day on which the request is received or, if later, on which payment is received.

(4)   If inspection of the copies or register is refused, or a copy requested is not sent within the time specified above–
    (a) the limited liability partnership and every member of it who is in default is liable to a fine, and
    (b) the court may by order compel an immediate inspection of the copies or register or, as the case may be, direct that the copy be sent immediately.

413 Charges associated with debentures

(1)   The holding of debentures entitling the holder to a charge on land is not, for the purposes of section 410, deemed to be an interest in land.

(2)   Where a series of debentures containing, or giving by reference to any other instrument, any charge to the benefit of which the debenture holders of

that series are entitled pari passu, is created by a limited liability partnership, it is sufficient for purposes of section 410 if there are delivered to or received by the registrar of companies within 21 days after the execution of the deed containing the charge or if there is no such deed, after the execution of any debentures of the series, the following particulars in the prescribed form–

    (a) the total amount secured by the whole series,

    (b) the dates of the [determinations of the limited liability partnership] authorising the issue of the series and the date of the covering deed (if any) by which the security is created or defined,

    (c) a general description of the property charged,

    (d) the names of the trustees (if any) for the debenture holders, and

    (e) in the case of a floating charge, a statement of any provisions of the charge and of any instrument relating to it which prohibit or restrict or regulate the power of the limited liability partnership to grant further securities ranking in priority to, or pari passu with, the floating charge, or which vary or otherwise regulate the order of ranking of the floating charge in relation to subsisting securities,

together with a copy of the deed containing the charge or, if there is no such deed, of one of the debentures of the series:

Provided that where more than one issue is made of debentures in the series, there shall be sent to the registrar of companies for entry in the register particulars (in the prescribed form) of the date and amount of each issue of debentures of the series, but any omission to do this does not affect the validity of any of those debentures.

(3)   Where any commission, allowance or discount has been paid or made, either directly or indirectly, by a limited liability partnership to any person in consideration of his subscribing or agreeing to subscribe, whether absolutely or conditionally, for any debentures of the limited liability partnership, or procuring or agreeing to procure subscriptions (whether absolute or conditional) for any such debentures, the particulars required to be sent for registration under section 410 include particulars as to the amount or rate per cent of the commission, discount or allowance so paid or made; but any omission to do this does not affect the validity of the debentures issued.

The deposit of any debentures as security for any debt of the limited liability partnership is not, for purposes of this subsection, treated as the issue of the debentures at a discount.

414 Charge by way of ex facie absolute disposition, etc

(1)   For the avoidance of doubt, it is hereby declared that, in the case of a charge created by way of an ex facie absolute disposition or assignation qualified by a back letter or other agreement, or by a standard security qualified by an agreement, compliance with section 410(2) does not of itself render the charge unavailable as security for indebtedness incurred after the date of compliance.

(2)   Where the amount secured by a charge so created is purported to be increased by a further back letter or agreement, a further charge is held to have been created by the ex facie absolute disposition or assignation or (as the case

may be) by the standard security, as qualified by the further back letter or agreement; and the provisions of this Chapter apply to the further charge as if–

> (a) references in this Chapter (other than in this section) to the charge were references to the further charge, and
>
> (b) references to the date of the creation of the charge were references to the date on which the further back letter or agreement was executed.

415 Limited liability partnership's duty to register charges created by it

(1) It is a limited liability partnership's duty to send to the registrar of companies for registration the particulars of every charge created by the limited liability partnership and of the issues of debentures of a series requiring registration under sections 410 to 414; but registration of any such charge may be effected on the application of any person interested in it.

(2) Where registration is effected on the application of some person other than the limited liability partnership, that person is entitled to recover from the limited liability partnership the amount of any fees properly paid by him to the registrar on the registration.

(3) If a limited liability partnership makes default in sending to the registrar for registration the particulars of any charge created by the limited liability partnership or of the issues of debentures of a series requiring registration as above mentioned, then, unless the registration has been effected on the application of some other person, the limited liability partnership and every member of it who is in default is liable to a fine and, for continued contravention, a daily default fine.

416 Duty to register charges existing on property acquired

(1) Where a limited liability partnership acquires any property which is subject to a charge of any kind as would, if it had been created by the limited liability partnership after the acquisition of the property, have been required to be registered under this Chapter, the limited liability partnership shall cause the prescribed particulars of the charge, together with a copy (certified in the prescribed manner to be a correct copy) of the instrument (if any) by which the charge was created or is evidenced, to be delivered to the registrar of companies for registration in the manner required by this Chapter within 21 days after the date on which the transaction was settled.

(2) If, however, the property is situated and the charge was created outside Great Britain, 21 days after the date on which the copy of the instrument could (in due course of post, and if despatched with due diligence) have been received in the United Kingdom are substituted for 21 days after the settlement of the transaction as the time within which the particulars and the copy of the instrument are to be delivered to the registrar.

(3) If default is made in complying with this section, the limited liability partnership and every member of it who is in default is liable to a fine.

417 Register of charges to be kept by registrar of companies

(1) The registrar of companies shall keep, with respect to each limited liability partnership, a register in the prescribed form of all the charges requiring registration under this Chapter, and shall enter in the register with respect to such charges the particulars specified below.

(2) In the case of a charge to the benefit of which the holders of a series of debentures are entitled, there shall be entered in the register the particulars specified in section 413(2).

(3) In the case of any other charge there shall be entered–
  (a) if it is a charge created by the limited liability partnership, the date of its creation, and if it was a charge existing on property acquired by the limited liability partnership, the date of the acquisition of the property,
  (b) the amount secured by the charge,
  (c) short particulars of the property charged,
  (d) the persons entitled to the charge, and
  (e) in the case of a floating charge, a statement of any of the provisions of the charge and of any instrument relating to it which prohibit or restrict or regulate the limited liability partnership's power to grant further securities ranking in priority to, or pari passu with, the floating charge, or which vary or otherwise regulate the order of ranking of the floating charge in relation to subsisting securities.

(4) The register kept in pursuance of this section shall be open to inspection by any person.

418 Certificate of registration to be issued

(1) The registrar of companies shall give a certificate of the registration of any charge registered in pursuance of this Chapter.

(2) The certificate–
  (a) shall be either signed by the registrar, or authenticated by his official seal,
  (b) shall state the name of the limited liability partnership and the person first-named in the charge among those entitled to the benefit of the charge (or, in the case of a series of debentures, the name of the holder of the first such debenture to be issued) and the amount secured by the charge, and
  (c) is conclusive evidence that the requirements of this Chapter as to registration have been complied with.

419 Entries of satisfaction and relief

(1) Subject to subsections (1A) and (1B), the registrar of companies, on application being made to him in the prescribed form, and on receipt of a statutory declaration in the prescribed form verifying, with respect to any registered charge–

289

(a)   that the debt for which the charge was given has been paid or satisfied in whole or in part, or

(b)   that part of the property charged has been released from the charge or has ceased to form part of the limited liability partnership's property,

may enter on the register a memorandum of satisfaction (in whole or in part) regarding that fact.

(1A)   On an application being made to him in the prescribed form, the registrar of companies may make any such entry as is mentioned in subsection (1) where, instead of receiving such a statutory declaration as is mentioned in that subsection, he receives a statement by a director, secretary, liquidator, receiver or administrator of the company [or a designated member, liquidator, receiver or administrative receiver of the limited liability partnership] which is contained in an electronic communication and that statement–

(a)   verifies the matters set out in paragraph (a) or (b) of that subsection,

(b)   contains a description of the charge,

(c)   states the date of creation of the charge and the date of its registration under this Chapter,

(d)   states the name and address of the chargee or, in the case of a debenture, trustee, and

(e)   where paragraph (b) of subsection (1) applies, contains short particulars of the property which has been released from the charge, or which has ceased to form part of the limited liability partnership's property (as the case may be).

(1B)   Where the statement under subsection (1A) concerns the satisfaction of a floating charge, then there shall be delivered to the registrar a further statement which–

(a)   is made by the creditor entitled to the benefit of the floating charge or a person authorised to act on his behalf;

(b)   is incorporated into, or logically associated with, the electronic communication containing the statement; and

(c)   certifies that the particulars contained in the statement are correct.

(2)   Where the registrar enters a memorandum of satisfaction in whole, he shall, if required, furnish the limited liability partnership with a copy of the memorandum.

(3)   Without prejudice to the registrar's duty under this section to require to be satisfied as above mentioned, he shall not be so satisfied unless–

(a)   the creditor entitled to the benefit of the floating charge, or a person authorised to do so on his behalf, certifies as correct the particulars submitted to the registrar with respect to the entry on the register of a memorandum under this section, or

(b)   the court, on being satisfied that such certification cannot readily be obtained, directs him accordingly.

(4)   Nothing in this section requires the limited liability partnership to submit particulars with respect to the entry in the register of a memorandum of

satisfaction where the limited liability partnership, having created a floating charge over all or any part of its property, disposes of part of the property subject to the floating charge.

(5)   A memorandum or certification required for the purposes of this section shall be in such form as may be prescribed.

(5A)   Any person who makes a false statement under subsection (1A) or (1B) which he knows to be false or does not believe to be true is liable to imprisonment or a fine, or both.

420 Rectification of register

The court, on being satisfied that the omission to register a charge within the time required by this Act or that the omission or mis-statement of any particular with respect to any such charge or in a memorandum of satisfaction was accidental, or due to inadvertence or to some other sufficient cause, or is not of a nature to prejudice the position of creditors ... of the limited liability partnership, or that it is on other grounds just and equitable to grant relief, may, on the application of the limited liability partnership or any person interested, and on such terms and conditions as seem to the court just and expedient, order that the time for registration shall be extended or (as the case may be) that the omission or mis-statement shall be rectified.

421 Copies of instruments creating charges to be kept by limited liability partnership

(1)   Every limited liability partnership shall cause a copy of every instrument creating a charge requiring registration under this Chapter to be kept at the limited liability partnership's registered office.

(2)   In the case of a series of uniform debentures, a copy of one debenture of the series is sufficient.

422 Limited liability partnership's register of charges

(1)   Every limited liability partnership shall keep at its registered office a register of charges and enter in it all charges specifically affecting property of the limited liability partnership, and all floating charges on any property of the limited liability partnership.

(2)   There shall be given in each case a short description of the property charged, the amount of the charge and, except in the case of securities to bearer, the names of the persons entitled to it.

(3)   If a member of the limited liability partnership knowingly and wilfully authorises or permits the omission of an entry required to be made in pursuance of this section, he is liable to a fine.

423 Right to inspect copies of instruments, and limited liability partnership's register

(1)   The copies of instruments creating charges requiring registration under this Chapter with the registrar of companies, and the register of charges kept in pursuance of section 422, shall be open during business hours (but subject to such reasonable restrictions as the limited liability partnership … may impose, so that not less than two hours in each day be allowed for inspection) to the inspection of any creditor or member of the limited liability partnership without fee.

(2)   The register of charges shall be open to the inspection of any other person on payment of such fee, not exceeding 5 pence for each inspection, as the limited liability partnership may prescribe.

(3)   If inspection of the copies or register is refused, every member of the limited liability partnership who is in default is liable to a fine.

(4)   If such a refusal occurs in relation to a limited liability partnership, the court may by order compel an immediate inspection of the copies or register.

424

PART XIII
ARRANGEMENTS AND RECONSTRUCTIONS

425 Power of limited liability partnership to compromise with creditors and members

(1)   Where a compromise or arrangement is proposed between a limited liability partnership and its creditors, or any class of them, or between the limited liability partnership and its members, or any class of them, the court may on the application of the limited liability partnership or any creditor or member of it, or in the case of a limited liability partnership being wound up or an administration order being in force in relation to a limited liability partnership, of the liquidator or administrator, order a meeting of the creditors or class of creditors, or of the members of the limited liability partnership or class of members (as the case may be), to be summoned in such manner as the court directs.

(2)   If a majority in number representing three-fourths in value of the creditors or class of creditors or members or class of members (as the case may be), present and voting either in person or by proxy at the meeting, agree to any compromise or arrangement, the compromise or arrangement, if sanctioned by the court, is binding on all creditors or the class of creditors or on the members or class of members (as the case may be), and also on the limited liability partnership or, in the case of a limited liability partnership in the course of being wound up, on the liquidator and contributories of the limited liability partnership.

(3)   The court's order under subsection (2) has no effect until an office copy of it has been delivered to the registrar of companies for registration …

(4)   If a limited liability partnership makes default in complying with subsection (3), the limited liability partnership and every member of it who is in default is liable to a fine.

(5)   An order under subsection (1) pronounced in Scotland by the judge acting as vacation judge in pursuance of section 4 of the Administration of Justice (Scotland) Act 1933 is not subject to review, reduction, suspension or stay of execution.

(6)   ...

426 Information as to compromise to be circulated

(1)   The following applies where a meeting of creditors or any class of creditors, or of members or any class of members, is summoned under section 425.

(2)   With every notice summoning the meeting which is sent to a creditor or member there shall be sent also a statement explaining the effect of the compromise or arrangement and in particular stating any material interests of the members of the limited liability partnership (whether ... as members or as creditors of the limited liability partnership or otherwise) and the effect on those interests of the compromise or arrangement, in so far as it is different from the effect on the like interests of other persons.

(3)   In every notice summoning the meeting which is given by advertisement there shall be included either such a statement as above-mentioned or a notification of the place at which, and the manner in which, creditors or members entitled to attend the meeting may obtain copies of the statement.

(4)   Where the compromise or arrangement affects the rights of debenture holders of the limited liability partnership, the statement shall give the like explanation as respects the trustees of any deed for securing the issue of the debentures as it is required to give as respects the limited liability partnership's members.

(5)   Where a notice given by advertisement includes a notification that copies of a statement explaining the effect of the compromise or arrangement proposed can be obtained by creditors or members entitled to attend the meeting, every such creditor or member shall, on making application in the manner indicated by the notice, be furnished by the limited liability partnership free of charge with a copy of the statement.

(6)   If a limited liability partnership makes default in complying with any requirement of this section, the limited liability partnership and every member of it who is in default is liable to a fine; and for this purpose a liquidator or administrator of the limited liability partnership and a trustee of a deed for securing the issue of debentures of the limited liability partnership is deemed an member of it.
    However, a person is not liable under this subsection if he shows that the default was due to the refusal of another person, being a member or trustee for debenture holders, to supply the necessary particulars of his interests.

(7)   It is the duty of any member of the limited liability partnership, and of any trustee for its debenture holders, to give notice to the limited liability partnership of such matters relating to himself as may be necessary for purposes of this section; and any person who makes default in complying with this subsection is liable to a fine.

427 Provisions for facilitating limited liability partnership reconstruction or amalgamation

(1)   The following applies where application is made to the court under section 425 for the sanctioning of a compromise or arrangement proposed between a limited liability partnership and any such persons as are mentioned in that section.

(2)   If it is shown–
    (a)   that the compromise or arrangement has been proposed for the purposes of, or in connection with, a scheme for the reconstruction of any limited liability partnership or limited liability partnerships, or the amalgamation of any two or more limited liability partnerships, and
    (b)   that under the scheme the whole or any part of the undertaking or the property of any limited liability partnership concerned in the scheme ("a transferor limited liability partnership") is to be transferred to another limited liability partnership ("the transferee limited liability partnership"),
the court may, either by the order sanctioning the compromise or arrangement or by any subsequent order, make provision for all or any of the following matters.

(3)   The matters for which the court's order may make provision are–
    (a)   the transfer to the transferee limited liability partnership of the whole or any part of the undertaking and of the property or liabilities of any transferor limited liability partnership,
    (b)   the allotting or appropriation by the transferee limited liability partnership of any shares, debentures, [policies, other like interests or, in the case of a limited liability partnership, property or interests in the limited liability partnership] in that limited liability partnership which under the compromise or arrangement are to be allotted or appropriated by that limited liability partnership to or for any person,
    (c)   the continuation by or against the transferee limited liability partnership of any legal proceedings pending by or against any transferor limited liability partnership,
    (d)   the dissolution, without winding up, of any transferor limited liability partnership,
    (e)   the provision to be made for any persons who, within such time and in such manner as the court directs, dissent from the compromise or arrangement,
    (f)   such incidental, consequential and supplemental matters as are necessary to secure that the reconstruction or amalgamation is fully and effectively carried out.

(4)   If an order under this section provides for the transfer of property or liabilities, then–

(a) that property is by virtue of the order transferred to, and vests in, the transferee limited liability partnership, and

(b) those liabilities are, by virtue of the order, transferred to and become liabilities of that limited liability partnership;

and property (if the order so directs) vests freed from any charge which is by virtue of the compromise or arrangement to cease to have effect.

(5) Where an order is made under this section, every limited liability partnership in relation to which the order is made shall cause an office copy of the order to be delivered to the registrar of companies for registration within seven days after its making; and if default is made in complying with this subsection, the limited liability partnership and every member of it who is in default is liable to a fine and, for continued contravention, to a daily default fine.

(6) In this section the expression "property" includes property, rights and powers of every description; the expression "liabilities" includes duties and ["company" includes only a company as defined in section 735(1) or a limited liability partnership].

427A–430F

PART XIV
INVESTIGATION OF LIMITED LIABILITY PARTNERSHIPS AND THEIR AFFAIRS; REQUISITION OF DOCUMENTS

431 Investigation of a limited liability partnership on its own application or that of its members

(1) The Secretary of State may appoint one or more competent inspectors to investigate the affairs of a limited liability partnership and to report on them in such manner as he may direct.

[(2) The appointment may be made on the application of the limited liability partnership or on the application of not less than one-fifth in number of those who appear from notifications made to the registrar of companies to be currently members of the limited liability partnership.]

(3) The application shall be supported by such evidence as the Secretary of State may require for the purpose of showing that the applicant or applicants have good reason for requiring the investigation.

(4) The Secretary of State may, before appointing inspectors, require the applicant or applicants to give security, to an amount not exceeding £5,000, or such other sum as he may by order specify, for payment of the costs of the investigation.

An order under this subsection shall be made by statutory instrument subject to annulment in pursuance of a resolution of either House of Parliament.

432 Other limited liability partnership investigations

(1) The Secretary of State shall appoint one or more competent inspectors to investigate the affairs of a limited liability partnership and report on them in

such manner as he directs, if the court by order declares that its affairs ought to be so investigated.

(2)   The Secretary of State may make such an appointment if it appears to him that there are circumstances suggesting–
- (a)   that the limited liability partnership's affairs are being or have been conducted with intent to defraud its creditors or the creditors of any other person, or otherwise for a fraudulent or unlawful purpose, or in a manner which is unfairly prejudicial to some part of its members, or
- (b)   that any actual or proposed act or omission of the limited liability partnership (including an act or omission on its behalf) is or would be so prejudicial, or that the limited liability partnership was formed for any fraudulent or unlawful purpose, or
- (c)   that persons concerned with the limited liability partnership's formation or the management of its affairs have in connection therewith been guilty of fraud, misfeasance or other misconduct towards it or towards its members, or
- (d)   that the limited liability partnership's members have not been given all the information with respect to its affairs which they might reasonably expect.

(2A)   Inspectors may be appointed under subsection (2) on terms that any report they may make is not for publication; and in such a case, the provisions of section 437(3) (availability and publication of inspectors' reports) do not apply.

(3)   Subsections (1) and (2) are without prejudice to the powers of the Secretary of State under section 431; and the power conferred by subsection (2) is exercisable with respect to a body corporate notwithstanding that it is in course of being voluntarily wound up.

(4)   The reference in subsection (2)(a) to a limited liability partnership's members includes any person who is not a member [but to whom a member's share in the limited liability partnership has been transferred or transmitted by operation of law.]

433 Inspectors' powers during investigation

(1)   If inspectors appointed under section 431 or 432 to investigate the affairs of a limited liability partnership think it necessary for the purposes of their investigation to investigate also the affairs of another body corporate which is or at any relevant time has been the limited liability partnership's subsidiary or holding company, or a subsidiary of its holding company or a holding company of its subsidiary, they have power to do so; and they shall report on the affairs of the other body corporate so far as they think that the results of their investigation of its affairs are relevant to the investigation of the affairs of the limited liability partnership first mentioned above.

434 Production of documents and evidence to inspectors

(1)   When inspectors are appointed under section 431 or 432, it is the duty of all members and agents of the limited liability partnership, and of all officers

and agents of any other body corporate whose affairs are investigated under section 433(1)–

    (a)   to produce to the inspectors all documents of or relating to the limited liability partnership or, as the case may be, the other body corporate which are in their custody or power,

    (b)   to attend before the inspectors when required to do so, and

    (c)   otherwise to give the inspectors all assistance in connection with the investigation which they are reasonably able to give.

(2)   If the inspectors consider that an member or agent of the limited liability partnership or other body corporate, or any other person, is or may be in possession of information relating to a matter which they believe to be relevant to the investigation, they may require him–

    (a)   to produce to them any documents in his custody or power relating to that matter,

    (b)   to attend before them, and

    (c)   otherwise to give them all assistance in connection with the investigation which he is reasonably able to give;

and it is that person's duty to comply with the requirement.

(3)   An inspector may for the purposes of the investigation examine any person on oath, and may administer an oath accordingly.

(4)   In this section a reference to members or to agents includes past, as well as present, members or agents (as the case may be); and "agents", in relation to a limited liability partnership or other body corporate, includes its bankers and solicitors and persons employed by it as auditors, whether these persons are or are not members of the limited liability partnership or other body corporate.

(5)   An answer given by a person to a question put to him in exercise of powers conferred by this section (whether as it has effect in relation to an investigation under any of sections 431 to 433, or as applied by any other section in this Part) may be used in evidence against him.

(5A) However, in criminal proceedings in which that person is charged with an offence to which this subsection applies–

    (a)   no evidence relating to the answer may be adduced, and

    (b)   no question relating to it may be asked,

by or on behalf of the prosecution, unless evidence relating to it is adduced, or a question relating to it is asked, in the proceedings by or on behalf of that person.

(5B) Subsection (5A) applies to any offence other than–

    (a)   an offence under section 2 or 5 of the Perjury Act 1911 (false statements made on oath otherwise than in judicial proceedings or made otherwise than on oath); or

    (b)   an offence under section 44(1) or (2) of the Criminal Law (Consolidation)(Scotland) Act 1995 (false statements made on oath or otherwise than on oath).

(6)   In this section "documents" includes information recorded in any form; and, in relation to information recorded otherwise than in legible form, the power to require its production includes power to require the production of a copy of the information in legible form.

436 Obstruction of inspectors treated as contempt of court

(1)   If any person–
    (a)   fails to comply with section 434(1)(a) or (c),
    (b)   refuses to comply with a requirement under section 434(1)(b) or (2), or
    (c)   refuses to answer any question put to him by the inspectors for the purposes of the investigation,
the inspectors may certify that fact in writing to the court.

(3)   The court may thereupon enquire into the case; and, after hearing any witnesses who may be produced against or on behalf of the alleged offender and after hearing any statement which may be offered in defence, the court may punish the offender in like manner as if he had been guilty of contempt of the court.

437 Inspectors' reports

(1)   The inspectors may, and if so directed by the Secretary of State shall, make interim reports to the Secretary of State, and on the conclusion of their investigation shall make a final report to him.
Any such report shall be written or printed, as the Secretary of State directs.

(1A)   Any persons who have been appointed under section 431 or 432 may at any time and, if the Secretary of State directs them to do so, shall inform him of any matters coming to their knowledge as a result of their investigations.

(1B)   If it appears to the Secretary of State that matters have come to light in the course of the inspectors' investigation which suggest that a criminal offence has been committed, and those matters have been referred to the appropriate prosecuting authority, he may direct the inspectors to take no further steps in the investigation or to take only such further steps as are specified in the direction.

(1C)   Where an investigation is the subject of a direction under subsection (1B), the inspectors shall make a final report to the Secretary of State only where–
    (a)   they were appointed under section 432(1) (appointment in pursuance of an order of the court), or
    (b)   the Secretary of State directs them to do so.

(2)   If the inspectors were appointed under section 432 in pursuance of an order of the court, the Secretary of State shall furnish a copy of any report of theirs to the court.

(3)   In any case the Secretary of State may, if he thinks fit–
    (a)   forward a copy of any report made by the inspectors to the limited liability partnership's registered office,

(b) furnish a copy on request and on payment of the prescribed fee to–

    (i) any member of the limited liability partnership or other body corporate which is the subject of the report,

    (ii) any person whose conduct is referred to in the report,

    (iii) the auditors of that limited liability partnership or body corporate,

    (iv) the applicants for the investigation,

    (v) any other person whose financial interests appear to the Secretary of State to be affected by the matters dealt with in the report, whether as a creditor of the limited liability partnership or body corporate, or otherwise, and

(c) cause any such report to be printed and published.

438 Power to bring civil proceedings on limited liability partnership's behalf

(1) If from any report made or information obtained under this Part it appears to the Secretary of State that any civil proceedings ought in the public interest to be brought by any body corporate, he may himself bring such proceedings in the name and on behalf of the body corporate.

(2) The Secretary of State shall indemnify the body corporate against any costs or expenses incurred by it in or in connection with proceedings brought under this section.

439 Expenses of investigating a limited liability partnership's affairs

(1) The expenses of an investigation under any of the powers conferred by this Part shall be defrayed in the first instance by the Secretary of State, but he may recover those expenses from the persons liable in accordance with this section.

There shall be treated as expenses of the investigation, in particular, such reasonable sums as the Secretary of State may determine in respect of general staff costs and overheads.

(2) A person who is convicted on a prosecution instituted as a result of the investigation, or is ordered to pay the whole or any part of the costs of proceedings brought under section 438, may in the same proceedings be ordered to pay those expenses to such extent as may be specified in the order.

(3) A body corporate in whose name proceedings are brought under that section is liable to the amount or value of any sums or property recovered by it as a result of those proceedings; and any amount for which a body corporate is liable under this subsection is a first charge on the sums or property recovered.

(4) A body corporate dealt with by an inspector's report, where the inspectors were appointed otherwise than of the Secretary of State's own motion, is liable except where it was the applicant for the investigation, and except so far as the Secretary of State otherwise directs.

(5)   Where inspectors were appointed–
    (a)   under section 431, …
    (b)   …
the applicant or applicants for the investigation is or are liable to such extent (if any) as the Secretary of State may direct.

(6)   The report of inspectors appointed otherwise than of the Secretary of State's own motion may, if they think fit, and shall if the Secretary of State so directs, include a recommendation as to the directions (if any) which they think appropriate, in the light of their investigation, to be given under subsection (4) or (5) of this section.

(7)   For purposes of this section, any costs or expenses incurred by the Secretary of State in or in connection with proceedings brought under section 438 (including expenses incurred under subsection (2) of it) are to be treated as expenses of the investigation giving rise to the proceedings.

(8)   Any liability to repay the Secretary of State imposed by subsections (2) and (3) above is (subject to satisfaction of his right to repayment) a liability also to indemnify all persons against liability under subsections (4) and (5); and any such liability imposed by subsection (2) is (subject as mentioned above) a liability also to indemnify all persons against liability under subsection (3).

(9)   A person liable under any one of those subsections is entitled to contribution from any other person liable under the same subsection, according to the amount of their respective liabilities under it.

(10)   Expenses to be defrayed by the Secretary of State under this section shall, so far as not recovered under it, be paid out of money provided by Parliament.

441 Inspectors' report to be evidence

(1)   A copy of any report of inspectors appointed under this Part, certified by the Secretary of State to be a true copy, is admissible in any legal proceedings as evidence of the opinion of the inspectors in relation to any matter contained in the report and, in proceedings on an application under section 8 of the Company Directors Disqualification Act 1986, as evidence of any fact stated therein.

(2)   A document purporting to be such a certificate as is mentioned above shall be received in evidence and be deemed to be such a certificate, unless the contrary is proved.

442–446

447 Secretary of State's power to require production of documents

(2)   The Secretary of State may at any time, if he thinks there is good reason to do so, give directions to a limited liability partnership requiring it, at such time and place as may be specified in the directions, to produce such documents as may be so specified.

(3)   The Secretary of State may at any time, if he thinks there is good reason to do so, authorise an officer of his or any other competent person, on producing (if so required) evidence of his authority, to require a limited liability partnership to produce to him (the officer or other person) forthwith any documents which he (the officer or other person) may specify.

(4)   Where by virtue of subsection (2) or (3) the Secretary of State or an officer of his or other person has power to require the production of documents from a limited liability partnership, he or the officer or other person has the like power to require production of those documents from any person who appears to him or the officer to be in possession of them; but where any such person claims a lien on documents produced by him, the production is without prejudice to the lien.

(5)   The power under this section to require a limited liability partnership or other person to produce documents includes power–
    (a) if the documents are produced–
        (i) to take copies of them or extracts from them, and
        (ii) to require that person, or any other person who is a present or past member of, or is or was at any time employed by, the limited liability partnership in question, to provide an explanation of any of them;
    (b) if the documents are not produced, to require the person who was required to produce them to state, to the best of his knowledge and belief, where they are.

(6)   If the requirement to produce documents or provide an explanation or make a statement is not complied with, the limited liability partnership or other person on whom the requirement was so imposed is guilty of an offence and liable to a fine.
    Sections 732 (restriction on prosecutions), 733 (liability of individuals for corporate default) and 734 (criminal proceedings against unincorporated bodies) apply to this offence.

(7)   However, where a person is charged with an offence under subsection (6) in respect of a requirement to produce any documents, it is a defence to prove that they were not in his possession or under his control and that it was not reasonably practicable for him to comply with the requirement.

(8)   A statement made by a person in compliance with such a requirement may be used in evidence against him.

(8A) However, in criminal proceedings in which that person is charged with an offence to which this subsection applies–
    (a) no evidence relating to the statement may be adduced, and
    (b) no question relating to it may be asked,
by or on behalf of the prosecution, unless evidence relating to it is adduced, or a question relating to it is asked, in the proceedings by or on behalf of that person.

(8B)   Subsection (8A) applies to any offence other than–
   (a)   an offence under subsection (6) or section 451;
   (b)   an offence under section 5 of the Perjury Act 1911 (false statements made otherwise than on oath); or
   (c)   an offence under section 44(2) of the Criminal Law (Consolidation)(Scotland) Act 1995 (false statements made otherwise than on oath).

(9)   In this section "documents" includes information recorded in any form; and, in relation to information recorded otherwise than in legible form, the power to require its production includes power to require the production of a copy of it in legible form.

448 Entry and search of premises

(1)   A justice of the peace may issue a warrant under this section if satisfied on information on oath given by or on behalf of the Secretary of State, or by a person appointed or authorised to exercise powers under this Part, that there are reasonable grounds for believing that there are on any premises documents whose production has been required under this Part and which have not been produced in compliance with the requirement.

(2)   A justice of the peace may also issue a warrant under this section if satisfied on information on oath given by or on behalf of the Secretary of State, or by a person appointed or authorised to exercise powers under this Part–
   (a)   that there are reasonable grounds for believing that an offence has been committed for which the penalty on conviction on indictment is imprisonment for a term of not less than two years and that there are on any premises documents relating to whether the offence has been committed,
   (b)   that the Secretary of State, or the person so appointed or authorised, has power to require the production of the documents under this Part, and
   (c)   that there are reasonable grounds for believing that if production was so required the documents would not be produced but would be removed from the premises, hidden, tampered with or destroyed.

(3)   A warrant under this section shall authorise a constable, together with any other person named in it and any other constables–
   (a)   to enter the premises specified in the information, using such force as is reasonably necessary for the purpose;
   (b)   to search the premises and take possession of any documents appearing to be such documents as are mentioned in subsection (1) or (2), as the case may be, or to take, in relation to any such documents, any other steps which may appear to be necessary for preserving them or preventing interference with them;
   (c)   to take copies of any such documents; and
   (d)   to require any person named in the warrant to provide an explanation of them or to state where they may be found.

(4)   If in the case of a warrant under subsection (2) the justice of the peace is satisfied on information on oath that there are reasonable grounds for believing that there are also on the premises other documents relevant to the investigation, the warrant shall also authorise the actions mentioned in subsection (3) to be taken in relation to such documents.

(5)   A warrant under this section shall continue in force until the end of the period of one month beginning with the day on which it is issued.

(6)   Any documents of which possession is taken under this section may be retained–
    (a) for a period of three months; or
    (b) if within that period proceedings to which the documents are relevant are commenced against any person for any criminal offence, until the conclusion of those proceedings.

(7)   Any person who intentionally obstructs the exercise of any rights conferred by a warrant issued under this section or fails without reasonable excuse to comply with any requirement imposed in accordance with subsection (3)(d) is guilty of an offence and liable to a fine.

    Sections 732 (restrictions on prosecutions), 733 (liability of individuals for corporate default) and 734 (criminal proceedings against unincorporated bodies) apply to this offence.

(8)   For the purposes of sections 449 and 451A (provision for security of information) documents obtained under this section shall be treated as if they had been obtained under the provision of this Part under which their production was or, as the case may be, could have been required.

(9)   In the application of this section to Scotland for the references to a justice of the peace substitute references to a justice of the peace or a sheriff, and for the references to information on oath substitute references to evidence on oath.

(10)   In this section "document" includes information recorded in any form.

449 Provision for security of information obtained

(1)   No information or document relating to a limited liability partnership which has been obtained under section 447 shall, without the previous consent in writing of that limited liability partnership, be published or disclosed, except to a competent authority, unless the publication or disclosure is required–
    (a) with a view to the institution of or otherwise for the purposes of criminal proceedings;
    (ba) with a view to the institution of, or otherwise for the purposes of, any proceedings on an application under section 6, 7 or 8 of the Company Directors Disqualification Act 1986;
    (c) for the purposes of enabling or assisting any inspector appointed under this Part, or under section 94 or 177 of the Financial Services Act 1986, to discharge his functions;

(cc) for the purpose of enabling or assisting any person authorised to exercise powers or appointed under section 43A or 44 of the Insurance Companies Act 1982, section 447 of this Act, section 106 of the Financial Services Act 1986 or section 84 of the Companies Act 1989 to discharge his functions;

(d) for the purpose of enabling or assisting the Secretary of State or the Treasury to exercise any of their functions, under this Act, the insider dealing legislation, *the Prevention of Fraud (Investments) Act 1958*, the Insurance Companies Act 1982, the Insolvency Act 1986, the Company Directors Disqualification Act 1986 , the Financial Services Act 1986 or Part II, III or VII of the Companies Act 1989,

(dd) for the purpose of enabling or assisting the Department of Economic Development for Northern Ireland to exercise any powers conferred on it by the enactments relating to companies or insolvency or for the purpose of enabling or assisting any inspector appointed by it under the enactments relating to companies to discharge his functions

(de) for the purpose of enabling or assisting the Chief Registrar of friendly societies or the Assistant Registrar of friendly societies for Scotland to discharge his functions under the enactments relating to friendly societies;

(df) for the purpose of enabling or assisting the Friendly Societies Commission to discharge its functions under the Financial Services Act 1986,

(dg) for the purpose of enabling or assisting the Occupational Pensions Regulatory Authority to discharge their functions under the Pension Schemes Act 1993 or the Pensions Act 1995 or any enactment in force in Northern Ireland corresponding to either of them,

(f) for the purpose of enabling or assisting the Bank of England to discharge its functions,

(fa) for the purpose of enabling or assisting the Financial Services Authority to discharge–
    (i) any functions under the Financial Services Act 1986, other than as a designated agency within the meaning of that Act,
    (ii) its functions under the Banking Act 1987, or
    (iii) its functions under section 171 of the Companies Act 1989,

(g) for the purpose of enabling or assisting the Deposit Protection Board to discharge its functions under that Act,

(h) for any purpose mentioned in section 180(1)(b),(e),(h),or (n) of the Financial Services Act 1986,

(hh) for the purpose of enabling or assisting a body established by order under section 46 of the Companies Act 1989 to discharge its functions under Part II of that Act, or of enabling or assisting a recognised supervisory or qualifying body within the meaning of that Part to discharge its functions as such;

(i) for the purpose of enabling or assisting the Friendly Societies Commission to discharge its functions under the enactments relating to industrial assurance,

(j) for the purpose of enabling or assisting the Insurance Brokers Registration Council to discharge its functions under the Insurance Brokers (Registration) Act 1977,

    (k) for the purpose of enabling or assisting an official receiver to discharge his functions under the enactments relating to insolvency or for the purpose of enabling or assisting a body which is for the time being a recognised professional body for the purposes of section 391 of the Insolvency Act 1986 to discharge its functions as such,

    (l) with a view to the institution of, or otherwise for the purposes of, any disciplinary proceedings relating to the exercise by a solicitor, auditor, accountant, valuer or actuary of his professional duties,

    (ll) with a view to the institution of, or otherwise for the purposes of, any disciplinary proceedings relating to the discharge by a public servant of his duties;

    (m) for the purpose of enabling or assisting an overseas regulatory authority to exercise its regulatory functions.

(1A) In subsection (1)–

    (a) in paragraph (ll) "public servant" means an officer or servant of the Crown or of any public or other authority for the time being designated for the purposes of that paragraph by the Secretary of State by order made by statutory instrument; and

    (b) in paragraph (m) "overseas regulatory authority" and "regulatory functions" have the same meaning as in section 82 of the Companies Act 1989.

(1B) Subject to subsection (1C), subsection (1) shall not preclude publication or disclosure for the purpose of enabling or assisting any public or other authority for the time being designated for the purposes of this subsection by the Secretary of State by an order in a statutory instrument to discharge any functions which are specified in the order.

(1C) An order under subsection (1B) designating an authority for the purpose of that subsection may–

    (a) impose conditions subject to which the publication or disclosure of any information or document is permitted by that subsection; and

    (b) otherwise restrict the circumstances in which that subsection permits publication or disclosure.

(1D) Subsection (1) shall not preclude the publication or disclosure of any such information as is mentioned in section 180(5) of the Financial Services Act 1986 by any person who by virtue of that section is not precluded by section 179 of that Act from disclosing it.

(2)   A person who publishes or discloses any information or document in contravention of this section is guilty of an offence and liable to imprisonment or a fine, or both.

Sections 732 (restriction on prosecutions), 733 (liability of individuals for corporate default) and 734 (criminal proceedings against unincorporated bodies) apply to this offence.

(3)   For the purposes of this section each of the following is a competent authority–

(a)   the Secretary of State,

(b) an inspector appointed under this Part or under section 94 or 177 of the Financial Services Act 1986,

(c) any person authorised to exercise powers under section 44 of the Insurance Companies Act 1982, section 447 of this Act, section 106 of the Financial Services Act 1986 or section 84 of the Companies Act 1989,

(d) the Department of Economic Development in Northern Ireland,

(e) the Treasury,

(f) the Bank of England,

(g) the Lord Advocate,

(h) the Director of Public Prosecutions, and the Director of Public Prosecutions for Northern Ireland,

(ha) the Financial Services Authority, other than in its capacity as a designated agency within the meaning of the Financial Services Act 1986,

(i) any designated agency or transferee body within the meaning of the Financial Services Act 1986, and any body administering a scheme under section 54 of or paragraph 18 of Schedule 11 to that Act (schemes for compensation of investors),

(j) the Chief Registrar of friendly societies,

(jj) the Friendly Societies Commission,

(k) the Friendly Societies Commission,

(l) any constable,

(m) any procurator fiscal,

(n) the Scottish Ministers.

(3A) Any information which may by virtue of this section be disclosed to a competent authority may be disclosed to any officer or servant of the authority.

(4) A statutory instrument containing an order under subsection (1A)(a) or (1B) is subject to annulment in pursuance of a resolution of either House of Parliament.

450 Punishment for destroying, mutilating etc limited liability partnership documents

(1) A member of a limited liability partnership … who–
(a) destroys, mutilates or falsifies, or is privy to the destruction, mutilation or falsification of a document affecting or relating to the limited liability partnership's property or affairs, or
(b) makes, or is privy to the making of, a false entry in such a document,
is guilty of an offence, unless he proves that he had no intention to conceal the state of affairs of the limited liability partnership or to defeat the law.

(2) Such a person as above mentioned who fraudulently either parts with, alters or makes an omission in any such document or is privy to fraudulent parting with, fraudulent altering or fraudulent making of an omission in, any such document, is guilty of an offence.

(3) A person guilty of an offence under this section is liable to imprisonment or a fine, or both.

(4)   Sections 732 (restriction on prosecutions), 733 (liability of individuals for corporate default) and 734 (criminal proceedings against unincorporated bodies) apply to an offence under this section.

(5)   In this section "document" includes information recorded in any form.

451 Punishment for furnishing false information

A person who, in purported compliance with a requirement imposed under section 447 to provide an explanation or make a statement, provides or makes an explanation or statement which he knows to be false in a material particular or recklessly provides or makes an explanation or statement which is so false, is guilty of an offence and liable to imprisonment or a fine, or both.

Sections 732 (restriction on prosecutions), 733 (liability of individuals for corporate default) and 734 (criminal proceedings against unincorporated bodies) apply to this offence.

451A Disclosure of information by Secretary of State or inspector

(1)   This section applies to information obtained under sections [434 to 441].

(2)   The Secretary of State may, if he thinks fit–
   (a)   disclose any information to which this section applies to any person to whom, or for any purpose for which, disclosure is permitted under section 449, or
   (b)   authorise or require an inspector appointed under this Part to disclose such information to any such person or for any such purpose.

(3)   Information to which this section applies may also be disclosed by an inspector appointed under this Part to–
   (a)   another inspector appointed under this Part or an inspector appointed under section 94 or 177 of the Financial Services Act 1986, or
   (b)   a person authorised to exercise powers or appointed under section 43A or 44 of the Insurance Companies Act 1982, section 447 of this Act, section 106 of the Financial Services Act 1986 or section 84 of the Companies Act 1989.

(4)   Any information which may by virtue of subsection (3) be disclosed to any person may be disclosed to any officer or servant of that person.

(5)   ...

452 Privileged information

(1)   Nothing in sections [431 to 441] requires the disclosure to the Secretary of State or to an inspector appointed by him–
   (a)   by any person of information which he would in an action in the High Court or the Court of Session be entitled to refuse to disclose on grounds of legal professional privilege except, if he is a lawyer, the name and address of his client,

(1A)   Nothing in [section 434] requires a person (except as mentioned in subsection (1B) below) to disclose information or produce documents in respect of which he owes an obligation of confidence by virtue of carrying on the business of banking unless–

(a)   the person to whom the obligation of confidence is owed is the limited liability partnership or other body corporate under investigation,

(b)   the person to whom the obligation of confidence is owed consents to the disclosure or production, or

(c)   the making of the requirement is authorised by the Secretary of State.

(1B)   Subsection (1A) does not apply where the person owing the obligation of confidence is the limited liability partnership or other body corporate under investigation under section 431, 432 or 433.

(2)   Nothing in sections 447 to 451 compels the production by any person of a document which he would in an action in the High Court or the Court of Session be entitled to refuse to produce on grounds of legal professional privilege, or authorises the taking of possession of any such document which is in the person's possession.

(3)   The Secretary of State shall not under section 447 require, or authorise an officer of his or other person to require, the production by a person carrying on the business of banking of a document relating to the affairs of a customer of his unless either it appears to the Secretary of State that it is necessary to do so for the purpose of investigating the affairs of the first-mentioned person, or the customer is a person on whom a requirement has been imposed under that section, or under section 43A or 44(2) to (4) of the Insurance Companies Act 1982 (provision corresponding to section 447).

453–457

PART XVI
FRAUDULENT TRADING BY A LIMITED LIABILITY PARTNERSHIP

458 Punishment for fraudulent trading

If any business of a limited liability partnership is carried on with intent to defraud creditors of the limited liability partnership or creditors of any other person, or for any fraudulent purpose, every person who was knowingly a party to the carrying on of the business in that manner is liable to imprisonment or a fine, or both.

This applies whether or not the limited liability partnership has been, or is in the course of being, wound up.

PART XVII
PROTECTION OF LIMITED LIABILITY PARTNERSHIP'S MEMBERS
AGAINST UNFAIR PREJUDICE

459 Order on application of limited liability partnership member

(1)   [Subject to subsection (1A)] a member of a limited liability partnership may apply to the court by petition for an order under this Part on the ground that

the limited liability partnership's affairs are being or have been conducted in a manner which is unfairly prejudicial to the interests of its members generally or of some part of its members (including at least himself) or that any actual or proposed act or omission of the limited liability partnership (including an act or omission on its behalf) is or would be so prejudicial.

[(1A) The members of a limited liability partnership may by unanimous agreement exclude the right contained in subsection 459(1) for such period as shall be agreed. The agreement referred to in this subsection shall be recorded in writing.]

(2),(3) ...

460 Order on application of Secretary of State

(1)   If in the case of any limited liability partnership–
   (a) the Secretary of State has received a report under section 437, or exercised his powers under section 447 or 448 of this Act ..., and
   (b) it appears to him that the limited liability partnership's affairs are being or have been conducted in a manner which is unfairly prejudicial to the interests of its members generally or of some part of its members, or that any actual or proposed act or omission of the limited liability partnership (including an act or omission on its behalf) is or would be so prejudicial,

he may himself (in addition to or instead of presenting a petition or the winding up of the limited liability partnership) apply to the court by petition for an order under this Part.

(2)   ...

461 Provisions as to petitions and orders under this Part

(1)   If the court is satisfied that a petition under this Part is well founded, it may make such order as it thinks fit for giving relief in respect of the matters complained of.

(2)   Without prejudice to the generality of subsection (1), the court's order may–
   (a) regulate the conduct of the limited liability partnership's affairs in the future,
   (b) require the limited liability partnership to refrain from doing or continuing an act complained of by the petitioner or to do an act which the petitioner has complained it has omitted to do,
   (c) authorise civil proceedings to be brought in the name and on behalf of the limited liability partnership by such person or persons and on such terms as the court may direct,
   (d) provide for the purchase of [the shares of any members in the limited liability partnership by other members or by the limited liability partnership itself.]

(3)   If an order under this Part requires the limited liability partnership not to make any, or any specified, alteration in the [limited liability partnership agreement], the limited liability partnership does not then have power without leave of the court to make any such alteration in breach of that requirement.

(4)   [Any alteration in the limited liability partnership agreement made by virtue of an order under this Part is of the same effect as if duly agreed by the members of the limited liability partnership and the provisions of this Act apply to the limited liability partnership agreement as so altered accordingly.]

(5)   …

(6)   The power under section 411 of the Insolvency Act to make rules shall, so far as it relates to a winding-up petition, apply for the purposes of a petition under this Part.

PART XVIII
FLOATING CHARGES AND RECEIVERS (SCOTLAND)

CHAPTER I
FLOATING CHARGES

462 Power of limited liability partnership to create floating charge

(1)   It is competent under the law of Scotland for [a limited liability partnership], for the purpose of securing any debt or other obligation (including a cautionary obligation) incurred or to be incurred by, or binding upon, the company or any other person, to create in favour of the creditor in the debt or obligation a charge, in this Part referred to as a floating charge, over all or any part of the property … which may from time to time be comprised in its property and undertaking.

(4)   References in this Part to the instrument by which a floating charge was created are, in the case of a floating charge created by words in a bond or other written acknowledgment, references to the bond or, as the case may be, the other written acknowledgment.

(5)   Subject to this Act, a floating charge has effect in accordance with this Part and Part III of the Insolvency Act 1986 in relation to any heritable property in Scotland to which it relates, notwithstanding that the instrument creating it is not recorded in the Register of Sasines or, as appropriate, registered in accordance with the Land Registration (Scotland) Act 1979.

[Section 462, as modified by the Limited Liability Partnerships (Scotland) Regulations 2001]

463 Effect of floating charge on winding up

(1)   Where a company goes into liquidation within the meaning of section 247(2) of the Insolvency Act 1986, a floating charge created by the limited liability

partnership attaches to the property then comprised in the company's property and undertaking or, as the case may be, in part of that property and undertaking, but does so subject to the rights of any person who–

(a) has effectually executed diligence on the property or any part of it; or

(b) holds a fixed security over the property or any part of it ranking in priority to the floating charge; or

(c) holds over the property or any part of it another floating charge so ranking.

(2)   The provisions of Part IV of the Insolvency Act (except section 185) have effect in relation to a floating charge, subject to subsection (1), as if the charge were a fixed security over the property to which it has attached in respect of the principal of the debt or obligation to which it relates and any interest due or to become due thereon.

(3)   Nothing in this section derogates from the provisions of sections 53(7) and 54(6) of the Insolvency Act (attachment of floating charge on appointment of receiver), or prejudices the operation of sections 175 and 176 of that Act (payment of preferential debts in winding up).

(4)   Interest accrues, in respect of a floating charge which after 16th November 1972 attaches to the property of the company, until payment of the sum due under the charge is made.

[Section 463, as modified by the Limited Liability Partnerships (Scotland) Regulations 2001]

464 Ranking of floating charges

(1)   Subject to subsection (2), the instrument creating a floating charge over all or any part of the limited liability partnership's property under [the law of Scotland] may contain–

(a) provisions prohibiting or restricting the creation of any fixed security or any other floating charge having priority over, or ranking pari passu with, the floating charge; or

(b) with the consent of the holder of any subsisting floating charge or fixed security which would be adversely affected, provisions regulating the order in which the floating charge shall rank with any other subsisting or future floating charges or fixed securities over that property or any part of it.

(1A)   Where an instrument creating a floating charge contains any such provision as is mentioned in subsection (1)(a), that provision shall be effective to confer priority on the floating charge over any fixed security or floating charge created after the date of the instrument.

(2)   Where all or any part of the property of a limited liability partnership is subject both to a floating charge and to a fixed security arising by operation of law, the fixed security has priority over the floating charge.

(3)   The order of ranking of the floating charge with any other subsisting or future floating charges or fixed securities over all or any part of the limited liability partnership's property is determined in accordance with the provisions of subsections (4) and (5) except where it is determined in accordance with any provision such as is mentioned in paragraph (a) or (b) of subsection (1).

(4)   Subject to the provisions of this section–
  (a) a fixed security, the right to which has been constituted as a real right before a floating charge has attached to all or any part of the property of the limited liability partnership, has priority of ranking over the floating charge;
  (b) floating charges rank with one another according to the time of registration in accordance with Chapter II of Part XII;
  (c) floating charges which have been received by the registrar for registration by the same postal delivery rank with one another equally.

(5)   Where the holder of a floating charge over all or any part of the limited liability partnership's property which has been registered in accordance with Chapter II of Part XII has received intimation in writing of the subsequent registration in accordance with that Chapter of another floating charge over the same property or any part thereof, the preference in ranking of the first-mentioned floating charge is restricted to security for–
  (a) the holder's present advances;
  (b) future advances which he may be required to make under the instrument creating the floating charge or under any ancillary document;
  (c) interest due or to become due on all such advances;
  (d) any expenses or outlays which may reasonably be incurred by the holder; and
  (e) (in the case of a floating charge to secure a contingent liability other than a liability arising under any further advances made from time to time) the maximum sum to which that contingent liability is capable of amounting whether or not it is contractually limited.

(6)   This section is subject to Part XII and to sections 175 and 176 of the Insolvency Act.

465

466 Alteration of floating charges

(1)   The instrument creating a floating charge under section 462 or any ancillary document may be altered by the execution of an instrument of alteration by the limited liability partnership, the holder of the charge and the holder of any other charge (including a fixed security) which would be adversely affected by the alteration.

(2)   Without prejudice to any enactment or rule of law regarding the execution of documents, such an instrument of alteration is validly executed if it is executed–

(b)   where trustees for debenture holders are acting under and in accordance with a trust deed, by those trustees; or

(c)   where, in the case of a series of secured debentures, no such trustees are acting, by or on behalf of–

    (i)   a majority in nominal value of those present or represented by proxy and voting at a meeting of debenture holders at which the holders of at least one-third in nominal value of the outstanding debentures of the series are present or so represented; or

    (ii) where no such meeting is held, the holders of at least one-half in nominal value of the outstanding debentures of the series;

(3)   Section 464 applies to an instrument of alteration under this section as it applies to an instrument creating a floating charge.

(4)   Subject to the next subsection, section 410(2) and (3) and section 420 apply to an instrument of alteration under this section which–

(a)   prohibits or restricts the creation of any fixed security or any other floating charge having priority over, or ranking pari passu with, the floating charge; or

(b)   varies, or otherwise regulates the order of, the ranking of the floating charge in relation to fixed securities or to other floating charges; or

(c)   releases property from the floating charge; or

(d)   increases the amount secured by the floating charge.

(5)   Section 410(2) and (3) and section 420 apply to an instrument of alteration falling under subsection (4) of this section as if references in the said sections to a charge were references to an alteration to a floating charge, and as if in section 410(2) and (3)–

(a)   references to the creation of a charge were references to the execution of such alteration; and

(b)   for the words from the beginning of subsection (2) to the word "applies" there were substituted the words "Every alteration to a floating charge created by a limited liability partnership".

(6)   Any reference (however expressed) in any enactment, including this Act, to a floating charge is, for the purposes of this section and unless the context otherwise requires, to be construed as including a reference to the floating charge as altered by an instrument of alteration falling under subsection (4) of this section.

[Section 466(1)(2)(3)(6), as modified by the Limited Liability Partnerships (Scotland) Regulations 2001]

CHAPTER III
GENERAL

486 Interpretation for Part XVIII generally

(1)   In this Part, unless the context otherwise requires, the following expressions have the following meanings respectively assigned to them, that is to say–

"ancillary document" means–

    (a) a document which relates to the floating charge and which was executed by the debtor or creditor in the charge before the registration of the charge in accordance with Chapter II of Part XII; or

    (b) an instrument of alteration such as is mentioned in section 466 in this Part;

["company" means a limited liability partnership]

"fixed security", in relation to any property of a limited liability partnership, means any security, other than a floating charge or a charge having the nature of a floating charge, which on the winding up of the limited liability partnership in Scotland would be treated as an effective security over that property, and (without prejudice to that generality) includes a security over that property, being a heritable security within the meaning of section 9(8) of the Conveyancing and Feudal Reform (Scotland) Act 1970;

…

487 Extent of Part XVIII

This Part extends to Scotland only.

PART XX
WINDING UP OF LIMITED LIABILITY PARTNERSHIPS
REGISTERED UNDER THIS ACT

CHAPTER VI
MATTERS ARISING SUBSEQUENT TO WINDING UP

651 Power of court to declare dissolution of limited liability partnership void

(1)   Where a limited liability partnership has been dissolved, the court may, on an application made for the purpose by the liquidator of the limited liability partnership or by any other person appearing to the court to be interested, make an order, on such terms as the court thinks fit, declaring the dissolution to have been void.

(2)   Thereupon such proceedings may be taken as might have been taken if the limited liability partnership had not been dissolved.

(3)   It is the duty of the person on whose application the order was made, within seven days after its making (or such further time as the court may allow), to deliver to the registrar of companies for registration an office copy of the order.

    If the person fails to do so, he is liable to a fine and, for continued contravention, to a daily default fine.

(4)   Subject to the following provisions, an application under this section may not be made after the end of the period of two years from the date of the dissolution of the limited liability partnership.

(5)   An application for the purposes of bringing proceedings against the limited liability partnership–

> (a)   for damages in respect of personal injuries (including any sum claimed by virtue of section 1(2)(c) of the Law Reform (Miscellaneous Provisions) Act 1934 (funeral expenses)), or
>
> (b)   for damages under the Fatal Accidents Act 1976 or the Damages (Scotland) Act 1976,

may be made at any time; but no order shall be made on such an application if it appears to the court that the proceedings would fail by virtue of any enactment as to the time within which proceedings must be brought.

(6)   Nothing in subsection (5) affects the power of the court on making an order under this section to direct that the period between the dissolution of the limited liability partnership and the making of the order shall not count for the purposes of any such enactment.

(7)   In subsection (5)(a) "personal injuries" includes any disease and any impairment of a person's physical or mental condition.

652 Registrar may strike defunct limited liability partnership off register

(1)   If the registrar of companies has reasonable cause to believe that a limited liability partnership is not carrying on business or in operation, he may send to the limited liability partnership by post a letter inquiring whether the limited liability partnership is carrying on business or in operation.

(2)   If the registrar does not within one month of sending the letter receive any answer to it, he shall within 14 days after the expiration of that month send to the limited liability partnership by post a registered letter referring to the first letter, and stating that no answer to it has been received, and that if an answer is not received to the second letter within one month from its date, a notice will be published in the Gazette with a view to striking the limited liability partnership's name off the register.

(3)   If the registrar either receives an answer to the effect that the limited liability partnership is not carrying on business or in operation, or does not within one month after sending the second letter receive any answer, he may publish in the Gazette, and send to the limited liability partnership by post, a notice that at the expiration of three months from the date of that notice the name of the limited liability partnership mentioned in it will, unless cause is shown to the contrary, be struck off the register and the limited liability partnership will be dissolved.

(4)   If, in a case where a limited liability partnership is being wound up, the registrar has reasonable cause to believe either that no liquidator is acting, or that the affairs of the limited liability partnership are fully wound up, and the returns required to be made by the liquidator have not been made for a period of six consecutive months, the registrar shall publish in the Gazette and send to the limited liability partnership or the liquidator (if any) a like notice as is provided in subsection (3).

(5)   At the expiration of the time mentioned in the notice the registrar may, unless cause to the contrary is previously shown by the limited liability partnership, strike its name off the register, and shall publish notice of this in the Gazette; and on the publication of that notice in the Gazette the limited liability partnership is dissolved.

(6)   However–
- (a) the liability (if any) of every ... member of the limited liability partnership continues and may be enforced as if the limited liability partnership had not been dissolved, and
- (b) nothing in subsection (5) affects the power of the court to wind up a limited liability partnership the name of which has been struck off the register.

(7)   A notice to be sent to a liquidator under this section may be addressed to him at his last known place of business; and a letter or notice to be sent under this section to a limited liability partnership may be addressed to the limited liability partnership at its registered office or, if no office has been registered, to the care of some member of the limited liability partnership.

If there is no member of the limited liability partnership whose name and address are known to the registrar of companies, the letter or notice may be sent to each of the persons who subscribed the incorporation document, addressed to him at the address mentioned in the incorporation document.

652A Registrar may strike limited liability partnership off register on application

(1)   [On application by two or more designated members of a limited liability partnership, the registrar of companies may strike the limited liability partnership's name off the register.]

(2)   An application by a limited liability partnership under this section shall–
- (a) ...
- (b) be [made] in the prescribed form, and
- (c) contain the prescribed information.

(3)   The registrar shall not strike a limited liability partnership off under this section until after the expiration of three months from the publication by him in the Gazette of a notice–
- (a) stating that he may exercise his power under this section in relation to the limited liability partnership, and
- (b) inviting any person to show cause why he should not do so.

(4)   Where the registrar strikes a limited liability partnership off under this section, he shall publish notice of that fact in the Gazette.

(5)   On the publication in the Gazette of a notice under subsection (4), the limited liability partnership to which the notice relates is dissolved.

(6)   However, the liability (if any) of every … and member of the limited liability partnership continues and may be enforced as if the limited liability partnership had not been dissolved.

(7)   Nothing in this section affects the power of the court to wind up a limited liability partnership the name of which has been struck off the register.

652B Duties in connection with making application under section 652A

(1)   A person shall not make an application under section 652A on behalf of a limited liability partnership if, at any time in the previous three months, the limited liability partnership has–
- (a)   changed its name,
- (b)   traded or otherwise carried on business,
- (c)   made a disposal for value of property or rights which, immediately before ceasing to trade or otherwise carry on business, it held for the purpose of disposal for gain in the normal course of trading or otherwise carrying on business, or
- (d)   engaged in any other activity, except one which is–
    - (i)   necessary or expedient for the purpose of making an application under section 652A, or deciding whether to do so,
    - (ii)   necessary or expedient for the purpose of concluding the affairs of the limited liability partnership,
    - (iii)   necessary or expedient for the purpose of complying with any statutory requirement, or
    - (iv)   specified by the Secretary of State by order for the purposes of this sub-paragraph.

(2)   For the purposes of subsection (1), a limited liability partnership shall not be treated as trading or otherwise carrying on business by virtue only of the fact that it makes a payment in respect of a liability incurred in the course of trading or otherwise carrying on business.

(3)   A person shall not make an application under section 652A on behalf of a limited liability partnership at a time when any of the following is the case–
- (a)   an application has been made to the court under section 425 on behalf of the limited liability partnership for the sanctioning of a compromise or arrangement and the matter has not been finally concluded;
- (b)   a voluntary arrangement in relation to the limited liability partnership has been proposed under Part I of the Insolvency Act 1986 and the matter has not been finally concluded;
- (c)   an administration order in relation to the limited liability partnership is in force under Part II of that Act or a petition for such an order has been presented and not finally dealt with or withdrawn;
- (d)   the limited liability partnership is being wound up under Part IV of that Act, whether voluntarily or by the court, or a petition under that Part for the winding up of the limited liability partnership by the court has been presented and not finally dealt with or withdrawn;

   (e) there is a receiver or manager of the limited liability partnership's
        property;

   (f) the limited liability partnership's estate is being administered by a
        judicial factor.

(4) For the purposes of subsection (3)(a), the matter is finally concluded if–

   (a) the application has been withdrawn,

   (b) the application has been finally dealt with without a compromise or
        arrangement being sanctioned by the court, or

   (c) a compromise or arrangement has been sanctioned by the court and has,
        together with anything required to be done under any provision made
        in relation to the matter by order of the court, been fully carried out.

(5) For the purposes of subsection (3)(b), the matter is finally concluded if–

   (a) [no meeting is] to be summoned under section 3 of the Insolvency
        Act 1986,

   (b) [the meeting summoned under that section fails] to approve the
        arrangement with no, or the same, modifications,

   (c) an arrangement approved by [a meeting] summoned under that section,
        or in consequence of a direction under section 6(4)(b) of that Act, has
        been fully implemented, or

   (d) the court makes an order under subsection (5) of section 6 of that
        Act revoking approval given [at a previous meeting] and, if the court
        gives any directions under subsection (6) of that section, the limited
        liability partnership has done whatever it is required to do under
        those directions.

(6) A person who makes an application under section 652A on behalf of a
limited liability partnership shall secure that a copy of the application is given,
within seven days from the day on which the application is made, to every person
who, at any time on that day, is–

   (a) a member of the limited liability partnership,

   (b) an employee of the limited liability partnership,

   (c) a creditor of the limited liability partnership,

   (d) …

   (e) a manager or trustee of any pension fund established for the benefit of
        employees of the limited liability partnership, or

   (f) a person of a description specified for the purposes of this paragraph
        by regulations made by the Secretary of State.

(7) Subsection (6) shall not require a copy of the application to be given to a
member who is a party to the application.

(8) The duty imposed by subsection (6) shall cease to apply if the application is
withdrawn before the end of the period for giving the copy application.

(9) The Secretary of State may by order amend subsection (1) for the purpose
of altering the period in relation to which the doing of the things mentioned in
paragraphs (a) to (d) of that subsection is relevant.

652C Members' duties following application under section 652A

(1)   Subsection (2) applies in relation to any time after the day on which a limited liability partnership makes an application under section 652A and before the day on which the application is finally dealt with or withdrawn.

(2)   A person who [is a designated member of the limited liability partnership] at the end of a day on which a person other than himself becomes–

    (a)   a member of the limited liability partnership,

    (b)   an employee of the limited liability partnership,

    (c)   a creditor of the limited liability partnership,

    (d)   …

    (e)   a manager or trustee of any pension fund established for the benefit of employees of the limited liability partnership, or

    (f)   a person of a description specified for the purposes of this paragraph by regulations made by the Secretary of State,

shall secure that a copy of the application is given to that person within seven days from that day.

(3)   The duty imposed by subsection (2) shall cease to apply if the application is finally dealt with or withdrawn before the end of the period for giving the copy application.

(4)   Subsection (5) applies where, at any time on or after the day on which a limited liability partnership makes an application under section 652A and before the day on which the application is finally dealt with or withdrawn–

    (a)   the limited liability partnership–

        (i)   changes its name,

        (ii)   trades or otherwise carries on business,

        (iii)   makes a disposal for value of any property or rights other than those which it was necessary or expedient for it to hold for the purpose of making, or proceeding with, an application under section 652A, or

        (iv)   engages in any other activity, except one to which subsection (6) applies;

    (b)   an application is made to the court under section 425 on behalf of the limited liability partnership for the sanctioning of a compromise or arrangement;

    (c)   a voluntary arrangement in relation to the limited liability partnership is proposed under Part I of the Insolvency Act 1986;

    (d)   a petition is presented for the making of an administration order under Part II of that Act in relation to the limited liability partnership;

    (e)   there arise any of the circumstances in which, under section 84(1) of that Act, the limited liability partnership may be voluntarily wound up;

    (f)   a petition is presented for the winding up of the limited liability partnership by the court under Part IV of that Act;

    (g)   a receiver or manager of the limited liability partnership's property is appointed; or

(h)   a judicial factor is appointed to administer the limited liability partnership's estate.

(5)   A person who, at the end of a day on which an event mentioned in any of paragraphs (a) to (h) of subsection (4) occurs, [is a designated member of the limited liability partnership] shall secure that the limited liability partnership's application is withdrawn forthwith.

(6)   This subsection applies to any activity which is–
(a)   necessary or expedient for the purpose of making, or proceeding with, an application under section 652A,
(b)   necessary or expedient for the purpose of concluding affairs of the limited liability partnership which are outstanding because of what has been necessary or expedient for the purpose of making, or proceeding with, such an application,
(c)   necessary or expedient for the purpose of complying with any statutory requirement, …
(d)   …

(7)   For the purposes of subsection (4)(a), a limited liability partnership shall not be treated as trading or otherwise carrying on business by virtue only of the fact that it makes a payment in respect of a liability incurred in the course of trading or otherwise carrying on business.

652D   Sections 652B and 652C: supplementary provisions

(1)   For the purposes of sections 652B(6) and 652C(2), a document shall be treated as given to a person if it is delivered to him or left at his proper address or sent by post to him at that address.

(2)   For the purposes of subsection (1) and section 7 of the Interpretation Act 1978 (which relates to the service of documents by post) in its application to that subsection, the proper address of any person shall be his last known address, except that–
(a)   in the case of a body corporate, other than one to which subsection (3) applies, it shall be the address of its registered or principal office,
(b)   in the case of a partnership, other than one to which subsection (3) applies, it shall be the address of its principal office, and
(c)   in the case of a body corporate or partnership to which subsection (3) applies, it shall be the address of its principal office in the United Kingdom.

(3)   This subsection applies to a body corporate or partnership which–
(a)   is incorporated or formed under the law of a country or territory outside the United Kingdom, and
(b)   has a place of business in the United Kingdom.

(4)   Where a creditor of the limited liability partnership has more than one place of business, subsection (1) shall have effect, so far as concerns the giving of

a document to him, as if for the words from "delivered" to the end there were substituted "left, or sent by post to him, at each place of business of his with which the limited liability partnership has had dealings in relation to a matter by virtue of which he is a creditor of the limited liability partnership."

(5)   Any power to make an order or regulations under section 652B or 652C shall–

    (a)   include power to make different provision for different cases or classes of case,

    (b)   include power to make such transitional provisions as the Secretary of State considers appropriate, and

    (c)   be exercisable by statutory instrument subject to annulment in pursuance of a resolution of either House of Parliament.

(6)   For the purposes of sections 652B and 652C, an application under section 652A is withdrawn if notice of withdrawal in the prescribed form is given to the registrar of companies.

(7)   In sections 652B and 652C, "disposal" includes part disposal.

(8)   In sections 652B and 652C and this section, "creditor" includes a contingent or prospective creditor.

652E Sections 652B and 652C: enforcement

(1)   A person who breaches or fails to perform a duty imposed on him by section 652B or 652C is guilty of an offence and liable to a fine.

(2)   A person who fails to perform a duty imposed on him by section 652B(6) or 652C(2) with the intention of concealing the making of the application in question from the person concerned is guilty of an offence and liable to imprisonment or a fine, or both.

(3)   In any proceedings for an offence under subsection (1) consisting of breach of a duty imposed by section 652B(1) or (3), it shall be a defence for the accused to prove that he did not know, and could not reasonably have known, of the existence of the facts which led to the breach.

(4)   In any proceedings for an offence under subsection (1) consisting of failure to perform the duty imposed by section 652B(6), it shall be a defence for the accused to prove that he took all reasonable steps to perform the duty.

(5)   In any proceedings for an offence under subsection (1) consisting of failure to perform a duty imposed by section 652C(2) or (5), it shall be a defence for the accused to prove–

    (a)   that at the time of the failure he was not aware of the fact that the limited liability partnership had made an application under section 652A, or

    (b)   that he took all reasonable steps to perform the duty.

652F Other offences connected with section 652A

(1)   Where a limited liability partnership makes an application under section 652A, any person who, in connection with the application, knowingly or recklessly furnishes any information to the registrar of companies which is false or misleading in a material particular is guilty of an offence and liable to a fine.

(2)   Any person who knowingly or recklessly makes an application to the registrar of companies which purports to be an application under section 652A, but which is not, is guilty of an offence and liable to a fine.

653 Objection to striking off by person aggrieved

(1)   Subsection (2) applies if a limited liability partnership or any member or creditor of it feels aggrieved by the limited liability partnership having been struck off the register under section 652.

(2)   The court, on an application by the limited liability partnership or the member or creditor made before the expiration of 20 years from publication in the Gazette of notice under section 652, may, if satisfied that the limited liability partnership was at the time of the striking off carrying on business or in operation, or otherwise that it is just that the limited liability partnership be restored to the register, order the limited liability partnership's name to be restored.

(2A)   Subsections (2B) and (2D) apply if a limited liability partnership has been struck off the register under section 652A.

(2B)   The court, on an application by a notifiable person made before the expiration of 20 years from publication in the Gazette of notice under section 652A(4), may, if satisfied–
- (a)   that any duty under section 652B or 652C with respect to the giving to that person of a copy of the limited liability partnership's application under section 652A was not performed,
- (b)   that the making of the limited liability partnership's application under section 652A involved a breach of duty under section 652B(1) or (3), or
- (c)   that it is for some other reason just to do so,

order the limited liability partnership's name to be restored to the register.

(2C)   In subsection (2B), "notifiable person" means a person to whom a copy of the limited liability partnership's application under section 652A was required to be given under section 652B or 652C.

(2D)   The court, on an application by the Secretary of State made before the expiration of 20 years from publication in the Gazette of notice under section 652A(4), may, if satisfied that it is in the public interest to do so, order the limited liability partnership's name to be restored.

(3)   On an office copy of an order under subsection (2), (2B) or (2D) being delivered to the registrar of companies for registration the limited liability

partnership to which the order relates is deemed to have continued in existence as if its name had not been struck off; and the court may by the order give such directions and make such provisions as seem just for placing the limited liability partnership and all other persons in the same position (as nearly as may be) as if the limited liability partnership's name had not been struck off.

654 Property of dissolved limited liability partnership to be bona vacantia

(1)   When a limited liability partnership is dissolved, all property and rights whatsoever vested in or held on trust for the limited liability partnership immediately before its dissolution (including leasehold property, but not including property held by the limited liability partnership on trust for any other person) are deemed to be bona vacantia and–
- (a)   accordingly belong to the Crown, or to the Duchy of Lancaster or to the Duke of Cornwall for the time being (as the case may be), and
- (b)   vest and may be dealt with in the same manner as other bona vacantia accruing to the Crown, to the Duchy of Lancaster or to the Duke of Cornwall.

(2)   Except as provided by the section next following, the above has effect subject and without prejudice to any order made by the court under section 651 or 653.

655 Effect on s 654 of limited liability partnership's revival after dissolution

(1)   The person in whom any property or right is vested by section 654 may dispose of, or of an interest in, that property or right notwithstanding that an order may be made under section 651 or 653.

(2)   Where such an order is made–
- (a)   it does not affect the disposition (but without prejudice to the order so far as it relates to any other property or right previously vested in or held on trust for the limited liability partnership), and
- (b)   the Crown or, as the case may be, the Duke of Cornwall shall pay to the limited liability partnership an amount equal to–
  - (i)   the amount of any consideration received for the property or right, or interest therein, or
  - (ii)   the value of any such consideration at the time of the disposition,
or, if no consideration was received, an amount equal to the value of the property, right or interest disposed of, as at the date of the disposition.

(3)   Where a liability accrues under subsection (2) in respect of any property or right which, before the order under section 651 or 653 was made, had accrued as bona vacantia to the Duchy of Lancaster, the Attorney General of the Duchy shall represent Her Majesty in any proceedings arising in connection with that liability.

(4)   Where a liability accrues under subsection (2) in respect of any property or right which, before the order under section 651 or 653 was made, had accrued as

bona vacantia to the Duchy of Cornwall, such persons as the Duke of Cornwall (or other possessor for the time being of the Duchy) may appoint shall represent the Duke (or other possessor) in any proceedings arising out of that liability.

(5)   This section applies in relation to the disposition of any property, right or interest on or after 22nd December 1981, whether the limited liability partnership concerned was dissolved before, on or after that day.

656 Crown disclaimer of property vesting as bona vacantia

(1)   Where property vests in the Crown under section 654, the Crown's title to it under that section may be disclaimed by a notice signed by the Crown representative, that is to say the Treasury Solicitor, or, in relation to property in Scotland, the Queen's and Lord Treasurer's Remembrancer.

(2)   The right to execute a notice of disclaimer under this section may be waived by or on behalf of the Crown either expressly or by taking possession or other act evincing that intention.

(3)   A notice of disclaimer under this section is of no effect unless it is executed–
   (a)   within twelve months of the date on which the vesting of the property under section 654 came to the notice of the Crown representative, or
   (b)   if an application in writing is made to the Crown representative by any person interested in the property requiring him to decide whether he will or will not disclaim, within a period of three months after the receipt of the application or such further period as may be allowed by the court which would have had jurisdiction to wind up the limited liability partnership if it had not been dissolved.

(4)   A statement in a notice of disclaimer of any property under this section that the vesting of it came to the notice of the Crown representative on a specified date, or that no such application as above mentioned was received by him with respect to the property before a specified date, is sufficient evidence of the fact stated, until the contrary is proved.

(5)   A notice of disclaimer under this section shall be delivered to the registrar of companies and retained and registered by him; and copies of it shall be published in the Gazette and sent to any persons who have given the Crown representative notice that they claim to be interested in the property.

(6)   This section applies to property vested in the Duchy of Lancaster or the Duke of Cornwall under section 654 as if for references to the Crown and the Crown representative there were respectively substituted references to the Duchy of Lancaster and to the Solicitor to that Duchy, or to the Duke of Cornwall and to the Solicitor to the Duchy of Cornwall, as the case may be.

657 Effect of Crown disclaimer under s 656

(1)   Where notice of disclaimer is executed under section 656 as respects any property, that property is deemed not to have vested in the Crown under section 654.

(2)   As regards property in England and Wales, section 178(4) and sections 179 to 182 of the Insolvency Act shall apply as if the property had been disclaimed by the liquidator under the said section 91 immediately before the dissolution of the limited liability partnership.

(3)   As regards property in Scotland, the following four subsections apply.

(4)   The Crown's disclaimer operates to determine, as from the date of the disclaimer, the rights, interests and liabilities of the limited liability partnership, and the property of the limited liability partnership, in or in respect of the property disclaimed; but it does not (except so far as is necessary for the purpose of releasing the limited liability partnership and its property from liability) affect the rights or liabilities of any other person.

(5)   The court may, on application by a person who either claims an interest in disclaimed property or is under a liability not discharged by this Act in respect of disclaimed property, and on hearing such persons as it thinks fit, make an order for the vesting of the property in or its delivery to any persons entitled to it, or to whom it may seem just that the property should be delivered by way of compensation for such liability, or a trustee for him, and on such terms as the court thinks just.

(6)   On such a vesting order being made, the property comprised in it vests accordingly in the person named in that behalf in the order, without conveyance or assignation for that purpose.

(7)   Part II of Schedule 20 has effect for the protection of third parties where the property disclaimed is held under a lease.

658 Liability for rentcharge on limited liability partnership's land after dissolution

(1)   Section 180 of the Insolvency Act shall apply to land in England and Wales which by operation of law vests subject to a rentcharge in the Crown or any other person on the dissolution of a limited liability partnership as it applies to land so vesting on a disclaimer under that section.

(2)   In this section "company" includes any body corporate.

675–690

PART XXIII
OVERSEA LIMITED LIABILITY PARTNERSHIPS

CHAPTER I
REGISTRATION, ETC

690A–692A

693 Obligation to state name and other particulars

(1)   [Every oversea limited liability partnership shall–
    (a)   in every prospectus inviting subscriptions for its debentures in Great Britain, state the country in which the limited liability partnership is incorporated,
    (b)   conspicuously exhibit on every place where it carries on business in Great Britain the name of the limited liability partnership and the country in which it is incorporated,
    (c)   cause the name of the limited liability partnership and the country in which it is incorporated to be stated in legible characters in all bill heads, letter paper, and in all notices and other official publications and communications of the limited liability partnership.]

(2)   [For the purposes of this section "oversea limited liability partnership" means a body incorporated or otherwise established outside Great Britain whose name under its law of incorporation or establishment includes the words "limited liability partnership".]

(3),(4) …

694–703R

PART XXIV
THE REGISTRAR OF COMPANIES, HIS FUNCTIONS AND OFFICES

704 Registration offices

(1)   For the purposes of the registration of limited liability partnerships under the Companies Acts, there shall continue to be offices in England and Wales and in Scotland, at such places as the Secretary of State thinks fit.

(2)   The Secretary of State may appoint such registrars, assistant registrars, clerks and servants as he thinks necessary for that purpose, and may make regulations with respect to their duties, and may remove any persons so appointed.

(3)   The salaries of the persons so appointed continue to be fixed by the Secretary of State, with the concurrence of the Treasury, and shall be paid out of money provided by Parliament.

(4)   The Secretary of State may direct a seal or seals to be prepared for the authentication of documents required for or in connection with the registration of limited liability partnerships; and any seal so prepared is referred to in this Act as the registrar's official seal.

(5)   Wherever any act is by the Companies Acts directed to be done to or by the registrar of companies, it shall (until the Secretary of State otherwise directs) be done to or by the existing registrar of companies in England and Wales or in Scotland (as the case may be), or to or by such person as the Secretary of State may for the time being authorise.

(6)   In the event of the Secretary of State altering the constitution of the existing registration offices or any of them, any such act shall be done to or by such officer and at such place with reference to the local situation of the registered offices of the limited liability partnerships to be registered as the Secretary of State may appoint.

(7)   Subsection (8) below applies where by virtue of an order made under section 69 of the Deregulation and Contracting Out Act 1994 a person is authorised by the registrar of companies to accept delivery of any class of documents which are under any provision of the Companies Acts to be delivered to the registrar.

(8)   If–
   (a)   the registrar directs that documents of that class shall be delivered to a specified address of the authorised person; and
   (b)   the direction is printed and made available to the public (with or without payment),
any document of that class which is delivered to an address other than the specified address shall be treated for the purposes of those Acts as not having been delivered.

705 Limited liability partnerships' registered numbers

(1)   The registrar shall allocate to every limited liability partnership a number, which shall be known as the limited liability partnership's registered number.

(2)   Limited liability partnerships' registered numbers shall be in such form, consisting of one or more sequences of figures or letters, as the registrar may from time to time determine.

(3)   The registrar may upon adopting a new form of registered number make such changes of existing registered numbers as appear to him necessary.

(4)   A change of a limited liability partnership's registered number has effect from the date on which the limited liability partnership is notified by the registrar of the change; but for a period of three years beginning with the date on which that notification is sent by the registrar the requirement of section 351(1)(a) as to the use of the limited liability partnership's registered number on business letters and order forms is satisfied by the use of either the old number or the new.

(5)   …

705A

706 Delivery to the registrar of documents in legible form

(1)   This section applies to the delivery to the registrar under any provision of the Companies Acts of documents in legible form.

(2)   The document must–
   (a)   state in a prominent position the registered number of the limited liability partnership to which it relates …,

(b) satisfy any requirements prescribed by regulations for the purposes of this section, and

(c) conform to such requirements as the registrar may specify for the purpose of enabling him to copy the document.

(3) If a document is delivered to the registrar which does not comply with the requirements of this section, he may serve on the person by whom the document was delivered (or, if there are two or more such persons, on any of them) a notice indicating the respect in which the document does not comply.

(4) Where the registrar serves such a notice, then, unless a replacement document–

(a) is delivered to him within 14 days after the service of the notice, and

(b) complies with the requirements of this section (or section 707B) or is not rejected by him for failure to comply with those requirements,

the original document shall be deemed not to have been delivered to him.

But for the purposes of any enactment imposing a penalty for failure to deliver, so far as it imposes a penalty for continued contravention, no account shall be taken of the period between the delivery of the original document and the end of the period of 14 days after service of the registrar's notice.

(5) Regulations made for the purposes of this section may make different provision with respect to different descriptions of document.

707

707A The keeping of limited liability partnership records by the registrar

(1) The information contained in a document delivered to the registrar under the Companies Acts may be recorded and kept by him in any form he thinks fit, provided it is possible to inspect the information and to produce a copy of it in legible form.

This is sufficient compliance with any duty of his to keep, file or register the document.

(2) The originals of documents delivered to the registrar in legible form shall be kept by him for ten years, after which they may be destroyed.

(3) Where a limited liability partnership has been dissolved, the registrar may, at any time after the expiration of two years from the date of the dissolution, direct that any records in his custody relating to the limited liability partnership may be removed to the Public Record Office; and records in respect of which such a direction is given shall be disposed of in accordance with the enactments relating to that Office and the rules made under them.

This subsection does not extend to Scotland.

(4) …

707B Delivery to the registrar using electronic communications

(1)   Electronic communications may be used for the delivery of any document to the registrar under any provision of the Companies Acts (including delivery of a document in the prescribed form), provided that such delivery is in such form and manner as is directed by the registrar.

(2)   Where the document is required under any provision of the Companies Acts to be signed or sealed, it shall instead be authenticated in such manner as is directed by the registrar.

(3)   The document must contain in a prominent position–
    (a)   the name and registered number of the limited liability partnership to which it relates ...
    (b)   ...

(4)   If a document is delivered to the registrar which does not comply with the requirements imposed by or under this section, he may serve on the person by whom the document was delivered (or, if there are two or more such persons, on any of them) a notice indicating the respect in which the document does not comply.

(5)   Where the registrar serves such a notice, then unless a replacement document–
    (a)   is delivered to him within 14 days after the service of the notice, and
    (b)   complies with the requirements of this section (or section 706) or is not rejected by him for failure to comply with those requirements,
the original document shall be deemed not to have been delivered to him.

    But for the purposes of any enactment imposing a penalty for failure to deliver, so far as it imposes a penalty for continued contravention, no account shall be taken of the period between the delivery of the original document and the end of the period of 14 days after service of the registrar's notice.

(6)   In this section references to the delivery of a document include references to the forwarding, lodging, registering, sending or submission of a document and to the giving of a notice, and cognate expressions are to be construed accordingly.

708 Fees payable to registrar

(1)   The Secretary of State may by regulations made by statutory instrument require the payment to the registrar of companies of such fees as may be specified in the regulations in respect of–
    (a)   the performance by the registrar of such functions under the Companies Acts as may be so specified, including the receipt by him of any document which under those Acts is required to be delivered to him,
    (b)   the inspection of documents kept by him under those Acts.

(2)   A statutory instrument containing regulations under this section requiring the payment of a fee in respect of a matter for which no fee was previously

payable, or increasing a fee, shall be laid before Parliament after being made and shall cease to have effect at the end of the period of 28 days beginning with the day on which the regulations were made (but without prejudice to anything previously done under the regulations or to the making of further regulations) unless in that period the regulations are approved by resolution of each House of Parliament.

In reckoning that period of 28 days no account is to be taken of any time during which Parliament is dissolved or prorogued or during which both Houses are adjourned for more than four days.

(3)   A statutory instrument containing regulations under this section, where subsection (2) does not apply, is subject to annulment in pursuance of a resolution of either House of Parliament.

(4)   Fees paid to the registrar under the Companies Acts shall be paid into the Consolidated Fund.

(5)   It is hereby declared that the registrar may charge a fee for any services provided by him otherwise than in pursuance of an obligation imposed on him by law.

709 Inspection, &c of records kept by the registrar

(1)   Any person may inspect any records kept by the registrar for the purposes of the Companies Acts and may require–
    (a)   a copy, in such form as the registrar considers appropriate, of any information contained in those records, or
    (b)   a certified copy of, or extract from, any such record.

(2)   The right of inspection extends to the originals of documents delivered to the registrar in legible form only where the record kept by the registrar of the contents of the document is illegible or unavailable.

(3)   A copy of or extract from a record kept at any of the offices for the registration of limited liability partnerships in England and Wales or Scotland, certified in writing by the registrar (whose official position it is unnecessary to prove) to be an accurate record of the contents of any document delivered to him under the Companies Acts, is in all legal proceedings admissible in evidence as of equal validity with the original document and as evidence of any fact stated therein of which direct oral evidence would be admissible.

(4)   Copies of or extracts from records furnished by the registrar may, instead of being certified by him in writing to be an accurate record, be sealed with his official seal.

(5)   No process for compelling the production of a record kept by the registrar shall issue from any court except with the leave of the court; and any such process shall bear on it a statement that it is issued with the leave of the court.

710 Certificate of incorporation

Any person may require a certificate of the incorporation of a limited liability partnership, signed by the registrar or authenticated by his official seal.

710A Provision and authentication by registrar of documents in non-legible form

(1)   Any requirement of the Companies Acts as to the supply by the registrar of a document may, if the registrar thinks fit, be satisfied by the communication by the registrar of the requisite information in any non-legible form prescribed for the purposes of this section by regulations or approved by him.

(2)   Where the document is required to be signed by him or sealed with his official seal, it shall instead be authenticated in such manner as may be prescribed by regulations or approved by the registrar.

710B Documents relating to Welsh limited liability partnerships

(1)   This section applies to any document which–
    (a)   is delivered to the registrar under this Act or the Insolvency Act 1986, and
    (b)   relates to a limited liability partnership (whether already registered or to be registered) whose incorporation document states that its registered office is to be situated in Wales.

(2)   A document to which this section applies may be in Welsh but, subject to subsection (3), shall on delivery to the registrar be accompanied by a certified translation into English.

(3)   The requirement for a translation imposed by subsection (2) shall not apply–
    (a)   to documents of such descriptions as may be prescribed for the purposes of this paragraph, or
    (b)   to documents in a form prescribed in Welsh (or partly in Welsh and partly in English) by virtue of section 26 of the Welsh Language Act 1993.

(4)   Where by virtue of subsection (3) the registrar receives a document in Welsh without a certified translation into English, he shall, if that document is to be available for inspection, himself obtain such a translation; and that translation shall be treated as delivered to him in accordance with the same provision as the original.

(5)   A limited liability partnership whose incorporation document states that its registered office is to be situated in Wales may deliver to the registrar a certified translation into Welsh of any document in English which relates to the limited liability partnership and which is or has been delivered to the registrar.

(6)   The provisions within subsection (7) (which require certified translations into English of certain documents delivered to the registrar) shall not apply

where a translation is required by subsection (2) or would be required but for subsection (3).

(7)   The provisions within this subsection are section 228(2)(f), the second sentence of section 242(1), sections 243(4) …

(8)   In this section "certified translation" means a translation certified in the prescribed manner to be a correct translation.

711 Public notice by registrar of receipt and issue of certain documents

(1)   The registrar of companies shall cause to be published in the Gazette notice of the issue or receipt by him of documents of any of the following descriptions (stating in the notice the name of the limited liability partnership, the description of document and the date of issue or receipt)–
  (a)   any certificate of incorporation of a limited liability partnership,
  (b)   any document making or evidencing an alteration in a limited liability partnership's incorporation document …,
  (c)   any notification of a change among the members of a limited liability partnership,
  (d),(e),(f),(g),(h),(j)   …
  (k)   any documents delivered by a limited liability partnership under section 242(1) (accounts and reports),
  (l),(m)   …
  (n)   any notice of a change in the situation of a limited liability partnership's registered office,
  (p)   any copy of a winding-up order in respect of a limited liability partnership,
  (q)   any order for the dissolution of a limited liability partnership on a winding up,
  (r)   any return by a liquidator of the final meeting of a limited liability partnership on a winding up.
  (s),(u),(v),(w),(x),(y),(z)   …

(2)   In section 42 "official notification" means–
  (a)   in relation to anything stated in a document of any of the above descriptions, the notification of that document in the Gazette under this section, and
  (b)   in relation to the appointment of a liquidator in a voluntary winding up, the notification of it in the Gazette under section 109 of the Insolvency Act;
and "officially notified" is to be construed accordingly.

711A

713 Enforcement of limited liability partnership's duty to make returns

(1)   If a limited liability partnership, having made default in complying with any provision of the Companies Acts which requires it to deliver a document to

the registrar of companies, or to give notice to him of any matter, fails to make good the default within 14 days after the service of a notice on the limited liability partnership requiring it to do so, the court may, on an application made to it by any member or creditor of the limited liability partnership or by the registrar of companies, make an order directing the limited liability partnership and [any designated member] of it to make good the default within such time as may be specified in the order.

(2)   The court's order may provide that all costs of and incidental to the application shall be borne by the limited liability partnership or by any [designated members] of it responsible for the default.

(3)   Nothing in this section prejudices the operation of any enactment imposing penalties on a limited liability partnership or its [designated members] in respect of any such default as is mentioned above.

714 Registrar's index of limited liability partnership and corporate names

(1)   The registrar of companies shall keep an index of the names of the following bodies–
- (a) companies as defined by this Act,
- (aa) companies incorporated outside the United Kingdom and Gibraltar which have complied with paragraph 1 of Schedule 21A and which do not appear to the registrar of companies not to have a branch in Great Britain,
- (b) companies incorporated outside Great Britain which have complied with section 691 and which do not appear to the registrar of companies not to have a place of business in Great Britain,
- (c) incorporated and unincorporated bodies to which any provision of this Act applies by virtue of section 718 (unregistered companies),
- (d) limited partnerships registered under the Limited Partnerships Act 1907,
- (da) limited liability partnerships incorporated under the Limited Liability Partnerships Act 2000,
- (e) companies within the meaning of the Companies Act (Northern Ireland) 1960,
- (f) companies incorporated outside Northern Ireland which have complied with section 356 of that Act (which corresponds with section 691 of this Act), and which do not appear to the registrar not to have a place of business in Northern Ireland, and
- (g) societies registered under the Industrial and Provident Societies Act 1965 or the Industrial and Provident Societies Act (Northern Ireland) 1969.

(2)   The Secretary of State may by order in a statutory instrument vary subsection (1) by the addition or deletion of any class of body, except any within paragraph (a) or (b) of the subsection, whether incorporated or unincorporated; and any such statutory instrument is subject to annulment in pursuance of a resolution of either House of Parliament.

715A Interpretation

(1)   In this Part–

"document" includes information recorded in any form; and

"legible", in the context of documents in legible or non-legible form, means capable of being read with the naked eye.

(2)   References in this Part to delivering a document include sending, forwarding, producing or (in the case of a notice) giving it.

PART XXV
MISCELLANEOUS AND SUPPLEMENTARY PROVISIONS

716–720

721 Production and inspection of books where offence suspected

(1)   The following applies if on an application made–
    (a)   in England and Wales, to a judge of the High Court by the Director of Public Prosecutions, the Secretary of State or a chief officer of police, or
    (b)   in Scotland, to one of the Lords Commissioners of Justiciary by the Lord Advocate,
there is shown to be reasonable cause to believe that any person has, while a member of a limited liability partnership, committed an offence in connection with the management of the limited liability partnership's affairs and that evidence of the commission of the offence is to be found in any books or papers of or under the control of the limited liability partnership.

(2)   An order may be made–
    (a)   authorising any person named in it to inspect the books or papers in question, or any of them, for the purpose of investigating and obtaining evidence of the offence, or
    (b)   requiring [such] member of it as may be named in the order to produce the books or papers (or any of them) to a person named in the order at a place so named.

(3)   The above applies also in relation to any books or papers of a person carrying on the business of banking so far as they relate to the limited liability partnership's affairs, as it applies to any books or papers of or under the control of the limited liability partnership, except that no such order as is referred to in subsection (2)(b) shall be made by virtue of this subsection.

(4)   The decision of a judge of the High Court or of any of the Lords Commissioners of Justiciary on an application under this section is not appealable.

722 Form of limited liability partnership registers, etc

(1)   Any register, index, minute book or accounting record, required by the Companies Acts to be kept by a limited liability partnership may be kept either by making entries in bound books or by recording the matters in question in any other manner.

(2)   Where any such register, index, minute book or accounting record is not kept by making entries in a bound book, but by some other means, adequate precautions shall be taken for guarding against falsification and facilitating its discovery.

(3)   If default is made in complying with subsection (2), the limited liability partnership and every member of it who is in default is liable to a fine and, for continued contravention, to a daily default fine.

723 Use of computers for limited liability partnership records

(1)   The power conferred on a limited liability partnership by section 722(1) to keep a register or other record by recording the matters in question otherwise than by making entries in bound books includes power to keep the register or other record by recording those matters otherwise than in a legible form, so long as the recording is capable of being reproduced in a legible form.

(2)   ...

(3)   If any such register or other record of a limited liability partnership as is mentioned in section 722(1), or a register of holders of a limited liability partnership's debentures, is kept by the limited liability partnership by recording the matters in question otherwise than in a legible form, any duty imposed on the limited liability partnership by this Act to allow inspection of, or to furnish a copy of, the register or other record or any part of it is to be treated as a duty to allow inspection of, or to furnish, a reproduction of the recording or of the relevant part of it in a legible form.

(4)   The Secretary of State may by regulations in a statutory instrument make such provision in addition to subsection (3) as he considers appropriate in connection with such registers or other records as are mentioned in that subsection, and are kept as so mentioned; and the regulations may make modifications of provisions of this Act relating to such registers or other records.

(5)   A statutory instrument under subsection (4) is subject to annulment in pursuance of a resolution of either House of Parliament.

723A Obligations of limited liability partnership as to inspection of registers, &c

(1)   The Secretary of State may make provision by regulations as to the obligations of a limited liability partnership which is required by any provision of this Act—

(a)   to make available for inspection any register, index or document, or

(b)   to provide copies of any such register, index or document, or part of it;
and a limited liability partnership which fails to comply with the regulations shall be deemed to have refused inspection or, as the case may be, to have failed to provide a copy.

(2)   The regulations may make provision as to the time, duration and manner of inspection, including the circumstances in which and extent to which the copying of information is permitted in the course of inspection.

(3)   The regulations may define what may be required of the limited liability partnership as regards the nature, extent and manner of extracting or presenting any information for the purposes of inspection or the provision of copies.

(4)   Where there is power to charge a fee, the regulations may make provision as to the amount of the fee and the basis of its calculation.

(5)   Regulations under this section may make different provision for different classes of case.

(6)   Nothing in any provision of this Act or in the regulations shall be construed as preventing a limited liability partnership from affording more extensive facilities than are required by the regulations or, where a fee may be charged, from charging a lesser fee than that prescribed or no fee at all.

(7)   Regulations under this section shall be made by statutory instrument which shall be subject to annulment in pursuance of a resolution of either House of Parliament.

725 Service of documents

(1)   A document may be served on a limited liability partnership by leaving it at, or sending it by post to, the limited liability partnership's registered office.

(2)   Where a limited liability partnership registered in Scotland carries on business in England and Wales, the process of any court in England and Wales may be served on the limited liability partnership by leaving it at, or sending it by post to, the limited liability partnership's principal place of business in England and Wales, addressed to the manager or [a designated member] in England and Wales of the limited liability partnership.

(3)   Where process is served on a limited liability partnership under subsection (2), the person issuing out the process shall send a copy of it by post to the limited liability partnership's registered office.

726 Costs and expenses in actions by certain limited liability partnerships

(1)   Where in England and Wales a limited liability partnership is plaintiff in an action or other legal proceeding, the court having jurisdiction in the matter may,

if it appears by credible testimony that there is reason to believe that the limited liability partnership will be unable to pay the defendant's costs if successful in his defence, require sufficient security to be given for those costs, and may stay all proceedings until the security is given.

(2) Where in Scotland a limited liability partnership is pursuer in an action or other legal proceeding, the court having jurisdiction in the matter may, if it appears by credible testimony that there is reason to believe that the limited liability partnership will be unable to pay the defender's expenses if successful in his defence, order the limited liability partnership to find caution and sist the proceedings until caution is found.

727 Power of court to grant relief in certain cases

(1) If in any proceedings for negligence, default, breach of duty or breach of trust against ... a person employed by a limited liability partnership as auditor (whether he is or is not a member of the limited liability partnership) it appears to the court hearing the case that that ... person is or may be liable in respect of the negligence, default, breach of duty or breach of trust, but that he has acted honestly and reasonably, and that having regard to all the circumstances of the case (including those connected with his appointment) he ought fairly to be excused for the negligence, default, breach of duty or breach of trust, that court may relieve him, either wholly or partly, from his liability on such terms as it thinks fit.

(2) If any such ... person as above-mentioned has reason to apprehend that any claim will or might be made against him in respect of any negligence, default, breach of duty or breach of trust, he may apply to the court for relief; and the court on the application has the same power to relieve him as under this section it would have had if it had been a court before which proceedings against that person for negligence, default, breach of duty or breach of trust had been brought.

(3) Where a case to which subsection (1) applies is being tried by a judge with a jury, the judge, after hearing the evidence, may, if he is satisfied that the defendant or defender ought in pursuance of that subsection to be relieved either in whole or in part from the liability sought to be enforced against him, withdraw the case in whole or in part from the jury and forthwith direct judgment to be entered for the defendant or defender on such terms as to costs or otherwise as the judge may think proper.

728 Enforcement of High Court orders

Orders made by the High Court under this Act may be enforced in the same manner as orders made in an action pending in that court.

729 Annual report by Secretary of State

The Secretary of State shall cause a general annual report of matters within the Companies Acts to be prepared and laid before both Houses of Parliament.

730 Punishment of offences

(1)   Schedule 24 to this Act has effect with respect to the way in which offences under this Act are punishable on conviction.

(2)   In relation to an offence under a provision of this Act specified in the first column of the Schedule (the general nature of the offence being described in the second column), the third column shows whether the offence is punishable on conviction on indictment, or on summary conviction, or either in the one way or the other.

(3)   The fourth column of the Schedule shows, in relation to an offence, the maximum punishment by way of fine or imprisonment under this Act which may be imposed on a person convicted of the offence in the way specified in relation to it in the third column (that is to say, on indictment or summarily), a reference to a period of years or months being to a term of imprisonment of that duration.

(4)   The fifth column shows (in relation to an offence for which there is an entry in that column) that a person convicted of the offence after continued contravention is liable to a daily default fine; that is to say, he is liable on a second or subsequent summary conviction of the offence to the fine specified in that column for each day on which the contravention is continued (instead of the penalty specified for the offence in the fourth column of the Schedule).

(5)   For the purpose of any enactment in the Companies Acts which provides that a member of a limited liability partnership or other body who is in default is liable to a fine or penalty, the expression "member who is in default" means any member of the limited liability partnership or other body who knowingly and wilfully authorises or permits the default, refusal or contravention mentioned in the enactment.

731 Summary proceedings

(1)   Summary proceedings for any offence under the Companies Acts may (without prejudice to any jurisdiction exercisable apart from this subsection) be taken against a body corporate at any place at which the body has a place of business, and against any other person at any place at which he is for the time being.

(2)   Notwithstanding anything in section 127(1) of the Magistrates' Courts Act 1980, an information relating to an offence under the Companies Acts which is triable by a magistrates' court in England and Wales may be so tried if it is laid at any time within three years after the commission of the offence and within twelve months after the date on which evidence sufficient in the opinion of the Director of Public Prosecutions or the Secretary of State (as the case may be) to justify the proceedings comes to his knowledge.

(3)   Summary proceedings in Scotland for an offence under the Companies Acts shall not be commenced after the expiration of three years from the commission of the offence.

Subject to this (and notwithstanding anything in section 136 of the Criminal Procedure (Scotland) Act 1995), such proceedings may (in Scotland) be commenced at any time within twelve months after the date on which evidence sufficient in the Lord Advocate's opinion to justify the proceedings came to his knowledge or, where such evidence was reported to him by the Secretary of State, within twelve months after the date on which it came to the knowledge of the latter; and subsection (3) of that section applies for the purpose of this subsection as it applies for the purpose of that section.

(4) For purposes of this section, a certificate of the Director of Public Prosecutions, the Lord Advocate or the Secretary of State (as the case may be) as to the date on which such evidence as is referred to above came to his knowledge is conclusive evidence.

732 Prosecution by public authorities

(1) In respect of an offence under any of sections ... 447 to 451 ..., proceedings shall not, in England and Wales, be instituted except by or with the consent of the appropriate authority.

(2) That authority is–
  (a) ...
  (b) for an offence under any of sections 447 to 451, [either the Secretary of State, the Director of Public Prosecutions] or the Friendly Societies Commission ...
  (c) ...

(3) ...

733 Offences by bodies corporate

(1) The following applies to offences under any of sections ... 394A(1) and 447 to 451.

(2) Where a body corporate is guilty of such an offence and it is proved that the offence occurred with the consent or connivance of, or was attributable to any neglect on the part of any director, manager ... or other similar officer of the body, or any person who was purporting to act in any such capacity, he as well as the body corporate is guilty of that offence and is liable to be proceeded against and punished accordingly.

(3) ...

(4) In this section "director", in relation to an offence under any of sections 447 to 451, includes a shadow director.

734 Criminal proceedings against unincorporated bodies

(1) Proceedings for an offence alleged to have been committed under section 389A(3) or section 394A(1) or any of sections 447 to 451 by an unincorporated

body shall be brought in the name of that body (and not in that of any of its members), and for the purposes of any such proceedings, any rules of court relating to the service of documents apply as if that body were a corporation.

(2)   A fine imposed on an unincorporated body on its conviction of such an offence shall be paid out of the funds of that body.

(3)   In a case in which an unincorporated body is charged in England and Wales with such an offence, section 33 of the Criminal Justice Act 1925 and Schedule 3 to the Magistrates' Courts Act 1980 (procedure on charge of an offence against a corporation) have effect in like manner as in the case of a corporation so charged.

(4)   In relation to proceedings on indictment in Scotland for such an offence alleged to have been committed by an unincorporated body, section 70 of the Criminal Procedure (Scotland) Act 1995 (proceedings on indictment against bodies corporate) has effect as if that body were a body corporate.

(5)   Where such an offence committed by a partnership is proved to have been committed with the consent or connivance of, or to be attributable to any neglect on the part of, a partner, he as well as the partnership is guilty of the offence and liable to be proceeded against and punished accordingly.

(6)   Where such an offence committed by an unincorporated body (other than a partnership) is proved to have been committed with the consent or connivance of, or to be attributable to any neglect on the part of, any officer of the body or any member of its governing body, he as well as the body is guilty of the offence and liable to be proceeded against and punished accordingly.

PART XXVI
INTERPRETATION

735

735A Relationship of this Act to Insolvency Act

(1)   In this Act "the Insolvency Act" means the Insolvency Act 1986; and in the following provisions of this Act, namely, sections … 425(6)(a), 460(2) [and] 728 …, the words "this Act" are to be read as including Parts I to VII of that Act, sections 411, 413, 414, 416 and 417 in Part XV of that Act, and also the Company Directors Disqualifications Act 1986.

(2)   In sections 704(5), (7) and (8), 706(1), 707A(1), 707B(1), 708(1)(a) and (4), 709(1) and (3), 710A, 713(1), 729 and 732(3) references to the Companies Acts include Parts I to VII of the Insolvency Act, sections 411, 413, 414, 416 and 417 in Part XV of that Act, and also the Company Directors Disqualification Act 1986.

(3)   Subsections (1) and (2) apply unless the contrary intention appears.

340

736 "Subsidiary", "holding company" and "wholly owned subsidiary"

[(1)   Subject to subsection (1A) a company is a "subsidiary" of a limited liability partnership, its "holding company", if that limited liability partnership–
  (a)   holds a majority of the voting rights in it, or
  (b)   is a member of it and has the right to appoint or remove a majority of its board of directors, or
  (c)   is a member of it and controls alone, pursuant to an agreement with other shareholders or members, a majority of the voting rights in it,
or if it is a subsidiary of a company or limited liability partnership which is itself a subsidiary of that other company.]

[(1A) A limited liability partnership is a subsidiary of a company or a subsidiary of another limited liability partnership (such company or limited liability partnership being referred to in this section as its "holding company") if that company or limited liability partnership–
  (a)   holds a majority of the voting rights in it;
  (b)   is a member of it and has the right to appoint or remove a majority of other members; or
  (c)   is a member of it and controls, alone or pursuant to an agreement with other members, a majority of voting rights in it,
or if it is a subsidiary of a company or limited liability partnership which is itself a subsidiary of that holding company.]

(2)   [A company or a limited liability partnership is a "wholly-owned subsidiary" of another company or limited liability partnership if it has no members except that other and that other's wholly-owned subsidiaries or persons acting on behalf of that other or its wholly-owned subsidiaries.]

(3)   In this section "company" includes any body corporate.

736A Provisions supplementing s 736

(1)   The provisions of this section explain expressions used in section 736 and otherwise supplement that section.

[(1A) In section 736(1A)(a) and (c) the references to the voting rights in a limited liability partnership are to the rights conferred on members in respect of their interest in the limited liability partnership to vote on those matters which are to be decided upon by a vote of the members of the limited liability partnership.]

(2)   In section 736(1)(a) and (c) the references to the voting rights in a company are to the rights conferred on shareholders in respect of their shares or, in the case of a company not having a share capital, on members, to vote at general meetings of the company on all, or substantially all, matters.

[(2A) In section 736(1A)(b) the reference to the right to appoint or remove a majority of the members of the limited liability partnership is to the right to appoint or remove members holding a majority of the voting rights referred to in subsection (1A) and for this purpose–

(a) the person shall be treated as having the right to appoint a member if
   (i)   a person's appointment as member results directly from his appointment as a director or member of the holding company, or
   (ii) the member of the limited liability partnership is the company or limited liability partnership which is the holding company; and
(b) a right to appoint or remove which is exercisable only with the consent or concurrence of another person shall be left out of account.]

(3)   In section 736(1)(b) the reference to the right to appoint or remove a majority of the board of directors is to the right to appoint or remove directors holding a majority of the voting rights at meetings of the board on all, or substantially all, matters; and for the purposes of that provision–
(a) a company shall be treated as having the right to appoint to a directorship if–
   (i)   a person's appointment to it follows necessarily from his appointment as director of the company, or
   (ii) the directorship is held by the company itself; and
(b) a right to appoint or remove which is exercisable only with the consent or concurrence of another person shall be left out of account unless no other person has a right to appoint or, as the case may be, remove in relation to that directorship.

(4)   Rights which are exercisable only in certain circumstances shall be taken into account only–
(a) when the circumstances have arisen, and for so long as they continue to obtain, or
(b) when the circumstances are within the control of the person having the rights;
and rights which are normally exercisable but are temporarily incapable of exercise shall continue to be taken into account.

(5)   Rights held by a person in a fiduciary capacity shall be treated as not held by him.

(6)   Rights held by a person as nominee for another shall be treated as held by the other; and rights shall be regarded as held as nominee for another if they are exercisable only on his instructions or with his consent or concurrence.

(7)   Rights attached to shares [or to a member's interest in a limited liability partnership] held by way of security shall be treated as held by the person providing the security–
(a) where apart from the right to exercise them for the purpose of preserving the value of the security, or of realising it, the rights are exercisable only in accordance with his instructions;
(b) where the shares are held in connection with the granting of loans as part of normal business activities and apart from the right to exercise them for the purpose of preserving the value of the security, or of realising it, the rights are exercisable only in his interests.

(8)   Rights shall be treated as held by a company [or a limited liability partnership] if they are held by any of its subsidiaries; and nothing in subsection (6) or (7) shall be construed as requiring rights held by a company [or a limited liability partnership] to be treated as held by any of its subsidiaries.

(9)   For the purposes of subsection (7) rights shall be treated as being exercisable in accordance with the instructions or in the interests of a company [or a limited liability partnership] if they are exercisable in accordance with the instructions of or, as the case may be, in the interests of–

    (a)   any subsidiary or holding company of that company [or the limited liability partnership], or

    (b)   any subsidiary of a holding company of that company [or the limited liability partnership].

(10)   The voting rights in a company [or a limited liability partnership] shall be reduced by any rights held by the company [or the limited liability partnership] itself.

(11)   References in any provision of subsections (5) to (10) to rights held by a person include rights falling to be treated as held by him by virtue of any other provision of those subsections but not rights which by virtue of any such provision are to be treated as not held by him.

(12)   [In this section "company" includes a body corporate other than a limited liability partnership.]

736B–738

739 "Non-cash asset"

(1)   In this Act "non-cash asset" means any property or interest in property other than cash; and for this purpose "cash" includes foreign currency.

(2)   A reference to the transfer or acquisition of a non-cash asset includes the creation or extinction of an estate or interest in, or a right over, any property and also the discharge of any person's liability, other than a liability for a liquidated sum.

740 "Body corporate" and "corporation"

References in this Act to a body corporate or to a corporation do not include a corporation sole, but include a company incorporated elsewhere than in Great Britain.

    Such references to a body corporate do not include a Scottish firm.

741 "Member" and "shadow member"

(1)   In this Act, "member" includes any person occupying the position of member, by whatever name called.

(2)   In relation to a limited liability partnership, "shadow member" means a person in accordance with whose directions or instructions the members of the limited liability partnership are accustomed to act.

However, a person is not deemed a shadow member by reason only that the members act on advice given by him in a professional capacity.

(3)   …

742 Expressions used in connection with accounts

(1)   In this Act, unless a contrary intention appears, the following expressions have the same meaning as in Part VII (accounts)–

"annual accounts",

"accounting reference date" and "accounting reference period",

"balance sheet" and "balance sheet date",

"current assets",

"financial year", in relation to a limited liability partnership,

"fixed assets",

"parent company" and "parent undertaking",

"profit and loss account", and

"subsidiary undertaking".

(2)   References in this Act to "realised profits" and "realised losses", in relation to a company's accounts, shall be construed in accordance with section 262(3).

(2A)   References in this Act to sending or sending out copies of any of the documents referred to in section 238(1) include sending or sending out such copies in accordance with section 238(4A) or (4B).

743

743A Meaning of "office copy" in Scotland

References in this Act to an office copy of a court order shall be construed, as respects Scotland, as references to a certified copy interlocutor.

744 Expressions used generally in this Act

In this Act, unless the contrary intention appears, the following definitions apply–

"agent" does not include a person's counsel acting as such;

"bank holiday" means a holiday under the Banking and Financial Dealings Act 1971;

"banking company" means a company which is authorised under the Banking Act 1987;

"books and papers" and "books or papers" include accounts, deeds, writings and documents;

"communication" means the same as in the Electronic Communications Act 2000;

"the Companies Acts" means this Act, the insider dealing legislation and the Consequential Provisions Act;

"the Consequential Provisions Act" means the Companies Consolidation (Consequential Provisions) Act 1985;

"the court", in relation to a limited liability partnership, means the court having jurisdiction to wind up the limited liability partnership;

"debenture" includes debenture stock, bonds and any other securities of a limited liability partnership, whether constituting a charge on the assets of the limited liability partnership or not;

"document" includes summons, notice, order, and other legal process, and registers;

"EEA State" means a State which is a Contracting Party to the Agreement on the European Economic Area signed at Oporto on 2nd May 1992 as adjusted by the Protocol signed at Brussels on 17th March 1993;

"electronic communication" means the same as in the Electronic Communications Act 2000;

"expert" has the meaning given by section 62;

"floating charge" includes a floating charge within the meaning given by section 462;

"the Gazette" means, as respects limited liability partnerships registered in England and Wales, the London Gazette and, as respects limited liability partnerships registered in Scotland, the Edinburgh Gazette;

"hire-purchase agreement" has the same meaning as in the Consumer Credit Act 1974;

"incorporation document", in relation to a limited liability partnership, means its incorporation document, as originally framed or as altered in pursuance of any enactment;

"insurance company" means the same as in the Insurance Companies Act 1982;

"limited liability partnership" has the meaning given it in section 1(2) of the Limited Liability Partnerships Act 2001

"number", in relation to shares, includes amount, where the context admits of the reference to shares being construed to include stock;

"officer", in relation to a body corporate, includes a director, manager or secretary;

"official seal", in relation to the registrar of companies, means a seal prepared under section 704(4) for the authentication of documents required for or in connection with the registration of limited liability partnerships;

"oversea company" means–
- (a) a company incorporated elsewhere than in Great Britain which, after the commencement of this Act, establishes a place of business in Great Britain, and
- (b) a company so incorporated which has, before that commencement, established a place of business and continues to have an established place of business in Great Britain at that commencement;

"place of business" includes a share transfer or share registration office;

"prescribed" means–
- (a) as respects provisions of this Act relating to winding up, prescribed by general rules, and
- (b) otherwise, prescribed by statutory instrument made by the Secretary of State;

"the registrar of companies" and "the registrar" mean the registrar or other officer performing under this Act the duty of registration of companies in England and Wales or in Scotland, as the case may require;

"shadow member" has the same meaning as it has in the Limited Liability Partnerships Regulations 2000.

744A Index of defined expressions

The following Table shows provisions defining or otherwise explaining expressions for the purposes of this Act generally–

accounting reference date, accounting reference period	sections 224 and 742(1)
acquisition (in relation to a non-cash asset)	section 739(2)
agent	section 744
annual accounts	sections 261(2), 262(1) and 742(1)
annual return	section 363

balance sheet and balance sheet date	sections 261(2), 262(1) and 742(1)
bank holiday	section 744
banking company	section 744
body corporate	section 740
books and papers, books or papers	section 744
communication	section 744
the Companies Acts	section 744
companies charges register	section 397
company	section 735(1)
the Consequential Provisions Act	section 744
corporation	section 740
the court (in relation to a limited liability partnership)	section 744
current assets	sections 262(1) and 742(1)
debenture	section 744
member	section 741(1)
document	section 744
EEA State	section 744
electronic communication	section 744
financial year (of a limited liability partnership)	sections 223 and 742(1)
fixed assets	sections 262(1) and 742(1)
floating charge (in Scotland)	section 462
the Gazette	section 744
hire-purchase agreement	section 744
holding company	section 736
the Insolvency Act	section 735A(1)
insurance company	section 744
limited company	section 1(2)
member (of a company)	section 22
incorporation document (in relation to a limited liability partnership)	section 744
non-cash asset	section 739(1)
office copy (in relation to a court order in Scotland)	section 743A
officer (in relation to a body corporate)	section 744
official seal (in relation to the registrar of companies)	section 744
oversea company	section 744
parent company and parent undertaking	sections 258 and 742(1)
place of business	section 744
prescribed	section 744
private company	section 1(3)
profit and loss account	sections 261(2), 262(1) and 742(1)
realised profits or losses	sections 262(3) and 742(2)
registered number (of a limited liability partnership)	section 705(1)

registrar and registrar of companies	section 744
shadow member	section 741(2) and (3)
subsidiary	section 736
subsidiary undertaking	sections 258 and 742(1)
transfer (in relation to a non-cash asset)	section 739(2)
undistributable reserves	section 264(3)
wholly-owned subsidiary	section 736(2)

Schedules 1–3

SCHEDULE 4
FORM AND CONTENT OF LIMITED LIABILITY PARTNERSHIP
ACCOUNTS

PART I
GENERAL RULES AND FORMATS

Section A
General Rules

1 – (1)   Subject to the following provisions of this Schedule–
   (a)   every balance sheet of a limited liability partnership shall show the items listed in either of the balance sheet formats set out below in section B of this Part; and
   (b)   every profit and loss account of a limited liability partnership shall show the items listed in [either of] the profit and loss account formats so set out;
in either case in the order and under the headings and sub-headings given in the format adopted.

(2)   Sub-paragraph (1) above is not to be read as requiring the heading or sub-heading for any item to be distinguished by any letter or number assigned to that item in the format adopted.

2 – (1)   Where in accordance with paragraph 1 a limited liability partnership's balance sheet or profit and loss account for any financial year has been prepared by reference to one of the formats set out in section B below, the members of the limited liability partnership shall adopt the same format in preparing the accounts for subsequent financial years of the limited liability partnership unless in their opinion there are special reasons for a change.

(2)   Particulars of any change in the format adopted in preparing a limited liability partnership's balance sheet or profit and loss account in accordance with paragraph 1 shall be disclosed, and the reasons for the change shall be explained, in a note to the accounts in which the new format is first adopted.

3 – (1)   Any item required in accordance with paragraph 1 to be shown in a limited liability partnership's balance sheet or profit and loss account may be shown in greater detail than required by the format adopted.

(2)   A limited liability partnership's balance sheet or profit and loss account may include an item representing or covering the amount of any asset or liability, income or expenditure not otherwise covered by any of the items listed in the format adopted, but the following shall not be treated as assets in any limited liability partnership's balance sheet–
  (a)   preliminary expenses;
  (b)   expenses of and commission on any issue of ... debentures; and
  (c)   costs of research.

(3)   In preparing a limited liability partnership's balance sheet or profit and loss account the members of the limited liability partnership shall adapt the arrangement and headings and sub-headings otherwise required by paragraph 1 in respect of items to which an Arabic number is assigned in the format adopted, in any case where the special nature of the limited liability partnership's business requires such adaptation.

(4)   Items to which Arabic numbers are assigned in any of the formats set out in section B below may be combined in a limited liability partnership's accounts for any financial year if either–
  (a)   their individual amounts are not material to assessing the state of affairs or profit or loss of the limited liability partnership for that year; or
  (b)   the combination facilitates that assessment;
but in a case within paragraph (b) the individual amounts of any items so combined shall be disclosed in a note to the accounts.

(5)   Subject to paragraph 4(3) below, a heading or sub-heading corresponding to an item listed in the format adopted in preparing a limited liability partnership's balance sheet or profit and loss account shall not be included if there is no amount to be shown for that item in respect of the financial year to which the balance sheet or profit and loss account relates.

(6)   Every profit and loss account of a limited liability partnership shall show the amount of the limited liability partnership's profit or loss on ordinary activities before taxation.

(7)   Every profit and loss account of a limited liability partnership shall show separately as additional items–
  (a)   any amount set aside or proposed to be set aside to, or withdrawn or proposed to be withdrawn from, reserves;
  (b),(c)   ...

4 – (1)   In respect of every item shown in a limited liability partnership's balance sheet or profit and loss account the corresponding amount for the financial year immediately preceding that to which the balance sheet or profit and loss account relates shall also be shown.

(2)   Where that corresponding amount is not comparable with the amount to be shown for the item in question in respect of the financial year to which the balance sheet or profit and loss account relates, the former amount shall be adjusted

and particulars of the adjustment and the reasons for it shall be disclosed in a note to the accounts.

(3)   Paragraph 3(5) does not apply in any case where an amount can be shown for the item in question in respect of the financial year immediately preceding that to which the balance sheet or profit and loss account relates, and that amount shall be shown under the heading or sub-heading required by paragraph 1 for that item.

5   Amounts in respect of items representing assets or income may not be set off against amounts in respect of items representing liabilities or expenditure (as the case may be), or vice versa.

Section B
The Required Formats for Accounts

Preliminary

6   References in this Part of this Schedule to the items listed in any of the formats set out below are to those items read together with any of the notes following the formats which apply to any of those items, and the requirement imposed by paragraph 1 to show the items listed in any such format in the order adopted in the format is subject to any provision in those notes for alternative positions for any particular items.

7   A number in brackets following any item in any of the formats set out below is a reference to the note of that number in the notes following the formats.

8   In the notes following the formats–
   (a)   the heading of each note gives the required heading or sub-heading for the item to which it applies and a reference to any letters and numbers assigned to that item in the formats set out below (taking a reference in the case of Format 2 of the balance sheet formats to the item listed under "Assets" or under "Liabilities" as the case may require); and
   (b)   references to a numbered format are to the balance sheet format or (as the case may require) to the profit and loss account format of that number set out below.

Balance sheet formats
Format 1

A. ...
B. Fixed assets
    I Intangible assets
        1. Development costs
        2. Concessions, patents, licences, trade marks and similar rights and assets *(2)*
        3. Goodwill *(3)*

350

        4. Payments on account
    II Tangible assets
        1. Land and buildings
        2. Plant and machinery
        3. Fixtures, fittings, tools and equipment
        4. Payments on account and assets in course of construction
    III Investments
        1. Shares in group undertakings
        2. Loans to group undertakings
        3. Participating interests
        4. Loans to undertakings in which the limited liability partnership has a participating interest
        5. Other investments other than loans
        6. Other loans
        7. …
C. Current assets
    I Stocks
        1. Raw materials and consumables
        2. Work in progress
        3. Finished goods and goods for resale
        4. Payments on account
    II Debtors *(5)*
        1. Trade debtors
        2. Amounts owed by group undertakings
        3. Amounts owed by undertakings in which the limited liability partnership has a participating interest
        4. Other debtors
        5. …
        6. Prepayments and accrued income *(6)*
    III Investments
        1. Shares in group undertakings
        2. …
        3. Other investments
    IV Cash at bank and in hand
D. Prepayments and accrued income *(6)*
E. Creditors: amounts falling due within one year
        1. Debenture loans *(7)*
        2. Bank loans and overdrafts
        3. Payments received on account *(8)*
        4. Trade creditors
        5. Bills of exchange payable
        6. Amounts owed to group undertakings
        7. Amounts owed to undertakings in which the limited liability partnership has a participating interest
        8. Other creditors including taxation and social security *(9)*
        9. Accruals and deferred income *(10)*
F. Net current assets (liabilities) *(11)*
G. Total assets less current liabilities
H. Creditors: amounts falling due after more than one year

1. Debenture loans *(7)*
2. Bank loans and overdrafts
3. Payments received on account *(8)*
4. Trade creditors
5. Bills of exchange payable
6. Amounts owed to group undertakings
7. Amounts owed to undertakings in which the limited liability partnership has a participating interest
8. Other creditors including taxation and social security *(9)*
9. Accruals and deferred income *(10)*

I. Provisions for liabilities and charges
1. Pensions and similar obligations
2. Taxation, including deferred taxation
3. Other provisions

J. Accruals and deferred income *(10)*
[K. Loans and other debts due to members *(12)*
L. Members' other interests
I Members' capital
II Revaluation reserve
III Other reserves]

Balance sheet formats
Format 2

ASSETS
A. …
B. Fixed assets
I Intangible assets
1. Development costs
2. Concessions, patents, licences, trade marks and similar rights and assets *(2)*
3. Goodwill *(3)*
4. Payments on account
II Tangible assets
1. Land and buildings
2. Plant and machinery
3. Fixtures, fittings, tools and equipment
4. Payments on account and assets in course of construction
III Investments
1. Shares in group undertakings
2. Loans to group undertakings
3. Participating interests
4. Loans to undertakings in which the limited liability partnership has a participating interest
5. Other investments other than loans
6. Other loans
7. …
C. Current assets
I Stocks

    1. Raw materials and consumables
    2. Work in progress
    3. Finished goods and goods for resale
    4. Payments on account
  II Debtors *(5)*
    1. Trade debtors
    2. Amounts owed by group undertakings
    3. Amounts owed by undertakings in which the limited liability partnership has a participating interest
    4. Other debtors
    5. …
    6. Prepayments and accrued income *(6)*
  III Investments
    1. Shares in group undertakings
    2. …
    3. Other investments
  IV Cash at bank and in hand
D. Prepayments and accrued income *(6)*

LIABILITIES
[A. Loans and other debts due to members *(12)*
AA Members' other interests
  I Members' capital
  II Revaluation reserve
  III Other reserves]
B. Provisions for liabilities and charges
    1. Pensions and similar obligations
    2. Taxation including deferred taxation
    3. Other provisions
C. Creditors *(13)*
    1. Debenture loans (7)
    2. Bank loans and overdrafts
    3. Payments received on account *(8)*
    4. Trade creditors
    5. Bills of exchange payable
    6. Amounts owed to group undertakings
    7. Amounts owed to undertakings in which the limited liability partnership has a participating interest
    8. Other creditors including taxation and social security *(9)*
    9. Accruals and deferred income *(10)*
D. Accruals and deferred income *(10)*

Notes on the balance sheet formats

(1)   …

(2)   *Concessions, patents, licences, trade marks and similar rights and assets*
(Formats 1 and 2, item B.I.2.)
    Amounts in respect of assets shall only be included in a limited liability partnership's balance sheet under this item if either–

    (a)   the assets were acquired for valuable consideration and are not required to be shown under goodwill; or

    (b)   the assets in question were created by the limited liability partnership itself.

(3)   Goodwill
(Formats 1 and 2, item B.I.3.)
    Amounts representing goodwill shall only be included to the extent that the goodwill was acquired for valuable consideration.

(4)   ...

(5)   Debtors
(Formats 1 and 2, items C.II.1 to 6.)
    The amount falling due after more than one year shall be shown separately for each item included under debtors.

(6)   Prepayments and accrued income
(Formats 1 and 2, items C.II.6 and D.)
    This item may be shown in either of the two positions given in Formats 1 and 2.

(7)   Debenture loans
(Format 1, items E.1 and H.1 and Format 2, item C.1.)
    The amount of any convertible loans shall be shown separately.

(8)   Payments received on account
(Format 1, items E.3 and H.3 and Format 2, item C.3.)
    Payments received on account of orders shall be shown for each of these items in so far as they are not shown as deductions from stocks.

(9)   Other creditors including taxation and social security
(Format 1, items E.8 and H.8 and Format 2, item C.8.)
    The amount for creditors in respect of taxation and social security shall be shown separately from the amount for other creditors.

(10)   Accruals and deferred income
(Format 1, items E.9, H.9 and J and Format 2, items C.9 and D.)
    The two positions given for this item in Format 1 at E.9 and H.9 are an alternative to the position at J, but if the item is not shown in a position corresponding to that at J it may be shown in either or both of the other two positions (as the case may require).
    The two positions given for this item in Format 2 are alternatives.

(11)   Net current assets (liabilities)
(Format 1, item F.)
    In determining the amount to be shown for this item any amount shown under "prepayments and accrued income" shall be taken into account wherever shown.

[*(12) Loans and other debts due to members*
(Format 1, item K. and Format 2, item A.)
The following amounts shall be shown separately under this item–
(a) the aggregate amount of money advanced to the limited liability partnership by the members by way of loan,
(b) the aggregate amount of money owed to members by the limited liability partnership in respect of profits,
(c) any other amounts.]

(13) Creditors
(Format 2, items C.1 to 9.)
Amounts falling due within one year and after one year shall be shown separately for each of these items and for the aggregate of all of these items.

Profit and loss account formats
Format 1
(see note *(17)* below)

1. Turnover
2. Cost of sales *(14)*
3. Gross profit or loss
4. Distribution costs *(14)*
5. Administrative expenses *(14)*
6. Other operating income
7. Income from shares in group undertakings
8. Income from participating interests
9. Income from other fixed asset investments *(15)*
10. Other interest receivable and similar income *(15)*
11. Amounts written off investments
12. Interest payable and similar charges *(16)*
13. Tax on profit or loss on ordinary activities
14. Profit or loss on ordinary activities after taxation
15. Extraordinary income
16. Extraordinary charges
17. Extraordinary profit or loss
18. Tax on extraordinary profit or loss
19. Other taxes not shown under the above items
[20. Profit or loss for the financial year before members' remuneration and profit shares]

Profit and loss account formats
Format 2

1. Turnover
2. Change in stocks of finished goods and in work in progress
3. Own work capitalised
4. Other operating income
5. – (a) Raw materials and consumables
      (b) Other external charges

6. Staff costs:
   (a) wages and salaries
   (b) social security costs
   (c) other pension costs
7. – (a)   Depreciation and other amounts written off tangible and intangible fixed assets
   (b) Exceptional amounts written off current assets
8. Other operating charges
9. Income from shares in group undertakings
10. Income from participating interests
11. Income from other fixed asset investments *(15)*
12. Other interest receivable and similar income *(15)*
13. Amounts written off investments
14. Interest payable and similar charges *(16)*
15. Tax on profit or loss on ordinary activities
16. Profit or loss on ordinary activities after taxation
17. Extraordinary income
18. Extraordinary charges
19. Extraordinary profit or loss
20. Tax on extraordinary profit or loss
21. Other taxes not shown under the above items
[22. Profit or loss for the financial year before members' remuneration and profit shares]

Profit and loss account formats
Format 3

…

Profit and loss account formats
Format 4

…

Notes on the profit and loss account formats

(14)   Cost of sales: distribution costs: administrative expenses
(Format 1, items 2, 4 and 5 …)
      These items shall be stated after taking into account any necessary provisions for depreciation or diminution in value of assets.

(15)   Income from other fixed asset investments: other interest receivable and similar income
(Format 1, items 9 and 10: Format 2, items 11 and 12 …)
      Income and interest derived from group undertakings shall be shown separately from income and interest derived from other sources. [Interest receivable from members shall not be included under this item.]

(16)   Interest payable and similar charges
(Format 1, item 12: Format 2, item 14 …)

The amount payable to group undertakings shall be shown separately. [Interest payable to members shall not be included under this item.]

(17) Format 1 ...

The amount of any provisions for depreciation and diminution in value of tangible and intangible fixed assets falling to be shown under items 7(a) and A.4(a) respectively in Format 2 ... shall be disclosed in a note to the accounts in any case where the profit and loss account is prepared by reference to Format 1...

PART II
ACCOUNTING PRINCIPLES AND RULES

Section A
Accounting Principles

Preliminary

9 Subject to paragraph 15 below, the amounts to be included in respect of all items shown in a limited liability partnership's accounts shall be determined in accordance with the principles set out in paragraphs 10 to 14.

Accounting principles

10 The limited liability partnership shall be presumed to be carrying on business as a going concern.

11 Accounting policies shall be applied consistently within the same accounts and from one financial year to the next.

12 The amount of any item shall be determined on a prudent basis, and in particular–

(a) only profits realised at the balance sheet date shall be included in the profit and loss account; and

(b) all liabilities and losses which have arisen or are likely to arise in respect of the financial year to which the accounts relate or a previous financial year shall be taken into account, including those which only become apparent between the balance sheet date and the date on which it is signed ... in pursuance of section 233 of this Act.

13 All income and charges relating to the financial year to which the accounts relate shall be taken into account, without regard to the date of receipt or payment.

14 In determining the aggregate amount of any item the amount of each individual asset or liability that falls to be taken into account shall be determined separately.

Departure from the accounting principles

15 If it appears to the designated members of a limited liability partnership that there are special reasons for departing from any of the principles stated above in preparing the limited liability partnership's accounts in respect of any financial year they may do so, but particulars of the departure, the reasons for it and its effect shall be given in a note to the accounts.

Section B
Historical Cost Accounting Rules

Preliminary

16   Subject to section C of this Part of this Schedule, the amounts to be included in respect of all items shown in a limited liability partnership's accounts shall be determined in accordance with the rules set out in paragraphs 17 to 28.

Fixed assets

17   Subject to any provision for depreciation or diminution in value made in accordance with paragraph 18 or 19 the amount to be included in respect of any fixed asset shall be its purchase price or production cost.

18   In the case of any fixed asset which has a limited useful economic life, the amount of–
    (a)   its purchase price or production cost; or
    (b)   where it is estimated that any such asset will have a residual value at the end of the period of its useful economic life, its purchase price or production cost less that estimated residual value;
shall be reduced by provisions for depreciation calculated to write off that amount systematically over the period of the asset's useful economic life.

19 – (1)   Where a fixed asset investment of a description falling to be included under item B.III of either of the balance sheet formats set out in Part I of this Schedule has diminished in value provisions for diminution in value may be made in respect of it and the amount to be included in respect of it may be reduced accordingly; and any such provisions which are not shown in the profit and loss account shall be disclosed (either separately or in aggregate) in a note to the accounts.

(2)   Provisions for diminution in value shall be made in respect of any fixed asset which has diminished in value if the reduction in its value is expected to be permanent (whether its useful economic life is limited or not), and the amount to be included in respect of it shall be reduced accordingly; and any such provisions which are not shown in the profit and loss account shall be disclosed (either separately or in aggregate) in a note to the accounts.

(3)   Where the reasons for which any provision was made in accordance with sub-paragraph (1) or (2) have ceased to apply to any extent, that provision shall be written back to the extent that it is no longer necessary; and any amounts written back in accordance with this sub-paragraph which are not shown in the profit and loss account shall be disclosed (either separately or in aggregate) in a note to the accounts.

20 – (1)   Notwithstanding that an item in respect of "development costs" is included under "fixed assets" in the balance sheet formats set out in Part I of this Schedule, an amount may only be included in a limited liability partnership's balance sheet in respect of development costs in special circumstances.

(2)   If any amount is included in a limited liability partnership's balance sheet in respect of development costs the following information shall be given in a note to the accounts–

    (a)   the period over which the amount of those costs originally capitalised is being or is to be written off; and

    (b)   the reasons for capitalising the development costs in question.

21 – (1)   The application of paragraphs 17 to 19 in relation to goodwill (in any case where goodwill is treated as an asset) is subject to the following provisions of this paragraph.

(2)   Subject to sub-paragraph (3) below, the amount of the consideration for any goodwill acquired by a limited liability partnership shall be reduced by provisions for depreciation calculated to write off that amount systematically over a period chosen by the members of the limited liability partnership.

(3)   The period chosen shall not exceed the useful economic life of the goodwill in question.

(4)   In any case where any goodwill acquired by a limited liability partnership is shown or included as an asset in the limited liability partnership's balance sheet the period chosen for writing off the consideration for that goodwill and the reasons for choosing that period shall be disclosed in a note to the accounts.

Current assets

22   Subject to paragraph 23, the amount to be included in respect of any current asset shall be its purchase price or production cost.

23 – (1)   If the net realisable value of any current asset is lower than its purchase price or production cost the amount to be included in respect of that asset shall be the net realisable value.

(2)   Where the reasons for which any provision for diminution in value was made in accordance with sub-paragraph (1) have ceased to apply to any extent, that provision shall be written back to the extent that it is no longer necessary.

Miscellaneous and supplementary provisions

24 – (1)   Where the amount repayable on any debt owed by a limited liability partnership is greater than the value of the consideration received in the transaction giving rise to the debt, the amount of the difference may be treated as an asset.

(2)   Where any such amount is so treated–

(a) it shall be written off by reasonable amounts each year and must be completely written off before repayment of the debt; and

(b) if the current amount is not shown as a separate item in the limited liability partnership's balance sheet it must be disclosed in a note to the accounts.

25 – (1) Subject to the following sub-paragraph, assets which fall to be included–

(a) amongst the fixed assets of a limited liability partnership under the item "tangible assets"; or

(b) amongst the current assets of a limited liability partnership under the item "raw materials and consumables";

may be included at a fixed quantity and value.

(2) Sub-paragraph (1) applies to assets of a kind which are constantly being replaced, where–

(a) their overall value is not material to assessing the limited liability partnership's state of affairs; and

(b) their quantity, value and composition are not subject to material variation.

26 – (1) The purchase price of an asset shall be determined by adding to the actual price paid any expenses incidental to its acquisition.

(2) The production cost of an asset shall be determined by adding to the purchase price of the raw materials and consumables used the amount of the costs incurred by the limited liability partnership which are directly attributable to the production of that asset.

(3) In addition, there may be included in the production cost of an asset–

(a) a reasonable proportion of the costs incurred by the limited liability partnership which are only indirectly attributable to the production of that asset, but only to the extent that they relate to the period of production; and

(b) interest on capital borrowed to finance the production of that asset, to the extent that it accrues in respect of the period of production;

provided, however, in a case within paragraph (b) above, that the inclusion of the interest in determining the cost of that asset and the amount of the interest so included is disclosed in a note to the accounts.

(4) In the case of current assets distribution costs may not be included in production costs.

27 – (1) Subject to the qualification mentioned below, the purchase price or production cost of–

(a) any assets which fall to be included under any item shown in a limited liability partnership's balance sheet under the general item "stocks"; and

(b) any assets which are fungible assets (including investments);

may be determined by the application of any of the methods mentioned in sub-paragraph (2) below in relation to any such assets of the same class.

The method chosen must be one which appears to the members to be appropriate in the circumstances of the limited liability partnership.

(2)   Those methods are–
- (a)   the method known as "first in, first out" (FIFO);
- (b)   the method known as "last in, first out" (LIFO);
- (c)   a weighted average price; and
- (d)   any other method similar to any of the methods mentioned above.

(3)   Where in the case of any limited liability partnership–
- (a)   the purchase price or production cost of assets falling to be included under any item shown in the limited liability partnership's balance sheet has been determined by the application of any method permitted by this paragraph; and
- (b)   the amount shown in respect of that item differs materially from the relevant alternative amount given below in this paragraph;

the amount of that difference shall be disclosed in a note to the accounts.

(4)   Subject to sub-paragraph (5) below, for the purposes of sub-paragraph (3)(b) above, the relevant alternative amount, in relation to any item shown in a limited liability partnership's balance sheet, is the amount which would have been shown in respect of that item if assets of any class included under that item at an amount determined by any method permitted by this paragraph had instead been included at their replacement cost as at the balance sheet date.

(5)   The relevant alternative amount may be determined by reference to the most recent actual purchase price or production cost before the balance sheet date of assets of any class included under the item in question instead of by reference to their replacement cost as at that date, but only if the former appears to the members of the limited liability partnership to constitute the more appropriate standard of comparison in the case of assets of that class.

(6)   For the purposes of this paragraph, assets of any description shall be regarded as fungible if assets of that description are substantially indistinguishable one from another.

28   Where there is no record of the purchase price or production cost of any asset of a limited liability partnership or of any price, expenses or costs relevant for determining its purchase price or production cost in accordance with paragraph 26, or any such record cannot be obtained without unreasonable expense or delay, its purchase price or production cost shall be taken for the purposes of paragraphs 17 to 23 to be the value ascribed to it in the earliest available record of its value made on or after its acquisition or production by the limited liability partnership.

Section C
Alternative Accounting Rules

Preliminary

29 – (1)   The rules set out in section B are referred to below in this Schedule as the historical cost accounting rules.

(2)   Those rules, with the omission of paragraphs 16, 21 and 25 to 28, are referred to below in this Part of this Schedule as the depreciation rules; and references below in this Schedule to the historical cost accounting rules do not include the depreciation rules as they apply by virtue of paragraph 32.

30   Subject to paragraphs 32 to 34, the amounts to be included in respect of assets of any description mentioned in paragraph 31 may be determined on any basis so mentioned.

Alternative accounting rules

31 – (1)   Intangible fixed assets, other than goodwill, may be included at their current cost.

(2)   Tangible fixed assets may be included at a market value determined as at the date of their last valuation or at their current cost.

(3)   Investments of any description falling to be included under item B.III of either of the balance sheet formats set out in Part I of this Schedule may be included either–
   (a)   at a market value determined as at the date of their last valuation; or
   (b)   at a value determined on any basis which appears to the members to be appropriate in the circumstances of the limited liability partnership;
but in the latter case particulars of the method of valuation adopted and of the reasons for adopting it shall be disclosed in a note to the accounts.

(4)   Investments of any description falling to be included under item C.III of either of the balance sheet formats set out in Part I of this Schedule may be included at their current cost.

(5)   Stocks may be included at their current cost.

Application of the depreciation rules

32 – (1)   Where the value of any asset of a limited liability partnership is determined on any basis mentioned in paragraph 31, that value shall be, or (as the case may require) be the starting point for determining, the amount to be included in respect of that asset in the limited liability partnership's accounts, instead of its purchase price or production cost or any value previously so determined for that asset; and the depreciation rules shall apply accordingly in relation to any such asset with the substitution for any reference to its purchase price or production cost of a reference to the value most recently determined for that asset on any basis mentioned in paragraph 31.

(2)   The amount of any provision for depreciation required in the case of any fixed asset by paragraph 18 or 19 as it applies by virtue of sub-paragraph (1) is referred to below in this paragraph as the adjusted amount, and the amount of any provision which would be required by that paragraph in the case of that asset according to the historical cost accounting rules is referred to as the historical cost amount.

(3)   Where sub-paragraph (1) applies in the case of any fixed asset the amount of any provision for depreciation in respect of that asset–

> (a)   included in any item shown in the profit and loss account in respect of amounts written off assets of the description in question; or
>
> (b)   taken into account in stating any item so shown which is required by note (14) of the notes on the profit and loss account formats set out in Part I of this Schedule to be stated after taking into account any necessary provisions for depreciation or diminution in value of assets included under it;

may be the historical cost amount instead of the adjusted amount, provided that the amount of any difference between the two is shown separately in the profit and loss account or in a note to the accounts.

Additional information to be provided in case of departure from historical cost accounting rules

33 – (1)   This paragraph applies where the amounts to be included in respect of assets covered by any items shown in a limited liability partnership's accounts have been determined on any basis mentioned in paragraph 31.

(2)   The items affected and the basis of valuation adopted in determining the amounts of the assets in question in the case of each such item shall be disclosed in a note to the accounts.

(3)   In the case of each balance sheet item affected (except stocks) either–

> (a)   the comparable amounts determined according to the historical cost accounting rules; or
>
> (b)   the differences between those amounts and the corresponding amounts actually shown in the balance sheet in respect of that item;

shall be shown separately in the balance sheet or in a note to the accounts.

(4)   In sub-paragraph (3) above, references in relation to any item to the comparable amounts determined as there mentioned are references to–

> (a)   the aggregate amount which would be required to be shown in respect of that item if the amounts to be included in respect of all the assets covered by that item were determined according to the historical cost accounting rules; and
>
> (b)   the aggregate amount of the cumulative provisions for depreciation or diminution in value which would be permitted or required in determining those amounts according to those rules.

Revaluation reserve

34 – (1) With respect to any determination of the value of an asset of a limited liability partnership on any basis mentioned in paragraph 31, the amount of any profit or loss arising from that determination (after allowing, where appropriate, for any provisions for depreciation or diminution in value made otherwise than by reference to the value so determined and any adjustments of any such provisions made in the light of that determination) shall be credited or (as the case may be) debited to a separate reserve ("the revaluation reserve").

(2)   The amount of the revaluation reserve shall be shown in the limited liability partnership's balance sheet under a separate sub-heading in the position given for the item "revaluation reserve" in Format 1 or 2 of the balance sheet formats set out in Part I of this Schedule, but need not be shown under that name.

(3),(3A),(3B) …

(4)   The treatment for taxation purposes of amounts credited or debited to the revaluation reserve shall be disclosed in a note to the accounts.

PART III
NOTES TO THE ACCOUNTS

Preliminary

35   Any information required in the case of any limited liability partnership by the following provisions of this Part of this Schedule shall (if not given in the limited liability partnership's accounts) be given by way of a note to those accounts.

Disclosure of accounting policies

36   The accounting policies adopted by the limited liability partnership in determining the amounts to be included in respect of items shown in the balance sheet and in determining the profit or loss of the limited liability partnership shall be stated (including such policies with respect to the depreciation and diminution in value of assets).

36A   It shall be stated whether the accounts have been prepared in accordance with applicable accounting standards and particulars of any material departure from those standards and the reasons for it shall be given.

Information supplementing the balance sheet

37   Paragraphs [41 to 51(1)] require information which either supplements the information given with respect to any particular items shown in the balance sheet or is otherwise relevant to assessing the limited liability partnership's state of affairs in the light of the information so given.

[*Loans and other debts due to members*

37A The following information shall be given–
- (a) the aggregate amounts of loans and other debts due to members as at the date of the beginning of the financial year,
- (b) the aggregate amounts contributed by members during the financial year,
- (c) the aggregate amounts transferred to or from the profit and loss account during that year,
- (d) the aggregate amounts withdrawn by members or applied on behalf of members during that year,
- (e) the aggregate amounts of loans and other debts due to members as at the balance sheet date, and
- (f) the aggregate amounts of loans and other debts due to members that fall due after one year.]

38, 39, 40 ...

41 – (1) If the limited liability partnership has issued any debentures during the financial year to which the accounts relate, the following information shall be given–
- (b) the classes of debentures issued; and
- (c) as respects each class of debentures, the amount issued and the consideration received by the limited liability partnership for the issue.

(3) Where any of the limited liability partnership's debentures are held by a nominee of or trustee for the limited liability partnership, the nominal amount of the debentures and the amount at which they are stated in the accounting records kept by the limited liability partnership in accordance with section 221 of this Act shall be stated.

42 – (1) In respect of each item which is or would but for paragraph 3(4)(b) be shown under the general item "fixed assets" in the limited liability partnership's balance sheet the following information shall be given–
- (a) the appropriate amounts in respect of that item as at the date of the beginning of the financial year and as at the balance sheet date respectively;
- (b) the effect on any amount shown in the balance sheet in respect of that item of–
  - (i) any revision of the amount in respect of any assets included under that item made during that year on any basis mentioned in paragraph 31;
  - (ii) acquisitions during that year of any assets;
  - (iii) disposals during that year of any assets; and
  - (iv) any transfers of assets of the limited liability partnership to and from that item during that year.

(2) The reference in sub-paragraph (1)(a) to the appropriate amounts in respect of any item as at any date there mentioned is a reference to amounts representing

the aggregate amounts determined, as at that date, in respect of assets falling to be included under that item on either of the following bases, that is to say–
    (a) on the basis of purchase price or production cost (determined in accordance with paragraphs 26 and 27); or
    (b) on any basis mentioned in paragraph 31,
(leaving out of account in either case any provisions for depreciation or diminution in value).

(3)   In respect of each item within sub-paragraph (1)–
    (a) the cumulative amount of provisions for depreciation or diminution in value of assets included under that item as at each date mentioned in sub-paragraph (1)(a);
    (b) the amount of any such provisions made in respect of the financial year;
    (c) the amount of any adjustments made in respect of any such provisions during that year in consequence of the disposal of any assets; and
    (d) the amount of any other adjustments made in respect of any such provisions during that year;
shall also be stated.

43   Where any fixed assets of the limited liability partnership (other than listed investments) are included under any item shown in the limited liability partnership's balance sheet at an amount determined on any basis mentioned in paragraph 31, the following information shall be given–
    (a) the years (so far as they are known to the members) in which the assets were severally valued and the several values; and
    (b) in the case of assets that have been valued during the financial year, the names of the persons who valued them or particulars of their qualifications for doing so and (whichever is stated) the bases of valuation used by them.

44   In relation to any amount which is or would but for paragraph 3(4)(b) be shown in respect of the item "land and buildings" in the limited liability partnership's balance sheet there shall be stated–
    (a) how much of that amount is ascribable to land of freehold tenure and how much to land of leasehold tenure; and
    (b) how much of the amount ascribable to land of leasehold tenure is ascribable to land held on long lease and how much to land held on short lease.

45 – (1)   In respect of the amount of each item which is or would but for paragraph 3(4)(b) be shown in the limited liability partnership's balance sheet under the general item "investments" (whether as fixed assets or as current assets) there shall be stated–
    (a) how much of that amount is ascribable to listed investments;

(2)   Where the amount of any listed investments is stated for any item in accordance with sub-paragraph (1)(a), the following amounts shall also be stated–
    (a) the aggregate market value of those investments where it differs from the amount so stated; and

    (b)   both the market value and the stock exchange value of any investments of which the former value is, for the purposes of the accounts, taken as being higher than the latter.

46 – (1)   Where any amount is transferred–

    (a)   to or from any reserves; or

    (b)   to any provisions for liabilities and charges; or

    (c)   from any provision for liabilities and charges otherwise than for the purpose for which the provision was established;

and the reserves or provisions are or would but for paragraph 3(4)(b) be shown as separate items in the limited liability partnership's balance sheet, the information mentioned in the following sub-paragraph shall be given in respect of the aggregate of reserves or provisions included in the same item.

(2)   That information is–

    (a)   the amount of the reserves or provisions as at the date of the beginning of the financial year and as at the balance sheet date respectively;

    (b)   any amounts transferred to or from the reserves or provisions during that year; and

    (c)   the source and application respectively of any amounts so transferred.

(3)   Particulars shall be given of each provision included in the item "other provisions" in the limited liability partnership's balance sheet in any case where the amount of that provision is material.

47   The amount of any provision for deferred taxation shall be stated separately from the amount of any provision for other taxation.

48 – (1)   In respect of each item shown under "creditors" in the limited liability partnership's balance sheet there shall be stated the aggregate of the following amounts, that is to say–

    (a)   the amount of any debts included under that item which are payable or repayable otherwise than by instalments and fall due for payment or repayment after the end of the period of five years beginning with the day next following the end of the financial year; and

    (b)   in the case of any debts so included which are payable or repayable by instalments, the amount of any instalments which fall due for payment after the end of that period.

(2)   Subject to sub-paragraph (3), in relation to each debt falling to be taken into account under sub-paragraph (1), the terms of payment or repayment and the rate of any interest payable on the debt shall be stated.

(3)   If the number of debts is such that, in the opinion of the members, compliance with sub-paragraph (2) would result in a statement of excessive length, it shall be sufficient to give a general indication of the terms of payment or repayment and the rates of any interest payable on the debts.

(4)   In respect of each item shown under "creditors" in the limited liability partnership's balance sheet there shall be stated–

(a) the aggregate amount of any debts included under that item in respect of which any security has been given by the limited liability partnership; and

(b) an indication of the nature of the securities so given.

(5) References above in this paragraph to an item shown under "creditors" in the limited liability partnership's balance sheet include references, where amounts falling due to creditors within one year and after more than one year are distinguished in the balance sheet–

(a) in a case within sub-paragraph (1), to an item shown under the latter of those categories; and

(b) in a case within sub-paragraph (4), to an item shown under either of those categories;

and references to items shown under "creditors" include references to items which would but for paragraph 3(4)(b) be shown under that heading.

49   …

50 – (1) Particulars shall be given of any charge on the assets of the limited liability partnership to secure the liabilities of any other person, including, where practicable, the amount secured.

(2) The following information shall be given with respect to any other contingent liability not provided for–

(a) the amount or estimated amount of that liability;

(b) its legal nature; and

(c) whether any valuable security has been provided by the limited liability partnership in connection with that liability and if so, what.

(3) There shall be stated, where practicable–

(a) the aggregate amount or estimated amount of contracts for capital expenditure, so far as not provided for;

(4) Particulars shall be given of–

(a) any pension commitments included under any provision shown in the limited liability partnership's balance sheet; and

(b) any such commitments for which no provision has been made;

and where any such commitment relates wholly or partly to pensions payable to past members of the limited liability partnership separate particulars shall be given of that commitment so far as it relates to such pensions.

(5) Particulars shall also be given of any other financial commitments which–

(a) have not been provided for; and

(b) are relevant to assessing the limited liability partnership's state of affairs.

51 – (1) Particulars shall be given of any case where the purchase price or production cost of any asset is for the first time determined under paragraph 28.

(2)   …

Information supplementing the profit and loss account

52   Paragraphs 53 to 57 require information which either supplements the information given with respect to any particular items shown in the profit and loss account or otherwise provides particulars of income or expenditure of the limited liability partnership or of circumstances affecting the items shown in the profit and loss account.

53 – (1)   Subject to the following provisions of this paragraph, each of the amounts mentioned below shall be stated.

(2)   The amount of the interest on or any similar charges in respect of–
   (a)   bank loans and overdrafts; and
   (b)   loans of any other kind made to the limited liability partnership.
   This sub-paragraph does not apply to interest or charges on loans to the limited liability partnership from group undertakings, but, with that exception, it applies to interest or charges on all loans, whether made on the security of debentures or not.

54 – (2)   Particulars shall be given of any special circumstances which affect liability in respect of taxation of profits, income or capital gains for the financial year or liability in respect of taxation of profits, income or capital gains for succeeding financial years.

(3)   The following amounts shall be stated–
   (a)   the amount of the charge for United Kingdom corporation tax;
   (b)   if that amount would have been greater but for relief from double taxation, the amount which it would have been but for such relief;
   (c)   the amount of the charge for United Kingdom income tax; and
   (d)   the amount of the charge for taxation imposed outside the United Kingdom of profits, income and (so far as charged to revenue) capital gains.
   These amounts shall be stated separately in respect of each of the amounts which is or would but for paragraph 3(4)(b) be shown under the following items in the profit and loss account, that is to say "tax on profit or loss on ordinary activities" and "tax on extraordinary profit or loss".

55 – (1)   If in the course of the financial year the limited liability partnership has carried on business of two or more classes that, in the opinion of the members, differ substantially from each other, there shall be stated in respect of each class (describing it)–
   (a)   the amount of the turnover attributable to that class;

(2)   If in the course of the financial year the limited liability partnership has supplied markets that, in the opinion of the members, differ substantially from each other, the amount of the turnover attributable to each such market shall also be stated.
   In this paragraph "market" means a market delimited by geographical bounds.

(3)   In analysing for the purposes of this paragraph the source (in terms of business or in terms of market) of turnover, the members of the limited liability partnership shall have regard to the manner in which the limited liability partnership's activities are organised.

(4)   For the purposes of this paragraph–
    (a) classes of business which, in the opinion of the members, do not differ substantially from each other shall be treated as one class; and
    (b) markets which, in the opinion of the members, do not differ substantially from each other shall be treated as one market;
and any amounts properly attributable to one class of business or (as the case may be) to one market which are not material may be included in the amount stated in respect of another.

(5)   Where in the opinion of the designated members the disclosure of any information required by this paragraph would be seriously prejudicial to the interests of the limited liability partnership, that information need not be disclosed, but the fact that any such information has not been disclosed must be stated.

56 – (1)   The following information shall be given with respect to the employees of the limited liability partnership–
    (a) the average number of persons employed by the limited liability partnership in the financial year; and
    (b) the average number of persons so employed within each category of persons employed by the limited liability partnership.

(2)   The average number required by sub-paragraph (1)(a) or (b) shall be determined by dividing the relevant annual number by the number of months in the financial year.

(3)   The relevant annual number shall be determined by ascertaining for each month in the financial year–
    (a) for the purposes of sub-paragraph (1)(a), the number of persons employed under contracts of service by the limited liability partnership in that month(whether throughout the month or not);
    (b) for the purposes of sub-paragraph (1)(b), the number of persons in the category in question of persons so employed;
and, in either case, adding together all the monthly numbers.

(4)   In respect of all persons employed by the limited liability partnership during the financial year who are taken into account in determining the relevant annual number for the purposes of sub-paragraph (1)(a) there shall also be stated the aggregate amounts respectively of–
    (a) wages and salaries paid or payable in respect of that year to those persons;
    (b) social security costs incurred by the limited liability partnership on their behalf; and
    (c) other pension costs so incurred;
save in so far as those amounts or any of them are stated in the profit and loss account.

(5)   The categories of persons employed by the limited liability partnership by reference to which the number required to be disclosed by sub-paragraph (1)(b) is to be determined shall be such as the members may select, having regard to the manner in which the limited liability partnership's activities are organised.

[Particulars of members

56A – (1)   Particulars shall be given of the average number of members of the limited liability partnership in the financial year, which number shall be determined by dividing the relevant annual number by the number of months in the financial year.

(2)   The relevant annual number shall be determined by ascertaining for each month in the financial year the number of members of the limited liability partnership for all or part of that month, and adding together all the monthly numbers.

(3)   Where the amount of the profit of the limited liability partnership for the financial year before members' remuneration and profit shares exceeds £200,000, there shall be disclosed the amount of profit (including remuneration) which is attributable to the member with the largest entitlement to profit (including remuneration).

For the purpose of determining the amount to be disclosed, "remuneration" includes any emoluments specified in paragraph 1(1)(a), (c) or (d) of Schedule 6 to this Act which are paid by or receivable from–
  (i)   the limited liability partnership; and
  (ii)   the limited liability partnership's subsidiary undertakings; and
  (iii) any other person.]

[The emoluments specified in paragraph 1(1)(a),(c) and (d) of Schedule 6 to the Companies Act 1985 are as follows (note that Schedule 6 does not otherwise apply to LLPs, and is therefore not reproduced):

  '(a) the aggregate amount of emoluments paid to or receivable by members in respect of qualifying services;

  ...

  (c)   the aggregate of the following, namely–
    (i)   the amount of money paid to or receivable by members under long-term incentive schemes in respect of qualifying services, and
    (ii)   the net value of assets (other than money and share options) received or receivable by members under such schemes in respect of such services;
  (d)   the aggregate value of any company contributions paid, or treated as paid, to a pension scheme in respect of directors' qualifying services, being contributions by reference to which the rate or amount of any money purchase benefits that may become payable will be calculated.']

57 – (1)   Where any amount relating to any preceding financial year is included in any item in the profit and loss account, the effect shall be stated.

(2)   Particulars shall be given of any extraordinary income or charges arising in the financial year.

(3)   The effect shall be stated of any transactions that are exceptional by virtue of size or incidence though they fall within the ordinary activities of the limited liability partnership.

General

58 – (1)   Where sums originally denominated in foreign currencies have been brought into account under any items shown in the balance sheet or profit and loss account, the basis on which those sums have been translated into sterling shall be stated.

(2)   Subject to the following sub-paragraph, in respect of every item stated in a note to the accounts the corresponding amount for the financial year immediately preceding that to which the accounts relate shall also be stated and where the corresponding amount is not comparable, it shall be adjusted and particulars of the adjustment and the reasons for it shall be given.

(3)   Sub-paragraph (2) does not apply in relation to any amounts stated by virtue of any of the following provisions of this Act–
  (a)   paragraph 13 of Schedule 4A (details of accounting treatment of acquisitions),
  (b)   paragraphs 2, 8(3), 16, 21(1)(d), 22(4) and (5), 24(3) and (4) and 27(3) and (4) of Schedule 5 (shareholdings in other undertakings),
  (c)   …

Dormant limited liability partnerships acting as agents

58A   Where the members of a limited liability partnership take advantage of the exemption conferred by section 249AA, and the limited liability partnership has during the financial year in question acted as an agent for any person, the fact that it has so acted must be stated.

PART IV
SPECIAL PROVISIONS WHERE LIMITED LIABILITY PARTNERSHIP IS A PARENT LIMITED LIABILITY PARTNERSHIP OR SUBSIDIARY UNDERTAKING

Limited liability partnership's own accounts

59A   Commitments within any of sub-paragraphs (1) to (5) of paragraph 50 (guarantees and other financial commitments) which are undertaken on behalf of or for the benefit of–
  (a)   any parent undertaking or fellow subsidiary undertaking, or
  (b)   any subsidiary undertaking of the limited liability partnership,
shall be stated separately from the other commitments within that sub-paragraph, and commitments within paragraph (a) shall also be stated separately from those within paragraph (b).

71, 72, 73 ...

PART VII
INTERPRETATION OF SCHEDULE

76   The following paragraphs apply for the purposes of this Schedule and its interpretation.

82   References to the historical cost accounting rules shall be read in accordance with paragraph 29.

83 – (1)   "Long lease" means a lease in the case of which the portion of the term for which it was granted remaining unexpired at the end of the financial year is not less than 50 years.

(2)   "Short lease" means a lease which is not a long lease.

(3)   "Lease" includes an agreement for a lease.

84   "Listed investment" means an investment as respects which there has been granted a listing on a recognised investment exchange other than an overseas investment exchange within the meaning of the Financial Services Act 1986 or on any stock exchange of repute outside Great Britain.

85   A loan is treated as falling due for repayment, and an instalment of a loan is treated as falling due for payment, on the earliest date on which the lender could require repayment or (as the case may be) payment, if he exercised all options and rights available to him.

86   Amounts which in the particular context of any provision of this Schedule are not material may be disregarded for the purposes of that provision.

88 – (1)   References to provisions for depreciation or diminution in value of assets are to any amount written off by way of providing for depreciation or diminution in value of assets.

(2)   Any reference in the profit and loss account formats set out in Part I of this Schedule to the depreciation of, or amounts written off, assets of any description is to any provision for depreciation or diminution in value of assets of that description.

89   References to provisions for liabilities or charges are to any amount retained as reasonably necessary for the purpose of providing for any liability or loss which is either likely to be incurred, or certain to be incurred but uncertain as to amount or as to the date on which it will arise.

93   In the application of this Schedule to Scotland, "land of freehold tenure" means land in respect of which the limited liability partnership is the proprietor of the dominium utile or, in the case of land not held on feudal tenure, is the owner;"land of leasehold tenure" means land of which the limited liability partnership is the tenant under a lease; and the reference to ground-rents, rates and other outgoings includes feu-duty and ground annual.

94 – (1)   "Social security costs" means any contributions by the limited liability partnership to any state social security or pension scheme, fund or arrangement.

(2)   "Pension costs" includes any costs incurred by the limited liability partnership in respect of any pension scheme established for the purpose of providing pensions for persons currently or formerly employed by the limited liability partnership, any sums set aside for the future payment of pensions directly by the limited liability partnership to current or former employees and any pensions paid directly to such persons without having first been set aside.

(3)   Any amount stated in respect of the item "social security costs" or in respect of the item "wages and salaries" in the limited liability partnership's profit and loss account shall be determined by reference to payments made or costs incurred in respect of all persons employed by the limited liability partnership during the financial year who are taken into account in determining the relevant annual number for the purposes of paragraph 56(1)(a).

SCHEDULE 4A
FORM AND CONTENT OF GROUP ACCOUNTS

1 – (1)   Group accounts shall comply so far as practicable with the provisions of section 390A(3) (amount of auditors' remuneration) and Schedule 4 (form and content of limited liability partnership accounts) as if the undertakings included in the consolidation ("the group") were a single limited liability partnership.

(3)   ...

2 – (1)   The consolidated balance sheet and profit and loss account shall incorporate in full the information contained in the individual accounts of the undertakings included in the consolidation, subject to the adjustments authorised or required by the following provisions of this Schedule and to such other adjustments (if any) as may be appropriate in accordance with generally accepted accounting principles or practice.

(2)   If the financial year of a subsidiary undertaking included in the consolidation does not end with that of the parent limited liability partnership, the group accounts shall be made up–
  (a)   from the accounts of the subsidiary undertaking for its financial year last ending before the end of the parent limited liability partnership's financial year, provided that year ended no more than three months before that of the parent limited liability partnership, or
  (b)   from interim accounts prepared by the subsidiary undertaking as at the end of that parent limited liability partnership's financial year.

3 – (1)   Where assets and liabilities to be included in the group accounts have been valued or otherwise determined by undertakings according to accounting rules differing from those used for the group accounts, the values or amounts shall be adjusted so as to accord with the rules used for the group accounts.

(2)   If it appears to the members of the parent limited liability partnership that there are special reasons for departing from sub-paragraph (1) they may do so, but particulars of any such departure, the reasons for it and its effect shall be given in a note to the accounts.

(3)   The adjustments referred to in this paragraph need not be made if they are not material for the purpose of giving a true and fair view.

4   Any differences of accounting rules as between a parent limited liability partnership's individual accounts for a financial year and its group accounts shall be disclosed in a note to the latter accounts and the reasons for the difference given.

5   Amounts which in the particular context of any provision of this Schedule are not material may be disregarded for the purposes of that provision.

6 – (1)   Debts and claims between undertakings included in the consolidation, and income and expenditure relating to transactions between such undertakings, shall be eliminated in preparing the group accounts.

(2)   Where profits and losses resulting from transactions between undertakings included in the consolidation are included in the book value of assets, they shall be eliminated in preparing the group accounts.

(3)   The elimination required by sub-paragraph (2) may be effected in proportion to the group's interest in the shares of the undertakings.

(4)   Sub-paragraphs (1) and (2) need not be complied with if the amounts concerned are not material for the purpose of giving a true and fair view.

7 – (1)   The following provisions apply where an undertaking becomes a subsidiary undertaking of the parent limited liability partnership.

(2)   That event is referred to in those provisions as an "acquisition", and references to the "undertaking acquired" shall be construed accordingly.

8   An acquisition shall be accounted for by the acquisition method of accounting unless the conditions for accounting for it as a merger are met and the merger method of accounting is adopted.

9 – (1)   The acquisition method of accounting is as follows.

(2)   The identifiable assets and liabilities of the undertaking acquired shall be included in the consolidated balance sheet at their fair values as at the date of acquisition.
    In this paragraph the "identifiable" assets or liabilities of the undertaking acquired means the assets or liabilities which are capable of being disposed of or discharged separately, without disposing of a business of the undertaking.

(3)   The income and expenditure of the undertaking acquired shall be brought into the group accounts only as from the date of the acquisition.

(4)   There shall be set off against the acquisition cost of the interest in the shares of the undertaking held by the parent limited liability partnership and its subsidiary undertakings the interest of the parent limited liability partnership and its subsidiary undertakings in the adjusted capital and reserves of the undertaking acquired.
       For this purpose–

"the acquisition cost" means the amount of any cash consideration and the fair value of any other consideration, together with such amount (if any) in respect of fees and other expenses of the acquisition as the limited liability partnership may determine, and

"the adjusted capital and reserves" of the undertaking acquired means its capital and reserves at the date of the acquisition after adjusting the identifiable assets and liabilities of the undertaking to fair values as at that date.

(5)   The resulting amount if positive shall be treated as goodwill, and if negative as a negative consolidation difference.

10 – (1)   The conditions for accounting for an acquisition as a merger are–
       (a),(b),(c)   ...
       (d)   that adoption of the merger method of accounting accords with generally accepted accounting principles or practice.

(2)   ...

11 – [(1) Where a limited liability partnership adopts the merger method of accounting, it must comply with this paragraph, and with generally accepted accounting principles or practice.]

(2)   The assets and liabilities of the undertaking acquired shall be brought into the group accounts at the figures at which they stand in the undertaking's accounts, subject to any adjustment authorised or required by this Schedule.

(3)   The income and expenditure of the undertaking acquired shall be included in the group accounts for the entire financial year, including the period before the acquisition.

(4)   The group accounts shall show corresponding amounts relating to the previous financial year as if the undertaking acquired had been included in the consolidation throughout that year.

(5),(6),(7)   ...

12 – (1)   Where a group is acquired, paragraphs 9 to 11 apply with the following adaptations.

(2)   References to shares of the undertaking acquired shall be construed as references to shares of the parent undertaking of the group.

(3)   Other references to the undertaking acquired shall be construed as references to the group; and references to the assets and liabilities, income and expenditure and capital and reserves of the undertaking acquired shall be construed as references to the assets and liabilities, income and expenditure and capital and reserves of the group after making the set-offs and other adjustments required by this Schedule in the case of group accounts.

13 – (1)   The following information with respect to acquisitions taking place in the financial year shall be given in a note to the accounts.

(2)   There shall be stated–
- (a)   the name of the undertaking acquired or, where a group was acquired, the name of the parent undertaking of that group, and
- (b)   whether the acquisition has been accounted for by the acquisition or the merger method of accounting;

and in relation to an acquisition which significantly affects the figures shown in the group accounts, the following further information shall be given.

(3)   The composition and fair value of the consideration for the acquisition given by the parent limited liability partnership and its subsidiary undertakings shall be stated.

(5)   Where the acquisition method of accounting has been adopted, the book values immediately prior to the acquisition, and the fair values at the date of acquisition, of each class of assets and liabilities of the undertaking or group acquired shall be stated in tabular form, including a statement of the amount of any goodwill or negative consolidation difference arising on the acquisition, together with an explanation of any significant adjustments made.

(6)   Where the merger method of accounting has been adopted, an explanation shall be given of any significant adjustments made in relation to the amounts of the assets and liabilities of the undertaking or group acquired, together with a statement of any resulting adjustment to the consolidated reserves (including the re-statement of opening consolidated reserves).

(7)   In ascertaining for the purposes of sub-paragraph (5) or (6) the profit or loss of a group, the book values and fair values of assets and liabilities of a group or the amount of the assets and liabilities of a group, the set-offs and other adjustments required by this Schedule in the case of group accounts shall be made.

14 – (1)   There shall also be stated in a note to the accounts the cumulative amount of goodwill resulting from acquisitions in that and earlier financial years which has been written off otherwise than in the consolidated profit and loss account for that or any earlier financial year.

(2)   That figure shall be shown net of any goodwill attributable to subsidiary undertakings or businesses disposed of prior to the balance sheet date.

15   Where during the financial year there has been a disposal of an undertaking or group which significantly affects the figures shown in the group accounts, there shall be stated in a note to the accounts–
  (a)   the name of that undertaking or, as the case may be, of the parent undertaking of that group, and
  (b)   the extent to which the profit or loss shown in the group accounts is attributable to profit or loss of that undertaking or group.

16   The information required by paragraph 13, 14 or 15 above need not be disclosed with respect to an undertaking which–
  (a)   is established under the law of a country outside the United Kingdom, or
  (b)   carries on business outside the United Kingdom,
if in the opinion of the members of the parent limited liability partnership the disclosure would be seriously prejudicial to the business of that undertaking or to the business of the parent limited liability partnership or any of its subsidiary undertakings and the Secretary of State agrees that the information should not be disclosed.

17 – (1)   The formats set out in Schedule 4 have effect in relation to group accounts with the following additions.

(2)   In the Balance Sheet Formats a further item headed "Minority interests" shall be added–
  (a)   in Format 1, either after item J or at the end (after [item L]), and
  (b)   in Format 2, under the general heading "LIABILITIES", between [item AA];
and under that item shall be shown the amount of capital and reserves attributable to shares in subsidiary undertakings included in the consolidation held by or on behalf of persons other than the parent limited liability partnership and its subsidiary undertakings.

(3)   In the Profit and Loss Account Formats a further item headed "Minority interests" shall be added–
  (a)   in Format 1, between items 14 and 15,
  (b)   in Format 2, between items 16 and 17,
  (c),(d)   ...
and under that item shall be shown the amount of any profit or loss on ordinary activities attributable to shares in subsidiary undertakings included in the consolidation held by or on behalf of persons other than the parent limited liability partnership and its subsidiary undertakings.

(4)   In the Profit and Loss Account Formats a further item headed "Minority interests" shall be added–
  (a)   in Format 1, between items 18 and 19,
  (b)   in Format 2, between items 20 and 21,
  (c),(d)   ...

and under that item shall be shown the amount of any profit or loss on extraordinary activities attributable to shares in subsidiary undertakings included in the consolidation held by or on behalf of persons other than the parent limited liability partnership and its subsidiary undertakings.

(5)   For the purposes of paragraph 3(3) and (4) of Schedule 4 (power to adapt or combine items)–

    (a)   the additional item required by sub-paragraph (2) above shall be treated as one to which a letter is assigned, and

    (b)   the additional items required by sub-paragraphs (3) and (4) above shall be treated as ones to which an Arabic number is assigned.

18   The interest of the group in subsidiary undertakings excluded from consolidation under section 229(4) (undertakings with activities different from those of undertakings included in the consolidation), and the amount of profit or loss attributable to such an interest, shall be shown in the consolidated balance sheet or, as the case may be, in the consolidated profit and loss account by the equity method of accounting (including dealing with any goodwill arising in accordance with paragraphs 17 to 19 and 21 of Schedule 4).

19 – (1)   Where an undertaking included in the consolidation manages another undertaking jointly with one or more undertakings not included in the consolidation, that other undertaking ("the joint venture") may, if it is not–

    (a)   a body corporate, or

    (b)   a subsidiary undertaking of the parent limited liability partnership,

be dealt with in the group accounts by the method of proportional consolidation.

(2)   The provisions of this Schedule relating to the preparation of consolidated accounts apply, with any necessary modifications, to proportional consolidation under this paragraph.

20 – (1)   An "associated undertaking" means an undertaking in which an undertaking included in the consolidation has a participating interest and over whose operating and financial policy it exercises a significant influence, and which is not–

    (a)   a subsidiary undertaking of the parent limited liability partnership, or

    (b)   a joint venture dealt with in accordance with paragraph 19.

(2)   Where an undertaking holds 20 per cent or more of the voting rights in another undertaking, it shall be presumed to exercise such an influence over it unless the contrary is shown.

(3)   The voting rights in an undertaking means the rights conferred on shareholders in respect of their shares or, in the case of an undertaking not having a share capital, on members, to vote at general meetings of the undertaking on all, or substantially all, matters.

(4)   The provisions of paragraphs 5 to 11 of Schedule 10A (rights to be taken into account and attribution of rights) apply in determining for the purposes of

this paragraph whether an undertaking holds 20 per cent or more of the voting rights in another undertaking.

21 – (1) The formats set out in Schedule 4 have effect in relation to group accounts with the following modifications.

(2)   In the Balance Sheet Formats the items headed "Participating interests", that is–
  (a) in Format 1, item B.III.3, and
  (b) in Format 2, item B.III.3 under the heading "ASSETS",
shall be replaced by two items, "Interests in associated undertakings" and "Other participating interests".

(3)   In the Profit and Loss Account Formats, the items headed "Income from participating interests", that is–
  (a) in Format 1, item 8,
  (b) in Format 2, item 10,
  (c),(d) …
shall be replaced by two items, "Income from interests in associated undertakings" and "Income from other participating interests".

22 – (1) The interest of an undertaking in an associated undertaking, and the amount of profit or loss attributable to such an interest, shall be shown by the equity method of accounting (including dealing with any goodwill arising in accordance with paragraphs 17 to 19 and 21 of Schedule 4).

(2)   Where the associated undertaking is itself a parent undertaking, the net assets and profits or losses to be taken into account are those of the parent and its subsidiary undertakings (after making any consolidation adjustments).

(3)   The equity method of accounting need not be applied if the amounts in question are not material for the purpose of giving a true and fair view.

SCHEDULE 5
DISCLOSURE OF INFORMATION: RELATED UNDERTAKINGS

PART I
LIMITED LIABILITY PARTNERSHIPS NOT REQUIRED TO
PREPARE GROUP ACCOUNTS

1 – (1)   The following information shall be given where at the end of the financial year the limited liability partnership has subsidiary undertakings.

(2)   The name of each subsidiary undertaking shall be stated.

(3)   There shall be stated with respect to each subsidiary undertaking–
  (a) if it is incorporated outside Great Britain, the country in which it is incorporated;
  (c) if it is unincorporated, the address of its principal place of business.

(4)   The reason why the limited liability partnership is not required to prepare group accounts shall be stated.

(5)   If the reason is that all the subsidiary undertakings of the limited liability partnership fall within the exclusions provided for in section 229, it shall be stated with respect to each subsidiary undertaking which of those exclusions applies.

2 – (1)   There shall be stated in relation to shares of each class held by the limited liability partnership in a subsidiary undertaking–
   (a)   the identity of the class, and
   (b)   the proportion of the nominal value of the shares of that class represented by those shares.

(2)   The shares held by or on behalf of the limited liability partnership itself shall be distinguished from those attributed to the limited liability partnership which are held by or on behalf of a subsidiary undertaking.

3 – (1)   There shall be disclosed with respect to each subsidiary undertaking–
   (a)   the aggregate amount of its capital and reserves as at the end of its relevant financial year, and
   (b)   its profit or loss for that year.

(2)   That information need not be given if the limited liability partnership is exempt by virtue of section 228 from the requirement to prepare group accounts (parent limited liability partnership included in accounts of larger group).

(2A)   That information need not be given if the limited liability partnership's investment in the subsidiary undertaking is included in the limited liability partnership's accounts by way of the equity method of valuation.

(3)   That information need not be given if–
   (a)   the subsidiary undertaking is not required by any provision of this Act to deliver a copy of its balance sheet for its relevant financial year and does not otherwise publish that balance sheet in Great Britain or elsewhere, and
   (b)   the limited liability partnership's holding is less than 50 per cent of the nominal value of the shares in the undertaking.

(4)   Information otherwise required by this paragraph need not be given if it is not material.

(5)   For the purposes of this paragraph the "relevant financial year" of a subsidiary undertaking is–
   (a)   if its financial year ends with that of the limited liability partnership, that year, and
   (b)   if not, its financial year ending last before the end of the limited liability partnership's financial year.

4   Where–
   (a)   disclosure is made under paragraph 3(1) with respect to a subsidiary
         undertaking, and
   (b)   that undertaking's financial year does not end with that of the limited
         liability partnership,
there shall be stated in relation to that undertaking the date on which its last
financial year ended (last before the end of the limited liability partnership's financial
year).

6   . . .

7 – (1)   The information required by paragraphs 8 and 9 shall be given where
at the end of the financial year the limited liability partnership has a significant
holding in an undertaking which is not a subsidiary undertaking of the limited
liability partnership.

(2)   A holding is significant for this purpose if–
   (a)   it amounts to 20 per cent or more of the nominal value of any class of
         shares in the undertaking, or
   (b)   the amount of the holding (as stated or included in the limited liability
         partnership's accounts) exceeds one-fifth of the amount (as so stated)
         of the limited liability partnership's assets.

8 – (1)   The name of the undertaking shall be stated.

(2)   There shall be stated–
   (a)   if the undertaking is incorporated outside Great Britain, the country
         in which it is incorporated;
   (c)   if it is unincorporated, the address of its principal place of business.

(3)   There shall also be stated–
   (a)   the identity of each class of shares in the undertaking held by the
         limited liability partnership, and
   (b)   the proportion of the nominal value of the shares of that class represented
         by those shares.

9 – (1)   There shall also be stated–
   (a)   the aggregate amount of the capital and reserves of the undertaking as
         at the end of its relevant financial year, and
   (b)   its profit or loss for that year.

(2)   That information need not be given if–
   (a)   the limited liability partnership is exempt by virtue of section 228
         from the requirement to prepare group accounts (parent limited liability
         partnership included in accounts of larger group), and
   (b)   the investment of the limited liability partnership in all undertakings
         in which it has such a holding as is mentioned in sub-paragraph (1) is
         shown, in aggregate, in the notes to the accounts by way of the equity
         method of valuation.

(3) That information need not be given in respect of an undertaking if–
   (a) the undertaking is not required by any provision of this Act to deliver a copy of its balance sheet for its relevant financial year and does not otherwise publish that balance sheet in Great Britain or elsewhere, and
   (b) the limited liability partnership's holding is less than 50 per cent of the nominal value of the shares in the undertaking.

(4) Information otherwise required by this paragraph need not be given if it is not material.

(5) For the purposes of this paragraph the "relevant financial year" of an undertaking is–
   (a) if its financial year ends with that of the limited liability partnership, that year, and
   (b) if not, its financial year ending last before the end of the limited liability partnership's financial year.

9A ...

11 – (1) Where the limited liability partnership is a subsidiary undertaking, the following information shall be given with respect to the parent undertaking of–
   (a) the largest group of undertakings for which group accounts are drawn up and of which the limited liability partnership is a member, and
   (b) the smallest such group of undertakings.

(2) The name of the parent undertaking shall be stated.

(3) There shall be stated–
   (a) if the undertaking is incorporated outside Great Britain, the country in which it is incorporated;
   (c) if it is unincorporated, the address of its principal place of business.

(4) If copies of the group accounts referred to in sub-paragraph (1) are available to the public, there shall also be stated the addresses from which copies of the accounts can be obtained.

12 – (1) Where the limited liability partnership is a subsidiary undertaking, the following information shall be given with respect to the company (if any) regarded by the members as being the limited liability partnership's ultimate parent company.

(2) The name of that company shall be stated.

(3) If known to the members, there shall be stated–
   (a) if that company is incorporated outside Great Britain, the country in which it is incorporated;

(4) In this paragraph "company" includes any body corporate.

13 – (1) References in this Part of this Schedule to shares held by a limited liability partnership shall be construed as follows.

(2) For the purposes of paragraphs 2 to 4 (information about subsidiary undertakings)–
- (a) there shall be attributed to the limited liability partnership any shares held by a subsidiary undertaking, or by a person acting on behalf of the limited liability partnership or a subsidiary undertaking; but
- (b) there shall be treated as not held by the limited liability partnership any shares held on behalf of a person other than the limited liability partnership or a subsidiary undertaking.

(3) For the purposes of paragraphs 7 to 9 (information about undertakings other than subsidiary undertakings)–
- (a) there shall be attributed to the limited liability partnership shares held on its behalf by any person; but
- (b) there shall be treated as not held by a limited liability partnership shares held on behalf of a person other than the limited liability partnership.

(4) For the purposes of any of those provisions, shares held by way of security shall be treated as held by the person providing the security–
- (a) where apart from the right to exercise them for the purpose of preserving the value of the security, or of realising it, the rights attached to the shares are exercisable only in accordance with his instructions, and
- (b) where the shares are held in connection with the granting of loans as part of normal business activities and apart from the right to exercise them for the purpose of preserving the value of the security, or of realising it, the rights attached to the shares are exercisable only in his interests.

PART II

LIMITED LIABILITY PARTNERSHIPS REQUIRED TO PREPARE
GROUP ACCOUNTS

14 In this Part of this Schedule "the group" means the group consisting of the parent limited liability partnership and its subsidiary undertakings.

15 – (1) The following information shall be given with respect to the undertakings which are subsidiary undertakings of the parent limited liability partnership at the end of the financial year.

(2) The name of each undertaking shall be stated.

(3) There shall be stated–
- (a) if the undertaking is incorporated outside Great Britain, the country in which it is incorporated;
- (c) if it is unincorporated, the address of its principal place of business.

(4)   It shall also be stated whether the subsidiary undertaking is included in the consolidation and, if it is not, the reasons for excluding it from consolidation shall be given.

(5)   It shall be stated with respect to each subsidiary undertaking by virtue of which of the conditions specified in section 258(2) or (4) it is a subsidiary undertaking of its immediate parent undertaking.

That information need not be given if the relevant condition is that specified in subsection (2)(a) of that section (holding of a majority of the voting rights) and the immediate parent undertaking holds the same proportion of the shares in the undertaking as it holds voting rights.

16 – (1)   The following information shall be given with respect to the shares of a subsidiary undertaking held–

     (a)   by the parent limited liability partnership, and

     (b)   by the group;

and the information under paragraphs (a) and (b) shall (if different) be shown separately.

(2)   There shall be stated–

     (a)   the identity of each class of shares held, and

     (b)   the proportion of the nominal value of the shares of that class represented by those shares.

17 – (1)   There shall be shown with respect to each subsidiary undertaking not included in the consolidation–

     (a)   the aggregate amount of its capital and reserves as at the end of its relevant financial year, and

     (b)   its profit or loss for that year.

(2)   That information need not be given if the group's investment in the undertaking is included in the accounts by way of the equity method of valuation or if–

     (a)   the undertaking is not required by any provision of this Act to deliver a copy of its balance sheet for its relevant financial year and does not otherwise publish that balance sheet in Great Britain or elsewhere, and

     (b)   the holding of the group is less than 50 per cent of the nominal value of the shares in the undertaking.

(3)   Information otherwise required by this paragraph need not be given if it is not material.

(4)   For the purposes of this paragraph the "relevant financial year" of a subsidiary undertaking is–

     (a)   if its financial year ends with that of the limited liability partnership, that year, and

     (b)   if not, its financial year ending last before the end of the limited liability partnership's financial year.

20   ...

21 – (1)   The following information shall be given where an undertaking is dealt with in the consolidated accounts by the method of proportional consolidation in accordance with paragraph 19 of Schedule 4A (joint ventures)–
   (a)   the name of the undertaking;
   (b)   the address of the principal place of business of the undertaking;
   (c)   the factors on which joint management of the undertaking is based; and
   (d)   the proportion of the capital of the undertaking held by undertakings included in the consolidation.

(2)   Where the financial year of the undertaking did not end with that of the limited liability partnership, there shall be stated the date on which a financial year of the undertaking last ended before that date.

22 – (1)   The following information shall be given where an undertaking included in the consolidation has an interest in an associated undertaking.

(2)   The name of the associated undertaking shall be stated.

(3)   There shall be stated–
   (a)   if the undertaking is incorporated outside Great Britain, the country in which it is incorporated;
   (c)   if it is unincorporated, the address of its principal place of business.

(4)   The following information shall be given with respect to the shares of the undertaking held–
   (a)   by the parent limited liability partnership, and
   (b)   by the group;
and the information under paragraphs (a) and (b) shall be shown separately.

(5)   There shall be stated–
   (a)   the identity of each class of shares held, and
   (b)   the proportion of the nominal value of the shares of that class represented by those shares.

(6)   In this paragraph "associated undertaking" has the meaning given by paragraph 20 of Schedule 4A; and the information required by this paragraph shall be given notwithstanding that paragraph 22(3) of that Schedule (materiality) applies in relation to the accounts themselves.

23 – (1)   The information required by paragraphs 24 and 25 shall be given where at the end of the financial year the parent limited liability partnership has a significant holding in an undertaking which is not one of its subsidiary undertakings and does not fall within paragraph 21 (joint ventures) or paragraph 22 (associated undertakings).

(2)   A holding is significant for this purpose if–
   (a)   it amounts to 20 per cent or more of the nominal value of any class of shares in the undertaking, or

(b) the amount of the holding (as stated or included in the limited liability partnership's individual accounts) exceeds one-fifth of the amount of its assets (as so stated).

24 – (1) The name of the undertaking shall be stated.

(2) There shall be stated–
    (a) if the undertaking is incorporated outside Great Britain, the country in which it is incorporated;
    (c) if it is unincorporated, the address of its principal place of business.

(3) The following information shall be given with respect to the shares of the undertaking held by the parent limited liability partnership.

(4) There shall be stated–
    (a) the identity of each class of shares held, and
    (b) the proportion of the nominal value of the shares of that class represented by those shares.

25 – (1) There shall also be stated–
    (a) the aggregate amount of the capital and reserves of the undertaking as at the end of its relevant financial year, and
    (b) its profit or loss for that year.

(2) That information need not be given in respect of an undertaking if–
    (a) the undertaking is not required by any provision of this Act to deliver a copy of its balance sheet for its relevant financial year and does not otherwise publish that balance sheet in Great Britain or elsewhere, and
    (b) the limited liability partnership's holding is less than 50 per cent of the nominal value of the shares in the undertaking.

(3) Information otherwise required by this paragraph need not be given if it is not material.

(4) For the purposes of this paragraph the "relevant financial year" of an undertaking is–
    (a) if its financial year ends with that of the limited liability partnership, that year, and
    (b) if not, its financial year ending last before the end of the limited liability partnership's financial year.

26 – (1) The information required by paragraphs 27 and 28 shall be given where at the end of the financial year the group has a significant holding in an undertaking which is not a subsidiary undertaking of the parent limited liability partnership and does not fall within paragraph 21 (joint ventures) or paragraph 22 (associated undertakings).

(2) A holding is significant for this purpose if–
    (a) it amounts to 20 per cent or more of the nominal value of any class of shares in the undertaking, or

(b) the amount of the holding (as stated or included in the group accounts) exceeds one-fifth of the amount of the group's assets (as so stated).

27 – (1)   The name of the undertaking shall be stated.

(2)   There shall be stated–
   (a) if the undertaking is incorporated outside Great Britain, the country in which it is incorporated;
   (c) if it is unincorporated, the address of its principal place of business.

(3)   The following information shall be given with respect to the shares of the undertaking held by the group.

(4)   There shall be stated–
   (a) the identity of each class of shares held, and
   (b) the proportion of the nominal value of the shares of that class represented by those shares.

28 – (1)   There shall also be stated–
   (a) the aggregate amount of the capital and reserves of the undertaking as at the end of its relevant financial year, and
   (b) its profit or loss for that year.

(2)   That information need not be given if–
   (a) the undertaking is not required by any provision of this Act to deliver a copy of its balance sheet for its relevant financial year and does not otherwise publish that balance sheet in Great Britain or elsewhere, and
   (b) the holding of the group is less than 50 per cent of the nominal value of the shares in the undertaking.

(3)   Information otherwise required by this paragraph need not be given if it is not material.

(4)   For the purposes of this paragraph the "relevant financial year" of an outside undertaking is–
   (a) if its financial year ends with that of the parent limited liability partnership, that year, and
   (b) if not, its financial year ending last before the end of the parent limited liability partnership's financial year.

28A …

30 – (1)   Where the parent limited liability partnership is itself a subsidiary undertaking, the following information shall be given with respect to that parent undertaking of the limited liability partnership which heads–
   (a) the largest group of undertakings for which group accounts are drawn up and of which that limited liability partnership is a member, and
   (b) the smallest such group of undertakings.

(2)   The name of the parent undertaking shall be stated.

(3)   There shall be stated–
    (a)   if the undertaking is incorporated outside Great Britain, the country in which it is incorporated;
    (c)   if it is unincorporated, the address of its principal place of business.

(4)   If copies of the group accounts referred to in sub-paragraph (1) are available to the public, there shall also be stated the addresses from which copies of the accounts can be obtained.

31 – (1)   Where the parent limited liability partnership is itself a subsidiary undertaking, the following information shall be given with respect to the limited liability partnership (if any) regarded by the members as being that limited liability partnership's ultimate parent limited liability partnership.

(2)   The name of that limited liability partnership shall be stated.

(3)   If known to the members, there shall be stated–
    (a)   if that limited liability partnership is incorporated outside Great Britain, the country in which it is incorporated;

(4)   In this paragraph "limited liability partnership" includes any body corporate.

32 – (1)   References in this Part of this Schedule to shares held by the parent limited liability partnership or group shall be construed as follows.

(2)   For the purposes of paragraphs 16, 22(4) and (5) and 23 to 25 (information about holdings in subsidiary and other undertakings)–
    (a)   there shall be attributed to the parent limited liability partnership shares held on its behalf by any person; but
    (b)   there shall be treated as not held by the parent limited liability partnership shares held on behalf of a person other than the limited liability partnership.

(3)   References to shares held by the group are to any shares held by or on behalf of the parent limited liability partnership or any of its subsidiary undertakings; but there shall be treated as not held by the group any shares held on behalf of a person other than the parent limited liability partnership or any of its subsidiary undertakings.

(4)   Shares held by way of security shall be treated as held by the person providing the security–
    (a)   where apart from the right to exercise them for the purpose of preserving the value of the security, or of realising it, the rights attached to the shares are exercisable only in accordance with his instructions, and
    (b)   where the shares are held in connection with the granting of loans as part of normal business activities and apart from the right to exercise them for the purpose of preserving the value of the security, or of realising it, the rights attached to the shares are exercisable only in his interests.

SCHEDULE 8
FORM AND CONTENT OF ACCOUNTS PREPARED BY SMALL LIMITED LIABILITY PARTNERSHIPS

PART I
GENERAL RULES AND FORMATS

Section A
General Rules

1 – (1)   Subject to the following provisions of this Schedule–
  (a) every balance sheet of a small limited liability partnership shall show the items listed in either of the balance sheet formats set out below in section B of this Part; and
  (b) every profit and loss account of a small limited liability partnership shall show the items listed in [either of] the profit and loss account formats so set out;
in either case in the order and under the headings and sub-headings given in the format adopted.

(2)   Sub-paragraph (1) above is not to be read as requiring the heading or sub-heading for any item to be distinguished by any letter or number assigned to that item in the format adopted.

2 – (1)   Where in accordance with paragraph 1 a small limited liability partnership's balance sheet or profit and loss account for any financial year has been prepared by reference to one of the formats set out in section B below, the members of the limited liability partnership shall adopt the same format in preparing the accounts for subsequent financial years of the limited liability partnership unless in their opinion there are special reasons for a change.

(2)   Particulars of any change in the format adopted in preparing a small limited liability partnership's balance sheet or profit and loss account in accordance with paragraph 1 shall be disclosed, and the reasons for the change shall be explained, in a note to the accounts in which the new format is first adopted.

3 – (1)   Any item required in accordance with paragraph 1 to be shown in a small limited liability partnership's balance sheet or profit and loss account may be shown in greater detail than required by the format adopted.

(2)   A small limited liability partnership's balance sheet or profit and loss account may include an item representing or covering the amount of any asset or liability, income or expenditure not otherwise covered by any of the items listed in the format adopted, but the following shall not be treated as assets in any small limited liability partnership's balance sheet–
  (a) preliminary expenses;
  (b) expenses of and commission on any issue of … debentures; and
  (c) costs of research.

(3)   In preparing a small limited liability partnership's balance sheet or profit and loss account the members of the limited liability partnership shall adapt the arrangement and headings and sub-headings otherwise required by paragraph 1 in respect of items to which an Arabic number is assigned in the format adopted, in any case where the special nature of the limited liability partnership's business requires such adaptation.

(4)   Items to which Arabic numbers are assigned in any of the formats set out in section B below may be combined in a small limited liability partnership's accounts for any financial year if either–

(a)   their individual amounts are not material to assessing the state of affairs or profit or loss of the limited liability partnership for that year; or

(b)   the combination facilitates that assessment;

but in a case within paragraph (b) the individual amounts of any items so combined shall be disclosed in a note to the accounts.

(5)   Subject to paragraph 4(3) below, a heading or sub-heading corresponding to an item listed in the format adopted in preparing a small limited liability partnership's balance sheet or profit and loss account shall not be included if there is no amount to be shown for that item in respect of the financial year to which the balance sheet or profit and loss account relates.

(6)   Every profit and loss account of a small limited liability partnership shall show the amount of the limited liability partnership's profit or loss on ordinary activities before taxation.

(7)   Every profit and loss account of a small limited liability partnership shall show separately as additional items–

(a)   any amount set aside or proposed to be set aside to, or withdrawn or proposed to be withdrawn from, reserves;

(b)   ...

4 – (1)   In respect of every item shown in a small limited liability partnership's balance sheet or profit and loss account the corresponding amount for the financial year immediately preceding that to which the balance sheet or profit and loss account relates shall also be shown.

(2)   Where that corresponding amount is not comparable with the amount to be shown for the item in question in respect of the financial year to which the balance sheet or profit and loss account relates, the former amount shall be adjusted and particulars of the adjustment and the reasons for it shall be disclosed in a note to the accounts.

(3)   Paragraph 3(5) does not apply in any case where an amount can be shown for the item in question in respect of the financial year immediately preceding that to which the balance sheet or profit and loss account relates, and that amount shall be shown under the heading or sub-heading required by paragraph 1 for that item.

5   Amounts in respect of items representing assets or income may not be set off against amounts in respect of items representing liabilities or expenditure (as the case may be), or vice versa.

Section B
The Required Formats For Accounts

Preliminary

6   References in this Part of this Schedule to the items listed in any of the formats set out below are to those items read together with any of the notes following the formats which apply to any of those items, and the requirement imposed by paragraph 1 to show the items listed in any such format in the order adopted in the format is subject to any provision in those notes for alternative positions for any particular items.

7   A number in brackets following any item in any of the formats set out below is a reference to the note of that number in the notes following the formats.

8   In the notes following the formats–
(a)   the heading of each note gives the required heading or sub-heading for the item to which it applies and a reference to any letters and numbers assigned to that item in the formats set out below (taking a reference in the case of Format 2 of the balance sheet formats to the item listed under "Assets" or under "Liabilities" as the case may require); and
(b)   references to a numbered format are to the balance sheet format or (as the case may require) to the profit and loss account format of that number set out below.

Balance sheet formats
Format 1

A. …
B. Fixed assets
　　I Intangible assets
　　　　1. Goodwill *(2)*
　　　　2. Other intangible assets *(3)*
　　II Tangible assets
　　　　1. Land and buildings
　　　　2. Plant and machinery etc
　　III Investments
　　　　1. Shares in group undertakings and participating interests
　　　　2. Loans to group undertakings and undertakings in which the limited liability partnership has a participating interest
　　　　3. Other investments other than loans
　　　　4. Other investments *(4)*
C. Current assets
　　I Stocks

    1. Stocks

    2. Payments on account

II Debtors *(5)*

    1. Trade debtors

    2. Amounts owed by group undertakings and undertakings in which the limited liability partnership has a participating interest

    3. Other debtors

III Investments

    1. Shares in group undertakings

    2. Other investments

IV Cash at bank and in hand

D. Prepayments and accrued income *(6)*

E. Creditors: amounts falling due within one year

    1. Bank loans and overdrafts

    2. Trade creditors

    3. Amounts owed to group undertakings and undertakings in which the limited liability partnership has a participating interest

    4. Other creditors *(7)*

F. Net current assets (liabilities) *(8)*

G. Total assets less current liabilities

H. Creditors: amounts falling due after more than one year

    1. Bank loans and overdrafts

    2. Trade creditors

    3. Amounts owed to group undertakings and undertakings in which the limited liability partnership has a participating interest

    4. Other creditors *(7)*

I. Provisions for liabilities and charges

J. Accruals and deferred income *(7)*

[K. Loans and other debts due to members *(9)*

L. Members' other interests

    I Members' capital

    II Revaluation reserve

    III Other reserves]

Balance sheet formats
Format 2

ASSETS

A. ...

B. Fixed assets

    I Intangible assets

        1. Goodwill *(2)*

        2. Other intangible assets *(3)*

    II Tangible assets

        1. Land and buildings

        2. Plant and machinery etc

    III Investments

        1. Shares in group undertakings and participating interests

        2. Loans to group undertakings and undertakings in which the limited liability partnership has a participating interest

3. Other investments other than loans

4. Other investments *(4)*

C. Current assets

    I Stocks

        1. Stocks

        2. Payments on account

    II Debtors *(5)*

        1. Trade debtors

        2. Amounts owed by group undertakings and undertakings in which the limited liability partnership has a participating interest

        3. Other debtors

    III Investments

        1. Shares in group undertakings

        2. Other investments

    IV Cash at bank and in hand

D. Prepayments and accrued income *(6)*

LIABILITIES

[A. Loans and other debts due to members

AA. Members' other interests

    I Members' capital

    II Revaluation reserve

    III Other reserves]

B. Provisions for liabilities and charges

C. Creditors *(10)*

        1. Bank loans and overdrafts

        2. Trade creditors

        3. Amounts owed to group undertakings and undertakings in which the limited liability partnership has a participating interest

        4. Other creditors *(7)*

D. Accruals and deferred income *(7)*

Notes on the balance sheet formats

(1) ...

(2) Goodwill

(Formats 1 and 2, item B I 1.)

    Amounts representing goodwill shall only be included to the extent that the goodwill was acquired for valuable consideration.

(3) Other intangible assets

(Formats 1 and 2, item B I 2.)

    Amounts in respect of concessions, patents, licences, trade marks and similar rights and assets shall only be included in a limited liability partnership's balance sheet under this item if either–

    (a)   the assets were acquired for valuable consideration and are not required to be shown under goodwill; or

    (b)   the assets in question were created by the limited liability partnership itself.

(4) ...

(5) Debtors
(Formats 1 and 2, items C II 1 to 3.)
The amount falling due after more than one year shall be shown separately for each item included under debtors unless the aggregate amount of debtors falling due after more than one year is disclosed in the notes to the accounts.

(6) Prepayments and accrued income
(Formats 1 and 2, item D.)
This item may alternatively be included under item C II 3 in Format 1 or 2.

(7) Other creditors
(Format 1, items E 4, H 4 and J and Format 2, items C 4 and D.)
There shall be shown separately–
(a) the amount of any convertible loans, and
(b) the amount for creditors in respect of taxation and social security.
Payments received on account of orders shall be included in so far as they are not shown as deductions from stocks.
In Format 1, accruals and deferred income may be shown under item J or included under item E 4 or H 4, or both (as the case may require). In Format 2, accruals and deferred income may be shown under item D or within item C 4 under Liabilities.

(8) Net current assets (liabilities)
(Format 1, item F.)
In determining the amount to be shown under this item any prepayments and accrued income shall be taken into account wherever shown.

[(9) Loans and other debts due to members
(Format 1, item K and Format 2, item A.)
The following amounts shall be shown separately under this item–
(a) the aggregate amount of money advanced to the limited liability partnership by the members by way of loan,
(b) the aggregate amount of money owed to members by the limited liability partnership in respect of profits,
(c) any other amounts.]

(10) Creditors
(Format 2, items C I to 4.)
Amounts falling due within one year and after one year shall be shown separately for each of these items and for the aggregate of all of these items unless the aggregate amount of creditors falling due within one year and the aggregate amount of creditors falling due after more than one year is disclosed in the notes to the accounts.

Profit and loss account formats
Format 1
(see note *(14)* below)

1. Turnover
2. Cost of sales *(11)*
3. Gross profit or loss
4. Distribution costs *(11)*
5. Administrative expenses *(11)*
6. Other operating income
7. Income from shares in group undertakings
8. Income from participating interests
9. Income from other fixed asset investments *(12)*
10. Other interest receivable and similar income *(12)*
11. Amounts written off investments
12. Interest payable and similar charges *(13)*
13. Tax on profit or loss on ordinary activities
14. Profit or loss on ordinary activities after taxation
15. Extraordinary income
16. Extraordinary charges
17. Extraordinary profit or loss
18. Tax on extraordinary profit or loss
19. Other taxes not shown under the above items
[20. Profit or loss for the financial year before members' remuneration and profit shares]

Profit and loss account formats
Format 2

1. Turnover
2. Change in stocks of finished goods and in work in progress
3. Own work capitalised
4. Other operating income
5. – (a) Raw materials and consumables
    (b) Other external charges
6. Staff costs:
    (a) wages and salaries
    (b) social security costs
    (c) other pension costs
7. – (a) Depreciation and other amounts written off tangible and intangible fixed assets
    (b) Exceptional amounts written off current assets
8. Other operating charges
9. Income from shares in group undertakings
10. Income from participating interests
11. Income from other fixed asset investments *(12)*
12. Other interest receivable and similar income *(12)*
13. Amounts written off investments
14. Interest payable and similar charges *(13)*

15. Tax on profit or loss on ordinary activities
16. Profit or loss on ordinary activities after taxation
17. Extraordinary income
18. Extraordinary charges
19. Extraordinary profit or loss
20. Tax on extraordinary profit or loss
21. Other taxes not shown under the above items
[22. Profit or loss for the financial year before members' remuneration and profit shares]

Profit and loss account formats
Format 3

...

Profit and loss account formats
Format 4

...

Notes on the profit and loss account formats

(11) Cost of sales: distribution costs: administrative expenses
(Format 1, items 2, 4 and 5 ...)
These items shall be stated after taking into account any necessary provisions for depreciation or diminution in value of assets.

(12) Income from other fixed asset investments: other interest receivable and similar income
(Format 1, items 9 and 10: Format 2, items 11 and 12 ...)
Income and interest derived from group undertakings shall be shown separately from income and interest derived from other sources.

(13) Interest payable and similar charges
(Format 1, item 12: Format 2, item 14 ...)
The amount payable to group undertakings shall be shown separately.

(14) Format 1 ...
The amount of any provisions for depreciation and diminution in value of tangible and intangible fixed assets falling to be shown under items 7(a) in Format 2 ... shall be disclosed in a note to the accounts in any case where the profit and loss account is prepared by reference to Format 1 ...

PART II
ACCOUNTING PRINCIPLES AND RULES

Section A
Accounting Principles

Preliminary

9   Subject to paragraph 15 below, the amounts to be included in respect of all items shown in a small limited liability partnership's accounts shall be determined in accordance with the principles set out in paragraphs 10 to 14.

Accounting principles

10   The limited liability partnership shall be presumed to be carrying on business as a going concern.

11   Accounting policies shall be applied consistently within the same accounts and from one financial year to the next.

12   The amount of any item shall be determined on a prudent basis, and in particular–
  (a)   only profits realised at the balance sheet date shall be included in the profit and loss account; and
  (b)   all liabilities and losses which have arisen or are likely to arise in respect of the financial year to which the accounts relate or a previous financial year shall be taken into account, including those which only become apparent between the balance sheet date and the date on which it is signed … in pursuance of section 233 of this Act.

13   All income and charges relating to the financial year to which the accounts relate shall be taken into account, without regard to the date of receipt or payment.

14   In determining the aggregate amount of any item the amount of each individual asset or liability that falls to be taken into account shall be determined separately.

Departure from the accounting principles

15   If it appears to the members of a small limited liability partnership that there are special reasons for departing from any of the principles stated above in preparing the limited liability partnership's accounts in respect of any financial year they may do so, but particulars of the departure, the reasons for it and its effect shall be given in a note to the accounts.

Section B
Historical Cost Accounting Rules

Preliminary

16   Subject to section C of this Part of this Schedule, the amounts to be included in respect of all items shown in a small limited liability partnership's accounts shall be determined in accordance with the rules set out in paragraphs 17 to 28.

Fixed assets

17   Subject to any provision for depreciation or diminution in value made in accordance with paragraph 18 or 19 the amount to be included in respect of any fixed asset shall be its purchase price or production cost.

18   In the case of any fixed asset which has a limited useful economic life, the amount of–
   (a)   its purchase price or production cost; or
   (b)   where it is estimated that any such asset will have a residual value at the end of the period of its useful economic life, its purchase price or production cost less that estimated residual value;
shall be reduced by provisions for depreciation calculated to write off that amount systematically over the period of the asset's useful economic life.

19 – (1)   Where a fixed asset investment of a description falling to be included under item B III of either of the balance sheet formats set out in Part I of this Schedule has diminished in value provisions for diminution in value may be made in respect of it and the amount to be included in respect of it may be reduced accordingly; and any such provisions which are not shown in the profit and loss account shall be disclosed (either separately or in aggregate) in a note to the accounts.

(2)   Provisions for diminution in value shall be made in respect of any fixed asset which has diminished in value if the reduction in its value is expected to be permanent (whether its useful economic life is limited or not), and the amount to be included in respect of it shall be reduced accordingly; and any such provisions which are not shown in the profit and loss account shall be disclosed (either separately or in aggregate) in a note to the accounts.

(3)   Where the reasons for which any provision was made in accordance with sub-paragraph (1) or (2) have ceased to apply to any extent, that provision shall be written back to the extent that it is no longer necessary; and any amounts written back in accordance with this sub-paragraph which are not shown in the profit and loss account shall be disclosed (either separately or in aggregate) in a note to the accounts.

20 – (1)   Notwithstanding that an item in respect of "development costs" is included under "fixed assets" in the balance sheet formats set out in Part I of this Schedule, an amount may only be included in a small limited liability partnership's balance sheet in respect of development costs in special circumstances.

(2)   If any amount is included in a small limited liability partnership's balance sheet in respect of development costs the following information shall be given in a note to the accounts–
  (a)   the period over which the amount of those costs originally capitalised is being or is to be written off; and
  (b)   the reasons for capitalising the development costs in question.

21 – (1)   The application of paragraphs 17 to 19 in relation to goodwill (in any case where goodwill is treated as an asset) is subject to the following provisions of this paragraph.

(2)   Subject to sub-paragraph (3) below, the amount of the consideration for any goodwill acquired by a small limited liability partnership shall be reduced by provisions for depreciation calculated to write off that amount systematically over a period chosen by the members of the limited liability partnership.

(3)   The period chosen shall not exceed the useful economic life of the goodwill in question.

(4)   In any case where any goodwill acquired by a small limited liability partnership is shown or included as an asset in the limited liability partnership's balance sheet the period chosen for writing off the consideration for that goodwill and the reasons for choosing that period shall be disclosed in a note to the accounts.

Current assets

22   Subject to paragraph 23, the amount to be included in respect of any current asset shall be its purchase price or production cost.

23 – (1)   If the net realisable value of any current asset is lower than its purchase price or production cost the amount to be included in respect of that asset shall be the net realisable value.

(2)   Where the reasons for which any provision for diminution in value was made in accordance with sub-paragraph (1) have ceased to apply to any extent, that provision shall be written back to the extent that it is no longer necessary.

Miscellaneous and supplementary provisions

24 – (1)   Where the amount repayable on any debt owed by a small limited liability partnership is greater than the value of the consideration received in the transaction giving rise to the debt, the amount of the difference may be treated as an asset.

(2)   Where any such amount is so treated–
  (a)   it shall be written off by reasonable amounts each year and must be completely written off before repayment of the debt; and
  (b)   if the current amount is not shown as a separate item in the limited liability partnership's balance sheet it must be disclosed in a note to the accounts.

25 – (1) Subject to the following sub-paragraph, assets which fall to be included–
  (a) amongst the fixed assets of a small limited liability partnership under the item "tangible assets"; or
  (b) amongst the current assets of a small limited liability partnership under the item "raw materials and consumables";
may be included at a fixed quantity and value.

(2) Sub-paragraph (1) applies to assets of a kind which are constantly being replaced, where–
  (a) their overall value is not material to assessing the limited liability partnership's state of affairs; and
  (b) their quantity, value and composition are not subject to material variation.

26 – (1) The purchase price of an asset shall be determined by adding to the actual price paid any expenses incidental to its acquisition.

(2) The production cost of an asset shall be determined by adding to the purchase price of the raw materials and consumables used the amount of the costs incurred by the limited liability partnership which are directly attributable to the production of that asset.

(3) In addition, there may be included in the production cost of an asset–
  (a) a reasonable proportion of the costs incurred by the limited liability partnership which are only indirectly attributable to the production of that asset, but only to the extent that they relate to the period of production; and
  (b) interest on capital borrowed to finance the production of that asset, to the extent that it accrues in respect of the period of production;
provided, however, in a case within paragraph (b) above, that the inclusion of the interest in determining the cost of that asset and the amount of the interest so included is disclosed in a note to the accounts.

(4) In the case of current assets distribution costs may not be included in production costs.

27 – (1) Subject to the qualification mentioned below, the purchase price or production cost of–
  (a) any assets which fall to be included under any item shown in a small limited liability partnership's balance sheet under the general item "stocks"; and
  (b) any assets which are fungible assets (including investments);
may be determined by the application of any of the methods mentioned in sub-paragraph (2) below in relation to any such assets of the same class.
  The method chosen must be one which appears to the members to be appropriate in the circumstances of the limited liability partnership.

(2) Those methods are–
  (a) the method known as "first in, first out"(FIFO);

  (b) the method known as "last in, first out"(LIFO);
  (c) a weighted average price; and
  (d) any other method similar to any of the methods mentioned above.

(3) For the purposes of this paragraph, assets of any description shall be regarded as fungible if assets of that description are substantially indistinguishable one from another.

28 Where there is no record of the purchase price or production cost of any asset of a small limited liability partnership or of any price, expenses or costs relevant for determining its purchase price or production cost in accordance with paragraph 26, or any such record cannot be obtained without unreasonable expense or delay, its purchase price or production cost shall be taken for the purposes of paragraphs 17 to 23 to be the value ascribed to it in the earliest available record of its value made on or after its acquisition or production by the limited liability partnership.

Section C
Alternative Accounting Rules

Preliminary

29 – (1) The rules set out in section B are referred to below in this Schedule as the historical cost accounting rules.

(2) Those rules, with the omission of paragraphs 16, 21 and 25 to 28, are referred to below in this Part of this Schedule as the depreciation rules; and references below in this Schedule to the historical cost accounting rules do not include the depreciation rules as they apply by virtue of paragraph 32.

30 Subject to paragraphs 32 to 34, the amounts to be included in respect of assets of any description mentioned in paragraph 31 may be determined on any basis so mentioned.

Alternative accounting rules

31 – (1) Intangible fixed assets, other than goodwill, may be included at their current cost.

(2) Tangible fixed assets may be included at a market value determined as at the date of their last valuation or at their current cost.

(3) Investments of any description falling to be included under item B III of either of the balance sheet formats set out in Part I of this Schedule may be included either–
  (a) at a market value determined as at the date of their last valuation; or
  (b) at a value determined on any basis which appears to the members to
    be appropriate in the circumstances of the limited liability partnership;
but in the latter case particulars of the method of valuation adopted and of the reasons for adopting it shall be disclosed in a note to the accounts.

(4)   Investments of any description falling to be included under item C III of either of the balance sheet formats set out in Part I of this Schedule may be included at their current cost.

(5)   Stocks may be included at their current cost.

Application of the depreciation rules

32 – (1)   Where the value of any asset of a small limited liability partnership is determined on any basis mentioned in paragraph 31, that value shall be, or (as the case may require) be the starting point for determining, the amount to be included in respect of that asset in the limited liability partnership's accounts, instead of its purchase price or production cost or any value previously so determined for that asset; and the depreciation rules shall apply accordingly in relation to any such asset with the substitution for any reference to its purchase price or production cost of a reference to the value most recently determined for that asset on any basis mentioned in paragraph 31.

(2)   The amount of any provision for depreciation required in the case of any fixed asset by paragraph 18 or 19 as it applies by virtue of sub-paragraph (1) is referred to below in this paragraph as the adjusted amount, and the amount of any provision which would be required by that paragraph in the case of that asset according to the historical cost accounting rules is referred to as the historical cost amount.

(3)   Where sub-paragraph (1) applies in the case of any fixed asset the amount of any provision for depreciation in respect of that asset–
  (a)   included in any item shown in the profit and loss account in respect of amounts written off assets of the description in question; or
  (b)   taken into account in stating any item so shown which is required by note (11) of the notes on the profit and loss account formats set out in Part I of this Schedule to be stated after taking into account any necessary provision for depreciation or diminution in value of assets included under it;
may be the historical cost amount instead of the adjusted amount, provided that the amount of any difference between the two is shown separately in the profit and loss account or in a note to the accounts.

Additional information to be provided in case of departure from historical cost accounting rules

33 – (1)   This paragraph applies where the amounts to be included in respect of assets covered by any items shown in a small limited liability partnership's accounts have been determined on any basis mentioned in paragraph 31.

(2)   The items affected and the basis of valuation adopted in determining the amounts of the assets in question in the case of each such item shall be disclosed in a note to the accounts.

(3)   In the case of each balance sheet item affected (except stocks) either–
    (a)   the comparable amounts determined according to the historical cost accounting rules; or
    (b)   the differences between those amounts and the corresponding amounts actually shown in the balance sheet in respect of that item;
shall be shown separately in the balance sheet or in a note to the accounts.

(4)   In sub-paragraph (3) above, references in relation to any item to the comparable amounts determined as there mentioned are references to–
    (a)   the aggregate amount which would be required to be shown in respect of that item if the amounts to be included in respect of all the assets covered by that item were determined according to the historical cost accounting rules; and
    (b)   the aggregate amount of the cumulative provisions for depreciation or diminution in value which would be permitted or required in determining those amounts according to those rules.

Revaluation reserve

34 – (1)   With respect to any determination of the value of an asset of a small limited liability partnership on any basis mentioned in paragraph 31, the amount of any profit or loss arising from that determination (after allowing, where appropriate, for any provisions for depreciation or diminution in value made otherwise than by reference to the value so determined and any adjustments of any such provisions made in the light of that determination) shall be credited or (as the case may be) debited to a separate reserve ("the revaluation reserve").

(2)   The amount of the revaluation reserve shall be shown in the limited liability partnership's balance sheet under a separate sub-heading in the position given for the item "revaluation reserve" in Format 1 or 2 of the balance sheet formats set out in Part I of this Schedule, but need not be shown under that name.

(3),(4),(5)   …

(6)   The treatment for taxation purposes of amounts credited or debited to the revaluation reserve shall be disclosed in a note to the accounts.

PART III
NOTES TO THE ACCOUNTS

Preliminary

35   Any information required in the case of any small limited liability partnership by the following provisions of this Part of this Schedule shall (if not given in the limited liability partnership's accounts) be given by way of a note to those accounts.

Disclosure of accounting policies

36   The accounting policies adopted by the limited liability partnership in determining the amounts to be included in respect of items shown in the balance sheet and in determining the profit or loss of the limited liability partnership shall be stated (including such policies with respect to the depreciation and diminution in value of assets).

Information supplementing the balance sheet

37 Paragraphs [40 to 47] require information which either supplements the information given with respect to any particular items shown in the balance sheet or is otherwise relevant to assessing the limited liability partnership's state of affairs in the light of the information so given.

[Loans and other debts due to members

37A The following information shall be given–
- (a) the aggregate amount of loans and other debts due to members as at the date of the beginning of the financial year,
- (b) the aggregate amounts contributed by members during the financial year,
- (c) the aggregate amounts transferred to or from the profit and loss account during that year,
- (d) the aggregate amounts withdrawn by members or applied on behalf of members during that year,
- (e) the aggregate amount of loans and other debts due to members as at the balance sheet date, and
- (f) the aggregate amount of loans and other debts due to members that fall due after one year.

38, 39 …

40 – (1) In respect of each item which is or would but for paragraph 3(4)(b) be shown under the general item "fixed assets" in the limited liability partnership's balance sheet the following information shall be given–
- (a) the appropriate amounts in respect of that item as at the date of the beginning of the financial year and as at the balance sheet date respectively;
- (b) the effect on any amount shown in the balance sheet in respect of that item of–
  - (i) any revision of the amount in respect of any assets included under that item made during that year on any basis mentioned in paragraph 31;
  - (ii) acquisitions during that year of any assets;
  - (iii) disposals during that year of any assets; and
  - (iv) any transfers of assets of the limited liability partnership to and from that item during that year.

(2) The reference in sub-paragraph (1)(a) to the appropriate amounts in respect of any item as at any date there mentioned is a reference to amounts representing the aggregate amounts determined, as at that date, in respect of assets falling to be included under that item on either of the following bases, that is to say–

(a) on the basis of purchase price or production cost (determined in accordance with paragraphs 26 and 27); or

(b) on any basis mentioned in paragraph 31,

(leaving out of account in either case any provisions for depreciation or diminution in value).

(3) In respect of each item within sub-paragraph (1)–

(a) the cumulative amount of provisions for depreciation or diminution in value of assets included under that item as at each date mentioned in sub-paragraph (1)(a);

(b) the amount of any such provisions made in respect of the financial year;

(c) the amount of any adjustments made in respect of any such provisions during that year in consequence of the disposal of any assets; and

(d) the amount of any other adjustments made in respect of any such provisions during that year;

shall also be stated.

41 Where any fixed assets of the limited liability partnership (other than listed investments) are included under any item shown in the limited liability partnership's balance sheet at an amount determined on any basis mentioned in paragraph 31, the following information shall be given–

(a) the years (so far as they are known to the members) in which the assets were severally valued and the several values; and

(b) in the case of assets that have been valued during the financial year, the names of the persons who valued them or particulars of their qualifications for doing so and (whichever is stated) the bases of valuation used by them.

42 – (1) In respect of the amount of each item which is or would but for paragraph 3(4)(b) be shown in the limited liability partnership's balance sheet under the general item "investments" (whether as fixed assets or as current assets) there shall be stated how much of that amount is ascribable to listed investments.

(2) Where the amount of any listed investments is stated for any item in accordance with sub-paragraph (1), the following amounts shall also be stated–

(a) the aggregate market value of those investments where it differs from the amount so stated; and

(b) both the market value and the stock exchange value of any investments of which the former value is, for the purposes of the accounts, taken as being higher than the latter.

43 – (1) Where any amount is transferred–

(a) to or from any reserves; or

(b) to any provisions for liabilities and charges; or

(c) from any provision for liabilities and charges otherwise than for the purpose for which the provision was established;

and the reserves or provisions are or would but for paragraph 3(4)(b) be shown as separate items in the limited liability partnership's balance sheet, the information mentioned in the following sub-paragraph shall be given in respect of the aggregate of reserves or provisions included in the same item.

(2)   That information is–
- (a)   the amount of the reserves or provisions as at the date of the beginning of the financial year and as at the balance sheet date respectively;
- (b)   any amounts transferred to or from the reserves or provisions during that year; and
- (c)   the source and application respectively of any amounts so transferred.

(3)   Particulars shall be given of each provision included in the item "other provisions" in the limited liability partnership's balance sheet in any case where the amount of that provision is material.

44 – (1)   For the aggregate of all items shown under "creditors" in the limited liability partnership's balance sheet there shall be stated the aggregate of the following amounts, that is to say–
- (a)   the amount of any debts included under "creditors" which are payable or repayable otherwise than by instalments and fall due for payment or repayment after the end of the period of five years beginning with the day next following the end of the financial year; and
- (b)   in the case of any debts so included which are payable or repayable by instalments, the amount of any instalments which fall due for payment after the end of that period.

(2)   In respect of each item shown under "creditors" in the limited liability partnership's balance sheet there shall be stated the aggregate amount of any debts included under that item in respect of which any security has been given by the limited liability partnership.

(3)   References above in this paragraph to an item shown under "creditors" in the limited liability partnership's balance sheet include references, where amounts falling due to creditors within one year and after more than one year are distinguished in the balance sheet–
- (a)   in a case within sub-paragraph (1), to an item shown under the latter of those categories; and
- (b)   in a case within sub-paragraph (2), to an item shown under either of those categories;

and references to items shown under "creditors" include references to items which would but for paragraph 3(4)(b) be shown under that heading.

45   ...

46 – (1)   Particulars shall be given of any charge on the assets of the limited liability partnership to secure the liabilities of any other person, including, where practicable, the amount secured.

(2)   The following information shall be given with respect to any other contingent liability not provided for–

    (a)   the amount or estimated amount of that liability;

    (b)   its legal nature; and

    (c)   whether any valuable security has been provided by the limited liability partnership in connection with that liability and if so, what.

(3)   There shall be stated, where practicable, the aggregate amount or estimated amount of contracts for capital expenditure, so far as not provided for.

(4)   Particulars shall be given of–

    (a)   any pension commitments included under any provision shown in the limited liability partnership's balance sheet; and

    (b)   any such commitments for which no provision has been made;

and where any such commitment relates wholly or partly to pensions payable to past members of the limited liability partnership separate particulars shall be given of that commitment so far as it relates to such pensions.

(5)   Particulars shall also be given of any other financial commitments which–

    (a)   have not been provided for; and

    (b)   are relevant to assessing the limited liability partnership's state of affairs.

(6)   Commitments within any of sub-paragraphs (1) to (5) which are undertaken on behalf of or for the benefit of–

    (a)   any parent undertaking or fellow subsidiary undertaking, or

    (b)   any subsidiary undertaking of the limited liability partnership,

shall be stated separately from the other commitments within that sub-paragraph, and commitments within paragraph (a) shall also be stated separately from those within paragraph (b).

47   Particulars shall be given of any case where the purchase price or production cost of any asset is for the first time determined under paragraph 28.

Information supplementing the profit and loss account

48   Paragraphs 49 and 50 require information which either supplements the information given with respect to any particular items shown in the profit and loss account or otherwise provides particulars of income or expenditure of the limited liability partnership or of circumstances affecting the items shown in the profit and loss account.

49 – (1)   If the limited liability partnership has supplied geographical markets outside the United Kingdom during the financial year in question, there shall be stated the percentage of its turnover that, in the opinion of the members, is attributable to those markets.

(2)   In analysing for the purposes of this paragraph the source of turnover, the members of the limited liability partnership shall have regard to the manner in which the limited liability partnership's activities are organised.

50 – (1)   Where any amount relating to any preceding financial year is included in any item in the profit and loss account, the effect shall be stated.

(2)   Particulars shall be given of any extraordinary income or charges arising in the financial year.

(3)   The effect shall be stated of any transactions that are exceptional by virtue of size or incidence though they fall within the ordinary activities of the limited liability partnership.

General

51 – (1)   Where sums originally denominated in foreign currencies have been brought into account under any items shown in the balance sheet or profit and loss account, the basis on which those sums have been translated into sterling shall be stated.

(2)   Subject to the following sub-paragraph, in respect of every item stated in a note to the accounts the corresponding amount for the financial year immediately preceding that to which the accounts relate shall also be stated and where the corresponding amount is not comparable, it shall be adjusted and particulars of the adjustment and the reasons for it shall be given.

(3)   Sub-paragraph (2) does not apply in relation to any amounts stated by virtue of any of the following provisions of this Act–
  (a)   paragraph 13 of Schedule 4A (details of accounting treatment of acquisitions),
  (b)   paragraphs 2, 8(3), 16, 21(1)(d), 22(4) and (5), 24(3) and (4) and 27(3) and (4) of Schedule 5 (shareholdings in other undertakings),
  (c)   …
  (d)   paragraphs 40 and 43 above (fixed assets and reserves and provisions).

Dormant limited liability partnerships acting as agents

51A   Where the members of a limited liability partnership take advantage of the exemption conferred by section 249AA, and the limited liability partnership has during the financial year in question acted as an agent for any person, the fact that it has so acted must be stated.

PART IV
INTERPRETATION OF SCHEDULE

52   The following paragraphs apply for the purposes of this Schedule and its interpretation.

53   References to the historical cost accounting rules shall be read in accordance with paragraph 29.

54   "Listed investment" means an investment as respects which there has been granted a listing on a recognised investment exchange other than an overseas investment exchange within the meaning of the Financial Services Act 1986 or on any stock exchange of repute outside Great Britain.

55   A loan is treated as falling due for repayment, and an instalment of a loan is treated as falling due for payment, on the earliest date on which the lender could require repayment or (as the case may be) payment, if he exercised all options and rights available to him.

56   Amounts which in the particular context of any provision of this Schedule are not material may be disregarded for the purposes of that provision.

57 – (1)   References to provisions for depreciation or diminution in value of assets are to any amount written off by way of providing for depreciation or diminution in value of assets.

(2)   Any reference in the profit and loss account formats set out in Part I of this Schedule to the depreciation of, or amounts written off, assets of any description is to any provision for depreciation or diminution in value of assets of that description.

58   References to provisions for liabilities or charges are to any amount retained as reasonably necessary for the purpose of providing for any liability or loss which is either likely to be incurred, or certain to be incurred but uncertain as to amount or as to the date on which it will arise.

59 – (1)   "Social security costs" means any contributions by the limited liability partnership to any state social security or pension scheme, fund or arrangement.

(2)   "Pension costs" includes any costs incurred by the limited liability partnership in respect of any pension scheme established for the purpose of providing pensions for persons currently or formerly employed by the limited liability partnership, any sums set aside for the future payment of pensions directly by the limited liability partnership to current or former employees and any pensions paid directly to such persons without having first been set aside.

(3)   Any amount stated in respect of the item "social security costs" or in respect of the item "wages and salaries" in the limited liability partnership's profit and loss account shall be determined by reference to payments made or costs incurred in respect of all persons employed by the limited liability partnership during the financial year under contracts of service.

SCHEDULE 8A
FORM AND CONTENT OF ABBREVIATED ACCOUNTS OF SMALL
LIMITED LIABILITY PARTNERSHIPS DELIVERED TO REGISTRAR

PART I
BALANCE SHEET FORMATS

1   A small limited liability partnership may deliver to the registrar a copy of the balance sheet showing the items listed in either of the balance sheet formats set out in paragraph 2 below in the order and under the headings and sub-headings given in the format adopted, but in other respects corresponding to the full balance sheet.

2   The formats referred to in paragraph 1 are as follows–

Balance sheet formats

Format 1

A. ...
B. Fixed assets
    I Intangible assets
    II Tangible assets
    III Investments
C. Current assets
    I Stocks
    II Debtors *(1)*
    III Investments
    IV Cash at bank and in hand
D. Prepayments and accrued income
E. Creditors: amounts falling due within one year
F. Net current assets (liabilities)
G. Total assets less current liabilities
H. Creditors: amounts falling due after more than one year
I. Provisions for liabilities and charges
J. Accruals and deferred income
[K. Loans and other debts due to members
L. Members' other interests
    I Members' capital
    II Revaluation reserve
    III Other reserves]

Balance sheet formats

Format 2

ASSETS
A. ...
B. Fixed assets
    I Intangible assets
    II Tangible assets
    III Investments
C. Current assets
    I Stocks
    II Debtors *(1)*
    III Investments
    IV Cash at bank and in hand
D. Prepayments and accrued income

LIABILITIES
[A. Loans and other debts due to members
AA. Members' other interests
    I Members' capital
    II Revaluation reserve

411

III Other reserves
B. Provisions for liabilities and charges
C. Creditors *(2)*
D. Accruals and deferred income

Notes on the balance sheet formats

(1) Debtors
(Formats 1 and 2, item C II.)
  The aggregate amount of debtors falling due after more than one year shall be shown separately, unless it is disclosed in the notes to the accounts.

(2) Creditors
(Format 2, Liabilities item C.)
  The aggregate amount of creditors falling due within one year and of creditors falling due after more than one year shall be shown separately, unless it is disclosed in the notes to the accounts.

PART II
NOTES TO THE ACCOUNTS

Preliminary

3 Any information required in the case of any small limited liability partnership by the following provisions of this Part of this Schedule shall (if not given in the limited liability partnership's accounts) be given by way of a note to those accounts.

Disclosure of accounting policies

4 The accounting policies adopted by the limited liability partnership in determining the amounts to be included in respect of items shown in the balance sheet and in determining the profit or loss of the limited liability partnership shall be stated (including such policies with respect to the depreciation and diminution in value of assets).

Information supplementing the balance sheet

5, 6 ...

7 – (1) In respect of each item to which a letter or Roman number is assigned under the general item "fixed assets" in the limited liability partnership's balance sheet the following information shall be given–
  (a) the appropriate amounts in respect of that item as at the date of the beginning of the financial year and as at the balance sheet date respectively;
  (b) the effect on any amount shown in the balance sheet in respect of that item of–
    (i) any revision of the amount in respect of any assets included under that item made during that year on any basis mentioned in paragraph 31 of Schedule 8;

(ii) acquisitions during that year of any assets;

(iii) disposals during that year of any assets; and

(iv) any transfers of assets of the limited liability partnership to and from that item during that year.

(2)   The reference in sub-paragraph (1)(a) to the appropriate amounts in respect of any item as at any date there mentioned is a reference to amounts representing the aggregate amounts determined, as at that date, in respect of assets falling to be included under that item on either of the following bases, that is to say–

(a) on the basis of purchase price or production cost (determined in accordance with paragraphs 26 and 27 of Schedule 8); or

(b) on any basis mentioned in paragraph 31 of that Schedule,

(leaving out of account in either case any provisions for depreciation or diminution in value).

(3)   In respect of each item within sub-paragraph (1)–

(a) the cumulative amount of provisions for depreciation or diminution in value of assets included under that item as at each date mentioned in sub-paragraph (1)(a);

(b) the amount of any such provisions made in respect of the financial year;

(c) the amount of any adjustments made in respect of any such provisions during that year in consequence of the disposal of any assets; and

(d) the amount of any other adjustments made in respect of any such provisions during that year;

shall also be stated.

8 – (1)   For the aggregate of all items shown under "creditors" in the limited liability partnership's balance sheet there shall be stated the aggregate of the following amounts, that is to say–

(a) the amount of any debts included under "creditors" which are payable or repayable otherwise than by instalments and fall due for payment or repayment after the end of the period of five years beginning with the day next following the end of the financial year; and

(b) in the case of any debts so included which are payable or repayable by instalments, the amount of any instalments which fall due for payment after the end of that period.

(2)   In respect of each item shown under "creditors" in the limited liability partnership's balance sheet there shall be stated the aggregate amount of any debts included under that item, in respect of which any security has been given by the limited liability partnership.

General

9 – (1)   Where sums originally denominated in foreign currencies have been brought into account under any items shown in the balance sheet or profit and loss account, the basis on which those sums have been translated into sterling shall be stated.

(2)   Subject to the following sub-paragraph, in respect of every item required to be stated in a note to the accounts by or under any provision of this Act, the corresponding amount for the financial year immediately preceding that to which the accounts relate shall also be stated and where the corresponding amount is not comparable, it shall be adjusted and particulars of the adjustment and the reasons for it shall be given.

(3)   Sub-paragraph (2) does not apply in relation to any amounts stated by virtue of any of the following provisions of this Act–

    (a)   paragraph 13 of Schedule 4A (details of accounting treatment of acquisitions),

    (b)   paragraphs 2, 8(3), 16, 21(1)(d), 22(4) and (5), 24(3) and (4) and 27(3) and (4) of Schedule 5 (shareholdings in other undertakings),

    (c)   …

    (d)   paragraph 7 above (fixed assets).

Dormant limited liability partnerships acting as agents

9A   Where the members of a limited liability partnership take advantage of the exemption conferred by section 249AA, and the limited liability partnership has during the financial year in question acted as an agent for any person, the fact that it has so acted must be stated.

Schedules 9–23

SCHEDULE 24

[Please see the following pages]

Schedule 25

SCHEDULE 24
PUNISHMENT OF OFFENCES UNDER THIS ACT

Section of Act creating offence	General nature of offence	Mode of prosecution	Punishment	Daily default fine (where applicable)
...				
191(4)	Refusal of inspection or copy of register of debenture holders, etc.	Summary.	One-fifth of the statutory maximum.	One-fiftieth of the statutory maximum.
...				
221(5) or 222(4)	Limited liability partnership failing to keep accounting records (liability of members).	1. On indictment. 2. Summary.	2 years or a fine; or both. 6 months or the statutory maximum; or both.	
222(6)	Member of limited liability partnership failing to secure compliance with, or intentionally causing default under section 222(5) (preservation of accounting records for requisite number of years).	1. On indictment. 2. Summary.	2 years or a fine; or both. 6 months or the statutory maximum; or both.	
231(6)	Limited liability partnership failing to annex to its annual return certain particulars required by Schedule 5 and not included in annual accounts.	Summary.	One-fifth of the statutory maximum.	One-fiftieth of the statutory maximum.

Section of Act creating offence	General nature of offence	Mode of prosecution	Punishment	Daily default fine (where applicable)
...				
233(5)	Approving defective accounts.	1. On indictment. 2. Summary.	A fine. The statutory maximum.	
233(6)	Laying or delivery of unsigned balance sheet; circulating copies of balance sheet without signature.	Summary.	One-fifth of the statutory maximum.	
...				
236(4)	Laying, circulating or delivering auditors' report without required signature.	Summary.	One-fifth of the statutory maximum.	
238(5)	Failing to send limited liability partnership's annual accounts, members' report and auditors' report to those entitled to receive them.	1. On indictment. 2. Summary.	A fine. The statutory maximum.	
239(3)	Limited liability partnership failing to supply copy of accounts and reports to member on demand.	Summary.	One-fifth of the statutory maximum.	
240(6)	Failure to comply with requirements in connection with publication of accounts.	Summary.	One-fifth of the statutory maximum.	One-fiftieth of the statutory maximum.

Section of Act creating offence	General nature of offence	Mode of prosecution	Punishment	Daily default fine (where applicable)
...				
348(2)	Limited liability partnership failing to paint or affix name; failing to keep it painted or affixed.	Summary.	One–fifth of the statutory maximum.	In the case of failure to keep the name painted or affixed, one-fiftieth of the statutory maximum.
349(2)	Limited liability partnership failing to have name on business correspondence, invoices, etc.	Summary.	One–fifth of the statutory maximum.	
349(3)	Member of limited liability partnership issuing business letter or document not bearing limited liability partnership's name.	Summary.	One–fifth of the statutory maximum.	
349(4)	Member of limited liability partnership signing cheque, bill of exchange, etc on which limited liability partnership's name not mentioned.	Summary.	One–fifth of the statutory maximum.	
350(1)	Limited liability partnership failing to have its name engraved on limited liability partnership seal.	Summary.	One–fifth of the statutory maximum.	

417

Appendix 2 – CA 1985 as modified

Section of Act creating offence	General nature of offence	Mode of prosecution	Punishment	Daily default fine (where applicable)
350(2)	Member of limited liability partnership, etc, using limited liability partnership seal without name engraved on it.	Summary.	One-fifth of the statutory maximum.	
351(5)(a)	Limited liability partnership failing to comply with section 351(1) or (2) (matters to be stated on business correspondence, etc).	Summary.	One-fifth of the statutory maximum.	
351(5)(b)	Member or agent of limited liability partnership issuing, or authorising issue of, business document not complying with those subsections.	Summary.	One-fifth of the statutory maximum.	
351(5)(c)	Contravention of section 351(3) or (4) (information in English to be stated on Welsh limited liability partnership's business correspondence, etc).	Summary.	One-fifth of the statutory maximum.	For contravention of section 351(3), one-fiftieth of the statutory maximum.
...				
363(3)	Limited liability partnership failing to make annual return.	Summary.	The statutory maximum.	One-tenth of the statutory maximum.
...				

418

Section of Act creating offence	General nature of offence	Mode of prosecution	Punishment	Daily default fine (where applicable)
387(2) ...	Limited liability partnership failing to give Secretary of State notice of non-appointment of auditors.	Summary.	One-fifth of the statutory maximum.	One-fiftieth of the statutory maximum.
389A(2)	Member of limited liability partnership making false, misleading or deceptive statement to auditors.	1. On indictment. 2. Summary.	2 years or a fine; or both. 6 months or the statutory maximum; or both.	
389A(3)	Subsidiary undertaking or its auditor failing to give information to auditors of parent limited liability partnership.	Summary.	One-fifth of the statutory maximum.	
389A(4)	Parent limited liability partnership failing to obtain from subsidiary undertaking information for purposes of audit.	Summary.	One-fifth of the statutory maximum.	
391(2)	Failing to give notice to registrar of removal of auditor.	Summary.	One-fifth of the statutory maximum.	One-fiftieth of the statutory maximum.
392(3)	Limited liability partnership failing to forward notice of auditor's resignation to registrar.	1. On indictment. 2. Summary.	A fine. The statutory maximum.	One-tenth of the statutory maximum.

419

Section of Act creating offence	General nature of offence	Mode of prosecution	Punishment	Daily default fine (where applicable)
392A(5)	Members failing to convene meeting requisitioned by resigning auditor.	1. On indictment. 2. Summary.	A fine. The statutory maximum.	
394A(1)	Person ceasing to hold office as auditor failing to deposit statement as to circumstances.	1. On indictment. 2. Summary.	A fine. The statutory maximum.	
394A(4)	Limited liability partnership failing to comply with requirements as to statement of person ceasing to hold office as auditor.	1. On indictment. 2. Summary.	A fine. The statutory maximum.	One-tenth of the statutory maximum.
399(3)	Limited liability partnership failing to send to registrar particulars of charge created by it, or of issue of debentures which requires registration.	1. On indictment. 2. Summary.	A fine. The statutory maximum.	One-tenth of the statutory maximum.
400(4)	Limited liability partnership failing to send to registrar particulars of charge on property acquired.	1. On indictment. 2. Summary.	A fine. The statutory maximum.	One-tenth of the statutory maximum.
402(3)	Authorising or permitting delivery of debenture or certificate of debenture stock, without endorsement on it of certificate of registration of charge.	Summary.	One-fifth of the statutory maximum.	

Section of Act creating offence	General nature of offence	Mode of prosecution	Punishment	Daily default fine (where applicable)
403(2A)	Person making false statement under section 403(1A) which he knows to be false or does not believe to be true.	1. On indictment. 2. Summary.	2 years or a fine; or both. 6 months or the statutory maximum; or both.	
405(4)	Failure to give notice to registrar of appointment of receiver or manager, or of his ceasing to act.	Summary.	One-fifth of the statutory maximum.	One-fiftieth of the statutory maximum.
407(3)	Authorising or permitting omission from limited liability partnership register of charges.	1. On indictment. 2. Summary.	A fine. The statutory maximum.	
408(3)	Member of limited liability partnership refusing inspection of charging instrument, or of register of charges.	Summary.	One-fifth of the statutory maximum.	One-fiftieth of the statutory maximum.
415(3)	Scottish limited liability partnership failing to send to registrar particulars of charge created by it, or of issue of debentures which requires registration.	1. On indictment. 2. Summary.	A fine. The statutory maximum.	One-tenth of the statutory maximum.
416(3)	Scottish limited liability partnership failing to send to registrar particulars of charge on property acquired by it.	1. On indictment. 2. Summary.	A fine. The statutory maximum.	One-tenth of the statutory maximum.

Section of Act creating offence	General nature of offence	Mode of prosecution	Punishment	Daily default fine (where applicable)
419(5A)	Person making false statement under section 419(1A) or (1B) which he knows to be false or does not believe to be true.	1. On indictment. 2. Summary.	2 years or a fine; or both. 6 months or the statutory maximum; or both.	
422(3)	Scottish limited liability partnership authorising or permitting omission from its register of charges.	1. On indictment. 2. Summary.	A fine. The statutory maximum.	
423(3)	Member of Scottish limited liability refusing inspection of charging instrument, or of a register of charges.	Summary.	One-fifth of the statutory maximum.	One-fiftieth partnership of the statutory maximum.
425(4)	Limited liability partnership failing to annex to memorandum court order sanctioning compromise or arrangement with creditors.	Summary.	One-fifth of the statutory maximum.	
426(6)	Limited liability partnership failing to comply with requirements of section 426 (information to members and creditors about compromise or arrangement.)	1. On indictment. 2. Summary.	A fine. The statutory maximum.	
426(7)	Member or trustee for debenture holders failing to give notice to limited liability partnership of matters necessary for purposes of section 426.	Summary.	One-fifth of the statutory maximum.	

Section of Act creating offence	General nature of offence	Mode of prosecution	Punishment	Daily default fine (where applicable)
427(5)	Failure to deliver to registrar office copy of court order under section 427 (limited liability partnership reconstruction or amalgamation).	Summary.	One-fifth of the statutory maximum.	One-fiftieth of the statutory maximum.
...				
447(6)	Failure to comply with requirement to produce documents imposed by Secretary of State under section 447.	1. On indictment. 2. Summary.	A fine. The statutory maximum.	
448(7)	Obstructing the exercise of any rights conferred by a warrant or failing to comply with a requirement imposed under subsection (3)(d).	1. On indictment. 2. Summary.	A fine. The statutory maximum.	
449(2)	Wrongful disclosure of information or document obtained under section 447 or 448.	1. On indictment. 2. Summary.	2 years, or a fine; or both. 6 months or the statutory maximum; or both.	
450	Destroying or mutilating limited liability partnership documents; falsifying such documents or making false entries; parting with such documents or altering them or making omissions.	1. On indictment. 2. Summary.	7 years, or a fine; or both. 6 months, or the statutory maximum; or both.	

Section of Act creating offence	General nature of offence	Mode of prosecution	Punishment	Daily default fine (where applicable)
451	Making false statement or explanation in purported compliance with section 447.	1. On indictment. 2. Summary.	2 years, or a fine; or both. 6 months, or the statutory maximum; or both.	
⋮				
458	Being a party to carrying on limited liability partnership's business with intent to defraud creditors, or for any fraudulent purpose.	1. On indictment. 2. Summary.	7 years or a fine; or both. 6 months or the statutory maximum; or both.	
⋮				
651(3)	Person obtaining court order to declare limited liability partnership's dissolution void, then failing to register the order.	Summary.	One-fifth of the statutory maximum.	One-fiftieth of the statutory maximum.
652E(1)	Person breaching or failing to perform duty imposed by section 652B or 652C.	1. On indictment. 2. Summary.	A fine. The statutory maximum.	
652E(2)	Person failing to perform duty imposed by section 652B(6) or 652C(2) with intent to conceal the making of application under section 652A.	1. On indictment. 2. Summary.	7 years or a fine; or both. 6 months or the statutory maximum; or both.	

Section of Act creating offence	General nature of offence	Mode of prosecution	Punishment	Daily default fine (where applicable)
652F(1)	Person furnishing false or misleading information in connection with application under section 652A.	1. On indictment. 2. Summary.	A fine. The statutory maximum.	
652F(2) ⋮	Person making false application under section 652A.	1. On indictment. 2. Summary.	A fine. The statutory maximum.	
722(3) ⋮	Limited liability partnership failing to comply with section 722(2), as regards the manner of keeping registers, minute books and accounting records.	Summary.	One-fifth of the statutory maximum.	One fiftieth of the statutory maximum.

Company Directors Disqualification Act 1986

1986 Chapter 40

Provisions of the Company Directors Disqualification Act 1986 with modifications as they apply to Limited Liability Partnerships

1 Disqualification orders: general

(1)   In the circumstances specified below in this Act a court may, and under section 6 shall, make against a person a disqualification order, that is to say an order that for a period specified in the order–

    (a)   he shall not be a member of a limited liability partnership, act as receiver of a limited liability partnership's property or in any way, whether directly or indirectly, be concerned or take part in the promotion, formation or management of a limited liability partnership unless (in each case) he has the leave of the court, and

    (b)   he shall not act as an insolvency practitioner.

(2)   In each section of this Act which gives to a court power or, as the case may be, imposes on it the duty to make a disqualification order there is specified the maximum (and, in section 6, the minimum) period of disqualification which may or (as the case may be) must be imposed by means of the order and, unless the court otherwise orders, the period of disqualification so imposed shall begin at the end of the period of 21 days beginning with the date of the order.

(3)   Where a disqualification order is made against a person who is already subject to such an order or to a disqualification undertaking, the periods specified in those orders or, as the case may be, in the order and the undertaking shall run concurrently.

(4)   A disqualification order may be made on grounds which are or include matters other than criminal convictions, notwithstanding that the person in respect of whom it is to be made may be criminally liable in respect of those matters.

1A Disqualification undertakings: general

(1)   In the circumstances specified in sections 7 and 8 the Secretary of State may accept a disqualification undertaking, that is to say an undertaking by any person that, for a period specified in the undertaking, the person–

    (a)   will not be a member of a limited liability partnership, act as receiver of a limited liability partnership's property or in any way, whether directly or indirectly, be concerned or take part in the promotion, formation or management of a limited liability partnership unless (in each case) he has the leave of a court, and

(b) will not act as an insolvency practitioner.

(2)   The maximum period which may be specified in a disqualification undertaking is 15 years; and the minimum period which may be specified in a disqualification undertaking under section 7 is two years.

(3)   Where a disqualification undertaking by a person who is already subject to such an undertaking or to a disqualification order is accepted, the periods specified in those undertakings or (as the case may be) the undertaking and the order shall run concurrently.

(4)   In determining whether to accept a disqualification undertaking by any person, the Secretary of State may take account of matters other than criminal convictions, notwithstanding that the person may be criminally liable in respect of those matters.

2 Disqualification on conviction of indictable offence

(1)   The court may make a disqualification order against a person where he is convicted of an indictable offence (whether on indictment or summarily) in connection with the promotion, formation, management, liquidation or striking off of a limited liability partnership, with the receivership of a limited liability partnership's property or with his being an administrative receiver of a limited liability partnership.

(2)   "The court" for this purpose means–
(a) any court having jurisdiction to wind up the limited liability partnership in relation to which the offence was committed, or
(b) the court by or before which the person is convicted of the offence, or
(c) in the case of a summary conviction in England and Wales, any other magistrates' court acting for the same petty sessions area;
and for the purposes of this section the definition of "indictable offence" in Schedule 1 to the Interpretation Act 1978 applies for Scotland as it does for England and Wales.

(3)   The maximum period of disqualification under this section is–
(a) where the disqualification order is made by a court of summary jurisdiction, five years, and
(b) in any other case, 15 years.

3 Disqualification for persistent breaches of companies legislation

(1)   The court may make a disqualification order against a person where it appears to it that he has been persistently in default in relation to provisions of the companies legislation requiring any return, account or other document to be filed with, delivered or sent, or notice of any matter to be given, to the registrar of companies.

(2)   On an application to the court for an order to be made under this section, the fact that a person has been persistently in default in relation to such provisions as are mentioned above may (without prejudice to its proof in any other manner) be conclusively proved by showing that in the five years ending with the date of the application he has been adjudged guilty (whether or not on the same occasion) of three or more defaults in relation to those provisions.

(3)   A person is to be treated under subsection (2) as being adjudged guilty of a default in relation to any provision of that legislation if–

    (a) he is convicted (whether on indictment or summarily) of an offence consisting in a contravention of or failure to comply with that provision (whether on his own part or on the part of any limited liability partnership), or

    (b) a default order is made against him, that is to say an order under any of the following provisions–

        (i)   section 242(4) of the Companies Act (order requiring delivery of limited liability partnership accounts),

        (ia) section 245B of that Act (order requiring preparation of revised accounts),

        (ii) section 713 of that Act (enforcement of limited liability partnership's duty to make returns),

        (iii) section 41 of the Insolvency Act (enforcement of receiver's or manager's duty to make returns), or

        (iv) section 170 of that Act (corresponding provision for liquidator in winding up),

in respect of any such contravention of or failure to comply with that provision (whether on his own part or on the part of any limited liability partnership).

(4)   In this section "the court" means any court having jurisdiction to wind up any of the limited liability partnerships in relation to which the offence or other default has been or is alleged to have been committed.

(5)   The maximum period of disqualification under this section is five years.

4 Disqualification for fraud, etc, in winding up

(1)   The court may make a disqualification order against a person if, in the course of the winding up of a limited liability partnership, it appears that he–

    (a) has been guilty of an offence for which he is liable (whether he has been convicted or not) under section 458 of the Companies Act (fraudulent trading), or

    (b) has otherwise been guilty, while a member or liquidator of the limited liability partnership receiver of the limited liability partnership's property or administrative receiver of the limited liability partnership, of any fraud in relation to the limited liability partnership or of any breach of his duty as such member, liquidator, receiver or administrative receiver.

(2)   In this section "the court" means any court having jurisdiction to wind up any of the limited liability partnerships in relation to which the offence or other

default has been or is alleged to have been committed; and "member" includes a shadow member.

(3)   The maximum period of disqualification under this section is 15 years.

5 Disqualification on summary conviction

(1)   An offence counting for the purposes of this section is one of which a person is convicted (either on indictment or summarily) in consequence of a contravention of, or failure to comply with, any provision of the companies legislation requiring a return, account or other document to be filed with, delivered or sent, or notice of any matter to be given, to the registrar of companies (whether the contravention or failure is on the person's own part or on the part of any limited liability partnership).

(2)   Where a person is convicted of a summary offence counting for those purposes, the court by which he is convicted (or, in England and Wales, any other magistrates' court acting for the same petty sessions area) may make a disqualification order against him if the circumstances specified in the next subsection are present.

(3)   Those circumstances are that, during the five years ending with the date of the conviction, the person has had made against him, or has been convicted of, in total not less than three default orders and offences counting for the purposes of this section; and those offences may include that of which he is convicted as mentioned in subsection (2) and any other offence of which he is convicted on the same occasion.

(4)   For the purposes of this section–
    (a)   the definition of "summary offence" in Schedule 1 to the Interpretation Act 1978 applies for Scotland as for England and Wales, and
    (b)   "default order" means the same as in section 3(3)(b).

(5)   The maximum period of disqualification under this section is five years.

6 Duty of court to disqualify unfit members of insolvent limited liability partnerships

(1)   The court shall make a disqualification order against a person in any case where, on an application under this section, it is satisfied–
    (a)   that he is or has been a member of a limited liability partnership which has at any time become insolvent (whether while he was a member or subsequently), and
    (b)   that his conduct as a member of that limited liability partnership (either taken alone or taken together with his conduct as a member of any other limited liability partnership or limited liability partnerships) makes him unfit to be concerned in the management of a limited liability partnership.

(2)   For the purposes of this section and the next, a limited liability partnership becomes insolvent if–

(a) the limited liability partnership goes into liquidation at a time when its assets are insufficient for the payment of its debts and other liabilities and the expenses of the winding up,

(b) an administration order is made in relation to the limited liability partnership, or

(c) an administrative receiver of the limited liability partnership is appointed;

and references to a person's conduct as a member of any limited liability partnership or limited liability partnerships include, where that limited liability partnership or any of those limited liability partnerships has become insolvent, that person's conduct in relation to any matter connected with or arising out of the insolvency of that limited liability partnership.

(3) In this section and section 7(2), "the court" means–

(a) where the limited liability partnership in question is being or has been wound up by the court, that court,

(b) where the limited liability partnership in question is being or has been wound up voluntarily, any court which has or (as the case may be) had jurisdiction to wind it up,

(c) where neither of the preceding paragraphs applies but an administration order has at any time been made, or an administrative receiver has at any time been appointed, in relation to the limited liability partnership in question, any court which has jurisdiction to wind it up.

(3A) Sections 117 and 120 of the Insolvency Act 1986 (jurisdiction) shall apply for the purposes of subsection (3) as if the references in the definitions of "registered office" to the presentation of the petition for winding up were references–

(a) in a case within paragraph (b) of that subsection, to the passing of the resolution for voluntary winding up,

(b) in a case within paragraph (c) of that subsection, to the making of the administration order or (as the case may be) the appointment of the administrative receiver.

(3B) Nothing in subsection (3) invalidates any proceedings by reason of their being taken in the wrong court; and proceedings–

(a) for or in connection with a disqualification order under this section, or

(b) in connection with a disqualification undertaking accepted under section 7,

may be retained in the court in which the proceedings were commenced, although it may not be the court in which they ought to have been commenced.

(3C) In this section and section 7, "member" includes a shadow member".

(4) Under this section the minimum period of disqualification is two years, and the maximum period is 15 years.

7 Disqualification order or undertaking; and reporting provisions

(1) If it appears to the Secretary of State that it is expedient in the public interest that a disqualification order under section 6 should be made against any

person, an application for the making of such an order against that person may be made–
(a) by the Secretary of State, or
(b) if the Secretary of State so directs in the case of a person who is or has been a member of a limited liability partnership which is being or has been wound up by the court in England and Wales, by the official receiver.

(2) Except with the leave of the court, an application for the making under that section of a disqualification order against any person shall not be made after the end of the period of two years beginning with the day on which the limited liability partnership of which that person is or has been a member became insolvent.

(2A) If it appears to the Secretary of State that the conditions mentioned in section 6(1) are satisfied as respects any person who has offered to give him a disqualification undertaking, he may accept the undertaking if it appears to him that it is expedient in the public interest that he should do so (instead of applying, or proceeding with an application, for a disqualification order).

(3) If it appears to the office-holder responsible under this section, that is to say–
(a) in the case of a limited liability partnership which is being wound up by the court in England and Wales, the official receiver,
(b) in the case of a limited liability partnership which is being wound up otherwise, the liquidator,
(c) in the case of a limited liability partnership in relation to which an administration order is in force, the administrator, or
(d) in the case of a limited liability partnership of which there is an administrative receiver, that receiver,
that the conditions mentioned in section 6(1) are satisfied as respects a person who is or has been a member of that limited liability partnership, the office-holder shall forthwith report the matter to the Secretary of State.

(4) The Secretary of State or the official receiver may require the liquidator, administrator or administrative receiver of a limited liability partnership, or the former liquidator, administrator or administrative receiver of a limited liability partnership–
(a) to furnish him with such information with respect to any person's conduct as a member of the limited liability partnership, and
(b) to produce and permit inspection of such books, papers and other records relevant to that person's conduct as such a member,
as the Secretary of State or the official receiver may reasonably require for the purpose of determining whether to exercise, or of exercising, any function of his under this section.

8 Disqualification after investigation of limited liability partnership

(1) If it appears to the Secretary of State from a report made by inspectors under section 437 of the Companies Act or section 94 or 177 of the Financial

Services Act 1986, or from information or documents obtained under section 447 or 448 of the Companies Act or section 105 of the Financial Services Act 1986 or section 2 of the Criminal Justice Act 1987 or section 28 of the Criminal Law (Consolidation) (Scotland) Act 1995 or section 83 of the Companies Act 1989, that it is expedient in the public interest that a disqualification order should be made against any person who is or has been a member or shadow member of any limited liability partnership, he may apply to the court for such an order to be made against that person.

(2)   The court may make a disqualification order against a person where, on an application under this section, it is satisfied that his conduct in relation to the limited liability partnership makes him unfit to be concerned in the management of a limited liability partnership.

(2A)   Where it appears to the Secretary of State from such report, information or documents that, in the case of a person who has offered to give him a disqualification undertaking–
   (a)   the conduct of the person in relation to a company of which the person is or has been a director or shadow director makes him unfit to be concerned in the management of a company, and
   (b)   it is expedient in the public interest that he should accept the undertaking (instead of applying, or proceeding with an application, for a disqualification order),
he may accept the undertaking.

(3)   In this section "the court" means the High Court or, in Scotland, the Court of Session.

(4)   The maximum period of disqualification under this section is 15 years.

8A Variation etc of disqualification undertaking

(1)   The court may, on the application of a person who is subject to a disqualification undertaking–
   (a)   reduce the period for which the undertaking is to be in force, or
   (b)   provide for it to cease to be in force.

(2)   On the hearing of an application under subsection (1), the Secretary of State shall appear and call the attention of the court to any matters which seem to him to be relevant, and may himself give evidence or call witnesses.

(3)   In this section "the court" has the same meaning as in section 7(2) or (as the case may be) 8.

9 Matters for determining unfitness of members

(1)   Where it falls to a court to determine whether a person's conduct as a member of any particular limited liability partnership or limited liability partnerships makes him unfit to be concerned in the management of a limited

liability partnership, the court shall, as respects his conduct as a member of that limited liability partnership or, as the case may be, each of those limited liability partnerships, have regard in particular–

    (a)   to the matters mentioned in Part I of Schedule 1 to this Act, and

    (b)   where the limited liability partnership has become insolvent, to the matters mentioned in Part II of that Schedule;

and references in that Schedule to the member and the limited liability partnership are to be read accordingly.

(1A)   In determining whether he may accept a disqualification undertaking from any person the Secretary of State shall, as respects the person's conduct as a member of any limited liability partnership concerned, have regard in particular–

    (a)   to the matters mentioned in Part I of Schedule 1 to this Act, and

    (b)   where the limited liability partnership has become insolvent, to the matters mentioned in Part II of that Schedule;

and references in that Schedule to the member and the limited liability partnership are to be read accordingly.

(2)   Section 6(2) applies for the purposes of this section and Schedule 1 as it applies for the purposes of sections 6 and 7 and in this section and that Schedule "member" includes a shadow member.

(3)   Subject to the next subsection, any reference in Schedule 1 to an enactment contained in the Companies Act or the Insolvency Act includes, in relation to any time before the coming into force of that enactment, the corresponding enactment in force at that time.

(4)   The Secretary of State may by order modify any of the provisions of Schedule 1; and such an order may contain such transitional provisions as may appear to the Secretary of State necessary or expedient.

(5)   The power to make orders under this section is exercisable by statutory instrument subject to annulment in pursuance of a resolution of either House of Parliament.

10 Participation in wrongful trading

(1)   Where the court makes a declaration under section 213 or 214 of the Insolvency Act that a person is liable to make a contribution to a limited liability partnership's assets, then, whether or not an application for such an order is made by any person, the court may, if it thinks fit, also make a disqualification order against the person to whom the declaration relates.

(2)   The maximum period of disqualification under this section is 15 years.

11 Undischarged bankrupts

(1)   It is an offence for a person who is an undischarged bankrupt to act as member of, or directly or indirectly to take part in or be concerned in the

promotion, formation or management of, a limited liability partnership, except with the leave of the court.

(2) "The court" for this purpose is the court by which the person was adjudged bankrupt or, in Scotland, sequestration of his estates was awarded.

(3) In England and Wales, the leave of the court shall not be given unless notice of intention to apply for it has been served on the official receiver; and it is the latter's duty, if he is of opinion that it is contrary to the public interest that the application should be granted, to attend on the hearing of the application and oppose it.

12 Failure to pay under county court administration order

(1) The following has effect where a court under section 429 of the Insolvency Act revokes an administration order under Part VI of the County Courts Act 1984.

(2) A person to whom that section applies by virtue of the order under section 429(2)(b) shall not, except with the leave of the court which made the order, act as member or liquidator of, or directly or indirectly take part or be concerned in the promotion, formation or management of, a limited liability partnership.

12A Northern Irish disqualification orders

(1) A person subject to a disqualification order under Part II of the Companies (Northern Ireland) Order 1989–
    (a) shall not be a member of a limited liability partnership, act as receiver of a limited liability partnership's property or in any way, whether directly or indirectly, be concerned or take part in the promotion, formation or management of a limited liability partnership unless (in each case) he has the leave of the High Court of Northern Ireland, and
    (b) shall not act as an insolvency practitioner.

(2) If provision is made in relation to Northern Ireland for undertakings corresponding to the disqualification undertakings provided for by section 6, the Secretary of State may by order made by statutory instrument make any modifications of the Company Directors Disqualification Act 1986, or any enactment amended by Part II of Schedule 4, which he considers necessary or expedient to give effect to those undertakings in relation to Great Britain.

(3) A statutory instrument containing an order under this section is to be subject to annulment in pursuance of a resolution of either House of Parliament.

13 Criminal penalties

If a person acts in contravention of a disqualification order or disqualification undertaking or in contravention of section 12(2) or 12A, or is guilty of an offence under section 11, he is liable–

(a) on conviction on indictment, to imprisonment for not more than two years or a fine, or both; and

(b) on summary conviction, to imprisonment for not more than six months or a fine not exceeding the statutory maximum, or both.

14 Offences by body corporate

(1) Where a body corporate is guilty of an offence of acting in contravention of a disqualification order or disqualification undertaking or in contravention of section 12A, and it is proved that the offence occurred with the consent or connivance of, or was attributable to any neglect on the part of any director, manager, secretary or other similar officer of the body corporate, or any person who was purporting to act in any such capacity he, as well as the body corporate, is guilty of the offence and liable to be proceeded against and punished accordingly.

(2) Where the affairs of a body corporate are managed by its members, subsection (1) applies in relation to the acts and defaults of a member in connection with his functions of management as if he were a director of the body corporate.

15 Personal liability for limited liability partnership's debts where person acts while disqualified

(1) A person is personally responsible for all the relevant debts of a limited liability partnership if at any time–
  (a) in contravention of a disqualification order or disqualification undertaking or in contravention of section 11 or 12A of this Act he is involved in the management of the limited liability partnership, or
  (b) as a person who is involved in the management of the limited liability partnership, he acts or is willing to act on instructions given without the leave of the court by a person whom he knows at that time to be the subject of a disqualification order or disqualification undertaking or a disqualification order under Part II of the Companies (Northern Ireland) Order 1989 or to be an undischarged bankrupt.

(2) Where a person is personally responsible under this section for the relevant debts of a limited liability partnership, he is jointly and severally liable in respect of those debts with the limited liability partnership and any other person who, whether under this section or otherwise, is so liable.

(3) For the purposes of this section the relevant debts of a limited liability partnership are–
  (a) in relation to a person who is personally responsible under paragraph (a) of subsection (1), such debts and other liabilities of the limited liability partnership as are incurred at a time when that person was involved in the management of the limited liability partnership, and
  (b) in relation to a person who is personally responsible under paragraph (b) of that subsection, such debts and other liabilities of the limited liability partnership as are incurred at a time when that person was acting or was willing to act on instructions given as mentioned in that paragraph.

(4)   For the purposes of this section, a person is involved in the management of a limited liability partnership if he is a member of the limited liability partnership or if he is concerned, whether directly or indirectly, or takes part, in the management of the limited liability partnership.

(5)   For the purposes of this section a person who, as a person involved in the management of a limited liability partnership, has at any time acted on instructions given without the leave of the court by a person whom he knew at that time to be the subject of a disqualification order or disqualification undertaking or a disqualification order under Part II of the Companies (Northern Ireland) Order 1989 or to be an undischarged bankrupt is presumed, unless the contrary is shown, to have been willing at any time thereafter to act on any instructions given by that person.

16 Application for disqualification order

(1)   A person intending to apply for the making of a disqualification order by the court having jurisdiction to wind up a limited liability partnership shall give not less than ten days' notice of his intention to the person against whom the order is sought; and on the hearing of the application the last-mentioned person may appear and himself give evidence or call witnesses.

(2)   An application to a court with jurisdiction to wind up limited liability partnerships for the making against any person of a disqualification order under any of sections 2 to 4 may be made by the Secretary of State or the official receiver, or by the liquidator or any past or present member or creditor of any limited liability partnership in relation to which that person has committed or is alleged to have committed an offence or other default.

(3)   On the hearing of any application under this Act made by the Secretary of State or the official receiver or the liquidator, the applicant shall appear and call the attention of the court to any matters which seem to him to be relevant, and may himself give evidence or call witnesses.

17 Application for leave under an order or undertaking

(1)   Where a person is subject to a disqualification order made by a court having jurisdiction to wind up limited liability partnerships, any application for leave for the purposes of section 1(1)(a) shall be made to that court.

(2)   Where–
(a) a person is subject to a disqualification order made under section 2 by a court other than a court having jurisdiction to wind up limited liability partnerships, or
(b) a person is subject to a disqualification order made under section 5,
any application for leave for the purposes of section 1(1)(a) shall be made to any court which, when the order was made, had jurisdiction to wind up the limited liability partnership (or, if there is more than one such limited liability partnership, any of the limited liability partnerships) to which the offence (or any of the offences) in question related.

(3)   Where a person is subject to a disqualification undertaking accepted at any time under section 7 or 8, any application for leave for the purposes of section 1A(1)(a) shall be made to any court to which, if the Secretary of State had applied for a disqualification order under the section in question at that time, his application could have been made.

(4)   But where a person is subject to two or more disqualification orders or undertakings (or to one or more disqualification orders and to one or more disqualification undertakings), any application for leave for the purposes of section 1(1)(a) or 1A(1)(a) shall be made to any court to which any such application relating to the latest order to be made, or undertaking to be accepted, could be made.

(5)   On the hearing of an application for leave for the purposes of section 1(1)(a) or 1A(1)(a), the Secretary of State shall appear and call the attention of the court to any matters which seem to him to be relevant, and may himself give evidence or call witnesses."

18 Register of disqualification orders and undetakings

(1)   The Secretary of State may make regulations requiring officers of courts to furnish him with such particulars as the regulations may specify of cases in which–
    (a) a disqualification order is made, or
    (b) any action is taken by a court in consequence of which such an order or a disqualification undertaking is varied or ceases to be in force, or
    (c) leave is granted by a court for a person subject to such an order to do any thing which otherwise the order prohibits him from doing; or
    (d) leave is granted by a court for a person subject to such an undertaking to do anything which otherwise the undertaking prohibits him from doing;
and the regulations may specify the time within which, and the form and manner in which, such particulars are to be furnished.

(2)   The Secretary of State shall, from the particulars so furnished, continue to maintain the register of orders, and of cases in which leave has been granted as mentioned in subsection (1)(c), which was set up by him under section 29 of the Companies Act 1976 and continued under section 301 of the Companies Act 1985.

(2A) The Secretary of State shall include in the register such particulars as he considers appropriate of disqualification undertakings accepted by him under section 7 or 8 and of cases in which leave has been granted as mentioned in subsection (1)(d).

(3)   When an order or undertaking of which entry is made in the register ceases to be in force, the Secretary of State shall delete the entry from the register and all particulars relating to it which have been furnished to him under this section or any previous corresponding provision and, in the case of a disqualification undertaking, any other particulars he has included in the register.

(4)   The register shall be open to inspection on payment of such fee as may be specified by the Secretary of State in regulations.

(4A)   Regulations under this section may extend the preceding provisions of this section, to such extent and with such modifications as may be specified in the regulations, to disqualification orders made under Part II of the Companies (Northern Ireland) Order 1989.

(5)   Regulations under this section shall be made by statutory instrument subject to annulment in pursuance of a resolution of either House of Parliament.

19 Special savings from repealed enactments

(1)   Schedule 2 to this Act has effect–
   (a)   in connection with certain transitional cases arising under sections 93 and 94 of the Companies Act 1981, so as to limit the power to make a disqualification order, or to restrict the duration of an order, by reference to events occurring or things done before the sections came into force,
   (b)   to preserve orders made under section 28 of the Companies Act 1976 (repealed by the Act of 1981), and
   (c)   to preclude any applications for a disqualification order under section 6 or 8, where the relevant limited liability partnership went into liquidation before 28th April 1986.

20 Admissibility in evidence of statements

(1)   In any proceedings (whether or not under this Act), any statement made in pursuance of a requirement imposed by or under sections 6 to 10, 15 or 19(c) of, or Schedule 1 to, this Act, or by or under rules made for the purposes of this Act under the Insolvency Act, may be used in evidence against any person making or concurring in making the statement.

(2)   However, in criminal proceedings in which any such person is charged with an offence to which this subsection applies–
   (a)   no evidence relating to the statement may be adduced, and
   (b)   no question relating to it may be asked,
by or on behalf of the prosecution, unless evidence relating to it is adduced, or a question relating to it is asked, in the proceedings by or on behalf of that person.

(3)   Subsection (2) applies to any offence other than–
   (a)   an offence which is–
      (i)   created by rules made for the purposes of this Act under the Insolvency Act, and
      (ii) designated for the purposes of this subsection by such rules or by regulations made by the Secretary of State;
   (b)   an offence which is–
      (i)   created by regulations made under any such rules, and
      (ii) designated for the purposes of this subsection by such regulations;

(c) an offence under section 5 of the Perjury Act 1911 (false statements made otherwise than on oath); or

(d) an offence under section 44(2) of the Criminal Law (Consolidation)(Scotland) Act 1995 (false statements made otherwise than on oath).

(4)   Regulations under subsection (3)(a)(ii) shall be made by statutory instrument and, after being made, shall be laid before each House of Parliament.

21 Interaction with Insolvency Act 1986

(1)   References in this Act to the official receiver, in relation to the winding up of a limited liability partnership or the bankruptcy of an individual, are to any person who, by virtue of section 399 of the Insolvency Act, is authorised to act as the official receiver in relation to that winding up or bankruptcy; and, in accordance with section 401(2) of that Act, references in this Act to an official receiver includes a person appointed as his deputy.

(2)   Sections 1A, 6 to 10, 13, 14, 15, 19(c) and 20 of, and Schedule 1 to, this Act and sections 1 and 17 of this Act as they apply for the purposes of those provisions are deemed included in Parts I to VII of the Insolvency Act for the purposes of the following sections of that Act–
      section 411 (power to make insolvency rules);
      section 414 (fees orders).

(3)   Section 434 of that Act (Crown application) applies to sections 1A, 6 to 10, 13, 14, 15, 19(c) and 20 of, and Schedule 1 to, this Act and sections 1 and 17 of this Act as they apply for the purposes of those provisions as it does to the provisions of that Act which are there mentioned.

(4)   For the purposes of summary proceedings in Scotland, section 431 of that Act applies to summary proceedings for an offence under section 11 or 13 of this Act as it applies to summary proceedings for an offence under Parts I to VII of that Act.

22 Interpretation

(1)   This section has effect with respect to the meaning of expressions used in this Act, and applies unless the context otherwise requires.

(2)   The expression "limited liability partnership"–
      (a) in section 11, includes a limited liability partnership incorporated outside Great Britain which has an established place of business in Great Britain.

(3)   Section 247 in Part VII of the Insolvency Act (interpretation for the first Group of Parts to that Act) applies as regards references to a limited liability partnership's insolvency and to its going into liquidation; and "administrative receiver" has the meaning given by section 251 of that Act and references to

acting as an insolvency practitioner are to be read in accordance with section 388 of that Act.

(4)   "Member" includes any person occupying the position of member, by whatever name called.

(5)   "Shadow member", in relation to a limited liability partnership, means a person in accordance with whose directions or instructions the members of the limited liability partnership are accustomed to act (but so that a person is not deemed a shadow member by reason only that the members act on advice given by him in a professional capacity).

(6)   Section 740 of the Companies Act applies as regards the meaning of "body corporate"; and "officer" has the meaning given by section 744 of that Act.

(7)   In references to legislation other than this Act–

"the Companies Act" means the Companies Act 1985;

"the Companies Acts" has the meaning given by section 744 of that Act; and

"the Insolvency Act" means the Insolvency Act 1986;

and in sections 3(1) and 5(1) of this Act "the companies legislation" means the Companies Acts (except the Insider Dealing Act), Parts I to VII of the Insolvency Act and, in Part XV of that Act, sections 411, 413, 414, 416 and 417.

(8)   Any reference to provisions, or a particular provision, of the Companies Acts or the Insolvency Act includes the corresponding provisions or provision of the former Companies Acts (as defined by section 735(1)(c) of the Companies Act, but including also that Act itself) or, as the case may be, the Insolvency Act 1985.

(9)   Any expression for whose interpretation provision is made by Part XXVI of the Companies Act (and not by subsections (3) to (8) above) is to be construed in accordance with that provision.

(10)   Any reference to acting as receiver–
        (a)   includes acting as manager or as both receiver and manager, but
        (b)   does not include acting as administrative receiver;
and "receivership" is to be read accordingly.

22A Application of Act to building societies

(1)   This Act applies to building societies as it applies to limited liability partnerships.

(2)   References in this Act to a limited liability partnership, or to a member of a limited liability partnership include, respectively, references to a building society within the meaning of the Building Societies Act 1986 or to a director or officer, within the meaning of that Act, of a building society.

(3)   In relation to a building society the definition of "shadow member" in section 22(5) applies with the substitution of "building society" for "limited liability partnership".

(4)   In the application of Schedule 1 to the directors of a building society, references to provisions of the Insolvency Act or the Companies Act include references to the corresponding provisions of the Building Societies Act 1986.

22B Application of Act to incorporated friendly societies

(1)   This Act applies to incorporated friendly societies as it applies to limited liability partnerships.

(2)   References in this Act to a limited liability partnership, or to a member of a limited liability partnership include, respectively, references to an incorporated friendly society within the meaning of the Friendly Societies Act 1992 or to a member of the committee of management or officer, within the meaning of the Act, of an incorporated friendly society.

(3)   In relation to an incorporated friendly society every reference to a shadow director shall be omitted.

(4)   In the application of Schedule 1 to the members of the committee of management of an incorporated friendly society, references to provisions of the Insolvency Act or the Companies Act include references to the corresponding provisions of the Friendly Societies Act 1992.

23 Transitional provisions, savings, repeals

(1)   The transitional provisions and savings in Schedule 3 to this Act have effect, and are without prejudice to anything in the Interpretation Act 1978 with regard to the effect of repeals.

(2)   The enactments specified in the second column of Schedule 4 to this Act are repealed to the extent specified in the third column of that Schedule.

24 Extent

(1)   This Act extends to England and Wales and to Scotland.

(2)   Nothing in this Act extends to Northern Ireland.

25 Commencement

This Act comes into force simultaneously with the Insolvency Act 1986.

26 Citation

This Act may be cited as the Company Directors Disqualification Act 1986.

SCHEDULE 1
MATTERS FOR DETERMINING UNFITNESS OF DIRECTORS

PART I
MATTERS APPLICABLE IN ALL CASES

1   Any misfeasance or breach of any fiduciary or other duty by the member in relation to the limited liability partnership.

2   Any misapplication or retention by the member of, or any conduct by the member giving rise to an obligation to account for, any money or other property of the limited liability partnership.

3   The extent of the member's responsibility for the limited liability partnership entering into any transaction liable to be set aside under Part XVI of the Insolvency Act (provisions against debt avoidance).

4   The extent of the member's responsibility for any failure by the limited liability partnership to comply with any of the following provisions of the Companies Act, namely–
  (a)   section 221 (limited liability partnerships to keep accounting records);
  (b)   section 222 (where and for how long records to be kept);
  (c)   section 288 (register of directors and secretaries);
  (h)   sections 399 and 415 (limited liability partnership's duty to register charges it creates).

5   The extent of the member's responsibility for any failure by the members of the limited liability partnership to comply with–
  (a)   section 226 or 227 of the Companies Act (duty to prepare annual accounts), or
  (b)   section 233 of that Act (approval and signature of accounts).

5A   In the application of this Part of this Schedule in relation to any person who is a director of an investment company with variable capital, any reference to a provision of the Companies Act shall be taken to be a reference to the corresponding provision of the Open-Ended Investment Companies (Investment Companies with Variable Capital) Regulations 1996 or of any regulations made under regulation 6 of those Regulations (SIB regulations).

PART II
MATTERS APPLICABLE WHERE LIMITED LIABILITY
PARTNERSHIP HAS BECOME INSOLVENT

6   The extent of the member's responsibility for the causes of the limited liability partnership becoming insolvent.

7   The extent of the member's responsibility for any failure by the limited liability partnership to supply any goods or services which have been paid for (in whole or in part).

8   The extent of the member's responsibility for the limited liability partnership entering into any transaction or giving any preference, being a transaction or preference–
  (a) liable to be set aside under section 127 or sections 238 to 240 of the Insolvency Act, or
  (b) challengeable under section 242 or 243 of that Act or under any rule of law in Scotland.

[8A   The extent of the member's and shadow member's responsibility for events leading to a member or shadow member, whether himself or some other member or shadow member, being declared by the court to be liable to make a contribution of the assets of the limited liability partnership under section 214A of the Insolvency Act 1986.]

9   The extent of the member's responsibility for any failure by the members of the limited liability partnership to comply with section 98 of the Insolvency Act (duty to call creditors' meeting in creditors' voluntary winding up).

10   Any failure by the member to comply with any obligation imposed on him by or under any of the following provisions of the Insolvency Act–
  (a) section 22 (limited liability partnership's statement of affairs in administration);
  (b) section 47 (statement of affairs to administrative receiver);
  (c) section 66 (statement of affairs in Scottish receivership);
  (d) section 99 (members' duty to attend meeting; statement of affairs in creditors' voluntary winding up);
  (e) section 131 (statement of affairs in winding up by the court);
  (f) section 234 (duty of any one with limited liability partnership property to deliver it up);
  (g) section 235 (duty to co-operate with liquidator, etc).

SCHEDULE 2
SAVINGS FROM COMPANIES ACT 1981 SS 93, 94, AND
INSOLVENCY ACT 1985 SCHEDULE 9

1   Sections 2 and 4(1)(b) do not apply in relation to anything done before 15th June 1982 by a person in his capacity as liquidator of a limited liability partnership or as receiver or manager of a limited liability partnership's property.

2   Subject to paragraph 1–
  (a) section 2 applies in a case where a person is convicted on indictment of an offence which he committed (and, in the case of a continuing offence, has ceased to commit) before 15th June 1982; but in such a case a disqualification order under that section shall not be made for a period in excess of five years;
  (b) that section does not apply in a case where a person is convicted summarily–
    (i)   in England and Wales, if he had consented so to be tried before that date, or
    (ii) in Scotland, if the summary proceedings commenced before that date.

3 Subject to paragraph 1, section 4 applies in relation to an offence committed or other thing done before 15th June 1982; but a disqualification order made on the grounds of such an offence or other thing done shall not be made for a period in excess of five years.

4 The powers of a court under section 5 are not exercisable in a case where a person is convicted of an offence which he committed (and, in the case of a continuing offence, had ceased to commit) before 15th June 1982.

5 For purposes of section 3(1) and section 5, no account is to be taken of any offence which was committed, or any default order which was made, before 1st June 1977.

6 An order made under section 28 of the Companies Act 1976 has effect as if made under section 3 of this Act; and an application made before 15th June 1982 for such an order is to be treated as an application for an order under the section last mentioned.

7 Where–
  (a) an application is made for a disqualification order under section 6 of this Act by virtue of paragraph (a) of subsection (2) of that section, and
  (b) the limited liability partnership in question went into liquidation before 28th April 1986 (the coming into force of the provision replaced by section 6),
the court shall not make an order under that section unless it could have made a disqualification order under section 300 of the Companies Act as it had effect immediately before the date specified in sub-paragraph (b) above.

8 An application shall not be made under section 8 of this Act in relation to a report made or information or documents obtained before 28th April 1986.

SCHEDULE 3
TRANSITIONAL PROVISIONS AND SAVINGS

1 In this Schedule, "the former enactments" means so much of the Companies Act, and so much of the Insolvency Act, as is repealed and replaced by this Act; and "the appointed day" means the day on which this Act comes into force.

2 So far as anything done or treated as done under or for the purposes of any provision of the former enactments could have been done under or for the purposes of the corresponding provision of this Act, it is not invalidated by the repeal of that provision but has effect as if done under or for the purposes of the corresponding provision; and any order, regulation, rule or other instrument made or having effect under any provision of the former enactments shall, insofar as its effect is preserved by this paragraph, be treated for all purposes as made and having effect under the corresponding provision.

3 Where any period of time specified in a provision of the former enactments is current immediately before the appointed day, this Act has effect as if the

445

corresponding provision had been in force when the period began to run; and (without prejudice to the foregoing) any period of time so specified and current is deemed for the purposes of this Act–

(a) to run from the date or event from which it was running immediately before the appointed day, and

(b) to expire (subject to any provision of this Act for its extension) whenever it would have expired if this Act had not been passed;

and any rights, priorities, liabilities, reliefs, obligations, requirements, powers, duties or exemptions dependent on the beginning, duration or end of such a period as above mentioned shall be under this Act as they were or would have been under the former enactments.

4   Where in any provision of this Act there is a reference to another such provision, and the first-mentioned provision operates, or is capable of operating, in relation to things done or omitted, or events occurring or not occurring, in the past (including in particular past acts of compliance with any enactment, failures of compliance, contraventions, offences and convictions of offences) the reference to the other provision is to be read as including a reference to the corresponding provision of the former enactments.

5   Offences committed before the appointed day under any provision of the former enactments may, notwithstanding any repeal by this Act, be prosecuted and punished after that day as if this Act had not passed.

6   A reference in any enactment, instrument or document (whether express or implied, and in whatever phraseology) to a provision of the former enactments (including the corresponding provision of any yet earlier enactment) is to be read, where necessary to retain for the enactment, instrument or document the same force and effect as it would have had but for the passing of this Act, as, or as including, a reference to the corresponding provision by which it is replaced in this Act.

SCHEDULE 4
REPEALS

Chapter	Short title	Extent of repeal
1985 c 6	The Companies Act 1985	Sections 295 to 299. Section 301. Section 302. In Schedule 24, the entries relating to sections 295(7) and 302(1).
1985 c 65	The Insolvency Act 1985	Sections 12 to 14. Section 16. Section 18. Schedule 12. Section 108(2). Schedule 2. In Schedule 6, paragraphs 1, 2, 7, and 14. In Schedule 9, paragraphs 2 and 3.

Insolvency Act 1986

1986 Chapter 45

Provisions of the Insolvency Act 1986 with modifications as they apply to Limited Liability Partnerships

THE FIRST GROUP OF PARTS
LIMITED LIABILITY PARTNERSHIP INSOLVENCY; LIMITED
LIABILITY PARTNERSHIPS WINDING UP

PART I
LIMITED LIABILITY PARTNERSHIP VOLUNTARY
ARRANGEMENTS

1 Those who may propose an arrangement

(1)   [A limited liability partnership] (other than one for which an administration order is in force, or which is being wound up) may make a proposal under this Part ... to its creditors for a composition in satisfaction of its debts or a scheme of arrangement of its affairs (from here on referred to, in either case, as a "voluntary arrangement").

(2)   A proposal under this Part is one which provides for some person ("the nominee") to act in relation to the voluntary arrangement either as trustee or otherwise for the purpose of supervising its implementation; and the nominee must be a person who is qualified to act as an insolvency practitioner in relation to the limited liability partnership.

(3)   Such a proposal may also be made–
    (a)   where an administration order is in force in relation to the limited liability partnership, by the administrator, and
    (b)   where the limited liability partnership is being wound up, by the liquidator
[but where a proposal is so made it must also be made to the limited liability partnership].

[The following modifications to sections 2 to 7 apply where a proposal under section 1 has been made by the limited liability partnership.]

2 Procedure where nominee is not the liquidator or administrator

(1)   This section applies where the nominee under section 1 is not the liquidator or administrator of the limited liability partnership.

(2)   The nominee shall, within 28 days (or such longer period as the court may allow) after he is given notice of the proposal for a voluntary arrangement, submit a report to the court stating–

    (a) whether, in his opinion, [a meeting of the creditors of the limited liability partnership] should be summoned to consider the proposal, and

    (b) if in his opinion such [a meeting] should be summoned, the date on which, and time and place at which, he proposes the [meeting] should be held.

(3)   For the purposes of enabling the nominee to prepare his report, [the designated members of the limited liability partnership] shall submit to the nominee–

    (a) a document setting out the terms of the proposed voluntary arrangement, and

    (b) a statement of the limited liability partnership's affairs containing–

        (i) such particulars of its creditors and of its debts and other liabilities and of its assets as may be prescribed, and

       (ii) such other information as may be prescribed.

(4)   The court may, on an application made by [the designated members of the limited liability partnership], in a case where the nominee has failed to submit the report required by this section, direct that the nominee be replaced as such by another person qualified to act as an insolvency practitioner in relation to the limited liability partnership.

3 Summoning of meetings

(1)   Where the nominee under section 1 is not the liquidator or administrator, and it has been reported to the court that [a meeting of creditors] should be summoned, the person making the report shall (unless the court otherwise directs) summon [that meeting] for the time, date and place proposed in the report.

(2)   ...

(3)   The persons to be summoned to a creditors' meeting under this section are every creditor of the limited liability partnership of whose claim and address the person summoning the meeting is aware.

4 Decisions of meetings

(1)   The [meeting] summoned under section 3 shall decide whether to approve the proposed voluntary arrangement (with or without modifications).

(2)   The modifications may include one conferring the functions proposed to be conferred on the nominee on another person qualified to act as an insolvency practitioner in relation to the limited liability partnership.
But they shall not include any modification by virtue of which the proposal ceases to be a proposal such as is mentioned in section 1.

(3)   A meeting so summoned shall not approve any proposal or modification which affects the right of a secured creditor of the limited liability partnership to enforce his security, except with the concurrence of the creditor concerned.

(4)   Subject as follows, a meeting so summoned shall not approve any proposal or modification under which–
  (a)   any preferential debt of the limited liability partnership is to be paid otherwise than in priority to such of its debts as are not preferential debts, or
  (b)   a preferential creditor of the limited liability partnership is to be paid an amount in respect of a preferential debt that bears to that debt a smaller proportion than is borne to another preferential debt by the amount that is to be paid in respect of that other debt.
However, the meeting may approve such a proposal or modification with the concurrence of the preferential creditor concerned.

(5)   Subject as above, [the meeting] shall be conducted in accordance with the rules.

[(5A) If modifications to the proposal are proposed at the meeting the chairman of the meeting shall, before the conclusion of the meeting, ascertain from the limited liability partnership whether or not it accepts the proposed modifications; and if at that conclusion the limited liability partnership has failed to respond to the proposed modification it shall be presumed not to have agreed to it.]

(6)   After the conclusion of [the] meeting in accordance with the rules, the chairman of the meeting shall report the result of the meeting [(including, where modifications to the proposal were proposed at the meeting, the response to those proposed modifications made by the limited liability partnership)] to the court, and, immediately after reporting to the court, shall give notice of the result of the meeting to such persons as may be prescribed [and to the limited liability partnership].

(7)   References in this section to preferential debts and preferential creditors are to be read in accordance with section 386 in Part XII of this Act.

5 Effect of approval

(1)   This section has effect where [the meeting] summoned under section 3 approves the proposed voluntary arrangement either [with modifications agreed to by the limited liability partnership] or without modifications.

(2)   The approved voluntary arrangement–
  (a)   takes effect as if made by the limited liability partnership at the creditors' meeting, and
  (b)   binds every person who in accordance with the rules had notice of, and was entitled to vote at, that meeting (whether or not he was present or represented at the meeting) as if he were a party to the voluntary arrangement.

(3)   Subject as follows, if the limited liability partnership is being wound up or an administration order is in force, the court may do one or both of the following, namely–

    (a) by order stay or sist all proceedings in the winding up or discharge the administration order;

    (b) give such directions with respect to the conduct of the winding up or the administration as it thinks appropriate for facilitating the implementation of the approved voluntary arrangement.

(4)   The court shall not make an order under subsection (3)(a)–

    (a) at any time before the end of the period of 28 days beginning with the first day on which [the report] required by section 4(6) has been made to the court, or

    (b) at any time when an application under the next section or an appeal in respect of such an application is pending, or at any time in the period within which such an appeal may be brought.

6 Challenge of decisions

(1)   Subject to this section, an application to the court may be made, by any of the persons specified below, on one or both of the following grounds, namely–

    (a) that a voluntary arrangement approved at the [meeting] summoned under section 3 unfairly prejudices the interests of a creditor, member or contributory of the limited liability partnership;

    (b) that there has been some material irregularity at or in relation to [the meeting].

(2)   The persons who may apply under this section are–

    (a) a person entitled, in accordance with the rules, to vote at [the meeting];

    [(aa) any member of the limited liability partnership; and]

    (b) the nominee or any person who has replaced him under section 2(4) or 4(2); …

    (c) …

(3)   An application under this section shall not be made after the end of the period of 28 days beginning with the first day on which [the report] required by section 4(6) has been made to the court.

[(4)   Where on such an application the court is satisfied as to either of the grounds mentioned in subsection (1), it may do one or both of the following, namely–

    (a) revoke or suspend the approval given by the meeting;

    (b) give a direction to any person for the summoning of a further meeting to consider any revised proposal the limited liability partnership may make or, in a case falling within subsection (1)(b), a further meeting to consider the original proposal.]

(5)   Where at any time after giving a direction under subsection (4)(b) for the summoning of [a meeting] to consider a revised proposal the court is satisfied that the [limited liability partnership] does not intend to submit a revised proposal, the court shall revoke the direction and revoke or suspend any approval given at the previous [meeting].

(6)   In a case where the court, on an application under this section with respect to any meeting–
  (a)   gives a direction under subsection (4)(b), or
  (b)   revokes or suspends an approval under subsection (4)(a) or (5),
the court may give such supplemental directions as it thinks fit and, in particular, directions with respect to things done since the meeting under any voluntary arrangement approved by the meeting.

(7)   Except in pursuance of the preceding provisions of this section, an approval given at a meeting summoned under section 3 is not invalidated by any irregularity at or in relation to the meeting.

7 Implementation of proposal

(1)   This section applies where a voluntary arrangement approved by the [meeting] summoned under section 3 has taken effect.

(2)   The person who is for the time being carrying out in relation to the voluntary arrangement the functions conferred–
  (a)   by virtue of the approval on the nominee, or
  (b)   by virtue of section 2(4) or 4(2) on a person other than the nominee,
shall be known as the supervisor of the voluntary arrangement.

(3)   If any of the limited liability partnership's creditors or any other person is dissatisfied by any act, omission or decision of the supervisor, he may apply to the court; and on the application the court may–
  (a)   confirm, reverse or modify any act or decision of the supervisor,
  (b)   give him directions, or
  (c)   make such other order as it thinks fit.

(4)   The supervisor–
  (a)   may apply to the court for directions in relation to any particular matter arising under the voluntary arrangement, and
  (b)   is included among the persons who may apply to the court for the winding up of the limited liability partnership or for an administration order to be made in relation to it.

(5)   The court may, whenever–
  (a)   it is expedient to appoint a person to carry out the functions of the supervisor, and
  (b)   it is inexpedient, difficult or impracticable for an appointment to be made without the assistance of the court,
make an order appointing a person who is qualified to act as an insolvency practitioner in relation to the limited liability partnership, either in substitution for the existing supervisor or to fill a vacancy.

(6)   The power conferred by subsection (5) is exercisable so as to increase the number of persons exercising the functions of supervisor or, where there is more than one person exercising those functions, so as to replace one or more of those persons.

[The following modifications apply to sections 2 and 3 where a proposal under section 1 has been made, where an administration order is in force in relation to the limited liability partnership, by the administrator or, where the limited liability partnership is being wound up, by the liquidator.]

2 Procedure where nominee is not the liquidator or administrator

(1)   This section applies where the nominee under section 1 is not the liquidator or administrator of the limited liability partnership.

(2)   The nominee shall, within 28 days (or such longer period as the court may allow) after he is given notice of the proposal for a voluntary arrangement, submit a report to the court stating–
   (a)   whether, in his opinion, [meetings of the members of the limited liability partnership] and of its creditors should be summoned to consider the proposal, and
   (b)   if in his opinion such meetings should be summoned, the date on which, and time and place at which, he proposes the meetings should be held.

(3)   For the purposes of enabling the nominee to prepare his report, the person intending to make the proposal shall submit to the nominee–
   (a)   a document setting out the terms of the proposed voluntary arrangement, and
   (b)   a statement of the limited liability partnership's affairs containing–
      (i)   such particulars of its creditors and of its debts and other liabilities and of its assets as may be prescribed, and
      (ii)   such other information as may be prescribed.

(4)   The court may, on an application made by the person intending to make the proposal, in a case where the nominee has failed to submit the report required by this section, direct that the nominee be replaced as such by another person qualified to act as an insolvency practitioner in relation to the limited liability partnership.

3 Summoning of meetings

(1)   Where the nominee under section 1 is not the liquidator or administrator, and it has been reported to the court that such meetings as are mentioned in section 2(2) should be summoned, the person making the report shall (unless the court otherwise directs) summon those meetings for the time, date and place proposed in the report.

(2)   Where the nominee is the liquidator or administrator, he shall summon [a meeting of the members of the limited liability partnership] and of its creditors to consider the proposal for such a time, date and place as he thinks fit.

(3)   The persons to be summoned to a creditors' meeting under this section are every creditor of the limited liability partnership of whose claim and address the person summoning the meeting is aware.

PART II
ADMINISTRATION ORDERS

8 Power of court to make order

(1) Subject to this section, if the court–
   (a) is satisfied that a limited liability partnership is or is likely to become unable to pay its debts (within the meaning given to that expression by section 123 of this Act), and
   (b) considers that the making of an order under this section would be likely to achieve one or more of the purposes mentioned below,
the court may make an administration order in relation to the limited liability partnership.

(2) An administration order is an order directing that, during the period for which the order is in force, the affairs, business and property of the limited liability partnership shall be managed by a person ("the administrator") appointed for the purpose by the court.

(3) The purposes for whose achievement an administration order may be made are–
   (a) the survival of the limited liability partnership, and the whole or any part of its undertaking, as a going concern;
   (b) the approval of a voluntary arrangement under Part I;
   (c) the sanctioning under section 425 of the Companies Act of a compromise or arrangement between the limited liability partnership and any such persons as are mentioned in that section; and
   (d) a more advantageous realisation of the limited liability partnership's assets than would be effected on a winding up;
and the order shall specify the purpose or purposes for which it is made.

(4) ...

9 Application for order

(1) An application to the court for an administration order shall be by petition presented either by the limited liability partnership ..., or by a creditor or creditors (including any contingent or prospective creditor or creditors), or by the clerk of a magistrates' court in the exercise of the power conferred by section 87A of the Magistrates' Courts Act 1980 (enforcement of fines imposed on companies) or by all or any of those parties, together or separately.

(2) Where a petition is presented to the court–
   (a) notice of the petition shall be given forthwith to any person who has appointed, or is or may be entitled to appoint, an administrative receiver of the limited liability partnership, and to such other persons as may be prescribed, and
   (b) the petition shall not be withdrawn except with the leave of the court.

(3)   Where the court is satisfied that there is an administrative receiver of the limited liability partnership, the court shall dismiss the petition unless it is also satisfied either–

      (a) that the person by whom or on whose behalf the receiver was appointed has consented to the making of the order, or

      (b) that, if an administration order were made, any security by virtue of which the receiver was appointed would–

          (i)   be liable to be released or discharged under sections 238 to 240 in Part VI (transactions at an undervalue and preferences),

          (ii) be avoided under section 245 in that Part (avoidance of floating charges), or

          (iii) be challengeable under section 242 (gratuitous alienations) or 243 (unfair preferences) in that Part, or under any rule of law in Scotland.

(4)   Subject to subsection (3), on hearing a petition the court may dismiss it, or adjourn the hearing conditionally or unconditionally, or make an interim order or any other order that it thinks fit.

(5)   Without prejudice to the generality of subsection (4), an interim order under that subsection may restrict the exercise of any powers of the members or of the limited liability partnership (whether by reference to the consent of the court or of a person qualified to act as an insolvency practitioner in relation to the limited liability partnership, or otherwise).

10 Effect of application

(1)   During the period beginning with the presentation of a petition for an administration order and ending with the making of such an order or the dismissal of the petition–

      (a) [no determination may be made or order made for the winding up of the limited liability partnership];

      (aa) no landlord or other person to whom rent is payable may exercise any right of forfeiture by peaceable re-entry in relation to premises let to the limited liability partnership in respect of a failure by the limited liability partnership to comply with any term or condition of its tenancy of such premises, except with the leave of the court and subject to such terms as the court may impose;

      (b) no steps may be taken to enforce any security over the limited liability partnership's property, or to repossess goods in the limited liability partnership's possession under any hire-purchase agreement, except with the leave of the court and subject to such terms as the court may impose; and

      (c) no other proceedings and no execution or other legal process may be commenced or continued, and no distress may be levied, against the limited liability partnership or its property except with the leave of the court and subject to such terms as aforesaid.

(2)   Nothing in subsection (1) requires the leave of the court–

      (a) for the presentation of a petition for the winding up of the limited liability partnership,

(b) for the appointment of an administrative receiver of the company, or

(c) for the carrying out by such a receiver (whenever appointed) of any of his functions.

(3) Where–

(a) a petition for an administration order is presented at a time when there is an administrative receiver of the limited liability partnership, and

(b) the person by or on whose behalf the receiver was appointed has not consented to the making of the order,

the period mentioned in subsection (1) is deemed not to begin unless and until that person so consents.

(4) References in this section and the next to hire-purchase agreements include conditional sale agreements, chattel leasing agreements and retention of title agreements.

(5) In the application of this section and the next to Scotland, references to execution being commenced or continued include references to diligence being carried out or continued, and references to distress being levied shall be omitted.

11 Effect of order

(1) On the making of an administration order–

(a) any petition for the winding up of the limited liability partnership shall be dismissed, and

(b) any administrative receiver of the limited liability partnership shall vacate office.

(2) Where an administration order has been made, any receiver of part of the limited liability partnership's property shall vacate office on being required to do so by the administrator.

(3) During the period for which an administration order is in force–

(a) [no determination may be made or order made for the winding up of the limited liability partnership];

(b) no administrative receiver of the limited liability partnership may be appointed;

(ba) no landlord or other person to whom rent is payable may exercise any right of forfeiture by peaceable re-entry in relation to premises let to the limited liability partnership in respect of a failure by the limited liability partnership to comply with any term or condition of its tenancy of such premises, except with the consent of the administrator or the leave of the court and subject (where the court gives leave) to such terms as the court may impose;

(c) no other steps may be taken to enforce any security over the limited liability partnership's property, or to repossess goods in the limited liability partnership's possession under any hire-purchase agreement, except with the consent of the administrator or the leave of the court and subject (where the court gives leave) to such terms as the court may impose; and

(d) no other proceedings and no execution or other legal process may be commenced or continued, and no distress may be levied, against the limited liability partnership or its property except with the consent of the administrator or the leave of the court and subject (where the court gives leave) to such terms as aforesaid.

(4)   Where at any time an administrative receiver of the limited liability partnership has vacated office under subsection (1)(b), or a receiver of part of the limited liability partnership's property has vacated office under subsection (2)–
(a) his remuneration and any expenses properly incurred by him, and
(b) any indemnity to which he is entitled out of the assets of the limited liability partnership,
shall be charged on and (subject to subsection (3) above) paid out of any property of the limited liability partnership which was in his custody or under his control at that time in priority to any security held by the person by or on whose behalf he was appointed.

(5)   Neither an administrative receiver who vacates office under subsection (1)(b) nor a receiver who vacates office under subsection (2) is required on or after so vacating office to take any steps for the purpose of complying with any duty imposed on him by section 40 or 59 of this Act (duty to pay preferential creditors).

12 Notification of order

(1)   Every invoice, order for goods or business letter which, at a time when an administration order is in force in relation to a limited liability partnership, is issued by or on behalf of the limited liability partnership or the administrator, being a document on or in which the limited liability partnership's name appears, shall also contain the administrator's name and a statement that the affairs, business and property of the limited liability partnership are being managed by the administrator.

(2)   If default is made in complying with this section, the limited liability partnership and any of the following persons who without reasonable excuse authorises or permits the default, namely, the administrator and any member of the limited liability partnership, is liable to a fine.

13 Appointment of administrator

(1)   The administrator of a limited liability partnership shall be appointed either by the administration order or by an order under the next subsection.

(2)   If a vacancy occurs by death, resignation or otherwise in the office of the administrator, the court may by order fill the vacancy.

(3)   An application for an order under subsection (2) may be made–
(a) by any continuing administrator of the limited liability partnership; or
(b) where there is no such administrator, by a creditors' committee established under section 26 below; or

(c)   where there is no such administrator and no such committee, by the limited liability partnership ... or by any creditor or creditors of the limited liability partnership.

14 General powers

(1)   The administrator of a limited liability partnership–
   (a)   may do all such things as may be necessary for the management of the affairs, business and property of the limited liability partnership, and
   (b)   without prejudice to the generality of paragraph (a), has the powers specified in Schedule 1 to this Act;
and in the application of that Schedule to the administrator of a limited liability partnership the words "he" and "him" refer to the administrator.

(2)   The administrator also has power–
   [(a)   to prevent any person from taking part in the management of the business of the limited liability partnership and to appoint any person to be a manager of that business, and]
   (b)   to call any meeting of the members or creditors of the limited liability partnership.
[Subsections (3) and (4) of section 92 shall apply for the purposes of this subsection as they apply for the purposes of that section.]

(3)   The administrator may apply to the court for directions in relation to any particular matter arising in connection with the carrying out of his functions.

(4)   Any power conferred on the limited liability partnership or its members, whether by this Act or the Companies Act or by the limited liability partnership agreement, which could be exercised in such a way as to interfere with the exercise by the administrator of his powers is not exercisable except with the consent of the administrator, which may be given either generally or in relation to particular cases.

(5)   In exercising his powers the administrator is deemed to act as the limited liability partnership's agent.

(6)   A person dealing with the administrator in good faith and for value is not concerned to inquire whether the administrator is acting within his powers.

15 Power to deal with charged property, etc

(1)   The administrator of a limited liability partnership may dispose of or otherwise exercise his powers in relation to any property of the limited liability partnership which is subject to a security to which this subsection applies as if the property were not subject to the security.

(2)   Where, on an application by the administrator, the court is satisfied that the disposal (with or without other assets) of–
   (a)   any property of the limited liability partnership subject to a security to which this subsection applies, or

    (b)   any goods in the possession of the limited liability partnership under a hire-purchase agreement,

would be likely to promote the purpose or one or more of the purposes specified in the administration order, the court may by order authorise the administrator to dispose of the property as if it were not subject to the security or to dispose of the goods as if all rights of the owner under the hire-purchase agreement were vested in the limited liability partnership.

(3)   Subsection (1) applies to any security which, as created, was a floating charge; and subsection (2) applies to any other security.

(4)   Where property is disposed of under subsection (1), the holder of the security has the same priority in respect of any property of the limited liability partnership directly or indirectly representing the property disposed of as he would have had in respect of the property subject to the security.

(5)   It shall be a condition of an order under subsection (2) that–
    (a)   the net proceeds of the disposal, and
    (b)   where those proceeds are less than such amount as may be determined by the court to be the net amount which would be realised on a sale of the property or goods in the open market by a willing vendor, such sums as may be required to make good the deficiency,

shall be applied towards discharging the sums secured by the security or payable under the hire-purchase agreement.

(6)   Where a condition imposed in pursuance of subsection (5) relates to two or more securities, that condition requires the net proceeds of the disposal and, where paragraph (b) of that subsection applies, the sums mentioned in that paragraph to be applied towards discharging the sums secured by those securities in the order of their priorities.

(7)   An office copy of an order under subsection (2) shall, within 14 days after the making of the order, be sent by the administrator to the registrar of companies.

(8)   If the administrator without reasonable excuse fails to comply with subsection (7), he is liable to a fine and, for continued contravention, to a daily default fine.

(9)   References in this section to hire-purchase agreements include conditional sale agreements, chattel leasing agreements and retention of title agreements.

16 Operation of s 15 in Scotland

(1)   Where property is disposed of under section 15 in its application to Scotland, the administrator shall grant to the disponee an appropriate document of transfer or conveyance of the property, and–
    (a)   that document, or
    (b)   where any recording, intimation or registration of the document is a legal requirement for completion of title to the property, that recording, intimation or registration,

has the effect of disencumbering the property of or, as the case may be, freeing the property from the security.

(2)   Where goods in the possession of the limited liability partnership under a hire-purchase agreement, conditional sale agreement, chattel leasing agreement or retention of title agreement are disposed of under section 15 in its application to Scotland, the disposal has the effect of extinguishing, as against the disponee, all rights of the owner of the goods under the agreement.

17 General duties

(1)   The administrator of a limited liability partnership shall, on his appointment, take into his custody or under his control all the property to which the limited liability partnership is or appears to be entitled.

(2)   The administrator shall manage the affairs, business and property of the limited liability partnership–
   (a)   at any time before proposals have been approved (with or without modifications) under section 24 below, in accordance with any directions given by the court, and
   (b)   at any time after proposals have been so approved, in accordance with those proposals as from time to time revised, whether by him or a predecessor of his.

(3)   The administrator shall summon a meeting of the limited liability partnership's creditors if–
   (a)   he is requested, in accordance with the rules, to do so by one-tenth, in value, of the company's creditors, or
   (b)   he is directed to do so by the court.

18 Discharge or variation of administration order

(1)   The administrator of a limited liability partnership may at any time apply to the court for the administration order to be discharged, or to be varied so as to specify an additional purpose.

(2)   The administrator shall make an application under this section if–
   (a)   it appears to him that the purpose or each of the purposes specified in the order either has been achieved or is incapable of achievement, or
   (b)   he is required to do so by a meeting of the limited liability partnership's creditors summoned for the purpose in accordance with the rules.

(3)   On the hearing of an application under this section, the court may by order discharge or vary the administration order and make such consequential provision as it thinks fit, or adjourn the hearing conditionally or unconditionally, or make an interim order or any other order it thinks fit.

(4)   Where the administration order is discharged or varied the administrator shall, within 14 days after the making of the order effecting the discharge or variation, send an office copy of that order to the registrar of companies.

(5)   If the administrator without reasonable excuse fails to comply with subsection (4), he is liable to a fine and, for continued contravention, to a daily default fine.

19 Vacation of office

(1)   The administrator of a limited liability partnership may at any time be removed from office by order of the court and may, in the prescribed circumstances, resign his office by giving notice of his resignation to the court.

(2)   The administrator shall vacate office if–
  (a)   he ceases to be qualified to act as an insolvency practitioner in relation to the limited liability partnership, or
  (b)   the administration order is discharged.

(3)   Where at any time a person ceases to be administrator, the following subsections apply.

(4)   His remuneration and any expenses properly incurred by him shall be charged on and paid out of any property of the limited liability partnership which is in his custody or under his control at that time in priority to any security to which section 15(1) then applies.

(5)   Any sums payable in respect of debts or liabilities incurred, while he was administrator, under contracts entered into by him or a predecessor of his in the carrying out of his or the predecessor's functions shall be charged on and paid out of any such property as is mentioned in subsection (4) in priority to any charge arising under that subsection.

(6)   Any sums payable in respect of liabilities incurred, while he was administrator, under contracts of employment adopted by him or a predecessor of his in the carrying out of his or the predecessor's functions shall, to the extent that the liabilities are qualifying liabilities, be charged on and paid out of any such property as is mentioned in subsection (4) and enjoy the same priority as any sums to which subsection (5) applies.
    For this purpose, the administrator is not to be taken to have adopted a contract of employment by reason of anything done or omitted to be done within 14 days after his appointment.

(7)   For the purposes of subsection (6), a liability under a contract of employment is a qualifying liability if–
  (a)   it is a liability to pay a sum by way of wages or salary or contribution to an occupational pension scheme, and
  (b)   it is in respect of services rendered wholly or partly after the adoption of the contract.

(8)   There shall be disregarded for the purposes of subsection (6) so much of any qualifying liability as represents payment in respect of services rendered before the adoption of the contract.

(9)   For the purposes of subsections (7) and (8)–
  (a)   wages or salary payable in respect of a period of holiday or absence from work through sickness or other good cause are deemed to be wages or (as the case may be) salary in respect of services rendered in that period, and
  (b)   a sum payable in lieu of holiday is deemed to be wages or (as the case may be) salary in respect of services rendered in the period by reference to which the holiday entitlement arose.

(10)   In subsection (9)(a), the reference to wages or salary payable in respect of a period of holiday includes any sums which, if they had been paid, would have been treated for the purposes of the enactments relating to social security as earnings in respect of that period.

20 Release of administrator

(1)   A person who has ceased to be the administrator of a limited liability partnership has his release with effect from the following time, that is to say–
  (a)   in the case of a person who has died, the time at which notice is given to the court in accordance with the rules that he has ceased to hold office;
  (b)   in any other case, such time as the court may determine.

(2)   Where a person has his release under this section, he is, with effect from the time specified above, discharged from all liability both in respect of acts or omissions of his in the administration and otherwise in relation to his conduct as administrator.

(3)   However, nothing in this section prevents the exercise, in relation to a person who has had his release as above, of the court's powers under section 212 in Chapter X of Part IV (summary remedy against delinquent members, liquidators, etc.).

21 Information to be given by administrator

(1)   Where an administration order has been made, the administrator shall–
  (a)   forthwith send to the limited liability partnership and publish in the prescribed manner a notice of the order, and
  (b)   within 28 days after the making of the order, unless the court otherwise directs, send such a notice to all creditors of the limited liability partnership (so far as he is aware of their addresses).

(2)   Where an administration order has been made, the administrator shall also, within 14 days after the making of the order, send an office copy of the order to the registrar of companies and to such other persons as may be prescribed.

(3)   If the administrator without reasonable excuse fails to comply with this section, he is liable to a fine and, for continued contravention, to a daily default fine.

22 Statement of affairs to be submitted to administrator

(1)   Where an administration order has been made, the administrator shall forthwith require some or all of the persons mentioned below to make out and

submit to him a statement in the prescribed form as to the affairs of the limited liability partnership.

(2)   The statement shall be verified by affidavit by the persons required to submit it and shall show–
    (a)   particulars of the limited liability partnership's assets, debts and liabilities;
    (b)   the names and addresses of its creditors;
    (c)   the securities held by them respectively;
    (d)   the dates when the securities were respectively given; and
    (e)   such further or other information as may be prescribed.

(3)   The persons referred to in subsection (1) are–
    (a)   those who are or have been members of the limited liability partnership;
    (b)   those who have taken part in the limited liability partnership's formation at any time within one year before the date of the administration order;
    (c)   those who are in the limited liability partnership's employment or have been in its employment within that year, and are in the administrator's opinion capable of giving the information required;
    (d)   those who are or have been within that year members of or in the employment of a limited liability partnership which is, or within that year was, a member of the limited liability partnership.
    In this subsection "employment" includes employment under a contract for services.

(4)   Where any persons are required under this section to submit a statement of affairs to the administrator, they shall do so (subject to the next subsection) before the end of the period of 21 days beginning with the day after that on which the prescribed notice of the requirement is given to them by the administrator.

(5)   The administrator, if he thinks fit, may–
    (a)   at any time release a person from an obligation imposed on him under subsection (1) or (2), or
    (b)   either when giving notice under subsection (4) or subsequently, extend the period so mentioned;
and where the administrator has refused to exercise a power conferred by this subsection, the court, if it thinks fit, may exercise it.

(6)   If a person without reasonable excuse fails to comply with any obligation imposed under this section, he is liable to a fine and, for continued contravention, to a daily default fine.

23 Statement of proposals

(1)   Where an administration order has been made, the administrator shall, within three months (or such longer period as the court may allow) after the making of the order–
    (a)   send to the registrar of companies and (so far as he is aware of their addresses) to all creditors a statement of his proposals for achieving the purpose or purposes specified in the order, and

(b) lay a copy of the statement before a meeting of the limited liability partnership's creditors summoned for the purpose on not less than 14 days' notice.

(2) The administrator shall also, within three months (or such longer period as the court may allow) after the making of the order, either–

(a) send a copy of the statement (so far as he is aware of their addresses) to all members of the limited liability partnership, or

(b) publish in the prescribed manner a notice stating an address to which members of the limited liability partnership should write for copies of the statement to be sent to them free of charge.

(3) If the administrator without reasonable excuse fails to comply with this section, he is liable to a fine and, for continued contravention, to a daily default fine.

24 Consideration of proposals by creditors' meeting

(1) A meeting of creditors summoned under section 23 shall decide whether to approve the administrator's proposals.

(2) The meeting may approve the proposals with modifications, but shall not do so unless the administrator consents to each modification.

(3) Subject as above, the meeting shall be conducted in accordance with the rules.

(4) After the conclusion of the meeting in accordance with the rules, the administrator shall report the result of the meeting to the court and shall give notice of that result to the registrar of companies and to such persons as may be prescribed.

(5) If a report is given to the court under subsection (4) that the meeting has declined to approve the administrator's proposals (with or without modifications), the court may by order discharge the administration order and make such consequential provision as it thinks fit, or adjourn the hearing conditionally or unconditionally, or make an interim order or any other order that it thinks fit.

(6) Where the administration order is discharged, the administrator shall, within 14 days after the making of the order effecting the discharge, send an office copy of that order to the registrar of companies.

(7) If the administrator without reasonable excuse fails to comply with subsection (6), he is liable to a fine and, for continued contravention, to a daily default fine.

25 Approval of substantial revisions

(1) This section applies where–

(a) proposals have been approved (with or without modifications) under section 24, and

(b) the administrator proposes to make revisions of those proposals which appear to him substantial.

(2) The administrator shall–
  (a) send to all creditors of the limited liability partnership (so far as he is aware of their addresses) a statement in the prescribed form of his proposed revisions, and
  (b) lay a copy of the statement before a meeting of the limited liability partnership's creditors summoned for the purpose on not less than 14 days' notice;
and he shall not make the proposed revisions unless they are approved by the meeting.

(3) The administrator shall also either–
  (a) send a copy of the statement (so far as he is aware of their addresses) to all members of the limited liability partnership, or
  (b) publish in the prescribed manner a notice stating an address to which members of the limited liability partnership should write for copies of the statement to be sent to them free of charge.

(4) The meeting of creditors may approve the proposed revisions with modifications, but shall not do so unless the administrator consents to each modification.

(5) Subject as above, the meeting shall be conducted in accordance with the rules.

(6) After the conclusion of the meeting in accordance with the rules, the administrator shall give notice of the result of the meeting to the registrar of companies and to such persons as may be prescribed.

26 Creditors' committee

(1) Where a meeting of creditors summoned under section 23 has approved the administrator's proposals (with or without modifications), the meeting may, if it thinks fit, establish a committee ("the creditor's committee") to exercise the functions conferred on it by or under this Act.

(2) If such a committee is established, the committee may, on giving not less than seven days' notice, require the administrator to attend before it at any reasonable time and furnish it with such information relating to the carrying out of his functions as it may reasonably require.

27 Protection of interests of creditors and members

(1) At any time when an administration order is in force, a creditor or member of the limited liability partnership may apply to the court by petition for an order under this section on the ground–
  (a) that the limited liability partnership's affairs, business and property are being or have been managed by the administrator in a manner which is unfairly prejudicial to the interests of its creditors or members generally, or of some part of its creditors or members (including at least himself), or

(b) that any actual or proposed act or omission of the administrator is or would be so prejudicial.

(2) On an application or an order under this section the court may, subject as follows, make such order as it thinks fit for giving relief in respect of the matters complained of, or adjourn the hearing conditionally or unconditionally, or make an interim order or any other order that it thinks fit.

(3) An order under this section shall not prejudice or prevent–
   (a) the implementation of a voluntary arrangement approved under section 4 in Part I, or any compromise or arrangement sanctioned under section 425 of the Companies Act; or
   (b) where the application for the order was made more than 28 days after the approval of any proposals or revised proposals under section 24 or 25, the implementation of those proposals or revised proposals.

(4) Subject as above, an order under this section may in particular–
   (a) regulate the future management by the administrator of the limited liability partnership's affairs, business and property;
   (b) require the administrator to refrain from doing or continuing an act complained of by the petitioner, or to do an act which the petitioner has complained he has omitted to do;
   (c) require the summoning of a meeting of creditors or members for the purpose of considering such matters as the court may direct;
   (d) discharge the administration order and make such consequential provision as the court thinks fit.

(5) Nothing in section 15 or 16 is to be taken as prejudicing applications to the court under this section.

(6) Where the administration order is discharged, the administrator shall, within 14 days after the making of the order effecting the discharge, send an office copy of that order to the registrar of companies; and if without reasonable excuse he fails to comply with this subsection, he is liable to a fine and, for continued contravention, to a daily default fine.

PART III
RECEIVERSHIP

CHAPTER I
RECEIVERS AND MANAGERS (ENGLAND AND WALES)

28 Extent of this Chapter

This Chapter does not apply to receivers appointed under Chapter II of this Part (Scotland).

29 Definitions

(1) It is hereby declared that, except where the context otherwise requires–

(a) any reference in the Companies Act or this Act to a receiver or manager of the property of a limited liability partnership, or to a receiver of it, includes a receiver or manager, or (as the case may be) a receiver of part only of that property and a receiver only of the income arising from the property or from part of it; and

(b) any reference in the Companies Act or this Act to the appointment of a receiver or manager under powers contained in an instrument includes an appointment made under powers which, by virtue of any enactment, are implied in and have effect as if contained in an instrument.

(2) In this Chapter "administrative receiver" means–

(a) a receiver or manager of the whole (or substantially the whole) of a limited liability partnership's property appointed by or on behalf of the holders of any debentures of the limited liability partnership secured by a charge which, as created, was a floating charge, or by such a charge and one or more other securities; or

(b) a person who would be such a receiver or manager but for the appointment of some other person as the receiver of part of the limited liability partnership's property.

30 Disqualification of body corporate from acting as receiver

A body corporate is not qualified for appointment as receiver of the property of a limited liability partnership, and any body corporate which acts as such a receiver is liable to a fine.

31 Disqualification of undischarged bankrupt

If a person being an undischarged bankrupt acts as receiver or manager of the property of a limited liability partnership on behalf of debenture holders, he is liable to imprisonment or a fine, or both.

This does not apply to a receiver or a manager acting under an appointment made by the court.

32 Power for court to appoint official receiver

Where application is made to the court to appoint a receiver on behalf of the debenture holders or other creditors of a limited liability partnership which is being wound up by the court, the official receiver may be appointed.

33 Time for which appointment is effective

(1) The appointment of a person as a receiver or manager of a limited liability partnership's property under powers contained in an instrument–

(a) is of no effect unless it is accepted by that person before the end of the business day next following that on which the instrument of appointment is received by him or on his behalf, and

(b) subject to this, is deemed to be made at the time at which the instrument of appointment is so received.

(2)   This section applies to the appointment of two or more persons as joint receivers or managers of a limited liability partnership's property under powers contained in an instrument, subject to such modifications as may be prescribed by the rules.

34 Liability for invalid appointment

Where the appointment of a person as the receiver or manager of a limited liability partnership's property under powers contained in an instrument is discovered to be invalid (whether by virtue of the invalidity of the instrument or otherwise), the court may order the person by whom or on whose behalf the appointment was made to indemnify the person appointed against any liability which arises solely by reason of the invalidity of the appointment.

35 Application to court for directions

(1)   A receiver or manager of the property of a limited liability partnership appointed under powers contained in an instrument, or the persons by whom or on whose behalf a receiver or manager has been so appointed, may apply to the court for directions in relation to any particular matter arising in connection with the performance of the functions of the receiver or manager.

(2)   On such an application, the court may give such directions, or may make such order declaring the rights of persons before the court or otherwise, as it thinks just.

36 Court's power to fix remuneration

(1)   The court may, on an application made by the liquidator of a limited liability partnership, by order fix the amount to be paid by way of remuneration to a person who, under powers contained in an instrument, has been appointed receiver or manager of the limited liability partnership's property.

(2)   The court's power under subsection (1), where no previous order has been made with respect thereto under the subsection–
(a)   extends to fixing the remuneration for any period before the making of the order or the application for it,
(b)   is exercisable notwithstanding that the receiver or manager has died or ceased to act before the making of the order or the application, and
(c)   where the receiver or manager has been paid or has retained for his remuneration for any period before the making of the order any amount in excess of that so fixed for that period, extends to requiring him or his personal representatives to account for the excess or such part of it as may be specified in the order.

But the power conferred by paragraph (c) shall not be exercised as respects any period before the making of the application for the order under this section, unless in the court's opinion there are special circumstances making it proper for the power to be exercised.

(3)   The court may from time to time on an application made either by the liquidator or by the receiver or manager, vary or amend an order made under subsection (1).

37 Liability for contracts, etc

(1)   A receiver or manager appointed under powers conferred in an instrument (other than an administrative receiver) is, to the same extent as if he had been appointed by order of the court–
   (a) personally liable on any contract entered into by him in the performance of his functions (except in so far as the contract otherwise provides) and on any contract of employment adopted by him in the performance of those functions, and
   (b) entitled in respect of that liability to indemnity out of the assets.

(2)   For the purposes of subsection (1)(a), the receiver or manager is not to be taken to have adopted a contract of employment by reason of anything done or omitted to be done within 14 days after his appointment.

(3)   Subsection (1) does not limit any right to indemnity which the receiver or manager would have apart from it, nor limit his liability on contracts entered into without authority, nor confer any right to indemnity in respect of that liability.

(4)   Where at any time the receiver or manager so appointed vacates office–
   (a) his remuneration and any expenses properly incurred by him, and
   (b) any indemnity to which he is entitled out of the assets of the limited liability partnership,
shall be charged on and paid out of any property of the limited liability partnership which is in his custody or under his control at that time in priority to any charge or other security held by the person by or on whose behalf he was appointed.

38 Receivership accounts to be delivered to registrar

(1)   Except in the case of an administrative receiver, every receiver or manager of a limited liability partnership's property who has been appointed under powers contained in an instrument shall deliver to the registrar of companies for registration the requisite accounts of his receipts and payments.

(2)   The accounts shall be delivered within one month (or such longer period as the registrar may allow) after the expiration of twelve months from the date of his appointment and of every subsequent period of six months, and also within one month after he ceases to act as receiver or manager.

(3)   The requisite accounts shall be an abstract in the prescribed form showing–
   (a) receipts and payments during the relevant period of twelve or six months, or
   (b) where the receiver or manager ceases to act, receipts and payments during the period from the end of the period of twelve or six months to which the last preceding abstract related (or, if no preceding abstract

has been delivered under this section, from the date of his appointment) up to the date of his so ceasing, and the aggregate amount of receipts and payments during all preceding periods since his appointment.

(4)   In this section "prescribed" means prescribed by regulations made by statutory instrument by the Secretary of State.

(5)   A receiver or manager who makes default in complying with this section is liable to a fine and, for continued contravention, to a daily default fine.

39 Notification that receiver or manager appointed

(1)   When a receiver or manager of the property of a limited liability partnership has been appointed, every invoice, order for goods or business letter issued by or on behalf of the limited liability partnership or the receiver or manager or the liquidator of the limited liability partnership, being a document on or in which the limited liability partnership's name appears, shall contain a statement that a receiver or manager has been appointed.

(2)   If default is made in complying with this section, the limited liability partnership and any of the following persons, who knowingly and wilfully authorises or permits the default, namely, any member of the limited liability partnership, any liquidator of the limited liability partnership and any receiver or manager, is liable to a fine.

40 Payment of debts out of assets subject to floating charge

(1)   The following applies, in the case of a limited liability partnership, where a receiver is appointed on behalf of the holders of any debentures of the limited liability partnership secured by a charge which, as created, was a floating charge.

(2)   If the limited liability partnership is not at the time in course of being wound up, its preferential debts (within the meaning given to that expression by section 386 in Part XII) shall be paid out of the assets coming to the hands of the receiver in priority to any claims for principal or interest in respect of the debentures.

(3)   Payments made under this section shall be recouped, as far as may be, out of the assets of the limited liability partnership available for payment of general creditors.

41 Enforcement of duty to make returns

(1)   If a receiver or manager of a limited liability partnership's property–
  (a)   having made default in filing, delivering or making any return, account or other document, or in giving any notice, which a receiver or manager is by law required to file, deliver, make or give, fails to make good the default within 14 days after the service on him of a notice requiring him to do so, or

(b) having been appointed under powers contained in an instrument, has, after being required at any time by the liquidator of the limited liability partnership to do so, failed to render proper accounts of his receipts and payments and to vouch them and pay over to the liquidator the amount properly payable to him,

the court may, on an application made for the purpose, make an order directing the receiver or manager (as the case may be) to make good the default within such time as may be specified in the order.

(2) In the case of the default mentioned in subsection (1)(a), application to the court may be made by any member or creditor of the limited liability partnership or by the registrar of companies; and in the case of the default mentioned in subsection (1)(b), the application shall be made by the liquidator.

In either case the court's order may provide that all costs of and incidental to the application shall be borne by the receiver or manager, as the case may be.

(3) Nothing in this section prejudices the operation of any enactment imposing penalties on receivers in respect of any such default as is mentioned in subsection (1).

42 General powers

(1) The powers conferred on the administrative receiver of a limited liability partnership by the debentures by virtue of which he was appointed are deemed to include (except in so far as they are inconsistent with any of the provisions of those debentures) the powers specified in Schedule 1 to this Act.

(2) In the application of Schedule 1 to the administrative receiver of a limited liability partnership–
(a) the words "he" and "him" refer to the administrative receiver, and
(b) references to the property of the limited liability partnership are to the property of which he is or, but for the appointment of some other person as the receiver of part of the limited liability partnership's property, would be the receiver or manager.

(3) A person dealing with the administrative receiver in good faith and for value is not concerned to inquire whether the receiver is acting within his powers.

43 Power to dispose of charged property, etc

(1) Where, on an application by the administrative receiver, the court is satisfied that the disposal (with or without other assets) of any relevant property which is subject to a security would be likely to promote a more advantageous realisation of the limited liability partnership's assets than would otherwise be effected, the court may by order authorise the administrative receiver to dispose of the property as if it were not subject to the security.

(2) Subsection (1) does not apply in the case of any security held by the person by or on whose behalf the administrative receiver was appointed, or of any security to which a security so held has priority.

(3)   It shall be a condition of an order under this section that–
  (a) the net proceeds of the disposal, and
  (b) where those proceeds are less than such amount as may be determined by the court to be the net amount which would be realised on a sale of the property in the open market by a willing vendor, such sums as may be required to make good the deficiency,
shall be applied towards discharging the sums secured by the security.

(4)   Where a condition imposed in pursuance of subsection (3) relates to two or more securities, that condition shall require the net proceeds of the disposal and, where paragraph (b) of that subsection applies, the sums mentioned in that paragraph to be applied towards discharging the sums secured by those securities in the order of their priorities.

(5)   An office copy of an order under this section shall, within 14 days of the making of the order, be sent by the administrative receiver to the registrar of companies.

(6)   If the administrative receiver without reasonable excuse fails to comply with subsection (5), he is liable to a fine and, for continued contravention, to a daily default fine.

(7)   In this section "relevant property", in relation to the administrative receiver, means the property of which he is or, but for the appointment of some other person as the receiver of part of the limited liability partnership's property, would be the receiver or manager.

44 Agency and liability for contracts

(1)   The administrative receiver of a limited liability partnership–
  (a) is deemed to be the limited liability partnership's agent, unless and until the limited liability partnership goes into liquidation;
  (b) is personally liable on any contract entered into by him in the carrying out of his functions (except in so far as the contract otherwise provides) and, to the extent of any qualifying liability, on any contract of employment adopted by him in the carrying out of those functions; and
  (c) is entitled in respect of that liability to an indemnity out of the assets of the limited liability partnership.

(2)   For the purposes of subsection (1)(b) the administrative receiver is not to be taken to have adopted a contract of employment by reason of anything done or omitted to be done within 14 days after his appointment.

(2A) For the purposes of subsection (1)(b), a liability under a contract of employment is a qualifying liability if–
  (a) it is a liability to pay a sum by way of wages or salary or contribution to an occupational pension scheme,
  (b) it is incurred while the administrative receiver is in office, and

(c) it is in respect of services rendered wholly or partly after the adoption of the contract.

(2B)   Where a sum payable in respect of a liability which is a qualifying liability for the purposes of subsection (1)(b) is payable in respect of services rendered partly before and partly after the adoption of the contract, liability under subsection (1)(b) shall only extend to so much of the sum as is payable in respect of services rendered after the adoption of the contract.

(2C) For the purposes of subsections (2A) and (2B)–
    (a) wages or salary payable in respect of a period of holiday or absence from work through sickness or other good cause are deemed to be wages or (as the case may be) salary in respect of services rendered in that period, and
    (b) a sum payable in lieu of holiday is deemed to be wages or (as the case may be) salary in respect of services rendered in the period by reference to which the holiday entitlement arose.

(2D)   In subsection (2C)(a), the reference to wages or salary payable in respect of a period of holiday includes any sums which, if they had been paid, would have been treated for the purposes of the enactments relating to social security as earnings in respect of that period.

(3)   This section does not limit any right to indemnity which the administrative receiver would have apart from it, nor limit his liability on contracts entered into or adopted without authority, nor confer any right to indemnity in respect of that liability.

45 Vacation of office

(1)   An administrative receiver of a limited liability partnership may at any time be removed from office by order of the court (but not otherwise) and may resign his office by giving notice of his resignation in the prescribed manner to such persons as may be prescribed.

(2)   An administrative receiver shall vacate office if he ceases to be qualified to act as an insolvency practitioner in relation to the limited liability partnership.

(3)   Where at any time an administrative receiver vacates office–
    (a) his remuneration and any expenses properly incurred by him, and
    (b) any indemnity to which he is entitled out of the assets of the limited liability partnership,
shall be charged on and paid out of any property of the limited liability partnership which is in his custody or under his control at that time in priority to any security held by the person by or on whose behalf he was appointed.

(4)   Where an administrative receiver vacates office otherwise than by death, he shall, within 14 days after his vacation of office, send a notice to that effect to the registrar of companies.

(5)   If an administrative receiver without reasonable excuse fails to comply with subsection (4), he is liable to a fine and, for continued contravention, to a daily default fine.

46 Information to be given by administrative receiver

(1)   Where an administrative receiver is appointed, he shall–
- (a)   forthwith send to the limited liability partnership and publish in the prescribed manner a notice of his appointment, and
- (b)   within 28 days after his appointment, unless the court otherwise directs, send such a notice to all the creditors of the limited liability partnership (so far as he is aware of their addresses).

(2)   This section and the next do not apply in relation to the appointment of an administrative receiver to act–
- (a)   with an existing administrative receiver, or
- (b)   in place of an administrative receiver dying or ceasing to act,

except that, where they apply to an administrative receiver who dies or ceases to act before they have been fully complied with, the references in this section and the next to the administrative receiver include (subject to the next subsection) his successor and any continuing administrative receiver.

(3)   If the limited liability partnership is being wound up, this section and the next apply notwithstanding that the administrative receiver and the liquidator are the same person, but with any necessary modifications arising from that fact.

(4)   If the administrative receiver without reasonable excuse fails to comply with this section, he is liable to a fine and, for continued contravention, to a daily default fine.

47 Statement of affairs to be submitted

(1)   Where an administrative receiver is appointed, he shall forthwith require some or all of the persons mentioned below to make out and submit to him a statement in the prescribed form as to the affairs of the limited liability partnership.

(2)   A statement submitted under this section shall be verified by affidavit by the persons required to submit it and shall show–
- (a)   particulars of the limited liability partnership's assets, debts and liabilities;
- (b)   the names and addresses of its creditors;
- (c)   the securities held by them respectively;
- (d)   the dates when the securities were respectively given; and
- (e)   such further or other information as may be prescribed.

(3)   The persons referred to in subsection (1) are–
- (a)   those who are or have been members of the limited liability partnership;
- (b)   those who have taken part in the limited liability partnership's formation at any time within one year before the date of the appointment of the administrative receiver;

(c) those who are in the limited liability partnership's employment, or have been in its employment within that year, and are in the administrative receiver's opinion capable of giving the information required;

(d) those who are or have been within that year members of or in the employment of a limited liability partnership which is, or within that year was, a member of the limited liability partnership.

In this subsection "employment" includes employment under a contract for services.

(4) Where any persons are required under this section to submit a statement of affairs to the administrative receiver, they shall do so (subject to the next subsection) before the end of the period of 21 days beginning with the day after that on which the prescribed notice of the requirement is given to them by the administrative receiver.

(5) The administrative receiver, if he thinks fit, may–

(a) at any time release a person from an obligation imposed on him under subsection (1) or (2), or

(b) either when giving notice under subsection (4) or subsequently, extend the period so mentioned;

and where the administrative receiver has refused to exercise a power conferred by this subsection, the court, if it thinks fit, may exercise it.

(6) If a person without reasonable excuse fails to comply with any obligation imposed under this section, he is liable to a fine and, for continued contravention, to a daily default fine.

48 Report by administrative receiver

(1) Where an administrative receiver is appointed, he shall, within three months (or such longer period as the court may allow) after his appointment, send to the registrar of companies, to any trustees for secured creditors of the limited liability partnership and (so far as he is aware of their addresses) to all such creditors a report as to the following matters, namely–

(a) the events leading up to his appointment, so far as he is aware of them;

(b) the disposal or proposed disposal by him of any property of the limited liability partnership and the carrying on or proposed carrying on by him of any business of the limited liability partnership;

(c) the amounts of principal and interest payable to the debenture holders by whom or on whose behalf he was appointed and the amounts payable to preferential creditors; and

(d) the amount (if any) likely to be available for the payment of other creditors.

(2) The administrative receiver shall also, within three months (or such longer period as the court may allow) after his appointment, either–

(a) send a copy of the report (so far as he is aware of their addresses) to all unsecured creditors of the limited liability partnership; or

(b) publish in the prescribed manner a notice stating an address to which unsecured creditors of the limited liability partnership should write for copies of the report to be sent to them free of charge,

and (in either case), unless the court otherwise directs, lay a copy of the report before a meeting of the limited liability partnership's unsecured creditors summoned for the purpose on not less than 14 days' notice.

(3) The court shall not give a direction under subsection (2) unless–

(a) the report states the intention of the administrative receiver to apply for the direction, and

(b) a copy of the report is sent to the persons mentioned in paragraph (a) of that subsection, or a notice is published as mentioned in paragraph (b) of that subsection, not less than 14 days before the hearing of the application.

(4) Where the limited liability partnership has gone or goes into liquidation, the administrative receiver–

(a) shall, within seven days after his compliance with subsection (1) or, if later, the nomination or appointment of the liquidator, send a copy of the report to the liquidator, and

(b) where he does so within the time limited for compliance with subsection (2), is not required to comply with that subsection.

(5) A report under this section shall include a summary of the statement of affairs made out and submitted to the administrative receiver under section 47 and of his comments (if any) upon it.

(6) Nothing in this section is to be taken as requiring any such report to include any information the disclosure of which would seriously prejudice the carrying out by the administrative receiver of his functions.

(7) Section 46(2) applies for the purposes of this section also.

(8) If the administrative receiver without reasonable excuse fails to comply with this section, he is liable to a fine and, for continued contravention, to a default fine.

49 Committee of creditors

(1) Where a meeting of creditors is summoned under section 48, the meeting may, if it thinks fit, establish a committee ("the creditors' committee") to exercise the functions conferred on it by or under this Act.

(2) If such a committee is established, the committee may, on giving not less than seven days' notice, require the administrative receiver to attend before it at any reasonable time and furnish it with such information relating to the carrying out by him of his functions as it may reasonably require.

CHAPTER II
RECEIVERS (SCOTLAND)

50 Extent of this Chapter

This Chapter extends to Scotland only.

51 Power to appoint receiver

(1) It is competent under the law of Scotland for the holder of a floating charge over all or any part of the property (including uncalled capital), which may from time to time be comprised in the property and undertaking of an incorporated limited liability partnership (whether a limited liability partnership within the meaning of the Act or not) which the Court of Session has jurisdiction to wind up, to appoint a receiver of such part of the property of the limited liability partnership as is subject to the charge.

(2) It is competent under the law of Scotland for the court, on the application of the holder of such a floating charge, to appoint a receiver of such part of the property of the limited liability partnership as is subject to the charge.

(3) The following are disqualified from being appointed as receiver–
(a) a body corporate;
(b) an undischarged bankrupt; and
(c) a firm according to the law of Scotland.

(4) A body corporate or a firm according to the law of Scotland which acts as a receiver is liable to a fine.

(5) An undischarged bankrupt who so acts is liable to imprisonment or a fine, or both.

(6) In this section, "receiver" includes joint receivers.

52 Circumstances justifying appointment

(1) A receiver may be appointed under section 51(1) by the holder of the floating charge on the occurrence of any event which, by the provisions of the instrument creating the charge, entitles the holder of the charge to make that appointment and, in so far as not otherwise provided for by the instrument, on the occurrence of any of the following events, namely–
(a) the expiry of a period of 21 days after the making of a demand for payment of the whole or any part of the principal sum secured by the charge, without payment having been made;
(b) the expiry of a period of two months during the whole of which interest due and payable under the charge has been in arrears;
(c) the making of an order or the passing of a resolution to wind up the limited liability partnership;
(d) the appointment of a receiver by virtue of any other floating charge created by the limited liability partnership.

(2)   A receiver may be appointed by the court under section 51(2) on the occurrence of any event which, by the provisions of the instrument creating the floating charge, entitles the holder of the charge to make that appointment and, in so far as not otherwise provided for by the instrument, on the occurrence of any of the following events, namely–

(a)   where the court, on the application of the holder of the charge, pronounces itself satisfied that the position of the holder of the charge is likely to be prejudiced if no such appointment is made;

(b)   any of the events referred to in paragraphs (a) to (c) of subsection (1).

53 Mode of appointment by holder of charge

(1)   The appointment of a receiver by the holder of the floating charge under section 51(1) shall be by means of an instrument subscribed in accordance with the Requirements of Writing (Scotland) Act 1995 ("the instrument of appointment"), a copy (certified in the prescribed manner to be a correct copy) whereof shall be delivered by or on behalf of the person making the appointment to the registrar of companies for registration within seven days of its execution and shall be accompanied by a notice in the prescribed form.

(2)   If any person without reasonable excuse makes default in complying with the requirements of subsection (1), he is liable to a fine and, for continued contravention, to a daily default fine.

(4)   If the receiver is to be appointed by the holders of a series of secured debentures, the instrument of appointment may be executed on behalf of the holders of the floating charge by any person authorised by resolution of the debenture holders to execute the instrument.

(5)   On receipt of the certified copy of the instrument of appointment in accordance with subsection (1), the registrar shall, on payment of the prescribed fee, enter the particulars of the appointment in the register of charges.

(6)   The appointment of a person as a receiver by an instrument of appointment in accordance with subsection (1)–

(a)   is of no effect unless it is accepted by that person before the end of the business day next following that on which the instrument of appointment is received by him or on his behalf, and

(b)   subject to paragraph (a), is deemed to be made on the day on and at the time at which the instrument of appointment is so received, as evidenced by a written docket by that person or on his behalf;

and this subsection applies to the appointment of joint receivers subject to such modifications as may be prescribed.

(7)   On the appointment of a receiver under this section, the floating charge by virtue of which he was appointed attaches to the property then subject to the charge; and such attachment has effect as if the charge was a fixed security over the property to which it has attached.

54 Appointment by court

(1)   Application for the appointment of a receiver by the court under section 51(2) shall be by petition to the court, which shall be served on the limited liability partnership.

(2)   On such an application, the court shall, if it thinks fit, issue an interlocutor making the appointment of the receiver.

(3)   A copy (certified by the clerk of the court to be a correct copy) of the court's interlocutor making the appointment shall be delivered by or on behalf of the petitioner to the registrar of companies for registration, accompanied by a notice in the prescribed form, within seven days of the date of the interlocutor or such longer period as the court may allow.
    If any person without reasonable excuse makes default in complying with the requirements of this subsection, he is liable to a fine and, for continued contravention, to a daily default fine.

(4)   On receipt of the certified copy interlocutor in accordance with subsection (3), the registrar shall, on payment of the prescribed fee, enter the particulars of the appointment in the register of charges.

(5)   The receiver is to be regarded as having been appointed on the date of his being appointed by the court.

(6)   On the appointment of a receiver under this section, the floating charge by virtue of which he was appointed attaches to the property then subject to the charge; and such attachment has effect as if the charge were a fixed security over the property to which it has attached.

(7)   In making rules of court for the purposes of this section, the Court of Session shall have regard to the need for special provision for cases which appear to the court to require to be dealt with as a matter of urgency.

55 Powers of receiver

(1)   Subject to the next subsection, a receiver has in relation to such part of the property of the limited liability partnership as is attached by the floating charge by virtue of which he was appointed, the powers, if any, given to him by the instrument creating that charge.

(2)   In addition, the receiver has under this Chapter the powers as respects that property (in so far as these are not inconsistent with any provision contained in that instrument) which are specified in Schedule 2 to this Act.

(3)   Subsections (1) and (2) apply–
    (a) subject to the rights of any person who has effectually executed diligence on all or any part of the property of the limited liability partnership prior to the appointment of the receiver, and

(b) subject to the rights of any person who holds over all or any part of the property of the limited liability partnership a fixed security or floating charge having priority over, or ranking pari passu with, the floating charge by virtue of which the receiver was appointed.

(4) A person dealing with a receiver in good faith and for value is not concerned to enquire whether the receiver is acting within his powers.

56 Precedence among receivers

(1) Where there are two or more floating charges subsisting over all or any part of the property of the limited liability partnership, a receiver may be appointed under this Chapter by virtue of each such charge; but a receiver appointed by, or on the application of, the holder of a floating charge having priority of ranking over any other floating charge by virtue of which a receiver has been appointed has the powers given to a receiver by section 55 and Schedule 2 to the exclusion of any other receiver.

(2) Where two or more floating charges rank with one another equally, and two or more receivers have been appointed by virtue of such charges, the receivers so appointed are deemed to have been appointed as joint receivers.

(3) Receivers appointed, or deemed to have been appointed, as joint receivers shall act jointly unless the instrument of appointment or respective instruments of appointment otherwise provide.

(4) Subject to subsection (5) below, the powers of a receiver appointed by, or on the application of, the holder of a floating charge are suspended by, and as from the date of, the appointment of a receiver by, or on the application of, the holder of a floating charge having priority of ranking over that charge to such extent as may be necessary to enable the receiver second mentioned to exercise his powers under section 55 and Schedule 2; and any powers so suspended take effect again when the floating charge having priority of ranking ceases to attach to the property then subject to the charge, whether such cessation is by virtue of section 62(6) or otherwise.

(5) The suspension of the powers of a receiver under subsection (4) does not have the effect of requiring him to release any part of the property (including any letters or documents) of the limited liability partnership from his control until he receives from the receiver superseding him a valid indemnity (subject to the limit of the value of such part of the property of the limited liability partnership as is subject to the charge by virtue of which he was appointed) in respect of any expenses, charges and liabilities he may have incurred in the performance of his functions as receiver.

(6) The suspension of the powers of a receiver under subsection (4) does not cause the floating charge by virtue of which he was appointed to cease to attach to the property to which it attached by virtue of section 53(7) or 54(6).

(7)   Nothing in this section prevents the same receiver being appointed by virtue of two or more floating charges.

57 Agency and liability of receiver for contracts

(1)   A receiver is deemed to be the agent of the limited liability partnership in relation to such property of the limited liability partnership as is attached by the floating charge by virtue of which he was appointed.

(1A)   Without prejudice to subsection (1), a receiver is deemed to be the agent of the limited liability partnership in relation to any contract of employment adopted by him in the carrying out of his functions.

(2)   A receiver (including a receiver whose powers are subsequently suspended under section 56) is personally liable on any contract entered into by him in the performance of his functions, except in so far as the contract otherwise provides, and, to the extent of any qualifying liability, on any contract of employment adopted by him in the carrying out of those functions.

(2A)   For the purposes of subsection (2), a liability under a contract of employment is a qualifying liability if–
   (a)   it is a liability to pay a sum by way of wages or salary or contribution to an occupational pension scheme,
   (b)   it is incurred while the receiver is in office, and
   (c)   it is in respect of services rendered wholly or partly after the adoption of the contract.

(2B)   Where a sum payable in respect of a liability which is a qualifying liability for the purposes of subsection (2) is payable in respect of services rendered partly before and partly after the adoption of the contract, liability under that subsection shall only extend to so much of the sum as is payable in respect of services rendered after the adoption of the contract.

(2C)   For the purposes of subsections (2A) and (2B)–
   (a)   wages or salary payable in respect of a period of holiday or absence from work through sickness or other good cause are deemed to be wages or (as the case may be) salary in respect of services rendered in that period, and
   (b)   a sum payable in lieu of holiday is deemed to be wages or (as the case may be) salary in respect of services rendered in the period by reference to which the holiday entitlement arose.

(2D)   In subsection (2C)(a), the reference to wages or salary payable in respect of a period of holiday includes any sums which, if they had been paid, would have been treated for the purposes of the enactments relating to social security as earnings in respect of that period.

(3)   A receiver who is personally liable by virtue of subsection (2) is entitled to be indemnified out of the property in respect of which he was appointed.

(4)   Any contract entered into by or on behalf of the limited liability partnership prior to the appointment of a receiver continues in force (subject to its terms) notwithstanding that appointment, but the receiver does not by virtue only of his appointment incur any personal liability on any such contract.

(5)   For the purposes of subsection (2), a receiver is not to be taken to have adopted a contract of employment by reason of anything done or omitted to be done within 14 days after his appointment.

(6)   This section does not limit any right to indemnity which the receiver would have apart from it, nor limit his liability on contracts entered into or adopted without authority, nor confer any right to indemnity in respect of that liability.

(7)   Any contract entered into by a receiver in the performance of his functions continues in force (subject to its terms) although the powers of the receiver are subsequently suspended under section 56.

58 Remuneration of receiver

(1)   The remuneration to be paid to a receiver is to be determined by agreement between the receiver and the holder of the floating charge by virtue of which he was appointed.

(2)   Where the remuneration to be paid to the receiver has not been determined under subsection (1), or where it has been so determined but is disputed by any of the persons mentioned in paragraphs (a) to (d) below, it may be fixed instead by the Auditor of the Court of Session on application made to him by–
  (a)   the receiver;
  (b)   the holder of any floating charge or fixed security over all or any part of the property of the limited liability partnership;
  (c)   the limited liability partnership; or
  (d)   the liquidator of the limited liability partnership.

(3)   Where the receiver has been paid or has retained for his remuneration for any period before the remuneration has been fixed by the Auditor of the Court of Session under subsection (2) any amount in excess of the remuneration so fixed for that period, the receiver or his personal representatives shall account for the excess.

59 Priority of debts

(1)   Where a receiver is appointed and the limited liability partnership is not at the time of the appointment in course of being wound up, the debts which fall under subsection (2) of this section shall be paid out of any assets coming to the hands of the receiver in priority to any claim for principal or interest by the holder of the floating charge by virtue of which the receiver was appointed.

(2)   Debts falling under this subsection are preferential debts (within the meaning given by section 386 in Part XII) which, by the end of a period of six months

after advertisement by the receiver for claims in the Edinburgh Gazette and in a newspaper circulating in the district where the limited liability partnership carries on business either–

    (i)   have been intimated to him, or

    (ii) have become known to him.

(3)   Any payments made under this section shall be recouped as far as may be out of the assets of the limited liability partnership available for payment of ordinary creditors.

60 Distribution of moneys

(1)   Subject to the next section, and to the rights of any of the following categories of persons (which rights shall, except to the extent otherwise provided in any instrument, have the following order of priority), namely–

    (a)   the holder of any fixed security which is over property subject to the floating charge and which ranks prior to, or pari passu with, the floating charge;

    (b)   all persons who have effectually executed diligence on any part of the property of the limited liability partnership which is subject to the charge by virtue of which the receiver was appointed;

    (c)   creditors in respect of all liabilities, charges and expenses incurred by or on behalf of the receiver;

    (d)   the receiver in respect of his liabilities, expenses and remuneration, and any indemnity to which he is entitled out of the property of the limited liability partnership; and

    (e)   the preferential creditors entitled to payment under section 59,

the receiver shall pay moneys received by him to the holder of the floating charge by virtue of which the receiver was appointed in or towards satisfaction of the debt secured by the floating charge.

(2)   Any balance of moneys remaining after the provisions of subsection (1) and section 61 below have been satisfied shall be paid in accordance with their respective rights and interests to the following persons, as the case may require–

    (a)   any other receiver;

    (b)   the holder of a fixed security which is over property subject to the floating charge;

    (c)   the limited liability partnership or its liquidator, as the case may be.

(3)   Where any question arises as to the person entitled to a payment under this section, or where a receipt or a discharge of a security cannot be obtained in respect of any such payment, the receiver shall consign the amount of such payment in any joint stock bank of issue in Scotland in name of the Accountant of Court for behoof of the person or persons entitled thereto.

61 Disposal of interest in property

(1)   Where the receiver sells or disposes, or is desirous of selling or disposing, of any property or interest in property of the limited liability partnership which is

subject to the floating charge by virtue of which the receiver was appointed and which is–

    (a)   subject to any security or interest of, or burden or encumbrance in favour of, a creditor the ranking of which is prior to, or pari passu with, or postponed to the floating charge, or

    (b)   property or an interest in property affected or attached by effectual diligence executed by any person,

and the receiver is unable to obtain the consent of such creditor or, as the case may be, such person to such a sale or disposal, the receiver may apply to the court for authority to sell or dispose of the property or interest in property free of such security, interest, burden, encumbrance or diligence.

(2)   Subject to the next subsection, on such an application the court may, if it thinks fit, authorise the sale or disposal of the property or interest in question free of such security, interest, burden, encumbrance or diligence, and such authorisation may be on such terms or conditions as the court thinks fit.

(3)   In the case of an application where a fixed security over the property or interest in question which ranks prior to the floating charge has not been met or provided for in full, the court shall not authorise the sale or disposal of the property or interest in question unless it is satisfied that the sale or disposal would be likely to provide a more advantageous realisation of the limited liability partnership's assets than would otherwise be effected.

(4)   It shall be a condition of an authorisation to which subsection (3) applies that–

    (a)   the net proceeds of the disposal, and

    (b)   where those proceeds are less than such amount as may be determined by the court to be the net amount which would be realised on a sale of the property or interest in the open market by a willing seller, such sums as may be required to make good the deficiency,

shall be applied towards discharging the sums secured by the fixed security.

(5)   Where a condition imposed in pursuance of subsection (4) relates to two or more such fixed securities, that condition shall require the net proceeds of the disposal and, where paragraph (b) of that subsection applies, the sums mentioned in that paragraph to be applied towards discharging the sums secured by those fixed securities in the order of their priorities.

(6)   A copy of an authorisation under subsection (2) certified by the clerk of court shall, within 14 days of the granting of the authorisation, be sent by the receiver to the registrar of companies.

(7)   If the receiver without reasonable excuse fails to comply with subsection (6), he is liable to a fine and, for continued contravention, to a daily default fine.

(8)   Where any sale or disposal is effected in accordance with the authorisation of the court under subsection (2), the receiver shall grant to the purchaser or disponee an appropriate document of transfer or conveyance of the property or

interest in question, and that document has the effect, or, where recording, intimation or registration of that document is a legal requirement for completion of title to the property or interest, then that recording, intimation or registration (as the case may be) has the effect, of–

    (a) disencumbering the property or interest of the security, interest, burden or encumbrance affecting it, and

    (b) freeing the property or interest from the diligence executed upon it.

(9)   Nothing in this section prejudices the right of any creditor of the limited liability partnership to rank for his debt in the winding up of the limited liability partnership.

62 Cessation of appointment of receiver

(1)   A receiver may be removed from office by the court under subsection (3) below and may resign his office by giving notice of his resignation in the prescribed manner to such persons as may be prescribed.

(2)   A receiver shall vacate office if he ceases to be qualified to act as an insolvency practitioner in relation to the limited liability partnership.

(3)   Subject to the next subsection, a receiver may, on application to the court by the holder of the floating charge by virtue of which he was appointed, be removed by the court on cause shown.

(4)   Where at any time a receiver vacates office–

    (a) his remuneration and any expenses properly incurred by him, and

    (b) any indemnity to which he is entitled out of the property of the limited liability partnership,

shall be paid out of the property of the limited liability partnership which is subject to the floating charge and shall have priority as provided for in section 60(1).

(5)   When a receiver ceases to act as such otherwise than by death he shall, and, when a receiver is removed by the court, the holder of the floating charge by virtue of which he was appointed shall, within 14 days of the cessation or removal (as the case may be) give the registrar of companies notice to that effect, and the registrar shall enter the notice in the register of charges.

    If the receiver or the holder of the floating charge (as the case may require) makes default in complying with the requirements of this subsection, he is liable to a fine and, for continued contravention, to a daily default fine.

(6)   If by the expiry of a period of one month following upon the removal of the receiver or his ceasing to act as such no other receiver has been appointed, the floating charge by virtue of which the receiver was appointed–

    (a) thereupon ceases to attach to the property then subject to the charge, and

    (b) again subsists as a floating charge;

and for the purposes of calculating the period of one month under this subsection no account shall be taken of any period during which an administration order under Part II of this Act is in force.

63 Powers of court

(1)   The court on the application of–
    (a)   the holder of a floating charge by virtue of which a receiver was appointed, or
    (b)   a receiver appointed under section 51,
may give directions to the receiver in respect of any matter arising in connection with the performance by him of his functions.

(2)   Where the appointment of a person as a receiver by the holder of a floating charge is discovered to be invalid (whether by virtue of the invalidity of the instrument or otherwise), the court may order the holder of the floating charge to indemnify the person appointed against any liability which arises solely by reason of the invalidity of the appointment.

64 Notification that receiver appointed

(1)   Where a receiver has been appointed, every invoice, order for goods or business letter issued by or on behalf of the limited liability partnership or the receiver or the liquidator of the limited liability partnership, being a document on or in which the name of the limited liability partnership appears, shall contain a statement that a receiver has been appointed.

(2)   If default is made in complying with the requirements of this section, the limited liability partnership and any of the following persons who knowingly and wilfully authorises or permits the default, namely any member of the limited liability partnership, any liquidator of the limited liability partnership and any receiver, is liable to a fine.

65 Information to be given by receiver

(1)   Where a receiver is appointed, he shall–
    (a)   forthwith send to the limited liability partnership and publish notice of his appointment, and
    (b)   within 28 days after his appointment, unless the court otherwise directs, send such notice to all the creditors of the limited liability partnership (so far as he is aware of their addresses).

(2)   This section and the next do not apply in relation to the appointment of a receiver to act–
    (a)   with an existing receiver, or
    (b)   in place of a receiver who has died or ceased to act,
except that, where they apply to a receiver who dies or ceases to act before they have been fully complied with, the references in this section and the next to the receiver include (subject to subsection (3) of this section) his successor and any continuing receiver.

(3)   If the limited liability partnership is being wound up, this section and the next apply notwithstanding that the receiver and the liquidator are the same person, but with any necessary modifications arising from that fact.

(4)   If a person without reasonable excuse fails to comply with this section, he is liable to a fine and, for continued contravention, to a daily default fine.

66 Limited liability partnership's statement of affairs

(1)   Where a receiver of a limited liability partnership is appointed, the receiver shall forthwith require some or all of the persons mentioned in subsection (3) below to make out and submit to him a statement in the prescribed form as to the affairs of the limited liability partnership.

(2)   A statement submitted under this section shall be verified by affidavit by the persons required to submit it and shall show–
    (a)   particulars of the limited liability partnership's assets, debts and liabilities;
    (b)   the names and addresses of its creditors;
    (c)   the securities held by them respectively;
    (d)   the dates when the securities were respectively given; and
    (e)   such further or other information as may be prescribed.

(3)   The persons referred to in subsection (1) are–
    (a)   those who are or have been members of the limited liability partnership;
    (b)   those who have taken part in the limited liability partnership's formation at any time within one year before the date of the appointment of the receiver;
    (c)   those who are in the limited liability partnership's employment or have been in its employment within that year, and are in the receiver's opinion capable of giving the information required;
    (d)   those who are or have been within that year members of or in the employment of a limited liability partnership which is, or within that year was, a member of the limited liability partnership.
In this subsection "employment" includes employment under a contract for services.

(4)   Where any persons are required under this section to submit a statement of affairs to the receiver they shall do so (subject to the next subsection) before the end of the period of 21 days beginning with the day after that on which the prescribed notice of the requirement is given to them by the receiver.

(5)   The receiver, if he thinks fit, may–
    (a)   at any time release a person from an obligation imposed on him under subsection (1) or (2), or
    (b)   either when giving the notice mentioned in subsection (4) or subsequently extend the period so mentioned,
and where the receiver has refused to exercise a power conferred by this subsection, the court, if it thinks fit, may exercise it.

(6)   If a person without reasonable excuse fails to comply with any obligation imposed under this section, he is liable to a fine and, for continued contravention, to a daily default fine.

67 Report by receiver

(1)   Where a receiver is appointed under section 51, he shall within three months (or such longer period as the court may allow) after his appointment, send to the registrar of companies, to the holder of the floating charge by virtue of which he was appointed and to any trustees for secured creditors of the limited liability partnership and (so far as he is aware of their addresses) to all such creditors a report as to the following matters, namely–

(a)   the events leading up to his appointment, so far as he is aware of them;

(b)   the disposal or proposed disposal by him of any property of the limited liability partnership and the carrying on or proposed carrying on by him of any business of the limited liability partnership;

(c)   the amounts of principal and interest payable to the holder of the floating charge by virtue of which he was appointed and the amounts payable to preferential creditors; and

(d)   the amount (if any) likely to be available for the payment of other creditors.

(2)   The receiver shall also, within three months (or such longer period as the court may allow) after his appointment, either–

(a)   send a copy of the report (so far as he is aware of their addresses) to all unsecured creditors of the limited liability partnership, or

(b)   publish in the prescribed manner a notice stating an address to which unsecured creditors of the limited liability partnership should write for copies of the report to be sent to them free of charge,

and (in either case), unless the court otherwise directs, lay a copy of the report before a meeting of the limited liability partnership's unsecured creditors summoned for the purpose on not less than 14 days' notice.

(3)   The court shall not give a direction under subsection (2) unless–

(a)   the report states the intention of the receiver to apply for the direction; and

(b)   a copy of the report is sent to the persons mentioned in paragraph (a) of that subsection, or a notice is published as mentioned in paragraph (b) of that subsection, not less than 14 days before the hearing of the application.

(4)   Where the limited liability partnership has gone or goes into liquidation, the receiver–

(a)   shall, within seven days after his compliance with subsection (1) or, if later, the nomination or appointment of the liquidator, send a copy of the report to the liquidator, and

(b)   where he does so within the time limited for compliance with subsection (2), is not required to comply with that subsection.

(5)   A report under this section shall include a summary of the statement of affairs made out and submitted under section 66 and of his comments (if any) on it.

(6)   Nothing in this section shall be taken as requiring any such report to include any information the disclosure of which would seriously prejudice the carrying out by the receiver of his functions.

(7)   Section 65(2) applies for the purposes of this section also.

(8)   If a person without reasonable excuse fails to comply with this section, he is liable to a fine and, for continued contravention, to a daily default fine.

(9)   In this section "secured creditor", in relation to a limited liability partnership, means a creditor of the limited liability partnership who holds in respect of his debt a security over property of the limited liability partnership, and "unsecured creditor" shall be construed accordingly.

68 Committee of creditors

(1)   Where a meeting of creditors is summoned under section 67, the meeting may, if it thinks fit, establish a committee ("the creditors' committee") to exercise the functions conferred on it by or under this Act.

(2)   If such a committee is established, the committee may on giving not less than seven days' notice require the receiver to attend before it at any reasonable time and furnish it with such information relating to the carrying out by him of his functions as it may reasonably require.

69 Enforcement of receiver's duty to make returns, etc

(1)   If any receiver–
   (a) having made default in filing, delivering or making any return, account or other document, or in giving any notice, which a receiver is by law required to file, deliver, make or give, fails to make good the default within 14 days after the service on him of a notice requiring him to do so; or
   (b) has, after being required at any time by the liquidator of the limited liability partnership so to do, failed to render proper accounts of his receipts and payments and to vouch the same and to pay over to the liquidator the amount properly payable to him,
the court may, on an application made for the purpose, make an order directing the receiver to make good the default within such time as may be specified in the order.

(2)   In the case of any such default as is mentioned in subsection (1)(a), an application for the purposes of this section may be made by any member or creditor of the limited liability partnership or by the registrar of companies; and, in the case of any such default as is mentioned in subsection (1)(b), the application shall be made by the liquidator; and, in either case, the order may provide that all expenses of and incidental to the application shall be borne by the receiver.

(3)   Nothing in this section prejudices the operation of any enactments imposing penalties on receivers in respect of any such default as is mentioned in subsection (1).

70 Interpretation for Chapter II

(1)   In this Chapter, unless the contrary intention appears, the following expressions have the following meanings respectively assigned to them–

"limited liability partnership" means an incorporated limited liability partnership (whether or not a limited liability partnership within the meaning of the Act) which the Court of Session has jurisdiction to wind up;

"fixed security", in relation to any property of a limited liability partnership, means any security, other than a floating charge or a charge having the nature of a floating charge, which on the winding up of the limited liability partnership in Scotland would be treated as an effective security over that property, and (without prejudice to that generality) includes a security over that property, being a heritable security within the meaning of the Conveyancing and Feudal Reform (Scotland) Act 1970;

"instrument of appointment" has the meaning given by section 53(1);

"prescribed" means prescribed by regulations made under this Chapter by the Secretary of State;

"receiver" means a receiver of such part of the property of the limited liability partnership as is subject to the floating charge by virtue of which he has been appointed under section 51;

"register of charges" means the register kept by the registrar of companies for the purposes of Chapter II of Part XII of the Companies Act;

"secured debenture" means a bond, debenture, debenture stock or other security which, either itself or by reference to any other instrument, creates a floating charge over all or any part of the property of the limited liability partnership, but does not include a security which creates no charge other than a fixed security; and

"series of secured debentures" means two or more secured debentures created as a series by the limited liability partnership in such a manner that the holders thereof are entitled pari passu to the benefit of the floating charge.

(2)   Where a floating charge, secured debenture or series of secured debentures has been created by the limited liability partnership, then, except where the context otherwise requires, any reference in this Chapter to the holder of the floating charge shall–

(a)   where the floating charge, secured debenture or series of secured debentures provides for a receiver to be appointed by any person or body, be construed as a reference to that person or body;

(b)   where, in the case of a series of secured debentures, no such provision has been made therein but–

(i)   there are trustees acting for the debenture holders under and in accordance with a trust deed, be construed as a reference to those trustees, and

(ii)   where no such trustees are acting, be construed as a reference to–

(aa)   a majority in nominal value of those present or represented by proxy and voting at a meeting of debenture holders at which the holders of at least one-third in nominal value of the outstanding debentures of the series are present or so represented, or (bb) where no such meeting is held, the holders of at least one-half in nominal value of the outstanding debentures of the series.

(3) Any reference in this Chapter to a floating charge, secured debenture, series of secured debentures or instrument creating a charge includes, except where the context otherwise requires, a reference to that floating charge, debenture, series of debentures or instrument as varied by any instrument.

(4) References in this Chapter to the instrument by which a floating charge was created are, in the case of a floating charge created by words in a bond or other written acknowledgement, references to the bond or, as the case may be, the other written acknowledgement.

71 Prescription of forms etc; regulations

(1) The notice referred to in section 62(5), and the notice referred to in section 65(1)(a) shall be in such form as may be prescribed.

(2) Any power conferred by this Chapter on the Secretary of State to make regulations is exercisable by statutory instrument; and a statutory instrument made in the exercise of the power so conferred to prescribe a fee is subject to annulment in pursuance of a resolution of either House of Parliament.

CHAPTER III
RECEIVERS' POWERS IN GREAT BRITAIN AS A WHOLE

72 Cross-border operation of receivership provisions

(1) A receiver appointed under the law of either part of Great Britain in respect of the whole or any part of any property or undertaking of a limited liability partnership and in consequence of the limited liability partnership having created a charge which, as created, was a floating charge may exercise his powers in the other part of Great Britain so far as their exercise is not inconsistent with the law applicable there.

(2) In subsection (1) "receiver" includes a manager and a person who is appointed both receiver and manager.

PART IV
WINDING UP OF LIMITED LIABILITY PARTNERSHIPS
REGISTERED UNDER THE ACT

CHAPTER I
PRELIMINARY

73 Alternative modes of winding up

(1) The winding up of a limited liability partnership … may be either voluntary (Chapters II, III, IV and V in this Part) or by the court (Chapter VI).

(2)   This Chapter, and Chapters VII to X, relate to winding up generally, except where otherwise stated.

74 Liability as contributories of present and past members

[When a limited liability partnership is wound up every present and past member of the limited liability partnership who has agreed with the other members or with the limited liability partnership that he will, in circumstances which have arisen, be liable to contribute to the assets of the limited liability partnership in the event that the limited liability partnership goes into liquidation is liable, to the extent that he has agreed, to contribute to its assets to any amount sufficient for payment of its debts and liabilities, and the expenses of the winding up, and for the adjustment of the rights of the contributories among themselves.

However, a past member shall only be liable if the obligation arising from such agreement survived his ceasing to be a member of the limited liability partnership.]

75, 76, 77, 78   ...

79 Meaning of "contributory"

(1)   In this Act and the Companies Act the expression "contributory" means [(a) every present member of the limited liability partnership and (b) every past member of the limited liability partnership] liable to contribute to the assets of a limited liability partnership in the event of its being wound up, and for the purposes of all proceedings for determining, and all proceedings prior to the final determination of, the persons who are to be deemed contributories, includes any person alleged to be a contributory.

(2)   The reference in subsection (1) to persons liable to contribute to the assets does not include a person so liable by virtue of a declaration by the court under section 213 (imputed responsibility for limited liability partnership's fraudulent trading) or section 214 (wrongful trading) [or 214A (adjustment of withdrawals)] in Chapter X of this Part.

(3)   ...

80 Nature of contributory's liability

The liability of a contributory creates a debt (in England and Wales in the nature of a specialty) accruing due from him at the time when his liability commenced, but payable at the times when calls are made for enforcing the liability.

81 Contributories in case of death of a member

(1)   If a contributory dies either before or after he has been placed on the list of contributories, his personal representatives, and the heirs and legatees of heritage of his heritable estate in Scotland, are liable in a due course of administration to contribute to the assets of the limited liability partnership in discharge of his liability and are contributories accordingly.

(2)   Where the personal representatives are placed on the list of contributories, the heirs or legatees of heritage need not be added, but they may be added as and when the court thinks fit.

(3)   If in England and Wales the personal representatives make default in paying any money ordered to be paid by them, proceedings may be taken for administering the estate of the deceased contributory and for compelling payment out of it of the money due.

82 Effect of contributory's bankruptcy

(1)   The following applies if a contributory becomes bankrupt, either before or after he has been placed on the list of contributories.

(2)   His trustee in bankruptcy represents him for all purposes of the winding up, and is a contributory accordingly.

(3)   The trustee may be called on to admit to proof against the bankrupt's estate, or otherwise allow to be paid out of the bankrupt's assets in due course of law, any money due from the bankrupt in respect of his liability to contribute to the limited liability partnership's assets.

(4)   There may be proved against the bankrupt's estate the estimated value of his liability to future calls as well as calls already made.

83   …

CHAPTER II
VOLUNTARY WINDING UP (INTRODUCTORY AND
GENERAL)

84 Circumstances in which limited liability partnership may be wound up voluntarily

[1]   A limited liability partnership may be wound up voluntarily when it determines that it is to be wound up voluntarily.]

(2)   …

[(3)   Within 15 days after a limited liability partnership has determined that it be wound up there shall be forwarded to the registrar of companies either a printed copy or else a copy in some other form approved by the registrar of the determination.]

[If a limited liability partnership fails to comply with this regulation, the limited liability partnership and every designated member of it who is in default is liable on summary conviction to a fine not exceeding level 3 on the standard scale.]

85 Notice of resolution to wind up

[(1)   When a limited liability partnership has determined that it shall be wound up voluntary, it shall within 14 days after the making of the determination give notice of the determination by advertisement in the Gazette.]

(2)   If default is made in complying with this section, the limited liability partnership and every member of it who is in default is liable to a fine and, for continued contravention, to a daily default fine.

For the purposes of this subsection the liquidator is deemed a member of the limited liability partnership.

86 Commencement of winding up

[A voluntary winding up is deemed to commence at the time when the limited liability partnership determines that it be wound up voluntarily.]

87 Effect on business and status of limited liability partnership

(1)   In case of a voluntary winding up, the limited liability partnership shall from the commencement of the winding up cease to carry on its business, except so far as may be required for its beneficial winding up.

(2)   However, the corporate state and corporate powers of the limited liability partnership, notwithstanding anything to the contrary in its [limited liability partnership agreement], continue until the limited liability partnership is dissolved.

88 Avoidance of share transfers, etc after winding-up resolution

Any transfer of [the interest of any member in the property of the limited liability partnership], not being a transfer made to or with the sanction of the liquidator, and any alteration in the status of the limited liability partnership's members, made after the commencement of a voluntary winding up, is void.

89 Statutory declaration of solvency

(1)   Where it is proposed to wind up a limited liability partnership voluntarily, the [designated members] (or, in the case of a limited liability partnership having more than two [designated members], the majority of them) may at a [designated members'] meeting make a statutory declaration to the effect that they have made a full inquiry into the limited liability partnership's affairs and that, having done so, they have formed the opinion that the limited liability partnership will be able to pay its debts in full, together with interest at the official rate (as defined in section 251), within such period, not exceeding twelve months from the commencement of the winding up, as may be specified in the declaration.

(2)   Such a declaration by the [designated members] has no effect for purposes of this Act unless–

[(a) it is made within the five weeks immediately preceding the date when the limited liability partnership determined that it be wound up voluntarily or on that date but before the making of the determination, and]

(b) it embodies a statement of the limited liability partnership's assets and liabilities as at the latest practicable date before the making of the declaration.

(3) The declaration shall be delivered to the registrar of companies before the expiration of 15 days immediately following the date on which the [limited liability partnership determined that it be wound up voluntarily].

(4) A [designated member] making a declaration under this section without having reasonable grounds for the opinion that the limited liability partnership will be able to pay its debts in full, together with interest at the official rate, within the period specified is liable to imprisonment or a fine, or both.

(5) If the limited liability partnership is wound up [voluntarily] within five weeks after the making of the declaration, and its debts (together with interest at the official rate) are not paid or provided for in full within the period specified, it is to be presumed (unless the contrary is shown) that the [designated member] did not have reasonable grounds for his opinion.

(6) If a declaration required by subsection (3) to be delivered to the registrar is not so delivered within the time prescribed by that subsection, the limited liability partnership and every member in default is liable to a fine and, for continued contravention, to a daily default fine.

90 Distinction between "members'" and "creditors'" voluntary winding up

A winding up in the case of which a [designated members'] statutory declaration under section 89 has been made is a "members' voluntary winding up"; and a winding up in the case of which such a declaration has not been made is a "creditors' voluntary winding up".

CHAPTER III
MEMBERS' VOLUNTARY WINDING UP

91 Appointment of liquidator

(1) In a members' voluntary winding up, the limited liability partnership ... shall appoint one or more liquidators for the purpose of winding up the limited liability partnership's affairs and distributing its assets.

[(2) On the appointment of a liquidator the powers of the members of the limited liability partnership shall cease except to the extent that a meeting of the members of the limited liability partnership summoned for the purpose or the liquidator sanctions its continuance.]

[(3)   Subsections (3) and (4) of section 92 shall apply for the purposes of this section as they apply for the purposes of that section.]

92 Power to fill vacancy in office of liquidator

(1)   If a vacancy occurs by death, resignation or otherwise in the office of liquidator appointed by the limited liability partnership, [a meeting of the members of the limited liability partnership summoned for the purpose] may, subject to any arrangement with its creditors, fill the vacancy.

(2)   For that purpose [a meeting of the members of the limited liability partnership] may be convened by any contributory or, if there were more liquidators than one, by the continuing liquidators.

(3)   The meeting shall be held in manner provided by this Act or by the [limited liability partnership agreement], or in such manner as may, on application by any contributory or by the continuing liquidators, be determined by the court.

[(4)   The quorum required for a meeting of the members of the limited liability partnership shall be any quorum required by the limited liability partnership agreement for meetings of the members of the limited liability partnership and if no requirement for a quorum has been agreed upon the quorum shall be two members.]

93 General limited liability partnership meeting at each year's end

(1)   Subject to sections 96 and 102, in the event of the winding up continuing for more than one year, the liquidator shall summon [a meeting of the members of the limited liability partnership] at the end of the first year from the commencement of the winding up, and of each succeeding year, or at the first convenient date within three months from the end of the year or such longer period as the Secretary of State may allow.

(2)   The liquidator shall lay before the meeting an account of his acts and dealings, and of the conduct of the winding up, during the preceding year.

(3)   If the liquidator fails to comply with this section, he is liable to a fine.

[(4)   Subsections (3) and (4) of section 92 shall apply for the purposes of this section as they apply for the purposes of that section.]

94 Final meeting prior to dissolution

(1)   As soon as the limited liability partnership's affairs are fully wound up, the liquidator shall make up an account of the winding up, showing how it has been conducted and the limited liability partnership's property has been disposed of, and thereupon shall call [a meeting of the members of the limited liability partnership] for the purpose of laying before it the account, and giving an explanation of it.

(2)   The meeting shall be called by advertisement in the Gazette, specifying its time, place and object and published at least one month before the meeting.

(3)   Within one week after the meeting, the liquidator shall send to the registrar of companies a copy of the account, and shall make a return to him of the holding of the meeting and of its date.

(4)   If the copy is not sent or the return is not made in accordance with subsection (3), the liquidator is liable to a fine and, for continued contravention, to a daily default fine.

(5)   If a quorum is not present at the meeting, the liquidator shall, in lieu of the return mentioned above, make a return that the meeting was duly summoned and that no quorum was present; and upon such a return being made, the provisions of subsection (3) as to the making of the return are deemed complied with.

[(5A) Subsections (3) and (4) of section 92 shall apply for the purposes of this section as they apply for the purposes of that section.]

(6)   If the liquidator fails to call [a meeting of the members of the limited liability partnership] as required by subsection (1), he is liable to a fine.

95 Effect of limited liability partnership's insolvency

(1)   This section applies where the liquidator is of the opinion that the limited liability partnership will be unable to pay its debts in full (together with interest at the official rate) within the period stated in the [designated members'] declaration under section 89.

(2)   The liquidator shall–
  (a)   summon a meeting of creditors for a day not later than the 28th day after the day on which he formed that opinion;
  (b)   send notices of the creditors' meeting to the creditors by post not less than seven days before the day on which that meeting is to be held;
  (c)   cause notice of the creditors' meeting to be advertised once in the Gazette and once at least in two newspapers circulating in the relevant locality (that is to say the locality in which the limited liability partnership's principal place of business in Great Britain was situated during the relevant period); and
  (d)   during the period before the day on which the creditors' meeting is to be held, furnish creditors free of charge with such information concerning the affairs of the limited liability partnership as they may reasonably require;
and the notice of the creditors' meeting shall state the duty imposed by paragraph (d) above.

(3)   The liquidator shall also–
  (a)   make out a statement in the prescribed form as to the affairs of the limited liability partnership;

(b) lay that statement before the creditors' meeting; and

(c) attend and preside at that meeting.

(4) The statement as to the affairs of the limited liability partnership shall be verified by affidavit by the liquidator and shall show–

(a) particulars of the limited liability partnership's assets, debts and liabilities;

(b) the names and addresses of the limited liability partnership's creditors;

(c) the securities held by them respectively;

(d) the dates when the securities were respectively given; and

(e) such further or other information as may be prescribed.

(5) Where the limited liability partnership's principal place of business in Great Britain was situated in different localities at different times during the relevant period, the duty imposed by subsection (2)(c) applies separately in relation to each of those localities.

(6) Where the limited liability partnership had no place of business in Great Britain during the relevant period, references in subsections (2)(c) and (5) to the limited liability partnership's principal place of business in Great Britain are replaced by references to its registered office.

[(7) In this section "the relevant period" means the period of six months immediately preceding the date on which the limited liability partnership determined that it be wound up voluntarily.]

(8) If the liquidator without reasonable excuse fails to comply with this section, he is liable to a fine.

96 Conversion to creditors' voluntary winding up

As from the day on which the creditors' meeting is held under section 95, this Act has effect as if–

(a) the [designated members'] declaration under section 89 had not been made; and

[(b) the creditors' meeting was the meeting mentioned in section 98 in the next Chapter;]

and accordingly the winding up becomes a creditors' voluntary winding up.

CHAPTER IV
CREDITORS' VOLUNTARY WINDING UP

97 Application of this Chapter

(1) Subject as follows, this Chapter applies in relation to a creditors' voluntary winding up.

(2) Sections 98 and 99 do not apply where, under section 96 in Chapter III, a members' voluntary winding up has become a creditors' voluntary winding up.

98 Meeting of creditors

(1)   The limited liability partnership shall–

[(a) cause a meeting of its creditors to be summoned for a day not later than the 14th day after the day on which the limited liability partnership determined that it be wound up voluntarily;]

(b) cause the notices of the creditors' meeting to be sent by post to the creditors not less than seven days before the day on which that meeting is to be held; and

(c) cause notice of the creditors' meeting to be advertised once in the Gazette and once at least in two newspapers circulating in the relevant locality (that is to say the locality in which the limited liability partnership's principal place of business in Great Britain was situated during the relevant period).

(2)   The notice of the creditors' meeting shall state either–

(a) the name and address of a person qualified to act as an insolvency practitioner in relation to the limited liability partnership who, during the period before the day on which that meeting is to be held, will furnish creditors free of charge with such information concerning the limited liability partnership's affairs as they may reasonably require; or

(b) a place in the relevant locality where, on the two business days falling next before the day on which that meeting is to be held, a list of the names and addresses of the limited liability partnership's creditors will be available for inspection free of charge.

(3)   Where the limited liability partnership's principal place of business in Great Britain was situated in different localities at different times during the relevant period, the duties imposed by subsections (1)(c) and (2)(b) above apply separately in relation to each of those localities.

(4)   Where the limited liability partnership had no place of business in Great Britain during the relevant period, references in subsections (1)(c) and (3) to the limited liability partnership's principal place of business in Great Britain are replaced by references to its registered office.

(5)   In this section "the relevant period" means the period of six months immediately preceding the day on which [the limited liability partnership determined that it be wound up voluntarily].

(6)   If the limited liability partnership without reasonable excuse fails to comply with subsection (1) or (2), it is guilty of an offence and liable to a fine.

99 Members to lay statement of affairs before creditors

(1)   [The designated members] shall–

(a) make out a statement in the prescribed form as to the affairs of the limited liability partnership;

(b) cause that statement to be laid before the creditors' meeting under section 98; and

(c) appoint one of their number to preside at that meeting;
and it is the duty of [the designated member so appointed] to attend the meeting and preside over it.

(2) The statement as to the affairs of the limited liability partnership shall be verified by affidavit by some or all of the [designated members] and shall show–
  (a) particulars of the limited liability partnership's assets, debts and liabilities;
  (b) the names and addresses of the limited liability partnership's creditors;
  (c) the securities held by them respectively;
  (d) the dates when the securities were respectively given; and
  (e) such further or other information as may be prescribed.

(3) If–
  (a) the [designated members] without reasonable excuse fail to comply with subsection (1) or (2); or
  (b) any [designated member] without reasonable excuse fails to comply with subsection (1), so far as requiring him to attend and preside at the creditors' meeting,
the [designated members] are or (as the case may be) the [designated member] is guilty of an offence and liable to a fine.

100 Appointment of liquidator

(1) [The creditors at their meeting mentioned in section 98 and the limited liability partnership] may nominate a person to be liquidator for the purpose of winding up the limited liability partnership's affairs and distributing its assets.

(2) The liquidator shall be the person nominated by the creditors or, where no person has been so nominated, the person (if any) nominated by the limited liability partnership.

(3) In the case of different persons being nominated, any ... member or creditor of the limited liability partnership may, within seven days after the date on which the nomination was made by the creditors, apply to the court for an order either–
  (a) directing that the person nominated as liquidator by the limited liability partnership shall be liquidator instead of or jointly with the person nominated by the creditors, or
  (b) appointing some other person to be liquidator instead of the person nominated by the creditors.

101 Appointment of liquidation committee

(1) The creditors at the meeting to be held under section 98 or at any subsequent meeting may, if they think fit, appoint a committee ("the liquidation committee") of not more than five persons to exercise the functions conferred on it by or under this Act.

[(2) If such a committee is appointed, the limited liability partnership may, when it determines that it be wound up voluntarily or at any time thereafter, appoint such number of persons as they think fit to act as members of the committee, not exceeding five.]

(3)   However, the creditors may, if they think fit, resolve that all or any of the persons so appointed by the limited liability partnership ought not to be members of the liquidation committee; and if the creditors so resolve–
> (a) the persons mentioned in the resolution are not then, unless the court otherwise directs, qualified to act as members of the committee; and
> (b) on any application to the court under this provision the court may, if it thinks fit, appoint other persons to act as such members in place of the persons mentioned in the resolution.

(4)   In Scotland, the liquidation committee has, in addition to the powers and duties conferred and imposed on it by this Act, such of the powers and duties of commissioners on a bankrupt estate as may be conferred and imposed on liquidation committees by the rules.

102 Creditors' meeting where winding up converted under s 96

Where, in the case of a winding up which was, under section 96 in Chapter III, converted to a creditors' voluntary winding up, a creditors' meeting is held in accordance with section 95, any appointment made or committee established by that meeting is deemed to have been made or established by a meeting held in accordance with section 98 in this Chapter.

103 Cesser of members' powers

On the appointment of a liquidator, all the powers of the members cease, except so far as the liquidation committee (or, if there is no such committee, the creditors) sanction their continuance.

104 Vacancy in office of liquidator

If a vacancy occurs, by death, resignation or otherwise, in the office of a liquidator (other than a liquidator appointed by, or by the direction of, the court) the creditors may fill the vacancy.

105 Meetings of limited liability partnership and creditors at each year's end

(1)   If the winding up continues for more than one year, the liquidator shall summon [a meeting of the members of the limited liability partnership] and a meeting of the creditors at the end of the first year from the commencement of the winding up, and of each succeeding year, or at the first convenient date within three months from the end of the year or such longer period as the Secretary of State may allow.

(2)   The liquidator shall lay before each of the meetings an account of his acts and dealings and of the conduct of the winding up during the preceding year.

(3)   If the liquidator fails to comply with this section, he is liable to a fine.

(4)   Where under section 96 a members' voluntary winding up has become a creditors' voluntary winding up, and the creditors' meeting under section 95 is held three months or less before the end of the first year from the commencement of the winding up, the liquidator is not required by this section to summon a meeting of creditors at the end of that year.

[(5)   Subsections (3) and (4) of section 92 shall apply for the purposes of this section as they apply for the purposes of that section.]

106 Final meeting prior to dissolution

(1)   As soon as the limited liability partnership's affairs are fully wound up, the liquidator shall make up an account of the winding up, showing how it has been conducted and the limited liability partnership's property has been disposed of, and thereupon shall call [a meeting of the members of the limited liability partnership] and a meeting of the creditors for the purpose of laying the account before the meetings and giving an explanation of it.

(2)   Each such meeting shall be called by advertisement in the Gazette specifying the time, place and object of the meeting, and published at least one month before it.

(3)   Within one week after the date of the meetings (or, if they are not held on the same date, after the date of the later one) the liquidator shall send to the registrar of companies a copy of the account, and shall make a return to him of the holding of the meetings and of their dates.

(4)   If the copy is not sent or the return is not made in accordance with subsection (3), the liquidator is liable to a fine and, for continued contravention, to a daily default fine.

(5)   However, if a quorum is not present at either such meeting, the liquidator shall, in lieu of the return required by subsection (3), make a return that the meeting was duly summoned and that no quorum was present; and upon such return being made the provisions of that subsection as to the making of the return are, in respect of that meeting, deemed complied with.

[(5A) Subsections (3) and (4) of section 92 shall apply for the purposes of this section as they apply for the purposes of that section.]

(6)   If the liquidator fails to call [a meeting of the members of the limited liability partnership] or a meeting of the creditors as required by this section, he is liable to a fine.

CHAPTER V
PROVISIONS APPLYING TO BOTH KINDS OF VOLUNTARY
WINDING UP

107 Distribution of limited liability partnership's property

Subject to the provisions of this Act as to preferential payments, the limited liability partnership's property in a voluntary winding up shall on the winding up be applied in satisfaction of the limited liability partnership's liabilities pari passu and, subject to that application, shall (unless the limited liability partnership agreement otherwise provides) be distributed among the members according to their rights and interests in the limited liability partnership.

108 Appointment or removal of liquidator by the court

(1)   If from any cause whatever there is no liquidator acting, the court may appoint a liquidator.

(2)   The court may, on cause shown, remove a liquidator and appoint another.

109 Notice by liquidator of his appointment

(1)   The liquidator shall, within 14 days after his appointment, publish in the Gazette and deliver to the registrar of companies for registration a notice of his appointment in the form prescribed by statutory instrument made by the Secretary of State.

(2)   If the liquidator fails to comply with this section, he is liable to a fine and, for continued contravention, to a daily default fine.

110 Acceptance of shares, etc, as consideration for sale of limited liability partnership property

[(1)   This section applies, in the case of a limited liability partnership proposed to be, or being, wound up voluntarily, where the whole or part of the limited liability partnership's business or property is proposed to be transferred or sold to another company whether or not the latter is a company within the meaning of the Companies Act ("the transferee company") or to a limited liability partnership ("the transferee limited liability partnership").

(2)   With the requisite sanction, the liquidator of the limited liability partnership being, or proposed to be, wound up ("the transferor limited liability partnership") may receive, in compensation or part compensation for the transfer or sale, shares, policies or other like interests in the transferee company or transferee limited liability partnership for distribution among the members of the transferor limited liability partnership.

(3)   The sanction required under subsection (2) is–
    (a)   in the case of a members' voluntary winding up, that of a determination of the limited liability partnership at a meeting of the members of the

limited liability partnership conferring either a general authority on the liquidator or an authority in respect of any particular arrangement (subsections (3) and (4) of section 92 to apply for this purpose as they apply for the purposes of that section), and

(b) in the case of a creditors' voluntary winding up, that of either the court or the liquidation committee.

(4) Alternatively to subsection (2), the liquidator may (with the sanction) enter into any other arrangement whereby the members of the transferor limited liability partnership may, in lieu of receiving cash, shares, policies or other like interests (or in addition thereto), participate in the profits, or receive any other benefit from the transferee company or the transferee limited liability partnership.

(5) A sale or arrangement in pursuance of this section is binding on members of the transferor limited liability partnership.

(6) A determination by the limited liability partnership is not invalid for purposes of this section by reason that it is made before or concurrently with a determination by the limited liability partnership that it be wound up voluntarily or for appointing liquidators; but, if an order is made within a year for winding up the limited liability partnership by the court, the determination by the limited liability partnership is not valid unless sanctioned by the court.]

111 Dissent from arrangement under s 110

[(1) This section applies in the case of a voluntary winding up where, for the purposes of section 110(2) or (4), a determination of the limited liability partnership has provided the sanction requisite for the liquidator under that section.

(2) If a member of the transferor limited liability partnership who did not vote in favour of providing the sanction required for the liquidator under section 110 expresses his dissent from it in writing addressed to the liquidator and left at the registered office of the limited liability partnership within seven days after the date on which that sanction was given, he may require the liquidator either to abstain from carrying the arrangement so sanctioned into effect or to purchase his interest at a price to be determined by agreement or by arbitration under this section.

(3) If the liquidator elects to purchase the member's interest, the purchase money must be paid before the limited liability partnership is dissolved and be raised by the liquidator in such manner as may be determined by the limited liability partnership.]

(4) ...

112 Reference of questions to court

(1) The liquidator or any contributory or creditor may apply to the court to determine any question arising in the winding up of a limited liability partnership, or to exercise, as respects the enforcing of calls or any other matter, all or any of the powers which the court might exercise if the limited liability partnership were being wound up by the court.

(2)   The court, if satisfied that the determination of the question or the required exercise of power will be just and beneficial, may accede wholly or partially to the application on such terms and conditions as it thinks fit, or may make such other order on the application as it thinks just.

(3)   A copy of an order made by virtue of this section staying the proceedings in the winding up shall forthwith be forwarded by the limited liability partnership, or otherwise as may be prescribed, to the registrar of companies, who shall enter it in his records relating to the limited liability partnership.

113 Court's power to control proceedings (Scotland)

If the court, on the application of the liquidator in the winding up of a limited liability partnership registered in Scotland, so directs, no action or proceeding shall be proceeded with or commenced against the limited liability partnership except by leave of the court and subject to such terms as the court may impose.

114 No liquidator appointed or nominated by limited liability partnership

(1)   This section applies where, in the case of a voluntary winding up, no liquidator has been appointed or nominated by the limited liability partnership.

(2)   The powers of the members shall not be exercised, except with the sanction of the court or (in the case of a creditors' voluntary winding up) so far as may be necessary to secure compliance with sections 98 (creditors' meeting) and 99 (statement of affairs), during the period before the appointment or nomination of a liquidator of the limited liability partnership.

(3)   Subsection (2) does not apply in relation to the powers of the members–
   (a)   to dispose of perishable goods and other goods the value of which is likely to diminish if they are not immediately disposed of, and
   (b)   to do all such other things as may be necessary for the protection of the limited liability partnership's assets.

(4)   If the members of the limited liability partnership without reasonable excuse fail to comply with this section, they are liable to a fine.

115 Expenses of voluntary winding up

All expenses properly incurred in the winding up, including the remuneration of the liquidator, are payable out of the limited liability partnership's assets in priority to all other claims.

116 Saving for certain rights

The voluntary winding up of a limited liability partnership does not bar the right of any creditor or contributory to have it wound up by the court; but in the case of an application by a contributory the court must be satisfied that the rights of the contributories will be prejudiced by a voluntary winding up.

CHAPTER VI
WINDING UP BY THE COURT

117 High Court and county court jurisdiction

(1)   The High Court has jurisdiction to wind up any limited liability partnership registered in England and Wales.

(2)   ... the county court of the district in which the limited liability partnership's registered office is situated has concurrent jurisdiction with the High Court to wind up the limited liability partnership.

(3)   ...

(4)   The Lord Chancellor may by order in a statutory instrument exclude a county court from having winding-up jurisdiction, and for the purposes of that jurisdiction may attach its district, or any part thereof, to any other county court, and may by statutory instrument revoke or vary any such order.
    In exercising the powers of this section, the Lord Chancellor shall provide that a county court is not to have winding-up jurisdiction unless it has for the time being jurisdiction for the purposes of Parts VIII to XI of this Act (individual insolvency).

(5)   Every court in England and Wales having winding-up jurisdiction has for the purposes of that jurisdiction all the powers of the High Court; and every prescribed officer of the court shall perform any duties which an officer of the High Court may discharge by order of a judge of that court or otherwise in relation to winding up.

(6)   For the purposes of this section, a limited liability partnership's "registered office" is the place which has longest been its registered office during the six months immediately preceding the presentation of the petition for winding up.

118 Proceedings taken in wrong court

(1)   Nothing in section 117 invalidates a proceeding by reason of its being taken in the wrong court.

(2)   The winding up of a limited liability partnership by the court in England and Wales, or any proceedings in the winding up, may be retained in the court in which the proceedings were commenced, although it may not be the court in which they ought to have been commenced.

119 Proceedings in county court; case stated for High Court

(1)   If any question arises in any winding-up proceedings in a county court which all the parties to the proceedings, or which one of them and the judge of the court, desire to have determined in the first instance in the High Court, the judge shall state the facts in the form of a special case for the opinion of the High Court.

(2)   Thereupon the special case and the proceedings (or such of them as may be required) shall be transmitted to the High Court for the purposes of the determination.

120 Court of Session and sheriff court jurisdiction

(1)   The Court of Session has jurisdiction to wind up any limited liability partnership registered in Scotland.

(2)   When the Court of Session is in vacation, the jurisdiction conferred on that court by this section may (subject to the provisions of this Part) be exercised by the judge acting as vacation judge

(3)   … the sheriff court of the sheriffdom in which the limited liability partnership's registered office is situated has concurrent jurisdiction with the Court of Session to wind up the limited liability partnership; but–
    (a) the Court of Session may, if it thinks expedient having regard to the amount of the limited liability partnership's assets to do so–
        (i)   remit to sheriff court any petition presented to the Court of Session for winding up such a limited liability partnership, or
        (ii) require such a petition presented to a sheriff court to be remitted to the Court of Session; and
    (b) the Court of Session may require any such petition as above-mentioned presented to one sheriff court to be remitted to another sheriff court; and
    (c) in a winding up in the sheriff court the sheriff may submit a stated case for the opinion of the Court of Session on any question of law arising in that winding up.

(4)   For purposes of this section, the expression "registered office" means the place which has longest been the limited liability partnership's registered office during the six months immediately preceding the presentation of the petition for winding up.

(5)   …

121 Power to remit winding up to Lord Ordinary

(1)   The Court of Session may, by Act of Sederunt, make provision for the taking of proceedings in a winding up before one of the Lords Ordinary; and, where provision is so made, the Lord Ordinary has, for the purposes of the winding up, all the powers and jurisdiction of the court.

(2)   However, the Lord Ordinary may report to the Inner House any matter which may arise in the course of a winding up.

122 Circumstances in which limited liability partnership may be wound up by the court

[(1)   A limited liability partnership may be wound up by the court if–
    (a) the limited liability partnership has determined that the limited liability partnership be wound up by the court,

    (b) the limited liability partnership does not commence its business within a year from its incorporation or suspends its business for a whole year,

    (c) the number of members is reduced below two,

    (d) the limited liability partnership is unable to pay its debts, or

    (e) the court is of the opinion that it is just and equitable that the limited liability partnership should be wound up.

(2)   In Scotland, a limited liability partnership which the Court of Session has jurisdiction to wind up may be wound up by the Court if there is subsisting a floating charge over property comprised in the limited liability partnership's property and undertaking, and the court is satisfied that the security of the creditor entitled to the benefit of the floating charge is in jeopardy.

    For this purpose a creditor's security is deemed to be in jeopardy if the Court is satisfied that events have occurred or are about to occur which render it unreasonable in the creditor's interests that the limited liability partnership should retain power to dispose of the property which is subject to the floating charge.

123 Definition of inability to pay debts

(1)   A limited liability partnership is deemed unable to pay its debts–

    (a) if a creditor (by assignment or otherwise) to whom the limited liability partnership is indebted in a sum exceeding £750 then due has served on the limited liability partnership, by leaving it at the limited liability partnership's registered office, a written demand (in the prescribed form) requiring the limited liability partnership to pay the sum so due and the limited liability partnership has for three weeks thereafter neglected to pay the sum or to secure or compound for it to the reasonable satisfaction of the creditor, or

    (b) if, in England and Wales, execution or other process issued on a judgment, decree or order of any court in favour of a creditor of the limited liability partnership is returned unsatisfied in whole or in part, or

    (c) if, in Scotland, the induciae of a charge for payment on an extract decree, or an extract registered bond, or an extract registered protest, have expired without payment being made, or

    (d) if, in Northern Ireland, a certificate of unenforceability has been granted in respect of a judgment against the limited liability partnership, or

    (e) if it is proved to the satisfaction of the court that the limited liability partnership is unable to pay its debts as they fall due.

(2)   A limited liability partnership is also deemed unable to pay its debts if it is proved to the satisfaction of the court that the value of the limited liability partnership's assets is less than the amount of its liabilities, taking into account its contingent and prospective liabilities.

(3)   The money sum for the time being specified in subsection (1)(a) is subject to increase or reduction by order under section 416 in Part XV.

124 Application for winding up

(1)   Subject to the provisions of this section, an application to the court for the winding up of a limited liability partnership shall be by petition presented either by the limited liability partnership, or the members, or by any creditor or creditors (including any contingent or prospective creditor or creditors), contributory or contributories or by the clerk of a magistrates' court in the exercise of the power conferred by section 87A of the Magistrates' Courts Act 1980 (enforcement of fines imposed on companies), or by all or any of those parties, together or separately.

(2),(3) …

(4)   A winding-up petition may be presented by the Secretary of State–
    (a)   …
    (b)   in a case falling within section 124A below.

(5)   Where a limited liability partnership is being wound up voluntarily in England and Wales, a winding-up petition may be presented by the official receiver attached to the court as well as by any other person authorised in that behalf under the other provisions of this section; but the court shall not make a winding-up order on the petition unless it is satisfied that the voluntary winding up cannot be continued with due regard to the interests of the creditors or contributories.

124A Petition for winding up on grounds of public interest

(1)   Where it appears to the Secretary of State from–
    (a)   any report made or information obtained under Part XIV of the Companies Act 1985 (limited liability partnership investigations, &c.),
    (b)   …
    (c)   any information obtained under section 2 of the Criminal Justice Act 1987 or section 52 of the Criminal Justice (Scotland) Act 1987 (fraud investigations), or
    (d)   any information obtained under section 83 of the Companies Act 1989 (powers exercisable for purpose of assisting overseas regulatory authorities),
that it is expedient in the public interest that a limited liability partnership should be wound up, he may present a petition for it to be wound up if the court thinks it just and equitable for it to be so.

(2)   This section does not apply if the limited liability partnership is already being wound up by the court.

125 Powers of court on hearing of petition

(1)   On hearing a winding-up petition the court may dismiss it, or adjourn the hearing conditionally or unconditionally, or make an interim order, or any other order that it thinks fit; but the court shall not refuse to make a winding-up order on the ground only that the limited liability partnership's assets have been mortgaged to an amount equal to or in excess of those assets, or that the limited liability partnership has no assets.

(2)   If the petition is presented by members of the limited liability partnership as contributories on the ground that it is just and equitable that the limited liability partnership should be wound up, the court, if it is of opinion–

(a)   that the petitioners are entitled to relief either by winding up the limited liability partnership or by some other means, and

(b)   that in the absence of any other remedy it would be just and equitable that the limited liability partnership should be wound up,

shall make a winding-up order; but this does not apply if the court is also of the opinion both that some other remedy is available to the petitioners and that they are acting unreasonably in seeking to have the limited liability partnership wound up instead of pursuing that other remedy.

126 Power to stay or restrain proceedings against limited liability partnership

(1)   At any time after the presentation of a winding-up petition, and before a winding-up order has been made, the limited liability partnership, or any creditor or contributory, may–

(a)   where any action or proceeding against the limited liability partnership is pending in the High Court or Court of Appeal in England and Wales or Northern Ireland, apply to the court in which the action or proceeding is pending for a stay of proceedings therein, and

(b)   where any other action or proceeding is pending against the limited liability partnership, apply to the court having jurisdiction to wind up the limited liability partnership to restrain further proceedings in the action or proceeding;

and the court to which application is so made may (as the case may be) stay, sist or restrain the proceedings accordingly on such terms as it thinks fit.

(2)   ...

127 Avoidance of property dispositions, etc

In a winding up by the court, any disposition of the limited liability partnership's property, and [any transfer by a member of the limited liability partnership of his interest in the property of the limited liability partnership], or alteration in the status of the limited liability partnership's members, made after the commencement of the winding up is, unless the court otherwise orders, void.

128 Avoidance of attachments, etc

(1)   Where a limited liability partnership registered in England and Wales is being wound up by the court, any attachment, sequestration, distress or execution put in force against the estate or effects of the limited liability partnership after the commencement of the winding up is void.

(2)   This section, so far as relates to any estate or effects of the limited liability partnership situated in England and Wales, applies in the case of a limited liability partnership registered in Scotland as it applies in the case of a limited liability partnership registered in England and Wales.

129 Commencement of winding up by the court

(1)   If, before the presentation of a petition for the winding up of a limited liability partnership by the court, [a determination has been made] for voluntary winding up, the winding up of the limited liability partnership is deemed to have commenced [at the time of that determination]; and unless the court, on proof of fraud or mistake, directs otherwise, all proceedings taken in the voluntary winding up are deemed to have been validly taken.

(2)   In any other case, the winding up of a limited liability partnership by the court is deemed to commence at the time of the presentation of the petition for winding up.

130 Consequences of winding-up order

(1)   On the making of a winding-up order, a copy of the order must forthwith be forwarded by the limited liability partnership (or otherwise as may be prescribed) to the registrar of companies, who shall enter it in his records relating to the limited liability partnership.

(2)   When a winding-up order has been made or a provisional liquidator has been appointed, no action or proceeding shall be proceeded with or commenced against the limited liability partnership or its property, except by leave of the court and subject to such terms as the court may impose.

(3)   …

(4)   An order for winding up a limited liability partnership operates in favour of all the creditors and of all contributories of the limited liability partnership as if made on the joint petition of a creditor and of a contributory.

131 Limited liability partnership's statement of affairs

(1)   Where the court has made a winding-up order or appointed a provisional liquidator, the official receiver may require some or all of the persons mentioned in subsection (3) below to make out and submit to him a statement in the prescribed form as to the affairs of the limited liability partnership.

(2)   The statement shall be verified by affidavit by the persons required to submit it and shall show–
   (a)   particulars of the limited liability partnership's assets, debts and liabilities;
   (b)   the names and addresses of the limited liability partnership's creditors;
   (c)   the securities held by them respectively;
   (d)   the dates when the securities were respectively given; and
   (e)   such further or other information as may be prescribed or as the official receiver may require.

(3)   The persons referred to in subsection (1) are–
   (a)   those who are or have been members of the limited liability partnership;

(b) those who have taken part in the formation of the limited liability partnership at any time within one year before the relevant date;

(c) those who are in the limited liability partnership's employment, or have been in its employment within that year, and are in the official receiver's opinion capable of giving the information required;

(d) those who are or have been within that year members of, or in the employment of, a limited liability partnership which is, or within that year was, a member of the limited liability partnership.

(4) Where any persons are required under this section to submit a statement of affairs to the official receiver, they shall do so (subject to the next subsection) before the end of the period of 21 days beginning with the day after that on which the prescribed notice of the requirement is given to them by the official receiver.

(5) The official receiver, if he thinks fit, may–

(a) at any time release a person from an obligation imposed on him under subsection (1) or (2) above; or

(b) either when giving the notice mentioned in subsection (4) or subsequently, extend the period so mentioned;

and where the official receiver has refused to exercise a power conferred by this subsection, the court, if it thinks fit, may exercise it.

(6) In this section–

"employment" includes employment under a contract for services; and

"the relevant date" means–

(a) in a case where a provisional liquidator is appointed, the date of his appointment; and

(b) in a case where no such appointment is made, the date of the winding-up order.

(7) If a person without reasonable excuse fails to comply with any obligation imposed under this section, he is liable to a fine and, for continued contravention, to a daily default fine.

(8) In the application of this section to Scotland references to the official receiver are to the liquidator or, in a case where a provisional liquidator is appointed, the provisional liquidator.

132 Investigation by official receiver

(1) Where a winding-up order is made by the court in England and Wales, it is the duty of the official receiver to investigate–

(a) if the limited liability partnership has failed, the causes of the failure; and

(b) generally, the promotion, formation, business, dealings and affairs of the limited liability partnership,

and to make such report (if any) to the court as he thinks fit.

(2) The report is, in any proceedings, prima facie evidence of the facts stated in it.

133 Public examination of members

(1)   Where a limited liability partnership is being wound up by the court, the official receiver or, in Scotland, the liquidator may at any time before the dissolution of the limited liability partnership apply to the court for the public examination of any person who–
   (a)   is or has been a member of the limited liability partnership; or
   (b)   has acted as liquidator or administrator of the limited liability partnership or as receiver or manager or, in Scotland, receiver of its property; or
   (c)   not being a person falling within paragraph (a) or (b), is or has been concerned, or has taken part, in the promotion, formation or management of the limited liability partnership.

(2)   Unless the court otherwise orders, the official receiver or, in Scotland, the liquidator shall make an application under subsection (1) if he is requested in accordance with the rules to do so by–
   (a)   one-half, in value, of the limited liability partnership's creditors; or
   (b)   three-quarters, in value, of the limited liability partnership's contributories.

(3)   On an application under subsection (1), the court shall direct that a public examination of the person to whom the application relates shall be held on a day appointed by the court; and that person shall attend on that day and be publicly examined as to the promotion, formation or management of the limited liability partnership or as to the conduct of its business and affairs, or his conduct or dealings in relation to the limited liability partnership.

(4)   The following may take part in the public examination of a person under this section and may question that person concerning the matters mentioned in subsection (3), namely–
   (a)   the official receiver;
   (b)   the liquidator of the limited liability partnership;
   (c)   any person who has been appointed as special manager of the limited liability partnership's property or business;
   (d)   any creditor of the limited liability partnership who has tendered a proof or, in Scotland, submitted a claim in the winding up;
   (e)   any contributory of the limited liability partnership.

134 Enforcement of s 133

(1)   If a person without reasonable excuse fails at any time to attend his public examination under section 133, he is guilty of a contempt of court and liable to be punished accordingly.

(2)   In a case where a person without reasonable excuse fails at any time to attend his examination under section 133 or there are reasonable grounds for believing that a person has absconded, or is about to abscond, with a view to avoiding or delaying his examination under that section, the court may cause a warrant to be issued to a constable or prescribed member of the court–

(a) for the arrest of that person; and

(b) for the seizure of any books, papers, records, money or goods in that person's possession.

(3) In such a case the court may authorise the person arrested under the warrant to be kept in custody, and anything seized under such a warrant to be held, in accordance with the rules, until such time as the court may order.

135 Appointment and powers of provisional liquidator

(1) Subject to the provisions of this section, the court may, at any time after the presentation of a winding-up petition, appoint a liquidator provisionally.

(2) In England and Wales, the appointment of a provisional liquidator may be made at any time before the making of a winding-up order; and either the official receiver or any other fit person may be appointed.

(3) In Scotland, such an appointment may be made at any time before the first appointment of liquidators.

(4) The provisional liquidator shall carry out such functions as the court may confer on him.

(5) When a liquidator is provisionally appointed by the court, his powers may be limited by the order appointing him.

136 Functions of official receiver in relation to office of liquidator

(1) The following provisions of this section have effect, subject to section 140 below, on a winding-up order being made by the court in England and Wales.

(2) The official receiver, by virtue of his office, becomes the liquidator of the limited liability partnership and continues in office until another person becomes liquidator under the provisions of this Part.

(3) The official receiver is, by virtue of his office, the liquidator during any vacancy.

(4) At any time when he is the liquidator of the limited liability partnership, the official receiver may summon separate meetings of the limited liability partnership's creditors and contributories for the purpose of choosing a person to be liquidator of the limited liability partnership in place of the official receiver.

(5) It is the duty of the official receiver–

(a) as soon as practicable in the period of twelve weeks beginning with the day on which the winding-up order was made, to decide whether to exercise his power under subsection (4) to summon meetings, and

(b) if in pursuance of paragraph (a) he decides not to exercise that power, to give notice of his decision, before the end of that period, to the court and to the limited liability partnership's creditors and contributories, and

(c) (whether or not he has decided to exercise that power) to exercise his power to summon meetings under subsection (4) if he is at any time requested, in accordance with the rules, to do so by one-quarter, in value, of the limited liability partnership's creditors;

and accordingly, where the duty imposed by paragraph (c) arises before the official receiver has performed a duty imposed by paragraph (a) or (b), he is not required to perform the latter duty.

(6)   A notice given under subsection (5)(b) to the limited liability partnership's creditors shall contain an explanation of the creditors' power under subsection (5)(c) to require the official receiver to summon meetings of the limited liability partnership's creditors and contributories.

137 Appointment by Secretary of State

(1)   In a winding up by the court in England and Wales the official receiver may, at any time when he is the liquidator of the limited liability partnership, apply to the Secretary of State for the appointment of a person as liquidator in his place.

(2)   If meetings are held in pursuance of a decision under section 136(5)(a), but no person is chosen to be liquidator as a result of those meetings, it is the duty of the official receiver to decide whether to refer the need for an appointment to the Secretary of State.

(3)   On an application under subsection (1), or a reference made in pursuance of a decision under subsection (2), the Secretary of State shall either make an appointment or decline to make one.

(4)   Where a liquidator has been appointed by the Secretary of State under subsection (3), the liquidator shall give notice of his appointment to the limited liability partnership's creditors or, if the court so allows, shall advertise his appointment in accordance with the directions of the court.

(5)   In that notice or advertisement the liquidator shall–
   (a) state whether he proposes to summon a general meeting of the limited liability partnership's creditors under section 141 below for the purpose of determining (together with any meeting of contributories) whether a liquidation committee should be established under that section, and
   (b) if he does not propose to summon such a meeting, set out the power of the limited liability partnership's creditors under that section to require him to summon one.

138 Appointment of liquidator in Scotland

(1)   Where a winding-up order is made by the court in Scotland, a liquidator shall be appointed by the court at the time when the order is made.

(2)   The liquidator so appointed (here referred to as "the interim liquidator") continues in office until another person becomes liquidator in his place under this section or the next.

(3)   The interim liquidator shall (subject to the next subsection) as soon as practicable in the period of 28 days beginning with the day on which the winding-up order was made or such longer period as the court may allow, summon separate meetings of the limited liability partnership's creditors and contributories for the purpose of choosing a person (who may be the person who is the interim liquidator) to be liquidator of the limited liability partnership in place of the interim liquidator.

(4)   If it appears to the interim liquidator, in any case where a limited liability partnership is being wound up on grounds including its inability to pay its debts, that it would be inappropriate to summon under subsection (3) a meeting of the limited liability partnership's contributories, he may summon only a meeting of the limited liability partnership's creditors for the purpose mentioned in that subsection.

(5)   If one or more meetings are held in pursuance of this section but no person is appointed or nominated by the meeting or meetings, the interim liquidator shall make a report to the court which shall appoint either the interim liquidator or some other person to be liquidator of the limited liability partnership.

(6)   A person who becomes liquidator of the limited liability partnership in place of the interim liquidator shall, unless he is appointed by the court, forthwith notify the court of that fact.

139 Choice of liquidator at meetings of creditors and contributories

(1)   This section applies where a limited liability partnership is being wound up by the court and separate meetings of the limited liability partnership's creditors and contributories are summoned for the purpose of choosing a person to be liquidator of the limited liability partnership.

(2)   The creditors and the contributories at their respective meetings may nominate a person to be liquidator.

(3)   The liquidator shall be the person nominated by the creditors or, where no person has been so nominated, the person (if any) nominated by the contributories.

(4)   In the case of different persons being nominated, any contributory or creditor may, within seven days after the date on which the nomination was made by the creditors, apply to the court for an order either–
    (a)   appointing the person nominated as liquidator by the contributories to be a liquidator instead of, or jointly with, the person nominated by the creditors; or
    (b)   appointing some other person to be liquidator instead of the person nominated by the creditors.

140 Appointment by the court following administration or voluntary arrangement

(1)   Where a winding-up order is made immediately upon the discharge of an administration order, the court may appoint as liquidator of the limited liability

partnership the person who has ceased on the discharge of the administration order to be the administrator of the limited liability partnership.

(2)　Where a winding-up order is made at a time when there is a supervisor of a voluntary arrangement approved in relation to the limited liability partnership under Part I, the court may appoint as liquidator of the limited liability partnership the person who is the supervisor at the time when the winding-up order is made.

(3)　Where the court makes an appointment under this section, the official receiver does not become the liquidator as otherwise provided by section 136(2), and he has no duty under section 136(5)(a) or (b) in respect of the summoning of creditors' or contributories' meetings.

141 Liquidation committee (England and Wales)

(1)　Where a winding-up order has been made by the court in England and Wales and separate meetings of creditors and contributories have been summoned for the purpose of choosing a person to be liquidator, those meetings may establish a committee ("the liquidation committee") to exercise the functions conferred on it by or under this Act.

(2)　The liquidator (not being the official receiver) may at any time, if he thinks fit, summon separate general meetings of the limited liability partnership's creditors and contributories for the purpose of determining whether such a committee should be established and, if it is so determined, of establishing it.
The liquidator (not being the official receiver) shall summon such a meeting if he is requested, in accordance with the rules, to do so by one-tenth, in value, of the limited liability partnership's creditors.

(3)　Where meetings are summoned under this section, or for the purpose of choosing a person to be liquidator, and either the meeting of creditors or the meeting of contributories decides that a liquidation committee should be established, but the other meeting does not so decide or decides that a committee should not be established, the committee shall be established in accordance with the rules, unless the court otherwise orders.

(4)　The liquidation committee is not to be able or required to carry out its functions at any time when the official receiver is liquidator; but at any such time its functions are vested in the Secretary of State except to the extent that the rules otherwise provide.

(5)　Where there is for the time being no liquidation committee, and the liquidator is a person other than the official receiver, the functions of such a committee are vested in the Secretary of State except to the extent that the rules otherwise provide.

142 Liquidation committee (Scotland)

(1)　Where a winding-up order has been made by the court in Scotland and separate meetings of creditors and contributories have been summoned for the purpose of choosing a person to be liquidator or, under section 138(4), only a meeting of creditors has been summoned for that purpose, those meetings or (as the case may be) that meeting may establish a committee ("the liquidation committee") to exercise the functions conferred on it by or under this Act.

(2)   The liquidator may at any time, if he thinks fit, summon separate general meetings of the limited liability partnership's creditors and contributories for the purpose of determining whether such a committee should be established and, if it is so determined, of establishing it.

(3)   The liquidator, if appointed by the court otherwise than under section 139(4)(a), is required to summon meetings under subsection (2) if he is requested, in accordance with the rules, to do so by one-tenth, in value, of the limited liability partnership's creditors.

(4)   Where meetings are summoned under this section, or for the purpose of choosing a person to be liquidator, and either the meeting of creditors or the meeting of contributories decides that a liquidation committee should be established, but the other meeting does not so decide or decides that a committee should not be established, the committee shall be established in accordance with the rules, unless the court otherwise orders.

(5)   Where in the case of any winding up there is for the time being no liquidation committee, the functions of such a committee are vested in the court except to the extent that the rules otherwise provide.

(6)   In addition to the powers and duties conferred and imposed on it by this Act, a liquidation committee has such of the powers and duties of commissioners in a sequestration as may be conferred and imposed on such committees by the rules.

143 General functions in winding up by the court

(1)   The functions of the liquidator of a limited liability partnership which is being wound up by the court are to secure that the assets of the limited liability partnership are got in, realised and distributed to the limited liability partnership's creditors and, if there is a surplus, to the persons entitled to it.

(2)   It is the duty of the liquidator of a limited liability partnership which is being wound up by the court in England and Wales, if he is not the official receiver–
    (a)   to furnish the official receiver with such information,
    (b)   to produce to the official receiver, and permit inspection by the official receiver of, such books, papers and other records, and
    (c)   to give the official receiver such other assistance,
as the official receiver may reasonably require for the purposes of carrying out his functions in relation to the winding up.

144 Custody of limited liability partnership's property

(1)   When a winding-up order has been made, or where a provisional liquidator has been appointed, the liquidator or the provisional liquidator (as the case may be)

shall take into his custody or under his control all the property and things in action to which the limited liability partnership is or appears to be entitled.

(2) In a winding up by the court in Scotland, if and so long as there is no liquidator, all the property of the limited liability partnership is deemed to be in the custody of the court.

145 Vesting of limited liability partnership property in liquidator

(1) When a limited liability partnership is being wound up by the court, the court may on the application of the liquidator by order direct that all or any part of the property of whatsoever description belonging to the limited liability partnership or held by trustees on its behalf shall vest in the liquidator by his official name; and thereupon the property to which the order relates vests accordingly.

(2) The liquidator may, after giving such indemnity (if any) as the court may direct, bring or defend in his official name any action or other legal proceeding which relates to that property or which it is necessary to bring or defend for the purpose of effectually winding up the limited liability partnership and recovering its property.

146 Duty to summon final meeting

(1) Subject to the next subsection, if it appears to the liquidator of a limited liability partnership which is being wound by the court that the winding up of the limited liability partnership is for practical purposes complete and the liquidator is not the official receiver, the liquidator shall summon a final general meeting of the limited liability partnership's creditors which–
 (a) shall receive the liquidator's report of the winding up, and
 (b) shall determine whether the liquidator should have his release under section 174 in Chapter VII of this Part.

(2) The liquidator may, if he thinks fit, give the notice summoning the final general meeting at the same time as giving notice of any final distribution of the limited liability partnership's property but, if summoned for an earlier date, that meeting shall be adjourned (and, if necessary, further adjourned) until a date on which the liquidator is able to report to the meeting that the winding up of the limited liability partnership is for practical purposes complete.

(3) In the carrying out of his functions in the winding up it is the duty of the liquidator to retain sufficient sums from the limited liability partnership's property to cover the expenses of summoning and holding the meeting required by this section.

147 Power to stay or sist winding up

(1) The court may at any time after an order for winding up, on the application either of the liquidator or the official receiver or any creditor or contributory, and on proof to the satisfaction of the court that all proceedings in the winding up ought to

be stayed or sisted, make an order staying or sisting the proceedings, either altogether or for a limited time, on such terms and conditions as the court thinks fit.

(2)   The court may, before making an order, require the official receiver to furnish to it a report with respect to any facts or matters which are in his opinion relevant to the application.

(3)   A copy of every order made under this section shall forthwith be forwarded by the limited liability partnership, or otherwise as may be prescribed, to the registrar of companies, who shall enter it in his records relating to the limited liability partnership.

148 Settlement of list of contributories and application of assets

(1)   As soon as may be after making a winding-up order, the court shall settle a list of contributories, ... and shall cause the limited liability partnership's assets to be collected, and applied in discharge of its liabilities.

(2)   If it appears to the court that it will not be necessary to make calls on or adjust the rights of contributories, the court may dispense with the settlement of a list of contributories.

(3)   In settling the list, the court shall distinguish between persons who are contributories in their own right and persons who are contributories as being representatives of or liable for the debts of others.

149 Debts due from contributory to limited liability partnership

(1)   The court may, at any time after making a winding-up order, make an order on any contributory for the time being on the list of contributories to pay, in manner directed by the order, any money due from him (or from the estate of the person who he represents) to the limited liability partnership, exclusive of any money payable by him or the estate by virtue of any call in pursuance of ... this Act.

(2)   ...

(3)   In the case of any limited liability partnership ... when all the creditors are paid in full (together with interest at the official rate), any money due on any account whatever to a contributory from the limited liability partnership may be allowed to him by way of set-off against any subsequent call.

150 Power to make calls

(1)   The court may, at any time after making a winding-up order, and either before or after it has ascertained the sufficiency of the limited liability partnership's assets, make calls on all or any of the contributories for the time being settled on the list of the contributories to the extent of their liability, for payment of any money which the court considers necessary to satisfy the limited liability partnership's debts and liabilities, and the expenses of winding up, and for the

adjustment of the rights of the contributories among themselves, and make an order for payment of any calls so made.

(2)   In making a call the court may take into consideration the probability that some of the contributories may partly or wholly fail to pay it.

151 Payment into bank of money due to limited liability partnership

(1)   The court may order any contributory, purchaser or other person from whom money is due to the limited liability partnership to pay the amount due into the Bank of England (or any branch of it) to the account of the liquidator instead of to the liquidator, and such an order may be enforced in the same manner as if it had directed payment to the liquidator.

(2)   All money and securities paid or delivered into the Bank of England (or branch) in the event of a winding up by the court are subject in all respects to the orders of the court.

152 Order on contributory to be conclusive evidence

(1)   An order made by the court on a contributory is conclusive evidence that the money (if any) thereby appearing to be due or ordered to be paid is due, but subject to any right of appeal.

(2)   All other pertinent matters stated in the order are to be taken as truly stated as against all persons and in all proceedings except proceedings in Scotland against the heritable estate of a deceased contributory; and in that case the order is only prima facie evidence for the purpose of charging his heritable estate, unless his heirs or legatees of heritage were on the list of contributories at the time of the order being made.

153 Power to exclude creditors not proving in time

The court may fix a time or times within which creditors are to prove their debts or claims or to be excluded from the benefit of any distribution made before those debts are proved.

154 Adjustment of rights of contributories

The court shall adjust the rights of the contributories among themselves and distribute any surplus among the persons entitled to it.

155 Inspection of books by creditors, etc

(1)   The court may, at any time after making a winding-up order, make such order for inspection of the limited liability partnership's books and papers by creditors and contributories as the court thinks just; and any books and papers in the limited liability partnership's possession may be inspected by creditors and contributories accordingly, but not further or otherwise.

(2)   Nothing in this section excludes or restricts any statutory rights of a government department or person acting under the authority of a government department.

(3)   For the purposes of subsection (2) above, references to a government department shall be construed as including references to any part of the Scottish Administration.

156 Payment of expenses of winding up

The court may, in the event of the assets being insufficient to satisfy the liabilities, make an order as to the payment out of the assets of the expenses incurred in the winding up in such order of priority as the court thinks just.

157 Attendance at limited liability partnership meetings (Scotland)

In the winding up by the court of a limited liability partnership registered in Scotland, the court has power to require the attendance of any member of the limited liability partnership at any meeting of creditors or of contributories, or of a liquidation committee, for the purpose of giving information as to the trade, dealings, affairs or property of the limited liability partnership.

158 Power to arrest absconding contributory

The court, at any time either before or after making a winding-up order, on proof of probable cause for believing that a contributory is about to quit the United Kingdom or otherwise to abscond or to remove or conceal any of his property for the purpose of evading payment of calls, may cause the contributory to be arrested and his books and papers and movable personal property to be seized and him and them to be kept safely until such time as the court may order.

159 Powers of court to be cumulative

Powers conferred by this Act and the Companies Act on the court are in addition to, and not in restriction of, any existing powers of instituting proceedings against a contributory or debtor of the limited liability partnership, or the estate of any contributory or debtor, for the recovery of any call or other sums.

160 Delegation of powers to liquidator (England and Wales)

(1)   Provision may be made by rules for enabling or requiring all or any of the powers and duties conferred and imposed on the court in England and Wales by the Companies Act and this Act in respect of the following matters–
    (a)   the holding and conducting of meetings to ascertain the wishes of creditors and contributories,
    (b)   the settling of lists of contributories ... where required, and the collection and application of the assets,
    (c)   the payment, delivery, conveyance, surrender or transfer of money, property, books or papers to the liquidator,

(d)   the making of calls,

(e)   the fixing of a time within which debts and claims must be proved,

to be exercised or performed by the liquidator as an officer of the court, and subject to the court's control.

[(2)   But the liquidator shall not make any call without the special leave of the court or the sanction of the liquidation committee.]

161 Orders for calls on contributories (Scotland)

(1)   In Scotland, where an order, interlocutor or decree has been made for winding up a limited liability partnership by the court, it is competent to the court, on production by the liquidators of a list certified by them of the names of the contributories liable in payment of any calls, and of the amount due by each contributory, and of the date when that amount became due, to pronounce forthwith a decree against those contributories for payment of the sums so certified to be due, with interest from that date until payment (at 5 per cent per annum) in the same way and to the same effect as if they had severally consented to registration for execution, on a charge of six days, of a legal obligation to pay those calls and interest.

(2)   The decree may be extracted immediately, and no suspension of it is competent, except on caution or consignation, unless with special leave of the court.

162 Appeals from orders in Scotland

(1)   Subject to the provisions of this section and to rules of court, an appeal from any order or decision made or given in the winding up of a limited liability partnership by the court in Scotland under this Act lies in the same manner and subject to the same conditions as an appeal from an order or decision of the court in cases within its ordinary jurisdiction.

(2)   In regard to orders or judgments pronounced by the judge acting as vacation judge–

(a)   none of the orders specified in Part I of Schedule 3 to this Act are subject to review, reduction, suspension or stay of execution, and

(b)   every other order or judgment (except as mentioned below) may be submitted to review by the Inner House by reclaiming motion enrolled within 14 days from the date of the order or judgment.

(3)   However, an order being one of those specified in Part II of that Schedule shall, from the date of the order and notwithstanding that it has been submitted to review as above, be carried out and receive effect until the Inner House have disposed of the matter.

(4)   In regard to orders or judgments pronounced in Scotland by a Lord Ordinary before whom proceedings in a winding up are being taken, any such order or judgment may be submitted to review by the Inner House by reclaiming motion enrolled within 14 days from its date; but should it not be so submitted to review

during session, the provisions of this section in regard to orders or judgments pronounced by the judge acting as vacation judge apply.

(5)   Nothing in this section affects provisions of the Companies Act or this Act in reference to decrees in Scotland for payment of calls in the winding up of limited liability partnerships, whether voluntary or by the court.

CHAPTER VII

LIQUIDATORS

163 Style and title of liquidators

The liquidator of a limited liability partnership shall be described–
  (a)   where a person other than the official receiver is liquidator, by the style of "the liquidator" of the particular limited liability partnership, or
  (b)   where the official receiver is liquidator, by the style of "the official receiver and liquidator" of the particular limited liability partnership;
and in neither case shall he be described by an individual name.

164 Corrupt inducement affecting appointment

A person who gives, or agrees or offers to give, to any member or creditor of a limited liability partnership any valuable consideration with a view to securing his own appointment or nomination, or to securing or preventing the appointment or nomination of some person other than himself, as the limited liability partnership's liquidator is liable to a fine.

165 Voluntary winding up

(1)   This section has effect where a limited liability partnership is being wound up voluntarily, but subject to section 166 below in the case of a creditors' voluntary winding up.

(2)   The liquidator may–
  (a)   in the case of a member's voluntary winding up, with the sanction of [a determination by a meeting of the members of the limited liability partnership], and
  (b)   in the case of a creditors' voluntary winding up, with the sanction of the court or the liquidation committee (or, if there is no such committee, a meeting of the limited liability partnership's creditors),
exercise any of the powers specified in Part I of Schedule 4 to this Act (payment of debts, compromise of claims, etc.).

(3)   The liquidator may, without sanction, exercise either of the powers specified in Part II of that Schedule (institution and defence of proceedings; carrying on the business of the limited liability partnership) and any of the general powers specified in Part III of that Schedule.

(4)   The liquidator may–

(a) exercise the court's power of settling a list of contributories (which list is prima facie evidence of the liability of the persons named in it to be contributories),

(b) exercise the court's power of making calls,

[(c) summon meetings of the members of the limited liability partnership for the purpose of obtaining their sanction or for any other purpose he may think fit.]

[(4A) Subsections (3) and (4) of section 92 shall apply for the purposes of this section as they apply for the purposes of that section.]

(5) The liquidator shall pay the limited liability partnership's debts and adjust the rights of the contributories among themselves.

(6) Where the liquidator in exercise of the powers conferred on him by this Act disposes of any property of the limited liability partnership to a person who is connected with the limited liability partnership (within the meaning of section 249 in Part VII), he shall, if there is for the time being a liquidation committee, give notice to the committee of that exercise of his powers.

166 Creditors' voluntary winding up

(1) This section applies where, in the case of a creditors' voluntary winding up, a liquidator has been nominated by the limited liability partnership.

(2) The powers conferred on the liquidator by section 165 shall not be exercised, except with the sanction of the court, during the period before the holding of the creditors' meeting under section 98 in Chapter IV.

(3) Subsection (2) does not apply in relation to the power of the liquidator–

(a) to take into his custody or under his control all the property to which the limited liability partnership is or appears to be entitled;

(b) to dispose of perishable goods and other goods the value of which is likely to diminish if they are not immediately disposed of; and

(c) to do all such other things as may be necessary for the protection of the limited liability partnership's assets.

(4) The liquidator shall attend the creditors' meeting held under section 98 and shall report to the meeting on any exercise by him of his powers (whether or not under this section or under section 112 or 165).

(5) If default is made–

(a) by the limited liability partnership in complying with subsection (1) or (2) of section 98, or

(b) by the [designated members] in complying with subsection (1) or (2) of section 99,

the liquidator shall, within seven days of the relevant day, apply to the court for directions as to the manner in which that default is to be remedied.

(6)   "The relevant day" means the day on which the liquidator was nominated by the limited liability partnership or the day on which he first became aware of the default, whichever is the later.

(7)   If the liquidator without reasonable excuse fails to comply with this section, he is liable to a fine.

167 Winding up by the court

(1)   Where a limited liability partnership is being wound up by the court, the liquidator may–
  (a) with the sanction of the court or the liquidation committee, exercise any of the powers specified in Parts I and II of Schedule 4 to this Act (payment of debts; compromise of claims, etc; institution and defence of proceedings; carrying on of the business of the limited liability partnership), and
  (b) with or without that sanction, exercise any of the general powers specified in Part III of that Schedule.

(2)   Where the liquidator (not being the official receiver), in exercise of the powers conferred on him by this Act–
  (a) disposes of any property of the limited liability partnership to a person who is connected with the limited liability partnership (within the meaning of section 249 in Part VII), or
  (b) employs a solicitor to assist him in the carrying out of his functions,
he shall, if there is for the time being a liquidation committee, give notice to the committee of that exercise of his powers.

(3)   The exercise by the liquidator in a winding up by the court of the powers conferred by this section is subject to the control of the court, and any creditor or contributory may apply to the court with respect to any exercise or proposed exercise of any of those powers.

168 Supplementary powers (England and Wales)

(1)   This section applies in the case of a limited liability partnership which is being wound up by the court in England and Wales.

(2)   The liquidator may summon general meetings of the creditors or contributories for the purpose of ascertaining their wishes; and it is his duty to summon meetings at such times as the creditors or contributories by resolution (either at the meeting appointing the liquidator or otherwise) may direct, or whenever requested in writing to do so by one-tenth in value of the creditors or contributories (as the case may be).

(3)   The liquidator may apply to the court (in the prescribed manner) for directions in relation to any particular matter arising in the winding up.

(4)   Subject to the provisions of this Act, the liquidator shall use his own discretion in the management of the assets and their distribution among the creditors.

(5)   If any person is aggrieved by an act or decision of the liquidator, that person may apply to the court; and the court may confirm, reverse or modify the act or decision complained of, and make such order in the case as it thinks just.

(5A)   Where at any time after a winding-up petition has been presented to the court against any person (including an insolvent partnership or other body which may be wound up under Part V of the Act as an unregistered company), whether by virtue of the provisions of the Insolvent Partnerships Order 1994 or not, the attention of the court is drawn to the fact that the person in question is a member of an insolvent partnership, the court may make an order as to the future conduct of the insolvency proceedings and any such order may apply any provisions of that Order with any necessary modifications.

(5B)   Any order or directions under subsection (5A) may be made or given on the application of the official receiver, any responsible insolvency practitioner, the trustee of the partnership or any other interested person and may include provisions as to the administration of the joint estate of the partnership, and in particular how it and the separate estate of any member are to be administered.

(5C)   Where the court makes an order under section 72(1)(a) of the Financial Services Act 1986 or section 92(1)(a) of the Banking Act 1987 for the winding up of an insolvent partnership, the court may make an order as to the future conduct of the winding-up proceedings, and any such order may apply any provisions of the Insolvent Partnerships Order 1994 with any necessary modifications.

169 Supplementary powers (Scotland)

(1)   In the case of a winding up in Scotland, the court may provide by order that the liquidator may, where there is no liquidation committee, exercise any of the following powers, namely–
  (a)   to bring or defend any action or other legal proceeding in the name and on behalf of the limited liability partnership, or
  (b)   to carry on the business of the limited liability partnership so far as may be necessary for its beneficial winding up,
without the sanction or intervention of the court.

(2)   In a winding up by the court in Scotland, the liquidator has (subject to the rules) the same powers as a trustee on a bankrupt estate.

170 Enforcement of liquidator's duty to make returns, etc

(1)   If a liquidator who has made any default–
  (a)   in filing, delivering or making any return, account or other document, or
  (b)   in giving any notice which he is by law required to file, deliver, make or give,
fails to make good the default within 14 days after the service on him of a notice requiring him to do so, the court has the following powers.

(2)   On an application made by any creditor or contributory of the limited liability partnership, or by the registrar of companies, the court may make an order directing the liquidator to make good the default within such time as may be specified in the order.

(3)   The court's order may provide that all costs of and incidental to the application shall be borne by the liquidator.

(4)   Nothing in this section prejudices the operation of any enactment imposing penalties on a liquidator in respect of any such default as is mentioned above.

171 Removal, etc (voluntary winding up)

(1)   This section applies with respect to the removal from office and vacation of office of the liquidator of a limited liability partnership which is being wound up voluntarily.

(2)   Subject to the next subsection, the liquidator may be removed from office only by an order of the court or–
- [(a) in the case of a members' voluntary winding up, by a meeting of the members of the limited liability partnership summoned specially for that purpose, or]
- (b) in the case of a creditors' voluntary winding up, by a general meeting of the limited liability partnership's creditors summoned specially for that purpose in accordance with the rules.

(3)   Where the liquidator was appointed by the court under section 108 in Chapter V, a meeting such as is mentioned in subsection (2) above shall be summoned for the purpose of replacing him only if he thinks fit or the court so directs or the meeting is requested, in accordance with the rules–
- (a) in the case of a members' voluntary winding up, by members representing not less than one-half of the total voting rights of all the members having at the date of the request a right to vote at the meeting, or
- (b) in the case of a creditors' voluntary winding up, by not less than one-half, in value, of the limited liability partnership's creditors.

(4)   A liquidator shall vacate office if he ceases to be a person who is qualified to act as an insolvency practitioner in relation to the limited liability partnership.

(5)   A liquidator may, in the prescribed circumstances, resign his office by giving notice of his resignation to the registrar of companies.

(6)   Where–
- (a) in the case of a members' voluntary winding up, a [final meeting of the members of the limited liability partnership] has been held under section 94 in Chapter III, or
- (b) in the case of a creditors' voluntary winding up, [final meetings of the members of the limited liability partnership] and of the creditors have been held under section 106 in Chapter IV,

the liquidator whose report was considered at the meeting or meetings shall vacate office as soon as he has complied with subsection (3) of that section and has given notice to the registrar of companies that the meeting or meetings have been held and of the decisions (if any) of the meeting or meetings.

[(7)   Subsections (3) and (4) of section 92 shall apply for the purposes of this section as they apply for the purposes of that section.]

172 Removal, etc (winding up by the court)

(1)   This section applies with respect to the removal from office and vacation of office of the liquidator of a limited liability partnership which is being wound up by the court, or of a provisional liquidator.

(2)   Subject as follows, the liquidator may be removed from office only by an order of the court or by a general meeting of the limited liability partnership's creditors summoned specially for that purpose in accordance with the rules; and a provisional liquidator may be removed from office only by an order of the court.

(3)   Where–
    (a)   the official receiver is liquidator otherwise than in succession under section 136(3) to a person who held office as a result of a nomination by a meeting of the limited liability partnership's creditors or contributories, or
    (b)   the liquidator was appointed by the court otherwise than under section 139(4)(a) or 140(1), or was appointed by the Secretary of State,
a general meeting of the limited liability partnership's creditors shall be summoned for the purpose of replacing him only if he thinks fit, or the court so directs, or the meeting is requested, in accordance with the rules, by not less that one-quarter, in value, of the creditors.

(4)   If appointed by the Secretary of State, the liquidator may be removed from office by a direction of the Secretary of State.

(5)   A liquidator or provisional liquidator, not being the official receiver, shall vacate office if he ceases to be a person who is qualified to act as an insolvency practitioner in relation to the limited liability partnership.

(6)   A liquidator may, in the prescribed circumstances, resign his office by giving notice of his resignation to the court.

(7)   Where an order is made under section 204 (early dissolution in Scotland) for the dissolution of the limited liability partnership, the liquidator shall vacate office when the dissolution of the limited liability partnership takes effect in accordance with that section.

(8)   Where a final meeting has been held under section 146 (liquidator's report on completion of winding up), the liquidator whose report was considered at the meeting shall vacate office as soon as he has given notice to the court and the

registrar of companies that the meeting has been held and of the decisions (if any) of the meeting.

173 Release (voluntary winding up)

(1)   This section applies with respect to the release of the liquidator of a limited liability partnership which is being wound up voluntarily.

(2)   A person who has ceased to be a liquidator shall have his release with effect from the following time, that is to say–
  (a)   in the case of a person who has been removed from office [a meeting of the members of the limited liability partnership] or by a general meeting of the limited liability partnership's creditors that has not resolved against his release or who has died, the time at which notice is given to the registrar of companies in accordance with the rules that that person has ceased to hold office;
  (b)   in the case of a person who has been removed from office by a general meeting of the limited liability partnership's creditors that has resolved against his release, or by the court, or who has vacated office under section 171(4) above, such time as the Secretary of State may, on the application of that person, determine;
  (c)   in the case of a person who has resigned, such time as may be prescribed;
  (d)   in the case of a person who has vacated office under subsection (6)(a) of section 171, the time at which he vacated office;
  (e)   in the case of a person who has vacated office under subsection (6)(b) of that section–
    (i)   if the final meeting of the creditors referred to in that subsection has resolved against that person's release, such time as the Secretary of State may, on an application by that person, determine, and
    (ii) if that meeting has not resolved against that person's release, the time at which he vacated office.

(3)   In the application of subsection (2) to the winding up of a limited liability partnership registered in Scotland, the references to a determination by the Secretary of State as to the time from which a person who has ceased to be liquidator shall have his release are to be read as references to such a determination by the Accountant of Court.

(4)   Where a liquidator has his release under subsection (2), he is, with effect from the time specified in that subsection, discharged from all liability both in respect of acts or omissions of his in the winding up and otherwise in relation to his conduct as liquidator.
    But nothing in this section prevents the exercise, in relation to a person who has had his release under subsection (2), of the court's powers under section 212 of this Act (summary remedy against delinquent members, liquidators, etc.).

174 Release (winding up by the court)

(1)   This section applies with respect to the release of the liquidator of a limited liability partnership which is being wound up by the court, or of a provisional liquidator.

(2)   Where the official receiver has ceased to be liquidator and a person becomes liquidator in his stead, the official receiver has his release with effect from the following time, that is to say–
    (a)   in a case where that person was nominated by a general meeting of creditors or contributories, or was appointed by the Secretary of State, the time at which the official receiver gives notice to the court that he has been replaced;
    (b)   in a case where that person is appointed by the court, such time as the court may determine.

(3)   If the official receiver while he is a liquidator gives notice to the Secretary of State that the winding up is for practical purposes complete, he has his release with effect from such time as the Secretary of State may determine.

(4)   A person other than the official receiver who has ceased to be a liquidator has his release with effect from the following time, that is to say–
    (a)   in the case of a person who has been removed from office by a general meeting of creditors that has not resolved against his release or who has died, the time at which notice is given to the court in accordance with the rules that that person has ceased to hold office;
    (b)   in the case of a person who has been removed from office by a general meeting of creditors that has resolved against his release, or by the court or the Secretary of State, or who has vacated office under section 172(5) or (7), such time as the Secretary of State may, on an application by that person, determine;
    (c)   in the case of a person who has resigned, such time as may be prescribed;
    (d)   in the case of a person who has vacated office under section 172(8)–
       (i)   if the final meeting referred to in that subsection has resolved against that person's release, such time as the Secretary of State may, on an application by that person, determine, and
      (ii)   if that meeting has not so resolved, the time at which that person vacated office.

(5)   A person who has ceased to hold office as a provisional liquidator has his release with effect from such time as the court may, on an application by him, determine.

(6)   Where the official receiver or a liquidator or provisional liquidator has his release under this section, he is, with effect from the time specified in the preceding provisions of this section, discharged from all liability both in respect of acts or omissions of his in the winding up and otherwise in relation to his conduct as liquidator or provisional liquidator.
    But nothing in this section prevents the exercise, in relation to a person who has had his release under this section, of the court's powers under section 212 (summary remedy against delinquent members, liquidators, etc.).

(7)   In the application of this section to a case where the order for winding up has been made by the court in Scotland, the references to a determination by the Secretary of State as to the time from which a person who has ceased to be liquidator has his release are to such a determination by the Accountant of Court.

CHAPTER VIII
PROVISIONS OF GENERAL APPLICATION IN WINDING UP

175 Preferential debts (general provision)

(1) In a winding up the limited liability partnership's preferential debts (within the meaning given by section 386 in Part XII) shall be paid in priority to all other debts.

(2) Preferential debts–
(a) rank equally among themselves after the expenses of the winding up and shall be paid in full, unless the assets are insufficient to meet them, in which case they abate in equal proportions; and
(b) so far as the assets of the limited liability partnership available for payment of general creditors are insufficient to meet them, have priority over the claims of holders of debentures secured by, or holders of, any floating charge created by the limited liability partnership, and shall be paid accordingly out of any property comprised in or subject to that charge.

176 Preferential charge on goods distrained

(1) This section applies where a limited liability partnership is being wound up by the court in England and Wales, and is without prejudice to section 128 (avoidance of attachments, etc.).

(2) Where any person (whether or not a landlord or person entitled to rent) has distrained upon the goods or effects of the limited liability partnership in the period of three months ending with the date of the winding-up order, those goods or effects, or the proceeds of their sale, shall be charged for the benefit of the limited liability partnership with the preferential debts of the limited liability partnership to the extent that the limited liability partnership's property is for the time being insufficient for meeting them.

(3) Where by virtue of a charge under subsection (2) any person surrenders any goods or effects to a limited liability partnership or makes a payment to a limited liability partnership, that person ranks, in respect of the amount of the proceeds of sale of those goods or effects by the liquidator or (as the case may be) the amount of the payment, as a preferential creditor of the limited liability partnership, except as against so much of the limited liability partnership's property as is available for the payment of preferential creditors by virtue of the surrender or payment.

177 Power to appoint special manager

(1) Where a limited liability partnership has gone into liquidation or a provisional liquidator has been appointed, the court may, on an application under this section, appoint any person to be the special manager of the business or property of the limited liability partnership.

(2)   The application may be made by the liquidator or provisional liquidator in any case where it appears to him that the nature of the business or property of the limited liability partnership, or the interests of the limited liability partnership's creditors or contributories or members generally, require the appointment of another person to manage the limited liability partnership's business or property.

(3)   The special manager has such powers as may be entrusted to him by the court.

(4)   The court's power to entrust powers to the special manager includes power to direct that any provision of this Act that has effect in relation to the provisional liquidator or liquidator of a limited liability partnership shall have the like effect in relation to the special manager for the purposes of the carrying out by him of any of the functions of the provisional liquidator or liquidator.

(5)   The special manager shall–
    (a)   give such security or, in Scotland, caution as may be prescribed;
    (b)   prepare and keep such accounts as may be prescribed; and
    (c)   produce those accounts in accordance with the rules to the Secretary of State or to such other persons as may be prescribed.

178 Power to disclaim onerous property

(1)   This and the next two sections apply to a limited liability partnership that is being wound up in England and Wales.

(2)   Subject as follows, the liquidator may, by the giving of the prescribed notice, disclaim any onerous property and may do so notwithstanding that he has taken possession of it, endeavoured to sell it, or otherwise exercised rights of ownership in relation to it.

(3)   The following is onerous property for the purposes of this section–
    (a)   any unprofitable contract, and
    (b)   any other property of the limited liability partnership which is unsaleable or not readily saleable or is such that it may give rise to a liability to pay money or perform any other onerous act.

(4)   A disclaimer under this section–
    (a)   operates so as to determine, as from the date of the disclaimer, the rights, interests and liabilities of the limited liability partnership in or in respect of the property disclaimed; but
    (b)   does not, except so far as is necessary for the purpose of releasing the limited liability partnership from any liability, affect the rights or liabilities of any other person.

(5)   A notice of disclaimer shall not be given under this section in respect of any property if–
    (a)   a person interested in the property has applied in writing to the liquidator or one of his predecessors as liquidator requiring the liquidator or that predecessor to decide whether he will disclaim or not, and

(b) the period of 28 days beginning with the day on which that application was made, or such longer period as the court may allow, has expired without a notice of disclaimer having been given under this section in respect of that property.

(6) Any person sustaining loss or damage in consequence of the operation of a disclaimer under this section is deemed a creditor of the limited liability partnership to the extent of the loss or damage and accordingly may prove for the loss or damage in the winding up.

179 Disclaimer of leaseholds

(1) The disclaimer under section 178 of any property of a leasehold nature does not take effect unless a copy of the disclaimer has been served (so far as the liquidator is aware of their addresses) on every person claiming under the limited liability partnership as underlessee or mortgagee and either–
   (a) no application under section 181 below is made with respect to that property before the end of the period of 14 days beginning with the day on which the last notice served under this subsection was served; or
   (b) where such an application has been made, the court directs that the disclaimer shall take effect.

(2) Where the court gives a direction under subsection (1)(b it may also, instead of or in addition to any order it makes under section 181, make such orders with respect to fixtures, tenant's improvements and other matters arising out of the lease as it thinks fit.

180 Land subject to rentcharge

(1) The following applies where, in consequence of the disclaimer under section 178 of any land subject to a rentcharge, that land vests by operation of law in the Crown or any other person (referred to in the next subsection as "the proprietor").

(2) The proprietor and the successors in title of the proprietor are not subject to any personal liability in respect of any sums becoming due under the rentcharge except sums becoming due after the proprietor, or some person claiming under or through the proprietor, has taken possession or control of the land or has entered into occupation of it.

181 Powers of court (general)

(1) This section and the next apply where the liquidator has disclaimed property under section 178.

(2) An application under this section may be made to the court by–
   (a) any person who claims an interest in the disclaimed property, or
   (b) any person who is under any liability in respect of the disclaimed property, not being a liability discharged by the disclaimer.

(3)   Subject as follows, the court may on the application make an order, on such terms as it thinks fit, for the vesting of the disclaimed property in, or for its delivery to–
  (a) a person entitled to it or a trustee for such a person, or
  (b) a person subject to such a liability as is mentioned in subsection (2)(b) or a trustee for such a person.

(4)   The court shall not make an order under subsection (3)(b) except where it appears to the court that it would be just to do so for the purpose of compensating the person subject to the liability in respect of the disclaimer.

(5)   The effect of any order under this section shall be taken into account in assessing for the purpose of section 178(6) the extent of any loss or damage sustained by any person in consequence of the disclaimer.

(6)   An order under this section vesting property in any person need not be completed by conveyance, assignment or transfer.

182 Powers of court (leaseholds)

(1)   The court shall not make an order under section 181 vesting property of a leasehold nature in any person claiming under the limited liability partnership as underlessee or mortgagee except on terms making that person–
  (a) subject to the same liabilities and obligations as the limited liability partnership was subject to under the lease at the commencement of the winding up, or
  (b) if the court thinks fit, subject to the same liabilities and obligations as that person would be subject to if the lease had been assigned to him at the commencement of the winding up.

(2)   For the purposes of an order under section 181 relating to only part of any property comprised in a lease, the requirements of subsection (1) apply as if the lease comprised only the property to which the order relates.

(3)   Where subsection (1) applies and no person claiming under the limited liability partnership as underlessee or mortgagee is willing to accept an order under section 181 on the terms required by virtue of that subsection, the court may, by order under that section, vest the limited liability partnership's estate or interest in the property in any person who is liable (whether personally or in a representative capacity, and whether alone or jointly with the limited liability partnership) to perform the lessee's covenants in the lease.
    The court may vest that estate and interest in such a person freed and discharged from all estates, incumbrances and interests created by the limited liability partnership.

(4)   Where subsection (1) applies and a person claiming under the limited liability partnership as underlessee or mortgagee declines to accept an order under section 181, that person is excluded from all interest in the property.

183 Effect of execution or attachment (England and Wales)

(1)   Where a creditor has issued execution against the goods or land of a limited liability partnership or has attached any debt due to it, and the limited liability partnership is subsequently wound up, he is not entitled to retain the benefit of the execution or attachment against the liquidator unless he has completed the execution or attachment before the commencement of the winding up.

(2)   However–
  (a)   ...
  (b)   a person who purchases in good faith under a sale by the sheriff any goods of a limited liability partnership on which execution has been levied in all cases acquires a good title to them against the liquidator; and
  (c)   the rights conferred by subsection (1) on the liquidator may be set aside by the court in favour of the creditor to such extent and subject to such terms as the court thinks fit.

(3)   For the purposes of this Act–
  (a)   an execution against goods is completed by seizure and sale, or by the making of a charging order under section 1 of the Charging Orders Act 1979;
  (b)   an attachment of a debt is completed by receipt of the debt; and
  (c)   an execution against land is completed by seizure, by the appointment of a receiver, or by the making of a charging order under section 1 of the Act above-mentioned.

(4)   In this section "goods" includes all chattels personal; and "the sheriff" includes any officer charged with the execution of a writ or other process.

(5)   This section does not apply in the case of a winding up in Scotland.

184 Duties of sheriff (England and Wales)

(1)   The following applies where a limited liability partnership's goods are taken in execution and, before their sale or the completion of the execution (by the receipt or recovery of the full amount of the levy), notice is served on the sheriff that a provisional liquidator has been appointed or that a winding-up order has been made, or [the limited liability partnership has determined that it be wound up voluntarily].

(2)   The sheriff shall, on being so required, deliver the goods and any money seized or received in part satisfaction of the execution to the liquidator; but the costs of execution are a first charge on the goods or money so delivered, and the liquidator may sell the goods, or a sufficient part of them, for the purpose of satisfying the charge.

(3)   If under an execution in respect of a judgment for a sum exceeding £500 a limited liability partnership's goods are sold or money is paid in order to avoid sale, the sheriff shall deduct the costs of the execution from the proceeds of sale or the money paid and retain the balance for 14 days.

(4)   …

(5)   The rights conferred by this section on the liquidator may be set aside by the court in favour of the creditor to such extent and subject to such terms as the court thinks fit.

(6)   In this section, "goods" includes all chattels personal; and "the sheriff" includes any officer charged with the execution of a writ or other process.

(7)   The money sum for the time being specified in subsection (3) is subject to increase or reduction by order under section 416 in Part XV.

(8)   This section does not apply in the case of a winding up in Scotland.

185 Effect of diligence (Scotland)

(1)   In the winding up of a limited liability partnership registered in Scotland, the following provisions of the Bankruptcy (Scotland) Act 1985–
   (a)   subsections (1) to (6) of section 37 (effect of sequestration on diligence); and
   (b)   subsections (3),(4),(7) and (8) of section 39 (realisation of estate),
apply, so far as consistent with this Act, in like manner as they apply in the sequestration of a debtor's estate, with the substitutions specified below and with any other necessary modifications.

(2)   The substitutions to be made in those sections of the Act of 1985 are as follows–
   (a)   for references to the debtor, substitute references to the limited liability partnership;
   (b)   for references to the sequestration, substitute references to the winding up;
   (c)   for references to the date of sequestration, substitute references to the commencement of the winding up of the limited liability partnership; and
   (d)   for references to the permanent trustee, substitute references to the liquidator.

(3)   In this section, "the commencement of the winding up of the limited liability partnership" means, where it is being wound up by the court, the day on which the winding-up order is made.

(4)   This section, so far as relating to any estate or effects of the limited liability partnership situated in Scotland, applies in the case of a limited liability partnership registered in England and Wales as in the case of one registered in Scotland.

186 Rescission of contracts by the court

(1)   The court may, on the application of a person who is, as against the liquidator, entitled to the benefit or subject to the burden of a contract made with the limited liability partnership, make an order rescinding the contract on such terms

as to payment by or to either party of damages for the non-performance of the contract, or otherwise as the court thinks just.

(2)   Any damages payable under the order to such a person may be proved by him as a debt in the winding up.

187 ...

188 Notification that limited liability partnership is in liquidation

(1)   When a limited liability partnership is being wound up, whether by the court or voluntarily, every invoice, order for goods or business letter issued by or on behalf of the limited liability partnership, or a liquidator of the limited liability partnership, or a receiver or manager of the limited liability partnership's property, being a document on or in which the name of the limited liability partnership appears, shall contain a statement that the limited liability partnership is being wound up.

(2)   If default is made in complying with this section, the limited liability partnership and any of the following persons who knowingly and wilfully authorises or permits the default, namely, any member of the limited liability partnership, any liquidator of the limited liability partnership and any receiver or manager, is liable to a fine.

189 Interest on debts

(1)   In a winding up interest is payable in accordance with this section on any debt proved in the winding up, including so much of any such debt as represents interest on the remainder.

(2)   Any surplus remaining after the payment of the debts proved in a winding up shall, before being applied for any other purpose, be applied in paying interest on those debts in respect of the periods during which they have been outstanding since the limited liability partnership went into liquidation.

(3)   All interest under this section ranks equally, whether or not the debts on which it is payable rank equally.

(4)   The rate of interest payable under this section in respect of any debt ("the official rate" for the purposes of any provision of this Act in which that expression is used) is whichever is the greater of–
    (a)   the rate specified in section 17 of the Judgments Act 1838 on the day on which the limited liability partnership went into liquidation, and
    (b)   the rate applicable to that debt apart from the winding up.

(5)   In the application of this section to Scotland–
    (a)   references to a debt proved in a winding up have effect as references to a claim accepted in a winding up, and
    (b)   the reference to section 17 of the Judgments Act 1838 has effect as a reference to the rules.

190 Documents exempt from stamp duty

(1)   In the case of a winding up by the court, or of a creditors' voluntary winding up, the following has effect as regards exemption from duties chargeable under the enactments relating to stamp duties.

(2)   If the limited liability partnership is registered in England and Wales, the following documents are exempt from stamp duty–
   (a)   every assurance relating solely to freehold or leasehold property, or to any estate, right or interest in, any real or personal property, which forms part of the limited liability partnership's assets and which, after the execution of the assurance, either at law or in equity, is or remains part of those assets, and
   (b)   every writ, order, certificate, or other instrument or writing relating solely to the property of any limited liability partnership which is being wound up as mentioned in subsection (1), or to any proceeding under such a winding up.
   "Assurance" here includes deed, conveyance, assignment and surrender.

(3)   If the limited liability partnership is registered in Scotland, the following documents are exempt from stamp duty–
   (a)   every conveyance relating solely to property which forms part of the limited liability partnership's assets and which, after the execution of the conveyance, is or remains the limited liability partnership's property for the benefit of its creditors,
   (b)   any articles of roup or sale, submission and every other instrument and writing whatsoever relating solely to the limited liability partnership's property, and
   (c)   every deed or writing forming part of the proceedings in the winding up.
   "Conveyance" here includes assignation, instrument, discharge, writing and deed.

191 Limited liability partnership's books to be evidence

Where a limited liability partnership is being wound up, all books and papers of the limited liability partnership and of the liquidators are, as between the contributories of the limited liability partnership, prima facie evidence of the truth of all matters purporting to be recorded in them.

192 Information as to pending liquidations

(1)   If the winding up of a limited liability partnership is not concluded within one year after its commencement, the liquidator shall, at such intervals as may be prescribed, until the winding up is concluded, send to the registrar of companies a statement in the prescribed form and containing the prescribed particulars with respect to the proceedings in, and position of, the liquidation.

(2)   If a liquidator fails to comply with this section, he is liable to a fine and, for continued contravention, to a daily default fine.

193 Unclaimed dividends (Scotland)

(1)   The following applies where a limited liability partnership registered in Scotland has been wound up, and is about to be dissolved.

(2)   The liquidator shall lodge in an appropriate bank or institution as defined in section 73(1) of the Bankruptcy (Scotland) Act 1985 (not being a bank or institution in or of which the liquidator is acting partner, manager, agent or cashier) in the name of the Accountant of Court the whole unclaimed dividends and unapplied or undistributable balances, and the deposit receipts shall be transmitted to the Accountant of Court.

(3)   The provisions of section 58 of the Bankruptcy (Scotland) Act 1985 (so far as consistent with this Act and the Companies Act) apply with any necessary modifications to sums lodged in a bank or institution under this section as they apply to sums deposited under section 57 of the Act first mentioned.

194 Resolutions passed at adjourned meetings

Where a resolution is passed at an adjourned meeting of a limited liability partnership's creditors or contributories [or of the members of a limited liability partnership], the resolution is treated for all purposes as having been passed on the date on which it was in fact passed, and not as having been passed on any earlier date.

195 Meetings to ascertain wishes of creditors or contributories

(1)   The court may—
    (a)   as to all matters relating to the winding up of a limited liability partnership, have regard to the wishes of the creditors or contributories (as proved to it by any sufficient evidence), and
    (b)   if it thinks fit, for the purpose of ascertaining those wishes, direct meetings of the creditors or contributories to be called, held and conducted in such manner as the court directs, and appoint a person to act as chairman of any such meeting and report the result of it to the court.

(2)   In the case of creditors, regard shall be had to the value of each creditor's debt.

(3)   In the case of contributories, regard shall be had to the number of votes conferred on each contributory by the … limited liability partnership agreement.

196 Judicial notice of court documents

In all proceedings under this Part, all courts, judges and persons judicially acting, and all officers, judicial or ministerial, of any court, or employed in enforcing the process of any court shall take judicial notice—
    (a)   of the signature of any officer of the High Court or of a county court in England and Wales, or of the Court of Session or a sheriff court in Scotland, or of the High Court in Northern Ireland, and also

(b) of the official seal or stamp of the several offices of the High Court in England and Wales or Northern Ireland, or of the Court of Session, appended to or impressed on any document made, issued or signed under the provisions of this Act or the Companies Act, or any official copy of such a document.

197 Commission for receiving evidence

(1) When a limited liability partnership is wound up in England and Wales or in Scotland, the court may refer the whole or any part of the examination of witnesses–
  (a) to a specified county court in England and Wales, or
  (b) to the sheriff principal for a special sheriffdom in Scotland, or
  (c) to the High Court in Northern Ireland or a specified Northern Ireland County Court,
("specified" meaning specified in the order of the winding-up court).

(2) Any person exercising jurisdiction as a judge of the court to which the reference is made (or, in Scotland, the sheriff principal to whom it is made) shall then, by virtue of this section, be a commissioner for the purpose of taking the evidence of those witnesses.

(3) The judge or sheriff principal has in the matter referred the same power of summoning and examining witnesses, of requiring the production and delivery of documents, of punishing defaults by witnesses, and of allowing costs and expenses to witnesses, as the court which made the winding-up order.

These powers are in addition to any which the judge or sheriff principal might lawfully exercise apart from this section.

(4) The examination so taken shall be returned or reported to the court which made the order in such manner as that court requests.

(5) This section extends to Northern Ireland.

198 Court order for examination of persons in Scotland

(1) The court may direct the examination in Scotland of any person for the time being in Scotland (whether a contributory of the limited liability partnership or not), in regard to the trade, dealings, affairs or property of any limited liability partnership in course of being wound up, or of any person being a contributory of the limited liability partnership, so far as the limited liability partnership may be interested by reason of his being a contributory.

(2) The order or commission to take the examination shall be directed to the sheriff principal of the sheriffdom in which the person to be examined is residing or happens to be for the time; and the sheriff principal shall summon the person to appear before him at a time and place to be specified in the summons for examination on oath as a witness or as a haver, and to produce any books or papers called for which are in his possession or power.

(3)   The sheriff principal may take the examination either orally or on written interrogatories, and shall report the same in writing in the usual form to the court, and shall transmit with the report the books and papers produced, if the originals are required and specified by the order or commission, or otherwise copies or extracts authenticated by the sheriff.

(4)   If a person so summoned fails to appear at the time and place specified, or refuses to be examined or to make the production required, the sheriff principal shall proceed against him as a witness or haver duly cited; and failing to appear or refusing to give evidence or make production may be proceeded against by the law of Scotland.

(5)   The sheriff principal is entitled to such fees, and the witness is entitled to such allowances, as sheriffs principal when acting as commissioners under appointment from the Court or Session and as witnesses and havers are entitled to in the like cases according to the law and practice of Scotland.

(6)   If any objection is stated to the sheriff principal by the witness, either on the ground of his incompetency as a witness, or as to the production required, or on any other ground, the sheriff principal may, if he thinks fit, report the objection to the court, and suspend the examination of the witness until it has been disposed of by the court.

199 Costs of application for leave to proceed (Scottish limited liability partnerships)

Where a petition or application for leave to proceed with an action or proceeding against a limited liability partnership which is being wound up in Scotland is unopposed and is granted by the court, the costs of the petition or application shall, unless the court otherwise directs, be added to the amount of the petitioner's or applicant's claim against the limited liability partnership.

200 Affidavits etc in United Kingdom and overseas

(1)   An affidavit required to be sworn under or for the purposes of this Part may be sworn in the United Kingdom, or elsewhere in Her Majesty's dominions, before any court, judge or person lawfully authorised to take and receive affidavits, or before any of Her Majesty's consuls or vice-consuls in any place outside Her dominions.

(2)   All courts, judges, justices, commissioners and persons acting judicially shall take judicial notice of the seal or stamp or signature (as the case may be) of any such court, judge, person, consul or vice-consul attached, appended or subscribed to any such affidavit, or to any other document to be used for the purposes of this Part.

CHAPTER IX
DISSOLUTION OF LIMITED LIABILITY PARTNERSHIPS AFTER
WINDING UP

201 Dissolution (voluntary winding up)

(1)   This section applies, in the case of a limited liability partnership wound up voluntarily, where the liquidator has sent to the registrar of companies his final account and return under section 94 (members' voluntary) or section 106 (creditors' voluntary).

(2)   The registrar on receiving the account and return shall forthwith register them; and on the expiration of three months from the registration of the return the limited liability partnership is deemed to be dissolved.

(3)   However, the court may, on the application of the liquidator or any other person who appears to the court to be interested, make an order deferring the date at which the dissolution of the limited liability partnership is to take effect for such time as the court thinks fit.

(4)   It is the duty of the person on whose application an order of the court under this section is made within seven days after the making of the order to deliver to the registrar an office copy of the order for registration; and if that person fails to do so he is liable to a fine and, for continued contravention, to a daily default fine.

202 Early dissolution (England and Wales)

(1)   This section applies where an order for the winding up of a limited liability partnership has been made by the court in England and Wales.

(2)   The official receiver, if–
    (a)   he is the liquidator of the limited liability partnership, and
    (b)   it appears to him–
        (i)   that the realisable assets of the limited liability partnership are insufficient to cover the expenses of the winding up, and
        (ii)   that the affairs of the limited liability partnership do not require any further investigation,
may at any time apply to the registrar of companies for the early dissolution of the limited liability partnership.

(3)   Before making that application, the official receiver shall give not less than 28 days' notice of his intention to do so to the limited liability partnership's creditors and contributories and, if there is an administrative receiver of the limited liability partnership, to that receiver.

(4)   With the giving of that notice the official receiver ceases (subject to any directions under the next section) to be required to perform any duties imposed on him in relation to the limited liability partnership, its creditors or contributories by virtue of any provision of this Act, apart from a duty to make an application under subsection (2) of this section.

(5)   On the receipt of the official receiver's application under subsection (2) the registrar shall forthwith register it and, at the end of the period of three months beginning with the day of the registration of the application, the limited liability partnership shall be dissolved.

However, the Secretary of State may, on the application of the official receiver or any other person who appears to the Secretary of State to be interested, give directions under section 203 at any time before the end of that period.

203 Consequence of notice under s 202

(1)   Where a notice has been given under section 202(3), the official receiver or any creditor or contributory of the limited liability partnership, or the administrative receiver of the limited liability partnership(if there is one) may apply to the Secretary of State for directions under this section.

(2)   The grounds on which that application may be made are–
(a)   that the realisable assets of the limited liability partnership are sufficient to cover the expenses of the winding up;
(b)   that the affairs of the limited liability partnership do require further investigation; or
(c)   that for any other reason the early dissolution of the limited liability partnership is inappropriate.

(3)   Directions under this section–
(a)   are directions making such provision as the Secretary of State thinks fit for enabling the winding up of the limited liability partnership to proceed as if no notice had been given under section 202(3), and
(b)   may, in the case of an application under section 202(5), include a direction deferring the date at which the dissolution of the limited liability partnership is to take effect for such period as the Secretary of State thinks fit.

(4)   An appeal to the court lies from any decision of the Secretary of State on an application for directions under this section.

(5)   It is the duty of the person on whose application any directions are given under this section, or in whose favour an appeal with respect to an application for such directions is determined, within seven days after the giving of the directions or the determination of the appeal, to deliver to the registrar of companies for registration such a copy of the directions or determination as is prescribed.

(6)   If a person without reasonable excuse fails to deliver a copy as required by subsection (5), he is liable to a fine and, for continued contravention, to a daily default fine.

204 Early dissolution (Scotland)

(1)   This section applies where a winding-up order has been made by the court in Scotland.

(2)   If after a meeting or meetings under section 138 (appointment of liquidator in Scotland) it appears to the liquidator that the realisable assets of the limited liability partnership are insufficient to cover the expenses of the winding up, he may apply to the court for an order that the limited liability partnership be dissolved.

(3)   Where the liquidator makes that application, if the court is satisfied that the realisable assets of the limited liability partnership are insufficient to cover the expenses of the winding up and it appears to the court appropriate to do so, the court shall make an order that the limited liability partnership be dissolved in accordance with this section.

(4)   A copy of the order shall within 14 days from its date be forwarded by the liquidator to the registrar of companies, who shall forthwith register it; and, at the end of the period of three months beginning with the day of the registration of the order, the limited liability partnership shall be dissolved.

(5)   The court may, on an application by any person who appears to the court to have an interest, order that the date at which the dissolution of the limited liability partnership is to take effect shall be deferred for such period as the court thinks fit.

(6)   It is the duty of the person on whose application an order is made under subsection (5), within seven days after the making of the order, to deliver to the registrar of companies such a copy of the order as is prescribed.

(7)   If the liquidator without reasonable excuse fails to comply with the requirements of subsection (4), he is liable to a fine and, for continued contravention, to a daily default fine.

(8)   If a person without reasonable excuse fails to deliver a copy as required by subsection (6), he is liable to a fine and, for continued contravention, to a daily default fine.

205 Dissolution otherwise than under ss 202–204

(1)   This section applies where the registrar of companies receives–
   (a)   a notice served for the purposes of section 172(8) (final meeting of creditors and vacation of office by liquidator), or
   (b)   a notice from the official receiver that the winding up of a limited liability partnership by the court is complete.

(2)   The registrar shall, on receipt of the notice, forthwith register it; and, subject as follows, at the end of the period of three months beginning with the day of the registration of the notice, the limited liability partnership shall be dissolved.

(3)   The Secretary of State may, on the application of the official receiver or any other person who appears to the Secretary of State to be interested, give a direction deferring the date at which the dissolution of the limited liability partnership is to take effect for such period as the Secretary of State thinks fit.

(4)   An appeal to the court lies from any decision of the Secretary of State on an application for a direction under subsection (3).

(5)   Subsection (3) does not apply in a case where the winding-up order was made by the court in Scotland, but in such a case the court may, on an application by any person appearing to the court to have an interest, order that the date at which the dissolution of the limited liability partnership is to take effect shall be deferred for such period as the court thinks fit.

(6)   It is the duty of the person–
    (a)   on whose application a direction is given under subsection (3);
    (b)   in whose favour an appeal with respect to an application for such a direction is determined; or
    (c)   on whose application an order is made under subsection (5),
within seven days after the giving of the direction, the determination of the appeal or the making of the order, to deliver to the registrar for registration such a copy of the direction, determination or order as is prescribed.

(7)   If a person without reasonable excuse fails to deliver a copy as required by subsection (6), he is liable to a fine and, for continued contravention to a daily default fine.

CHAPTER X

MALPRACTICE BEFORE AND DURING LIQUIDATION; PENALISATION OF LIMITED LIABILITY PARTNERSHIPS AND LIMITED LIABILITY PARTNERSHIP OFFICERS; INVESTIGATIONS AND PROSECUTIONS

206 Fraud, etc in anticipation of winding up

(1)   When a limited liability partnership is ordered to be wound up by the court, or [makes a determination that it be wound up voluntarily], any person, being a past or present member of the limited liability partnership, is deemed to have committed an offence if, within the twelve months immediately preceding the commencement of the winding up, he has–
    (a)   concealed any part of the limited liability partnership's property to the value of £500 or more, or concealed any debt due to or from the limited liability partnership, or
    (b)   fraudulently removed any part of the limited liability partnership's property to the value of £500 or more, or
    (c)   concealed, destroyed, mutilated or falsified any book or paper affecting or relating to the limited liability partnership's property or affairs, or
    (d)   made any false entry in any book or paper affecting or relating to the limited liability partnership's property or affairs, or
    (e)   fraudulently parted with, altered or made any omission in any document affecting or relating to the limited liability partnership's property or affairs, or
    (f)   pawned, pledged or disposed of any property of the limited liability partnership which has been obtained on credit and has not been paid

for (unless the pawning, pledging or disposal was in the ordinary way of the limited liability partnership's business).

(2)   Such a person is deemed to have committed an offence if within the period above mentioned he has been privy to the doing by others of any of the things mentioned in paragraphs (c),(d) and (e) of subsection (1); and he commits an offence if, at any time after the commencement of the winding up, he does any of the things mentioned in paragraphs (a) to (f) of that subsection, or is privy to the doing by others of any of the things mentioned in paragraphs (c) to (e) of it.

(3)   For purposes of this section, "member" includes a shadow member.

(4)   It is a defence–
   (a)   for a person charged under paragraph (a) or (f) of subsection (1) (or under subsection (2) in respect of the things mentioned in either of those two paragraphs) to prove that he had no intent to defraud, and
   (b)   for a person charged under paragraph (c) or (d) of subsection (1) (or under subsection (2) in respect of the things mentioned in either of those two paragraphs) to prove that he had no intent to conceal the state of affairs of the limited liability partnership or to defeat the law.

(5)   Where a person pawns, pledges or disposes of any property in circumstances which amount to an offence under subsection (1)(f), every person who takes in pawn or pledge, or otherwise receives, the property knowing it to be pawned, pledged or disposed of in such circumstances, is guilty of an offence.

(6)   A person guilty of an offence under this section is liable to imprisonment or a fine, or both.

(7)   The money sums specified in paragraphs (a) and (b) of subsection (1) are subject to increase or reduction by order under section 416 in Part XV.

207 Transactions in fraud of creditors

(1)   When a limited liability partnership is ordered to be wound up by the court or [makes a determination that it be wound up voluntarily], a person is deemed to have committed an offence if he, being at the time a member of the limited liability partnership–
   (a)   has made or caused to be made any gift or transfer of, or charge on, or has caused or connived at the levying of any execution against, the limited liability partnership's property, or
   (b)   has concealed or removed any part of the limited liability partnership's property since, or within two months before, the date of any unsatisfied judgment or order for the payment of money obtained against the limited liability partnership.

(2)   A person is not guilty of an offence under this section–
   (a)   by reason of conduct constituting an offence under subsection (1)(a) which occurred more than five years before the commencement of the winding up, or

(b) if he proves that, at the time of the conduct constituting the offence, he had no intent to defraud the limited liability partnership's creditors.

(3) A person guilty of an offence under this section is liable to imprisonment or a fine, or both.

208 Misconduct in course of winding up

(1) When a limited liability partnership is being wound up, whether by the court or voluntarily, any person, being a past or present member of the limited liability partnership, commits an offence if he—

(a) does not to the best of his knowledge and belief fully and truly discover to the liquidator all the limited liability partnership's property, and how and to whom and for what consideration and when the limited liability partnership disposed of any part of that property (except such part as has been disposed of in the ordinary way of the limited liability partnership's business), or

(b) does not deliver up to the liquidator (or as he directs) all such part of the limited liability partnership's property as is in his custody or under his control, and which he is required by law to deliver up, or

(c) does not deliver up to the liquidator (or as he directs) all books and papers in his custody or under his control belonging to the limited liability partnership and which he is required by law to deliver up, or

(d) knowing or believing that a false debt has been proved by any person in the winding up, fails to inform the liquidator as soon as practicable, or

(e) after the commencement of the winding up, prevents the production of any book or paper affecting or relating to the limited liability partnership's property or affairs.

(2) Such a person commits an offence if after the commencement of the winding up he attempts to account for any part of the limited liability partnership's property by fictitious losses or expenses; and he is deemed to have committed that offence if he has so attempted at any meeting of the limited liability partnership's creditors within the twelve months immediately preceding the commencement of the winding up.

(3) For purposes of this section, "member" includes a shadow member.

(4) It is a defence—

(a) for a person charged under paragraph (a),(b) or (c) of subsection (1) to prove that he had no intent to defraud, and

(b) for a person charged under paragraph (e) of that subsection to prove that he had no intent to conceal the state of affairs of the limited liability partnership or to defeat the law.

(5) A person guilty of an offence under this section is liable to imprisonment or a fine, or both.

209 Falsification of limited liability partnership's books

(1)   When a limited liability partnership is being wound up, a member or contributory of the limited liability partnership commits an offence if he destroys, mutilates, alters or falsifies any books, papers or securities, or makes or is privy to the making of any false or fraudulent entry in any register, book of account or document belonging to the limited liability partnership with intent to defraud or deceive any person.

(2)   A person guilty of an offence under this section is liable to imprisonment or a fine, or both.

210 Material omissions from statement relating to limited liability partnership's affairs

(1)   When a limited liability partnership is being wound up, whether by the court or voluntarily, any person, being a past or present member of the limited liability partnership, commits an offence if he makes any material omission in any statement relating to the limited liability partnership's affairs.

(2)   When a limited liability partnership has been ordered to be wound up by the court, or [made a determination that it be wound up voluntarily], any such person is deemed to have committed that offence if, prior to the winding up, he has made any material omission in any such statement.

(3)   For purposes of this section, "member" includes a shadow member.

(4)   It is a defence for a person charged under this section to prove that he had no intent to defraud.

(5)   A person guilty of an offence under this section is liable to imprisonment or a fine, or both.

211 False representations to creditors

(1)   When a limited liability partnership is being wound up, whether by the court or voluntarily, any person, being a past or present member of the limited liability partnership–
  (a)   commits an offence if he makes any false representation or commits any other fraud for the purpose of obtaining the consent of the limited liability partnership's creditors or any of them to an agreement with reference to the limited liability partnership's affairs or to the winding up, and
  (b)   is deemed to have committed that offence if, prior to the winding up, he has made any false representation, or committed any other fraud, for that purpose.

(2)   For purposes of this section, "member" includes a shadow member.

548

(3)   A person guilty of an offence under this section is liable to imprisonment or a fine, or both.

212 Summary remedy against delinquent members, liquidators, etc

(1)   This section applies if in the course of the winding up of a limited liability partnership it appears that a person who–
(a)   is or has been an member of the limited liability partnership,
(b)   has acted as liquidator, administrator or administrative receiver of the limited liability partnership, or
(c)   not being a person falling within paragraph (a) or (b), is or has been concerned, or has taken part, in the promotion, formation or management of the limited liability partnership,
has misapplied or retained, or become accountable for, any money or other property of the limited liability partnership, or been guilty of any misfeasance or breach of any fiduciary or other duty in relation to the limited liability partnership.

(2)   The reference in subsection (1) to any misfeasance or breach of any fiduciary or other duty in relation to the limited liability partnership includes, in the case of a person who has acted as liquidator or administrator of the limited liability partnership, any misfeasance or breach of any fiduciary or other duty in connection with the carrying out of his functions as liquidator or administrator of the limited liability partnership.

(3)   The court may, on the application of the official receiver or the liquidator, or of any creditor or contributory, examine into the conduct of the person falling within subsection (1) and compel him–
(a)   to repay, restore or account for the money or property or any part of it, with interest at such rate as the court thinks just, or
(b)   to contribute such sum to the limited liability partnership's assets by way of compensation in respect of the misfeasance or breach of fiduciary or other duty as the court thinks just.

(4)   The power to make an application under subsection (3) in relation to a person who has acted as liquidator or administrator of the limited liability partnership is not exercisable, except with the leave of the court, after that person has had his release.

(5)   The power of a contributory to make an application under subsection (3) is not exercisable except with the leave of the court, but is exercisable notwithstanding that he will not benefit from any order the court may make on the application.

213 Fraudulent trading

(1)   If in the course of the winding up of a limited liability partnership it appears that any business of the limited liability partnership has been carried on with intent to defraud creditors of the limited liability partnership or creditors of any other person, or for any fraudulent purpose, the following has effect.

(2)   The court, on the application of the liquidator may declare that any persons who were knowingly parties to the carrying on of the business in the manner above-mentioned are to be liable to make such contributions (if any) to the limited liability partnership's assets as the court thinks proper.

214 Wrongful trading

(1)   Subject to subsection (3) below, if in the course of the winding up of a limited liability partnership it appears that subsection (2) of this section applies in relation to a person who is or has been a member of the limited liability partnership, the court, on the application of the liquidator, may declare that that person is to be liable to make such contribution (if any) to the limited liability partnership's assets as the court thinks proper.

(2)   This subsection applies in relation to a person if–
    (a) the limited liability partnership has gone into insolvent liquidation,
    (b) at some time before the commencement of the winding up of the limited liability partnership, that person knew or ought to have concluded that there was no reasonable prospect that the limited liability partnership would avoid going into insolvent liquidation, and
    (c) that person was a member of the limited liability partnership at that time

…

(3)   The court shall not make a declaration under this section with respect to any person if it is satisfied that after the condition specified in subsection (2)(b) was first satisfied in relation to him that person took every step with a view to minimising the potential loss to the limited liability partnership's creditors as (assuming him to have known that there was no reasonable prospect that the limited liability partnership would avoid going into insolvent liquidation) he ought to have taken.

(4)   For the purposes of subsections (2) and (3), the facts which a member of a limited liability partnership ought to know or ascertain, the conclusions which he ought to reach and the steps which he ought to take are those which would be known or ascertained, or reached or taken, by a reasonably diligent person having both–
    (a) the general knowledge, skill and experience that may reasonably be expected of a person carrying out the same functions as are carried out by that member in relation to the limited liability partnership, and
    (b) the general knowledge, skill and experience that that member has.

(5)   The reference in subsection (4) to the functions carried out in relation to a limited liability partnership by a member of the limited liability partnership includes any functions which he does not carry out but which have been entrusted to him.

(6)   For the purposes of this section a limited liability partnership goes into insolvent liquidation if it goes into liquidation at a time when its assets are insufficient for the payment of its debts and other liabilities and the expenses of the winding up.

(7)   In this section "member" includes a shadow member.

(8)   This section is without prejudice to section 213.

[214A Adjustment of withdrawals

(1)   This section has effect in relation to a person who is or has been a member of a limited liability partnership where, in the course of the winding up of that limited liability partnership, it appears that subsection (2) of this section applies in relation to that person.

(2)   This subsection applies in relation to a person if–
  (a) within the period of two years ending with the commencement of the winding up, he was a member of the limited liability partnership who withdrew property of the limited liability partnership, whether in the form of a share of profits, salary, repayment of or payment of interest on a loan to the limited liability partnership or any other withdrawal of property, and
  (b) it is proved by the liquidator to the satisfaction of the court that at the time of the withdrawal he knew or had reasonable ground for believing that the limited liability partnership–
    (i)   was at the time of the withdrawal unable to pay its debts within the meaning of section 123, or
    (ii) would become so unable to pay its debts after the assets of the limited liability partnership had been depleted by that withdrawal taken together with all other withdrawals (if any) made by any members contemporaneously with that withdrawal or in contemplation when that withdrawal was made.

(3)   Where this section has effect in relation to any person the court, on the application of the liquidator, may declare that that person is to be liable to make such contribution (if any) to the limited liability partnership's assets as the court thinks proper.

(4)   The court shall not make a declaration in relation to any person the amount of which exceeds the aggregate of the amounts or values of all the withdrawals referred to in subsection (2) made by that person within the period of two years referred to in that subsection.

(5)   The court shall not make a declaration under this section with respect to any person unless that person knew or ought to have concluded that after each withdrawal referred to in subsection (2) there was no reasonable prospect that the limited liability partnership would avoid going into insolvent liquidation.

(6)   For the purposes of subsection (5) the facts which a member ought to know or ascertain and the conclusions which he ought to reach are those which would be known, ascertained, or reached by a reasonably diligent person having both–
  (a) the general knowledge, skill and experience that may reasonably be expected of a person carrying out the same functions as are carried out by that member in relation to the limited liability partnership, and
  (b) the general knowledge, skill and experience that that member has.

551

(7)   For the purposes of this section a limited liability partnership goes into insolvent liquidation if it goes into liquidation at a time when its assets are insufficient for the payment of its debts and other liabilities and the expenses of the winding up.

(8)   In this section "member" includes a shadow member.

(9)   This section is without prejudice to section 214.]

215 Proceedings under ss 213, 214

(1)   On the hearing of an application under section 213 … 214 [or 214A], the liquidator may himself give evidence or call witnesses.

(2)   Where under [any of those sections] the court makes a declaration, it may give such further directions as it thinks proper for giving effect to the declaration; and in particular, the court may–
(a)   provide for the liability of any person under the declaration to be a charge on any debt or obligation due from the limited liability partnership to him, or on any mortgage or charge or any interest in a mortgage or charge on assets of the limited liability partnership held by or vested in him, or any person on his behalf, or any person claiming as assignee from or through the person liable or any person acting on his behalf, and
(b)   from time to time make such further order as may be necessary for enforcing any charge imposed under this subsection.

(3)   For the purposes of subsection (2), "assignee"–
(a)   includes a person to whom or in whose favour, by the directions of the person made liable, the debt, obligation, mortgage or charge was created, issued or transferred or the interest created, but
(b)   does not include an assignee for valuable consideration (not including consideration by way of marriage) given in good faith and without notice of any of the matters on the ground of which the declaration is made.

(4)   Where the court makes a declaration under [any of those sections] in relation to a person who is a creditor of the limited liability partnership, it may direct that the whole or any part of any debt owed by the limited liability partnership to that person and any interest thereon shall rank in priority after all other debts owed by the limited liability partnership and after any interest on those debts.

(5)   [Sections 213, 214 or 214A] have effect notwithstanding that the person concerned may be criminally liable in respect of matters on the ground of which the declaration under the section is to be made.

216 Restriction on re-use of limited liability partnership names

(1)   This section applies to a person where a limited liability partnership ("the liquidating limited liability partnership") has gone into insolvent liquidation on

or after the appointed day and he was a member or shadow member of the limited liability partnership at any time in the period of twelve months ending with the day before it went into liquidation.

(2)   For the purposes of this section, a name is a prohibited name in relation to such a person if—

    (a)   it is a name by which the liquidating limited liability partnership was known at any time in that period of twelve months, or

    (b)   it is a name which is so similar to a name falling within paragraph (a) as to suggest an association with that limited liability partnership.

(3)   Except with leave of the court or in such circumstances as may be prescribed, a person to whom this section applies shall not at any time in the period of five years beginning with the day on which the liquidating limited liability partnership went into liquidation—

    (a)   be a member of any other limited liability partnership that is known by a prohibited name, or

    (b)   in any way, whether directly or indirectly, be concerned or take part in the promotion, formation or management of any such limited liability partnership, or

    (c)   in any way, whether directly or indirectly, be concerned or take part in the carrying on of a business carried on (otherwise than by a limited liability partnership) under a prohibited name.

(4)   If a person acts in contravention of this section, he is liable to imprisonment or a fine, or both.

(5)   In subsection (3) "the court" means any court having jurisdiction to wind up limited liability partnerships; and on an application for leave under that subsection, the Secretary of State or the official receiver may appear and call the attention of the court to any matters which seem to him to be relevant.

(6)   References in this section, in relation to any time, to a name by which a limited liability partnership is known are to the name of the limited liability partnership at that time or to any name under which the limited liability partnership carries on business at that time.

(7)   For the purposes of this section a limited liability partnership goes into insolvent liquidation if it goes into liquidation at a time when its assets are insufficient for the payment of its debts and other liabilities and the expenses of the winding up.

217 Personal liability for debts, following contravention of s 216

(1)   A person is personally responsible for all the relevant debts of a limited liability partnership if at any time—

    (a)   in contravention of section 216, he is involved in the management of the limited liability partnership, or

    (b)   as a person who is involved in the management of the limited liability partnership, he acts or is willing to act on instructions given (without the leave of the court) by a person whom he knows at that time to be in contravention in relation to the limited liability partnership of section 216.

(2)   Where a person is personally responsible under this section for the relevant debts of a limited liability partnership, he is jointly and severally liable in respect of those debts with the limited liability partnership and any other person who, whether under this section or otherwise, is so liable.

(3)   For the purposes of this section the relevant debts of a limited liability partnership are–
   (a)   in relation to a person who is personally responsible under paragraph (a) of subsection (1), such debts and other liabilities of the limited liability partnership as are incurred at a time when that person was involved in the management of the limited liability partnership, and
   (b)   in relation to a person who is personally responsible under paragraph (b) of that subsection, such debts and other liabilities of the limited liability partnership as are incurred at a time when that person was acting or was willing to act on instructions given as mentioned in that paragraph.

(4)   For the purposes of this section, a person is involved in the management of a limited liability partnership if he is a member of the limited liability partnership or if he is concerned, whether directly or indirectly, or takes part, in the management of the limited liability partnership.

(5)   For the purposes of this section a person who, as a person involved in the management of a limited liability partnership, has at any time acted on instructions given (without the leave of the court) by a person whom he knew at that time to be in contravention in relation to the limited liability partnership of section 216 is presumed, unless the contrary is shown, to have been willing at any time thereafter to act on any instructions given by that person.

218 Prosecution of delinquent members of limited liability partnership

(1)   If it appears to the court in the course of a winding up by the court that any past or present [member of the limited liability partnership] has been guilty of any offence in relation to the limited liability partnership for which he is criminally liable, the court may (either on the application of a person interested in the winding up or of its own motion) direct the liquidator to refer the matter–
   (a)   in the case of a winding up in England and Wales, to the Secretary of State, and
   (b)   in the case of a winding up in Scotland, to the Lord Advocate.

(3)   If in the case of a winding up by the court in England and Wales it appears to the liquidator, not being the official receiver, that any past or present [member of the limited liability partnership] has been guilty of an offence in relation to the limited liability partnership for which he is criminally liable, the liquidator shall report the matter to the official receiver.

(4)   If it appears to the liquidator in the course of a voluntary winding up that any past or present [member of the limited liability partnership] has been guilty of an offence in relation to the limited liability partnership for which he is criminally liable, he shall forthwith report the matter–

(a) in the case of a winding up in England and Wales, to the Secretary of State, and

(b) in the case of a winding up in Scotland, to the Lord Advocate,

and shall furnish to the Secretary of State or (as the case may be) the Lord Advocate such information and give to him such access to and facilities for inspecting and taking copies of documents (being information or documents in the possession or under the control of the liquidator and relating to the matter in question) as the Secretary of State or (as the case may be) the Lord Advocate requires.

(5)   Where a report is made to the Secretary of State under subsection (4) he may, for the purpose of investigating the matter reported to him and such other matters relating to the affairs of the limited liability partnership as appear to him to require investigation, exercise any of the powers which are exercisable by inspectors appointed under section 431 or 432 of the Companies Act to investigate a limited liability partnership's affairs.

(6)   If it appears to the court in the course of a voluntary winding up that–

(a) any past or present [member of the limited liability partnership] has been guilty as above-mentioned, and

(b) no report with respect to the matter has been made by the liquidator under subsection (4),

the court may (on the application of any person interested in the winding up or of its own motion) direct the liquidator to make such a report.

On a report being made accordingly, this section has effect as though the report had been made in pursuance of subsection (4).

219 Obligations arising under s 218

(1)   For the purpose of an investigation by the Secretary of State in consequence of a report made to him under section 218(4), any obligation imposed on a person by any provision of the Companies Act to produce documents or give information to, or otherwise to assist, inspectors appointed as mentioned in section 218(5) is to be regarded as an obligation similarly to assist the Secretary of State in his investigation.

(2)   An answer given by a person to a question put to him in exercise of the powers conferred by section 218(5) may be used in evidence against him.

(2A)   However, in criminal proceedings in which that person is charged with an offence to which this subsection applies–

(a) no evidence relating to the answer may be adduced, and

(b) no question relating to it may be asked,

by or on behalf of the prosecution, unless evidence relating to it is adduced, or a question relating to it is asked, in the proceedings by or on behalf of that person.

(2B)   Subsection (2A) applies to any offence other than–
  (a)   an offence under section 2 or 5 of the Perjury Act 1911 (false statements made on oath otherwise than in judicial proceedings or made otherwise than on oath), or
  (b)   an offence under section 44(1) or (2) of the Criminal Law (Consolidation)(Scotland) Act 1995 (false statements made on oath or otherwise than on oath).

(3)   Where criminal proceedings are instituted by the Director of Public Prosecutions, the Lord Advocate or the Secretary of State following any report or reference under section 218, it is the duty of the liquidator and every member and agent of the limited liability partnership past and present (other than the defendant or defender) to give to the Director of Public Prosecutions, the Lord Advocate or the Secretary of State (as the case may be) all assistance in connection with the prosecution which he is reasonably able to give.
  For this purpose "agent" includes any banker or solicitor of the limited liability partnership and any person employed by the limited liability partnership as auditor, whether that person is or is not a member of the limited liability partnership.

(4)   If a person fails or neglects to give assistance in the manner required by subsection (3), the court may, on the application of the prosecuting authority or the Secretary of State (as the case may be) direct the person to comply with that subsection; and if the application is made with respect to a liquidator, the court may (unless it appears that the failure or neglect to comply was due to the liquidator not having in his hands sufficient assets of the limited liability partnership to enable him to do so) direct that the costs shall be borne by the liquidator personally.

220–229

PART VI
MISCELLANEOUS PROVISIONS APPLYING TO LIMITED LIABILITY PARTNERSHIPS WHICH ARE INSOLVENT OR IN LIQUIDATION

230 Holders of office to be qualified insolvency practitioners

(1)   Where an administration order is made in relation to a limited liability partnership, the administrator must be a person who is qualified to act as an insolvency practitioner in relation to the limited liability partnership.

(2)   Where an administrative receiver of a limited liability partnership is appointed, he must be a person who is so qualified.

(3)   Where a limited liability partnership goes into liquidation, the liquidator must be a person who is so qualified.

(4)   Where a provisional liquidator is appointed, he must be a person who is so qualified.

(5)   Subsections (3) and (4) are without prejudice to any enactment under which the official receiver is to be, or may be, liquidator or provisional liquidator.

231 Appointment to office of two or more persons

(1)   This section applies if an appointment or nomination of any person to the office of administrator, administrative receiver, liquidator or provisional liquidator–
    (a)   relates to more than one person, or
    (b)   has the effect that the office is to be held by more than one person.

(2)   The appointment or nomination shall declare whether any act required or authorised under any enactment to be done by the administrator, administrative receiver, liquidator or provisional liquidator is to be done by all or any one or more of the persons for the time being holding the office in question.

232 Validity of office-holder's acts

The acts of an individual as administrator, administrative receiver, liquidator or provisional liquidator of a limited liability partnership are valid notwithstanding any defect in his appointment, nomination or qualifications.

233 Supplies of gas, water, electricity, etc

(1)   This section applies in the case of a limited liability partnership where–
    (a)   an administration order is made in relation to the limited liability partnership, or
    (b)   an administrative receiver is appointed, or
    [(c)   a voluntary arrangement under Part I has taken effect in accordance with section 5], or
    (d)   the limited liability partnership goes into liquidation, or
    (e)   a provisional liquidator is appointed;
and "the office-holder" means the administrator, the administrative receiver, the supervisor of the voluntary arrangement, the liquidator or the provisional liquidator, as the case may be.

(2)   If a request is made by or with the concurrence of the office-holder for the giving, after the effective date, of any of the supplies mentioned in the next subsection, the supplier–
    (a)   may make it a condition of the giving of the supply that the office-holder personally guarantees the payment of any charges in respect of the supply, but
    (b)   shall not make it a condition of the giving of the supply, or do anything which has the effect of making it a condition of the giving of the supply, that any outstanding charges in respect of a supply given to the limited liability partnership before the effective date are paid.

(3)   The supplies referred to in subsection (2) are–
    (a)   a supply of gas by a gas supplier within the meaning of Part I of the Gas Act 1986;

(b) a public supply of electricity,
(c) a supply of water by a water undertaker or, in Scotland, a water authority,
(d) a supply of telecommunication services by a public telecommunications operator.

(4) "The effective date" for the purposes of this section is whichever is applicable of the following dates–
(a) the date on which the administration order was made,
(b) the date on which the administrative receiver was appointed (or, if he was appointed in succession to another administrative receiver, the date on which the first of his predecessors was appointed),
[(c) the date on which the voluntary arrangement took effect in accordance with section 5],
(d) the date on which the limited liability partnership went into liquidation,
(e) the date on which the provisional liquidator was appointed.

(5) The following applies to expressions used in subsection (3)–
(b) "public supply of electricity" means a supply of electricity by a public electricity supplier within the meaning of Part I of the Electricity Act 1989;
(c) "water authority" means the same as in the Water (Scotland) Act 1980, and
(d) "telecommunication services" and "public telecommunications operator" mean the same as in the Telecommunications Act 1984, except that the former does not include local delivery services within the meaning of Part II of the Broadcasting Act 1990.

234 Getting in the limited liability partnership's property

(1) This section applies in the case of a limited liability partnership where–
(a) an administration order is made in relation to the limited liability partnership, or
(b) an administrative receiver is appointed, or
(c) the limited liability partnership goes into liquidation, or
(d) a provisional liquidator is appointed;
and "the office-holder" means the administrator, the administrative receiver, the liquidator or the provisional liquidator, as the case may be.

(2) Where any person has in his possession or control any property, books, papers or records to which the limited liability partnership appears to be entitled, the court may require that person forthwith (or within such period as the court may direct) to pay, deliver, convey, surrender or transfer the property, books, papers or records to the office-holder.

(3) Where the office-holder–
(a) seizes or disposes of any property which is not property of the limited liability partnership, and
(b) at the time of seizure or disposal believes, and has reasonable grounds for believing, that he is entitled (whether in pursuance of an order of the court or otherwise) to seize or dispose of that property,
the next subsection has effect.

(4) In that case the office-holder–
(a) is not liable to any person in respect of any loss or damage resulting from the seizure or disposal except in so far as that loss or damage is caused by the office-holder's own negligence, and
(b) has a lien on the property, or the proceeds of its sale, for such expenses as were incurred in connection with the seizure or disposal.

235 Duty to co-operate with office-holder

(1) This section applies as does section 234; and it also applies, in the case of a limited liability partnership in respect of which a winding-up order has been made by the court in England and Wales, as if references to the office-holder included the official receiver, whether or not he is the liquidator.

(2) Each of the persons mentioned in the next subsection shall–
(a) give to the office-holder such information concerning the limited liability partnership and its promotion, formation, business, dealings, affairs or property as the office-holder may at any time after the effective date reasonably require, and
(b) attend on the office-holder at such times as the latter may reasonably require.

(3) The persons referred to above are–
(a) those who are or have at any time been members of the limited liability partnership,
(b) those who have taken part in the formation of the limited liability partnership at any time within one year before the effective date,
(c) those who are in the employment of the limited liability partnership, or have been in its employment (including employment under a contract for services) within that year, and are in the office-holder's opinion capable of giving information which he requires,
(d) those who are, or have within that year been, officers of, or in the employment (including employment under a contract for services) of, another limited liability partnership which is, or within that year was, a member of the limited liability partnership in question, and
(e) in the case of a limited liability partnership being wound up by the court, any person who has acted as administrator, administrative receiver or liquidator of the limited liability partnership.

(4) For the purposes of subsections (2) and (3), "the effective date" is whichever is applicable of the following dates–
(a) the date on which the administration order was made,
(b) the date on which the administrative receiver was appointed or, if he was appointed in succession to another administrative receiver, the date on which the first of his predecessors was appointed,
(c) the date on which the provisional liquidator was appointed, and
(d) the date on which the limited liability partnership went into liquidation.

(5)   If a person without reasonable excuse fails to comply with any obligation imposed by this section, he is liable to a fine and, for contravention, to a daily default fine.

236 Inquiry into limited liability partnership's dealings, etc

(1)   This section applies as does section 234; and it also applies in the case of a limited liability partnership in respect of which a winding-up order has been made by the court in England and Wales as if references to the office-holder included the official receiver, whether or not he is the liquidator.

(2)   The court may, on the application of the office-holder, summon to appear before it–
    (a)   any member of the limited liability partnership,
    (b)   any person known or suspected to have in his possession any property of the limited liability partnership or supposed to be indebted to the limited liability partnership, or
    (c)   any person whom the court thinks capable of giving information concerning the promotion, formation, business, dealings, affairs or property of the limited liability partnership.

(3)   The court may require any such person as is mentioned in subsection (2)(a) to (c) to submit an affidavit to the court containing an account of his dealings with the limited liability partnership or to produce any books, papers or other records in his possession or under his control relating to the limited liability partnership or the matters mentioned in paragraph (c) of the subsection.

(4)   The following applies in a case where–
    (a)   a person without reasonable excuse fails to appear before the court when he is summoned to do so under this section, or
    (b)   there are reasonable grounds for believing that a person has absconded, or is about to abscond, with a view to avoiding his appearance before the court under this section.

(5)   The court may, for the purpose of bringing that person and anything in his possession before the court, cause a warrant to be issued to a constable or prescribed officer of the court–
    (a)   for the arrest of that person, and
    (b)   for the seizure of any books, papers, records, money or goods in that person's possession.

(6)   The court may authorise a person arrested under such a warrant to be kept in custody, and anything seized under such a warrant to be held, in accordance with the rules, until that person is brought before the court under the warrant or until such other time as the court may order.

237 Court's enforcement powers under s 236

(1)   If it appears to the court, on consideration of any evidence obtained under section 236 or this section, that any person has in his possession any

property of the limited liability partnership, the court may, on the application of the office-holder, order that person to deliver the whole or any part of the property to the office-holder at such time, in such manner and on such terms as the court thinks fit.

(2)   If it appears to the court, on consideration of any evidence so obtained, that any person is indebted to the limited liability partnership, the court may, on the application of the office-holder, order that person to pay to the office-holder, at such time and in such manner as the court may direct, the whole or any part of the amount due, whether in full discharge of the debt or otherwise, as the court thinks fit.

(3)   The court may, if it thinks fit, order that any person who if within the jurisdiction of the court would be liable to be summoned to appear before it under section 236 or this section shall be examined in any part of the United Kingdom where he may for the time being be, or in a place outside the United Kingdom.

(4)   Any person who appears or is brought before the court under section 236 or this section may be examined on oath, either orally or (except in Scotland) by interrogatories, concerning the limited liability partnership or the matters mentioned in section 236(2)(c).

238 Transactions at an undervalue (England and Wales)

(1)   This section applies in the case of a limited liability partnership where–
    (a)   an administration order is made in relation to the limited liability partnership, or
    (b)   the limited liability partnership goes into liquidation;
and "the office-holder" means the administrator or the liquidator, as the case may be.

(2)   Where the limited liability partnership has at a relevant time (defined in section 240) entered into a transaction with any person at an undervalue, the office-holder may apply to the court for an order under this section.

(3)   Subject as follows, the court shall, on such an application, make such order as it thinks fit for restoring the position to what it would have been if the limited liability partnership had not entered into that transaction.

(4)   For the purposes of this section and section 241, a limited liability partnership enters into a transaction with a person at an undervalue if–
    (a)   the limited liability partnership makes a gift to that person or otherwise enters into a transaction with that person on terms that provide for the limited liability partnership to receive no consideration, or
    (b)   the limited liability partnership enters into a transaction with that person for a consideration the value of which, in money or money's worth, is significantly less than the value, in money or money's worth, of the consideration provided by the limited liability partnership.

(5)   The court shall not make an order under this section in respect of a transaction at an undervalue if it is satisfied–
   (a)   that the limited liability partnership which entered into the transaction did so in good faith and for the purpose of carrying on its business, and
   (b)   that at the time it did so there were reasonable grounds for believing that the transaction would benefit the limited liability partnership.

239 Preferences (England and Wales)

(1)   This section applies as does section 238.

(2)   Where the limited liability partnership has at a relevant time (defined in the next section) given a preference to any person, the office-holder may apply to the court for an order under this section.

(3)   Subject as follows, the court shall, on such an application, make such order as it thinks fit for restoring the position to what it would have been if the limited liability partnership had not given that preference.

(4)   For the purposes of this section and section 241, a limited liability partnership gives a preference to a person if–
   (a)   that person is one of the limited liability partnership's creditors or a surety or guarantor for any of the limited liability partnership's debts or other liabilities, and
   (b)   the limited liability partnership does anything or suffers anything to be done which (in either case) has the effect of putting that person into a position which, in the event of the limited liability partnership going into insolvent liquidation, will be better than the position he would have been in if that thing had not been done.

(5)   The court shall not make an order under this section in respect of a preference given to any person unless the limited liability partnership which gave the preference was influenced in deciding to give it by a desire to produce in relation to that person the effect mentioned in subsection (4)(b).

(6)   A limited liability partnership which has given a preference to a person connected with the limited liability partnership (otherwise than by reason only of being its employee) at the time the preference was given is presumed, unless the contrary is shown, to have been influenced in deciding to give it by such a desire as is mentioned in subsection (5).

(7)   The fact that something has been done in pursuance of the order of a court does not, without more, prevent the doing or suffering of that thing from constituting the giving of a preference.

240 "Relevant time" under ss 238, 239

(1)   Subject to the next subsection, the time at which a limited liability partnership enters into a transaction at an undervalue or gives a preference is a relevant time if the transaction is entered into, or the preference given–

    (a)   in the case of a transaction at an undervalue or of a preference which is given to a person who is connected with the limited liability partnership (otherwise than by reason only of being its employee), at a time in the period of two years ending with the onset of insolvency (which expression is defined below),

    (b)   in the case of a preference which is not such a transaction and is not so given, at a time in the period of six months ending with the onset of insolvency, and

    (c)   in either case, at a time between the presentation of a petition for the making of an administration order in relation to the limited liability partnership and the making of such an order on that petition.

(2)   Where a limited liability partnership enters into a transaction at an undervalue or gives a preference at a time mentioned in subsection (1)(a) or (b), that time is not a relevant time for the purposes of section 238 or 239 unless the limited liability partnership–

    (a)   is at that time unable to pay its debts within the meaning of section 123 in Chapter VI of Part IV, or

    (b)   becomes unable to pay its debts within the meaning of that section in consequence of the transaction or preference;

but the requirements of this subsection are presumed to be satisfied, unless the contrary is shown, in relation to any transaction at an undervalue which is entered into by a limited liability partnership with a person who is connected with the limited liability partnership.

(3)   For the purposes of subsection (1), the onset of insolvency is–

    (a)   in a case where section 238 or 239 applies by reason of the making of an administration order or of a limited liability partnership going into liquidation immediately upon the discharge of an administration order, the date of the presentation of the petition on which the administration order was made, and

    (b)   in a case where the section applies by reason of a limited liability partnership going into liquidation at any other time, the date of the commencement of the winding up.

241 Orders under ss 238, 239

(1)   Without prejudice to the generality of sections 238(3) and 239(3), an order under either of those sections with respect to a transaction or preference entered into or given by a limited liability partnership may (subject to the next subsection)–

    (a)   require any property transferred as part of the transaction, or in connection with the giving of the preference, to be vested in the limited liability partnership,

    (b)   require any property to be so vested if it represents in any person's hands the application either of the proceeds of sale of property so transferred or of money so transferred,

    (c)   release or discharge (in whole or in part) any security given by the limited liability partnership,

(d) require any person to pay, in respect of benefits received by him from the limited liability partnership, such sums to the office-holder as the court may direct,

(e) provide for any surety or guarantor whose obligations to any person were released or discharged (in whole or in part) under the transaction, or by the giving of the preference, to be under such new or revived obligations to that person as the court thinks appropriate,

(f) provide for security to be provided for the discharge of any obligation imposed by or arising under the order, for such an obligation to be charged on any property and for the security or charge to have the same priority as a security or charge released or discharged (in whole or in part) under the transaction or by the giving of the preference, and

(g) provide for the extent to which any person whose property is vested by the order in the limited liability partnership, or on whom obligations are imposed by the order, is to be able to prove in the winding up of the limited liability partnership for debts or other liabilities which arose from, or were released or discharged (in whole or in part) under or by, the transaction or the giving of the preference.

(2) An order under section 238 or 239 may affect the property of, or impose any obligation on, any person whether or not he is the person with whom the limited liability partnership in question entered into the transaction or (as the case may be) the person to whom the preference was given; but such an order–

(a) shall not prejudice any interest in property which was acquired from a person other than the limited liability partnership and was acquired in good faith and for value, or prejudice any interest deriving from such an interest, and

(b) shall not require a person who received a benefit from the transaction or preference in good faith and for value to pay a sum to the office-holder, except where that person was a party to the transaction or the payment is to be in respect of a preference given to that person at a time when he was a creditor of the limited liability partnership.

(2A) Where a person has acquired an interest in property from a person other than the limited liability partnership in question, or has received a benefit from the transaction or preference, and at the time of that acquisition or receipt–

(a) he had notice of the relevant surrounding circumstances and of the relevant proceedings, or

(b) he was connected with, or was an associate of, either the limited liability partnership in question or the person with whom that limited liability partnership entered into the transaction or to whom that limited liability partnership gave the preference,

then, unless the contrary is shown, it shall be presumed for the purposes of paragraph (a) or (as the case may be) paragraph (b) of subsection (2) that the interest was acquired or the benefit was received otherwise than in good faith.

(3) For the purposes of subsection (2A)(a), the relevant surrounding circumstances are (as the case may require)–

(a) the fact that the limited liability partnership in question entered into the transaction at an undervalue; or
(b) the circumstances which amounted to the giving of the preference by the limited liability partnership in question;

and subsections (3A) to (3C) have effect to determine whether, for those purposes, a person has notice of the relevant proceedings.

(3A) In a case where section 238 or 239 applies by reason of the making of an administration order, a person has notice of the relevant proceedings if he has notice—
(a) of the fact that the petition on which the administration order is made has been presented; or
(b) of the fact that the administration order has been made.

(3B) In a case where section 238 or 239 applies by reason of the limited liability partnership in question going into liquidation immediately upon the discharge of an administration order, a person has notice of the relevant proceedings if he has notice—
(a) of the fact that the petition on which the administration order is made has been presented;
(b) of the fact that the administration order has been made; or
(c) of the fact that the limited liability partnership has gone into liquidation.

(3C) In a case where section 238 or 239 applies by reason of the limited liability partnership in question going into liquidation at any other time, a person has notice of the relevant proceedings if he has notice—
(a) where the limited liability partnership goes into liquidation on the making of a winding-up order, of the fact that the petition on which the winding-up order is made has been presented or of the fact that the limited liability partnership has gone into liquidation;
(b) in any other case, of the fact that the limited liability partnership has gone into liquidation.

(4) The provisions of sections 238 to 241 apply without prejudice to the availability of any other remedy, even in relation to a transaction or preference which the limited liability partnership had no power to enter into or give.

242 Gratuitous alienations (Scotland)

(1) Where this subsection applies and—
(a) the winding up of a limited liability partnership has commenced, an alienation by the limited liability partnership is challengeable by—
    (i) any creditor who is a creditor by virtue of a debt incurred on or before the date of such commencement, or
    (ii) the liquidator;
(b) an administration order is in force in relation to a limited liability partnership, an alienation by the limited liability partnership is challengeable by the administrator.

(2)   Subsection (1) applies where–
   (a) by the alienation, whether before or after 1st April 1986 (the coming into force of section 75 of the Bankruptcy (Scotland) Act 1985), any part of the limited liability partnership's property is transferred or any claim or right of the limited liability partnership is discharged or renounced, and
   (b) the alienation takes place on a relevant day.

(3)   For the purposes of subsection (2)(b), the day on which an alienation takes place is the day on which it becomes completely effectual; and in that subsection "relevant day" means, if the alienation has the effect of favouring–
   (a) a person who is an associate (within the meaning of the Bankruptcy (Scotland) Act 1985) of the limited liability partnership, a day not earlier than five years before the date on which–
      (i)   the winding up of the limited liability partnership commences, or
      (ii) as the case may be, the administration order is made; or
   (b) any other person, a day not earlier than two years before that date.

(4)   On a challenge being brought under subsection (1), the court shall grant decree of reduction or for such restoration of property to the limited liability partnership's assets or other redress as may be appropriate; but the court shall not grant such a decree if the person seeking to uphold the alienation establishes–
   (a) that immediately, or at any other time, after the alienation the limited liability partnership's assets were greater than its liabilities, or
   (b) that the alienation was made for adequate consideration, or
   (c) that the alienation–
      (i)   was a birthday, Christmas or other conventional gift, or
      (ii) was a gift made, for a charitable purpose, to a person who is not an associate of the limited liability partnership,
      which, having regard to all the circumstances, it was reasonable for the limited liability partnership to make;
   Provided that this subsection is without prejudice to any right or interest acquired in good faith and for value from or through the transferee in the alienation.

(5)   In subsection (4) above, "charitable purpose" means any charitable, benevolent or philanthropic purpose, whether or not it is charitable within the meaning of any rule of law.

(6)   For the purposes of the foregoing provisions of this section, an alienation in implementation of a prior obligation is deemed to be one for which there was no consideration or no adequate consideration to the extent that the prior obligation was undertaken for no consideration or no adequate consideration.

(7)   A liquidator and an administrator have the same right as a creditor has under any rule of law to challenge an alienation of a limited liability partnership made for no consideration or no adequate consideration.

(8)   This section applies to Scotland only.

243 Unfair preferences (Scotland)

(1)   Subject to subsection (2) below, subsection (4) below applies to a transaction entered into by a limited liability partnership, whether before or after 1st April 1986, which has the effect of creating a preference in favour of a creditor to the prejudice of the general body of creditors, being a preference created not earlier than six months before the commencement of the winding up of the limited liability partnership or the making of an administration order in relation to the limited liability partnership.

(2)   Subsection (4) below does not apply to any of the following transactions–
(a)   a transaction in the ordinary course of trade or business;
(b)   a payment in cash for a debt which when it was paid had become payable, unless the transaction was collusive with the purpose of prejudicing the general body of creditors;
(c)   a transaction whereby the parties to it undertake reciprocal obligations (whether the performance by the parties of their respective obligations occurs at the same time or at different times) unless the transaction was collusive as aforesaid;
(d)   the granting of a mandate by a limited liability partnership authorising an arrestee to pay over the arrested funds or part thereof to the arrester where–
(i)   there has been a decree for payment or a warrant for summary diligence, and
(ii)   the decree or warrant has been preceded by an arrestment on the dependence of the action or followed by an arrestment in execution.

(3)   For the purposes of subsection (1) above, the day on which a preference was created is the day on which the preference became completely effectual.

(4)   A transaction to which this subsection applies is challengeable by–
(a)   in the case of a winding up–
(i)   any creditor who is a creditor by virtue of a debt incurred on or before the date of commencement of the winding up, or
(ii)   the liquidator; and
(b)   in the case of an administration order, the administrator.

(5)   On a challenge being brought under subsection (4) above, the court, if satisfied that the transaction challenged is a transaction to which this section applies, shall grant decree of reduction or for such restoration of property to the limited liability partnership's assets or other redress as may be appropriate:
    Provided that this subsection is without prejudice to any right or interest acquired in good faith and for value from or through the creditor in whose favour the preference was created.

(6)   A liquidator and an administrator have the same right as a creditor has under any rule of law to challenge a preference created by a debtor.

(7)   This section applies to Scotland only.

244 Extortionate credit transactions

(1)   This section applies as does section 238, and where the limited liability partnership is, or has been, a party to a transaction for, or involving, the provision of credit to the limited liability partnership.

(2)   The court may, on the application of the office-holder, make an order with respect to the transaction if the transaction is or was extortionate and was entered into in the period of three years ending with the day on which the administration order was made or (as the case may be) the limited liability partnership went into liquidation.

(3)   For the purposes of this section a transaction is extortionate if, having regard to the risk accepted by the person providing the credit–
    (a) the terms of it are or were such as to require grossly exorbitant payments to be made (whether unconditionally or in certain contingencies) in respect of the provision of the credit, or
    (b) it otherwise grossly contravened ordinary principles of fair dealing;
and it shall be presumed, unless the contrary is proved, that a transaction with respect to which an application is made under this section is or, as the case may be, was extortionate.

(4)   An order under this section with respect to any transaction may contain such one or more of the following as the court thinks fit, that is to say–
    (a) provision setting aside the whole or part of any obligation created by the transaction,
    (b) provision otherwise varying the terms of the transaction or varying the terms on which any security for the purposes of the transaction is held,
    (c) provision requiring any person who is or was a party to the transaction to pay to the office-holder any sums paid to that person, by virtue of the transaction, by the limited liability partnership,
    (d) provision requiring any person to surrender to the office-holder any property held by him as security for the purposes of the transaction,
    (e) provision directing accounts to be taken between any persons.

(5)   The powers conferred by this section are exercisable in relation to any transaction concurrently with any powers exercisable in relation to that transaction as a transaction at an undervalue or under section 242 (gratuitous alienations in Scotland).

245 Avoidance of certain floating charges

(1)   This section applies as does section 238, but applies to Scotland as well as to England and Wales.

(2)   Subject as follows, a floating charge on the limited liability partnership's undertaking or property created at a relevant time is invalid except to the extent of the aggregate of–

(a) the value of so much of the consideration for the creation of the charge as consists of money paid, or goods or services supplied, to the limited liability partnership at the same time as, or after, the creation of the charge,

(b) the value of so much of that consideration as consists of the discharge or reduction, at the same time as, or after the creation of the charge, of any debt of the limited liability partnership, and

(c) the amount of such interest (if any) as is payable on the amount falling within paragraph (a) or (b) in pursuance of any agreement under which the money was so paid, the goods or services were so supplied or the debt was so discharged or reduced.

(3) Subject to the next subsection, the time at which a floating charge is created by a limited liability partnership is a relevant time for the purposes of this section if the charge is created—

(a) in the case of a charge which is created in favour of a person who is connected with the limited liability partnership, at a time in the period of two years ending with the onset of insolvency,

(b) in the case of a charge which is created in favour of any other person, at a time in the period of twelve months ending with the onset of insolvency, or

(c) in either case, at a time between the presentation of a petition for the making of an administration order in relation to the limited liability partnership and the making of such an order on that petition.

(4) Where a limited liability partnership creates a floating charge at a time mentioned in subsection (3)(b) and the person in favour of whom the charge is created is not connected with the limited liability partnership, that time is not a relevant time for the purposes of this section unless the limited liability partnership—

(a) is at that time unable to pay its debts within the meaning of section 123 in Chapter VI of Part IV, or

(b) becomes unable to pay its debts within the meaning of that section in consequence of the transaction under which the charge is created.

(5) For the purposes of subsection (3), the onset of insolvency is—

(a) in a case where this section applies by reason of the making of an administration order, the date of the presentation of the petition on which the order was made, and

(b) in a case where this section applies by reason of a limited liability partnership going into liquidation, the date of the commencement of the winding up.

(6) For the purposes of subsection (2)(a) the value of any goods or services supplied by way of consideration for a floating charge is the amount in money which at the time they were supplied could reasonably have been expected to be obtained for supplying the goods or services in the ordinary course of business and on the same terms (apart from the consideration) as those on which they were supplied to the limited liability partnership.

246 Unenforceability of liens on books, etc

(1)   This section applies in the case of a limited liability partnership where–
(a)   an administration order is made in relation to the limited liability partnership, or
(b)   the limited liability partnership goes into liquidation, or
(c)   a provisional liquidator is appointed;
and "the office-holder" means the administrator, the liquidator or the provisional liquidator, as the case may be.

(2)   Subject as follows, a lien or other right to retain possession of any of the books, papers or other records of the limited liability partnership is unenforceable to the extent that its enforcement would deny possession of any books, papers or other records to the office-holder.

(3)   This does not apply to a lien on documents which give a title to property and are held as such.

PART VII
INTERPRETATION FOR FIRST GROUP OF PARTS

247 "Insolvency" and "go into liquidation"

(1)   In this Group of Parts, except in so far as the context otherwise requires, "insolvency", in relation to a limited liability partnership, includes the approval of a voluntary arrangement under Part I, the making of an administration order or the appointment of an administrative receiver.

(2)   For the purposes of any provision in this Group of Parts, a limited liability partnership goes into liquidation if it [makes a determination that it be wound up voluntarily] or an order for its winding up is made by the court at a time when it has not already gone into liquidation by [making such a determination].

248 "Secured creditor", etc

In this Group of Parts, except in so far as the context otherwise requires–
(a)   "secured creditor", in relation to a limited liability partnership, means a creditor of the limited liability partnership who holds in respect of his debt a security over property of the limited liability partnership, and "unsecured creditor" is to be read accordingly; and
(b)   "security" means–
(i)   in relation to England and Wales, any mortgage, charge, lien or other security, and
(ii)   in relation to Scotland, any security (whether heritable or moveable), any floating charge and any right of lien or preference and any right of retention (other than a right of compensation or set off).

249 "Connected" with a limited liability partnership

[For the purposes of any provision in this Group of Parts, a person is connected with a company (including a limited liability partnership) if–
  (a) he is a director or shadow director of the company or an associate of such a director or shadow director (including a member or a shadow member of a limited liability partnership or an associate of such a member or shadow member); or
  (b) he is an associate of the company or of the limited liability partnership.]

250   ...

251 Expressions used generally

In this Group of Parts, except in so far as the context otherwise requires–

"administrative receiver" means–
  (a) an administrative receiver as defined by section 29(2) in Chapter I of Part III, or
  (b) a receiver appointed under section 51 in Chapter II of that Part in a case where the whole (or substantially the whole) of the limited liability partnership's property is attached by the floating charge;

"business day" means any day other than a Saturday, a Sunday, Christmas Day, Good Friday or a day which is a bank holiday in any part of Great Britain;

"chattel leasing agreement" means an agreement for the bailment or, in Scotland, the hiring of goods which is capable of subsisting for more than three months;

"contributory" has the meaning given by section 79;

"floating charge" means a charge which, as created, was a floating charge and includes a floating charge within section 462 of the Companies Act (Scottish floating charges);

"member" includes any person occupying the position of member, by whatever name called;

"office copy", in relation to Scotland, means a copy certified by the clerk of court;

"the official rate", in relation to interest, means the rate payable under section 189(4);

"prescribed" means prescribed by the rules;

"receiver", in the expression "receiver or manager", does not include a receiver appointed under section 51 in Chapter II of Part III;

"retention of title agreement" means an agreement for the sale of goods to a limited liability partnership, being an agreement–

(a) which does not constitute a charge on the goods, but
(b) under which, if the seller is not paid and the limited liability partnership is wound up, the seller will have priority over all other creditors of the limited liability partnership as respects the goods or any property representing the goods;

"the rules" means rules under section 411 in Part XV; ...

"shadow director", in relation to a company, means a person in accordance with whose directions or instructions the directors of the company are accustomed to act (but so that a person is not deemed a shadow director by reason only that the directors act on advice given by him in a professional capacity); [and

"shadow member", in relation to a limited liability partnership, means a person in accordance with whose directions or instructions the members of the limited liability partnership are accustomed to act (but so that a person is not deemed a shadow member by reason only that the members of the limited liability partnership act on advice given by him in a professional capacity);]

and any expression for whose interpretation provision is made by Part XXVI of the Companies Act, other than an expression defined above in this section, is to be construed in accordance with that provision.

252–385

THE THIRD GROUP OF PARTS
MISCELLANEOUS MATTERS BEARING ON BOTH LIMITED
LIABILITY PARTNERSHIP AND INDIVIDUAL INSOLVENCY;
GENERAL INTERPRETATION; FINAL PROVISIONS

PART XII
PREFERENTIAL DEBTS IN LIMITED LIABILITY PARTNERSHIP
AND INDIVIDUAL INSOLVENCY

386 Categories of preferential debts

(1)   A reference in this Act to the preferential debts of a limited liability partnership ... is to the debts listed in Schedule 6 to this Act (money owed to the Inland Revenue for income tax deducted at source; VAT, insurance premium tax, landfill tax, climate change levy, car tax, betting and gaming duties, beer duty, lottery duty, air passenger duty; social security and pension scheme contributions; remuneration etc of employees; levies on coal and steel production); and references to preferential creditors are to be read accordingly.

(2)   In that Schedule "the debtor" means the limited liability partnership ... concerned.

(3)   Schedule 6 is to be read with Schedule 4 to the Pension Schemes Act 1993 (occupational pension scheme contributions).

387 "The relevant date"

(1)   This section explains references in Schedule 6 to the relevant date (being the date which determines the existence and amount of a preferential debt).

(2)   For the purposes of section 4 in Part I (meetings to consider limited liability partnership voluntary arrangement), the relevant date in relation to a limited liability partnership which is not being wound up is–
 (a)   where an administration order is in force in relation to the limited liability partnership, the date of the making of that order, and
 (b)   where no such order has been made, the date of the approval of the voluntary arrangement.

(3)   In relation to a limited liability partnership which is being wound up, the following applies–
 (a)   if the winding up is by the court, and the winding-up order was made immediately upon the discharge of an administration order, the relevant date is the date of the making of the administration order;
 (b)   if the case does not fall within paragraph (a) and the limited liability partnership–
  (i)   is being wound up by the court, and
  (ii) had not commenced to be wound up voluntarily before the date of the making of the winding-up order,
  the relevant date is the date of the appointment (or first appointment) of a provisional liquidator or, if no such appointment has been made, the date of the winding-up order;
 (c)   if the case does not fall within either paragraph (a) or (b), the relevant date is the date of the [making of the determination by the limited liability partnership that it be wound up voluntarily].

(4)   In relation to a limited liability partnership in receivership (where section 40 or, as the case may be, section 59 applies), the relevant date is–
 (a)   in England and Wales, the date of the appointment of the receiver by debenture holders, and
 (b)   in Scotland, the date of the appointment of the receiver under section 53(6) or (as the case may be) 54(5).

(5),(6) …

PART XIII
INSOLVENCY PRACTITIONERS AND THEIR QUALIFICATION

388 Meaning of "act as insolvency practitioner"

(1)   A person acts as an insolvency practitioner in relation to a limited liability partnership by acting–
 (a)   as its liquidator, provisional liquidator, administrator or administrative receiver, or
 (b)   as supervisor of a voluntary arrangement approved by it under Part I.

(2)   ...

(2A)   A person acts as an insolvency practitioner in relation to an insolvent partnership by acting–
  (a)   as its liquidator, provisional liquidator or administrator, or
  (b)   as trustee of the partnership under article 11 of the Insolvent Partnerships Order 1994, or
  (c)   as supervisor of a voluntary arrangement approved in relation to it under Part I of this Act.

(3)   ...

(4)   In this section–

"administrative receiver" has the meaning given by section 251 in Part VII;
...

(5)   Nothing in this section applies to anything done by–
  (a)   the official receiver; or
  (b)   the Accountant in Bankruptcy (within the meaning of the Bankruptcy (Scotland) Act 1985).

389 Acting without qualification an offence

(1)   A person who acts as an insolvency practitioner in relation to a limited liability partnership ... at a time when he is not qualified to do so is liable to imprisonment or a fine, or to both.

(2)   This section does not apply to the official receiver or the Accountant in Bankruptcy (within the meaning of the Bankruptcy (Scotland) Act 1985.

390 Persons not qualified to act as insolvency practitioners

(1)   A person who is not an individual is not qualified to act as an insolvency practitioner.

(2)   A person is not qualified to act as an insolvency practitioner at any time unless at that time–
  (a)   he is authorised so to act by virtue of membership of a professional body recognised under section 391 below, being permitted so to act by or under the rules of that body, or
  (b)   he holds an authorisation granted by a competent authority under section 393.

(3)   A person is not qualified to act as an insolvency practitioner in relation to another person at any time unless–
  (a)   there is in force at that time security or, in Scotland, caution for the proper performance of his functions, and
  (b)   that security or caution meets the prescribed requirements with respect to his so acting in relation to that other person.

(4)   A person is not qualified to act as an insolvency practitioner at any time if at that time–
    (a)   he has been adjudged bankrupt or sequestration of his estate has been awarded and (in either case) he has not been discharged,
    (b)   he is subject to a disqualification order made or a disqualifcation undertaking accepted under the Company Directors Disqualification Act 1986 or to a disqualification order made under Part II of the Companies (Northern Ireland) Order 1989, or
    (c)   he is a patient within the meaning of Part VII of the Mental Health Act 1983 or section 125(1) of the Mental Health (Scotland) Act 1984.

391 Recognised professional bodies

(1)   The Secretary of State may by order declare a body which appears to him to fall within subsection (2) below to be a recognised professional body for the purposes of this section.

(2)   A body may be recognised if it regulates the practice of a profession and maintains and enforces rules for securing that such of its members as are permitted by or under the rules to act as insolvency practitioners–
    (a)   are fit and proper persons so to act, and
    (b)   meet acceptable requirements as to education and practical training and experience.

(3)   References to members of a recognised professional body are to persons who, whether members of that body or not, are subject to its rules in the practice of the profession in question.
        The reference in section 390(2) above to membership of a professional body recognised under this section is to be read accordingly.

(4)   An order made under subsection (1) in relation to a professional body may be revoked by a further order if it appears to the Secretary of State that the body no longer falls within subsection (2).

(5)   An order of the Secretary of State under this section has effect from such date as is specified in the order; and any such order revoking a previous order may make provision whereby members of the body in question continue to be treated as authorised to act as insolvency practitioners for a specified period after the revocation takes effect.

392 Authorisation by competent authority

(1)   Application may be made to a competent authority for authorisation to act as an insolvency practitioner.

(2)   The competent authorities for this purpose are–
    (a)   in relation to a case of any description specified in directions given by the Secretary of State, the body or person so specified in relation to cases of that description, and

(b) in relation to a case not falling within paragraph (a), the Secretary of State.

(3) The application–
(a) shall be made in such manner as the competent authority may direct,
(b) shall contain or be accompanied by such information as that authority may reasonably require for the purpose of determining the application, and
(c) shall be accompanied by the prescribed fee;
and the authority may direct that notice of the making of the application shall be published in such manner as may be specified in the direction.

(4) At any time after receiving the application and before determining it the authority may require the applicant to furnish additional information.

(5) Directions and requirements given or imposed under subsection (3) or (4) may differ as between different applications.

(6) Any information to be furnished to the competent authority under this section shall, if it so requires, be in such form or verified in such manner as it may specify.

(7) An application may be withdrawn before it is granted or refused.

(8) Any sums received under this section by a competent authority other than the Secretary of State may be retained by the authority; and any sums so received by the Secretary of State shall be paid into the Consolidated Fund.

393 Grant, refusal and withdrawal of authorisation

(1) The competent authority may, on an application duly made in accordance with section 392 and after being furnished with all such information as it may require under that section, grant or refuse the application.

(2) The authority shall grant the application if it appears to it from the information furnished by the applicant and having regard to such other information, if any, as it may have–
(a) that the applicant is a fit and proper person to act as an insolvency practitioner, and
(b) that the applicant meets the prescribed requirements with respect to education and practical training and experience.

(3) An authorisation granted under this section, if not previously withdrawn, continues in force for such period not exceeding the prescribed maximum as may be specified in the authorisation.

(4) An authorisation so granted may be withdrawn by the competent authority if it appears to it–
(a) that the holder of the authorisation is no longer a fit and proper person to act as an insolvency practitioner, or

(b) without prejudice to paragraph (a), that the holder–
   (i) has failed to comply with any provision of this Part or of any regulations made under this Part or Part XV, or
   (ii) in purported compliance with any such provision, has furnished the competent authority with false, inaccurate or misleading information.

(5)   An authorisation granted under this section may be withdrawn by the competent authority at the request or with the consent of the holder of the authorisation.

394 Notices

(1)   Where a competent authority grants an authorisation under section 393, it shall give written notice of that fact to the applicant, specifying the date on which the authorisation takes effect.

(2)   Where the authority proposes to refuse an application, or to withdraw an authorisation under section 393(4), it shall give the applicant or holder of the authorisation written notice of its intention to do so, setting out particulars of the grounds on which it proposes to act.

(3)   In the case of a proposed withdrawal the notice shall state the date on which it is proposed that the withdrawal should take effect.

(4)   A notice under subsection (2) shall give particulars of the rights exercisable under the next two sections by a person on whom the notice is served.

395 Right to make representations

(1)   A person on whom a notice is served under section 394(2) may within 14 days after the date of service make written representations to the competent authority.

(2)   The competent authority shall have regard to any representations so made in determining whether to refuse the application or withdraw the authorisation, as the case may be.

396 Reference to Tribunal

(1)   The Insolvency Practitioners Tribunal ("the Tribunal") continues in being; and the provisions of Schedule 7 apply to it.

(2)   Where a person is served with a notice under section 394(2), he may–
   (a) at any time within 28 days after the date of service of the notice, or
   (b) at any time after the making by him of representations under section 395 and before the end of the period of 28 days after the date of the service on him of a notice by the competent authority that the authority does not propose to alter its decision in consequence of the representations,
give written notice to the authority requiring the case to be referred to the Tribunal.

(3)   Where a requirement is made under subsection (2), then, unless the competent authority–
(a)   has decided or decides to grant the application or, as the case may be, not to withdraw the authorisation, and
(b)   within seven days after the date of the making of the requirement, gives written notice of that decision to the person by whom the requirement was made,
it shall refer the case to the Tribunal.

397 Action of Tribunal on reference

(1)   On a reference under section 396 the Tribunal shall–
(a)   investigate the case, and
(b)   make a report to the competent authority stating what would in their opinion be the appropriate decision in the matter and the reasons for that opinion,
and it is the duty of the competent authority to decide the matter accordingly.

(2)   The Tribunal shall send a copy of the report to the applicant or, as the case may be, the holder of the authorisation; and the competent authority shall serve him with a written notice of the decision made by it in accordance with the report.

(3)   The competent authority may, if he thinks fit, publish the report of the Tribunal.

398 Refusal or withdrawal without reference to Tribunal

Where in the case of any proposed refusal or withdrawal of an authorisation either–
(a)   the period mentioned in section 396(2)(a) has expired without the making of any requirement under that subsection or of any representations under section 395, or
(b)   the competent authority has given a notice such as is mentioned in section 396(2)(b) and the period so mentioned has expired without the making of any such requirement,
the competent authority may give written notice of the refusal or withdrawal to the person concerned in accordance with the proposal in the notice given under section 394(2).

PART XIV
PUBLIC ADMINISTRATION (ENGLAND AND WALES)

399 Appointment, etc of official receivers

(1)   For the purposes of this Act the official receiver, in relation to any bankruptcy or winding up, is any person who by virtue of the following provisions of this section or section 401 below is authorised to act as the official receiver in relation to that bankruptcy or winding up.

(2)   The Secretary of State may (subject to the approval of the Treasury as to numbers) appoint persons to the office of official receiver, and a person appointed to that office (whether under this section or section 70 of the Bankruptcy Act 1914)–

    (a)   shall be paid out of money provided by Parliament such salary as the Secretary of State may with the concurrence of the Treasury direct,

    (b)   shall hold office on such other terms and conditions as the Secretary of State may with the concurrence of the Treasury direct, and

    (c)   may be removed from office by a direction of the Secretary of State.

(3)   Where a person holds the office of official receiver, the Secretary of State shall from time to time attach him either to the High Court or to a county court having jurisdiction for the purposes of the second Group of Parts of this Act.

(4)   Subject to any directions under subsection (6) below, an official receiver attached to a particular court is the person authorised to act as the official receiver in relation to every bankruptcy or winding up falling within the jurisdiction of that court.

(5)   The Secretary of State shall ensure that there is, at all times, at least one official receiver attached to the High Court and at least one attached to each county court having jurisdiction for the purposes of the second Group of Parts; but he may attach the same official receiver to two or more different courts.

(6)   The Secretary of State may give directions with respect to the disposal of the business of official receivers, and such directions may, in particular–

    (a)   authorise an official receiver attached to one court to act as the official receiver in relation to any case or description of cases falling within the jurisdiction of another court;

    (b)   provide, where there is more than one official receiver authorised to act as the official receiver in relation to cases falling within the jurisdiction of any court, for the distribution of their business between or among themselves.

(7)   A person who at the coming into force of section 222 of the Insolvency Act 1985 (replaced by this section) is an official receiver attached to a court shall continue in office after the coming into force of that section as an official receiver attached to that court under this section.

400 Functions and status of official receivers

(1)   In addition to any functions conferred on him by this Act, a person holding the office of official receiver shall carry out such other functions as may from time to time be conferred on him by the Secretary of State.

(2)   In the exercise of the functions of his office a person holding the office of official receiver shall act under the general directions of the Secretary of State and shall also be an officer of the court in relation to which he exercises those functions.

(3)   Any property vested in his official capacity in a person holding the office of official receiver shall, on his dying, ceasing to hold office or being otherwise succeeded in relation to the bankruptcy or winding up in question by another official receiver, vest in his successor without any conveyance, assignment or transfer.

401 Deputy official receivers and staff

(1)   The Secretary of State may, if he thinks it expedient to do so in order to facilitate the disposal of the business of the official receiver attached to any court, appoint an officer of his department to act as deputy to that official receiver.

(2)   Subject to any directions given by the Secretary of State under section 399 or 400, a person appointed to act as deputy to an official receiver has, on such conditions and for such period as may be specified in the terms of his appointment, the same status and functions as the official receiver to whom he is appointed deputy.
     Accordingly, references in this Act (except section 399(1) to (5)) to an official receiver include a person appointed to act as his deputy.

(3)   An appointment made under subsection (1) may be terminated at any time by the Secretary of State.

(4)   The Secretary of State may, subject to the approval of the Treasury as to numbers and remuneration and as to the other terms and conditions of the appointments, appoint officers of his department to assist official receivers in the carrying out of their functions.

402   …

403 Insolvency Services Account

(1)   All money received by the Secretary of State in respect of proceedings under this Act as it applies to England and Wales shall be paid into the Insolvency Services Account kept by the Secretary of State with the Bank of England; and all payments out of money standing to the credit of the Secretary of State in that account shall be made by the Bank of England in such manner as he may direct.

(2)   Whenever the cash balance standing to the credit of the Insolvency Services Account is in excess of the amount which in the opinion of the Secretary of State is required for the time being to answer demands in respect of bankrupts' estates or limited liability partnerships' estates, the Secretary of State shall–
     (a)   notify the excess to the National Debt Commissioners, and
     (b)   pay into the Insolvency Services Investment Account ("the Investment Account") kept by the Commissioners with the Bank of England the whole or any part of the excess as the Commissioners may require for investment in accordance with the following provisions of this Part.

(3)   Whenever any part of the money so invested is, in the opinion of the Secretary of State, required to answer any demand in respect of bankrupt's estates

or limited liability partnerships' estates, he shall notify to the National Debt Commissioners the amount so required and the Commissioners—
  (a) shall thereupon repay to the Secretary of State such sum as may be required to the credit of the Insolvency Services Account, and
  (b) for that purpose may direct the sale of such part of the securities in which the money has been invested as may be necessary.

404 Investment Account

Any money standing to the credit of the Investment Account (including any money received by the National Debt Commissioners by way of interest on or proceeds of any investment under this section) may be invested by the Commissioners, in accordance with such directions as may be given by the Treasury, in any manner for the time being specified in Part II of Schedule 1 to the Trustee Investments Act 1961.

405 Application of income in Investment Account; adjustment of balances

(1)   Where the annual account to be kept by the National Debt Commissioners under section 409 below shows that in the year for which it is made up the gross amount of the interest accrued from the securities standing to the credit of the Investment Account exceeded the aggregate of—
  (a) a sum, to be determined by the Treasury, to provide against the depreciation in the value of the securities, and
  (b) the sums paid into the Insolvency Services Account in pursuance of the next section together with the sums paid in pursuance of that section to the Commissioners of Inland Revenue,
the National Debt Commissioners shall, within three months after the account is laid before Parliament, cause the amount of the excess to be paid out of the Investment Account into the Consolidated Fund in such manner as may from time to time be agreed between the Treasury and the Commissioners.

(2)   Where the said annual account shows that in the year for which it is made up the gross amount of interest accrued from the securities standing to the credit of the Investment Account was less than the aggregate mentioned in subsection (1), an amount equal to the deficiency shall, at such times as the Treasury direct, be paid out of the Consolidated Fund into the Investment Account.

(3)   If the Investment Account is insufficient to meet its liabilities the Treasury may, on being informed of the insufficiency by the National Debt Commissioners, issue the amount of the deficiency out of the Consolidated Fund and the Treasury shall certify the deficiency to Parliament.

406 Interest on money received by liquidators or trustees in bankruptcy and invested

Where under rules made by virtue of paragraph 16 of Schedule 8 to this Act (investment of money received by limited liability partnership's liquidators) or paragraph 21 of Schedule 9 to this Act (investment of money received by trustee in bankruptcy), a limited liability partnership or a bankrupt's estate has become entitled to any sum by way of interest, the Secretary of State shall certify that sum and the amount of tax payable on it to the National Debt Commissioners; and the Commissioners shall pay, out of the Investment Account–

    (a) into the Insolvency Services Account, the sum so certified less the amount of tax so certified, and

    (b) to the Commissioners of Inland Revenue, the amount of tax so certified.

407 Unclaimed dividends and undistributed balances

(1)   The Secretary of State shall from time to time pay into the Consolidated Fund out of the Insolvency Services Account so much of the sums standing to the credit of that Account as represents–

    (a) dividends which were declared before such date as the Treasury may from time to time determine and have not been claimed, and

    (b) balances ascertained before that date which are too small to be divided among the persons entitled to them.

(2)   For the purposes of this section the sums standing to the credit of the Insolvency Services Account are deemed to include any sums paid out of that Account and represented by any sums or securities standing to the credit of the Investment Account.

(3)   The Secretary of State may require the National Debt Commissioners to pay out of the Investment Account into the Insolvency Services Account the whole or part of any sum which he is required to pay out of that account under subsection (1); and the Commissioners may direct the sale of such securities standing to the credit of the Investment Account as may be necessary for that purpose.

408 Recourse to Consolidated Fund

If, after any repayment due to it from the Investment Account, the Insolvency Services Account is insufficient to meet its liabilities, the Treasury may, on being informed of it by the Secretary of State, issue the amount of the deficiency out of the Consolidated Fund, and the Treasury shall certify the deficiency to Parliament.

409 Annual financial statement and audit

(1)   The National Debt Commissioners shall for each year ending on 31st March prepare a statement of the sums credited and debited to the Investment Account in such form and manner as the Treasury may direct and shall transmit it to the Comptroller and Auditor General before the end of November next following the year.

(2)   The Secretary of State shall for each year ending 31st March prepare a statement of the sums received or paid by him under section 403 above in such form and manner as the Treasury may direct and shall transmit each statement to the Comptroller and Auditor General before the end of November next following the year.

(3) Every such statement shall include such additional information as the Treasury may direct.

(4) The Comptroller and Auditor General shall examine, certify and report on every such statement and shall lay copies of it, and of his report, before Parliament.

410 Extent of this Part

This Part of this Act extends to England and Wales only.

PART XV
SUBORDINATE LEGISLATION

411 Limited liability partnership insolvency rules

(1) Rules may be made—
    (a) in relation to England and Wales, by the Lord Chancellor with the concurrence of the Secretary of State, or
    (b) in relation to Scotland, by the Secretary of State,
for the purpose of giving effect to Parts I to VII of this Act.

(2) Without prejudice to the generality of subsection (1), or to any provision of those Parts by virtue of which rules under this section may be made with respect to any matter, rules under this section may contain—
    (a) any such provision as is specified in Schedule 8 to this Act or corresponds to provision contained immediately before the coming into force of section 106 of the Insolvency Act 1985 in rules made, or having effect as if made, under section 663(1) or (2) of the Companies Act (old winding-up rules), and
    (b) such incidental, supplemental and transitional provisions as may appear to the Lord Chancellor or, as the case may be, the Secretary of State necessary or expedient.

(3) In Schedule 8 to this Act "liquidator" includes a provisional liquidator; and references above in this section to Parts I to VII of this Act are to be read as including the Companies Act so far as relating to, and to matters connected with or arising out of, the insolvency or winding up of limited liability partnerships.

(4) Rules under this section shall be made by statutory instrument subject to annulment in pursuance of a resolution of either House of Parliament.

(5) Regulations made by the Secretary of State under a power conferred by rules under this section shall be made by statutory instrument and, after being made, shall be laid before each House of Parliament.

(6) Nothing in this section prejudices any power to make rules of court.

412 ...

413 Insolvency Rules Committee

(1)   The committee established under section 10 of the Insolvency Act 1976 (advisory committee on bankruptcy and winding-up rules) continues to exist for the purpose of being consulted under this section.

(2)   The Lord Chancellor shall consult the committee before making any rules under section 411 or 412 other than rules which contain a statement that the only provision made by the rules is provision applying rules made under section 411, with or without modifications, for the purposes of provision made by any of sections 23 to 26 of the Water Industry Act 1991 or Schedule 3 to that Act or by any of sections 59 to 65 of, or Schedule 6 or 7 to, the Railways Act 1993.

(3)   Subject to the next subsection, the committee shall consist of–
   (a)   a judge of the High Court attached to the Chancery Division;
   (b)   a circuit judge;
   (c)   a registrar in bankruptcy of the High Court;
   (d)   the registrar of a county court;
   (e)   a practising barrister;
   (f)   a practising solicitor; and
   (g)   a practising accountant;
and the appointment of any person as a member of the committee shall be made by the Lord Chancellor.

(4)   The Lord Chancellor may appoint as additional members of the committee any persons appearing to him to have qualifications or experience that would be of value to the committee in considering any matter with which it is concerned.

414 Fees orders (limited liability partnership insolvency proceedings)

(1)   There shall be paid in respect of–
   (a)   proceedings under any of Parts I to VII of this Act, and
   (b)   the performance by the official receiver or the Secretary of State of functions under those Parts,
such fees as the competent authority may with the sanction of the Treasury by order direct.

(2)   That authority is–
   (a)   in relation to England and Wales, the Lord Chancellor, and
   (b)   in relation to Scotland, the Secretary of State.

(3)   The Treasury may by order direct by whom and in what manner the fees are to be collected and accounted for.

(4)   The Lord Chancellor may, with the sanction of the Treasury, by order provide for sums to be deposited, by such persons, in such manner and in such circumstances as may be specified in the order, by way of security for fees payable by virtue of this section.

(5)　An order under this section may contain such incidental, supplemental and transitional provisions as may appear to the Lord Chancellor, the Secretary of State or (as the case may be) the Treasury necessary or expedient.

(6)　An order under this section shall be made by statutory instrument and, after being made, shall be laid before each House of Parliament.

(7)　Fees payable by virtue of this section shall be paid into the Consolidated Fund.

(8)　References in subsection (1) to Parts I to VII of this Act are to be read as including the Companies Act so far as relating to, and to matters connected with or arising out of, the insolvency or winding up of limited liability partnerships.

(9)　Nothing in this section prejudices any power to make rules of court; and the application of this section to Scotland is without prejudice to section 2 of the Courts of Law Fees (Scotland) Act 1895.

415 ...

416 Monetary limits (limited liability partnerships winding up)

(1)　The Secretary of State may by order in a statutory instrument increase or reduce any of the money sums for the time being specified in the following provisions in the first Group of Parts–

> ...
> section 123(1)(a) (minimum debt for service of demand on limited liability partnership by unpaid creditor);
> section 184(3) (minimum value of judgment, affecting sheriff's duties on levying execution);
> section 206(1)(a) and (b) (minimum value of limited liability partnership property concealed or fraudulently removed, affecting criminal liability of limited liability partnership's member).

(2)　An order under this section may contain such transitional provisions as may appear to the Secretary of State necessary or expedient.

(3)　No order under this section increasing or reducing any of the money sums for the time being specified in section ... 123(1)(a) shall be made unless a draft of the order has been laid before and approved by a resolution of each House of Parliament.

(4)　A statutory instrument containing an order under this section, other than an order to which subsection (3) applies, is subject to annulment in pursuance of a resolution of either House of Parliament.

417 Money sum in section 222

The Secretary of State may by regulations in a statutory instrument increase or reduce the money sum for the time being specified in section 222(1) (minimum debt for service of demand on unregistered company by unpaid creditor); but such regulations shall not be made unless a draft of the statutory instrument containing them has been approved by resolution of each House of Parliament.

418 ...

419 Regulations for purposes of Part XIII

(1)   The Secretary of State may make regulations for the purpose of giving effect to Part XIII of this Act; and "prescribed" in that Part means prescribed by regulations made by the Secretary of State.

(2)   Without prejudice to the generality of subsection (1) or to any provision of that Part by virtue of which regulations may be made with respect to any matter, regulations under this section may contain–
- (a)   provision as to the matters to be taken into account in determining whether a person is a fit and proper person to act as an insolvency practitioner;
- (b)   provision prohibiting a person from so acting in prescribed cases, being cases in which a conflict of interest will or may arise;
- (c)   provision imposing requirements with respect to–
  - (i)   the preparation and keeping by a person who acts as an insolvency practitioner of prescribed books, accounts and other records, and
  - (ii)   the production of those books, accounts and records to prescribed persons;
- (d)   provision conferring power on prescribed persons–
  - (i)   to require any person who acts or has acted as an insolvency practitioner to answer any inquiry in relation to a case in which he is so acting or has so acted, and
  - (ii)   to apply to a court to examine such a person or any other person on oath concerning such a case;
- (e)   provision making non-compliance with any of the regulations a criminal offence; and
- (f)   such incidental, supplemental and transitional provisions as may appear to the Secretary of State necessary or expedient.

(3)   Any power conferred by Part XIII or this Part to make regulations, rules or orders is exercisable by statutory instrument subject to annulment by resolution of either House of Parliament.

(4)   Any rule or regulation under Part XIII or this Part may make different provision with respect to different cases or descriptions of cases, including different provision for different areas.

420, 421, 422...

PART XVI
PROVISIONS AGAINST DEBT AVOIDANCE (ENGLAND AND WALES
ONLY)

423 Transactions defrauding creditors

(1)   This section relates to transactions entered into at an undervalue; and a person enters into such a transaction with another person if–
(a)   he makes a gift to the other person or he otherwise enters into a transaction with the other on terms that provide for him to receive no consideration;
(b)   he enters into a transaction with the other in consideration of marriage; or
(c)   he enters into a transaction with the other for a consideration the value of which, in money or money's worth, is significantly less than the value, in money or money's worth, of the consideration provided by himself.

(2)   Where a person has entered into such a transaction, the court may, if satisfied under the next subsection, make such order as it thinks fit for–
(a)   restoring the position to what it would have been if the transaction had not been entered into, and
(b)   protecting the interests of persons who are victims of the transaction.

(3)   In the case of a person entering into such a transaction, an order shall only be made if the court is satisfied that it was entered into by him for the purpose–
(a)   of putting assets beyond the reach of a person who is making, or may at some time make, a claim against him, or
(b)   of otherwise prejudicing the interests of such a person in relation to the claim which he is making or may make.

(4)   In this section "the court" means the High Court or–
(a)   if the person entering into the transaction is an individual, any other court which would have jurisdiction in relation to a bankruptcy petition relating to him;
(b)   if that person is a body capable of being wound up under Part IV or V of this Act, any other court having jurisdiction to wind it up.

(5)   In relation to a transaction at an undervalue, references here and below to a victim of the transaction are to a person who is, or is capable of being, prejudiced by it; and in the following two sections the person entering into the transaction is referred to as "the debtor".

424 Those who may apply for an order under s 423

(1)   An application for an order under section 423 shall not be made in relation to a transaction except–
(a)   in a case where the debtor has been adjudged bankrupt or is a body corporate which is being wound up or in relation to which an

administration order is in force, by the official receiver, by the trustee of the bankrupt's estate or the liquidator or administrator of the body corporate or (with the leave of the court) by a victim of the transaction;

(b) in a case where a victim of the transaction is bound by a voluntary arrangement approved under Part I or Part VIII of this Act, by the supervisor of the voluntary arrangement or by any person who (whether or not so bound) is such a victim; or

(c) in any other case, by a victim of the transaction.

(2) An application made under any of the paragraphs of subsection (1) is to be treated as made on behalf of every victim of the transaction.

425 Provision which may be made by order under s 423

(1) Without prejudice to the generality of section 423, an order made under that section with respect to a transaction may (subject as follows)–

(a) require any property transferred as part of the transaction to be vested in any person, either absolutely or for the benefit of all the persons on whose behalf the application for the order is treated as made;

(b) require any property to be so vested if it represents, in any person's hands, the application either of the proceeds of sale of property so transferred or of money so transferred;

(c) release or discharge (in whole or in part) any security given by the debtor;

(d) require any person to pay to any other person in respect of benefits received from the debtor such sums as the court may direct;

(e) provide for any surety or guarantor whose obligations to any person were released or discharged (in whole or in part) under the transaction to be under such new or revived obligations as the court thinks appropriate;

(f) provide for security to be provided for the discharge of any obligation imposed by or arising under the order, for such an obligation to be charged on any property and for such security or charge to have the same priority as a security or charge released or discharged (in whole or in part) under the transaction.

(2) An order under section 423 may affect the property of, or impose any obligation on, any person whether or not he is the person with whom the debtor entered into the transaction; but such an order–

(a) shall not prejudice any interest in property which was acquired from a person other than the debtor and was acquired in good faith, for value and without notice of the relevant circumstances, or prejudice any interest deriving from such an interest, and

(b) shall not require a person who received a benefit from the transaction in good faith, for value and without notice of the relevant circumstances to pay any sum unless he was a party to the transaction.

(3) For the purposes of this section the relevant circumstances in relation to a transaction are the circumstances by virtue of which an order under section 423 may be made in respect of the transaction.

(4) In this section "security" means any mortgage, charge, lien or other security.

PART XVII
MISCELLANEOUS AND GENERAL

426 Co-operation between courts exercising jurisdiction in relation to insolvency

(1)   An order made by a court in any part of the United Kingdom in the exercise of jurisdiction in relation to insolvency law shall be enforced in any other part of the United Kingdom as if it were made by a court exercising the corresponding jurisdiction in that other part.

(2)   However, without prejudice to the following provisions of this section, nothing in subsection (1) requires a court in any part of the United Kingdom to enforce, in relation to property situated in that part, any order made by a court in any other part of the United Kingdom.

(3)   The Secretary of State, with the concurrence in relation to property situated in England and Wales of the Lord Chancellor, may by order make provision for securing that a trustee or assignee under the insolvency law of any part of the United Kingdom has, with such modifications as may be specified in the order, the same rights in relation to any property situated in another part of the United Kingdom as he would have in the corresponding circumstances if he were a trustee or assignee under the insolvency law of that other part.

(4)   The courts having jurisdiction in relation to insolvency law in any part of the United Kingdom shall assist the courts having the corresponding jurisdiction in any other part of the United Kingdom or any relevant country or territory.

(5)   For the purposes of subsection (4) a request made to a court in any part of the United Kingdom by a court in any other part of the United Kingdom or in a relevant country or territory is authority for the court to which the request is made to apply, in relation to any matters specified in the request, the insolvency law which is applicable by either court in relation to comparable matters falling within its jurisdiction.
        In exercising its discretion under this subsection, a court shall have regard in particular to the rules of private international law.

(6)   Where a person who is a trustee or assignee under the insolvency law of any part of the United Kingdom claims property situated in any other part of the United Kingdom (whether by virtue of an order under subsection (3) or otherwise), the submission of that claim to the court exercising jurisdiction in relation to insolvency law in that other part shall be treated in the same manner as a request made by a court for the purpose of subsection (4).

(7)   Section 38 of the Criminal Law Act 1977 (execution of warrant of arrest throughout the United Kingdom) applies to a warrant which, in exercise of any jurisdiction in relation to insolvency law, is issued in any part of the United Kingdom for the arrest of a person as it applies to a warrant issued in that part of the United Kingdom for the arrest of a person charged with an offence.

(8)   Without prejudice to any power to make rules of court, any power to make provision by subordinate legislation for the purpose of giving effect in relation to limited liability partnerships or individuals to the insolvency law of any part of the United Kingdom includes power to make provision for the purpose of giving effect in that part to any provision made by or under the preceding provisions of this section.

(9)   An order under subsection (3) shall be made by statutory instrument subject to annulment in pursuance of a resolution of either House of Parliament.

(10)   In this section "insolvency law" means–
    (a)   in relation to England and Wales, provision extending to England and Wales and made by or under this Act or sections 1A, 6 to 10, 12 to 15, 19(c) and 20 (with Schedule 1) of the Company Directors Disqualification Act 1986 and sections 1 to 17 of that Act as they apply for the purposes of those provisions of that Act;
    (b)   in relation to Scotland, provision extending to Scotland and made by or under this Act, sections 1A, 6 to 10, 12 to 15, 19(c) and 20 (with Schedule 1) of the Company Directors Disqualification Act 1986, Part XVIII of the Companies Act or the Bankruptcy (Scotland) Act 1985 and sections 1 to 17 of that Act as they apply for the purposes of those provisions of that Act;
    (c)   in relation to Northern Ireland, provision made by or under the Insolvency (Northern Ireland) Order 1989;
    (d)   in relation to any relevant country or territory, so much of the law of that country or territory as corresponds to provisions falling within any of the foregoing paragraphs;
and references in this subsection to any enactment include, in relation to any time before the coming into force of that enactment the corresponding enactment in force at that time.

(11)   In this section "relevant country or territory" means–
    (a)   any of the Channel Islands or the Isle of Man, or
    (b)   any country or territory designated for the purposes of this section by the Secretary of State by order made by statutory instrument.

(12)   In the application of this section to Northern Ireland–
    (a)   for any reference to the Secretary of State there is substituted a reference to the Department of Economic Development in Northern Ireland;
    (b)   in subsection (3) for the words "another part of the United Kingdom" and the words "that other part" there are substituted the words "Northern Ireland";
    (c)   for subsection (9) there is substituted the following subsection–
    "(9) An order made under subsection (3) by the Department of Economic Development in Northern Ireland shall be a statutory rule for the purposes of the Statutory Rules (Northern Ireland) Order 1979 and shall be subject to negative resolution within the meaning of section 41(6) of the Interpretation Act (Northern Ireland) 1954.".

427 ...

428 Exemptions from Restrictive Trade Practices Act

(3)   In this section "insolvency services" means the services of persons acting as insolvency practitioners or carrying out under the law of Northern Ireland functions corresponding to those mentioned in section 388(1) or (2) in Part XIII, in their capacity as such .

429 ...

430 Provision introducing Schedule of punishments

(1)   Schedule 10 to this Act has effect with respect to the way in which offences under this Act are punishable on conviction.

(2)   In relation to an offence under a provision of this Act specified in the first column of the Schedule (the general nature of the offence being described in the second column), the third column shows whether the offence is punishable on conviction on indictment, or on summary conviction, or either in the one way or the other.

(3)   The fourth column of the Schedule shows, in relation to an offence, the maximum punishment by way of fine or imprisonment under this Act which may be imposed on a person convicted of the offence in the way specified in relation to it in the third column (that is to say, on indictment or summarily) a reference to a period of years or months being to a term of imprisonment of that duration.

(4)   The fifth column shows,(in relation to an offence for which there is an entry in that column) that a person convicted of the offence after continued contravention is liable to a daily default fine; that is to say, he is liable on a second or subsequent conviction of the offence to the fine specified in that column for each day on which the contravention is continued (instead of the penalty specified for the offence in the fourth column of the Schedule).

(5)   For the purpose of any enactment in this Act whereby a member of a limited liability partnership who is in default is liable to a fine or penalty, the expression "member who is in default" means any member of the limited liability partnership who knowingly and wilfully authorises or permits the default, refusal or contravention mentioned in the enactment.

431 Summary proceedings

(1)   Summary proceedings for any offence under any of Parts I to VII of this Act may (without prejudice to any jurisdiction exercisable apart from this subsection) be taken against a body corporate at any place at which the body has a place of business, and against any other person at any place at which he is for the time being.

(2)   Notwithstanding anything in section 127(1) of the Magistrates' Courts Act 1980, an information relating to such an offence which is triable by a magistrates' court in England and Wales may be so tried if it is laid at any time within three years after the commission of the offence and within twelve months after the date on which evidence sufficient in the opinion of the Director of Public Prosecutions or the Secretary of State (as the case may be) to justify the proceedings comes to his knowledge.

(3)   Summary proceedings in Scotland for such an offence shall not be commenced after the expiration of three years from the commission of the offence. Subject to this (and notwithstanding anything in section 136 of the Criminal Procedure (Scotland) Act 1995), such proceedings may (in Scotland) be commenced at any time within twelve months after the date on which evidence sufficient in the Lord Advocate's opinion to justify the proceedings came to his knowledge or, where such evidence was reported to him by the Secretary of State, within twelve months after the date on which it came to the knowledge of the latter; and subsection (3) of that section applies for the purpose of this subsection as it applies for the purpose of that section.

(4)   For purposes of this section, a certificate of the Director of Public Prosecutions, the Lord Advocate or the Secretary of State (as the case may be) as to the date on which such evidence as is referred to above came to his knowledge is conclusive evidence.

432 Offences by bodies corporate

(1)   This section applies to offences under this Act other than those excepted by subsection (4).

(2)   Where a body corporate is guilty of an offence to which this section applies and the offence is proved to have been committed with the consent or connivance of, or to be attributable to any neglect on the part of, any director, manager … or other similar officer of the body corporate or any person who was purporting to act in any such capacity he, as well as the body corporate, is guilty of the offence and liable to be proceeded against and punished accordingly.

(3)   Where the affairs of a body corporate are managed by its members, subsection (2) applies in relation to the acts and defaults of a member in connection with his functions of management as if he were a director of the body corporate.

(4)   The offences excepted from this section are those under sections 30, 39, 51, 53, 54, 62, 64, 66, 85, 89, 164, 188, 201, 206, 207, 208, 209, 210 and 211.

433 Admissibility in evidence of statements of affairs, etc

(1)   In any proceedings (whether or not under this Act)–
   (a)   a statement of affairs prepared for the purposes of any provision of this Act which is derived from the Insolvency Act 1985, and
   (b)   any other statement made in pursuance of a requirement imposed by or under any such provision or by or under rules made under this Act,

may be used in evidence against any person making or concurring in making the statement.

(2)   However, in criminal proceedings in which any such person is charged with an offence to which this subsection applies–
        (a)   no evidence relating to the statement may be adduced, and
        (b)   no question relating to it may be asked,
by or on behalf of the prosecution, unless evidence relating to it is adduced, or a question relating to it is asked, in the proceedings by or on behalf of that person.

(3)   Subsection (2) applies to any offence other than–
        (a)   an offence under section 22(6), 47(6), 48(8), 66(6), 67(8), 95(8), 98(6), 99(3)(a), 131(7), 192(2), 208(1)(a) or (d) or (2), 210, 235(5), 353(1), 354(1)(b) or (3) or 356(1) or (2)(a) or (b) or paragraph 4(3)(a) of Schedule 7;
        (b)   an offence which is–
              (i)   created by rules made under this Act, and
              (ii)   designated for the purposes of this subsection by such rules or by regulations made by the Secretary of State;
        (c)   an offence which is–
              (i)   created by regulations made under any such rules, and
              (ii)   designated for the purposes of this subsection by such regulations;
        (d)   an offence under section 1, 2 or 5 of the Perjury Act 1911 (false statements made on oath or made otherwise than on oath); or
        (e)   an offence under section 44(1) or (2) of the Criminal Law (Consolidation)(Scotland) Act 1995 (false statements made on oath or otherwise than on oath).

(4)   Regulations under subsection (3)(b)(ii) shall be made by statutory instrument and, after being made, shall be laid before each House of Parliament.

434 Crown application

For the avoidance of doubt it is hereby declared that provisions of this Act which derive from the Insolvency Act 1985 bind the Crown so far as affecting or relating to the following matters, namely–
        (a)   remedies against, or against the property of, limited liability partnerships or individuals;
        (b)   priorities of debts;
        (c)   transactions at an undervalue or preferences;
        (d)   voluntary arrangements approved under Part I or Part VIII, and
        (e)   discharge from bankruptcy.

PART XVIII
INTERPRETATION

435 Meaning of "associate"

(1)   For the purposes of this Act any question whether a person is an associate of another person is to be determined in accordance with the following provisions

of this section (any provision that a person is an associate of another person being taken to mean that they are associates of each other).

(2)   A person is an associate of an individual if that person is the individual's husband or wife, or is a relative, or the husband or wife of a relative, of the individual or of the individual's husband or wife.

(3)   A person is an associate of any person with whom he is in partnership, and of the husband or wife or a relative of any individual with whom he is in partnership; and a Scottish firm is an associate of any person who is a member of the firm.

[(3A) A member of a limited liability partnership is an associate of that limited liability partnership and of every other member of that limited liability partnership and of the husband or wife or relative of every other member of that limited liability partnership.]

(4)   A person is an associate of any person whom he employs or by whom he is employed.

(5)   A person in his capacity as trustee of a trust other than–
(a)   a trust arising under any of the second Group of Parts or the Bankruptcy (Scotland) Act 1985, or
(b)   a pension scheme or an employees' share scheme (within the meaning of the Companies Act),
is an associate of another person if the beneficiaries of the trust include, or the terms of the trust confer a power that may be exercised for the benefit of, that other person or an associate of that other person.

(6)   A limited liability partnership is an associate of another limited liability partnership–
(a)   if the same person has control of both, or a person has control of one and persons who are his associates, or he and persons who are his associates, have control of the other, or
(b)   if a group of two or more persons has control of each limited liability partnership, and the groups either consist of the same persons or could be regarded as consisting of the same persons by treating (in one or more cases) a member of either group as replaced by a person of whom he is an associate.

(7)   A limited liability partnership is an associate of another person if that person has control of it or if that person and persons who are his associates together have control of it.

(8)   For the purposes of this section a person is a relative of an individual if he is that individual's brother, sister, uncle, aunt, nephew, niece, lineal ancestor or lineal descendant, treating–
(a)   any relationship of the half blood as a relationship of the whole blood and the stepchild or adopted child of any person as his child, and

(b) an illegitimate child as the legitimate child of his mother and reputed father;

and references in this section to a husband or wife include a former husband or wife and a reputed husband or wife.

(9) For the purposes of this section any member of a limited liability partnership is to be treated as employed by that limited liability partnership.

(10) For the purposes of this section a person is to be taken as having control of a limited liability partnership if—

(a) the members of the limited liability partnership or of another limited liability partnership which has control of it (or any of them) are accustomed to act in accordance with his directions or instructions, or

(b) he is entitled to exercise, or control the exercise of, one third or more of the voting power at any general meeting of the limited liability partnership or of another limited liability partnership which has control of it;

and where two or more persons together satisfy either of the above conditions, they are to be taken as having control of the limited liability partnership.

[(11) In this section "limited liability partnership" includes any body corporate (whether incorporated in Great Britain or elsewhere); and references to members of a limited liability partnership and to voting power at any general meeting of a limited liability partnership have effect with any necessary modifications.]

436 Expressions used generally

In this Act, except in so far as the context otherwise requires (and subject to Parts VII and XI)–

"the appointed day" means the day on which this Act comes into force under section 443;

"associate" has the meaning given by section 435;

"business" includes a trade or profession;

"the Companies Act" means the Companies Act 1985;

"conditional sale agreement" and "hire-purchase agreement" have the same meanings as in the Consumer Credit Act 1974;

["designated member" has the same meaning as it has in the Limited Liability Partnerships Act 2000;

"limited liability partnership" means a limited liability partnership formed and registered under the Limited Liability Partnerships Act 2000;

"limited liability partnership agreement", in relation to a limited liability partnership, means any agreement, express or implied, made between the members of the limited liability partnership or between the limited liability partnership and the members of the limited liability partnership which determines the mutual rights and duties of the members, and their rights and duties in relation to the limited liability partnership;]

"modifications" includes additions, alterations and omissions and cognate expressions shall be construed accordingly;

"property" includes money, goods, things in action, land and every description of property wherever situated and also obligations and every description of interest, whether present or future or vested or contingent, arising out of, or incidental to, property;

"records" includes computer records and other non-documentary records;

"subordinate legislation" has the same meaning as in the Interpretation Act 1978; and

"transaction" includes a gift, agreement or arrangement, and references to entering into a transaction shall be construed accordingly.

PART XIX
FINAL PROVISIONS

437 ...

438 Repeals

The enactments specified in the second column of Schedule 12 to this Act are repealed to the extent specified in the third column of that Schedule.

439 Amendment of enactments

(1)   The Companies Act is amended as shown in Parts I and II of Schedule 13 to this Act, being amendments consequential on this Act and the Company Directors Disqualification Act 1986.

(2)   The enactments specified in the first column of Schedule 14 to this Act (being enactments which refer, or otherwise relate, to those which are repealed and replaced by this Act or the Company Directors Disqualification Act 1986) are amended as shown in the second column of that Schedule.

(3)   The Lord Chancellor may by order make such consequential modifications of any provision contained in any subordinate legislation made before the appointed day and such transitional provisions in connection with those modifications as appear to him necessary or expedient in respect of–
  (a)   any reference in that subordinate legislation to the Bankruptcy Act 1914;
  (b)   any reference in that subordinate legislation to any enactment repealed by Part III or IV of Schedule 10 to the Insolvency Act 1985; or
  (c)   any reference in that subordinate legislation to any matter provided for under the Act of 1914 or under any enactment so repealed.

(4)   An order under this section shall be made by statutory instrument subject to annulment in pursuance of a resolution of either House of Parliament.

440 Extent (Scotland)

(1)   Subject to the next subsection, provisions of this Act contained in the first Group of Parts extend to Scotland except where otherwise stated.

(2)   The following provisions of this Act do not extend to Scotland–
(a)   in the first Group of Parts–
section 43;
sections 238 to 241; and
section 246;
(b)   ...
(c)   in the third Group of Parts–
sections 399 to 402,
sections 412, 413, 415, 418, 420 and 421,
sections 423 to 425, and
section 429(1) and (2); and
(d)   in the Schedules–
Parts II and III of Schedule 11; and
Schedules 12 and 14 so far as they repeal or amend enactments which extend to England and Wales only.

441, 442   ...

443 Commencement

This Act comes into force on the day appointed under section 236(2) of the Insolvency Act 1985 for the coming into force of Part III of that Act (individual insolvency and bankruptcy), immediately after that Part of that Act comes into force for England and Wales.

444 Citation

This Act may be cited as the Insolvency Act 1986.

SCHEDULE 1
POWERS OF ADMINISTRATOR OR ADMINISTRATIVE
RECEIVER

1   Power to take possession of, collect and get in the property of the limited liability partnership and, for that purpose, to take such proceedings as may seem to him expedient.

2   Power to sell or otherwise dispose of the property of the limited liability partnership by public auction or private contract or, in Scotland, to sell, feu, hire out or otherwise dispose of the property of the limited liability partnership by public roup or private bargain.

3   Power to raise or borrow money and grant security therefor over the property of the limited liability partnership.

4   Power to appoint a solicitor or accountant or other professionally qualified person to assist him in the performance of his functions.

5   Power to bring or defend any action or other legal proceedings in the name and on behalf of the limited liability partnership.

6   Power to refer to arbitration any question affecting the limited liability partnership.

7   Power to effect and maintain insurances in respect of the business and property of the limited liability partnership.

8   Power to use the limited liability partnership's seal.

9   Power to do all acts and to execute in the name and on behalf of the limited liability partnership any deed, receipt or other document.

10   Power to draw, accept, make and endorse any bill of exchange or promissory note in the name and on behalf of the limited liability partnership.

11   Power to appoint any agent to do any business which he is unable to do himself or which can more conveniently be done by an agent and power to employ and dismiss employees.

12   Power to do all such things (including the carrying out of works) as may be necessary for the realisation of the property of the limited liability partnership.

13   Power to make any payment which is necessary or incidental to the performance of his functions.

14   Power to carry on the business of the limited liability partnership.

15   Power to establish subsidiaries of the limited liability partnership.

16   Power to transfer to subsidiaries of the limited liability partnership the whole or any part of the business and property of the limited liability partnership.

17   Power to grant or accept a surrender of a lease or tenancy of any of the property of the limited liability partnership, and to take a lease or tenancy of any property required or convenient for the business of the limited liability partnership.

18   Power to make any arrangement or compromise on behalf of the limited liability partnership.

[19   Power to enforce any rights the limited liability partnership has against the members under the terms of the limited liability partnership agreement.]

20   Power to rank and claim in the bankruptcy, insolvency, sequestration or liquidation of any person indebted to the limited liability partnership and to receive dividends, and to accede to trust deeds for the creditors of any such person.

21   Power to present or defend a petition for the winding up of the limited liability partnership.

22   Power to change the situation of the limited liability partnership's registered office.

23   Power to do all other things incidental to the exercise of the foregoing powers.

SCHEDULE 2
POWERS OF A SCOTTISH RECEIVER (ADDITIONAL TO THOSE CONFERRED ON HIM BY THE INSTRUMENT OF CHARGE)

1   Power to take possession of, collect and get in the property from the limited liability partnership or a liquidator thereof or any other person, and for that purpose, to take such proceedings as may seem to him expedient.

2   Power to sell, feu, hire out or otherwise dispose of the property by public roup or private bargain and with or without advertisement.

3   Power to raise or borrow money and grant security therefor over the property.

4   Power to appoint a solicitor or accountant or other professionally qualified person to assist him in the performance of his functions.

5   Power to bring or defend any action or other legal proceedings in the name and on behalf of the limited liability partnership.

6   Power to refer to arbitration all questions affecting the limited liability partnership.

7   Power to effect and maintain insurances in respect of the business and property of the limited liability partnership.

8   Power to use the limited liability partnership's seal.

9   Power to do all acts and to execute in the name and on behalf of the limited liability partnership any deed, receipt or other document.

10   Power to draw, accept, make and endorse any bill of exchange or promissory note in the name and on behalf of the limited liability partnership.

11   Power to appoint any agent to do any business which he is unable to do himself or which can more conveniently be done by an agent, and power to employ and dismiss employees.

12   Power to do all such things (including the carrying out of works), as may be necessary for the realisation of the property.

13   Power to make any payment which is necessary or incidental to the performance of his functions.

14   Power to carry on the business of the limited liability partnership or any part of it.

15   Power to grant or accept a surrender of a lease or tenancy of any of the property, and to take a lease or tenancy of any property required or convenient for the business of the limited liability partnership.

16   Power to make any arrangement or compromise on behalf of the limited liability partnership.

[17   Power to enforce any rights the limited liability partnership has against the members under the terms of the limited liability partnership agreement.]

[Schedule 2, paragraph 17, as modified by the Limited Liability Partnerships (Scotland) Regulations 2001]

18   Power to establish subsidiaries of the limited liability partnership.

19   Power to transfer to subsidiaries of the limited liability partnership the business of the limited liability partnership or any part of it and any of the property.

20   Power to rank and claim in the bankruptcy, insolvency, sequestration or liquidation of any person or company indebted to the limited liability partnership and to receive dividends, and to accede to trust deeds for creditors of any such person.

21   Power to present or defend a petition for the winding up of the limited liability partnership.

22   Power to change the situation of the limited liability partnership's registered office.

23   Power to do all other things incidental to the exercise of the powers mentioned in section 55(1) of this Act or above in this Schedule.

SCHEDULE 3
ORDERS IN COURSE OF WINDING UP PRONOUNCED IN
VACATION (SCOTLAND)

PART I
ORDERS WHICH ARE TO BE FINAL

Orders under section 153, as to the time for proving debts and claims.
Orders under section 195 as to meetings for ascertaining wishes of creditors or contributories.

Orders under section 198, as to the examination of witnesses in regard to the property or affairs of a limited liability partnership.

PART II
ORDERS WHICH ARE TO TAKE EFFECT UNTIL MATTER DISPOSED OF BY INNER HOUSE

Orders under section 126(1), 130(2) or (3), 147, 227 or 228, restraining or permitting the commencement or the continuance of legal proceedings.
Orders under section 135(5), limiting the powers of provisional liquidators.
Orders under section 108, appointing a liquidator to fill a vacancy.
Orders under section 167 or 169, sanctioning the exercise of any powers by a liquidator, other than the powers specified in paragraphs 1, 2 and 3 of Schedule 4 to this Act.
Orders under section 158, as to the arrest and detention of an absconding contributory and his property.

SCHEDULE 4
POWERS OF LIQUIDATOR IN A WINDING UP

PART I
POWERS EXERCISABLE WITH SANCTION

1   Power to pay any class of creditors in full.

2   Power to make any compromise or arrangement with creditors or persons claiming to be creditors, or having or alleging themselves to have any claim (present or future, certain or contingent, ascertained or sounding only in damages) against the limited liability partnership, or whereby the limited liability partnership may be rendered liable.

3   Power to compromise, on such terms as may be agreed–
   (a)   all calls and liabilities to calls, all debts and liabilities capable of resulting in debts, and all claims (present or future, certain or contingent, ascertained or sounding only in damages) subsisting or supposed to subsist between the limited liability partnership and a contributory or alleged contributory or other debtor or person apprehending liability to the limited liability partnership, and
   (b)   all questions in any way relating to or affecting the assets or the winding up of the limited liability partnership,
and take any security for the discharge of any such call, debt, liability or claim and give a complete discharge in respect of it.

PART II
POWERS EXERCISABLE WITHOUT SANCTION IN VOLUNTARY WINDING UP, WITH SANCTION IN WINDING UP BY THE COURT

4   Power to bring or defend any action or other legal proceeding in the name and on behalf of the limited liability partnership.

5   Power to carry on the business of the limited liability partnership so far as may be necessary for its beneficial winding up.

PART III
POWERS EXERCISABLE WITHOUT SANCTION IN ANY
WINDING UP

6   Power to sell any of the limited liability partnership's property by public auction or private contract with power to transfer the whole of it to any person or to sell the same in parcels.

7   Power to do all acts and execute, in the name and on behalf of the limited liability partnership, all deeds, receipts and other documents and for that purpose to use, when necessary, the limited liability partnership's seal.

8   Power to prove, rank and claim in the bankruptcy, insolvency or sequestration of any contributory for any balance against his estate, and to receive dividends in the bankruptcy, insolvency or sequestration in respect of that balance, as a separate debt due from the bankrupt or insolvent, and rateably with the other separate creditors.

9   Power to draw, accept, make and indorse any bill of exchange or promissory note in the name and on behalf of the limited liability partnership, with the same effect with respect to the limited liability partnership's liability as if the bill or note had been drawn, accepted, made or indorsed by or on behalf of the limited liability partnership in the course of its business.

10   Power to raise on the security of the assets of the limited liability partnership any money requisite.

11   Power to take out in his official name letters of administration to any deceased contributory, and to do in his official name any other act necessary for obtaining payment of any money due from a contributory or his estate which cannot conveniently be done in the name of the limited liability partnership.
In all such cases the money due is deemed, for the purpose of enabling the liquidator to take out the letters of administration or recover the money, to be due to the liquidator himself.

12   Power to appoint an agent to do any business which the liquidator is unable to do himself.

13   Power to do all such other things as may be necessary for winding up the limited liability partnership's affairs and distributing its assets.

Schedule 5

SCHEDULE 6
THE CATEGORIES OF PREFERENTIAL DEBTS

Category 1: Debts due to Inland Revenue

1 Sums due at the relevant date from the debtor on account of deductions of income tax from emoluments paid during the period of twelve months next before that date.

The deductions here referred to are those which the debtor was liable to make under section 203 of the Income and Corporation Taxes Act 1988(pay as you earn), less the amount of the repayments of income tax which the debtor was liable to make during that period.

2 Sums due at the relevant date from the debtor in respect of such deductions as are required to be made by the debtor for that period under section 559 of the Income and Corporation Taxes Act 1988(sub-contractors in the construction industry).

Category 2: Debts due to Customs and Excise

3 Any value added tax which is referable to the period of six months next before the relevant date (which period is referred to below as "the six-month period").

For the purposes of this paragraph–
(a) where the whole of the prescribed accounting period to which any value added tax is attributable falls within the six-month period, the whole amount of that tax is referable to that period; and
(b) in any other case the amount of any value added tax which is referable to the six-month period is the proportion of the tax which is equal to such proportion (if any) of the accounting reference period in question as falls within the six-month period;
and in sub-paragraph (a)"prescribed" means prescribed by regulations under the Value Added Tax Act 1994.

3A Any insurance premium tax which is referable to the period of six months next before the relevant date (which period is referred to below as "the six-month period").

For the purposes of this paragraph–
(a) where the whole of the accounting period to which any insurance premium tax is attributable falls within the six-month period, the whole amount of that tax is referable to that period; and
(b) in any other case the amount of any insurance premium tax which is referable to the six-month period is the proportion of the tax which is equal to such proportion (if any) of the accounting period in question as falls within the six-month period;
and references here to accounting periods shall be construed in accordance with Part III of the Finance Act 1994.

3B Any landfill tax which is referable to the period of six months next before the relevant date (which period is referred to below as "the six-month period").

For the purposes of this paragraph–

(a) where the whole of the accounting period to which any landfill tax is attributable falls within the six-month period, the whole amount of that tax is referable to that period; and

(b) in any other case the amount of any landfill tax which is referable to the six-month period is the proportion of the tax which is equal to such proportion (if any) of the accounting period in question as falls within the six-month period;

and references here to accounting periods shall be construed in accordance with Part III of the Finance Act 1996.

3C Any climate change levy which is referable to the period of six months next before the relevant date (which period is referred to below as "the six-month period").

For the purposes of this paragraph–

(a) where the whole of the accounting period to which any climate change levy is attributable falls within the six-month period, the whole amount of that levy is referable to that period; and

(b) in any other case the amount of any climate change levy which is referable to the six-month period is the proportion of the levy which is equal to such proportion (if any) of the accounting period in question as falls within the six-month period;

and references here to accounting periods shall be construed in accordance with Schedule 6 to the Finance Act 2000.

4 The amount of any car tax which is due at the relevant date from the debtor and which became due within a period of twelve months next before that date.

5 Any amount which is due–

(a) by way of general betting duty, bingo duty or gaming duty, or

(b) under section 12(1) of the Betting and Gaming Duties Act 1981 (general betting duty and pool betting duty recoverable from agent collecting stakes),

from the debtor at the relevant date and which became due within the period of twelve months next before that date.

5A The amount of any excise duty on beer which is due at the relevant date from the debtor and which became due within a period of six months next before that date.

5B Any amount which is due by way of lottery duty from the debtor at the relevant date and which became due within the period of twelve months next before that date.

5C Any amount which is due by way of air passenger duty from the debtor at the relevant date and which became due within the period of six months next before that date.

Category 3: Social security contributions

6   All sums which on the relevant date are due from the debtor on account of Class 1 or Class 2 contributions under the Social Security Contributions and Benefits Act 1992 or the Social Security (Northern Ireland) Act 1975 and which became due from the debtor in the twelve months next before the relevant date.

7   All sums which on the relevant date have been assessed on and are due from the debtor on account of Class 4 contributions under either of those Acts of 1975, being sums which–
   (a)   are due to the Commissioners of Inland Revenue (rather than to the Secretary of State or a Northern Ireland department), and
   (b)   are assessed on the debtor up to 5th April next before the relevant date,
but not exceeding, in the whole, any one year's assessment.

Category 4: Contributions to occupational pension schemes, etc

8   Any sum which is owed by the debtor and is a sum to which Schedule 4 to the Pension Schemes Act 1993 applies (contributions to occupational pension schemes and state scheme premiums).

Category 5: Remuneration, etc, of employees

9   So much of any amount which–
   (a)   is owed by the debtor to a person who is or has been an employee of the debtor, and
   (b)   is payable by way of remuneration in respect of the whole or any part of the period of four months next before the relevant date,
as does not exceed so much as may be prescribed by order made by the Secretary of State.

10   An amount owed by way of accrued holiday remuneration, in respect of any period of employment before the relevant date, to a person whose employment by the debtor has been terminated, whether before, on or after that date.

11   So much of any sum owed in respect of money advanced for the purpose as has been applied for the payment of a debt which, if it had not been paid, would have been a debt falling within paragraph 9 or 10.

12   So much of any amount which–
   (a)   is ordered (whether before or after the relevant date) to be paid by the debtor under the Reserve Forces (Safeguard of Employment) Act 1985, and
   (b)   is so ordered in respect of a default made by the debtor before that date in the discharge of his obligations under that Act,
as does no exceed such amount as may be prescribed by order made by the Secretary of State.

13 – (1)   For the purposes of paragraphs 9 to 12, a sum is payable by the debtor to a person by way of remuneration in respect of any period if–
    (a)   it is paid as wages or salary (whether payable for time or for piece work or earned wholly or partly by way of commission) in respect of services rendered to the debtor in that period, or
    (b)   it is an amount falling within the following sub-paragraph and is payable by the debtor in respect of that period.

(2)   An amount falls within this sub-paragraph if it is–
    (a)   a guarantee payment under Part III of the Employment Rights Act 1996 (employee without work to do);
    (b)   any payment for time off under section 53 (time off to look for work or arrange training) or section 56 (time off for ante-natal care) of that Act or under section 169 of the Trade Union and Labour Relations (Consolidation) Act 1992 (time off for carrying out trade union duties etc);
    (c)   remuneration on suspension on medical grounds, or on maternity grounds, under Part VII of the Employment Rights Act 1996; or
    (d)   remuneration under a protective award under section 189 of the Trade Union and Labour Relations (Consolidation) Act 1992 (redundancy dismissal with compensation).

14 – (1)   This paragraph relates to a case in which a person's employment has been terminated by or in consequence of his employer going into liquidation or being adjudged bankrupt or (his employer being a limited liability partnership not in liquidation) by or in consequence of–
    (a)   a receiver being appointed as mentioned in section 40 of this Act (debenture holders secured by floating charge), or
    (b)   the appointment of a receiver under section 53(6) or 54(5) of this Act (Scottish limited liability partnership with property subject to floating charge), or
    (c)   the taking of possession by debenture holders (so secured), as mentioned in section 196 of the Companies Act.

(2)   For the purposes of paragraphs 9 to 12, holiday remuneration is deemed to have accrued to that person in respect of any period of employment if, by virtue of his contract of employment or of any enactment that remuneration would have accrued in respect of that period if his employment had continued until he became entitled to be allowed the holiday.

(3)   The reference in sub-paragraph (2) to any enactment includes an order or direction made under an enactment.

15   Without prejudice to paragraphs 13 and 14–
    (a)   any remuneration payable by the debtor to a person in respect of a period of holiday or of absence from work through sickness or other good cause is deemed to be wages or (as the case may be) salary in respect of services rendered to the debtor in that period, and

(b) references here and in those paragraphs to remuneration in respect of a period of holiday include any sums which, if they had been paid, would have been treated for the purposes of the enactments to social security as earnings in respect of that period.

Category 6: Levies on coal and steel production

15A Any sums due at the relevant date from the debtor in respect of–
    (a) the levies on the production of coal and steel referred to in Articles 49 and 50 of the E.C.S.C. Treaty, or
    (b) any surcharge for delay provided for in Article 50(3) of that Treaty and Article 6 of Decision 3/52 of the High Authority of the Coal and Steel Community.

16 An order under paragraph 9 or 12–
    (a) may contain such transitional provisions as may appear to the Secretary of State necessary or expedient;
    (b) shall be made by statutory instrument subject to annulment in pursuance of a resolution of either House of Parliament.

SCHEDULE 7
INSOLVENCY PRACTITIONERS TRIBUNAL

1 – (1) The Secretary of State shall draw up and from time to time revise–
    (a) a panel of persons who
        (i) have a seven-year general qualification, within the meaning of section 71 of the Courts and Legal Services Act 1990;
        (ii) are advocates or solicitors in Scotland of at least seven years' standing, and are nominated for the purpose by the Lord Chancellor or the Lord President of the Court of Session, and
    (b) a panel of persons who are experienced in insolvency matters;
    and the members of the Tribunal shall be selected from those panels in accordance with this Schedule.

(2) The power to revise the panels includes power to terminate a person's membership of either of them, and is accordingly to that extent subject to section 7 of the Tribunals and Inquiries Act 1992 (which makes it necessary to obtain the concurrence of the Lord Chancellor and the Lord President of the Court of Session to dismissals in certain cases).

2 The Secretary of State may out of money provided by Parliament pay to members of the Tribunal such remuneration as he may with the approval of the Treasury determine; and such expenses of the Tribunal as the Secretary of State and the Treasury may approve shall be defrayed by the Secretary of State out of money so provided.

3 – (1) For the purposes of carrying out their functions in relation to any cases referred to them, the Tribunal may sit either as a single tribunal or in two or more divisions.

(2)   The functions of the Tribunal in relation to any case referred to them shall be exercised by three members consisting of–
(a)   a chairman selected by the Secretary of State from the panel drawn up under paragraph 1(1)(a) above, and
(b)   two other members selected by the Secretary of State from the panel drawn up under paragraph 1(1)(b).

4 – (1)   Any investigation by the Tribunal shall be so conducted as to afford a reasonable opportunity for representations to be made to the Tribunal by or on behalf of the person whose case is the subject of the investigation.

(2)   For the purposes of any such investigation, the Tribunal–
(a)   may by summons require any person to attend, at such time and place as is specified in the summons, to give evidence or to produce any books, papers and other records in his possession or under his control which the Tribunal consider it necessary for the purposes of the investigation to examine, and
(b)   may take evidence on oath, and for the purpose administer oaths, or may, instead of administering an oath, require the person examined to make and subscribe a declaration of the truth of the matter respecting which he is examined;
but no person shall be required, in obedience to such a summons, to go more than ten miles from his place of residence, unless the necessary expenses of his attendance are paid or tendered to him.

(3)   Every person who–
(a)   without reasonable excuse fails to attend in obedience to a summons issued under this paragraph, or refuses to give evidence, or
(b)   intentionally alters, suppresses, conceals or destroys or refuses to produce any document which he may be required to produce for the purpose of an investigation by the Tribunal,
is liable to a fine.

(4)   Subject to the provisions of this paragraph, the Secretary of State may make rules for regulating the procedure on any investigation by the Tribunal.

(5)   In their application to Scotland, sub-paragraphs (2) and (3) above have effect as if for any reference to a summons there were substituted a reference to a notice in writing.

SCHEDULE 8
PROVISIONS CAPABLE OF INCLUSION IN LIMITED LIABILITY
PARTNERSHIP INSOLVENCY RULES

1   Provision for supplementing, in relation to the insolvency or winding up of limited liability partnerships, any provision made by or under section 117 of this Act (jurisdiction in relation to winding up).

2   Provision for regulating the practice and procedure of any court exercising jurisdiction for the purposes of Parts I to VII of this Act or the Companies Act so far as relating to, and to matters connected with or arising out of, the insolvency or winding up of limited liability partnerships, being any provision that could be made by rules of court.

3 Provision requiring notice of any proceedings in connection with or arising out of the insolvency or winding up of a limited liability partnership to be given or published in the manner prescribed by the rules.

4 Provision with respect to the form, manner of serving, contents and proof of any petition, application, order, notice, statement or other document required to be presented, made, given, published or prepared under any enactment or subordinate legislation relating to, or to matters connected with or arising out of, the insolvency or winding up of limited liability partnerships.

5 Provisions specifying the persons to whom any notice is to be given.

6 Provision for the registration of voluntary arrangements approved under Part I of this Act, including provision for the keeping and inspection of a register.

7 Provision as to the manner in which a provisional liquidator appointed under section 135 is to carry out his functions.

8 Provision with respect to the certification of any person as, and as to the proof that a person is, the liquidator, administrator or administrative receiver of a limited liability partnership.

9 The following provision with respect to meetings of a limited liability partnership's creditors, contributories or members–
  (a) provision as to the manner of summoning a meeting (including provision as to how any power to require a meeting is to be exercised, provision as to the manner of determining the value of any debt or contribution for the purposes of any such power and provision making the exercise of any such power subject to the deposit of a sum sufficient to cover the expenses likely to be incurred in summoning and holding a meeting);
  (b) provision specifying the time and place at which a meeting may be held and the period of notice required for a meeting;
  (c) provision as to the procedure to be followed at a meeting (including the manner in which decisions may be reached by a meeting and the manner in which the value of any vote at a meeting is to be determined);
  (d) provision for requiring a person who is or has been a member of the limited liability partnership to attend a meeting;
  (e) provision creating, in the prescribed circumstances, a presumption that a meeting has been duly summoned and held;
  (f) provision as to the manner of proving the decisions of a meeting.

10 – (1) Provision as to the functions, membership and proceedings of a committee established under section 26, 49, 68, 101, 141 or 142 of this Act.

(2)   The following provision with respect to the establishment of a committee under section 101, 141 or 142 of this Act, that is to say–
- (a)   provision for resolving differences between a meeting of the limited liability partnership's creditors and a meeting of its contributories or members;
- (b)   provision authorising the establishment of the committee without a meeting of contributories in a case where a limited liability partnership is being wound up on grounds including its inability to pay its debts; and
- (c)   provision modifying the requirements of this Act with respect to the establishment of the committee in a case where a winding-up order has been made immediately upon the discharge of an administration order.

11   Provision as to the manner in which any requirement that may be imposed on a person under any of Parts I to VII of this Act by the official receiver, the liquidator, administrator or administrative receiver of a limited liability partnership or a special manager appointed under section 177 is to be so imposed.

12   Provision as to the debts that may be proved in a winding up, as to the manner and conditions of proving a debt and as to the manner and expenses of establishing the value of any debt or security.

13   Provision with respect to the manner of the distribution of the property of a limited liability partnership that is being wound up, including provision with respect to unclaimed funds and dividends.

14   Provision which, with or without modifications, applies in relation to the winding up of limited liability partnerships any enactment contained in Parts VIII to XI of this Act or in the Bankruptcy (Scotland) Act 1985.

15   Provision as to the amount, or manner of determining the amount, payable to the liquidator, administrator or administrative receiver of a limited liability partnership or a special manager appointed under section 177, by way of remuneration for the carrying out of functions in connection with or arising out of the insolvency or winding up of a limited liability partnership.

16   Provision with respect to the manner in which moneys received by the liquidator of a limited liability partnership in the course of carrying out his functions as such are to be invested or otherwise handled and with respect to the payment of interest on sums which, in pursuance of rules made by virtue of this paragraph, have been paid into the Insolvency Services Account.

17   Provision as to the fees, costs, charges and other expenses that may be treated as the expenses of a winding up.

18   Provision as to the fees, costs, charges and other expenses that may be treated as properly incurred by the administrator or administrative receiver of a limited liability partnership.

19   Provision as to the fees, costs, charges and other expenses that may be incurred for any of the purposes of Part I of this Act or in the administration of any voluntary arrangement approved under that Part.

20   Provision requiring registrars and other officers of courts having jurisdiction in England and Wales in relation to, or to matters connected with or arising out of, the insolvency or winding up of limited liability partnerships–
  (a)   to keep books and other records with respect to the exercise of that jurisdiction, and
  (b)   to make returns to the Secretary of State of the business of those courts.

21   Provision requiring a creditor, member or contributory, or such a committee as is mentioned in paragraph 10 above, to be supplied (on payment in prescribed cases of the prescribed fee) with such information and with copies of such documents as may be prescribed.

22   Provision as to the manner in which public examinations under sections 133 and 134 of this Act and proceedings under sections 236 and 237 are to be conducted, as to the circumstances in which records of such examinations or proceedings are to be made available to prescribed persons and as to the costs of such examinations and proceedings.

23   Provision imposing requirements with respect to–
  (a)   the preparation and keeping by the liquidator, administrator or administrative receiver of a limited liability partnership, or by the supervisor of a voluntary arrangement approved under Part I of this Act, of prescribed books, accounts and other records;
  (b)   the production of those books, accounts and records for inspection by prescribed persons;
  (c)   the auditing of accounts kept by the liquidator, administrator or administrative receiver of a limited liability partnership, or the supervisor of such a voluntary arrangement; and
  (d)   the issue by the administrator or administrative receiver of a limited liability partnership of such a certificate as is mentioned in section 22(3)(b) of the Value Added Tax Act 1983 (refund of tax in cases of bad debts) and the supply of copies of the certificate to creditors of the limited liability partnership.

24   Provision requiring the person who is the supervisor of a voluntary arrangement approved under Part I, when it appears to him that the voluntary arrangement has been fully implemented and that nothing remains to be done by him under the arrangement–
  (a)   to give notice of that fact to persons bound by the voluntary arrangement, and
  (b)   to report to those persons on the carrying out of the functions conferred on the supervisor of the arrangement.

25   Provision as to the manner in which the liquidator of a limited liability partnership is to act in relation to the books, papers and other records of the limited liability partnership, including provision authorising their disposal.

26 Provision imposing requirements in connection with the carrying out of functions under section 7(3) of the Company Directors Disqualification Act 1986 (including, in particular, requirements with respect to the making of periodic returns).

27 Provision conferring power on the Secretary of State to make regulations with respect to so much of any matter that may be provided for in the rules as relates to the carrying out of the functions of the liquidator, administrator or administrative receiver of a limited liability partnership.

28 Provision conferring a discretion on the court.

29 Provision conferring power on the court to make orders for the purpose of securing compliance with obligations imposed by or under section 22, 47, 66, 131, 143(2) or 235 of this Act or section 7(4) of the Company Directors Disqualification Act 1986.

30 Provision making non-compliance with any of the rules a criminal offence.

31 Provision making different provision for different cases or descriptions of cases, including different provisions for different areas.

SCHEDULE 9

...

SCHEDULE 10
[Please see following pages]

SCHEDULE 11

...

SCHEDULE 12

[Schedule 12 relates to repeals made by the Insolvency Act 1986 and is not reproduced here]

SCHEDULE 10
PUNISHMENT OF OFFENCES UNDER THIS ACT

Section of Act creating offence	General nature of offence	Mode of prosecution	Punishment	Daily default fine (where applicable)
12(2)	Limited liability partnership and others failing to state in correspondence, etc that administrator appointed.	Summary.	One-fifth of the statutory maximum.	
15(8)	Failure of administrator to register office copy of court order permitting disposal of charged property.	Summary.	One-fifth of the statutory maximum.	One-fiftieth of the statutory maximum.
18(5)	Failure of administrator to register office copy of court order varying or discharging administration order.	Summary.	One-fifth of the statutory maximum.	One-fiftieth of the statutory maximum.
21(3)	Administrator failing to register administration order and give notice of appointment.	Summary.	One-fifth of the statutory maximum.	One-fiftieth of the statutory maximum.
22(6)	Failure to comply with provisions relating to statement of affairs, where administrator appointed.	1. On indictment. 2. Summary.	A fine. The statutory maximum.	One-tenth of the statutory maximum.
23(3)	Administrator failing to send out, register and lay before creditors statement of his proposals.	Summary.	One-fifth of the statutory maximum.	One-fiftieth of the statutory maximum.

Section of Act creating offence	General nature of offence	Mode of prosecution	Punishment	Daily default fine (where applicable)
24(7)	Administrator failing to file court order discharging administration order under s 24.	Summary.	One-fifth of the statutory maximum.	One-fiftieth of the statutory maximum.
27(6)	Administrator failing to file court order discharging administration order under s 27.	Summary.	One-fifth of the statutory maximum.	One-fiftieth of the statutory maximum.
30	Body corporate acting as receiver.	1. On indictment. 2. Summary.	A fine. The statutory maximum.	
31	Undischarged bankrupt acting as receiver or manager.	1. On indictment. 2. Summary.	2 years or a fine, or both. 6 months or the statutory maximum, or both.	
38(5)	Receiver failing to deliver accounts to registrar.	Summary.	One-fifth of the statutory maximum.	One-fiftieth of the statutory maximum.
39(2)	Limited liability partnership and others failing to state in correspondence that receiver appointed.	Summary.	One-fifth of the statutory maximum.	
43(6)	Administrative receiver failing to file office copy of order permitting disposal of charged property.	Summary.	One-fifth of the statutory maximum.	One-fiftieth of the statutory maximum.

Section of Act creating offence	General nature of offence	Mode of prosecution	Punishment	Daily default fine (where applicable)
45(5)	Administrative receiver failing to file notice of vacation of office.	Summary.	One-fifth of the statutory maximum.	One-fiftieth of the statutory maximum.
46(4)	Administrative receiver failing to give notice of his appointment.	Summary.	One-fifth of the statutory maximum.	One-fiftieth of the statutory maximum.
47(6)	Failure to comply with provisions relating to statement of affairs, where administrative receiver appointed.	1. On indictment. 2. Summary.	A fine. The statutory maximum.	One-tenth of the statutory maximum.
48(8)	Administrative receiver failing to comply with requirements as to his report.	Summary.	One-fifth of the statutory maximum.	One-fiftieth of the statutory maximum.
51(4)	Body corporate or Scottish firm acting as receiver.	1. On indictment. 2. Summary.	A fine. The statutory maximum.	
51(5)	Undischarged bankrupt acting as receiver (Scotland).	1. On indictment. 2. Summary.	2 years or a fine, or both. 6 months or the statutory maximum, or both.	
53(2)	Failing to deliver to registrar copy of instrument of appointment of receiver.	Summary.	One-fifth of the statutory maximum.	One-fiftieth of the statutory maximum.
54(3)	Failing to deliver to registrar the court's interlocutor appointing receiver.	Summary.	One-fifth of the statutory maximum.	One-fiftieth of the statutory maximum.

Appendix 2 – IA 1986 as modified

Section of Act creating offence	General nature of offence	Mode of prosecution	Punishment	Daily default fine (where applicable)
61(7)	Receiver failing to send to registrar certified copy of court order authorising disposal of charged property.	Summary.	One-fifth of the statutory maximum.	One-fiftieth of the statutory maximum.
62(5)	Failing to give notice to registrar of cessation or removal of receiver.	Summary.	One-fifth of the statutory maximum.	One-fiftieth of the statutory maximum.
64(2)	Limited liability partnership and others failing to state on correspondence etc that receiver appointed.	Summary.	One-fifth of the statutory maximum.	
65(4)	Receiver failing to send or publish notice of his appointment.	Summary.	One-fifth of the statutory maximum.	One-fiftieth of the statutory maximum.
66(6)	Failing to comply with provisions concerning statement of affairs, where receiver appointed.	1. On indictment. 2. Summary.	A fine. The statutory maximum.	One-tenth of the statutory maximum.
67(8)	Receiver failing to comply with requirements as to his report.	Summary.	One-fifth of the statutory maximum.	One-fiftieth of the statutory maximum.
85(2)	Limited liability partnership failing to give notice in Gazette of [making a determination for voluntary winding up].	Summary.	One-fifth of the statutory maximum.	One-fiftieth of the statutory maximum.

Section of Act creating offence	General nature of offence	Mode of prosecution	Punishment	Daily default fine (where applicable)
89(4)	[Designated member] making statutory declaration of limited liability partnership's solvency without reasonable grounds for his opinion.	1. On indictment. 2. Summary.	2 years or a fine, or both. 6 months or the statutory maximum, or both.	
89(6)	Declaration under section 89 not delivered to registrar within prescribed time.	Summary.	One-fifth of the statutory maximum.	One-fiftieth of the statutory maximum.
93(3)	Liquidator failing to summon [meeting of members of the limited liability partnership] at each year's end.	Summary.	One-fifth of the statutory maximum.	
94(4)	Liquidator failing to send to registrar a copy of account of winding up and return of final meeting.	Summary.	One-fifth of the statutory maximum.	One-fiftieth of the statutory maximum.
94(6)	Liquidator failing to call final meeting.	Summary.	One-fifth of the statutory maximum.	
95(8)	Liquidator failing to comply with s 95, where limited liability partnership insolvent.	Summary.	The statutory maximum.	

Appendix 2 – IA 1986 as modified

Section of Act creating offence	General nature of offence	Mode of prosecution	Punishment	Daily default fine (where applicable)
98(6)	Limited liability partnership failing to comply with s 98 in respect of summoning and giving notice of creditors' meeting.	1. On indictment. 2. Summary.	A fine. The statutory maximum.	
99(3)	[Designated members] failing to attend and lay statement in prescribed form before creditors' meeting.	1. On indictment. 2. Summary.	A fine. The statutory maximum.	
105(3)	Liquidator failing to summon [meeting of the members of the limited liability partnership] and creditors' meeting at each year's end.	Summary.	One-fifth of the statutory maximum.	
106(4)	Liquidator failing to send to registrar account of winding up and return of final meetings.	Summary.	One-fifth of the statutory maximum.	One-fiftieth of the statutory maximum.
106(6)	Liquidator failing to call [final meeting of the members of the limited liability partnership] or creditors.	Summary.	One-fifth of the statutory maximum.	
109(2)	Liquidator failing to publish notice of his appointment.	Summary.	One-fifth of the statutory maximum.	One-fiftieth of the statutory maximum.

Section of Act creating offence	General nature of offence	Mode of prosecution	Punishment	Daily default fine (where applicable)
114(4)	Members exercising powers in breach of s 114, where no liquidator.	Summary.	The statutory maximum.	
131(7)	Failing to comply with requirements as to statement of affairs, where liquidator appointed.	1. On indictment. 2. Summary.	A fine. The statutory maximum.	One-tenth of the statutory maximum.
164	Giving, offering etc. corrupt inducement affecting appointment of liquidator.	1. On indictment. 2. Summary.	A fine. The statutory maximum.	
166(7)	Liquidator failing to comply with requirements of s 166 in creditors' voluntary winding up.	Summary.	The statutory maximum.	
188(2)	Default in compliance with s 188 as to notification that limited liability partnership being wound up.	Summary.	One-fifth of the statutory maximum.	
192(2)	Liquidator failing to notify registrar as to progress of winding up.	Summary.	One-fifth of the statutory maximum.	One-fiftieth of the statutory maximum.
201(4)	Failing to deliver to registrar office copy of court order deferring dissolution.	Summary.	One-fifth of the statutory maximum.	One-fiftieth of the statutory maximum.

Section of Act creating offence	General nature of offence	Mode of prosecution	Punishment	Daily default fine (where applicable)
203(6)	Failing to deliver to registrar copy of directions or result of appeal under s 203.	Summary.	One-fifth of the statutory maximum.	One-fiftieth of the statutory maximum.
204(7)	Liquidator failing to deliver to registrar copy of court order for early dissolution.	Summary.	One-fifth of the statutory maximum.	One-fiftieth of the statutory maximum.
204(8)	Failing to deliver to registrar copy of court order deferring early dissolution.	Summary.	One-fifth of the statutory maximum.	One-fiftieth of the statutory maximum.
205(7)	Failing to deliver to registrar copy of Secretary of State's directions or court order deferring dissolution.	Summary.	One-fifth of the statutory maximum.	One-fiftieth of the statutory maximum.
206(1)	Fraud etc. in anticipation of winding up.	1. On indictment. 2. Summary.	7 years or a fine, or both. 6 months or the statutory maximum, or both.	
206(2)	Privity to fraud in anticipation of winding up; fraud, or privity to fraud, after commencement of winding up.	1. On indictment. 2. Summary.	7 years or a fine, or both. 6 months or the statutory maximum, or both.	
206(5)	Knowingly taking in pawn or pledge, or otherwise receiving, limited liability partnership property.	1. On indictment. 2. Summary.	7 years or a fine, or both. 6 months or the statutory maximum, or both.	

Section of Act creating offence	General nature of offence	Mode of prosecution	Punishment	Daily default fine (where applicable)
207	Member of limited liability partnership entering into transaction in fraud of limited liability partnership's creditors.	1. On indictment. 2. Summary.	2 years or a fine, or both. 6 months or the statutory maximum, or both.	
208	Member of limited liability partnership misconducting himself in course of winding up.	1. On indictment. 2. Summary.	7 years or a fine, or both. 6 months or the statutory maximum, or both.	
209	Member or contributory destroying, falsifying, etc limited liability partnership's books.	1. On indictment. 2. Summary	7 years or a fine, or both. 6 months or the statutory maximum, or both.	
210	Member of limited liability partnership making material omission from statement relating to limited liability partnership's affairs.	1. On indictment. 2. Summary.	7 years or a fine, or both. 6 months or the statutory maximum, or both.	
211	False representation or fraud for purpose of obtaining creditors' consent to an agreement in connection with winding up.	1. On indictment. 2. Summary.	7 years or a fine, or both. 6 months or the statutory maximum, or both.	
216(4)	Contravening restrictions on re-use of name of limited liability partnership in insolvent liquidation.	1. On indictment. 2. Summary.	2 years or a fine, or both. 6 months or the statutory maximum, or both.	

621

Section of Act creating offence	General nature of offence	Mode of prosecution	Punishment	Daily default fine (where applicable)
235(5)	Failing to co-operate with office-holder.	1. On indictment. 2. Summary.	A fine. The statutory maximum.	One-tenth of the statutory maximum.
...				
389	Acting as insolvency practitioner when not qualified.	1. On indictment. 2. Summary.	2 years or a fine, or both. 6 months or the statutory maximum or both.	
...				
Sch 7, para 4(3)	Failure to attend and give evidence to Insolvency Practitioners Tribunal; suppressing, concealing, etc relevant documents.	Summary.	Level 3 on the standard scale within the meaning given by section 75 of the Criminal Justice Act 1982.	

Appendix 3

Companies House Forms

Form LLP2

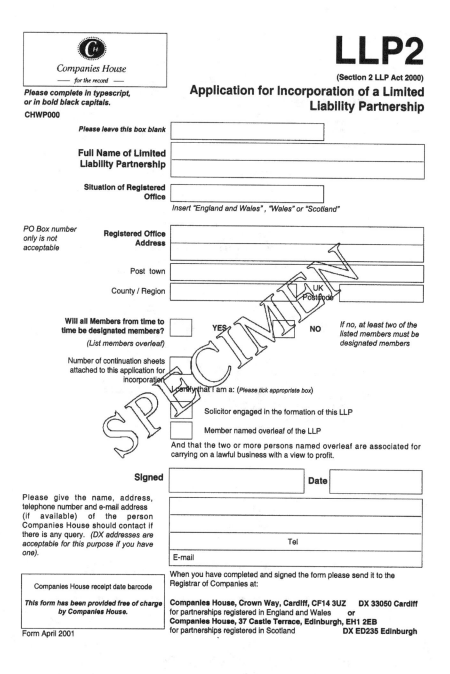

Form LLP2

List of Members on Incorporation

Peers or others known by a title may use the title instead of or in addition to their name

Surname or Corporate name

Forename(s)

Member Reference Number * (as advised by Companies House)

Date of Birth — Day Month Year

* Voluntary information

Usual Residential Address (or registered or principal office address in the case of a corporation or Scottish firm)

Post town

County / Region

UK Postcode

Country

I consent to act as a member of the limited liability partnership named on page 1

(*Please tick this box if consenting to act as a designated member*)

Signed _____ (*Member to sign and date*) **Date** _____

Peers or others known by a title may use the title instead of or in addition to their name

Surname or Corporate name

Forename(s)

Member Reference Number * (as advised by Companies House)

Date of Birth — Day Month Year

* Voluntary information

Usual Residential Address (or registered or principal office address in the case of a corporation or Scottish firm)

Post town

County / Region

UK Postcode

Country

I consent to act as a member of the limited liability partnership named on page 1

(*Please tick this box if consenting to act as a designated member*)

Signed _____ (*Member to sign and date*) **Date** _____

NOTE: Unless there are at least two designated members, all members will be designated members.

Page 2 (LLP2)

Form LLP2 cont

CHWP000

LLP2 cont

Full Name of Limited Liability Partnership

List of Members on Incorporation

Peers or others known by a title may use the title instead of or in addition to their name

Surname or Corporate name

Forename(s)

Member Reference Number *
(as advised by Companies House)

Date of Birth — Day Month Year

* Voluntary information

Usual Residential Address *(or registered or principal office address in the case of a corporation or Scottish firm)*

Post town

County / Region — UK Postcode

Country

I consent to act as a member of the limited liability partnership named on page 1

(Please tick this box if consenting to act as a designated member)

Signed **Date**

(Member to sign and date)

Peers or others known by a title may use the title instead of or in addition to their name

Surname or Corporate name

Forename(s)

Member Reference Number *
(as advised by Companies House)

Date of Birth — Day Month Year

* Voluntary information

Usual Residential Address *(or registered or principal office address in the case of a corporation or Scottish firm)*

Post town

County / Region — UK Postcode

Country

I consent to act as a member of the limited liability partnership named on page 1

(Please tick this box if consenting to act as a designated member)

Signed **Date**

(Member to sign and date)

Form April 2001   **NOTE: Unless there are at least two designated members, all members will be designated members.**

Form LLP2 cont

List of Members on Incorporation

Peers or others known by a title may use the title instead of or in addition to their name

Surname or Corporate name

Forename(s)

Member Reference Number * (as advised by Companies House)

* Voluntary information

Usual Residential Address (or registered or principal office address in the case of a corporation or Scottish firm)

	Date of Birth	Day	Month	Year

Post town

County / Region

UK Postcode

Country

I consent to act as a member of the limited liability partnership named on page 1

(Please tick this box if consenting to act as a designated member)

Signed

Date

(Member to sign and date)

Peers or others known by a title may use the title instead of or in addition to their name

Surname or Corporate name

Forename(s)

Member Reference Number * (as advised by Companies House)

* Voluntary information

Usual Residential Address (or registered or principal office address in the case of a corporation or Scottish firm)

	Date of Birth	Day	Month	Year

Post town

County / Region

UK Postcode

Country

I consent to act as a member of the limited liability partnership named on page 1

(Please tick this box if consenting to act as a designated member)

Signed

Date

(Member to sign and date)

Page 2 (LLP2cont)

Form LLP3

LLP3
(LLP Act 2000: Para 5 of Schedule)

Notice of Change of Name of a Limited Liability Partnership

LLP Number

Current Name of Limited Liability Partnership in full

Gives notice of a change of name in respect of the above named Limited Liability Partnership.

New Name of Limited Liability Partnership in full

Enter new name of LLP

A Designated Member must sign and date the form in the boxes below

Signed   **Date**

Designated Member

Please give the name, address, telephone number and e-mail (if available) of the person Companies House should contact if there is any query. *(DX addresses are acceptable for this purpose if you have one).*

Tel

E-mail

When you have completed and signed the form please send it to the Registrar of Companies at:
Companies House, Crown Way, Cardiff, CF14 3UZ   DX 33050 Cardiff
for partnerships registered in England and Wales
or
Companies House, 37 Castle Terrace, Edinburgh, EH1 2EB
for partnerships registered in Scotland   **DX ED235 Edinburgh**

Form LLP8

Companies House
— *for the record* —

Please complete in typescript,
or in bold black capitals.
CHFP000

LLP8

(Section 8 LLP Act 2000)

**Notice of Designated Member(s) of a
Limited Liability Partnership**

LLP Number

**Full Name of Limited
Liability Partnership**

Gives notice that : (tick appropriate box)

- Every person who from time to time is a member is a designated member

- Specified member(s) are now to be regarded as designated member(s)

Note: Please complete form LLP288c in respect of any existing member who changes their status as a consequence of this notice

A Designated Member must sign and date the form in the boxes below

Signed

Designated Member

Date

Please give the name, address, telephone number and e-mail (if available) of the person Companies House should contact if there is any query. *(DX addresses are acceptable for this purpose if you have one).*

Tel

E-mail

Companies House receipt date barcode

This form has been provided free of charge by Companies House.

Form April 2001

When you have completed and signed the form please send it to the Registrar of Companies at:

Companies House, Crown Way, Cardiff, CF14 3UZ   **DX 33050 Cardiff**
for partnerships registered in England and Wales
or
Companies House, 37 Castle Terrace, Edinburgh, EH1 2EB
for partnerships registered in Scotland   **DX ED235 Edinburgh**

Form LLP190

(G) *Companies House* — *for the record* —	**PART II**

Please complete in typescript, or in bold black capitals.

LLP190

Location of register of debenture holders of a Limited Liability Partnership

LLP Number

Full Name of Limited Liability Partnership

† Please delete as appropriate.

gives notice that [a register][registers][in duplicate form]† of holders of debentures of the company of the classes mentioned below †[is][are]kept at:

Address

Post town

County / region

UK Postcode

Please tick box if register of debenture holders is kept in non-legible (computer) form

Brief description of class of debentures

Signed

Date

† a designated member / member

Please give the name, address, telephone number and e-mail (if available) of the person Companies House should contact if there is any query. (DX addresses are acceptable for this purpose if you have one).

Tel

E-mail

Companies House receipt date barcode

When you have completed and signed the form please send it to the Registrar of Companies at:
Companies House, Crown Way, Cardiff, CF14 3UZ   **DX 33050 Cardiff**
for partnerships registered in England and Wales
or

Form April 2001

Companies House, 37 Castle Terrace, Edinburgh, EH1 2EB
for partnerships registered in Scotland   **DX ED235 Edinburgh**

Form LLP225

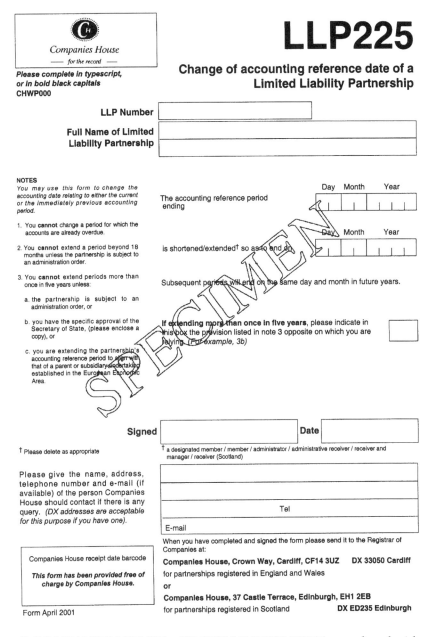

Form LLP244

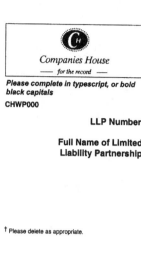

Companies House
— *for the record* —

Please complete in typescript, or bold black capitals

CHWP000

LLP244

Notice of claim to extension of period allowed for laying and delivering accounts - oversea business or interests of a Limited Liability Partnership

(See notes overleaf)

LLP Number

Full Name of Limited Liability Partnership

The members of this LLP give notice that the LLP is carrying on business, or has interests, outside the United Kingdom, the Channel Islands and the Isle of Man and claim an extension of three months to the period allowed under this section for laying and delivering accounts in relation to the financial year of the partnership [ending][which ended on]†

† Please delete as appropriate.

Day Month Year

Signed   Date

† a designated member / member / administrator / administrative receiver / receiver (Scotland)

Please give the name, address, telephone number and e-mail (if available) of the person Companies House should contact if there is any query. *(DX addresses are acceptable for this purpose if you have one).*

Tel

E-mail

Companies House receipt date barcode

This form has been provided free of charge by Companies House.

Form April 2001

When you have completed and signed the form please send it to the Registrar of Companies at:

Companies House, Crown Way, Cardiff, CF14 3UZ   **DX 33050 Cardiff**
for partnerships registered in England and Wales
or
Companies House, 37 Castle Terrace, Edinburgh, EH1 2EB
for partnerships registered in Scotland   **DX ED235 Edinburgh**

Form LLP244

Notes:

1. A LLP which carries on business or has interests outside the United Kingdom, the Channel Islands and the Isle of Man may, by using this form and delivering it to the Registrar of Companies under section 244(3) * of the Act, claim an extension of three months to the period which otherwise would be allowed for the laying and delivering of accounts under section 244(1) *.

2. Notice must be given before the expiry of that period which would otherwise be allowed under section 244(1) * of the Companies Act.

3. A seperate notice will be required for each period for which the claim is made.

* *As applied to LLPs by Schedule 1 of the Limited Liability Partnerships Regulations 2001*

Form LLP287

<table>
<tr>
<td>
©

Companies House
— *for the record* —

Please complete in typescript, or in bold black capitals.
CHWP000
</td>
<td>
LLP287

(LLP Act 2000 Schedule: paragraph 10)

Change in situation or address of Registered Office of a Limited Liability Partnership
</td>
</tr>
</table>

LLP Number	

Full Name of Limited Liability Partnership	

New situation of registered office

NOTE:

1. The change in the situation of the registered office does not take effect until the Registrar has registered this notice.

2. For 14 days beginning on the date that a change of registered office is registered at Companies House, a person may validly serve any document on the LLP at its previous registered office.

3. PO Box numbers only are not acceptable as a registered office address.

Address

Post town

County

Country

UK Postcode

Signed

Date

† Please delete as appropriate.

† designated member / administrator / administrative receiver / liquidator / receiver manager / receiver

Please give the name, address, telephone number and e-mail (if available) of the person Companies House should contact if there is any query. *(DX addresses are acceptable for this purpose if you have one).*

Tel

E-mail

Companies House receipt date barcode

This form has been provided free of charge by Companies House.

Form April 2001

When you have completed and signed the form please send it to the Registrar of Companies at:

Companies House, Crown Way, Cardiff, CF14 3UZ   **DX 33050 Cardiff**
for partnerships registered in England and Wales
or
Companies House, 37 Castle Terrace, Edinburgh, EH1 2EB
for partnerships registered in Scotland   **DX ED235 Edinburgh**

Form LLP287a

Companies House
— *for the record* —

Please complete in typescript,
or in bold black capitals.
CHFP000

LLP287a

(LLP Act 2000: Schedule: paragraph 9)

Notice that the Registered Office of a Limited Liability Partnership is Situated in Wales

LLP Number

Full Name of Limited Liability Partnership

Gives notice that the registered office of the above named Limited Liability Partnership is situated in Wales.

NOTE: *If the registered office address of the Limited Liability Partnership has changed or is to change as a result of this notice, please complete form LLP287*

A Designated Member must sign and date the form in the boxes below

Signed _____ **Date** _____

Designated Member

Please give the name, address, telephone number and e-mail (if available) of the person Companies House should contact if there is any query. *(DX addresses are acceptable for this purpose if you have one).*

Tel

E-mail

Companies House receipt date barcode

This form has been provided free of charge by Companies House.

Form April 2001

When you have completed and signed the form please send it to the Registrar of Companies at:

Companies House, Crown Way, Cardiff, CF14 3UZ   DX 33050 Cardiff for partnerships registered in England and Wales
or
Companies House, 37 Castle Terrace, Edinburgh, EH1 2EB for partnerships registered in Scotland   **DX ED235 Edinburgh**

© COMPANIES HOUSE – CROWN COPYRIGHT reproduced with the permission of the Controller of Her Majesty's Stationery Office.

Form LLP288a

Companies House
—— *for the record* ——

*Please complete in typescript,
or in bold black capitals.*
CHWP000

LLP288a

(LLP Act 2000 Section 9)

Appointment of a Member to a Limited Liability Partnership

*(NOT for terminating membership (use Form LLP288b)
or change of particulars (use Form LLP288c))*

LLP Number	
Full Name of Limited Liability Partnership	

Date of appointment — Day Month Year

* Voluntary Information — **Member Reference Number** * *(As advised by Companies House)*

Date of birth — Day Month Year

Peers or others known by a title may use the title instead of or in addition to their name — **Surname or Corporate name**

Forename(s)

Usual residential address *(or registered or principal office address in the case of a corporation or Scottish firm)*

Post town

UK Postcode

County / Region

Country

Designated member *(Please tick appropriate box)*   YES ☐   NO ☐

I consent to act as a member of the above named limited liability partnership

Consent signature | **Date**

Another Member being a Designated Member must sign and date the form in the boxes below.

Signed | **Date**

Designated Member

Please give the name, address, telephone number and e-mail (if available) of the person Companies House should contact if there is any query. *(DX addresses are acceptable for this purpose if you have one).*

Tel

E-mail

Companies House receipt date barcode

This form has been provided free of charge by Companies House.

Form April 2001

When you have completed and signed the form please send it to the Registrar of Companies at:
Companies House, Crown Way, Cardiff, CF14 3UZ   DX 33050 Cardiff
for partnerships registered in England and Wales
or
Companies House, 37 Castle Terrace, Edinburgh, EH1 2EB
for partnerships registered in Scotland   **DX ED235 Edinburgh**

Form LLP288b

Companies House
— *for the record* —

Please complete in typescript,
or in bold black capitals.
CHWP000

LLP288b
(LLP Act 2000 Section 9)

Terminating the Membership of a Member of a Limited Liability Partnership
(NOT for appointment (use Form LLP288a) or change of particulars (use Form LLP288c))

LLP Number

Full Name of Limited Liability Partnership

Date of termination of appointment

Day Month Year

Member Reference Number *
(As advised by Companies House)

Date of birth

Day Month Year

* Voluntary Information

Peers or other individuals known by a title may use the title instead of or in addition to their name

Surname or Corporate name

Forename(s)

Another Member being a Designated Member must sign and date the form in the boxes below.

Signed

Date

Designated Member

Please give the name, address, telephone number and e-mail (if available) of the person Companies House should contact if there is any query. *(DX addresses are acceptable for this purpose if you have one).*

Tel

E-mail

Companies House receipt date barcode

This form has been provided free of charge by Companies House.

Form April 2001

When you have completed and signed the form please send it to the Registrar of Companies at:

Companies House, Crown Way, Cardiff, CF14 3UZ   DX 33050 Cardiff
for partnerships registered in England and Wales
or
Companies House, 37 Castle Terrace, Edinburgh, EH1 2EB
for partnerships registered in Scotland   **DX ED235 Edinburgh**

Form LLP288c

LLP288c

(LLP Act 2000: Section 9)

Companies House
—— *for the record* ——

**Change of Particulars of a Member
of a Limited Liability Partnership**

Please complete in typescript,
or in bold black capitals.

CHWP000

(NOT for appointment (use Form LLP288a)
or terminating membership (use Form LLP288b))

LLP Number

**Full Name of Limited
Liability Partnership**

Current name
(complete in all cases) — Full name or Corporate name

* Voluntary
information — Member Reference Number *
(As advised by Companies House)

Date of Birth — Day Month Year

Date of change of particulars — Day Month Year

Change of status of member — The person named above is now a [designated member] [member] † of the above named limited liability partnership

† Delete as appropriate. — I consent to act as a member of the above named limited liability partnership

Consent Signature — **Date**

Change of name
(enter new name) — Full name or Corporate name

Peers or others known
by a title may use the
title instead of or in
addition to their name — Usual Residential Address

Change of address
(enter new address) — Post town

(or registered or
principal office
address in the case
of a corporation or
Scottish firm) — County / Region — UK Postcode

Country

Another Member being a Designated Member must sign and date the form in the boxes below.

Signed — **Date**

Designated Member

Please give the name, address,
telephone number and e-mail (if
available) of the person Companies
House should contact if there is any
query. (DX addresses are acceptable
for this purpose if you have one).

Tel

E-mail

Companies House receipt date barcode

This form has been provided free of charge
by Companies House.

Form April 2001

When you have completed and signed the form please send it to the
Registrar of Companies at:
Companies House, Crown Way, Cardiff, CF14 3UZ   DX 33050 Cardiff
for partnerships registered in England and Wales   **or**
Companies House, 37 Castle Terrace, Edinburgh, EH1 2EB
for partnerships registered in Scotland   **DX ED235 Edinburgh**

Form LLP363

LLP363

Please complete in typescript,
or in bold black capitals.

Annual Return of a Limited
Liability Partnership

LLP Number

**Full Name of Limited
Liability Partnership**

Date of this return
The information in this return
is made up to

Day   Month   Year

Date of next return
If you wish to make your next
return on a date earlier than
the anniversary of this return
please show the date here.

Day   Month   Year

Registered Office

Any change of
registered office
must be notified on
Form LLP287.

Show here the address
as **at the date of
this return.**

Post town

County

UK
Postcode

**Register of Debenture
Holders**

If there is a register of
debenture holders, or a
duplicate of any such
register or part of it,
which is not kept at the
registered office, state
here where it is kept

Post town

County

UK
Postcode

List members on page 2

Certificate   As a designated member I certify that the information given in this return is
true to the best of my knowledge and belief.

Signed   **Date**

Designated Member

When you have signed the return send it
with the fee of £15 to the Registrar of
Companies. Cheques should be made
payable to **Companies House.**

This return includes   continuation sheets.

(enter number)

Companies House receipt date barcode

When you have completed and signed the form please send it to the
Registrar of Companies at:
Companies House, Crown Way, Cardiff, CF14 3UZ   DX 33050 Cardiff
for partnerships registered in England and Wales
or
Companies House, 37 Castle Terrace, Edinburgh, EH1 2EB

Form April 2001

for partnerships registered in Scotland   **DX ED235 Edinburgh**

Page 1

Form LLP363

Members
Please list members in alphabetical order **Details of new members must be notified on form LLP288a**

In the case of a member that is a corporation or a Scottish firm, the name is the corporate or firm name.

Surname or Corporate Name

Forename(s)

Address

Usual residential address must be given. In the case of a corporation or a Scottish firm, give the registered or principal office address.

Post town

County / Region

Country

UK Postcode

Tick box if designated member

* Voluntary information

Member Reference Number * *(as advised by Companies House)*

Date of Birth

Day   Month   Year

Members
Please list members in alphabetical order **Details of new members must be notified on form LLP288a**

In the case of a member that is a corporation or a Scottish firm, the name is the corporate or firm name.

Surname or Corporate Name

Forename(s)

Address

Usual residential address must be given. In the case of a corporation or a Scottish firm, give the registered or principal office address.

Post town

County / Region

Country

UK Postcode

Tick box if designated member

* Voluntary information

Member Reference Number * *(as advised by Companies House)*

Date of Birth

Day   Month   Year

Members
Please list members in alphabetical order **Details of new members must be notified on form LLP288a**

In the case of a member that is a corporation or a Scottish firm, the name is the corporate or firm name.

Surname or Corporate Name

Forename(s)

Address

Usual residential address must be given. In the case of a corporation or a Scottish firm, give the registered or principal office address.

Post town

County / Region

Country

UK Postcode

Tick box if designated member

* Voluntary information

Member Reference Number * *(as advised by Companies House)*

Date of Birth

Day   Month   Year

Page 2

Form LLP363cont

Please complete in typescript,
or in bold black capitals.

LLP363 cont

Annual Return (continuation sheet)

LLP Number [   ]

Members

Please list members in alphabetical order   **Details of new members must be notified on form LLP288a**

In the case of a member that is a corporation or a Scottish firm, the name is the corporate or firm name.

Surname or Corporate Name [   ]

Forename(s) [   ]

Address [   ]

Usual residential address must be given. In the case of a corporation or a Scottish firm, give the registered or principal office address.

Post town [   ]

County / Region [   ]   UK Postcode [   ]

Country [   ]   Tick box if designated member [   ]

* Voluntary information

Member Reference Number * *(as advised by Companies House)* [   ]

Date of Birth   Day Month Year [| |]

Members

Please list members in alphabetical order   **Details of new members must be notified on form LLP288a**

In the case of a member that is a corporation or a Scottish firm, the name is the corporate or firm name.

Surname or Corporate Name [   ]

Forename(s) [   ]

Address [   ]

Usual residential address must be given. In the case of a corporation or a Scottish firm, give the registered or principal office address.

Post town [   ]

County / Region [   ]   UK Postcode [   ]

Country [   ]   Tick box if designated member [   ]

* Voluntary information

Member Reference Number * *(as advised by Companies House)* [   ]

Date of Birth   Day Month Year [| |]

Form LLP363cont

Members
Please list members in alphabetical order

Details of new members must be notified on form LLP288a

In the case of a member that is a corporation or a Scottish firm, the name is the corporate or firm name.

Surname or Corporate Name

Forename(s)

Address

Usual residential address must be given. In the case of a corporation or a Scottish firm, give the registered or principal office address.

Post town

County / Region

Country

UK Postcode

Tick box if designated member

* Voluntary information

Member Reference Number *(as advised by Companies House)

Date of Birth — Day Month Year

Members
Please list members in alphabetical order

Details of new members must be notified on form LLP288a

In the case of a member that is a corporation or a Scottish firm, the name is the corporate or firm name.

Surname or Corporate Name

Forename(s)

Address

Usual residential address must be given. In the case of a corporation or a Scottish firm, give the registered or principal office address.

Post town

County / Region

Country

UK Postcode

Tick box if designated member

* Voluntary information

Member Reference Number *(as advised by Companies House)

Date of Birth — Day Month Year

Members
Please list members in alphabetical order

Details of new members must be notified on form LLP288a

In the case of a member that is a corporation or a Scottish firm, the name is the corporate or firm name.

Surname or Corporate Name

Forename(s)

Address

Usual residential address must be given. In the case of a corporation or a Scottish firm, give the registered or principal office address.

Post town

County / Region

Country

UK Postcode

Tick box if designated member

* Voluntary information

Member Reference Number *(as advised by Companies House)

Date of Birth — Day Month Year

Page 2

Form LLP391

LLP391

Companies House
— *for the record* —

Please complete in typescript,
or in bold black capitals.

**Notice of removal of auditor from a
Limited Liability Partnership**

LLP Number

**Full Name of Limited
Liability Partnership**

	Day	Month	Year
Date of determination to remove auditor			

	Day	Month	Year
Date of removal			

Name of auditor removed from office

Name of Firm or Practise

Address

Post town

County / Region

UK
Postcode

SPECIMEN

A Designated Member must sign and date this form in the boxes below

Signed

Date

Designated Member

Please give the name, address, telephone number and e-mail (if available) of the person Companies House should contact if there is any query. *(DX addresses are acceptable for this purpose if you have one).*

Tel

E-mail

Companies House receipt date barcode

Form April 2001

When you have completed and signed the form please send it to the Registrar of Companies at:
Companies House, Crown Way, Cardiff, CF14 3UZ   **DX 33050 Cardiff**
for partnerships registered in England and Wales
or
Companies House, 37 Castle Terrace, Edinburgh, EH1 2EB
for partnerships registered in Scotland   **DX ED235 Edinburgh**

Form LLP395

M

CHWP000

*Please complete
in typescript, or
in bold black
capitals*

LLP395

Particulars of a mortgage or charge in respect
of a Limited Liability Partnership

A fee of £20 is payable to Companies House in respect of
each register entry for a mortgage or charge.

For official use

LLP Number

**Full Name of Limited
Liability Partnership**

Date of creation
of the charge

Description of the instrument
(if any) creating or evidencing
the charge (note 2)

Amount secured by the
mortgage or charge

Signed   **Date**

On behalf of [LLP][mortgagee/chargee] *(delete as appropriate)*

Please give the name, address,
telephone number and e-mail (if available) of the person Companies
House should contact if there is any
query. *(DX addresses are acceptable
for this purpose if you have one).*

Tel

E-mail

Companies House receipt date barcode

*This form has been provided free of charge
by Companies House.*

When you have completed and signed the form please send it to the
Registrar of Companies at:

Companies House, Crown Way, Cardiff, CF14 3UZ   DX 33050 Cardiff

Form April 2001

Form LLP395

Names and addresses
of the mortgagees or
persons entitled to
the charge

Short particulars of all the
property mortgaged
or charged

Particulars as to
commission allowance
or discount *(note 3)*

Notes

1   The original instrument (if any) creating or evidencing the charge, together with these prescribed particulars correctly completed must be delivered to the Registrar of Companies within 21 days after the date of creation of the charge (section 395 *). If the property is situated and the charge was created outside the United Kingdom delivery to the Registrar must be effected within 21 days after the date on which the instrument could in due course of post, and if dispatched with due diligence, have been received in the United Kingdom (section 398 *). A copy of the instrument creating the charge will be accepted where the property charged is situated and the charge was created outside the United Kingdom (section 398 *) and in such cases the copy must be verified to be a correct copy either by the company or by the person who has delivered or sent the copy to the registrar. The verification must be signed by or on behalf of the person giving the verification and where this is given by a body corporate it must be signed by an officer of that body. A verified copy will also be accepted where section 398(4) * applies (property situate in Scotland or Northern Ireland) and Form LLP398 is submitted.

2   A description of the instrument, eg "Trust Deed", "Debenture", "Mortgage", or "Legal Charge", etc, as the case may be, should be given.

3   In this section there should be inserted the amount or rate per cent. of the commission, allowance or discount (if any) paid or made either directly or indirectly by the LLP to any person in consideration of his:
      (a) subscribing or agreeing to subscribe, whether absolutely or conditionally, or
      (b) procuring or agreeing to procure subscriptions, whether absolute or conditional,
for any of the debentures included in this return. The rate of interest payable under the terms of the debentures should not be entered.

4   If any of the spaces in this form provide insufficient space the particulars must be entered on the Form LLP395 continuation sheet.

5   Cheques and Postal Orders must be made payable to **Companies House.**

*   As applied to LLPs by Schedule 2 of the Limited Liability Partnerships Regulations 2001

Page 2

646

Form LLP395

FORM LLP395 (Cont.) AND FORM LLP410 (Scot)(Cont.)

Particulars of a mortgage or charge (continued)

Continuation sheet No
to Form LLP395 and 410 (Scot)

LLP Number

Full Name of Limited Liability Partnership

Description of the instrument creating or evidencing the mortgage or charge (continued) (note 2)

Form LLP395

Amount due or owing on the mortgage or charge (continued)

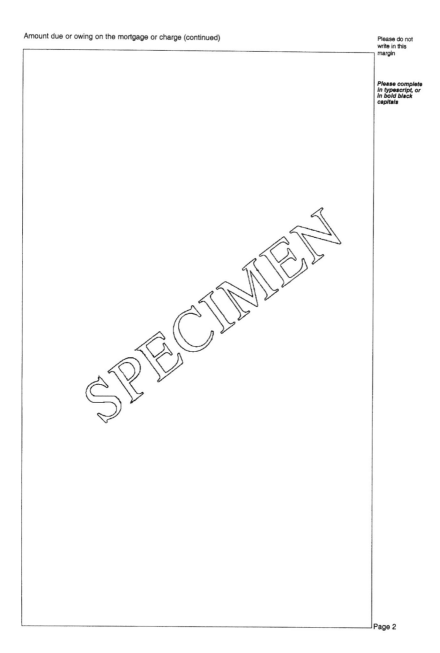

Page 2

Form LLP395

Please do not
write in this
margin

Names, addresses and descriptions of the mortgagees or persons entitled to the charge (continued)

*Please complete
in typescript, or
in bold black
capitals*

Page 3

Form LLP395

Short particulars of all the property mortgaged or charged (Continued)

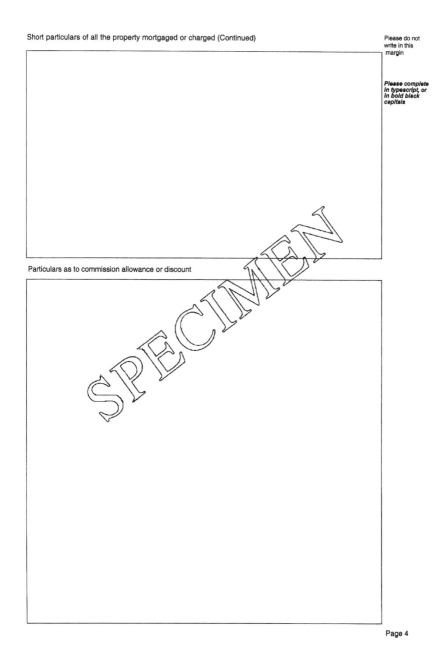

Particulars as to commission allowance or discount

Page 4

Form LLP397

M

LLP397

Particulars for the registration of a charge to secure a series of debentures in respect of a Limited Liability Partnership

A fee of £20 is payable to Companies House in respect of each register entry for a mortgage or charge.

For official use

LLP Number

Full Name of Limited Liability Partnership

Date of covering deed (if any) — Day Month Year

Total amount secured by the whole series

Date of present issue — Day Month Year

Amount of present issue (if any) of debentures of the series

Date(s) of determination(s) authorising the issue of the series

Names of the trustees (if any) for the debenture holders

General description of the property charged (continue overleaf if necessary)

Signed   **Date**

On behalf of [LLP][mortgagee/chargee] (delete as appropriate)

Please give the name, address, telephone number and e-mail (if available) of the person Companies House should contact if there is any query. *(DX addresses are acceptable for this purpose if you have one).*

Tel

E-mail

Companies House receipt date barcode

When you have completed and signed the form please send it to the Registrar of Companies at:

Companies House, Crown Way, Cardiff, CF14 3UZ   **DX 33050 Cardiff**

Form April 2001

651

Form LLP397

General description of the property charged (continued)

Particulars as to commission allowance or discount (note 3)

Notes

1 Particulars should be given on this form of a series of debentures containing (or giving by reference to any other instrument) any charge to the benefit of which the debenture holders of the series are entitled pari passu. This form is to be used for registration of particulars of the entire series, and may also be used when an issue of debentures is made at the same time as the series of debentures is created. All issues of debentures made after the registration of the series with the Registrar of Companies should be notified to the Registrar on Form No. LLP397a.

2 The date should be given of the covering deed (if any) by which the security is created or defined.

3 In this section there should be inserted the amount or rate per cent of the commission, allowance or discount (if any) paid or made either directly or indirectly by the LLP to any person in consideration of his

● subscribing or agreeing to subscribe, whether absolutely or conditionally, or

● procuring or agreeing to procure subscriptions, whether absolute or conditional,

for any of the debentures included in this return. The rate of interest payable under the terms of the debentures should not be entered.

4 The deed (if any) containing the charge must be delivered with these particulars correctly completed, to the Registrar within 21 days after its execution. If there is no such deed, one of the debentures must be so delivered within 21 days after the execution of any debenture of the series.

5 If the spaces in this form are insufficient, the particulars may be continued on a separate sheet.

6 Cheques and Postal Orders must be made payable to **Companies House.**

Form LLP397a

M

LLP397a

Particulars of an issue of secured debentures in a series in respect of a Limited Liability Partnership

Please complete in typescript, or in bold black capitals

For official use

LLP Number

Full Name of Limited Liability Partnership

Date of present issue

Note
Please read notes overleaf before completing this form

Amount of present issue

SPECIMEN

Particulars as to commission, allowance or discount (note 2)

Signed   **Date**

On behalf of [LLP][mortgagee/chargee] (delete as appropriate)

Please give the name, address, telephone number and e-mail (if available) of the person Companies House should contact if there is any query. *(DX addresses are acceptable for this purpose if you have one).*

Tel

E-mail

Companies House receipt date barcode

When you have completed and signed the form please send it to the Registrar of Companies at:

Companies House, Crown Way, Cardiff, CF14 3UZ   **DX 33050 Cardiff**

Form April 2001

Form LLP397a

Notes

1   This form is for use when an issue is made of debentures in a series; for registration of particulars of the entire series, Form No. LLP397 should be used.

2   In this space there should be inserted the amount or rate percent of the commission, allowance or discount (if any) paid or made either directly or indirectly by the LLP to any person in consideration of his

       (a) subscribing or agreeing to subscribe, whether absolutely or conditionally, or
       (b) procuring or agreeing to procure subscriptions, whether absolute or conditional

       for any of the debentures included in this form. The rate of interest payable under the terms of the debenture should not be entered.

Form LLP398

M FORM No. LLP398

LLP398

Limited Liability Partnership: Certificate of registration in Scotland or Northern Ireland of a charge comprising property situated there

Please complete in typescript, or in bold black capitals

LLP Number

Full Name of Limited Liability Partnership

I _____

of _____

* give date and parties to charge

certify that the charge *

of which a true copy is annexed to this form was presented for registration

† delete as appropriate

Day	Month	Year

on in [Scotland] [Northern Ireland] †

Signed **Date**

Please give the name, address, telephone number and e-mail (if available) of the person Companies House should contact if there is any query. *(DX addresses are acceptable for this purpose if you have one).*

Tel

E-mail

Companies House receipt date barcode

When you have completed and signed the form please send it to the Registrar of Companies at:
Companies House, Crown Way, Cardiff, CF14 3UZ   DX 33050 Cardiff
for partnerships registered in England and Wales
or
Companies House, 37 Castle Terrace, Edinburgh, EH1 2EB
for partnerships registered in Scotland   **DX ED235**

Form April 2001

© COMPANIES HOUSE – CROWN COPYRIGHT reproduced with the permission of the Controller of Her Majesty's Stationery Office.

Form LLP400

LLP400

Particulars of a mortgage or charge on a property that has been acquired by a Limited Liability Partnership

Please complete in typescript, or in bold black capitals

A fee of £20 is payable to Companies House in respect of each register entry for a mortgage or charge.

		For official use
LLP Number		

Full Name of Limited Liability Partnership	

Date and description of the instrument (if any) creating or evidencing the mortgage or charge (note 1)	
Amount secured by the mortgage or charge	
Names and addresses of the mortgagee or persons entitled to the mortgage or charge	
Short particulars of the property mortgaged or charged *(continue overleaf if necessary)*	

Date of the acquisition of the property	Day	Month	Year

Signed		Date	

designated member/ member / administrator / administrative receiver (delete as appropriate)

Please give the name, address, telephone number and e-mail (if available) of the person Companies House should contact if there is any query. *(DX addresses are acceptable for this purpose if you have one).*

	Tel
E-mail	

Companies House receipt date barcode

When you have completed and signed the form please send it to the Registrar of Companies at:

Companies House, Crown Way, Cardiff, CF14 3UZ   DX 33050 Cardiff

Form April 2001

Form LLP400

Short particulars of the property mortgaged or charged *(continued)*

Notes

1 A description of the instrument, eg, Trust Deed", Debenture", etc, as the case may be, should be given.

2 A verified copy of the instrument must be delivered with these particulars correctly completed to the Registrar of Companies within 21 days after the date of the completion of the acquisition of the property which is subject to the charge. The copy must be verified to be a correct copy either by the LLP or by the person who has delivered or sent the copy to the registrar. The verification must be signed by or on behalf of the person giving the verification and where this is given by a body corporate it must be signed by an officer of that body. If the property is situated and the charge was created outside Great Britain, they must be delivered within 21 days after the date on which the copy of the instrument could in due course of post, and if despatched with due diligence have been received in the United Kingdom.

3 Cheques and Postal Orders must be made payable to **Companies House.**

Page 2

Form LLP401

No. of Limited Liability Partnership

LLP401

> N.B. Searchers may find it helpful to
> refer to the mortgage documents
> for more detailed particulars

REGISTER
OF
Charges
Memoranda of Satisfaction
AND
Appointments and Cessations
of Receivers
OF

Form April 2001

Form LLP401

REGISTER of Charges,
Memoranda of Satisfaction and Receivers Details
N.B Searchers should refer to the mortgage documents for more detailed particulars

(1) Date of Registration		Serial No of Document on File	
(2) Charge Number			
(3) Date of Creation of the Charge and Description			
(4) Date of the Acquisition of the Property			
(5) Amount secured by the Charge			
(6) Short Particulars of the Property Charged			
(7) Names of the Persons Entitled to the Charge			

Particulars Relating to the Issues of Debentures of a Series

(8) Total Amount Secured by a Series of Debentures	(9)Dates and Amounts of Each Issue of the Series		(10)Dates of the Resolutions Authorising the Issue of the Series	(11) Date of the Covering Deed
	Date	Amount		
(12) General Description of the Property Charged				
(13) Names of the Trustees for the Debenture Holders				
(14) Amount or Rate per cent of the Commission Allowance or Discount				

(15) Memoranda of Satisfaction	Full/Partial		Date

(16) Receiver(s) or Manager(s)	Name	Date of Appointment	Date of Ceasing to Act

Page 1 of 1

Form LLP403a

M

LLP403a

Limited Liability Partnership: Declaration of satisfaction in full or in part of mortgage or charge

For official use

Please complete in typescript, or in bold black capitals

LLP Number

Full Name of Limited Liability Partnership

I,

of

[a designated member][a member][the administrator][the administrative receiver]† of the above LLP, do solemnly and sincerely declare that the debt for which the charge described below was given has been paid or satisfied in [full][part]†

Date and description of charge #

Date of registration ø

Name and address of [chargee][trustee for the debenture holders]†

Short particulars of property charged §

And I make this solemn declaration conscientiously believing the same to be true and by virtue of the provisions of the Statutory Declarations Act 1835.

† delete as appropriate

insert a description of the instrument(s) creating or evidencing the charge, eg 'Mortgage', 'Charge', 'Debenture' etc

ø the date of registration may be confirmed from the certificate

§ insert brief details of property

Declarant's signature

Declared at

Day Month Year

on

❶ Please print name

before me ❶

Signed

Date

† A *Commissioner for Oaths or Notary Public or Justic of the Peace or Solicitor*

Please give the name, address, telephone number and e-mail (if available) of the person Companies House should contact if there is any query. *(DX addresses are acceptable for this purpose if you have one).*

Tel

E-mail

Companies House receipt date barcode

When you have completed and signed the form please send it to the Registrar of Companies at:

Companies House, Crown Way, Cardiff, CF14 3UZ   DX 33050 Cardiff

Form April 2001

Form LLP403b

M

LLP403b

Declaration that part of the property or undertaking charged (a) has been released from the charge; (b) no longer forms part of the limited liability partnership's property or undertaking

Please complete in typescript, or in bold black capitals

For official use

LLP Number

Full Name of Limited Liability Partnership

I, _____

of _____

[designated member][member][the administrator][the administrative receiver]†
of the above LLP, do solemnly and sincerely declare that with respect to the
charge described below the part of the property or undertaking described [has
been released from the charge][has ceased to form part of the
LLP's property or undertaking]†

† delete as appropriate

Date and description of charge #

insert a description of the instrument(s) creating or evidencing the charge, eg 'Mortgage', 'Charge', 'Debenture' etc

Date of registration ø

Name and address of [chargee][trustee for the debenture holders]†

ø the date of registration may be confirmed from the certificate

Short particulars of property or undertaking released or no longer part of the limited liability partnership property or undertaking§

§ insert brief details of property

And I make this solemn declaration conscientiously believing the same to be
true and by virtue of the provisions of the Statutory Declarations Act 1835.

Declarant's signature

Declared at

Day   Month   Year

on

❶ Please print name

before me ❶

Signed   **Date**

Please give the name, address, telephone number and e-mail (if available) of the person Companies House should contact if there is any query. *(DX addresses are acceptable for this purpose if you have one).*

† A Commissioner for Oaths or Notary Public or Justic of the Peace or Solicitor

Tel

Companies House receipt date barcode

E-mail

When you have completed and signed the form please send it to the
Registrar of Companies at:

Companies House, Crown Way, Cardiff, CF14 3UZ   DX 33050 Cardiff

Form April 2001

Form LLP405(1)

M

LLP405(1)

Notice of appointment of receiver or manager in respect of Limited Liability Partnership

Please complete in typescript, or in bold black capitals

For official use

LLP Number

Full Name of Limited Liability Partnership

I / We †

of

give notice that *(insert name and address of receiver / manager in this box)*

† *delete as appropriate*

was appointed as [receiver][manager][receiver and manager]† of [all][part of] † the property of the limited liability partnership.

§ *name of court making the order*

The appointment was made by

[an order of the §

enter description and date of the instrument under which appointment is made, and state whether it is a debenture secured by a floating charge

made on]

[me / us † on _____ under the

powers contained in #]

Signed

Date

Please give the name, address, telephone number and e-mail (if available) of the person Companies House should contact if there is any query. *(DX addresses are acceptable for this purpose if you have one).*

Tel

E-mail

Companies House receipt date barcode

When you have completed and signed the form please send it to the Registrar of Companies at:

Companies House, Crown Way, Cardiff, CF14 3UZ   DX 33050 Cardiff
for partnerships registered in England and Wales
or
Companies House, 37 Castle Terrace, Edinburgh, EH1 2EB
for partnerships registered in Scotland   **DX ED235 Edinburgh**

Form April 2001

Form LLP405(2)

M

LLP405(2)

Notice of ceasing to act as receiver or manager
in respect of a Limited Liability Partnership

Please complete in typescript, or in bold black capitals

For official use

LLP Number

Full Name of Limited Liability Partnership

† *delete as appropriate*

I / We †

of

Postcode

give notice that I / we † ceased to act as [receiver][manager][receiver and manager] of the above LLP on

Day	Month	Year

Signed

Date

Please give the name, address, telephone number and e-mail (if available) of the person Companies House should contact if there is any query. *(DX addresses are acceptable for this purpose if you have one).*

Tel

E-mail

Companies House receipt date barcode

When you have completed and signed the form please send it to the Registrar of Companies at:
Companies House, Crown Way, Cardiff, CF14 3UZ   DX 33050 Cardiff
for partnerships registered in England and Wales
or
Companies House, 37 Castle Terrace, Edinburgh, EH1 2EB
for partnerships registered in Scotland   **DX ED235 Edinburgh**

Form April 2001

Form LLP410

M

CHWP000

Please complete in typescript, or in bold black capitals

FORM No. LLP 410(Scot)

LLP410
Particulars of a charge created by a Limited Liability Partnership registered in Scotland

A fee of £20 is payable to Companies House in respect of each register entry for a mortgage or charge

For official use

LLP Number

Full Name of Limited Liability Partnership

Date of creation of the charge (note 1)

Description of the instrument (if any) creating or evidencing the charge (note 1)

Amount secured by the charge

Names and addresses of the persons entitled to the charge

Signed

Date

On behalf of [LLP/chargee] *(delete as appropriate)*

Please give the name, address, telephone number and e-mail (if available) of the person Companies House should contact if there is any query. *(DX addresses are acceptable for this purpose if you have one).*

Companies House receipt date barcode

This form has been provided free of charge by Companies House.

Tel

E-mail

When you have completed and signed the form please send it to the Registrar of Companies at:

**Companies House, 37 Castle Terrace, Edinburgh EH1 2EB
DX ED235 Edinburgh 1**

Form April 2001

664

Form LLP410

Short particulars of all the property charged

Statement, in the case of a floating charge, as to any restrictions on power to grant further securities and any ranking provisions (note 2)

Particulars as to commission allowance or discount (note 3)

Notes

1. A description of the instrument e.g. "Standard Security" "Floating Charge" etc, should be given. For the date of creation of a charge see section 410(5) of the Act *. (Examples - date of signing of an Instrument of Charge; date of recording / registration of a Standard Security; date of intimation of an Assignation.)

2. In the case of a floating charge a statement should be given of (1) the restrictions, if any, on the power of the LLP to grant further securities ranking in priority to, or pari passu with the floating charge; and / or (2) the provisions, if any, regulating the order in which the floating charge shall rank with any other subsisting or future floating charges or fixed securities over the property which is the subject of the floating charge or any part of it.

3. A certified copy of the instrument, if any, creating or evidencing the charge, together with this form with the prescribed particulars correctly completed must be delivered to the Registrar of Companies within 21 days after the date of the creation of the charge. In the case of a charge created out of the United Kingdom comprising property situated outside the U.K., within 21 days after the date on which the copy of the instrument creating it could, in due course of post, and if despatched with due diligence, have been received in the U.K. Certified copies of any other documents relevant to the charge should also be delivered.

4. A certified copy must be signed by or on behalf of the person giving the certification and where this is a body corporate it must be signed by an officer of that body.

5. If there is insufficient space on this form please use form LLP395 (LLP410scot) continuation sheet.

6. Cheques and Postal Orders must be made payable to **Companies House.**

* **As applied to LLPs by Schedule 2 of the Limited Liability Partnerships Regulations 2001**

Page 2

Form LLP413

M

FORM No. LLP 413(Scot)

LLP413

Particulars for the registration of a charge to secure a series of debentures in respect of a Limited Liability Partnership *(note 1)*

Please complete in typescript, or in bold black capitals

A fee of £20 is payable to Companies House in respect of each register entry for a mortgage or charge.

For official use

LLP Number

Full Name of Limited Liability Partnership

Total amount secured by the whole series

Date of the present issue (if any) of the debentures of the series

Amount of the present issue (if any) of the debentures of the series

Date(s) of determination(s) authorising the issue of the series

Date of the covering deed (if any) (note 2)

General description of the property charged.

Names of trustees (if any) for the debenture holders

Postcode

Signed

Date

Please give the name, address, telephone number and e-mail (if available) of the person Companies House should contact if there is any query. *(DX addresses are acceptable for this purpose if you have one).*

On behalf of [LLP/chargee] (delete as appropriate)

Tel

E-mail

Companies House receipt date barcode

When you have completed and signed the form please send it to the Registrar of Companies at:

Companies House, 37 Castle Terrace, Edinburgh EH1 2EB
DX ED235 Edinburgh 1

Form April 2001

Form LLP413

Statement as to any restriction on power to grant further securities and any ranking provisions (note 3)

Particulars as to commission, allowance or discount paid (see section 413(3) *as applied to LLPs by Schedule 2 of the Limited Liability Partnerships Regulations 2001*)

Notes

1   Particulars should be given on this form of a series of debentures containing (or giving by reference to any other instrument) any charge to the benefit of which the debenture holders of the said series are entitled pari passu. The form is to be used for registration of particulars of the entire series, and may be used when an issue of debentures made thereunder is made at the same time as the series of debentures is created by the LLP. All issues of debentures in the series made after the registration of the series with the Registrar of Companies should be sent to the Registrar on Form LLP413a(Scot).

2   The date should be given of the covering deed (if any) by which the security is created or defined.

3   In the case of a floating charge a statement should be given of (1) the restrictions, if any, on the power of the LLP to grant further securities ranking in priority to, or pari passu with the floating charge; and/or (2) the provisions, if any, regulating the order in which the floating charge shall rank with any other subsisting or future floating charges or fixed securities over the property which is the subject of the floating charge or any part of it.

4   A certified copy of the instrument if any, creating or evidencing the charge, together with this form with the prescribed particulars correctly completed must be delivered to the Registrar within 21 days after the date of the creation of the charge, or in the case of a charge created out of the United Kingdom comprising property situated outside of U.K., within 21 days after the date on which the copy of the instrument creating it could, in due course of post, and if despatched with due diligence, have been received in the U.K. Certified copies of any other documents relevant to the charge should also be delivered.

5   A certified copy must be signed by or on behalf of the person giving the certification and where this is a body corporate it must be signed by an officer of that body.

6   Cheques and Postal Orders must be made payable to **Companies House**.

Page 2

Form LLP413a

M

FORM NO. LLP 413a(Scot)

LLP413a

Please complete
in typescript,
or in bold black
capitals.

Particulars of an issue of Debentures out of a series of secured Debentures in respect of a Limited Liability Partnership (note 1)

For official use

LLP Number

Full Name of Limited Liability Partnership

NOTE:
Please read notes
overleaf before
completing this form

Date of registration of the series (note 2)

Date of present issue

Amount of present issue

Particulars as to commission, allowance or discount paid

Signed   Date

a designated member / member / chargee *(delete as appropriate)*

Please give the name, address, telephone number and e-mail (if available) of the person Companies House should contact if there is any query. *(DX addresses are acceptable for this purpose if you have one).*

Tel

E-mail

Companies House receipt date barcode

When you have completed and signed the form please send it to the Registrar of Companies at:

Companies House, 37 Castle Terrace, Edinburgh, EH1 2EB
DX ED235 Edinburgh 1

Form April 2001

Form LLP413a

Notes

1   This form is for use when an issue is made of debentures in a series subsequent to the registration of that series with the Registrar of Companies. For registration of the entire series or an issue of debentures made thereunder at the same time as the series is created by the LLP, Form No. LLP413(Scot) should be used.

2   The date of the registration may be confirmed from the certificate of registration.

Form LLP416

M

FORM No. LLP 416(Scot)

LLP416

Particulars of a charge subject to which property has been acquired by a Limited Liability Partnership registered in Scotland

Please complete in typescript, or in bold black capitals

A fee of £20 is payable to Companies House in respect of each register entry for a mortgage or charge.

For official use

LLP Number

Full Name of Limited Liability Partnership

Date of creation of the charge
(note 1)

Description of the instrument (if any) creating or evidencing the charge (note 2)

Date of the acquisition of the property

Amount secured by the charge £

Names and addresses of the persons entitled to the charge

Signed   Date

† designated member / member / administrator / administrative receiver (delete as appropriate)

Please give the name, address, telephone number and e-mail (if available) of the person Companies House should contact if there is any query. *(DX addresses are acceptable for this purpose if you have one).*

Tel

Companies House receipt date barcode

E-mail

When you have completed and signed the form please send it to the Registrar of Companies at:

Companies House, 37 Castle Terrace, Edinburgh EH1 2EB
DX ED235 Edinburgh 1

Form April 2001

Form LLP416

Short particulars of all the property charged.

Notes

1. For the date of creation of a charge see section 410(5) of the Act *. (Examples - date of recording / registration of a Standard Security.)

2. A description of the instrument e.g. "Standard Security" should be given.

3. A certified copy of the instrument, if any, creating or evidencing the charge, together with this form with the prescribed particulars correctly completed must be delivered to the Registrar of Companies within 21 days after the date on which the transaction was settled or in the case of a charge created outside Great Britain comprising property situated outside Great Britain within 21 days after the date on which the copy of the instrument could, in due course of post, and if despatched with due diligence, have been received in U.K. Certified copies of any other documents relevant to the charge should also be delivered.

4. A certified copy must be signed by or on behalf of the person giving the certification and where this is a body corporate it must be signed by an officer of that body.

5. Cheques and Postal Orders must be made payable to **Companies House**.

* *As applied to LLPs by Schedule 2 of the Limited Liability Partnerships Regulations 2001*

Form LLP417(Scot)

No. of Limited Liability Partnership

LLP417(Scot)

N.B. Searchers may find it helpful to
refer to the mortgage documents
for more detailed particulars

REGISTER

OF

Charges

Memoranda of Satisfaction

AND

Appointments and Cessations

of Receivers

OF

Form April 2001

Form LLP417(Scot)

**REGISTER of Charges, Alterations to Charges,
Memoranda of Satisfaction and Receivers Details**

N.B Searchers should refer to the mortgage documents for more detailed particulars

CHARGE:

(1) Date of Registration		(2)Serial No of Document on File	

(3) Date of Creation of each Charge and Description of it.	
(4) Date of the Acquisition of the Property	
(5) Amount secured by the Charge	
(6) Short Particulars of the Property Charged	
(7) Names of the Persons Entitled to the Charge	
(8) In the case of a floating charge, a statement of the provisions, if any, prohibiting or restricting the creation by the limited liability partnership of any fixed security or any other floating charge having priority over, or ranking *pari passu* with the floating charge.	
(9) In the case of a floating charge, a statement of the provisions if any regulating the order in which the floating charge shall rank with any other subsisting or future floating charges or fixed securities over the property the subject of the floating charge or any part of it.	
(10) Amount or Rate per cent of the Commission Allowance or Discount	

(11) Memoranda of Satisfaction	Full/Partial		Date

(12) Receiver(s) or Manager(s)	Name	Date of Appointment	Date of Ceasing to Act

Instruments of Alteration to a Floating Charge

(13) Date of Execution	
(14) Names of the persons who have executed the instrument	
(15) The provisions, if any, prohibiting or restricting the creation by the LLP of any fixed security or any other floating charge having priority over, or ranking *pari passu* with the floating charge	

Page 1 of 2

673

Form LLP417(Scot)

REGISTER of Charges, Alterations to Charges, Memoranda of Satisfaction and Receivers Details (Cont.)

N.B Searchers should refer to the mortgage documents for more detailed particulars

CHARGE:

(16) The provisions, if any, varying or otherwise regulating the order of the ranking of the floating charge in relation to the fixed securities or to other floating charges.	
(17) Short particulars of any property released from the floating charge	
(18) The amount, if any, by which the amount secured by the floating charge has been increased	

Particulars Relating to the Issues of Debentures of a Series		
(19) Total Amount Secured by a Series of Debentures		
(20) Dates and Amounts of each Issue of the Series	Date	Amount
(21) Dates of the Resolutions authorising the Issues of the Series		
(22) Date of the Covering Deed		
(23) General Description of the Property Charged		
(24) Names of the Trustees for the Debenture Holders		
(25) Amount or Rate of per cent of the Commission Allowance or Discount		
(26) In the case of a floating charge, a statement of the provisions, if any, prohibiting or restricting the creation by the LLP of any fixed security or any other floating charge having priority over, or ranking *pari passu* with the floating charge.		
(27) In the case of a floating charge, a statement of the provision if any regulating the order in which the floating charge shall rank with any other subsisting or future floating charges or fixed securities over the property the subject of the floating charge or any part of it.		

Page 2 of 2

Form LLP419a

M

CHWP000

Please complete in typescript, or in bold black capitals

FORM No. LLP 419a(Scot)

LLP419a

Limited Liability Partnership: Memorandum of satisfaction in full or in part of a registered charge

For official use

LLP Number

Full Name of Limited Liability Partnership

† delete as appropriate

I, _____

of _____

[a designated member] [member] [the liquidator] [the receiver] [the administrator]†
of the limited liability partnership, do solemnly and sincerely declare that the debt
for which the charge described overleaf was given has been paid or satisfied in
[full] [part]†

And I make this solemn declaration conscientiously believing the same to be true
and by virtue of the provisions of the Statutory Declarations Act 1835.

Declarant's signature

Declared at

Day Month Year

on

❶ Please print name

before me ❶

Signed _____ **Date**

† A Commissioner for Oaths or Notary Public or Justic of the Peace or Solicitor

Please give the name, address, telephone number and e-mail (if available) of the person Companies House should contact if there is any query. *(DX addresses are acceptable for this purpose if you have one).*

Tel

E-mail

Companies House receipt date barcode

This form has been provided free of charge by Companies House.

When you have completed and signed the form please send it to the Registrar of Companies at:

Companies House, 37 Castle Terrace, Edinburgh, EH1 2EB
DX ED235 Edinburgh

Form April 2001

Form LLP419a

Particulars of the charge to which the application overleaf refers

Please complete in typescript, or in bold black capitals

Date of creation of the charge

Description of the instrument (if any) creating or evidencing the charge#

insert a description of the instruments creating or evidencing the charge eg 'Charge', 'Debenture' etc

Date of Registration *

* *the date of registration may be confirmed from the certificate*

Short particulars of all the property charged

Where a FLOATING CHARGE is being satisfied, the following Certificate MUST be completed:

CERTIFICATE

I _____

of _____

† delete as appropriate

being [the creditor] [a person authorised to act on behalf of the creditor]† entitled to the benefits of the floating charge specified above certify that the particulars above relating to the charge and the release of part of the property charged are correct.

Signature _____ Date _____

Page 2

Form LLP419b

M

CHWP000

Please complete
in typescript, or
in bold black
capitals

FORM No. LLP 419b(Scot)

LLP419b

Limited Liability Partnership: Memorandum of fact that part of a property charged (a) has been released from the charge; (b) no longer forms part of the LLP's property

For official use

LLP Number

Full Name of Limited Liability Partnership

I, _____

of _____

[a designated member] [member] [the liquidator] [the receiver] [the administrator]†
of the limited liability partnership, do solemnly and sincerely declare that the
particulars overleaf relating to the charge and the fact that part of the property or
undertaking charged [ceased to form part of] the LLP property or
undertaking] [was released from the charge] on _____
are true to the best of my knowledge and belief.

And I make this solemn declaration conscientiously believing the same to be true
and by virtue of the provisions of the Statutory Declarations Act 1835.

† delete as
appropriate

Declarant's signature

Declared at

Day   Month   Year

on

❶ Please print name

Before me †

Signed   Date

† *A Commissioner for Oaths or Notary Public or Justice of the Peace or Solicitor*

Please give the name, address,
telephone number and e-mail (if
available) of the person Companies
House should contact if there is any
query. *(DX addresses are acceptable
for this purpose if you have one).*

Tel

E-mail

Companies House receipt date barcode

*This form has been provided free of charge
by Companies House.*

When you have completed and signed the form please send it to the
Registrar of Companies at:

Companies House, 37 Castle Terrace, Edinburgh, EH1 2EB
DX ED235 Edinburgh

Form April 2001

Form LLP419b

Particulars of the charge to which the application overleaf refers

Please complete in typescript, or in bold black capitals

Date of creation of the charge

Description of the instrument (if any) creating or evidencing the charge#

 # insert a description of the instruments creating or evidencing the charge eg 'Charge', 'Debenture' etc

Date of Registration *

* the date of registration may be confirmed from the certificate

Short particulars of all the property charged

Where a FLOATING CHARGE is being satisfied, the following Certificate MUST be completed:

CERTIFICATE

I _____

of _____

† delete as appropriate

being [the creditor] [a person authorised to act on behalf of the creditor]† entitled to the benefits of the floating charge specified above certify that the particulars above relating to the charge and the release of part of the property charged are correct.

Signature _____   Date _____

Page 2

Form LLP466

M

FORM No. LLP 466(Scot)

LLP466

CHWP000

*Please complete
lin typescript, or in
bold black
capitals*

Particulars of an instrument of alteration to a floating charge created by a limited liability partnership registered in Scotland

A fee of £20 is payable to Companies House in respect of each register entry for a mortgage or charge.

LLP Number

For official use

Full Name of Limited Liability Partnership

Date of creation of the charge (note 1)

Description of the instrument creating or evidencing the charge or of any ancillary document which has been altered (note 1)

Names of the persons entitled to the charge

Short particulars of all the property charged

Please give the name, address, telephone number and e-mail (if available) of the person Companies House should contact if there is any query. *(DX addresses are acceptable for this purpose if you have one).*

Tel

E-mail

When you have completed and signed the form on page 4 please send it to the Registrar of Companies at:

**Companies House, 37 Castle Terrace, Edinburgh, EH1 2EB
DX ED235 Edinburgh**

Form April 2001

Page 1

Form LLP466

Names and addresses of the persons who have executed the instrument of alteration (note 2)

Please complete lin typescript, or in bold black capitals

Date(s) of execution of the instrument of alteration

A statement of the provisions, if any, imposed by the instrument of alteration prohibiting or restricting the creation by the LLP of any fixed security or any other floating charge having, priority over, or ranking pari passu with the floating charge

Short particulars of any property released from the floating charge

The amount, if any, by which the amount secured by the floating charge has been increased

Page 2

Form LLP466

Please complete **lin typescript, or in** **bold black** **capitals**

A statement of the provisions, if any, imposed by the instrument of alteration varying or otherwise regulating the order of the ranking of the floating charge in relation to fixed securities or to other floating charges

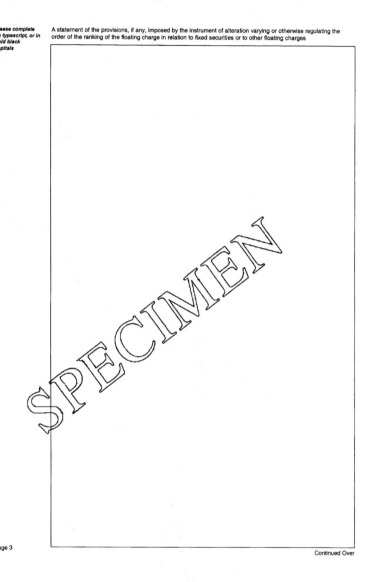

Page 3

Continued Over

Form LLP466

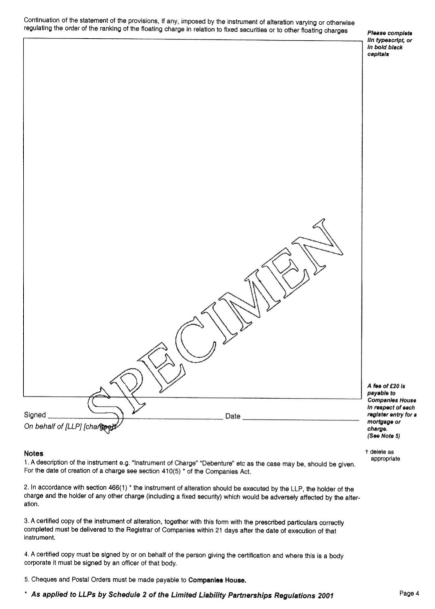

Continuation of the statement of the provisions, if any, imposed by the instrument of alteration varying or otherwise regulating the order of the ranking of the floating charge in relation to fixed securities or to other floating charges

Please complete lin typescript, or in bold black capitals

Signed _____ Date _____

On behalf of [LLP] [chargee]†

A fee of £20 is payable to Companies House in respect of each register entry for a mortgage or charge. (See Note 5)

† delete as appropriate

Notes

1. A description of the instrument e.g. "Instrument of Charge" "Debenture" etc as the case may be, should be given. For the date of creation of a charge see section 410(5) * of the Companies Act.

2. In accordance with section 466(1) * the instrument of alteration should be executed by the LLP, the holder of the charge and the holder of any other charge (including a fixed security) which would be adversely affected by the alteration.

3. A certified copy of the instrument of alteration, together with this form with the prescribed particulars correctly completed must be delivered to the Registrar of Companies within 21 days after the date of execution of that instrument.

4. A certified copy must be signed by or on behalf of the person giving the certification and where this is a body corporate it must be signed by an officer of that body.

5. Cheques and Postal Orders must be made payable to **Companies House.**

* *As applied to LLPs by Schedule 2 of the Limited Liability Partnerships Regulations 2001*

Page 4

Form LLP652a

Companies House
—— *for the record* ——

*Please complete in typescript,
or in bold black capitals*

CHWP000

LLP652a

Application for striking off a Limited
Liability Partnership

LLP Number

**Full Name of Limited
Liability Partnership**

I/We as designated member(s) apply for this LLP to be struck off the register.

The LLP is not the subject of, nor the proposed subject of, insolvency proceedings or a section 425 scheme and has not in the past three months:

- traded or otherwise carried on business, or changed its name;

- disposed of for value any property or rights which it would have disposed of for value in the normal course of trading or carrying on business; or

- engaged in any other activity except for the purpose of making this application, settling its affairs or meeting a statutory requirement.

I/We enclose the fee of £10 (made payable to Companies House).

Designated member signatures (use continuation sheet if necessary).

Name of Designated Member

Signed | Date

Name of Designated Member

Signed | Date

Name of Designated Member

Signed | Date

Please give the name, address, telephone number and e-mail (if available) of the person Companies House should contact if there is any query. *(DX addresses are acceptable for this purpose if you have one).*

Tel

E-mail

Companies House receipt date barcode

This form has been provided free of charge by Companies House.

Form April 2001

When you have signed the form send it with the fee to the Registrar of Companies at:

Companies House, Crown Way, Cardiff, CF14 3UZ DX 33050 Cardiff
for partnerships registered in England and Wales
or
Companies House, 37 Castle Terrace, Edinburgh, EH1 2EB
for partnerships registered in Scotland DX ED235 Edinburgh

Form LLP652a

Notes:

Guidance notes on all aspects of striking off are available from Companies House. You are advised to read them fully BEFORE completing and returning this for.

If the LLP ceases to be eligible for striking off at any time after the application is made, then the application must be withdrawn using form LLP652c. Failure to do so is an offence.

Copies of this application must be sent to all notifiable parties i.e. creditors, employees, pension managers or trustees and other members of the LLP within 7 days from the day on which the application is made. Copies must also be sent to anyone who later becomes a notifiable party within 7 days of becoming so. You should check the guidance notes which contain a full list of those who must be notified. Failure to notify interested parties is an offence. It is advisable to obtain and retain some proof of delivery or posting of copies to notifiable parties.

This form must be signed by both designated members if there are two, or by the majority if there are more than two. If more than three designated members' signatures are required, continuation sheets for this form are available from Companies House.

Form LLP652a cont

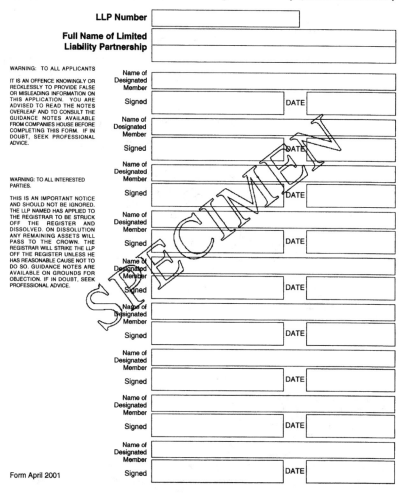

Please complete in typescript,
or in bold black capitals

LLP652a cont

Application for striking off a Limited Liability Partnership (continuation sheet)

LLP Number

Full Name of Limited Liability Partnership

WARNING: TO ALL APPLICANTS

IT IS AN OFFENCE KNOWINGLY OR RECKLESSLY TO PROVIDE FALSE OR MISLEADING INFORMATION ON THIS APPLICATION. YOU ARE ADVISED TO READ THE NOTES OVERLEAF AND TO CONSULT THE GUIDANCE NOTES AVAILABLE FROM COMPANIES HOUSE BEFORE COMPLETING THIS FORM. IF IN DOUBT, SEEK PROFESSIONAL ADVICE.

WARNING: TO ALL INTERESTED PARTIES.

THIS IS AN IMPORTANT NOTICE AND SHOULD NOT BE IGNORED. THE LLP NAMED HAS APPLIED TO THE REGISTRAR TO BE STRUCK OFF THE REGISTER AND DISSOLVED. ON DISSOLUTION ANY REMAINING ASSETS WILL PASS TO THE CROWN. THE REGISTRAR WILL STRIKE THE LLP OFF THE REGISTER UNLESS HE HAS REASONABLE CAUSE NOT TO DO SO. GUIDANCE NOTES ARE AVAILABLE ON GROUNDS FOR OBJECTION. IF IN DOUBT, SEEK PROFESSIONAL ADVICE.

Name of Designated Member

Signed   DATE

Name of Designated Member

Signed   DATE

Name of Designated Member

Signed   DATE

Name of Designated Member

Signed   DATE

Name of Designated Member

Signed   DATE

Name of Designated Member

Signed   DATE

Name of Designated Member

Signed   DATE

Name of Designated Member

Signed   DATE

Name of Designated Member

Signed   DATE

Form April 2001

Form LLP652c

Companies House
— *for the record* —

Please complete in typescript, or in bold black capitals

LLP652c

Withdrawal of application for striking off a Limited Liability Partnership

LLP Number	

Full Name of Limited Liability Partnership	

The designated members hereby withdraw the application dated

Day	Month	Year

in which it was requested that this LLP be struck off the register.

This form can be signed by any designated member of the Limited Liability Partnership.

Name of designated member	
Signed	Date

Please give the name, address, telephone number and e-mail (if available) of the person Companies House should contact if there is any query. *(DX addresses are acceptable for this purpose if you have one).*

Tel
E-mail

Companies House receipt date barcode

When you have signed the form send it to the Registrar of Companies at:

Companies House, Crown Way, Cardiff, CF14 3UZ   DX 33050 Cardiff
for partnerships registered in England and Wales
or
Companies House, 37 Castle Terrace, Edinburgh, EH1 2EB
for partnerships registered in Scotland   DX ED235 Edinburgh

Form April 2001

Table of Statutes

1890 Partnership Act
s 24 — 2.5

1963 Stock Transfer Act — 6.2

1982 Insurance Companies Act — 4.10

1984 Inheritance Tax
s 94 — 5.5
s 267A — 5.5, 5.6

1985 Business Names Act — 2.3, 2.7
ss 2, 3 — 2.7
s 4(1)(a)(b) — 2.7
(3A)(4A) — 2.7
(6)(7) — 2.7
s 5 — 2.7
s 7 — 2.7

1985 Companies Act
s 24 — 3.2
s 190 — 6.1
s 191 — 6.1, 6.4
ss 192, 193 — 6.1
s 194 — 6.1, 6.6
ss 195, 196 — 6.1
s 221 — 4.2
(5)(6) — 4.2
s 222(5) — 4.2
ss 223, 224 — 4.3
s 225 — 4.3, 4.9
(4) — 4.3
s 226 — 4.4
(2) — 4.4
(5) — 4.4
s 227 — 4.5
s 228(1) — 4.5
s 229 — 4.5
(2)–(4) — 4.5
s 230(3) — 4.7
s 233 — 4.6, 4.9
s 235(1)(2) — 4.7

1985 Companies Act
s 236 — 4.7
s 237(1)(2) — 4.8
s 238 — 4.9, 4.14, 4.25
s 239 — 4.9, 4.14
s 242(1)–(5) — 4.9
s 242A — 4.9
s 244(1)–(5) — 4.9
s 245 — 4.19
s 245A — 4.19
s 245B — 4.19
s 246 — 4.12
(6) — 4.24
s 246A(2)–(4) — 4.13
s 247(3) — 4.10
s 247A — 4.10
s 247B — 4.12, 4.13
s 248 — 4.5
(2) — 4.14, 4.22
s 249 — 4.14
(3)(4) — 4.11
s 249A — 4.10, 4.14, 4.18
(6A) — 4.16
s 249AA(2)–(5) — 4.18
(7) — 4.18
s 249B(1) — 4.14
(1A) — 4.15
(4)(5) — 4.17
s 249E — 4.14
s 258 — 4.5, 4.14
s 287 — 2.8
s 348 — 2.2, 2.8
s 349 — 2.2, 2.9
s 351 — 2.9
ss 363, 364 — 2.10
s 384 — 4.20
(4) — 4.21
(5) — 4.20, 4.21
s 385(2)–(4) — 4.20
ss 387, 388 — 4.20
s 388A — 4.14, 4.20, 4.22
(3)(5) — 4.22
s 389A(1)–(4) — 4.23
s 390(1) — 4.23

1985 *Companies Act*

s 390A(1)	4.24
(3)(5)	4.24
s 390B	4.24
s 391	4.28
(4)	4.29
s 391A(1)	4.29
(3)–(6)	4.29
s 392	4.27
(2)(3)	4.27
s 392A	4.27
(8)	4.27
s 394	4.27
(1)(2)	4.25
(3)	4.25
(b)	4.25, 4.26
(4)(6)	4.25
s 394A	4.27
(8)	4.27
s 395	6.1, 6.2, 6.7
(1)	6.3
s 396	6.1
s 397	6.1, 6.3
(1)	6.3
s 398	6.1
s 399	6.1, 6.3, 6.7
ss 400–402	6.1
s 403	6.1, 6.6
s 404	6.1, 6.9
s 405	6.1, 6.3
s 406	6.1, 6.10
s 407	6.1, 6.3, 6.10
s 408	6.1, 6.10
ss 409–423	6.1
s 425	7.23, 7.36
s 426	7.36
s 427	7.36, 7.37
s 458	3.10
s 459	3.12
(1A)	3.12
ss 460, 461	3.12
s 462	6.3, 7.19
ss 463–466	7.19
s 652A	7.18
s 652B	7.18
(6)	7.18
s 652C	7.18
s 693	2.2
s 714	2.3

1985 *Companies Act*

ss 736, 736A	4.5
s 744	6.2
Sch 4	4.1, 4.4
Sch 4A	4.1, 4.5, 4.11
Schs 5–7	4.1
Schs 8, 8A	4.1, 4.12
Sch 10A	4.1, 4.5, 4.14
Part VII	4.1
Part XI, Chapter V	4.1

1986 Company Directors Disqualification Act

	3.6, 7.10
s 2	3.8
s 3	3.9
s 4	3.10
s 5	3.9
s 6	3.7
s 7(3)	7.12, 7.27
s 8	3.11
Sch 1	3.7

1986 Financial Services Act

	4.10, 4.14, 4.18

1986 Insolvency Act

s 1	7.20
s 2	7.20, 7.21, 7.22
s 3	7.20
(1)	7.21
s 4	7.20, 7.21, 7.22
(5A)(6)	7.21
s 5	7.20
(2)(b)	7.21
s 6	7.20, 7.21
s 7	7.20, 7.22
(4)(b)	7.23
s 8	7.23
(2)(3)	7.23
s 9(1)–(3)	7.23
s 10(1)	7.23
s 11(1)–(3)	7.24
ss 14, 15	7.26
s 17	7.27
s 18	7.28
s 19	7.29
ss 23, 24	7.27

1986	Insolvency Act	
	s 30	7.30
	s 33	7.32
	s 36	7.30
	s 39(1)	7.32
	s 42	7.34
	s 43(1)	7.34
	s 44	7.33
	(1)	7.34
	s 46	7.32
	(1)	7.32
	s 47	7.32
	s 48(1)(2)	7.32
	(4)	7.32
	s 74	7.1
	s 79	7.8
	ss 84, 85	7.6
	s 86	7.2
	s 89	7.3, 7.6
	(4)(5)	7.3
	s 90	7.6
	s 91	7.3
	s 94	7.16
	ss 95, 96	7.3
	s 98	7.4, 7.6
	(1)(b)(c)	7.7
	ss 99–101	7.7
	s 103	7.7
	s 106(2)	7.16
	s 107	7.16
	s 109	7.6
	s 122	7.5
	s 123	7.5, 7.14, 7.23
	s 130(2)	7.9
	s 131	7.8
	s 136(2)(4)	7.8
	s 137	7.8
	s 139	7.8
	(4)	7.8
	s 141	7.11
	s 146	7.17
	s 165	7.11
	(4)	7.11
	ss 166–170	7.11
	s 175(2)(b)	7.16
	s 178	7.9
	s 201(2)	7.16
	s 212	7.13
	ss 213, 214	7.12, 7.13

1986	Insolvency Act	
	s 214A	7.1, 7.13, 7.14
	s 215	7.13
	s 218(4)	7.13
	ss 238, 239	7.13
	s 245	7.13
	ss 386, 387	7.16
	s 389	7.25, 7.30
	ss 390–394	7.10, 7.25, 7.30
	ss 395–398	7.10, 7.13, 7.25, 7.30
	ss 399–444	7.1
	s 416	7.19
	Sch 1	7.26
	Sch 4	7.11
	Sch 6	7.16, 7.35
	Parts I–IV	7.1
	Parts VI, VII	7.1

1987	**Banking Act**	4.10

1988	**Income and Corporation Taxes Act**	
	s 111	5.1
	s 114	5.1
	ss 117, 118	5.3
	ss 118ZA–118ZD	5.2, 5.3
	s 380	5.3
	s 381	5.3
	s 393A(1)	5.3
	s 403	5.3

1989	**Companies Act**	
	s 25(1)	4.21
	s 26(2)	4.20
	s 27(1)	4.21
	ss 92–104	6.1
	Part II	4.20, 4.21

1992	**Social Security Contributions and Benefits Act**	
	s 15(3A)	5.9

1992	**Social Security Contributions and Benefits (Northern Ireland) Act**	
	s 15(3A)	5.9

1992 Taxation of Chargeable Gains Act

ss 152, 153	5.4
s 154(2)	5.4
s 59A	5.2, 5.4
s 156A	5.2, 5.4

2000 Insolvency Act

	7.13, 7.23, 7.24

2000 Limited Liability Partnerships Act

ss 2, 3	2.4
s 4(1)	3.2
s 5(1)	3.1
s 6(1)–(4)	3.3

2000 Limited Liability Partnerships Act

s 8(1)(2)	3.5
(4)(5)	3.5
s 9	3.4
(1)(a)	3.4
(b)	3.5
s 10	5.2
s 11	5.1
ss 12, 13	5.1, 5.8
s 14	7.1
Sch, para 2	2.2
para 3(1)(2)	2.3
para 4(1)	2.6
(2)–(4)	2.3
paras 9, 10	2.8

Table of Statutory Instruments

1986 Insolvency Rules
SI 1986 No 1925

Rule 1.9	7.21
Rule 1.19(4)	7.21
Rule 1.21	7.21
Rule 1.28	7.22
Rule 1.29	7.22
Rule 2.2	7.23
Rules 2.18–2.30	7.27
Rules 2.32–2.46A	7.25
Rule 2.47	7.25
Rule 3(2)	7.32
Rules 4.73–4.85	7.15
Rule 4.125	7.17
Rule 4.126	7.16
Rule 4.218	7.16

1990 Companies (Revision of Defective Accounts and Report) Regulations

SI 1990 No 2570	4.19

1991 Companies Act 1985 (Disclosure of Remuneration for Non-Audit Work) Regulations

SI 1991 No 2128	4.24
Reg 4	4.24

1991 Companies (Inspection and Copying of Registers, Indices and Documents) Regulations

SI 1991 No 1998	6.4

2000 Limited Liability Partnerships Act 2000 (Commencement) Order

SI 2000 No 3316	1

2001 Limited Liability Partnerships (Fees) (No 2) Regulaions

SI 2001 No 969	1

2001 Limited Liability Partnerships (Forms) Regulations

SI 2001 No 927	1

2001 Limited Liability Partnerships Regulations

SI 2001 No 1090	1
Reg 4	3.6
(2)	7.12

2001	*Limited Liability Partnerships Regulations*	
	Reg 5	7.1
	(1)(2)	7.1
	Regs 7, 8	2.5, 3.1
	Sch 1	4.1, 4.17
	Sch 2	4.1, 7.19
	Part II	3.6
	Sch 3	7.1, 7.19, 7.20
	Sch 4	7.19
	Sch 5, paras 10, 11	2.3, 2.7
	Sch 6, Part II	7.15

2001	**Limited Liability Partnerships (Scotland) Regulations**	
	SSI 2001 No 128	**1**, 7.19
	Sch 1	6.3, 7.19

Index

Accounting records 4.2
Accounting reference date 4.3
Accounts and audit **4**
Accounts
  approval and signature 4.6
  exemptions
  —audit 4.14
  —medium-sized LLPs 4.13
  —small LLPs 4.12
  form and content 4.4
  group 4.5
  publication and delivery 4.9
  —unaudited accounts 4.17
  revisions 4.19
  small and medium-sized
  —groups 4.11
  —LLPs 4.10, 4.12, 4.13
Administration order
  discharge or variation 7.28
  effect 7.24
  introduction 7.23
Administrative receiver
  appointment by court 7.31
  appointment by debenture
    holders 7.32
  employees, position of 7.33
  duties 7.32
  funds, priority in distributing
    7.35
  liabilities 7.34
  powers 7.34
  qualification 7.30
  remuneration 7.30
Administrator
  duties 7.27
  powers 7.26
  qualification 7.25
  remuneration 7.25
  vacation of office 7.29
Annual return 2.10
Arrangement, scheme of 7.36
Audit exemption 4.14
  dormant LLPs 4.16
  dormant subsidiaries 4.15

Auditors
  appointment 4.20
  ceasing to hold office 4.25
  —notification to Companies
    House 4.27
  eligibility 4.21
  exemption from appointing 4.22
  removal or non re-appointment
    4.28
  —rights of auditor following
    4.29
  remuneration 4.24
  report 4.7, 4.8
  resignation 4.27
  rights 4.23
Business name 2.7
Capital gains tax 5.2–5.4
Charges **6**
  rectification of register 6.9
  register kept by LLP 6.10
  registration 6.6
  release of 6.8
  satisfaction of 6.8
Compromise 7.36
Court, winding up by
  distributions and release 7.17
  duties of liquidator 7.9
  initial procedures 7.8
  introduction 7.5
Creditors' voluntary winding up
  distributions and release 7.16
  introduction 7.4
  initial procedures 7.7
Criminal offences 7.13
Debentures (see also Charges)
  issue 6.1
  redemption 6.6
  secured 6.3
  stock 6.4
  types 6.2
  unsecured loan stock 6.5
Designated members 3.5
Disqualification of members
  conviction, on 3.8

fraudulent trading 3.10
public interest 3.11
statutory obligations, breach 3.9
unfitness 3.7
wrongful trading 3.10
Dormant LLPs 4.16, 4.18
Floating charge 6.3
Fixed charge 6.3
Fraud 7.13
General **1**
Income tax 5.2–5.4
Incorporation **2**
   matters to consider 2.1
   name 2.2
   —business 2.7
   —change of 2.6
   —control of LLP names 2.3
Inheritance tax 5.5, 5.6
Insolvency **6**
Letterheads 2.9
Liquidator
   duties and powers 7.11
   investigations by 7.13
   qualifications 7.10
   responsibilities
   —creditors' voluntary winding
     up 7.7
   —members' voluntary winding
     up 7.6
   —winding up by the court 7.9
Members 3.2
   assets, contribution to 7.14
   authority 3.3
   disqualification 3.6–3.11
   designated 3.5
   unfitness of 7.12
Membership **3**
Members' voluntary winding up
   distributions and release 7.16
   introduction 7.3
   initial procedures 7.6

Name 2.2, 2.3, 2.6, 2.7
National insurance 5.9
Partnership agreement 2.5
Preferences 7.13
Receiver (see Administrative receiver)
Reconstructions 7.37
Registered office 2.8
Registration 2.4
Scotland, winding up in 7.19
Stamp duty 5.8
Taxation **5**
   business, transfer of 5.7
   capital gains tax 5.2–5.4
   income tax 5.2–5.4
   inheritance tax 5.5, 5.6
   national insurance 5.9
   stamp duty 5.8
Unfair prejudice petition 3.12
Voluntary arrangements
   completion 7.22
   expenses 7.22
   introduction 7.20
   nominee 7.20–7.22
   procedure 7.21
   remuneration 7.22
   supervisor 7.22
Winding up
   court, by (see Court, winding up
     by)
   determination of creditors'
     claims 7.15
   dissolution of LLP without
     liquidation 7.18
   introduction 7.1
   investigations in 7.13
   methods 7.2
   Scotland, in 7.19
   voluntary (see Creditors' voluntary
     winding up *and* Members'
     voluntary winding up)